D0148936

Revolution, Reaction
and the
Triumph
of
Conservatism

Revolution, Reaction

and the Triumph

of

Conservatism

ENGLISH HISTORY, 1558–1700

MICHAEL A.R. GRAVES
AND
ROBIN H. SILCOCK

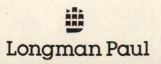

Longman Paul

LgBEM   11-4-84

Longman Paul Limited
182—190 Wairau Road
Auckland 10, New Zealand

Associated companies, branches and
representatives throughout the world

© Longman Paul Limited 1984
First published 1984

ISBN 0 582 68394 7

All rights reserved. No part of this publication
may be reproduced, stored in a retrieval system,
or transmitted in any form or by any means,
electronic, mechanical, photocopying, recording,
or otherwise, without the prior permission of
the Copyright owner.

The cover incorporates a view of the Great Fire of
London, 1666. Society of Antiquaries.

Printed in Hong Kong by
Quadrant Offset Printing Fty

DA 355
G73
1984

Contents

JUL 28 1986

Europe in 1558

SCOTLAND

IRELAND

NORTH SEA

ENGLAND

ATLANTIC OCEAN

FRANCE

NORWAY

SWEDEN

RUSSIA

NETHERLANDS

HOLY ROMAN EMPIRE

AUSTRIA

POLAND

HUNGARY

OTTOMAN

EMPIRE

PORTUGAL

SPAIN

Castile

Kingdom of Aragon

MEDITERRANEAN SEA

SWISS CONFEDERATION

Key
1 Genoa
2 Florence
3 Papal States
4 Venetian Republic
5 Naples
6 Sicily

Habsburg territory

Boundary of the Holy Roman Empire

Introduction

This book is not a grand narrative history. The reader who expects to find a comprehensive survey of the period 1558–1700, and a wealth of detail on every aspect of it, will be disappointed. To some extent, the decision to avoid such an ambitious venture was forced upon the authors by circumstances. The economics of present-day publishing prohibit this kind of treatment, which would consume so much print and paper and escalate the price of the finished product. Furthermore the exigencies of the school situation—in particular the limited time and resources available for the teaching of the subject—make it unrealistic and unhelpful to put on the market yet another bulky and expensive volume which treads a detailed narrative course through early modern England. Instead it was decided to structure the book in accordance with two principles.

1 It must be geared primarily, but by no means exclusively, to the needs of senior school pupils and teachers. The germ of inspiration for this volume was a questionnaire circulated around New Zealand secondary schools by Longman Paul. The response revealed that there was an overwhelming need for a book which catered for both teachers and pupils. It must not assume a knowledge of the functions, status and authority of institutions, or of technical terminology; and it must direct students of the period to other works which are important, accessible and reasonably priced, while possessing those qualities itself.

2 It should be structured thematically, not chronologically. The particular structure which has been adopted corresponds to the terms of reference of the New Zealand Entrance Scholarship and Bursary Examinations. Those are: changes in social and economic structure; problems of government and shifts of power; religion; Parliament and constitutional development; and personality and politics. However, it was decided that the section on personalities should be omitted, partly because it is not thematic, but especially because an adequate coverage would grossly enlarge the size and inflate the cost of the book. One further point should be stressed. The fact that this volume is designed, in the first instance, for New Zealand seventh formers

should not inhibit or discourage teachers elsewhere from using it. Its thematic structure is completely in accord with the common contemporary treatment of the period 1558–1700. Moreover, it is based not only upon the published results of recent research, but also on primary sources and unpublished theses which are normally unavailable to teachers and pupils alike. However, it has been the authors' intention throughout that a comprehensive coverage of the period should take second place to the clarity, continuity and cohesion of each theme.

In practical terms, therefore, the book sets out to satisfy these requirements which are lacking in the literature available at present:

1 To pursue each theme separately (while emphasising connection and overlap by frequent cross-references), checking and explaining the dynamics of change, and doing so with equal emphasis throughout the period, giving as much attention to the 1690s as to the 1560s. Fortunately the recent spate of monographs and general texts on the later seventeenth century has facilitated this.

2 To avoid lengthy narrative and descriptive excursions. Instead, and as a substitute, an extensive, annotated bibliography has been included. It directs the reader to appropriate and available works which can be purchased without auctioning off the staff or mortgaging the school. It is a waste of time to walk, say, the well-trodden path of S.T. Bindoff's *Tudor England* and G.E. Aylmer's *Struggle for the Constitution*, or to reproduce the uncontentious and descriptive aspects of, for example, J. Hurstfield's *Elizabeth I and the Unity of England*. Both in the text and (especially) the bibliography, the strengths and weaknesses of the available literature are evaluated. One consequence of this approach is that chapters vary dramatically in length. That is no indication of the relative importance of the subject under consideration, but rather a test of the quality of the available literature to which students can be directed.

3 To provide an historiographical structure for each theme, partly because it is important to be aware that history is not a static discipline, but also—and this is of more practical value here—because it will enable the student to identify where his particular text fits into the process of historiographical development, and the prejudices and position of its author. It should promote some critical awareness, at least in the more discerning student, and provide a practical purchasing guide for teachers. While acknowledging the difficulties involved, we cannot over-emphasise the need to keep pace with historiographical changes: examination papers will certainly continue to reflect such changes and examiners will expect candidates to display a knowledge of them.

In brief, this book is not a magic hold-all which students can take as their sole text; it must be used in conjunction with standard descriptive and narrative histories. Regard it as a working document which will provide teachers and pupils with the tools of thematic structure, historiography and bibiliography: what the priorities are within each theme; how the themes relate and where they coincide and overlap (for no one theme is exclusive); which books are most appropriate and when to apply caution, criticism and comparison; what is being modified and revised, where that revision can be read, and whether it is justified. These are practical questions, and yet they touch on some of the fundamentals of history as a discipline: the ceaseless questioning of sources, of other historians and, of course, of the motives and actions of those men and women whom we are studying. We have fulfilled our objective if we have provided a book which does more than merely inform. It must provoke the reader into a state of critical awareness. It should co-ordinate and evaluate the existing literature. It ought to guide the student on all manner of things, from sources and the historians who have used and misused them, to the evaluation of facts and the illumination of concepts.

Nor is this the end. This is the study of a changing society. When Elizabeth became queen in 1558 the idea was being mooted that obedience to the monarch was conditional. A godly Prince (defined according to one's own religious loyalties) was God's chosen one and ought to be obeyed. But the ungodly ruler might lawfully be resisted, deposed and even assassinated. As yet, however, few were ready to harbour and act upon such dangerous notions. More typical of contemporary attitudes were acceptance of the sanctity of kingship and the obligation to obey. In the 1530s bishops were preaching that, 'The King is to be obeyed, yea, and to be obeyed without exception'. Monarchy was part of the natural order of things, 'the supremest thing on earth'. What a revolution in thinking about fundamentals occurred in the next century and a half, when, early in the eighteenth century, Alexander Pope could write:

> For forms of government let fools contest,
> Whiche'er is best administered is best

Where was the 'Divine Right of Kings' now? Where was the belief that monarchy was the only right form of government? Gone. The student must ask why, and seek to discover how. Nor was change confined to political beliefs. In the economy, the structure of the State and its financing, religion, social habits and activities, there were dramatic transformations: as it is the student's task to understand the dynamics of such change, so it has been the authors' concern to assist in this.

The thematic structure which has been adopted in this book is an artificial framework, simply because it is impossible to compartmentalise the activities of human beings. An Elizabethan or Caroline gentleman, for example, might be a conforming Anglican (or a reforming Puritan, or a Catholic). He might also be a landlord or lessee, exploiting the opportunities afforded by inflation or suffering from its ill-effects. He may have been a Justice of the Peace (involved in law enforcement), a military man or a courtier. Perhaps he was a patron or a client involved in the faction politics of the Court or his county. Perhaps he sat in the Commons as a knight or burgess, or was raised to the Lords as a peer. Whatever his specific historical roles, his life was bound to have been the usual untidy disordered affair which most of us experience: financial problems, quarrelsome neighbours, disagreeable relatives, pressure of business and office. In other words, his life had many facets and he had many faces. Many of the more familiar faces of this age—William Cecil, Leicester, Buckingham— will make their presence felt in each of the following thematic studies. So too will many lesser mortals—Sir Thomas Tresham, for example. He was a recusant burdened with fines, a harsh commercial landlord, an aspiring gentleman building a magnificent house at Apethorpe. Thus if we generalise about such men—the greater and the lesser, the Cecils and the Treshams—and talk about 'society', we must not lose sight of the fact that humans cannot be described as exclusively economic animals or political creatures. Unconfined within the rigid framework of one particular theme, they spill messily out into the others. This should warn us not to label an individual as a kind of cardboard cut-out Puritan, parliamentarian, or royal servant. Inconvenient though we may find it, he will reappear wearing different hats: as a father, husband, owner of broad acres, magistrate or lawbreaker, a ruthless encloser or a gentle soul moved to pity and charity by the condition of the poor. Of more practical importance to most of those who will read this book, this means that individual themes cannot be isolated from the rest. Religion has a natural relationship with Parliament and politics, which, in turn, are interconnected with economics and society, and so on.

With regret, and in the cause of economy, we have had to put aside many of the sound and sensible proposals forwarded by teachers in response to the Longman Paul questionnaire. As a result, many will be dissatisfied on particular points. Nevertheless, we hope that the end-product is acceptable, not only to pupils and teachers in New Zealand, but anywhere that early modern history is taught in schools; and the more so because it is the work of two authors, not one. In many of the replies to the questionnaire, teachers expressed the opinion (often forcefully) that the author of such a work should be a schoolteacher; they felt that most 'ivory-tower' academics are out of touch with classroom requirements. Our response has been less a compromise than a merging of two streams of experience. One author is a schoolteacher, familiar with the hard realities of the 'frontline' situation, yet engaged in research and conversant with the most recent publications and the resources of English record offices. The other is a university lecturer, but hardly an 'armchair general'. He has been chief examiner of the University Entrance Scholarship examination for six of the last fourteen years, and an assistant Bursary examiner during the same period. He has travelled the country lecturing on topics within the examination prescription, and organised and participated in refresher courses for teachers. He was also a member of the committee which revised the Scholarship and Bursary history syllabus a few years ago. Together the authors can claim sound credentials and a rich diversity of experience.

Finally, we should add that we have endeavoured to avoid a scholarly work, in which pleasure is smothered by the academic weightiness of the text. History should be a serious study, but never a solemn one. After all, it is about people, and human beings have a talent for the impetuous and dramatic, the colourful and bizarre, the muddled, confused and downright silly. In this spirit, we considered it of prime importance to lace our thematic studies with examples of the thoughts and actions of Tudor and Stuart men (but rarely of women, which is a reflection of the 'chauvinistic' nature of a male-ordered society). If a number of these examples amuse as well as enlighten, all the better for that.

CHAPTER ONE

The social and economic structure, 1558–1700

The social structure and social mobility

There are several ways of identifying and describing social structure: for example, by wealth, occupational role, rank and status or, perhaps, by membership of a governed or governing class. All of these are applicable to some degree to Tudor and Stuart England. The fundamental divisions were of two kinds. One was the distinction between the governing and the governed. Not all members of the former actually held offices in local or central government at any given moment. In Elizabeth's reign, for example, the Crown disposed of about 2500 offices. Yet the governing class numbered at least 15–20 000 and probably many more. The qualification for inclusion in that class was not occupancy of office, but eligibility to serve—in other words, they possessed those qualities and characteristics which qualified them for office, if and when the Crown chose to employ them in its service.

In contrast the governed class had no recognised place in the State, except to serve and obey its superiors, and especially the monarch. Its political significance is confined to 'extra-legal' activities—riot and rebellion. It was also important because of the nervousness and even fear which it inspired in its governors. There is abundant evidence of this in the writings of gentlemen who variously described it as 'a ragged multitude of hinds and peasants, rude and merciless', 'the mad multitude' and an 'unruly sort of clowns'. Shakespeare condemned them as 'the many-headed multitude'. Early in the next century they were depicted as 'crabbed clowns', 'dunghill dogs' and 'peasants vile'. A Jacobean knight, Sir Thomas Browne, summed up the gentry's contempt for the governed when he scorned them in comprehensive terms as 'that great enemy of reason, virtue and religion, the multitude, that numerous piece of monstrosity which . . . confused together make but one great beast'. The governed class was to be treated with paternal care and charity, but only if it remained passive and obedient in its appointed place. (Quoted by C. Hill in Carter, 1965.)

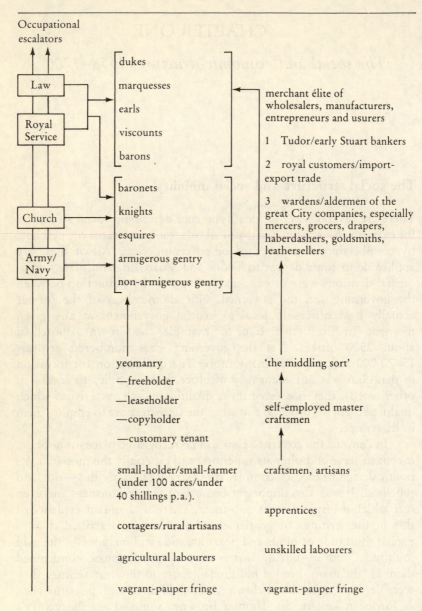

Occupational escalators

| Law |
| Royal Service |
| Church |
| Army/ Navy |

dukes
marquesses
earls
viscounts
barons

baronets
knights
esquires
armigerous gentry
non-armigerous gentry

merchant élite of wholesalers, manufacturers, entrepreneurs and usurers

1 Tudor/early Stuart bankers

2 royal customers/import-export trade

3 wardens/aldermen of the great City companies, especially mercers, grocers, drapers, haberdashers, goldsmiths, leathersellers

yeomanry
—freeholder
—leaseholder
—copyholder
—customary tenant

'the middling sort'

self-employed master craftsmen

small-holder/small-farmer (under 100 acres/under 40 shillings p.a.).

craftsmen, artisans

apprentices

cottagers/rural artisans

unskilled labourers

agricultural labourers

vagrant-pauper fringe

vagrant-pauper fringe

Social structure: a model

The other fundamental distinction was that between the gentle and the common (or mean and vulgar). The division was determined by the tests of gentle blood and pedigree, though as we shall see there were a number of ways of acquiring gentle status, and of doing so rapidly. The important point to remember is that, to a large extent, the dividing line between gentle and vulgar followed the boundary between governing and governed. In the following pages, most attention will be devoted to the upper sector of society, partly because relatively little is known about those whom they governed, and partly because the lower class had no constructive role to play in government.

The first task is to describe and analyse the governing class. Its largest, most powerful and status-conscious segment was the rural landed community. At the pinnacle of that segment was the *peerage*. It was numerically small: forty-nine in 1461, thirty-seven in 1485, forty-three in 1509, fifty-seven in 1558 and fifty-five in 1603. Thereafter the number rose. By 1641 the peerage had more than doubled to 121. In the 1690s it topped 160. Even then, peers were few on the ground compared to the 800 baronets and 16 000 gentry.

The peerage was organised in a graded hierarchy of five ranks: dukes, marquesses, earls, viscounts and barons. It is important to refer to these titleholders, collectively, as the peerage, although it is common to talk loosely about them as an *aristocracy* and as a *class*. Aristocracy is the historians' term for an élite. It should be used to describe peers only if the peerage (and the peerage alone) was the social and political élite. The term class should not be used at all in this context. The peerage was not a class, but a legal status group with hereditary titles, granted by the Crown, and certain legal privileges. These privileges, which marked the group off from the rest of the governing class, included the right to trial by their peers, freedom from arrest for debt and exemption from jury service. The vital privilege, the identifying mark of peerage status, was membership of the House of Lords. But in wealth, social practice, style of living, royal service and education, peers were indistinguishable from the greatest of the members of the social stratum beneath them, the gentry.

If the label of class is applied to the peerage, then peers ought to be coupled with gentlemen before that is done. The peerage and gentry comprised an homogeneous class, with similar social attitudes, practices and sources of wealth. They enjoyed the same kind of education; they acknowledged a similar obligation to dispense charity to the needy. In accordance with the will of the fourth Earl of Northumberland, 13 000 poor received a dole of twopence each at his funeral in 1489. A century later, in 1587, nearly 4000 of the lower classes were fed at the Earl of Rutland's funeral feast. On a smaller scale, many of the gentry performed in the same way. Members of this class also maintained 'open house' (hospitality) for their fellows. In 1561 the Earl of Derby, presiding over a household which was frequently inflated by the presence of guests, provided 672 sheep, sixty-six oxen and 49 000 gallons of beer at his table. Lower down the social scale, Sir William Holles, a Lincolnshire gentleman, kept open house over Christmas. His Christmas lasted from November until February! During that time any noble or gentleman could stay in his house for three days without being asked who he was or where he came from. Indeed his grandson, horrified by this lavish hospitality, complained that he had flushed the family fortunes down the privy. One obligation of hospitality no one could refuse was entertainment of the monarch— at considerable expense to the chosen hosts. When Elizabeth visited the Earl of Leicester in 1575, it cost him £6000.

The peerage and gentry constituted a class whose wealth was derived primarily, though not solely, from land. In other words, there was a common economic, as well as social, basis. It is true that the entire class was shot through with enmities, rivalries and all the other marks of an acquisitive, competitive society. For example, in Tudor and Stuart society, old families despised and resented the new. And always there were the conflicts of personality, parochial interests, status and power. Peers of ancient family and lineage worked to destroy new men who had risen to power and royal favour: they brought down Thomas Cromwell in 1540, and they tried the same (unsuccessfully) with William Cecil in 1570 and his son Robert in 1601. Lower down the social scale, there were county rivalries which were expressed in a number of ways: in contests for local offices, disputed parliamentary elections and even violent physical confrontations.

Despite this, there existed a powerful bonding class identity. All members of the class, no matter what rank they held, saw themselves in some sense as equal to others, because they were members of the same social group. When the gentility and pedigree of a mere gentleman, Richard Bertie, were impugned by the snobbish Henry FitzAlan, twelfth Earl of Arundel, he wrote to Burghley indignantly: 'My Lord of Arundel told the queen I was no gentleman. If I would, after the manner of the world, bring forth old abbey scrolls for matter of record, I am sure I can reach as far backward as FitzAlan'. Certainly contemporaries regarded peers and gentry as two tiers of essentially the same class. One, Dr Thomas Wilson, writing in 1600, described the peerage and bishops as *nobilitas major*, and the gentry, lawyers and lower clergy as 'the meaner nobility'. William Harrison, chaplain to an Elizabethan nobleman, described the peerage as 'gentlemen of the greater sort', and the gentry as 'they that are simply called gentlemen'.

Contemporary observers regarded the division between peers and gentry as one of degree. The former might be regarded as the uppermost step in a graded rural/gentle hierarchy. That hierarchy of ranks continued downwards through the gentry: knights (whose life-titles were created by the Crown), esquires (whose rank was awarded by royal heralds in the College of Arms) and armigerous gentry (that is, gentlemen with a shield of arms bestowed by the College, at a price. If the payment was handsome enough, the herald might be willing to trace back a man's gentle pedigree to the ancient British king, Brutus, or even to the survivors from ancient Troy—these were the contemporary ideals of respectable ancient pedigree). At the bottom was the plain gent. He had no shield of arms, but only an old gentle lineage as proof of his social respectability. There was no important modification of this hierarchical structure before 1700, except in 1611, when James I inserted between peers and gentlemen the new title of baronet, which was hereditary but not a rank of peerage.

The insignia of gentle blood, such as a title or shield of arms, and the possession of estates (landed property) were prerequisites of membership of the rural/landed governing class. However, the *amount* of wealth was also important, especially if those estates had been in the family's possession for generations. Burghley once described gentle status as 'nothing else but ancient riches'. On the other hand, the amount of wealth did not always correspond with rank. Peers were not necessarily wealthier than knights, knights than esquires, and so on. Any assumption that wealth followed rank requires modification in four particulars:

1 Many gentlemen were wealthier than the lower ranks of the peerage.

In 1600 Dr Thomas Wilson estimated that the average net income of 500 knights was equal to, or more than that of half the peerage. This agrees with Lawrence Stone's conclusions (see Bibliography). Some gentlemen were exceptionally wealthy. Robert Spencer, for example, had an annual income of £6500–£8000 in James I's reign. He was reputed, albeit incorrectly, to be the wealthiest person in the kingdom, but only two or three peers were wealthier. His social rise amply illustrates the importance of money in social mobility. Robert began as a prosperous yeoman (see page 14). His wealth led to a knighthood. In 1595 he paid the College of Arms to invent a pedigree establishing his descent from the great medieval house of Despenser, earls of Gloucester and Winchester. And in 1603 he was created a baron. His family origins—humble graziers in the fourteenth century—were concealed beneath the new shield of arms. But peers of ancient stock still scorned 'parvenu' (upstart) nobles ('gentlemen of the first head' they called them). In 1621 the Earl of Arundel reminded Baron Spencer in the House of Lords that, while his own ancestors were serving king and country, and suffering in the process, Spencer's were tending sheep. The important point to keep in mind here is that income did not necessarily distinguish peers from gentlemen, or individual ranks of peerage and gentry. The enormous range of income in the class is a matter of individual differences rather than of variations between ranks. Above all, money talked, as it has always done—it certainly enabled Spencer to buy his way rapidly up the social ladder.

2 The same is true at the lower end of the scale, in that blurred borderland between gentry and the highest non-gentle class, the yeomanry. Thomas Wilson pointed out that gentry incomes could fall as low as £300–400, while 'many yeoman in divers provinces in England are able yearly to spend betwixt £300 and £500 yearly by their lands and leases, and some twice and some thrice as much'.

3 In practice, primogeniture (by which title and property descended to the eldest child) was generally adopted in order to preserve estates intact. This meant that only the eldest son benefited substantially by inheritance. Younger sons might receive a pension or, more frequently, their education, apprenticeship in trade or training in law would be financed before they were left to fend for themselves. The younger sons of gentry families were landless, and they departed from rural society into the towns to study law or practise trade—what is termed horizontal mobility.

4 Wealth is relative. It is a point which Thomas Wilson was perceptive enough to grasp, but which H.R. Trevor-Roper missed. In 1953 he identified the cause of the English Civil War as a division between two groups of gentry. One consisted of those who could supplement their landed income from other sources (such as the Court, law and trade). Against them stood the 'mere' gentry whose income was confined to land and who, in an inflationary age, could not cope financially and so went into decline. In desperation they engineered the Civil War, which was an attempt by these 'mere' gentry to recoup their fortunes. Trevor-Roper points to small (which we are supposed to read as declining) incomes. However, there are two flaws in his argument. The mere gentry were thickest on the ground in the north and west, precisely those areas where support for the King was greatest. Furthermore, income must be related to environment, in particular to the cost structure, for example, of different counties. Let Thomas Wilson make the point: 'Especially about London and the counties adjoining, where lands are set to the highest [rent], he is not

counted of any great reckoning unless he be betwixt 1000 marks or £1000, but northward and far off a gentleman of good reputation may be content with £300 and £400 yearly'.

The rural landed class was therefore measured by its status and wealth—and, it should be repeated, chiefly, though not solely, landed wealth. Peers and gentlemen did supplement their revenues from mining, trade, Court office and law. But they performed no manual functions, unless fighting be accounted as such, for the third test of gentility, no less significant than wealth and the insignia of rank, was the style of living and the amount spent on it. Sir Thomas Smith, Elizabeth's Secretary of State, emphasised this qualification as the ultimate test of gentility: 'Whosoever studies the laws of the realm, who professes liberal sciences, who studies at the universities and to be short who can live idly and without manual labour, and will bear the port, charge and countenance of a gentleman, he shall be called master' (that is, gentleman).

The gentleman, and especially the great peer, was judged not by his savings or income but by his expenditure. The thrifty saver was a mortal of inferior mould. Only 'conspicuous consumption' marked a person off as a man of breeding: lavish expenditure on food, clothes, hospitality, houses, servants, funerals and tombs. For many there were also heavy Court expenses, because attendance there was necessary to secure offices and royal favours. One peer, Dudley Lord North, had an unusual explanation for his financially disastrous plunge into the pleasures and intrigues of Court life. It was an attempt, he said, to banish melancholy, brought on by an excessive consumption of treacle in early youth. 'Conspicuous consumption' was essential for the maintenance of status and prestige, even though it sometimes resulted in a slippery financial decline, even disaster if, in the words of Sir Thomas Smith, a gentleman 'perchance will bear a bigger sail than he is able to maintain'.

The rural landed class was not only the largest and the politically/socially predominant section of the governing class. It was also the focal point of society: the point at which most streams of social movement began or ended, and certainly to which all members of society aspired. There was movement in and out of the peerage and gentry on both an horizontal and vertical plane. Successful lawyers, especially the judges, and the rich merchants who governed the cities and towns, were, to a large extent, horizontal extensions of the landed governing class. The legal profession recruited many of its members from the younger sons of peers and gentlemen. To a lesser extent, this is also true of the urban communities. London and the other large cities were distinguished from those on the Continent because they rarely produced long-lived merchant dynasties—at the most two, three or four generations. The origins of English urban merchant families were frequently rural and gentle, and their aspirations were the same. When they were successful in business, they bought back into the countryside from which they or their forbears had come. John Isham's family, for example, had owned estates near Lamport in Northamptonshire since the twelfth century. John was a younger son, the fourth. In 1542 he was apprenticed to a London mercer (a dealer in fabrics) with £10 stock. By 1560 he was wealthy enough to buy Lamport, to which he moved in 1572. His son Thomas wrote that he 'would nott by any meanes be drawen agayn to dwell at London'. By 1582 he had held two royal offices in the county—a true gentleman. Isham's career illustrates an important social characteristic of the period: that there was no clear division between urban and rural communities. Peers and gentry did not scorn trade, industry or commerce. Instead they often engaged in it. And they sometimes married merchant heiresses, though not always with successful consequences. When extravagance threatened financial disaster to one Lincolnshire gentleman, he resolved to marry an ageing but rich widow, Catherine Needham. His descendant, Gervase Holles, told the story: '"Body of our Lord", quoth he, "I will go marry this old widow and pay my debts. Then, when I have buried her, I will marry a young wench and get children". This it seems was his design, but she deceived him, for she held him tug above thirty-eight years, and lived near twelve years after him'.

Of course social mobility was not only horizontal but also vertical. Indeed the latter movement was often dramatically swift. On the one hand, there was a regular fall-out through the extinction of male lines (a consequence of natural causes or execution), declining wealth or bankruptcy. On the other hand, there were what Lawrence Stone calls the 'occupational escalators'. These were the channels for recruitment to the governing class and for promotion within it. The four most important were the Church, the law, royal service and the army and navy. The Reformation, however, reduced the significance of the first of these. The clergy declined in status, and the prospects of power and wealth greatly diminished. The busiest escalators were the law and royal service, which often merged together. The Tudor State was seeking men of competence and expertise to cope with its expanding functions. The men equipped with the right educational qualifications—rhetoric (the art of public speaking), the classics, a modern language or two, and especially law—were ideal recruits. The sum total of all these movements, not only of men of ambition scrambling up the ladders of royal service, was considerable mobility in the governing class. However, there was no rise or fall of entire classes, as was once argued in the rise of the gentry' debate (Stone, 1965; note that, here and elsewhere, a shortened reference to author and date of publication will be used for works more fully described in the Bibliography, pages 491–502). Social movement, upwards, downwards or sideways was always an individual not a class experience.

In contrast to the relatively well-documented fates and fortunes of members of the governing class, their inferiors—the governed class—are much more difficult to identify and describe. For the most part one can do little more than single out their major occupational roles. It is pointless to apply the test of rank, because there were no visible insignia (marks of rank) among the governed. Status followed income and the prestige which particular occupations enjoyed (or lacked). It was also influenced by the degree of economic independence: the man who was self-employed or possessed property (whether shop, warehouse or smallholding). Nevertheless, it is possible to sketch broadly the structure of the urban and rural governed class. Beneath the merchant oligarchs (governors) of the cities and towns was a middle tier of manufacturers, wholesalers and entrepreneurs (middle men); below them, in descending order, were the retailers, craftsmen and artisans, unskilled labourers, and a vagrant/pauper fringe. The rural hierarchy proceeded downwards from the yeomanry, through small farmers, cottagers, artisans and labourers, many of whom combined domestic industry and smallhold farming with agrarian services to others.

The yeoman was by far the most important figure in the governed class, yet he remains an enigma. How to identify him? He was sometimes rich, but often of only moderate means, and even poor. He could be a freeholder, a leaseholder, a customary tenant, a copyholder, or a combination of these. He was a landlord; he was a tenant. He raised sheep, engaged in arable farming or mixed the two. In the 1580s Lord Cobham's chaplain described them as 'free men born English and may dispend of their own free land in yearly revenue to the sum of 40 shillings'. This may describe a lower limit, but it establishes no distinctive social or economic characteristics by which we can identify them. Mildred Campbell has devoted an entire volume to this problem without resolving it (M. Campbell, *The English Yeoman under Elizabeth and the Early Stuarts*, New Haven, 1942). Certainly contemporaries recognised the yeomanry with pride. To Thomas Wilson they were 'the glory of the country', while Harrison (Cobham's chaplain) extolled them as those 'that in times past made all France afraid'. All very patriotic, but not much help to us. Nevertheless, Harrison does hit upon that most common and distinguishing characteristic of the yeoman. Most of them were not landlords but farmers, often working land which they had leased from their social superiors. They lived thriftily, without the expensive social obligations of the gentle. They put their own hands to the plough. And, as Harrison tells us, they kept servants which were 'not idle servants, as the gentlemen do, but such as get both their own and part of their master's living'.

Many yeomen prospered. They, even more than the merchant élite, provided a recruiting ground for the gentry. This was so because many of them aspired to gentle status, and the line between gentry and yeomanry was a blurred one. Remember that gentle status was determined by wealth and style of living as well as by emblems of rank. Some yeomen were as wealthy, and even wealthier, than many lesser gentry. All that an aspiring, prosperous yeoman had to do was to transform his life-style: to educate himself or his sons, to adopt the gentleman's code of conduct, and perhaps to remodel and extend his cosy domestic house so that he could live the more public hospitable life of the gentry. Then an amenable herald, greedy for cash, might invent a pedigree and grant him a shield of arms—at a price. Thus the yeoman chrysalis emerges as the gentleman-butterfly!

This process occurred with sufficient frequency to evoke comment from contemporaries. Harrison observed that many yeomen 'are able and do buy the lands of unthrifty gentlemen'. They 'set their sons to the schools, to the universities, and to the Inns of Court, or, otherwise, leaving them sufficient lands whereupon they may live without labour, do make them by these means to become gentlemen'. Thomas Wilson was waspish about the matter, but he too reveals just how easily the change could be effected, if the money was there. The sons of yeomen 'not contented with the status of their fathers, to be counted yeomen, but must skip into his velvet breeches and silken doublet and, getting to be admitted into some Inn of Court, must ever after think scorn to be called any other than gentleman'.

It becomes clear, and not from the case of the yeomen alone, that there was a good deal of social mobility in early modern England. Society was neither caste-like nor rigid. If the degree of mobility was insignificant compared to the modern open society, it appears to have been much greater than in previous centuries. Yet, apart from the revolutionary decades of the mid-seventeenth century, this mobility neither undermined nor overthrew the existing social structure. In the previous pages a model of that structure has been established (see also page 2 for the model in diagrammatic form). It is not a neat and tidy model with classes moving up, down, or sideways in drilled battalions at the historian's command. It is a scrappy, untidy model, messy in the middle and frayed at the edges. The model has been based on individual and county case studies of family fortunes between 1558 and 1640. This has been made possible, partly by the chance survival of evidence but, more importantly, because historians have ransacked the records in order to explain the causes of the English Civil War. As a result there exists a very detailed picture of society between Mary I's death and the meeting of the Long Parliament. This obsession with the roots of the mid-seventeenth century upheaval, however, has done much more harm than good. In particular, it spawned the 'rise of the gentry' controversy, which died long ago, deserved only a decent burial and should not be disinterred. The chief antagonists were R.H. Tawney, L. Stone, H.R. Trevor-Roper and J.H. Hexter, although many others were drawn in. Their heated debate at least drew attention to the fact that, between 1558 and 1640, social mobility accelerated (partly because of inflation) and generated new tensions. It also placed a healthy emphasis on the relationship between social and economic change and politics. But the arguments were couched in terms of the rise and fall of classes, while the evidence was misused, misunderstood, or statistically assembled in a primitive and, at times, misleading manner.

Perhaps the most serious result was to over-simplify the processes of economic and social change. Elizabeth and the early Stuarts did not rule over a declining peerage, a desperate mere gentry or a rising gentry and yeomanry. Social mobility was a personal not a class experience. Each person responded to the current economic threats and opportunities of inflation in an individual way. As a general rule producers benefited from rising prices, while landlords (on fixed rents), wage-earners (whose income lagged behind rising prices) and consumers (especially the Crown) lost. Nevertheless, the fate of each peer, gentleman and merchant depended on a combination of circumstances peculiar only to him: the nature of his property (whether it was fertile and consolidated, or infertile and scattered), chance (bad harvests), inadequate fertility (no heirs), excessive fertility (an embarrassing number of children to provide for), estates encumbered with debts, thrift or extravagance—and so on. This is not an attempt to atomise history, to suggest that we can only study individual, not collective, experience; personal fortunes but not general trends. Indeed, there were such trends: in particular, inflation and accelerated mobility. However, they have nothing to do with the rise and fall of classes. The Marxist concern with class tensions and conflicts must be jettisoned, and attention switched to more meaningful and relevant economic developments: the hyperactive land market (stimulated by the sale of Crown and Church property), population growth (which increased the demand for goods), the European political situation (which often closed markets to English goods) and commercial farming practices (such as enclosures, rack-renting and evictions, all of which were responses to inflation and current market conditions).

We are faced with two extremes of interpretation: one is individualistic, the other is concerned with classes. As so often occurs, the most realistic approach lies somewhere in between. Consider, for example, one small manageable sample, the peerage. Every noble's experience differed from that of his fellows. And yet, through all the confusion of this diversity we can detect three broadly based movements. The wasters and spendthrifts declined: among them the seventeenth Earl of Oxford, spending his way through one of the richest inheritances in England. Henry, Lord Berkeley was almost as spectacular. As his steward lamented, he 'overran his purse' by 'cards, dice, tennis, bowling alley and hawking and hunting'. In his lifetime he sold lands worth £41 000, and made but one purchase—Canonbury manor for £5.11s.8d. Yet was he a declining peer? As a result of the industry of his steward, John Smyth, his remaining estates were still supporting him in the style to which he was accustomed, even at the very end of his life. On the other hand, Lord Vaux, who unlike Berkeley was not addicted to the 'good life', was in serious financial difficulties. In 1593 he could not even attend the opening of Parliament, because he could not afford to get his Parliament robes out of pawn. However, he was a recusant, crippled with the financial burdens of a devout Catholic.

The second form of mobility within the peerage was one of economic rise. The classic case is Henry, ninth Earl of Northumberland, who amply illustrates the uniqueness of each noble's experience. When he succeeded to his title, 'I was so well left for moveables [chattels such as furniture], as I was not worth a fire shovel or a pair of tongs: what was left me was wainscotts or things rivetted with nails, for wives commonly are great scratchers after their husbands' deaths, if things be loose'. However, worse was to come. His mother's looting was followed by his own extravagance: 'Then were my felicities, because I knew no better, hawks, hounds, horses, dice, cards, apparel, and all other riot of expense that follow them, were so far afoot and in excess, as I know not where I was, or what I did, till, out of my means of £3000 yearly, I had made shift in one year and an half to be £15 000 in debt'. Thereafter he made amends and efficiently administered his estates. On one occasion he wrote to a trusted servant about some of his properties, saying, 'I must know the uttermost value of them, because I will know what I do'. He conducted a continuous, personal supervision of his assets. Late in his life he wrote a revealing code of instructions for his son to observe when he inherited the family property: 'that you understand your estate better than any of your officers; [and] that you never suffer your wife to have power in the manage of your affairs [because some are] scratching kinds who have predominant power over the male'. He admonished his son to watch his servants, because 'all men love their own eases and themselves best'. Northumberland even advised him on the choice of a wife: that she 'should neither be ugly in body nor mind; that she should bring with her meat in her mouth to maintain her expense; and that her friends should be of that eminency, that they might appear to be steps for you to better your fortune'. By 1627–8, the Earl's care and efficiency had increased his income from £3000 to £16 000. Thus far he may seem to be just one of a common type: the conscientous, hardworking peer. But appearances are deceptive. Northumberland was imprisoned for many years for his supposed complicity in the Gunpowder Plot. He managed his estates from the Tower of London, and the fact that he lavished such attention on them was a simple consequence of his imprisonment—what else was there for a prisoner to do? Moreover, his confinement prevented the Earl from laying out large sums of money on forms of 'conspicuous consumption'. An apparently typical example of the 'rising' peers suddenly becomes unique. In any case it is probable that, with a few exceptions such as Northumberland, Oxford, Berkeley and Vaux, most members of the governing class (and not just the nobles) belong to the third stream of social mobility. In fact the term 'mobility' is a misnomer here, because this group did not move up or down. It remained in a static condition, in which income kept pace with rising prices, no more and no less.

Most of the fundamental characteristics of Elizabethan and early Stuart society endured until 1700 and beyond. It only remains to chart the changes which occurred in the last sixty years of the seventeenth century—changes which affected and modified, but did not destroy, the social fabric of Elizabethan and early Stuart England. Indeed, in some respects they simply reinforced those characteristics which had existed before the revolutionary years of the mid-century.

This political upheaval left its scars on the social structure. In the previous forty years there had been an escalation of social tensions as some of the new men rose and a number of the ancient families decayed. But it was not as simple as that. Elizabethan peers and great gentlemen, who were landlords rather than farmers, were caught between the millstones of inflation and increased expenditure. Some of them recovered under the early Stuarts, especially if they were favoured courtiers. Jacobean and Caroline generosity also resulted in the dramatic expansion of the peerage and the rank of knight, while James I reinforced the upper tiers of society with the new rank of baronet. This process injected both new tensions and new wealth into the élite. The dynamics of this change were a mixture of the political (royal patronage and the advancement of suitors by favourites), the social (the right qualifications or contacts) and the economic (the wealth to back one's aspirations and especially to buy titles and other honours). The novelty and magnitude of this process must not be exaggerated. There were always new men rising and old families decaying. When rich Jacobean merchants, such as William Cokayne, William Courteen and Baptist Hickes, seized estates for non-payment of debts, they were simply the latest examples of an old process of change. Moreover, it was a process which only affected a small proportion of the governing class, even if the scale and speed had increased by the early seventeenth century. The novelty lay not in the transformation of merchants and others into landowners, but in the fact that they could then use Court connections and money to acquire peerages, knighthoods and shields of arms. So Baptist Hickes, the moneylender, became a viscount and Robert Spencer, a wealthy sheep farmer from a family of yeoman stock, acquired a barony.

In the 1640s and 1650s, politics obtruded themselves in a new and dramatic way into the process of socio-economic change. Not only merchants, but also military commanders, some of whom were of humble origins, joined the ranks of the landed gentry. The estates of many royalist peers and gentlemen were confiscated or sold to pay heavy fines or taxes. The bishops were dispossessed when the Anglican Church was abolished. The pro-Court merchant élite in London and elsewhere were displaced in favour of men wedded to the parliamentary cause. Once again, the extent to which this happened should not be exaggerated. The effects were political rather than economic. In other words, the traditional governing class lost its political authority rather than its estates during the Interregnum. Even those royalist-Anglican landowners who were the victims of sequestration (seizure of property), heavy taxation, or the necessity to sell were not in every case permanently ruined. The peers were particularly successful in holding on to their estates and the majority of them managed to ride the economic shocks of the forties and fifties.

In any event, the Restoration was the salvation of many. Charles II, acting on the advice of Edward Hyde, left Parliament with the unenviable task of devising a land settlement. It proved to be, in large measure, an economic restoration of the old order. All royal and ecclesiastical lands were returned to Crown and Church. Sequestered estates went back to their original owners. Admittedly there were uncompensated victims—those who had sold their lands in order to meet the fines and taxes levied by the revolutionary regimes. However, after the Restoration the more fortunate were assisted and compensated with royal grants. Many of the newcomers to the old landed governing class, including those who had bought confiscated property in good faith and some of the Cromwellian army officers, rapidly disappeared. The governing class of the 1660s was not dramatically different from that which had administered the counties before 1640. The surviving newcomers simply represented a process of mobility which had been going on for a long time.

There were, however, significant shifts in emphasis within the socio-economic structure. Peers and gentry might lord it over their estates again. Bishops might administer their properties from their episcopal palaces once more, but the merchant community of London rapidly increased in importance in the later seventeenth century. That importance derived from two developments:

1 Its role in world-wide trading activities. By 1700 its shipping tonnage was more than eight times as great as Bristol, the second largest commercial centre in England (Wilson, 1971, page 162).

2 It became a more lucrative source of revenue to the Crown than the landed classes were. Other urban communities were thriving— Bristol with its involvement in the transatlantic trade and the African slave traffic, Newcastle's coal trade, developing industry in Liverpool and other cities—but only London with its commercial pre-eminence and unrivalled wealth could fund the loans required by the wartime government of William III.

Nevertheless, numerically and socially, England remained a rural society. The peers and gentry still dominated government, Parliament, and the counties. Their political pre-eminence may exaggerate and distort their economic importance, but the two are not entirely unrelated. Economic circumstances in the later seventeenth century favoured the greater landowners, peers and gentlemen alike: a spirit of commercial landlordism (a concern to maximise profits from one's estates), the end of feudal dues (which were not restored in 1660), advantageous market conditions and now agricultural techniques. Using estates as a security, great landowners borrowed in order to carry out improvements. Debt was not necessarily a sign of insolvency, any more than hire purchase is today. Frequently, it was a consequence of the growing practice of entail, which converted property into a perpetual family possession, and so prevented the current head of the family from selling or giving it away. Landowners with entailed estates could not dispose of them to resolve temporary financial difficulties. The only short-term alternative was to borrow and, as a credit economy developed, it became more acceptable to do so. The men with large estates were in the best position to do so. With their big rent rolls they could also absorb the additional burdens of the new land tax and the high poor rates of the 1690s. The conservative gentlemen with small estates, however, did not enjoy such advantages and they tended to be the victims rather than the beneficiaries of late seventeenth century conditions. The movement was not all downwards: some of the lesser gentry and leaseholding yeomen prospered; many more remained static, but there was a detectable movement of decline. However, this must be put in its right perspective and seen in the context of the general economic recovery of the post-Restoration governing class.

The political conditions of the Restoration also played their part. It was a socially conservative climate: a natural response to the radicalism of the 1640s and 1650s. The Cavalier Parliament legislated to prevent the physical movement of the governed class around the countryside. The élite which it represented also reacted against the educational 'expansiveness' of the previous century. By the 1650s, the ratio of schools to population was probably more impressive than at any time before the late nineteenth century. However, it was felt that education had given social 'inferiors' unhealthy and dangerous ideas above their station. Moreover, the biblical Protestantism of the Puritans had demanded at least a basic literacy, an ability to read the Scriptures. On both counts the governing class chose to restrict educational opportunities. At the same time the landed élite had secured political autonomy and freedom from royal interference in the counties. Thus the 1660s marked the dawning of an oligarchic golden age, politically and socially, as well as the economic resurgence of the old landed governing class.

The size of the community

Modern government needs information about the community if it is to govern effectively: the size of the population and its concentrations, the volume of trade and industrial output, the incidence and identification of common diseases, the number of working days lost through sickness, the number of families homeless, unemployed or in the care of social welfare agencies, the crime rate, and so on. Without such data, a government cannot decide its priorities and allocate its manpower and money to the most pressing problems of the day. Statistics have become a sophisticated tool enabling the State to fulfil its responsibilities more effectively, and to understand, and therefore tackle, social and economic problems. The national census is the classic example of such statistical information. It provides data not only on the size and distribution of population, but also about everything from religion to the number of houses without baths or indoor lavatories. However, it is only the most dramatic of the many streams of information which are fed into the various agencies of government. One of the simple end-products of this constant process is the information with which the public is bombarded by the news media: unemployment figures, inflation rates, productivity levels, incomes and crime statistics.

In early modern England such considerations were neglected through ignorance, or dealt with in an unsystematic, piecemeal, uncomprehending manner. Governments operated on the basis of rumour, hearsay, opinion and some observation, but not from data which had been systematically assembled and analysed. What is now known as 'political economy' did not exist in the sixteenth century. However, in the period 1558–1700 there was a silent revolution which laid the groundwork for modern political economy. A revival of interest in mathematics in the sixteenth century was followed, in the next hundred years, by its application to social and economic needs. Among the advocates and pioneers of what became known as 'political arithmetic' were William Petty and Gregory King. These men were representative of the ferment in ideas about government, administration and management of economy and society in the later seventeenth century. Petty, King and others had one common conviction: that government had to be informed about social and economic conditions, that these conditions could be measured in a quantitative way, and that the State should act on the basis of that information. So in 1667 Petty tried to persuade the government to lighten the tax burden on property owners by amassing statistical data on national income and the sources from which it derived. In William III's reign, King, like Petty a civil servant, had the same objective too: to assess the taxable capacity of the kingdom and decide which sectors of society could be most effectively tapped for revenue in support of William's wars. He supported his arguments with his own measured estimates of population in England and Wales in 1695. Not only was this the ancestor of the first official census in 1801, it also stands as a reasonably accurate measure of the number of the King's subjects. Beginning with the high-status groups (6400 in the peerage families) down through baronets, knights and esquires (50 600) to socio-economic groups such as merchants and traders (64 000), artisans (240 000) and 'labouring people' (over 1¼ million), altogether it added up to a population of five and a half millions.

If this was the size of the community in the closing years of the seventeenth century, how does it compare with England almost a century and a half before, when Elizabeth became queen? The question cannot be answered with confidence, since there were no Pettys or Kings. Political arithmetic was unknown. We can only lean on historians who, in turn, have made inspired guesses or used their imaginations. Nevertheless, there seems to be a general consensus of opinion that some two and a half million souls dwelt in Henry VII's kingdom in 1500. A hundred years later, it had increased to more than four million, although some estimates put it a million higher. One thing is certain: there was a sharp upward turn in the population graph, and numbers may have more than doubled between 1500 and 1700.

The distribution of population followed an ancient pattern. The greatest density and concentration was in London, and the bulk of the population lived in the southern counties, below a line drawn very roughly between Bristol and the Wash. Within that region there was no even distribution: it ranged from large agricultural populations, in Suffolk and Somerset, to the thinly populated Devon. As usual, the lowest densities were recorded in the north, Wales and the west. The Industrial Revolution in the eighteenth century would destroy this pattern, shifting the main concentrations of people to the north-east, Lancashire, the Black Country of the Midlands and the valley collieries of south Wales.

Both before and during that change, however, there was one constant: the growth of London. A town of 50 000 in 1500 had multiplied five-fold by James I's reign. By then it housed more than five per cent of the kingdom's population. Elizabethan and Jacobean governments were increasingly concerned by the phenomenon. Most Tudor cities were dense urban communities jammed into a very small area. The City of London occupied a single square mile, flanked by the Thames on the south and surrounded by a wall and moat on the landward side. As the population grew, however, it spilled over the walls into the extra-mural 'liberties' (suburbs outside the City proper but which were still subject to its government). In James I's reign over two-thirds of London's inhabitants dwelt in the liberties. Within or without the walls, they jostled out their lives in congestion, narrow streets, perpetual traffic jams of horse-drawn vehicles and the stench of accumulated rubbish, such as the offal thrown out by the butchers in St Paul's 'shambles' (the meat market). There was a constant and growing fear of disease (confirmed by the plague epidemics in 1603, 1625, 1636 and 1665), and of crime, fire and public disorder.

The growth of London seemed inevitable and irresistible. It stood at the centre of the economy, demanding ever more food, raw materials, manufactured and luxury goods; stimulating agriculture and industry by its ever-growing hunger, and acting as a magnet to the unemployed, the hungry and the ambitious. Growth was a conse-quence of both native reproduction and migration. Whatever the cause, it was a matter of concern to the government. James I fined the city heavily for ignoring the planning regulations, erecting unauthor-ised buildings and exceeding the limits laid down by royal decree. The Stuarts were no more successful than King Canute in stemming the tide. London's overspill had already engulfed Fleet Street, Holborn, Smithfield, Whitechapel and the other liberties. South of the river, Southwark became an industrial suburb of tanneries, soapworks and other noisome industries which might have fouled the London air. Not that it made much difference. As the century wore on, the air of the capital became smog-ridden from domestic hearths fired by sea coals, brought down the coast from Newcastle.

So London continued to grow, sucking in migrants, not only from the countryside, but also from abroad. In Elizabeth's reign, Dutch refugees settled in the City; the Scots came south under the early Stuarts, and in the late seventeenth century French Huguenots (Protestants) developed Spitalfields, to the north-east of the City, as an important silk-weaving centre. Throughout the period, London also expanded westwards from the commercial capital of the City to the political capital of Westminster. Nobles and gentry wanted to live near the Court, and property owners, such as the Earls of Bedford and Salisbury, saw the chance of a handsome profit. So did speculative builders such as Sir George Downing. There were, in fact, many reasons why London continued to sprawl. But grow it did, and by 1700 it housed ten per cent of the population.

London was unique. When its population was approaching a quarter of a million, near the end of Elizabeth's reign, the next cities of the kingdom—York, Norwich and Bristol—could boast of only fifteen or twenty thousand each. They were followed closely by Exeter. Exeter was the provincial capital and economic centre of the far west, diocesan seat of the bishop of Exeter, headquarters of the Lord Lieutenant and a flourishing port. In the mid-sixteenth century it had raised the revenue to dig a new river channel, and so overcome the threat to its trade from encroaching marshlands. Like London it was expanding and new suburbs were growing up outside the walls. Yet as late as 1600 one-third of the land within the walls was occupied by open gardens, church buildings and the property of the city's patron, the Earl of Bedford. It took little more than an hour to walk around the walls, and the inhabitants of Exeter numbered only 12 000.

As for the rest of the country there was, for a variety of reasons, extensive urban decay: silting harbours in the Cinque Ports; Yarmouth, adversely affected by rival fishing interests and derelict quays; the Cotswolds cloth towns suffering from trade restrictions and a change in fashion; and Southampton, whose economy was being undermined by London merchants, who feared a rival. London apart, England remained a rural community in which the majority were engaged in agriculture. In Gregory King's table of 1695, merchants, shopkeepers, traders and artisans, together with their families, totalled 484 000. In contrast, the landed peerage and gentry, freeholders, farmers, labourers and cottagers were well above three million in number. By 1700 trade was producing far more revenue per head than farming, but many more families lived on the land and many more men tilled the soil, supervised their toil, or collected farm rents.

Agriculture and agrarian problems

There is no doubt that agriculture was the foundation of life in early modern England. Not only was it the provider of food, but it was the source of nearly half the national income, the main area of employment and the source of most industrial raw materials. No one could escape the influence of agriculture in this profoundly agrarian society. The landowners were at the head of society and they were the greatest capitalists. Politically, they dominated both national and local government. Only in London and the largest towns were owners of other forms of wealth free from their overlordship. The state of the harvest was the most important single influence on the annual level of economic activity. It is doubtful if any major change in the economy or in society was possible without a major restructuring of agriculture (Clarkson, 1971, page 45).

Sixteenth and seventeenth century England can be compared with modern underdeveloped or pre-industrial societies. Its study can be an important part of understanding the forces which bring about economic change and lead to agricultural and industrial revolution. Perhaps paradoxically, an examination of England in the early modern period can be highly relevant to planners in pre-industrial societies today.

One of the fundamental questions one must ask about sixteenth and seventeenth century England is why it diverged from the rest of the world and led the way towards improvements and industrialisation which made it possible to support a vastly greater population at a standard of living superior to that of the past. Another is to identify when this divergence began. The traditional view is that the acceleration of economic development took place in the eighteenth century after many centuries in which there had been little change. Alternative opinions put forward for industry by J.U. Nef in the 1930s, and for agriculture by E. Kerridge in the 1950s and 60s, place the revolutionary divergence much earlier, in the late sixteenth and early seventeenth centuries. Whether these hypotheses are correct or not they have served a useful purpose in providing a starting point for most modern research into the economic history of the period.

Highland and lowland Britain

Agricultural practices in the sixteenth and seventeenth centuries displayed great diversity, and they were subject to considerable change. Soils, climate, drainage, aspect and other natural phenomena interacted with cultural traditions and market forces. Farming methods formed part of a total life-style which included settlement patterns, systems of landholding, class relationships, inheritance and even marriage customs among the peasantry.

The most fundamental division in agriculture and society was between highland and lowland Britain, two regions divided by a line running from Weymouth in the south-west to the mouth of the river Tees in the north-east. Pockets of lowland to the north-west of this line and hilly areas to the south-east had an agriculture and society more like that of the larger physiographic region they resembled than that of the nearer land with a different topography.

Lowland England consisted of the so-called 'champagne' country: flat land or gently undulating hill country. Farming concentrated on grain growing in an open-field system interspersed with nucleated villages, in which all aspects of life were under tight manorial control. Highland Britain, in contrast, was a land of stock rearing, dispersed settlement, enclosure, weak manorial structure and a high incidence of part-time industrial employment, especially in the wooded areas.

The classic manor of the lowlands in the sixteenth and seventeenth centuries consisted of at least three types of land: arable; pasture and meadow, sometimes with forests; heath and waste. The arable land was typically divided into three large fields, although there might be two or four. Each peasant had possession of at least one strip of land in each field. A strip was the amount of land an ox team could plough in a day. As an ox team was slow to turn, strips were long and narrow. The term 'furlong', representing a distance of 220 yards (approximately 200 metres), was originally 'furrow long', the length of an average strip of land in an open field. Each strip was divided from the others by marker stones, elevated grass strips known as baulks or, in low-lying areas, by ditches.

In the fertile areas of south-eastern England, the most common rotation in the three-field system was wheat, barley, then fallow. Fallow land was cultivated and kept weeded, but no crop was grown, thus allowing natural fertility to build up before planting wheat, a crop which makes high demands on the soil. There were many variations. Rye, oats, beans, peas, buckwheat, vetches, tares and lentils were sown, both to provide variety in the diet and because of physical conditions. Where soils were poor or wet, wheat could not be grown. Barley was the main breadcorn in many parts of England. Rye replaced barley in areas of sour soils, and oats became the main crop in the coldest and wettest areas. Especially near cities, specialist crops were grown to meet local demand—fruit, vegetables, and linen flax, for example; or potentially arable land was used for dairying or fattening animals for the butcher.

It was essential for open-field grain farmers to rear animals as well, and all holders of arable land had the right to run animals on the common pasture. The wealthier farmers who had their own plough needed to keep oxen or horses, and many peasants had at least one cow to produce their own milk, butter and cheese. By far the most numerous animals in the lowlands were sheep. Though they were important for their wool and their meat, it is arguable that their most important product was manure. Sheep were guarded by shepherds as they grazed the common land by day and enclosed in folds placed in a different piece of arable land each night. By the sixteenth century, most lowland manors had placed restrictions or 'stints' on the number of animals which tenants could run on the common. Farmers in the cool temperate zone usually had a surplus of fodder in the summer and a shortage in winter, something they tried to combat by making hay or growing special crops for winter feed. Hay was cut from the meadowland, the rich moist soil found near streams. When sold or rented separately, meadowland usually brought a higher price than arable.

Peasant farmers had other prerogatives which could be important to their standard of living. On many manors they had pannage rights: that is, permission to run pigs in the woodland, where they would live on the acorns or beech mast. The traditional obligation to repair their houses and outbuildings was matched by the custom of woodbote, which allowed them to cut the necessary timber in the woodland. Tenants usually had firebote (the right to break off deadwood 'by hook or by crook' and use it in their fires). By the late sixteenth century, the localised shortages of timber made such forest rights a frequent cause of litigation.

People in lowland Britain usually lived in nucleated villages: that is, central settlements from which they moved out daily to work their land. There was usually a resident lord of the manor and tight manorial control was exercised. A manor, it should be emphasised, was not just a piece of land (the site of the manor), but also a bundle of rights and privileges. In the Middle Ages, lords of manors had possessed important judicial powers which often included the right to impose the death sentence. By the sixteenth century, such powers had been assumed by the King's courts. However, many fees were still payable to the lord, and some received unclaimed lost goods and the property of convicted felons and suicides.

The manorial courts played a significant role in the life of the community. There were two types of court: the Court Baron and the Court Leet. The first regulated the issue, surrender and transfer of leases. Everything was decided by the steward, acting as judge, and a jury of tenants. The steward, usually an attorney (solicitor), ruled on the custom of the manor and presided over discussions about communal farming arrangements. These appear to have taken place in a very democratic way and lords of the manor were not usually able to dominate proceedings.

The Court Leet heard charges that people had breached manorial custom. These normally involved minor agricultural offences, such as failing to clear ditches, repair fences, join in communal road repair and so on. Such derelictions were usually punished by a fine of a few pence. Occasionally the Courts Leet heard charges of other types of anti-social behaviour. For example, one woman was charged in two Courts Leet with 'misbehaving her tongue towards her mother-in-law' and with being a common scold.

Decisions in the manorial courts were made on the basis of the customs of the manor. These had the same force within the manor as did the Common Law in England as a whole. The nature of the custom was decided from written records where these were adequate, or from the testimony of the oldest inhabitants where they were not. Manorial customs were enforceable in the King's courts. In lowland Britain, property was normally inherited by the oldest son of the deceased, rather than divided up among multiple heirs: this maintained the size of peasant holdings.

Highland life was quite different. Pastoral farming predominated and where tillage existed it was usually undertaken in enclosed fields. Highland areas were rarely self-sufficient in grain. Manors were usually large and incapable of enforcing strict control over farmers who were scattered in isolated farmsteads and tiny hamlets. Loyalty to clans (family groups) was usually stronger than to the squire. Perhaps because the highland zone was settled later than the lowland, and had developed its customs when land was still plentiful, partible inheritance (the division of land between heirs) was the norm and the immigration of poor people was not discouraged, something which caused problems when there was no longer a surplus of land.

The scattered communities of the highlands followed an infinite variety of farming techniques, but some generalisations can be made. In the far north of England, in Wales and in the West Country, cattle rearing was the main economic activity, though there were limited areas of arable land and meadows in the valleys. The cattle were usually sold to lowland farmers for fattening. In slightly easier land, such as that of the Lake District, sheep rearing for wool predominated. Flocks numbering in the thousands were run year-round in the fells and driven down to the valleys only for lambing and shearing. In the relatively fertile valleys of western England, the wood pasture pattern of farming developed on land cleared directly from woodland into enclosed pastoral farms. Market factors and land quality determined whether running store cattle or dairying would predominate.

Enclosure

Enclosure has often been seen as the ultimate evil in agricultural life, a device for breaking up rural communities. It is charged with causing depopulation, poverty, beggary and vagrancy for the peasantry, while raising their landlords to great wealth. On the other hand, enclosure has been seen as representing a victory of economic rationalism over medieval backwardness and the forces of inertia which made it impossible for agriculture to progress. The latter view sees the enclosure movement as a necessary step towards the agricultural revolution.

These two views can be reconciled by examining the types of enclosure and the way the motives and techniques of enclosure varied over time, and from place to place. There had been an enclosure movement in many areas before the end of the Middle Ages. Much, probably most, of this enclosure was carried out by agreement between tenants with the consent of the landlord and Court Baron. Strips were exchanged to allow some farmers to hold their land in compact blocks, rather than scattered throughout the open fields. The motive was usually a desire to save travelling time and to grow a specialist crop. This type of enclosure was common near cities and in areas where there was a demand for industrial crops, and the result was greater efficiency and greater diversity of crops. It did not affect traditional rights to use of the common and waste. Enclosure by agreement was, therefore, non-controversial. Such enclosure continued throughout the sixteenth and seventeenth centuries without attracting opposition.

More radical was the wholesale enclosure of an entire manor. This could be done by agreement registered in the Court of Chancery or by Act of Parliament. In some instances only the open-field land was

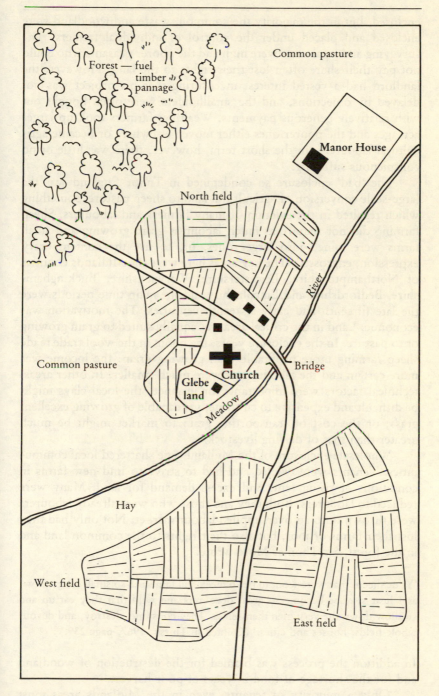

An open-field village

enclosed, but in the majority the common, waste and woodland were enclosed and placed under the control of individual farmers. The surveying and legal costs were high and the poorer peasants who could not pay their share often lost their rights to the land. However, the landlord had a vested interest in ensuring that his project was not delayed by objections, and the smallholders were often bought out with relatively generous payments. Wealthier farmers took up larger acreages and the poorer ones either moved elsewhere or became agricultural labourers. In the short term, however, there was little or no conspicuous suffering.

The 'bad' enclosure so condemned in Tudor England was the large-scale conversion of agricultural land to sheep pasture, something which resulted in the eviction of many farmers and labourers. Sheep farming did not require as much labour as grain growing and small farms were joined into larger ones, or, to use the contemporary expression, engrossed. The key areas here were the Midlands counties of Northamptonshire, Leicestershire, Warwickshire, Buckinghamshire, Bedfordshire and Lincolnshire and the main time periods were the late fifteenth and early sixteenth centuries. The motivation was economic. Land in the critical area was equally suited to grain growing or to pasture. In the enclosure years, the boom in the wool trade made sheep farming more profitable than growing grain: the income was more certain and the labour costs were much smaller. In other areas, technical factors were important: for instance, the local clays might be difficult and expensive to cultivate, yet capable of growing excellent grass; or the cost of transporting grain to market might be much greater than that of driving livestock.

Wholesale enclosure of the Midland type shattered local communities. Tenants were evicted and had to strive to find new farms in conditions of rising rents and excess demand for land. Many were reduced to labourers. Both they and those who were already labourers were thrown onto an oversupplied labour market. Not only had they lost their farms or jobs, but also their rights to the common land and in the forest. Sir Thomas More wrote:

'Your sheep, that were wont to be so meek and tame and so small eaters, now, as I hear say, be become so great devourers and wild that they eat up and swallow down the very men themselves. They consume, destroy, and devour whole fields, houses and cities.' (Quoted in Thirsk, 1967, page 239.)

In addition the process was blamed for the destruction of woodland and for the shortage of food in years of poor harvest.

Only a minority of tenants, even in the Midlands areas most affected by Tudor enclosure and conversion of arable to pasture, were at risk. In Lincolnshire, the county which was probably the most affected, only ten per cent of the arable land had been enclosed by 1607 (Coleman, 1977, page 39). The tenure by which they held their land could provide a legal barrier to the landlord's desires.

Those who held their land by free and common socage (the feudal tenure which was nearest to modern freehold) were almost completely safe. They paid only small and fixed headrents. For all practical purposes, they were owners. Copyholders are generally regarded as the next most secure. Their tenure was fixed and recorded in both the manorial records and their own copy, which they could produce in court to justify their title should it be challenged. Their title depended not only on their copy, but also on manorial custom. Customary tenants did not have the protection of their own certified copy of the court roll, but their position differed little from copyholders in other respects.

The actual tenures by which copyholders and customary tenants held their land varied from manor to manor. In many cases, land passed by hereditary succession. Tenants normally had to pay both an annual rental and a capital sum known as a fine on inheritance. This was usually equal to two years rent. The most fortunate tenants, in a time of rising prices, had both their rents and their fines fixed by the custom of the manor. Those a little less fortunate had fixed rents, but had to negotiate an entry fine with the landlord. Those in the weakest situation had to agree on both fine and rent. To use the language of the time, they were 'arbitrary at the will of the lord'. In practice, it was very difficult to make a large increase in either rent or fine. The latter, in particular, had, in law, to be 'reasonable' and both the manorial courts and the King's courts usually ruled in favour of a fine of about one and a half year's rent.

On the other hand, tenants who held land on short leases had no such security. Much demesne land, that is the land which had been assigned to the landlord to farm for himself, was leased for periods which ranged from one year to ninety-nine years, with twenty-one years being the most common. Copyholders or customary tenants with fixed rents, certain fines and rights of inheritance had a very secure title. Holders of short leases were obviously at risk, though only if they were poor. Wealthy agricultural capitalists who farmed leasehold land were in a strong bargaining position and could, in any case, easily move their interests (Kerridge, 1969, pages 32–93; Ramsay, 1972, pages 32–5).

Conversion from arable to pasture accompanied by wholesale eviction took place only where it could create more income for the landlord, and where the tenants had tenancies which denied them protection. Historians disagree about the proportion of tenants who were liable to eviction. Ramsay believes that a large proportion of tenants were at risk in the sixteenth century, while Kerridge states that 'security of tenure was firmly established in law and equity' (Ramsay, 1972, pages 35–6; Kerridge, 1969, page 94). The truth probably lies between these two extremes. A sufficient number of tenants were evicted to create a significant social problem, and their sufferings should not be minimised merely because we now know that their fate was not the central feature of sixteenth and seventeenth century agrarian history.

From the early seventeenth century, the motive for enclosure changed. It was now rarely undertaken to convert arable to pasture on a permanent basis; it was usually undertaken to allow innovations in farming practice and because it was generally believed to be more efficient than open-field farming. The encloser ceased to be the villain and became the hero in the eyes of most commentators on agriculture. Enclosure was credited with reducing costs, making possible more variety, using labour more efficiently and allowing greater modernisation.

Looked at as a whole, enclosure had both benefits and disadvantages. Especially in the sixteenth century, it was associated with depopulation, deserted villages, the displacement of smallholders, vagabondage, urban-drift and the possibly over-rapid shift of population to developing rural areas, such as the fens and woodlands. It contributed to the growth of a three-tier rural social structure with a hierarchy of landlord, prosperous farmer and labourer. Enclosure also contributed to changes in the appearance of the countryside. It sometimes increased the area under cultivation as hillsides, woods and wastelands were brought under the plough. It certainly created more hedges, ditches and fences, creating that checkerboard pattern of small fields which has been a characteristic of the English countryside from the time of enclosure until the present day. It altered the settlement pattern of lowland Britain as the nucleated villages lost population to new farm houses built on enclosed farms. Enclosure may, however, have been less important than the changes which accompanied it, changes which both encouraged the enclosure movement and were themselves stimulated by it.

Improvements in agriculture

The sixteenth and seventeenth centuries were times of change and opportunity for farmers. The sixteenth century and the first quarter of the seventeenth was a period of inflation, rising population and ever increasing demand for agricultural produce. In contrast, the later seventeenth century was a time of relatively stable demand and falling prices. Both economic situations provided an incentive to agricultural change, in the earlier period to maximise production, and in the later to reduce costs.

That landlords and more literate farmers were aware of the need to improve their techniques is suggested by the wide range of technical literature available for improving farmers. John Fitzherbert's *Boke of Husbandry*, published in 1523, paved the way for later works, such as Thomas Tusser, *A Hundred Good Pointes of Husbandrie* (1557) and *Five Hundred Good Pointes* in 1573; Barnaby Googe, *The Four Books of Husbandry* (1577), Sir Richard Weston's *Discourse of Husbandrie used in Brabant and Flanders* (1645), Walter Blith, *The English Improver* (1649) and John Worlidge, *Systema Agriculturae* (1669), and are but a small selection of the agricultural books published in this period. The quality of their advice varied. Googe's books brought the best in Dutch practices to the attention of English farmers, including the use of turnips as winter fodder. Some included much material about Mediterranean agriculture quite irrelevant to England, or laboured the author's untested theories. Tusser was not a success as a practical farmer.

In the sixteenth century, the problem was to increase grain production without extending acreage. As demand for foodstuffs rose with population, the first response was to cultivate more land. Waste land was brought into production, swamps drained, forests cleared and marginal lands put under the plough. By the late sixteenth century, there was limited scope for continuing this approach. The price of timber was rising in some areas owing to such clearances of forest.

The most spectacular increase in land under cultivation resulted from the fen drainage scheme of the Dutch engineer Cornelius Vermuyden. Nearly 400 000 acres of very rich soil was brought into cultivation as a result of the enterprise he began in 1634. However, the scope for large-scale and capital-intensive schemes such as this was very limited. If the amount of land under the plough was increased substantially in the existing agricultural areas, production fell because a reduced number of animals would be unable to provide sufficient manure. It was necessary to find a way of increasing production from the same area of land.

The first approach was to use more manure. Kerridge has found evidence that from the 1560s there was heavier use of compost, the ashes from soap boiling (where wood rather than coal was burned), marl and the organic waste from the towns. Sand was spread on clay soils to lighten them, clay on sandy soils to give them more body. Lime was used to a greater extent than it had been in the past, possibly because the use of coal in its processing had made it cheaper. These methods, however, involved heavy outlays of money and labour (Kerridge, 1967, pages 240–94). Especially in the west of England, the process known as 'denshiring' was adopted. Old turf was cut up, dried, burned and the ashes returned to the soil. The practice spread beyond the county which invented it with very beneficial effects.

Paradoxically, the way to increase grain production might be to keep more animals rather than fewer. If a greater number were available to manure the ground, crop yields per acre would be higher. Many of the improvements in the sixteenth and seventeenth century involved finding ways to keep more stock. One approach was to adopt convertible husbandry, also known as ley farming or up and down husbandry. In this system, land was kept in grass for seven to twelve years, then cropped, most commonly for five or seven years. Though three-quarters of the farm was in grass, corn output was maintained. That of meat, wool or dairy produce was increased as more animals were kept.

From the 1630s, ley farming was associated with the practice of sowing grass seed rather than waiting for self-sown grasses—rye grass, trefoil, lucerne, clover and sainfoin were all used. In the mid-seventeenth century there was a marked fall in the price of grass seed— clover seed fell from two shillings a pound in 1650 to seven pence in 1662—and this encouraged the use of the superior artificial grasses.

For all farmers in the cool temperate zone, the main obstacle to higher stocking rates is the need to carry animals through the winter. Hay-making is the traditional way of converting the spring and summer surplus into winter feed. Anything which will enable more hay to be grown, or the growth season to be extended, leads to more animals being kept and to more manure being available for the crops. One expensive method adopted in the seventeenth century was the water meadow. In valley bottoms, land was carefully levelled and the stream was dammed. In the winter, the grass was protected from the frost by a shallow covering of water. By March, when little or no grass was growing elsewhere, it would be five or six inches high. The meadow was then drained, and, after a day or two to dry, the ewes were turned onto it for their 'first bite' of the luxuriant, but stalky grass. Five hundred ewes with their lambs were fed on an acre of water meadow and then folded on an acre of crop land to manure it. By April the water meadow grass was eaten short, but by then other grass was available for the stock. The sluice gates were then closed and the grass covered for a few days to encourage regrowth for hay in June. The hay crop was reputed to be four times as heavy on a water meadow as on ordinary meadow. The capital cost was high, but, where the topography was suitable, so was the return. Rowland Vaughan, who pioneered the process in the 1580s, spent the enormous sum of £2000 on his first major work, but he reported that he had increased the income from his home farm seven or eight times. Coupled with his increased rent, he recouped his capital between four and six times over in the first four years. Much use of water meadows was made in the western valleys of England, especially those of Wiltshire and Herefordshire, (Kerridge, 1967, pages 251–67, especially page 259; Wilson, 1971, pages 29–30).

In the lighter soils of eastern England, an approach which could be more widely adopted was the growing of fodder crops. By the 1660s it was becoming common to plant turnips or carrots in mid-August, after the harvest of a grain crop. These were fed to stock in the critical month of March. Again the stocking rate was increased.

Perhaps the most significant result of the new fodder crops, ley farming and water meadows was that they made it possible to dispense with the time-honoured practice of fallowing. The increased use of clover, and the growing of more legumes, helped build up the nitrogen content of the soil, and the greater amount of manure produced by the larger numbers of stock had the same effect. The old system of three-field agriculture was no longer rational in those parts of the country where it was possible to adopt the new practices. All land which was not too steep could now be included in a pattern of cultivation, the growth of fodder crops and grassing. Production could be increased if the old distinction between permanent pasture and cultivated land was abandoned.

Though some areas of communal farming were willing to adopt new methods, it is obvious that the farmer who was keen to adopt the latest practices could do so more easily on his own enclosed farm. After 1660, especially, there was an increased trend for land to be enclosed to facilitate agricultural development. Though these changes did lead to many small farmers being reduced to farm labourers, it is probable that they increased the demand for labour. There is certainly no doubt that the improved farming methods increased production. Far from the former prohibitions on the export of grain and constant complaints about scarcity, the late seventeenth century was a time of over-supply and falling prices. Less efficient farmers could not pay their rent and had to leave the land. Landlords frequently had to reduce rents in order to get farmers to take the leases. In this environment of over-supply the government provided subsidies to encourage exports.

The new situation certainly favoured the consumer. Wheat bread was eaten rather than barley or rye, a matter of considerable dietary significance, owing to the higher protein content of wheat. Barley, which had been the main bread corn of the poor in southern England until at least the 1620s, was now used mainly for brewing or as a stock food. The much greater number of animals meant a rise in the consumption of meat and dairy products. The rise of specialist farming made more fruit and vegetables available at reasonable prices.

In addition to the greater production of the traditional products, late seventeenth century farmers turned to a wide range of industrial and specialised crops, usually on land not particularly suited to grain growing. Tobacco was widely grown until the English crop was displaced by the superior Virginia product. Dye plants, such as woad, weld, madder and saffron all employed a great deal of labour, as well as making high profits for a skilled farmer. Saffron could return a net profit of £20–30 an acre; liquorice, up to £100. Caraway seed, linseed, hops and coleseed all provided opportunities for those who would take them. Fruit farming, especially in Hereford, the Vale of Evesham and Kent, provided food for the table as well as cider and perry. A profitable form of small farming was market-gardening, especially near London. Undoubtedly the most lucrative in terms of profit per acre was growing vegetable seed. The most successful farmers were returning £100 an acre.

By 1700 the agricultural revolution was well under way. Certainly there were many areas in which conservatism prevailed, where mediaeval practices went unchallenged, but the achievements of the improvers had overcome the food shortage and injected a very potent agent for change into the economy. The fall in food prices was responsible for a slow but steady rise in real wages during the late seventeenth century. Discretionary income (that is, income left after necessities have been purchased) increased for the mass of the population and stimulated demand for industrial goods. In this increased purchasing power can be found one of the most important causes of the industrial revolution. In addition, the labour-saving methods adopted in agriculture freed workers for industrial employment, and the savings of those farmers and landlords who were successful in the new environment helped finance the eighteenth century economic revolution.

Trade

In discussing English trade during this period, it is important to start with the right perspective. Not even in 1700, and certainly not in 1558, was England the centre of the economic world. But change was afoot in the world economic order. By the end of the seventeenth century London had overtaken the cities of Italy, Antwerp, and even

Amsterdam, as the greatest entrepôt (central commercial market) of Europe, and therefore of the world. England's merchant marine had dramatically multiplied and its re-export trade was surging ahead of the Dutch. These must be numbered amongst the impressive end-products of 150 years of progress, which were nonetheless punctuated with violent fluctuations in trade and economic prosperity. Indeed it is important to express the nature and extent of that progress with care and caution. It is true that the total volume of England's trade had expanded enormously; it is easy to produce statistics to make the point: in the seventeenth century the volume of tobacco imports increased more than 700 times, two-thirds of which were re-exported to Europe; sugar more than doubled; Indian calicoes (cotton) tripled; the tonnage of English shipping to carry these commodities had already doubled by 1688; and so on and so on.

However, it was not an economic miracle, and the extent of the English achievement needs to be cut down to a realistic size. Even in 1700 much of England's expanding trade was internal. Too often historians, like economists and bureaucrats, are obsessed with the need to achieve a favourable balance of trade and to gauge national success in these terms. But much of the contemporary trading activity had nothing to do with this. It was internal trade—between towns, urban centres and their industrial hinterlands, counties and regions—or it was coastal. Colliers from Newcastle, for example, carried to London the sea coals which fuelled its domestic hearths and already contributed to the creation of the notorious London 'smog'. Secondly, cloth remained, as it always had been, the chief industry and article of trade. It was bartered internally and traded externally in 1700, just as it had been in 1558, although now it was sold not only in the traditional markets of the Low Countries and Germany, but also in Spain and the Mediterranean. Cloth remained the spearhead of trade. According to Charles Wilson it still accounted for between fifty and seventy-five per cent of all exports in value (Wilson, 1971, page 162). Yet such figures are deceptive, because they conceal changes of fundamental inportance: that the cloth trade, for example, no longer depended on one product, the traditional heavy broadcloth. It had diversified to meet the needs of changing fashions and new markets in warmer climes. Moreover, the late Stuart cloth industry must be set in the context of a more diversified economy and the availability of much more capital for investment in new ventures.

Elizabethan trade, 1558–1603

England's achievement by 1700 can only be measured by comparison with the economic insignificance of the country when Elizabeth became queen. Economically as well as geographically, the England of 1558 sat on the periphery of Europe. It had only one commodity to offer the Continent: if Elizabeth was queen, cloth was king. It dominated national industry and both internal and foreign trade. However, such dependence on one article of trade was dangerous: trade depressions, caused by over-production, foreign competition, or the dislocation of European markets as a result of war, were frequent. The mid-sixteenth century depression, Elizabeth's war with Spain and similar crises under James I and Charles I, wracked both the cloth industry and the cloth trade. Stocks of cloth rapidly accumulated, unemployment soared and cottage weavers found themselves without a vital source of income to supplement their often meagre earnings from farming. The English economy, so dependent on cloth, was in no position to counter depressions in the industry with profits and buoyancy in other manufactures. Even in the boom-times the biggest profits were creamed off by the Flemish and Dutch middlemen, not by the English producers. There was a simple reason for this. England was technologically backward; it lacked the facilities and skills to finish and dye the cloth which it manufactured. Instead it exported it in an 'undressed' and undyed condition to the Low Countries, which possessed the necessary expertise and amenities to produce a finished product, before re-exporting it at a handsome profit.

This harsh economic fact meant that England's prosperity rested precariously on the economic health, political stability and military security of the Low Countries, and above all of Antwerp. Nor was this the full extent of England's vulnerability. The great bulk of unfinished cloth passed abroad through one outlet—London. It was a kind of economic octopus, threatening to strangle the trade of provincial ports. It had fifteen or twenty times the population of Bristol, Norwich and York—the next cities in the kingdom—and it enjoyed a disproportionate share of the total export trade. Moreover the vital activity, the trade in cloth, was channelled through one commercial organisation, the merchant adventurers' company.

This company's unique position was chiefly the result of the State's financial interest in commerce. The fastest growing source of royal revenue in the second half of the sixteenth century derived from customs. Theoretically, that revenue was incidental to the Crown's right and duty to regulate trade in the interest of the nation's economic prosperity. However, to a poverty-stricken State, the financial motive inevitably loomed large, and it was anxious to promote and control commerce, if only to increase its revenue from levies on imports and exports. The most effective way of maintaining such control was to concentrate all trade in monopolistic companies. The small Tudor bureaucracy lacked the machinery, personnel, or information to supervise the trading activities of many merchants, each operating on his own. The only answer was to group them together in merchant companies, with whose governing bodies the State could deal directly. Because of London's commercial pre-eminence, and its close connections with the royal Court, it was natural that the company handling the staple export should be based there. Officially, the merchant adventurers' company was not a London company. Its headquarters were based in the Low Countries and its membership included merchants from other English ports. Yet, in practice, it became a London monopoly, drawing all trade to itself and squeezing out those who did not live and work there. It created a bitter hostility between the City and its lesser rivals, as it practised an exclusive commercial policy and shut out provincial ports.

London had unequalled advantages: its geographical position, which enabled it to carve out the lion's share of English trade in the Baltic (for naval supplies such as tar, hemp and timber) and above all with Antwerp; its proximity to the seat of government; and the ability of its merchants to raise loans for the Crown on the Antwerp money market. One prominent Elizabethan merchant, Thomas Gresham, became the government's chief financial agent in the Low Countries. He negotiated loans at reasonable rates of interest. In due course he reaped the rewards of his skill and loyal service: he enjoyed entrée at Court, he was knighted, and when he founded the Royal Exchange, where middlemen dealt between buyer and seller, its opening was graced by the Queen herself. Gresham epitomised the self-confidence of the London merchant, and the advantages of being one.

As London outstripped its provincial rivals, it attracted more and more business. The merchants of the Hanseatic League, a commercial confederation of North German cities, shifted from Hull and set up quarters at the Steelyard in London. The Italian community in Southampton transferred its activities to the City. This process benefited London, but not the country. Early Elizabethan England was a kingdom dependent on a single industry (cloth), a single city (London), a single company (the merchant adventurers) and a single market (Antwerp). This fragile economic structure rested on the unstable base of a small population, a limited home market, a dependence on foreign, especially Dutch, ships for its exports and imports, and an appalling, and deteriorating, network of roads, on which more people were drowned in winter quagmires than were knocked down in road accidents.

There was, however, cause for optimism. England was geographically well-placed as commerce moved westward with the opening up of transatlantic trade. The country was a free trade area without the internal customs barriers between provinces, as in France, or principalities, as in Germany. And, as if to compensate for the sad decay of the ancient network of Roman roads, it was blessed with a long coastline and many hundreds of miles of navigable rivers. During Elizabeth's reign, English merchant communities capitalised on these natural advantages and probed the existing frontiers of trade. It was not a period of dramatic growth or expansion, but rather one of change, which began to lessen the extreme vulnerability of the national economy. This process should not be exaggerated. The Hanse merchants enjoyed special trading privileges which were denied even to the English and which excluded them from the Baltic. The Dutch provided the ships which carried more and more goods to and from England, and Antwerp remained the chief outlet for English cloth. Meanwhile, many English merchants rested content with a safe market in Antwerp and were not prepared to accept the risks entailed in longer voyaging and the search for new trading contacts. It was only when this fragile economic structure crumbled under the strain of a series of crises that the English were forced into the adventurous courses which dramatically changed the economy.

These crises occurred in Elizabeth's reign. The most crucial was the collapse of the Antwerp market, caused largely by religious and political, rather than economic developments. Antwerp was the nerve centre, not only of Europe but also of the Habsburg empire. The Habsburgs were rulers of the Low Countries, Spain, the Holy Roman Empire, much of Italy and the silver-producing New World. They were also devout Catholics and the inheritors of the tradition of a united Christendom under the spiritual sway of the Pope. In the 1560s, Protestantism spread through the northern, Dutch provinces of the Low Countries, reinforcing their traditional autonomy, and precipitating a challenge both to the Catholic orthodoxy and the centralising policies of the Habsburgs. In 1572 tensions were transformed into open rebellion in the north—a revolt which was to last until 1610. By then Antwerp's economic pre-eminence and prosperity had been destroyed. This process was not entirely due to political events. Already English merchants had been trying to circumvent Antwerp's stranglehold on the finishing of cloth by using Hamburg or Emden instead. They had also become more adventurous, buying goods for import into England wherever they were produced, rather than, as in the past, purchasing them on the Antwerp market. However, the fundamental reasons for the collapse of England's chief outlet to the world were political and religious. The bankruptcy of both the Spanish and French Crowns in 1557 was a serious blow to the Antwerp money market. In 1576 the city was sacked by a mutinous unpaid Spanish army. When, in 1585, the Dutch closed the River Scheldt, Antwerp's access to the sea, it was ruined.

Antwerp's collapse was not the sole reason for the change in Elizabethan trading patterns, but it was by far the most important. It stimulated the search for new cloth markets in the Mediterranean and Baltic, and the hunt for alternative centres for the dyeing of English broadcloth. This led in turn to the growing export of other products, not only new kinds of cloth, such as worsteds and kerseys (the 'new draperies', lighter cloths more appropriate to warmer climates), but other commodities such as tin. Where cloth led, other English commodities followed. In the process, London's dominance lessened and provincial ports revived. So Hull and York carved out a profitable share of the Baltic trade in 'naval supplies' and other cities specialised in lighter, dressed and dyed cloth. Moreover, it should be remembered that trade was a two-way process, involving imports as well as exports. Merchants who returned with empty hulls were liable to sink—financially at least. Once they had shaken off the grip of Antwerp, they were ready to bargain with individual producers throughout Europe and beyond, and sail back home, laden with a wide variety of goods which economically backward England could not provide: French wines, Italian silks, metal products from Germany, salt and, from further afield, spices.

These activities depended upon private and personal initiatives: merchants who were prepared to take risks, deal in new commodities, accept the dangers from piracy and hostile foreign powers, sail uncharted seas and hazard their fortunes on long voyages. The Crown was always unhappy about this state of affairs. It preferred to organise merchants into companies with which it could deal directly and collectively, in order to regulate economic relations with other Powers and to ensure that it received what was due to it from customs duties. Two kinds of company were now in existence. The older type, representing an earlier stage of economic development, was the 'regulated' company. It did not have a stock of capital provided by members and used to finance collective trading enterprises. Individual merchants invested their own cash in their own commercial ventures. However, their governing body acted on their behalf, negotiating with both the English Crown and foreign governments for trading privileges, and sometimes even organising convoys for protection in time of war. This was the commonest form of Tudor company and, as mentioned above, one (regulated company), the merchant adventurers', dominated the nation's trade.

As English merchants searched for new markets and new commodities further afield, they were faced with the need for more capital than the individual or small partnership could provide. Voyages to the eastern Mediterranean, Russia, Africa and the East Indies were long, expensive and hazardous, and many months might pass before those merchants who had invested money realised any profits. So there emerged a new form of company, the joint stock company, in which members pooled their capital and used it to finance collective commercial ventures. The earliest was the Muscovy Company (1555), followed by the Levant (1581), East India (1601) and Royal African (1672) companies. These gave the financial backing necessary to enable English merchants to break away from the dependence on one centre, Antwerp, and on one commodity, cloth. But trading companies were unpopular. They were chartered by the Crown, enjoyed special trading privileges and tended to be monopolistic—even though their monopolies were often infringed by illegal poachers. During the seventeenth century, some companies, including the merchant adventurers', declined, while between 1660 and 1700 most of the joint stock companies (and the merchant adventurers) lost their exclusive membership and their monopolies.

The developments in Elizabethan trading organisations are another example of what was happening to the commerce of the nation. Cautious experiment was the keynote, not radical change or revolution. England was late in the field of exploration of new trade routes, the discovery of new markets and the settlement of colonies. When Elizabeth died, not a single colonial venture had succeeded. Much energy and expense had been directed into the fruitless search for north-east and north-west passages to the Indies. And during the long war with Spain, money was diverted from legitimate commerce into the 'get-rich-quick' lure of privateering. The capture of ships from the Spanish silver fleets, or Portuguese merchant vessels rich in prizes from the Far East—these were prospects which attracted courtiers and London merchants alike. Yet, despite spectacular successes, many lost their investments. The Earl of Cumberland's private squadron of ships, for example, simply burdened him with mounting debts. Merchants, attracted by the prospect of a 'quick kill', were distracted from the laborious search for new markets with their more distant and uncertain profits. Despite such distractions Elizabeth's reign provided a framework within which a healthier and more dynamic economy could develop. Dependence on one basic export, on one foreign market, on Flemish dyers and finishers, on London's dominance, and on one London-based company were all lessened or ended.

Crisis, 1603–1660

That forward impulse, however, was not immediately built on in the early seventeenth century. Instead, after the Elizabethan promise, the national economy was plunged into fifty years of varying stagnation, depression and crisis. There is no simple explanation for this, and no single cause. The continued vulnerability of an economy dependent on one commodity, international trade rivalry, foreign and civil wars: all played their part. So too did the continued technological backwardness of the country. These unfavourable conditions were worsened by the nature of government. As we have already seen, the Crown was always interested in commerce, but we should not be too cynical about its motives. It was genuinely anxious to promote economic prosperity, not merely to increase its profits from customs revenue or simply to prevent unemployment, hunger and poverty, because they might cause unrest and violent protest.

However, a government without enough money, or an adequate machinery, to restrain or coerce dissent, sedition, riot and rebellion, was bound to have a less altruistic interest in the financial possibilities of commerce. Under Elizabeth, the exploitation of trade as a source of patronage had caused resentments not only confined to the merchants most affected. In particular, the grant of harmful monopolies to courtiers and their clients resulted in the parliamentary rumblings of 1597 and the uproar of 1601. Despite Elizabeth's promise to cancel the most harmful of them, and to allow the rest to be examined in the Common Law courts, the grant of monopolies continued and even escalated under the early Stuarts—the Act of 1624, which prohibited them, made little practical difference. This was not the only way in which the Stuart monarchy interfered in the economy for immediate or personal reasons: for example, to reward a favourite or a courtier, or to squeeze a few thousand pounds more out of the merchant community. For such ends, trading companies were threatened with the loss of privileges and then reprieved only after payment of heavy fines. Charles I levied tunnage and poundage (see Appendix I, page 481) without parliamentary consent. Great courtiers looked to commerce and industry as a source of profit, and the merchant élite (who lent money to the Crown, enjoyed entrée at Court and had connections with privy councillors and favourites) used their position to benefit themselves and exclude others.

The worst, or at least the most dramatic, example of the Court's impact on trade was the Cokayne project. Sir William Cokayne, monopolist, speculator and moneylender, was the classic example of the London merchant with profitable connections at Court. He was the head of a merchant ring which persuaded James I to accept their proposal to increase English profits from the export of cloth. Nearly ninety per cent of commercial income derived from cloth, and the financially desperate King was willing to lend an ear to any scheme which might increase trade, and therefore customs revenue. The proposal was a simple one: the merchant adventurers' monopoly in unfinished cloth was to be suppressed; instead a new company, Cokayne's of course, would export cloth which was dyed and finished. This would deprive the Dutch and Flemings of the handsome profits which they received for carrying out these processes, and transfer them to the English instead, and at the same time the King would receive a much larger customs revenue. The temptation was irresistible and James I succumbed. The new scheme was put into operation, with disastrous effects. Everyone had overlooked two flaws in it: that England was not technologically equipped to dye and finish cloth, and that the Dutch and Flemings, the intended victims of the scheme, would not stand idly by without taking reprisals. The Dutch used their influence to ensure that all European markets were closed to the new company, and the result was a disastrous slump in the English cloth trade in 1616. It did not fully recover for almost fifty years. This prolonged depression was not the consequence of the Cokayne project alone. Plague, the dislocation of Continental markets by European wars (1618–60), the English Civil War (1642–6) and the disturbed political environment of the Interregnum: all played their part. In these circumstances the Crown's action in cancelling the Cokayne project had little effect on the depressed condition of the cloth trade.

The movement of English merchants into other commodities did not substantially compensate for this prolonged crisis. The 'new draperies' did not, as yet, offset the decline or loss of old markets for broadcloth. New companies, such as the East India Company, dealing in new products were not dramatic success stories. And everywhere, in the East and West Indies, North America and the markets of Europe, English merchants ran into a formidable obstacle: the Dutch. The fate of the East India Company's merchants in the Far East was typical. There the attempt to secure a share of the valuable spice trade ended with the 'Amboyna massacre' of English merchants in 1623.

Yet even during this period of crisis, when so many contemporaries were lamenting the decay of trade, there were three developments full of promise for the future. These built on the Elizabethan foundations and prepared the way for England's economic recovery and commercial expansion after 1660. One was the creation of a colonial empire (see pages 88–104). The second was the growth of naval power which enabled England to challenge the Dutch and even, in the 1650s, to defeat them. And the third was the evolution of a nationalistic economic thoery: mercantilism. It provided the moral justification for the use of force to protect and advance the country's economic interests. Mercantilism was not the brain-child of idealists and armchair philosophers, but of practical men-of-affairs, who were only too aware that England was in the depths of a prolonged economic crisis. The more perceptive of them recognised that the country must diversify its economic activities and lessen its dependence on cloth. There were obvious alternatives open to a nation with access to rich fisheries in the North Sea and off Newfoundland, with companies seeking new markets and new products in the Mediterranean, around Africa and India, and in the Far East, and with a growing colonial empire in North America and the West Indies. However, at every turn the English came up against the Dutch. Mercantilism was born out of the current long-term economic crisis and this rivalry with the Dutch republic. It was concerned above all with the interest of the State, especially its financial interest, but felt that this interest could best be served by benefiting the commonwealth (society) as a whole. The most effective way of achieving this was by promoting the right conditions for economic power and prosperity, and the most important precondition was a shift away from dependence on broadcloth to exploitation of new products and markets. On one hand, this meant protectionism: other countries were to be excluded from trade with the North American and West Indian colonies which, in turn, should not produce commodities in competition with the Mother Country (for example, coffee, sugar and tobacco were encouraged, but not textiles). English industries must be protected from foreign competition by means of tariffs (import duties). On the other hand, it meant aggression: that English merchants, supported by the State (with armed force when necessary), should compete with the Dutch for a greater share of the world market, for slaves from Africa, calicoes and silks from India, and spices from the Far East.

There was a good deal of muddled thinking in early mercantilist theory, especially the belief that wealth was to be equated in some way with the favourable movement of specie (coinage) and bullion (gold and silver) in and out of England. In other words, the value of imported coinage and precious metals must exceed the value of those exported. However, by the mid-seventeenth century this view was being displaced by the notion that what mattered was a favourable trade balance: more commodities exported than imported. If this was achieved, the flow of bullion would look after itself. But the pursuit of such a favourable trade balance still involved protectionism and aggression.

The first monument to these twin 'principles' was the Navigation Act of 1651 (see page 101). This Act also announced, for the first time, a national economic policy. In the past, the economic activities of royal government had not amounted to a coherent and consistent policy. They had been a mixture of *ad hoc* solutions to crises as they arose, grants of patronage (for example, licences permitting the export of prohibited goods) and actions designed to increase the State's revenue, or to favour vested interests (for example, monopolistic charters granted to groups of merchants, especially those of London). This was now replaced by a more coherent, national approach to the economy in the Act of 1651, and it was this Act, although not the direct occasion of the first Anglo-Dutch war (1652–4), which was the underlying cause of that conflict. It was a reaction against the way in which the Dutch traded with England's North American colonies, carried English goods, controlled English outlets to Europe and debarred English merchants from profitable trade in many parts of the world.

Revival and expansion, 1660–1700

The restoration of the Stuarts in 1660 did not, in some magical fashion, revive the national economy. Nevertheless, a revival did occur in the later seventeenth century and it is necessary to explain this phenomenon. To some extent it was mere coincidence. In the 1660s some long-term developments had their effect, such as the implementation of a coherent mercantilist policy, increased tobacco and cotton production in North America and the sugar revolution in the West Indies (see below, page 102). There was a recognition that the effective management of trade involved a combination of State regulation and support and individual merchant enterprise and initiative. The State could provide the legislation: for example, the Navigation Acts. The new laws formulated a national, protectionist economic policy: to make England self-sufficient, to expand trade, and to exclude foreign rivals from trade with its colonies and the carriage of its own goods. The arch-enemy was the Dutch republic, which even built many of the ships owned by English merchants. In order to break this economic stranglehold, the State was prepared to back legislation with armed force. So it went to war with the Dutch again in 1665–7 and, in alliance with France, in 1672–4. That these wars were much less successful than the first, in 1652–4, does not detract from the fact that the State was now prepared to give a much greater support to the merchant community than it had ever done before. This support should not be exaggerated or misunderstood. It was not always in the best interests of the economy: the third Anglo-Dutch war, for example, was the consequence of Charles II's pro-French and pro-Catholic policies. Charles's personal priorities, his short bursts of energy followed by lengthy periods of indolence, his over-riding concern to keep the political initiative no matter what it cost: they all tend to muddy the picture, because they made the government's economic policy less consistent than it might otherwise have been. But the general drift was unmistakeable: that the State was now throwing its weight behind the mercantile and industrial communities. Moreover, it lent its support in a variety of ways: with legislation, professional expertise and, if necessary, armed force.

It was also fortunate for English commerce that it benefited from two later seventeenth century developments. During the long reign of Louis XIV, France adopted policies which were expansionist and mercantilist. Its particular economic target was the Dutch Republic. So it sought to absorb the Spanish Netherlands (the buffer State between the French and Dutch) as a springboard to an invasion of the Dutch State. For much of the time between 1672 and 1713, the Dutch devoted their resources and energies to a struggle for survival against the French threat. Their worldwide commercial and colonial empire was threatened by both English and French rivals. By the end of Louis XIV's reign, England had superseded the Dutch as the world's greatest trading nation and London had overtaken Amsterdam as Europe's entrepôt.

The second development working in England's favour was the change in trading patterns. The country was shaking itself free from its traditional and dangerous dependence on cloth. North American, West Indian, Far Eastern and Indian products accounted for thirty-three per cent of all imports by 1700, and a large proportion of these (thirty per cent of all exports) was re-exported to hungry European markets. Between 1660 and 1700, an annual trade deficit of £300 000 was transformed into a favourable trade balance of over half a million. It was not dramatic, but it was healthy and it hinted at the commercial revolution which was to take place in the eighteenth century. Despite the intermittent but prolonged crisis in the first half of the seventeenth century, the significant economic developments which had begun in Elizabeth's reign were coming to fruition. The economy was becoming more diversified, and slumps in the cloth trade could be absorbed more easily by buoyancy and expansion in other sectors of the economy (for example, in the processing of tropical products and the re-export trade). London had replaced Continental cities such as Antwerp and Amsterdam as the entrepôt centre of Europe, and yet, at the same time, provincial centres were carving out a bigger slice of the growing trade and profit for themselves. Bristol, in particular, but also Liverpool and Glasgow, were all involved in the growing transatlantic trade.

The essence of the new expansion was an alliance and inter-relationship between the State and individual enterprise. The State was concerned with power and the revenue from commerce which helped to promote that power. The merchants were interested in profit. Unlike contemporary economic theorists, civil servants or the King, they were not interested in promoting favourable trade balances or boosting the Crown's income from customs revenue. They operated as individuals, concerned to maximise their profits. They exported what they could sell abroad and they imported what would be marketable at home. They were not willing and obedient servants of some official grand design to develop the national economy. Instead they carried into England goods which satisfied English consumer demand and brought an immediate profit, not raw materials which might engender and feed new industries, but which promised only long-term profits.

Nevertheless, the interests and skills of the State and the individual merchant combined effectively to promote economic growth. Gone were the days when the official attitude to commerce was determined simply by the profit motive of Crown and courtiers. To some extent this change was a legacy of the revolutionary decades of the 1640s and 1650s. Until then the monarch, Elizabeth as much as the early Stuarts, had treated the regulation of trade and customs revenue as 'mysteries of State' which were not open for discussion by the governing class. The Civil War and the Interregnum, however, opened up such matters for debate. Parliament had to raise money in order to conduct its war against Charles I, and afterwards the revolutionary regimes had to finance peacetime government and the maintenance of a large standing army. New forms of revenue were devised. New questions were raised: how to tap the wealth of society more effectively? Who should pay a larger share than before, the poor or the rich, the consumer or the producer, the landed gentry or the merchants?

In this ferment of experiment a new breed of royal bureaucrat emerged. Not the traditional courtier/civil servant, who was no more than an amateur appointed by the king or his favourite, but a professional. He was sometimes an economic theorist. He was interested, and increasingly skilled, in administration, organisation and the collection of statistics and other information. There was a strong recognition that government must be well-informed if its actions were to be effective. Some of these men were inherited by Charles II from the Interregnum; others were recruited into his service in the 1660s. They were not modern, professional civil servants, because they owed a personal allegiance to the King. Nevertheless, men like Samuel Pepys, Sir George Downing, William and Henry Coventry and Sir Leoline Jenkins provided a new expertise in economic matters. They were a buffer against the self-interest of courtiers who sought to exploit trade to their own profit, but at the same time they would not advise the Crown to back hare-brained, harmful or selfish schemes promoted by the merchants. They bridged the gap between the self-interest and profit motive of the State and the merchant communities. They also symbolised the alliance between State interest and individual merchant initiative which spelt the doom of the old monopolistic trading companies.

Industry

The coal industry

The coal industry was almost certainly the most rapidly expanding economic activity in Tudor and Stuart England. It was important in itself and it has been credited with producing widespread changes in other industries, in the transport system, in the growth of cities and in the improvement of domestic comfort. Even late seventeenth century improvements in agricultural output have been attributed to the use of coal, in this instance as a contributor to the reduced price of lime.

That there was a very large increase in coal production, and just as importantly in coal consumption, is not open to doubt. J.U. Nef has calculated that coal production increased fourteen-fold between 1551 and 1690 (J.U. Nef, *The Rise of the British Coal Industry*, London, 1932, I, page 19). Though his evidence was not strong enough to prove this precise figure, it is probably of the right order of magnitude. Both at the beginning and the end of this period, the most important coalfields were those of the north-eastern English counties, Northumberland and Durham. They were also the most rapidly developing of the major fields. Only Cumberland with its local industry and export trade to Ireland was expanding output more rapidly in percentage terms.

According to Nef, the increased importance of coal could be explained by the sixteenth century energy crisis. Rising population and increased industrial demand for fuel created an acute shortage of firewood and charcoal. Its place was taken by coal. In the growth of coal-mining and the spread of the use of coal, Nef saw the origins of an industrial revolution between 1540 and 1640. The use of coal in place of the traditional fuels, Nef claimed, stimulated very important technological innovations, which required far greater capital investment and larger scale industrial organisation. As a result of these improvements, there was a fall in the real price of industrial products and an even greater rise in profits. Enhanced profitability stimulated greater

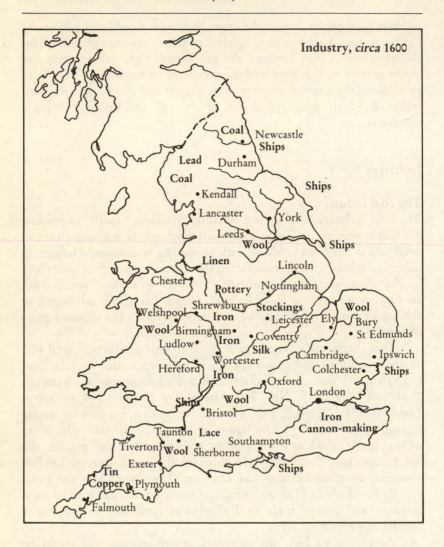

Industry, *circa* 1600

capital investment in industry and created in manufacturing the most important growth sector of the English economy.

Nef argued that the new industries introduced into England during the last sixty years of the sixteenth century—paper, cannon-making, zinc and copper mining—all required capitalist organisation, as the costs of establishing viable enterprises were far greater than could be met by groups of craftsmen working co-operatively. Older industries such as coalmining and iron-making adopted more advanced technology—deeper mines, pumps, drainage sloughs (drains cut horizontally into pits), blast furnaces and their more efficient water wheels—which required high capital investment. He claimed that, 'large-scale industry was thus becoming the normal form of enterprise, both in mining and metallurgy' (J.U. Nef, 'The Progress of Technology and the Growth of Large-Scale Industry in Great Britain, 1540–1640', in Carus-Wilson (editor) *Essays in Economic History*, London, 1954, page 97). Thirdly, new technical methods were developed to enable coal to be used in iron work, glass-making, brick manufacture and salt-boiling.

The introduction of new industries and of new machinery, tools and furnaces in old industries, had brought about technical changes in the methods of mining and manufacturing only less momentous than those associated with the great inventions of the late eighteenth and early nineteenth centuries . . . the striking changes in technique and the striking concentration of capital which began in the Elizabethan Age led directly to the rapid industrial progress of the late eighteenth and nineteenth centuries. (Nef, 'The Progress of Technology', page 105.)

Nef's revolutionary reappraisal of the development of British industry was never fully accepted by economic historians, but its sheer boldness, and the magnitude of the research on which it was based, have made comment on it the central theme of economic historiography relating to the century before the Civil War. Even in the 1930s, writers such as F.J. Fisher doubted that the advantages of large-scale economic organisation were as great as Nef claimed, except in mining and operations involving water. The cautious criticisms of Nef's younger contemporaries expanded into a full-scale reaction after the Second World War. D.C. Coleman, P. Deane and the, by then, more critical F.J. Fisher all denied that there was any discontinuity in economic growth of sufficient importance and breadth to warrant the use of the term 'Industrial Revolution' (Coleman, 'An Innovation and its Diffusion: The "New Draperies"', *Economic History Review*, second series, 22, 1969, pages 417–29; Deane, *The First Industrial Revolution*, 1965, pages 1–2; Fisher, 'Tawney's Century', in Fisher (editor), *Essays in the Economic and Social History of Tudor and Stuart England in Honour of R.H. Tawney*, 1961, page 2).

Nef's hypothesis served the very useful purpose of stimulating detailed research designed to verify or disprove its various ramifications. One of the most important of these is the investigation into his belief that there was a fuel crisis in the sixteenth century. C.H. Wilson adopted a moderately critical view.

The success with which coal was substituted for wood as fuel, and the growing output of the coal industry, must not be regarded as a *deus ex machina* which can be invoked to explain every development of British industry outside textiles. It was probably the factor of the economy of the early seventeenth century most favourable to expansion. The failure to substitute coal for wood in metal smelting was, conversely, a serious check to expansion in the mining and metallurgical industries. (Wilson, 1971 [paperback], page 85.)

D.C. Coleman holds similar views, claiming that the fuel crisis on which Nef placed so much stress was important only in particular localities. In fact, the prices of firewood and charcoal were rising less quickly than the average rate of inflation, though more rapidly than industrial prices (Coleman, 1973, 1977, pages 84–7). Hammersley has demonstrated that there was no general shortage of wood-based fuels, even in the iron industry (G. Hammersley, 'The Charcoal Iron Industry and its Fuel, 1540–1750', *Economic History Review*, second series, 26, 1973). Indeed, the reaction against Nef has proceeded so far that one of the most readily available short economic history books on this period, Sybil Jack's *Trade and Industry in Tudor and Stuart England* (see Bibliography), presents a devastatingly revisionist case which denies virtually all Nef's claims except that there was significant growth in the coal industry.

To return to the one aspect of Nef's work which is largely non-controversial, there is no doubt that coal production increased, and that it helped alleviate fuel shortages in some areas. There is no doubt that rising population, and the concomitant demand for food, reduced the supply of both full-grown trees and coppice timber as more land was cleared to grow grain. Coppice timber was grown specially for firewood. Suitable varieties were planted and cut off several feet above the ground when they reached suitable size. The trees regenerated from the stumps without the need for replanting.

The growth of cities, London in particular, exhausted those timber supplies which were within an economic transport distance. Coal, which could be produced without competition for the use of good agricultural land, and which had a higher heating value in relation to its transport cost, was substituted for wood and charcoal whenever the price, including freight charges, made it the better value for money.

The increasing importance of coal, and the belief of many contemporaries that it was a God-given substitute for timber, was expressed by the seventeenth century antiquary Thomas Habington who wrote:

Yet the stayned face of thys soyle supplyethe to vs in place of the Sun, for when wee are by the declination of thys Planet left to the coald wynter's rage wee have heere abundance of coles to defend vs agaynst that frosen adversary . . . thus hathe God . . . by the labor of theyse releyved our wantes out of the deapthe when wee by waste of our woodes have throwne our sealves into necessyties.

Habington's belief that coal was a replacement for timber was supported by West Midland experience. From the late fifteenth century, the city of Worcester showed its concern with the fuel shortage in passing strict laws against the theft of firewood, and local bequests often left funds to buy fuel for the poor. A rather wider concern at the timber shortage was demonstrated by the Parliamentary Act of 1559 which prohibited the cutting of timber for iron smelting within fourteen miles of the Severn. In an attempt to alleviate the fuel crisis, the city of Worcester invested in and operated its own coal mine between 1565 and 1574, apparently abandoning the venture thereafter, as commercially produced coal became available at a lower price. Further south, the acute fuel shortage of the Vale of Evesham was solved only by river improvements in the 1630s, which allowed barges to proceed far up the Avon.

Naturally enough, this expansion of coalmining was important not only to the consumers, but also to the producers. J.T. Cliffe (*The Yorkshire Gentry from the Reformation to the Civil War*, London, 1969, pages 57–62) has shown that coalmining was an importance source of income for many Yorkshire gentlemen. Even the small and shallow pits for which records survive could involve heavy expenditure. For example, Sir William Slingsby claimed to have invested £700 in his mines at Kippax, and in 1665 partners in a colliery at Seacroft were said to have spent £800 on making a sough (an underground drainage tunnel). The amount of capital and the risk sometimes led to gentlemen forming partnerships and bringing in an expert manager. Only a small number made large profits. Sir William Gascoigne of Sedbury owned mines in Durham which were said to bring him £400 a year in 1607 and it is believed that Sir William Slingsby had made £6000 from his Kippax mines over a twenty-year period ending in 1623. At that time his profit had been £600 a year for several years. Most gentleman colliers had a much smaller profit, with few netting more than £100 a year, and many received much less. Cliffe concluded that 'in general, coalmining profits were a useful supplement to the normal estate revenue, rather than a source of great wealth'.

It is quite clear that the coal industry was a major and growing force in the economy during the sixteenth and seventeenth centuries. It lowered the costs of home heating and cooking in areas of high firewood prices, it was a large employer of labour, it helped the development of certain industries, it stimulated investment and it did provide some high profits. In addition, it contributed to the development of a better transport system. To say this is not necessarily to agree with Nef that there was a coal-based industrial revolution. An examination of other sectors of the economy is necessary before any further comment can be made.

Other types of mining

Though coal was the most important mineral mined in Britain, a full analysis of the mining industry must include iron ore, copper, lead and tin. According to Nef, all of these experienced a significant increase in demand in the century after 1540 and an important trend towards the use of coal and more capital-intensive techniques of mining. Recent research does not confirm his views.

Iron ore was mined in all the iron-producing areas of the country. In the days of high transport costs, this industry could be established only where the basic ingredients of ore, timber to make charcoal and, once the blast furnace had been adopted, a stream to provide water-power, were at hand. Ore was mined, therefore, in the Weald of Kent and Sussex, the Forest of Dean, parts of Shropshire, Warwickshire and Worcestershire near to Birmingham, and in a few areas of the North. There is little to suggest any significant technical improvements or any very large expansion of output. Most English iron ore is low grade and the English iron industry was faced with so much foreign competition, especially from Sweden, that it was unable to pay the higher prices for ore which would have made deeper pits and larger scale production profitable. In the West Midlands at least, mining of new ore was supplemented by the re-working of Roman clinkers (ore from which some metal had been extracted), made worthwhile by the higher extraction rate of the new blast furnaces driven by the overshot water wheel (Jack, 1977, page 69).

Lead mining was probably the most profitable form of mining for metal ore in the sixteenth and seventeenth centuries. The expansion of cities created a continuing demand for roofing lead, which continued, owing to the trend to urbanisation, even after the slowing in the rate of population increase from the first third of the seventeenth century. The Great Fire of London (1666) was, of course, a boon to this industry. Lead mines were found in Derbyshire, the West Riding of Yorkshire, the Mendip Hills and at Aberystwyth in Wales.

Despite the increasing demand for lead, there was little technical innovation in mining until at least 1640. Open trenches, or meres, were worked by lighting fires on the solid rock and then pouring water on it, in order to produce the cracks which made it possible to work out the ore with hand tools. Productivity was low, two miners producing only about a ton a week, or, allowing for interruptions, approximately forty tons a year. This meant that there were a large number of miners wherever there was substantial production. In the early seventeenth century, there were 4000 miners in the Peak and Wirksworth areas of Derbyshire, which makes it one of the most highly industrialised areas of England. From 1640 water pumps and drainage soughs were becoming more common in lead mines, but these do not appear to have produced any increase in output per worker. This additional capital investment was more likely to have been required by the exhaustion of the more readily mined surface ores in some areas than by the hope of increasing profits by adopting larger scale organisation (Jack, 1977, pages 69–70).

In Yorkshire there were a considerable number of lead mines. By and large, these appear to have been operated by the county gentry, occasionally in partnerships, and could be a source of worthwhile profit. In 1573 Sir Henry Bewerley sold the lead mines on his manor to Thomas Benson, who was said to make an annual profit of £160 from them. The most profitable lead mines in Yorkshire appear to have been the Marrick mines in Swaledale, which were returning a clear income of nearly £1000 a year in the 1650s. This, it will be recalled, was an income sufficient to put a man into the 'greater gentry' category: lead mining could be highly profitable. It is worthy of note, however, that Yorkshire mining appears to have been financed by the gentry themselves, rather than by capitalist entrepreneurs from the City. It appears that the gentry were the risk-takers and active investors. If City money was needed, it was borrowed at a fixed rate of interest on the security of their land, rather than brought in as risk capital.

Copper was mined in Cumberland, but production was possible only with high capital investment, and the importation of foreign technology and workers. The quality of ore was low and the mine could not easily withstand the competition of more favoured Continental producers. It seems to have ceased production between 1640 and 1680.

Tin mining is one of the most ancient industrial activities in Britain. Indeed Britain was known to the Mediterranean world in the days before the Roman Empire as the 'Cassiterides', the remote island from which this necessary metal could be obtained (the type of tin ore found in England is known as cassiterite). In the sixteenth and seventeenth centuries, it was a major industry supporting a community of 10 000–12 000 people and blessed with considerable powers of self-regulation through the Stannary Courts. From the accession of Elizabeth until the middle of the seventeenth century, it was, however, a threatened industry. Accessible alluvial deposits had been largely worked out and the substitution of lode mining involved both high capital cost and technical difficulties. In addition, English pewter-makers, the main consumers of tin, were not as skillful as their Continental counterparts and could sell their wares only if they could buy the tin at a low price. Tin mining stagnated until the late seventeenth century when the ability of English pewter-makers to compete with foreign rivals improved, thus increasing their demand for tin (Jack, 1977, pages 70–1).

So apart from coal, mining in Britain was not experiencing a boom. It was usually small-scale in its operations. Heavy capital expenditure appears to have been a response to the exhaustion of accessible surface ores rather than a means of increasing productivity or meeting an ever-rising demand.

The iron industry

There is no doubt that the iron industry was both growing and experiencing technical innovation. The most recent research suggests that the output of iron rose rapidly from about 5000 tons a year in the 1550s to 15 000 tons a year in the 1570s, then more slowly to 20 000 tons in the 1630s. Output may have been as high as 24 000 tons per annum in the 1650s, but it did not exceed 30 000 tons until the middle of the next century. Furthermore, the production of bar iron in England could not keep up with demand and increasing quantities were imported. About 3000 tons were imported in the 1630s, up to 18 000 tons in the 1680s. This foreign, usually Swedish, iron was brought in both because the English product was regarded as unsuitable for steel-making and because Swedish iron was less expensive. English iron-masters did not yet have any superiority of technique which would enable them to offset the cheaper charcoal and lower wages of their northern rival.

Despite foreign competition, the iron industry spread geographically from the Weald to new locations in the Forest of Dean, the West Midlands and the North. The main technical innovation of the sixteenth century was the blast furnace which gradually ousted the older, slower and smaller scale bloomery process of making iron. The blast furnace had two main advantages: it extracted forty-six per cent of the iron in the ore, compared with thirty-three per cent in the bloomery process, and it was able to process at least seven times as much in a given time. On the other hand, the blast furnace required considerably greater capital expenditure and skills which were more difficult to acquire, especially in the sixteenth century. Unlike the bloomery method, which produced wrought iron in a single process, the blast furnace turned out brittle cast iron which had to be treated in a forge if it was to be used in any capacity which required tensile strength.

Only three blast furnaces are known to have existed in the 1530s, twenty-six in the 1560s, eighty-six ninety years later. As the number of blast furnaces increased, their geographical distribution became wider. In the mid-seventeenth century, half the blast furnaces were in areas other than the Weald. As the iron industry expanded into the newer areas, the Wealden iron-masters concentrated on their traditional skills in weapon-making, especially casting cannon. In the West Midlands, especially near Birmingham, a large domestic industry developed making small items, such as nails, wire, bolts, locks and agricultural implements. Despite the belief that West Midlands iron was too soft to be substituted for the Wealden product in weapon-making, a very significant part of the arms used by the royalist army in the Civil War was produced in the West Midlands. From the mid-seventeenth century, the number of blast furnaces fell, even though output increased. Their size and efficiency were increasing.

Once more the experiences of the Yorkshire gentry demonstrate that it was possible to make a good profit. The iron industry in that county was almost entirely in the hands of the nobility and gentry. Perhaps because many of them owned the ore, the forest, the land and the stream which was to be dammed as the source of power for the bellows, many appear to have done extremely well out of them.

It is clear, however, that investment in the iron industry was not the royal road to wealth. English iron-masters had difficulty in keeping down costs to a level where they could compete with foreigners. In many areas the relatively high cost of charcoal was a constraint and coal was gradually substituted for it in most aspects of smithy work. Attempts were made to use coal or coke in place of charcoal in the actual smelting, but despite the claims of Dud Dudley to have mastered the process in the 1630s, it was not until the early eighteenth century that the first useable iron was produced using coal. Though Dudley, one of the eleven illegitimate children of the Earl of Dudley, claimed to have perfected techniques of smelting with coal which he was prevented from implementing by floods, by the vandalism of jealous rival iron-masters and by the Civil War, it seems unlikely that he had, in fact, succeeded in this. An experiment conducted by the University of Birmingham in the 1920s, using Dudley's description of his methods, and the raw materials available in the area of his works, succeeded in producing iron, but of such low quality that it was totally useless.

Other metals and industrial processes

The technology of smelting other metals made some progress. Lead smelting changed from the primitive bole hill method to the use of furnaces, and experiments were made in the early seventeenth century with the use of coal as a fuel. Production increased to about 12 000 tons per annum in 1640 and about a third of this was exported. Lead, it must be recalled, was in constant and increasing demand as a roofing material, for the making of type in the printing industry, as bullets and shot and as a sheathing for the bottoms of men-of-war (Wilson, 1971, page 85). When faced with this increase in demand, the lead miners and refiners were able to improve their technology to meet it.

Copper, on the other hand, was no more successful at the smelting stage than at mining. Despite government help and the introduction of German specialists, the copper industry lost money. The increasing demand for copper had to be met by imports (Jack, 1977, pages 81–3).

The production of gunpowder had depended on the importation of saltpetre (potassium nitrate) until 1561. However, it is possible to make saltpetre artificially and in 1561 a German expert was brought in. Earth saturated with animal excrement was left in piles exposed to the air and wetted with urine until the saltpetre crystallised. The patentees were given the right to dig for 'earth' wherever they found suitable supplies, something which caused constant complaints and demands for compensation when barns collapsed because diggers for earth undermined their foundations. The operation was technically and financially successful, but it was never able to keep up with demand, owing to difficulties in finding sufficient raw material, and imports still had to be made, even though the imported product was more expensive (Jack, 1977, pages 83–4).

English salt was produced in two main ways: by the crystallisation of naturally occurring brine at Droitwich in Worcestershire, Nantwich, Middlewich and Northwich in Cheshire; and by the boiling of sea water in the north-east. There were, however, substantial imports of salt produced by solar evaporation of sea water in the Bay of Biscay and the Mediterranean. Salt-making was an important industry: its product was at that time the main preservative of food, and it was used in various industrial processes, such as glazing pottery.

Salt-boiling was a very energy-intensive industry and there were numerous complaints, in areas near the inland salt 'wyches', about the consumption of timber. Worcestershire and Cheshire salt production increased only slowly and met no more than the needs of local consumers. It was the sea-water based industry of north-eastern England and the coal-rich areas of Scotland which were expanding production. This type of industry demanded heavy capital investment in the large iron salt pans. In 1585 £4000 was invested in a single salt works. By the 1630s there may have been up to 250 salt pans, producing a total of more than 20 000 tons of salt a year. It is important to note, however, that the expanding English salt industry could not keep up with the increase in demand until after the Civil War. Large quantities continued to be imported (Jack, 1977, pages 19, 86–90; Wilson, 1971, pages 83, 201–2).

The glass industry is one of the success stories of sixteenth and seventeenth century technical innovation. The English makers of utility bottle and window glass expanded production rapidly from the 1560s and, despite paying high wages to their skilled workers, were able to reduce prices. Technicians in the glass industry were so well paid they were entitled to call themselves gentlemen. In 1612 a method of making glass, using coal rather than firewood, was patented and the making of glass quickly spread from the Weald, where its activities had competed with the iron industry for fuel, to coal-rich areas such as Newcastle on Tyne, Staffordshire and Stourbridge in Worcestershire.

So far we have concentrated on large-scale industries which produced for a national or international market. Despite their possibly growing importance, they were still less typical than small craft industries and those producing for local consumption. Food and drink processing, for example, must have constituted one of the largest industries of the day, but dispersal of the industry to meet the needs of local markets means that we have few records. Milling and baking went on in every town and every sizable village. Investment in mills and the profits of milling must have been considerable. Even bakers' ovens had a wider role in Tudor and Stuart Britain than they do today. Very few homes had ovens: meat was spit roasted, cakes and puddings had to be taken to the baker's oven.

More is known about brewing. Much was still carried on at home, or by small part-time operators, but, especially in London and the larger towns, large-scale malting and brewing was carried out, often with the use of coal as a fuel. As early as the reign of Elizabeth, one London brewer had £10 000 invested in his business (Jack, 1977, pages 111–12).

Soap was usually a domestic product, made by boiling tallow and wood ash, but commercial production was rising. Charles I thought it a sufficiently important industry to grant it to a monopolist.

Leather-making was an important industry, about which we know little. The main method of manufacture involved tanning with oak bark, and tanneries could be found wherever there was an ample supply of raw materials. Tanning was an industry no one wanted as a neighbour—hides were often soaked in a solution of chicken manure and the smells ensured that it was kept on the outskirts of towns.

Pottery was still a predominantly local industry. The manufacture of agricultural implements and harness was usually located in the buying area, something which contributed to the continuing existence of traditional apparatus in local areas. Blacksmiths could be found in all settlements of any size. Furniture-making appears to have been mainly the work of local craftsmen, and it must not be forgotten that the building and ancilliary trades were large employers of labour all over the country. The luxury trades were, of course, concentrated in London.

An examination of industry in the century before 1640 confirms some of the trends Nef describes. There was a fuel shortage, though it was much less serious and much more localised than he believed, and there was a rapid increase in coal production. There was a trend towards greater capital intensiveness in coalmining, iron-making, salt-boiling and glass-making. There was, however, no substantial increase in profits and there is certainly no evidence to support the view that technological innovations reduced costs to such an extent as to create a virtually unlimited market. England, furthermore, was not yet leading the world in technology, but still catching up with the Germans, the Dutch, the French and the Italians. Nef's century was certainly something more than part of a long industrial Dark Age which ended in the mid-eighteenth century, but it was not yet a century of industrial revolution.

Nef regarded the period between 1640 and the middle of the next century as one of stagnation, which grew out of the cessation of inflation, the end of rapid population growth, and the check to further coal-based developments until eighteenth century iron-masters had solved the problem of smelting with coke. Modern research suggests that the second half of the seventeenth century was a period of steady and unspectacular industrial developments, which helped pave the way for the Industrial Revolution of the eighteenth century. Coleman claims that the late seventeenth century was more conducive to the introduction of labour-saving machinery than was the preceding century, when rising population and falling wages had made investing capital to save labour of dubious value, in terms of both economics and social ethics. The stable population, possible labour shortage and higher real wages after 1660 provided a much greater incentive to change, and there was a steady rise in the issue of industrial patents (Coleman, 1977, page 154).

Coal production continued to rise and its widespread consumption encouraged transport improvements. By the late seventeenth century, it could undercut the price of wood or charcoal in almost every town. Landowners commented that, if it was not for the demands of iron-smelting, they would be unable to sell their coppice wood. Increased coal production meant larger and deeper pits and at the end of the seventeenth century there were a number of experiments using Newcomen-type atmospheric engines to pump water from pits. It was from these primitive pumping machines that James Watt developed the steam engine.

Iron-making and iron-based industries also showed technical improvements. As mentioned above, there was a considerable increase in the efficiency of blast furnaces. The wider use of the slitting mill in the West Midlands, and in the North, substantially reduced the price of nails and replaced the largest of the domestic iron industries with a capital-intensive one. By the end of the century it was possible to make large profits in the iron industry: the Foley family, for example, rose from rural obscurity in mid-century to a peerage before its end, thanks to profits in the iron industry. This is probably the first example of a peerage being granted to anyone whose wealth was derived from industry rather than trade.

The textile industry began to use more labour-saving machinery—Lombe's silk-throwing mill and the Dutch small ware's mill, for example—and improved methods in cloth spinning were said to double the amount of cloth which could be made from a pound of wool. The processing of agricultural products, both home-produced and colonial, became much more mechanised and efficient. Power-driven tobacco knives and larger scale sugar refineries made possible substantial reductions in the price of these imported products. Brewing, starch-making, soap and paper production all showed a marked trend towards more capital-intensive and large-scale production and the concentration of pottery-making in North Staffordshire was beginning (Coleman, 1977, pages 155–6, 164).

It is in the late seventeenth century that one detects an atmosphere of conscious modernity, of desire to change, and the beginnings of a rational and scientific approach to problems. The creation of the Royal Society was one response to the developing interest in science. Another was the application of scientific principles to industry and the willingness of academic scientists to investigate the principles underlying the pragmatically derived technology of the manufacturer: this pointed towards fruitful co-operation in the future. There was also a willingness to learn from foreigners: this was not new, but it may have become greater. English employers were willing to employ the French Huguenot refugees, and to invest in the businesses established by the more prosperous among them, especially when they brought French skills little known in England. An array of publications commended to Englishmen the technology, work habits and organisational methods of the Dutch. Of the many 'improvers' who published in the late seventeenth century, Andrew Yarranton was one of the foremost. The son of a yeoman, he was an advocate of Dutch farming techniques, enclosure, river improvements and German metal technology. Yarranton was no mere dreamer parading impractical ideas in print. He was an effective industrial spy, who gained knowledge of German technical secrets by travelling to Germany and feigning madness in order to gain access to a tin plate works, and he was an active partner in schemes to improve navigation in West Midland rivers.

At the very end of the seventeenth century, there was an important change in attitude towards technical improvement. Previously, England had been willing to copy and to acknowledge her role as a pupil in manufacturing techniques. By 1700 the Englishman had gained in confidence. Even if his conviction of technical superiority was premature, it was another pointer to the industrial revolution which lay ahead (Wilson, 1971, page 311; Coleman, 1977, pages 157–8: both give quotations from contemporary writers who praised England's leadership in mechanisation between 1695 and 1757). This progress in manufacturing was accompanied by changes in patterns of investment and in techniques of financial management.

Inflation

The inflation of the sixteenth century is a topic that exercised the minds of contemporaries and which still provokes debate among scholars today. Despite the attention given to it, this inflation was nothing like that of the Weimar Republic, in which prices rose by the hour, and went up forty-fold in a month. It was mild, to say the least, compared with that which has taken place in the Western World since 1945. If one takes the average level of prices between 1450 and 1499 as a base, agricultural prices had increased six-fold by the 1640s, timber prices had been increased by a factor of five and a quarter and industrial prices had trebled. Even the rate for agricultural prices reflects a compound rate of only 1.8 per cent per annum. At the fifteen per cent inflation experienced by New Zealand in the late 1970s and early 1980s, prices would double in less than six years and increase six-fold in thirteen.

What made the inflation such a focus of discussion was its duration, its harmful effects on particular groups of people, especially the poorest wage earners, and the contrast with the experience of the preceding 150 years. Though those who experienced the Tudor and early Stuart inflation could not know it at the time, a period of relative stability in long-term price trends was to follow and last until 1760. Attitudes towards inflation were coloured by the suffering caused when it reached its peak in the late 1540s, a maximum rate of 5.5 per cent per annum, and by the fact that the fastest rate of increase affected grain-based foods, the mainstay in the diet of the poor.

It must be admitted at once that our knowledge of sixteenth and seventeenth century prices is, at best, partial. Whole categories of prices important in everyday life are unknown to us. For example, fees for services were almost never recorded and actual retail prices for such basic commodities as bread, meat, beer and clothing can be discerned only occasionally. What we do have are reasonably complete records of certain wholesale prices. Even these have their problems: for example, the details of quality and quantity are often obscured by the use of forgotten or ambiguous technical terms. Items weighed in stones, for example, often cannot be assumed to have been measured in fourteen-pound units. In some parts of the country the stone was as low as eight pounds. References to cloths as 'short', 'long', 'fine' or 'coarse' tell us little today.

Despite these problems and uncertainties, reasonably accurate information can be obtained about the prices of certain basic commodities, such as wheat, other foodstuffs and clothing, from the records of institutional purchasers such as boarding schools and university colleges. Such records were used by J.E. Thorold Rogers in the nineteenth century, and by a team which Sir William Beveridge headed in the twentieth, to measure changes in prices from the Middle Ages until close to our own time. These studies had great scholarly value, but they told us little about the effect of such price rises on ordinary people, or on the relationship of price changes to movements in wages. In the 1950s Professor E.H. Phelps Brown and Miss Sheila V. Hopkins set out to provide the missing information. Surviving documents did not allow the construction of any index of average wages. They used the information which was available: the wages of building craftsmen in southern England whose wage rates were recorded in the surviving archives of certain cathedrals and colleges.

In order to make a comparison of changes in urban workers' purchasing power, Phelps Brown and Hopkins constructed a price index based on a basket of consumables divided into the six categories of grains, meat and fish, dairy produce, drink, fuel, light and textiles. The precise items included under each category were adjusted from time to time to allow for changes in purchasing patterns. The result was the famous Phelps Brown and Hopkins Index of prices and wages.

Its authors themselves have been very careful to point out its limitations. The prices in the index are wholesale prices: it was relatively easy to discover the price paid for a bushel of wheat or a sheep by an Oxford college, usually impossible to find how much the urban worker paid for his loaf of bread or his lamb chop. These large institutional purchasers probably made long-term purchasing contracts. These records, therefore, may not reflect short-term fluctuations. Wholesale prices, too, do not, in the short term, move at the same rate as retail prices. Despite these warnings, there can be no doubt that the Phelps Brown and Hopkins Index does provide good evidence of long-term changes in purchasing power.

Its other weakness, again pointed out by its authors, is that it is based on the purchasing pattern of urban workers. One must exercise the greatest caution in using this index as a guide to the living costs and expenses of farmers, wealthy merchants, noblemen or the Crown. As one moves to higher income levels in society, the proportion of total expenditure devoted to food will fall, that used to purchase luxury goods and services will rise. It is obvious, too, that an index giving a heavy weighting to food is inappropriate for rural inhabitants who produced most of their own.

The Phelps Brown and Hopkins Index shows a strong upward trend in prices, with the basket of consumables costing between six and seven times more in 1650 than in 1500. During this time, the wage rates for building craftsmen in southern England increased by only half as much. Although the provision of food for the workers, as well as the actual money wage, must have cushioned the effects to some extent, there can be no doubt that the inflation was accompanied by a marked fall in their standard of living.

Explanations for this inflation are still hotly debated. They fall into two broad camps, monetarist and real. The first makes money the prime cause of price fluctuations. Its increase in quantity or velocity of circulation will cause price increases; a decrease in quantity or velocity of circulation, a fall in prices. Real or physical explanations ascribe to money only a passive role. The primary reason for price movements is to be found in changes in demand, supply or the cost of production, which operate independently of monetary factors. The real factors may stimulate changes in the supply of money or the velocity of circulation. (Velocity of circulation, explained simply, is the speed with which money changes hands. If money tends to be hoarded for some time before being spent, velocity of circulation is low. If it is spent quickly by each person into whose hands it comes, velocity of circulation is high. A lowering in the velocity of circulation has the same effects as decreasing the supply; increasing it has the same consequences as putting additional money into the economy.) Today there is a third school, which combines real and monetarist factors in a multi-causal explanation.

Monetarist explanations can be divided into two, though they are not mutually exclusive. One stresses the increase in the quantity of money owing to debasement: that is, a reduction of the quantity of precious metal in the coinage usually accompanied by an increase in the volume of coins in circulation. The other stresses the increase in the amount of precious metals available for monetary purposes.

Contemporaries were, like modern economic historians, divided in their explanations. In France, Jean Bodin was a strong monetarist, attributing the inflation in his country to the influx of precious metal. In England, Sir Thomas Smith foreshadowed the two modern versions of monetarism by claiming that the inflation of the 1540s was the result of debasement of the currency, and that its continuation after 1562, when the currency was restored to almost its former silver content, was the result of the importation of Spanish silver (Hammarstrom in Ramsay, 1971, page 46; Outhwaite, 1969, page 22). In 1552 there were 1920 grains of silver to one pound sterling; in 1602, 1858. This quantity was not changed until 1861.

Modern monetarism was given its theoretical basis by the economist Irving Fisher. Fisher devised the equation $MV=PT$, in which M is equal to the total quantity of money in circulation, V the velocity of circulation, P the average level of prices and T the total number of trade transactions. In this form it is a truism, little more than a way of saying that the total money spent is equal to the amount received by the sellers of goods and services. Fisher extended the equation to a more controversial form: $P=MV \div T$, that is, the price level is equal to the total amount of money in circulation, multiplied by the velocity of circulation, divided by the total number of trade transactions. As neither Fisher nor his followers believed that either the total number of trade transactions, nor the velocity of circulation, changed significantly in the sixteenth and early seventeenth century, M, or the money supply, was left as the sole determinant of prices.

The monetarists of the early twentieth century, especially the American Earl J. Hamilton and the German Georg Wiebe, looked to the influx of silver from Mexico and Peru as the main fuel of the inflationary engine. The debate on the importance of these bullion imports in the later sixteenth century is discussed below. Critics pointed out, however, that little Spanish silver reached Europe before 1540 and that an inflationary trend was well-established before that time.

Rather than looking for non-monetarist explanations, most scholars investigated alternative sources of additional money. One was found in the expansion of silver production in Europe in the late fifteenth and early sixteenth centuries. This was believed to have stimulated prices in Continental European countries. However, the effect of this comparatively small increase in the European supply of silver can have been slight on English prices. In England, the main monetary factor in the price rise in the first half of the century was debasement of the currency.

There is a strong correlation between the period of greatest debasement and the period of most rapid price inflation. Between 1542 and 1551 the English silver coinage was debased by seventy-five per cent (that is, its silver content was reduced by the end of the period to one-quarter of what it had been at the beginning). Gold coinage was debased by twenty-five per cent. Despite this correlation, one must be careful to avoid accepting that debasement was either a sure recipe for rapid inflation, or that it was the sole, or even the main, cause of inflation in the 1540s. Earlier, though admittedly less severe, debasements had not produced any large increase in prices. The debasement of the 1540s was accompanied by other factors which would lead to an increase in prices: for example, war and a succession of poor harvests. In any case, the restoration of the coinage in 1562 did not stop price rises. Debasement may have been an important cause of inflation in the mid-sixteenth century, but it seems unlikely that it was the sole cause (Bowden in Thirsk, 1967, pages 593–4).

Monetarist economic historians attribute the continuing inflation of the late sixteenth and early seventeenth centuries to the importation of silver from Spanish America. There is no doubt that very large quantities of this silver reached Spain. According to Hamilton, it then pushed up prices throughout Europe as it flowed outwards to finance Spain's armies and to cover her trade deficit. This view was accepted orthodoxy until the last twenty years. Since then, a number of objections have been raised to it. Even in Continental Europe, the quantity of silver imported was insufficient to have created a price rise as great as the one which occurred. As far as England is concerned, there is little evidence to suggest an inflow of bullion. In the second half of the sixteenth century, England had a neutral or unfavourable trade balance and would not have gained specie (precious metals used as money) by trade. The capture of Spanish treasure ships did bring some silver into the country, but it was unlikely that the amount was sufficient to have led to an overall rise in prices. The possibility that there was an inflow of capital for investment which more than offset the negative balance of current trade cannot be discounted, but there is no proof that it took place on any large scale.

There is a further and theoretical objection to the American silver hypothesis, and, indeed, to any other explanation based on a quantity theory of money. From the 1930s, followers of J.M. Keynes have denied that there is any necessary connection between an increase in the quantity of money and the average level of prices. The injection of additional money into an economy where there was a high propensity to save and a low propensity to invest would result in hoarding, or the diversion of precious metals to non-monetary use. Thus the injection of extra money into the economy would be inflationary only if there were other factors at work as well.

It has been suggested that the movement in prices could not be a purely monetary phenomenon, owing to the differential movements in prices. This is probably an invalid criticism of monetarism. Owing to the varying elasticities (that is, sensitivity of supply and demand to price changes) of various commodities, inflation would result in uneven price movements. In any case, differential price movements occurred even in Sweden, one of the few countries in which average price levels remained stable during the Great Inflation.

The long-term movement most likely to have caused price inflation was the increase in population. This was a Europe-wide phenomenon throughout the whole period of inflation. This increase followed a century and a half of stable or falling prices, especially for agricultural products. The period of low prices was almost certainly the result of the Bubonic Plague of the mid-fourteenth century, which had halved the population of England and of most other European countries. The reduction in population had brought about a fall in prices and a rise in living standards in two ways. It had forced the landlords to take a lower return from their land, thus redistributing wealth to other sectors of society, and, secondly, by allowing marginal lands to be retired from cultivation. The lower real costs of producing basic foodstuffs when only good-quality land was used were passed on to the consumer. Wages remained high and tenants were able to obtain good terms from their landlords. In this 150 years of stable or falling prices, it is almost certain that a considerable amount of precious metal was converted to non-monetary uses.

With the rise in population in the early sixteenth century, the process was reversed. Increased demand for food by the greater population allowed higher profit-taking by commercial farmers, landlords and middlemen. Once more, it was necessary to bring back into cultivation inferior or distant land which could supply the market only at higher cost. As discussed in the section on agriculture, there was pressure to convert common and grazing land to tillage, thus reducing the number of sheep and thus the dung which had fertilised the fields. The felling of forests to make room for more cultivation may have helped create a timber and charcoal shortage and thus put up the price of these commodities. The profits from sheep rearing fell in relation to grain growing and the woollen industry could obtain its raw material only by paying higher prices.

In all this, the primacy of population pressure is suggested, firstly by the fact that food prices rose faster than any other prices and, secondly, by the decline in real wages. Furthermore, grain, which provided the staple food of the poor, rose in price more quickly than did meat and dairy produce. In other words, it was the items with the lowest price elasticity of demand which increased in price the most. Wages, on the other hand, rose much more slowly than the rate of price inflation. Indeed, the Phelps Brown and Hopkins Index shows that the purchasing power of a building worker's wages halved between 1500 and 1630, something which the authors of the Index regard as very strong evidence for population growth. Industrial prices did not rise as much as agricultural prices, because, firstly, the elasticity of demand for manufactured goods was lower than that for food, and, secondly, because the relatively slow growth in wage costs kept down prices. There is also the possibility that technical improvements reduced costs in manufacturing.

The real or physical explanation of the inflation is very logical, but in order for it to be convincing there has to be an examination of the mechanism which led to an overall price rise. The rise in population could, perhaps, have produced a large increase in the relative prices of foodstuffs while other prices fell, thus leaving average prices the same. Hammarstrom has answered this point by suggesting that the economic changes set in train by population growth and the enhanced demand for food brought about, firstly, an increase in the velocity of circulation, and, secondly, the reminting of precious metals withdrawn from monetary use in the low-price period following the Black Death. The shortage of money noted by many commentators in the early stages of the population increase sparked off debasement and the search for an increased supply of precious metals. Both the improved technology which allowed flooded European silver mines to resume production and the discoveries in America were, perhaps, direct responses to the increased demand created by population growth and the economic changes which followed it (Hammarstrom in Ramsay, 1971, pages 49–50, 56–7; Outhwaite, 1969, pages 50–1).

Real explanations do not deny the importance of changes in the supply of money or in the velocity of circulation. They differ from monetary explanations because they regard changes in demand or in the costs of production as the main determinants of price levels, and the monetary variations as secondary and usually derived from non-monetary first causes. To give a further example of this line of thinking, an economist of the real school would not deny the connection between debasement and the price increases of the 1540s. He would point out, however, that this was a period of war, with consequent high government expenditure and raised taxation. Debasement was an attempt to finance war by creating money. In addition, the years which showed the highest price increases were those of harvest failure rather than of the greatest debasement.

There is, of course, an alternative to both the monetarist and the real schools of thought. A multi-causal explanation will take into account both monetary and real factors and see them both as having an active and independent role. It is very probable that the best interpretations of the price rise are multi-causal. However, none has yet been able to command anything close to unanimous acceptance by economic historians. It is plausible, however, to see real factors, such as population growth, war and harvest failure, as the initiators of inflation. Attempts to meet the new prices by the increased coinage of existing stocks of gold and silver, and the discovery of these metals in the New World, eventually added an independent inflationary pressure. There is, of course, a parallel in the efforts of modern western countries to meet higher oil prices by expanding credit. Unfortunately there are still many unsolved problems which prevent conclusive proof. There is, for example, still the problem of showing that there was any significant influx of American silver into England. Certainly no economic historian of England has been as bold as Luigi Einaudi who calculated that 299.4 per cent out of a total price rise of 627 per cent in France between 1471 and 1598 could be attributed to the increase in stock of gold and silver.

Perhaps we could sum up by saying that an increased supply of money was a neccessary but not a sufficient cause for the inflation. Without accompanying real factors, it is unlikely that it would have produced a large rise in prices. However, in the absence of some increase in the quantity of money, it is unlikely that greater velocity of circulation alone could have produced such an increase in the average level of prices.

The consequences of inflation

Before proceeding to discuss the problems and benefits of inflation, we should first consider whether we are asking the right question. If the price rise was the passive product of independent changes in the economy, it could be more correct to discuss their consequences rather than those of inflation. Nevertheless, there were some direct and autonomous effects of rising prices, and in any case it may be convenient to discuss under this heading the major social and economic changes associated with price increases.

In the first place, the relative movements of prices placed unskilled workers, and indeed most landless workers, at a disadvantage. Though other factors may have cushioned the full impact of the rise relative to wage rates of the Phelps Brown and Hopkins basket of consumables, there can be no doubt that there was a marked fall in the living standards of the poor.

Secondly, there is the much more directly monetary problem created for large land owners, including the Crown. It took some time for peers, institutions and the Crown to adjust the rent on their land to prevailing values. Until they did—and there were often powerful legal barriers to so doing—they were faced with rising costs and a static income.

Thirdly, the Crown faced difficulties in its role as tax gatherer. Indirect taxes were usually specific: that is, charged at a fixed rate regardless of changes in the monetary value of the goods being taxed, and the taxes on land continued to be charged on values established in the time of Henry VI. In contrast, the main extraordinary expense of the Crown, war, continued to rise at a rate more rapid than that of general inflation.

Fourthly, the long-term price rise should be considered in association with the sharp short-term fluctuations in the price of grain. As prices rose higher, the degree to which they fluctuated from harvest to harvest increased too. This was not a directly monetary phenomenon, but a response to the increased urbanisation which accompanied the price rise. A higher urban population made more people dependent on the purchase of surplus grain from suppliers. Many peasant farmers operated at a near subsistence level and had only a small marketable surplus in years of average harvest size. Consider the case of a town depending for its supply of grain on peasant farmers who produce, in most years, twenty per cent more than their own requirements. If, in a poor harvest year, the farmers had a surplus of only ten per cent, the supply of grain to the town was halved. Prices soared as buyers competed for the available supply and remained very high, unless stocks could be brought in from alternative sources. In a good harvest year, on the contrary, when the peasants had thirty per cent more than their personal requirements, the town was flooded with one and a half times as much grain as it needed. Prices plummeted. It was the problems of the poor when food prices rose after harvest failure which created the most tragic aspect of the price rise period. Even though this was not, strictly speaking, caused by the long-term price rise, it is to this phenomenon which contemporaries often referred when complaining of inflation.

Finally, one may turn to the consequences of the price rise on economic development. Hamilton expressed what was to be ortho-doxy for a generation of economic historians when he argued that sixteenth century inflation had encouraged the development of capi-talism. The more rapid growth of prices than wages allowed indus-trialists to increase their profits and reinvest in larger scale enterprises. He also believed that rents remained low in relation to inflation and that there was, in consequence, a rise in the incomes and wealth of the middle class compared with those of the gentry.

Studies which have examined the rise in prices for particular commodities rather than the average level of inflation have shown that Hamilton's views can no longer be sustained. The price of industrial products rose little more quickly than wages and the slight advantage gained was almost certainly offset by the rising price of raw materials. It is now quite certain that the majority of gentlemen were able to increase their rents at a rate which at least kept up with inflation. The increase in profits to the larger farmers enabled many to expand their operations and then adopt the status and life-style of a gentleman. The changes in relative prices tended to direct funds into the building of country houses—the century in which inflation was most rapid was the one in which there was a rebuilding of rural England—and into agricultural improvements.

It is still possible, however, that both inflation acting directly and an associated phenomenon did encourage investment in industry. If money is invested to build, for example, a salt pan or a water wheel, both of which have a very long operating life, profits will increase with inflation, even though the original investment, or historic cost, remains the same. For example, if a water wheel cost £1000 and returned an annual profit equal to ten per cent of the cost of building it, the initial profit would be ten per cent. If, after several years, its current building cost has doubled with inflation and the return is still ten per cent of current cost, the profit margin is, in fact, twenty per cent when compared with the original investment.

This apparent increase in profits freed funds for investment and created a greater willingness to invest when there was the prospect of profits being enhanced by inflation. Second, the increase in the supply of money led to a fall in interest rates. In addition, the law relating to loans was changed to benefit the borrower and there was an increased social respectability in borrowing and lending. Entrepre-neurs were, therefore, able to borrow more freely than in the past. Inflation, of course, served to reduce the real rates of interest and the value of the capital repayment. In these ways, rather than in the manner argued by Hamilton, the price rise could have stimulated industrial investment (Gould in Ramsay, 1971, pages 99–116).

The end of inflation

Just as the origins of the inflationary century are confused by the near simultaneous emergence of real and monetary factors, so is its termination. By the 1630s the flow of American silver into Europe had slowed to a trickle. There is good reason to believe that the population increase slowed or even reversed itself at the same time. In addition, plague and war disrupted European markets. As a result, the rise in prices slowed in the 1640s and fell back in the 1650s to the level of the 1630s. The average agricultural prices of the 1640s were not exceeded until the 1690s. Industrial prices continued to rise slowly until the 1670s, regaining a little of the ground they had lost in the preceding century. The downward trend in the real wages of an urban workman was arrested, but only in the 1690s was there a significant improvement.

As the long-term movement in the general level of prices was no longer seen as a problem in the second half of the seventeenth century, it remains only to mention briefly why this was so. Certainly, the end to rapid population growth meant that there was no longer an ever-increasing demand for food. Secondly, technical improvements in both agriculture and industry led to a fall in the costs of production. Thirdly, the price trends of the late seventeenth century did not aggravate the sufferings of the poorest section of the community. Though the lot of the poor had improved little, at least it does not appear to have worsened.

The consequences of stable prices

Just as Hamilton and others saw the price rise in the century before 1640 as a factor stimulating investments and increasing profits, so they saw the rest of the seventeenth century as a period of depression, reduced demand and limited development. The twenty years of the Civil War and Interregnum were, of course, disrupted. The dislocation of war was followed by fourteen years of high taxation and uncertainty as the Interregnum governments attempted to establish stability. Economic developments in these years appear to have favoured military oriented industries. In the 1640s, poor harvests, military expenditure and the interference with normal trade patterns caused much suffering and depressed industry. Food prices were high.

After the Restoration, there was almost a century of stable, indeed slightly falling, prices. Prices were about three per cent lower in 1740–60 than they had been a century earlier. The reasons for this seem to have been the reverse of those which had caused the inflation. Silver imports into Spain began to decline from the 1590s, though this factor may have been more apparent than real in reducing the money supply in Europe. Instead of the trade deficit of Europe with Asia being met by American silver which first crossed the Atlantic before being sent to Asia, it was covered by bullion shipped directly across the Pacific. In addition, there was an increase in the use of paper bills, bonds, notes and cheques which had much the same effects as a greater supply of coin.

Almost certainly, the cessation of population increase and the possible slight decline was the main reason for the end of the price rise. Just as many of the consequences attributed to the price rise should, more correctly, be regarded as the result of rising population, so should many of those commonly associated with stable prices be seen as a response to demographic change. The 'terms of trade' between agricultural and industrial prices altered in just the way one would predict in a situation of static population.

After 1650 agricultural prices fell, while industrial prices continued a slow rise. Real wages for workers showed a significant improvement. The consequences of changing supply and demand were felt by both agriculture and industry. In the late seventeenth century, rents fell, yet it was not uncommon for farmers to be unable to pay them. Landlords found it hard to get and to keep good tenants. Manufacturers felt a profit squeeze and often complained about 'want of hands'.

It was long believed that the combination of stable population and mild deflation was sufficient to prevent economic growth. As will be discussed in more detail below, the challenge of lower prices and dearer labour provided farmers and manufacturers alike with an incentive to improve, to invest and to diversify. Deflation, as well as inflation, could be a potent agent of economic change.

Poverty, vagrancy and poor relief

Poverty

In early modern England there were three main types of poverty: chronic poverty, case poverty and crisis poverty. Though they overlapped to some extent, they were sufficiently distinct to be regarded as having separate causes and as requiring different treatments. The chronically poor were those who were more or less permanently unemployed, perhaps living as vagrants on the semi-criminal fringes of society. It was this group which was most feared by the authorities, and the treatment they received was often extremely harsh. Included in the category of those suffering from case poverty are widows, orphans, the indigent aged, the ill, the disabled and those who had suffered some personal economic misfortune. Society was fairly well attuned to the needs of the individual paupers. Attending to their needs was generally regarded as a family or neighbourly duty, and where organised assistance was required, the individual parishes were usually able to provide it. Crisis poverty was the most difficult problem because it plunged whole groups of people, often living in the same area, below the poverty line in times of plague, harvest failure or economic depression.

During the earlier part of Elizabeth's reign there was a considerable amount of mass poverty resulting from the actions of her predecessors. For example, the effects of the dissolution of the monasteries were still being felt. Many of the monks turned out into the world with pensions of £5 per annum were still alive, and their purchasing power was constantly being eroded by inflation. Surviving nuns, whose pensions were usually about half those awarded the monks, were likely to be in an even worse position, unless they had broken their vows and married. In addition, there were the approximately 80 000 monastic dependents who had been turned out to make their own living in a world of high unemployment. One must also take into account the position of people deprived of monastic charity, though the importance of this loss is debated by historians. Once regarded as a major cause of poverty, the dissolution of the monasteries is now regarded as having had only limited effects (Pound, 1971, pages 16–24).

Almost certainly more serious was the plight of the men who had been the armed retainers of great noblemen whose retinues had been broken up by Henry VII, and the plight of their fellow soldiers enlisted for the wars of the 1540s. There were no rehabilitation provisions for physically fit ex-servicemen in Tudor times and, as Sir Thomas More wrote, 'in the mean season they that be thus destitute of service either starve for hunger, or manfully play the thieves'. The situation was to emerge again after the Armada in 1588 when soldiers and sailors no longer needed, once the immediate crisis had passed, often starved in the streets. In the 1630s the government of Charles I was to face the same problem at the end of his wars with France and Spain, and the problem was to re-emerge on a much larger scale at the end of the Civil War and in the 1690s. Only a combination of aid and repression was able to reduce this problem to manageable proportions. From 1593, disbanded soldiers were entitled to receive pensions and licences to return home. Those who did not and took to begging and crime were likely to be dealt with by provost marshals, whose powers under military law extended to the infliction of a summary death penalty.

Important structural changes in the economy created a large pool of people who were rarely able to find work. In the second half of the sixteenth century, and in the first half of the seventeenth, the English cloth industry was faced with a period of long-term decline which affected the established broadcloth industry most of all. The contraction of employment opportunities drove many spinners and weavers into a frequently vain search for other employment, and kept others in the precarious position of finding work during favourable economic conditions and losing it during the frequent slumps. Especially in the 1540s, the enclosure of arable land in the Midlands and its conversion to sheep rearing drove many people from their land or their traditional employment. As is discussed elsewhere, the amount of land affected by this type of enclosure was small, but the concentration of change in such a small area magnified the problem of finding employment.

The concomitant agricultural changes taking place in an agrarian society which was becoming increasingly commercial, also displaced people and possibly reduced the total amount of employment. Engrossment, that is the joining together of previously separate farms, probably increased efficiency, but it deprived families of access to their own land after eviction and made them reliant solely on wages. The increasingly prevalent custom of gentlemen turning part of their estate into a deer park almost certainly reduced employment.

There can be little doubt that the most important cause of poverty was the increase in population and the pressure on resources which resulted. As population increased, so did demand for land. As discussed in more detail above, food prices rose in response to the need to cultivate poorer quality land. As the supply of labour rose relative to the demand for it, wages fell. All who had lost access to the land became part of an economically insecure class. Peter Laslett has written:

No sharper clash of interest, material, economic, or even biological, can be easily imagined than that between those with and those without access to the land. In an agrarian economy at times not far removed from the subsistence level in some areas, this might have meant that when harvests were bad some men could count on surviving whilst others, the landless, could not be so sure. (Laslett, 1965, page 37.)

Though rural labourers were entitled by law to four acres of land with their cottage, this law was often broken, the average allotment of those farm labourers studied by Alan Everitt (in Thirsk, 1967) being only an acre. Even this amount of land was useful, providing labourers with an opportunity to grow some of their own food. The position of the urban labourer was worse. Studies by Hoskins in Leicester, MacCaffrey in Exeter, Dyer in Worcester and Slack in Salisbury all found that urban poverty was a problem serious enough to dominate the activities of governing bodies. Hoskins and MacCaffrey both concluded that half the population of the cities they studied was living in poverty, and D.C. Coleman argues that between a quarter and half of the entire population of Stuart England was 'chronically below what contemporaries regarded as the official poverty line'. The people regarded as chronically poor in these studies were not necessarily in permanent receipt of poor relief, but they were liable to become dependent on public or private charity should the breadwinner become ill or suffer unemployment in a depression. Such people were exempt from both local and national taxation. An individual exemption certificate records that the person named on it was excused from paying hearth tax because his cottage was valued at less than one pound per annum:

and moreover, he is a very poore man, haveing a wife & a greate charge of children to maintain by his hard labour & very like to fall upon the parish charge.

Another person who had paid in the past was exempt as he had:

now . . . become poore by reason of the evill that is upon him and not able to work to maintain his family . . . is forced to receave alms of the parish.

The role of children in aggravating poverty is suggested in the certificates exempting a man who had 'little else but what he gaineth by his daily labour and having a wife and three small children to maintain out of it', and one who 'hath many small children to maintaine of his labour & is not able to pay'.

The relationship between access to land and poverty is suggested by the surviving records of poor law administration. At least before 1660, little formal aid to the poor was necessary in purely agricultural areas, even though urban parishes, and rural ones with a substantial industrial population, had trouble finding funds to meet their obligations.

Crisis poverty
The growing number of landless poor who were able to eke out a precarious living in more prosperous times were liable to destitution, not only if their personal circumstances changed for the worse, but whenever there was a downturn in the economy. The sixteenth and

seventeenth centuries were economically unstable. B.E. Supple has argued that the economic cycles of capitalism had not yet developed. Fluctuations were a response to random events—an outbreak of plague which disrupted markets, a war which shut off overseas trade, currency manipulations, government intervention and, the most common disrupter, a bad harvest. The first two could soon make workers unemployed by the direct stoppage of sales. The effects of a bad harvest were more subtle. It is clear that the sudden increase in food prices would have a particularly serious effect on the poor. In addition, it meant that even reasonably prosperous people who had to buy their food would have to postpone other purchases, such as new clothes, shoes or household goods.

The consequent fall in demand could lead to business failures and unemployment. It is true, of course, that poor harvests meant high prices and that farmers' incomes were greatest whenever production was below average, but not so low that they had no saleable surplus. Poor harvests, therefore, transferred income from the purchasers to the producers of food. Farmers are generally believed to have been more likely to save their additional income than were urban workers. To use economic jargon, they had a higher propensity to save. As a result, there was a lower velocity of circulation and a reduction in overall demand for goods and services.

In the sixteenth century, serious harvest failures were to cause economic disruption in 1573, 1586, and for the four consecutive years 1595–8. The most serious situation occurred when a major slump coincided with a harvest failure, something which happened twice in the early seventeenth century, in 1621–2 and in 1629–31. On both occasions, the combination of high food prices and unemployment created a crisis by making it necessary for many who normally contributed to the relief of the poor to seek aid for themselves (Thirsk 1967, page 820; Supple, 1959, pages 6–12, 16).

Vagrancy

The poor who were most feared by respectable society, and by the government, were the vagrants. They offended both the traditional concept of a static society, of a community in which every man had a place, and the newer ideas which made labour a virtue. Both the upholders of the old morality and the new could agree on the brutal treatment of the wandering poor.

Some of those who were forced from their home parish by economic changes or war were never resettled. These professional vagrants became self-perpetuating as they included women as well as men; their children grew up having known no other life. A whole literature developed concerning the vagrants. Perhaps the best known contemporary description was Thomas Dekker's *Bell-Man of London: A discovery of all the idle Vagabonds in England*, published in 1608. Dekker wrote of the way rogues simulated deformity in order to collect alms, then spent the proceeds on riotous living. Others managed to avoid punishment under the laws against sturdy beggars by having forged documents giving them permission to travel. Dekker wrote:

A rogue is known to all men by his name, but not to all men by his conditions: no puritan can dissemble more than he, for he will speak in a lamentable tune and crawl along the streets, (supporting his body by a staff) as if there were not life enough in him to put strength into his legs: his head shall be bound about with linen, loathsome to behold; . . . his apparel is all tattered . . . if they had better clothes given them, they would rather sell them . . . and wander up and down in that piteous manner, only to move people to compassion, and to be relieved with money, which being gotten, at night is spent as merrily and as lewdly as in the day it was won by counterfeit villainy.(Quoted in Pound, 1971, page 98.)

That this description was not purely imaginary is suggested by a legal deposition concerning a man who had pretended to be blind and crippled until he was given food and money; he then 'went away with a snail's pace halting downright and shaking and groping with his staffe till he thought he was out of sight and then he was an upright man on the sudden and without any lameness, blindness, quaking or quivering'.

In the Middle Ages the small number of vagrants had been tolerated: they did not represent any threat to society. In the sixteenth and seventeenth centuries they were seen as a pool of potential criminals and subversives, and harsh measures were taken against them. A statute of Henry VIII provided for the whipping of unlicensed beggars and the return to their place of birth, and an Act of Edward VI's first parliament permitted J.P.s to enslave sturdy beggars for two years, or for life if they ran away. Second offenders could be executed. Similar legislation was enacted under Elizabeth. An Act of 1572 empowered J.P.s to whip vagrants and to bore them through the ear for a first offence, condemn them as a felon for a second, and hang them for a third. This harsh law was enforced in full, at least in Middlesex. Between 1572 and 1575, forty-four vagabonds, who were second offenders reprieved from hanging, were sentenced to be branded, eight were set to service and five were hanged. In 1586 the hanging and ear-boring were repealed and the penalty for vagrancy, which was to remain in force throughout the rest of the sixteenth and the seventeenth century, was that a vagrant was to be whipped until 'his or her body be bloody', provided with a certificate of punishment and returned from constable to constable until he reached the parish in which he was legally settled. This provision was repeated by the statutes of 1598 and 1601 and there is ample evidence from county records that it was enforced as a matter of routine. In 1637 a parish constable noted laconically, 'I have stocked, whipped and passed five rogues'. At times when discharged soldiers reinforced the existing bands of vagrants, provost marshals were appointed to suppress them. In the seventeenth century, the Privy Council ordered the counties to employ them on at least six occasions. Their powers included the infliction of the death penalty.

Poor relief

In the early sixteenth century there was little organised relief for the poor. Help from family and neighbours, charitable aid from the squire or the monasteries, were usually sufficient. Where they were not, paupers might resort to begging. Even in the 1520s begging had become a sufficient problem in some of the cities for by-laws to be passed requiring beggars to be licensed. From the accession of Elizabeth, increased provision of official aid to the poor was necessary, and the legislation establishing the system of poor relief which was to last until the 1830s was passed in the last years of her reign. In the seventeenth century the administration of the Elizabethan laws was extended, refined and made more professional.

Elizabethan legislation showed a determination to check the economic trends which were believed to cause poverty, and to ensure that paupers were given at least minimum subsistence. In 1563 the Statute of Artificers reinforced apprenticeship requirements in an attempt to make the labour market more stable, and anti-enclosure laws were passed to limit rural depopulation. It was made compulsory for the more prosperous members of each parish to contribute to the relief of their own poor. In 1576 parishes were empowered to levy poor rates. (Note that the parliamentary committee which thrashed out the details of this Act was chaired by John Aldrich, the originator of the poor relief scheme operating in Norwich.) Also parishes and towns were instructed to provide special work schemes for the unemployed.

The Elizabethan Poor Laws culminated in the Acts of 1598 and 1601. Under their terms, each parish was empowered to appoint overseers of the poor, consisting of two churchwardens and four other 'substantial inhabitants', to control poor relief; the children of paupers were to be apprenticed, compulsorily if necessary, and the able-bodied poor were to be provided with work. The 1576 Act authorising poor rates was extended. J.P.s were empowered to impose a poor rate on a hundred (a major subdivision of a county which included several parishes), or even a whole county, if any parishes had so many poor that they could not provide for them out of their own resources. In general, poor relief was administered by parish officials, but their work was subject to supervision by the J.P.s. The most common reasons for intervention by a magistrate were the failure of local authorities to meet their obligations, and disputes between parishes over the responsibility to pay for particular paupers. Parishes were liable to pay relief to any paupers who were legally settled there, but what constituted legal settlement was often unclear. In one case, a pauper occupied a house which lay on the border between two parishes and they disputed liability:

Models of both the house and of the bed in which the pauper slept were laid before the Court that it might ascertain how much of his body lay in each parish. The Court held the pauper was settled where his head (being the nobler part) lay, though one of his legs at least, and a great part of his body, lay out of the parish'. (Quoted in Taylor, 1969, page 94.)

Parishes were liable to provide both a dwelling house and weekly maintenance to their poor. In purely rural parishes, there were few paupers and the problem was dealt with mainly by private charity until after the Restoration. Consequently, they lacked a well-developed administrative machinery. For example, the Worcestershire parish of Bransford does not appear to have paid regular maintenance money to its poor, though in 1616 and 1617 the parish paid the house rent of one Elizabeth Ball. In 1611 five shillings were distributed to unnamed unnumbered poor. In 1612 the parish provided one shilling's worth of food 'for the children of Jo. Holdship', and paid eight pence to a widow. The problem of poverty in this small rural parish was obviously of a different nature from that of the towns. Of seven Worcestershire parishes whose records survive from the seventeenth century, only one was making regular payments to the poor until after the Restoration.

In the towns, the problem of poverty was much more serious. Examination of the accounts of urban parishes indicates considerable truth in the report to the magistrates frequently made by constables that, 'the poor are weekly relieved'. The accounts of the suburban parish of St Michaels in Bedwardine show that the churchwardens were making regular payments to the poor from early Tudor times. Typical entries include 'Gyven to mother Walker in her sickness iis [two shillings]' (1569); 'Gyven to mother Margett at tymes iss vid'

(1569); 'Gyven to Thomas Flecher towards the cure in surgery of his sone Christofor Flecher xxs' (1582). Not all aid was as successful. In the same year, an entry recorded the payment of three pence to 'mother Clark'. The next line reads, 'Item gyven to burye her xvii Maii xiid'. Children were obvious recipients of help. In 1599 three pounds seventeen shillings were paid to 'widowe Elkynes for the keeping of a poor child'. Not all payments were made in selfless Christian charity. In the same year four pounds was 'geven to a poore woman which Henry Conway had taken in as tenant unto him, in consideracion that she should departe out of our parishe'. In the 1620s there were between ten and twenty persons regularly receiving alms, most of whom were women, a high proportion widows. In 1628 sixty-six payments were made, only ten to men. Occasionally, relief was given to poor families when the breadwinner was ill, to deserted wives and to orphans. One entry records, 'Given to Worralls wife & children at severall times (he being run away) 7/6'. The parish also bought a smock, stockings and shoes for this unfortunate family and paid for 'mending and makeing Cloathes for ye sayd Worralls daughter'.

The accounts of the churchwardens and overseers of the poor in the parish of St Andrews in the city of Worcester reveal a similar approach—regular maintenance money, occasional gifts of food and clothes. In St Nicholas, Worcester, an average of thirty-two people received regular monthly payments ranging from three pence to one shilling. In March 1634–5, £2.18s.8d was paid to thirty-two recipients. In the year ending March 1634, the parish disbursed £48.1s.4d in regular 'monthly pay' and in casual help to 'poor people not in the book'. Differing mainly in scale were the activities of the London parish of St Martin-in-the-Fields which spent £1876.16s.4d in 1714.

One of the more expensive obligations of the parish authorities was to provide housing. In rural areas, cottages were usually built on waste land at parish expense. Parish housing was often of a very low quality. On one occasion, a man was permitted to live in a sheep cote. Parishes did not provide housing for newly weds—they were expected to remain single until they could provide their own. In 1661 Justice Hyde made an assize ruling that 'lusty yong maried people . . . [were] to provide howses for themselves at their peril . . . yf yong men marry . . . before they have howses . . . let them lye under an oke'.

The problem of older pauper children was dealt with by compulsory apprenticeship. If parents did not arrange an apprentice-ship themselves, the churchwardens and the overseers of the poor could bring children before two J.P.s and, at the expense of the parish, bind any boy or girl aged between seven and fourteen to a master without the consent of either apprentice or employer. The period of indenture was usually until the age of twenty-one or, in the case of girls, until marriage. A typical agreement bound the apprentice to serve his master as 'a true and faithful servant ought to behave himself', and the master to teach his apprentice 'and in due manner to chastise him, findynge unto his said servant meate, drinke, linnen, woollen hose, shoes and all other things to him necessary'.

Apprenticeship could provide problems for the authorities, especially in times of trade depression when masters did not need any more labour. In many cases, orders of quarter sessions or assizes were needed to force compliance, and in the 1630s one refusal took the reluctant employer as far as the Star Chamber. Unfortunately, there were many examples of cruelty to unwanted apprentices.

The greater number of paupers in the towns and cities led to more elaborate systems of poor relief. By law, after 1598, towns had to build houses of correction, or bridewells, where the able-bodied poor were forced to work for a living. Sometimes, petty offenders were sentenced to join them. Conditions must have been harsh, for petitions to serve the rest of the sentence in the ordinary prison rather than the house of correction were not infrequent. In the late seventeenth century, the houses of correction came to be regarded as places of punishment for vagrants and petty offenders. Though not very common until after 1700, an increased number of workhouses were built to provide employment and minimum subsistence for other paupers.

Many cities adopted more far-reaching schemes than were required by law. Under Elizabeth, London, Ipswich, Gloucester, Cambridge and York all established compulsory poor rates, provided materials on which the poor were able to work, and built houses of correction, schools and hospitals. Perhaps the most ambitious scheme was that operated by Norwich. The city had been one of the earliest to adopt systematic poor relief, having instituted compulsory poor rates in 1549. In the 1570s over £500 a year was being spent on poor relief, more than was spent on all other city business (see Pound, 1977, pages 60–8, for an excellent case study). In the first half of the seventeenth century, the Puritan-dominated city of Salisbury combined harsh treatment of vagrants, over 600 of whom were whipped between 1598 and 1638, with the provision of work for its own able-bodied poor and a relatively generous system of relief payments to the infirm. The latter were made in the form of tokens exchangeable for food, drink and fuel at the public storehouse. Some education and job training was provided for poor children. To supplement the amount raised by the rates or available from charity, the corporation established a common brewhouse in 1623. The profits were used for 'the good and relyeffe of the poore of the workingehouse, and other poore of the Cittye'. Though the brewhouse operated on a large scale, the profits were less than expected and it was leased to private enterprise in 1646. The city workhouse was founded in 1602 and it continued to operate throughout the century. From the late 1630s, it seems to have operated more harshly. Idlers were whipped on admission and the poor children living there were to wear badges bearing the arms of the city and blue caps 'whereby they might be known the children of the workhouse and distinguished from all other children'. The disruption of city finances brought about by the Civil War led to Salisbury abandoning its attempt to do more than meet the requirements of the law.

There is no doubt that the scale of poor relief expanded during the seventeenth century. The population was rising more quickly than wealth was growing, until the 1620s. In addition, economic changes were disrupting traditional routines and forcing people away from the local communities in which they had sustenance and an established place. Perhaps as a result of this, there seems to have been a decline in the importance of personal face-to-face charity, and an increased willingness to rely on institutional relief rather than private aid to the poor. Indeed, there was a marked change of attitude from the Middle Ages and early sixteenth century, when giving alms to beggars was regarded as a meritorious act, to the seventeenth century Puritans who regarded such indiscriminate charity as an encouragement to indolence. By the seventeenth century, it was very rare for wealthy men to bequeath funds to be spent on doles to the poor at their funerals.

It has often been charged that the Puritans had a harsher attitude to the poor than did other Englishmen. Historians who see Puritanism as the ideology of a rising capitalist class expect to see an unfeeling attitude towards those who did not work, and who forced up the rates of taxation. This is only partly true. Puritans were very condemning of able-bodied paupers who did not seek to work. On the other hand, they were charitable to the disabled and unfortunate. The city schemes for poor relief, especially that of Salisbury, were devised by Puritans. In practice, the provision of public aid seems to have been determined more by need than by ideology. In his study of poor relief in Warwickshire, A.L. Beir (*Past and Present*, 35, 1966) found that both the number of persons requesting assistance and the amount provided was determined by the price of food and the level of employment, not the political or religious opinions of the county magistracy. The Interregnum governments were as concerned as their predecessors to establish a better system of poor relief, though like them they found it easier to enact measures for the suppression of vagrancy than for a national system of aid to the genuinely unemployed and disabled.

It is probable that attitudes to the poor became less humanitarian after the Restoration. Certainly the trend towards a more organised system of poor relief continued. Rating to provide funds became universal, even in purely agricultural areas. Perhaps as a result of the rising cost of poor relief, parishes became even more determined to exclude any poor but their own. The Act of Settlement of 1662 and its amendment in 1685 allowed anyone who occupied a tenement valued at less than £10 a year, or who seemed likely to be chargeable to the parish, to be returned to their last place of settlement. Vagabonds and sturdy beggers could be transported to the American colonies to work as unpaid indentured servants for seven years. A person moving for temporary work had to guard against arrest as a vagrant by obtaining a certificate from the minister of the parish, one of the churchwardens and one of the overseers of the poor. Perhaps the most unfeeling piece of legislation came in 1697 when those in receipt of parish relief were compelled to wear a badge on the shoulder of the right sleeve, 'a large Roman P, together with the first Letter of Name of Parish . . . cut either in red or blew cloth'. Those who refused to wear it were to be denied further assistance or even committed to the house of correction 'there to be whipt and kept at hard Labour' for up to twenty-one days (Taylor, 1969, pages 27–9, 104).

Though the system of parish poor relief was far from perfect, it does appear to have prevented outright starvation, except in a very small number of cases. In this at least it was superior to anything available in most Continental countries. In France many of the poor starved to death in years of poor harvests. On the other hand, the public system was minimalist in its assumptions—it was designed to provide only the bare necessities of life. The associated social policy can also be criticised. It tried to prevent poverty by restricting economic changes and by almost imprisoning workers in their home parish rather than by encouraging mobility of labour to growth areas, or by deliberately stimulating economic development in new industries with a capacity to employ additional labour.

The day to day charity provided by individuals is seldom recorded. Certainly, it is impossible to quantify. It was undoubtedly of great significance. However, one of the most important and most constructive types of poor relief was that provided by charitable bequests. These had been important ever since the Middle Ages and they were put on a firm legal footing by the Act of Charitable Uses in 1601. It remained in force until 1888 and the preamble of the Elizabethan Act was retained in its successor. The relief of the aged and sick, aid to students, the repair of roads, bridges and highways, help to young tradesmen, financial assistance 'for mariages of poore maides', and subsidies for those who were too poor to pay their taxes were among the wide-ranging activities regarded as charitable. (Quoted in Pound, 1977, page 56.)

W.K. Jordan (see Bibliography) has made the fullest study of charitable bequests. Some of his conclusions are now being questioned by other historians. In particular, his claim that charitable giving increased enormously between 1485 and 1600 is true only if one ignores inflation. If one takes rising prices into account, the amount left in wills for charitable purposes actually fell. Increased evidence of public poor relief has also thrown doubt on his assertion that bequest funds were more important than public money in poor relief. Despite these recent criticisms of Jordan's work, there is no doubt that endowment funds were tremendously important.

Jordan found that between 1480 and 1600 the proportion of bequest funds left for religious purposes showed a steady decline, while those willed to charity steadily increased. For example, before the Reformation forty-five per cent of London charity was devoted to religion; by 1600, only seven per cent. Money bequeathed to the poor could be used either to supplement public funds in providing minimum subsistence, or to pay for social rehabilitation schemes which, it was hoped, would enable beneficiaries to become economically productive citizens. The merchant class was particularly interested in this approach. Between 1561 and 1600, nearly eighty-seven per cent of merchants' charitable bequests were applied to social rehabilitation. Funds applied in this way helped combat the causes of poverty by making possible the education of poor boys. Schools and scholarships were common beneficiaries. An equally important approach was the provision of funds to provide low interest or interest-free loans to young men setting up in their first business. By investing in people, the merchant philanthropists made an important contribution towards the reduction of poverty. Had the public authorities adopted the same approach, instead of confining their activities to providing bare subsistence, the benefit to society would have been enormous.

Changes in economic organisation

Advances in financial organisation were one of the most important contributors to economic growth. It is more difficult to quantify their effects and to state precise benefits than it is to find evidence of expansion of trade, yet without a considerable modernisation in commercial practices, many significant material benefits could not have been financed.

One of the most significant developments, which made possible the transfer of money and even the expansion of credit, was the growth of banks. Before the 1650s, wealthy men who wished to borrow or lend money turned to the goldsmiths, brokers or scriveners. Scriveners and brokers simply placed out at interest the money of others. They were purely intermediaries: their role can, perhaps, be compared to that of an accountant or solicitor today, who arranges loans between private people, draws up the contract and takes a fee or commission. Goldsmiths, too, could work in this way, but they came to extend their operations beyond it. Because of the high value of their stock-in-trade, goldsmiths had to invest in elaborate security precautions and it was one of their early functions to provide a safe-deposit system for other peoples' valuables. They soon discovered that, when money was deposited with them, it was good business to use it to buy bills of exchange at a discount and then to repay the depositor with the proceeds of eventual sale. In addition, the receipt given the depositor could be passed from hand to hand as a substitute for coin, thus foreshadowing the banknote. Depositors could also write orders instructing the goldsmith to transfer parts of their deposit to a named person, thus providing the equivalent of a modern cheque.

From the 1650s, certain business houses, usually those which had engaged in the goldsmith business, took to full-time banking. By this time, they had learned one of the fundamental principles of banking: that it was possible to issue notes to a greater value than the funds deposited with the bank. This enabled the bank to increase its profits and it expanded the money supply. This system worked, provided that investors retained their confidence and did not attempt mass withdrawals, so forcing the collapse of the bank. By 1675 bankers were performing the three main functions of their modern equivalents: taking deposits, discounting bills and issuing notes (Wilson, 1971, pages 206–7, 329–33; Coleman, 1977, page 147).

One of the main functions of post-Restoration banks was to channel the funds of private investors into government hands. Many small investors were more willing to trust bankers than they were to trust the King, and the banks profited from their fears by re-lending their deposits at a higher rate of interest. The creation of the Bank of England in 1694 was an attempt to regulate and make more efficient a long-established custom, though one that had brought disaster to many bankers after the Stop on the Exchequer in 1672 (see chapter 3, page 187).

Though the banks developed overdraft facilities, in England they were not to become the main source of long-term loans for agricultural or industrial development. Methods of securing loans from one private individual to another were to experience significant development in the sixteenth and seventeenth centuries. One of the most important private contracts was the bill or bond. This was also known as the recognisance and statute, depending on small legal differences. All had in common that they were agreements to lend sums of money for short periods, usually six months. If the capital and interest were not repaid by the due date, the lender could prosecute the borrower in the Court of Common Pleas and ask either that goods be seized to pay the debt or that the debtor be imprisoned until he paid. There were considerable legal difficulties in enforcement and, as a result, bonds were usually for small amounts. Recognisances and statutes offered better legal protection for the lender to a peer or landed gentleman, as it enabled the debt to be recovered by seizure of rents. None of these variations on the bond were popular with the borrower, as failure to repay on due date made him liable for twice the sum borrowed.

Probably safer for both parties, if the borrower had a suitable security, was the pledge. Land, jewellery, plate, even the robes of a peer could be used as a pledge. This resort to pawning was, however, regarded as a last resort.

By the mid-seventeenth century the most satisfactory method of securing a substantial loan was the mortgage. Until about 1640, those who could not repay the money they had borrowed on mortgage were liable to lose the whole of the property against which the loan had been secured, even if it was considerably more valuable than the money owing. However, the Court of Chancery gradually moved against this practice by allowing late payers to regain their property if there was a good reason for the delay, and it became customary for the creditor to grant an extension of time if funds were not available at once. If foreclosure did take place, and the property was sold, any excess over capital, interest and expenses was usually returned to the borrower. These developments provided both borrower and lender with reasonable security when the loan was secured against landed property. Though there was no large increase in the amount lent once mortgages became safer, it is probable that funds raised in this way contributed to the rebuilding of rural England and to the financing of agricultural improvements. Where industrialists possessed suitable security, the mortgage may have contributed to the availability of funds for capital investment (Wilson, 1971, pages 207–8; Stones, 1981, pages 513–38).

Though forms of insurance were known in the Middle Ages, the direct forerunners of modern insurance were not to emerge in England until the middle or late seventeenth century. One of the problems was that the current state of both factual knowledge and mathematical skills made it difficult to compute premiums. There was some form of fire insurance in existence before the 1660s, but it was little used, and a rapid growth of interest only emerged after the Great Fire. The rebuilding of London in brick reduced the risk of fire and thus enabled premiums to be reduced. The first fire insurance office was the Hand in Hand Fire Office which was established in the 1690s.

For the first three-quarters of the seventeenth century, those English ship-owners and merchants who required insurance normally took advantage of the well-developed system established in Amsterdam. In the 1680s, however, a number of English marine underwriters began to accept risks. A large group of them took to meeting and exchanging news at Edward Lloyd's coffee house. In 1686 they established a formal club and in 1696 Lloyd himself published the first *Lloyd's News*. Lloyds was, and has remained, an association of underwriters rather than a company. Insurance was and is undertaken at Lloyds, not with Lloyds. Brokers arrange for the clients' premiums to be paid to an underwriter, or group of underwriters, who then accept the risk.

Life insurance of the modern type was another product of Dutch ingenuity. Once the idea spread to England in the late seventeenth century, it provided a challenge to the leading mathematicians— Graunt, Petty and Halley (the Astronomer Royal)—to develop means of making the actuarial calculations. By the end of the century, both life insurance (with the payment of a lump sum on the death of the person insured) and annuities (yearly payments in return for a capital sum) were readily available. The first specialist life insurance company, the Society for Assurance of Widows and Orphans, was established in 1699 (Wilson, 1971, pages 333–5).

All these forms of insurance helped reduce the investment risk to the individual: investors could ensure that they would not be left destitute by the sinking of their ship or the burning down of their mill; members of the middle class could make provision for the support of wives and children should they die prematurely. Insurance was a response to a more rational attitude to life, and as such it was often condemned as impious by religious people who believed that merchants should trust in God rather than in insurance companies. Insurance may, too, have been influenced by increasing urbanisation. To a rural man, so dependent on the vagaries of the seasons and the weather, risk was a part of life which he had always accepted as part of the natural order. City dwellers, with their capital invested in assets less durable than land, wanted greater security. It is possible, too, that the growth of insurance encouraged investment in non-landed property and thus contributed to industrial growth.

Another means of spreading risk was the development of the joint stock company. Despite claims by Nef that joint stock companies were characteristic of the sixteenth and early seventeenth centuries, recent scholarship suggests that they were neither common nor appropriate, except in special areas of the economy. Foreign trade, especially trans-oceanic ventures to areas outside Europe, was a particularly appropriate activity for joint stock companies for, as a contemporary wrote, 'private men cannot extend to making such long, adventurous and costly voyages'. (Quoted in Wilson, 1971, pages 172–3.) Even trade with the rest of Europe was in the hands of the regulated companies owned by a limited number of men.

By the end of the seventeenth century, the transoceanic trading companies had a very large amount of capital invested in them. The East India Company had £400 000 in paid up capital in 1660, £1.6 million in 1703. In addition, its rival the New East India Company, with which it was to merge in 1708, had £2.3 million invested in it, making a total of £3.8 million in the two companies. The Royal Africa Company had over £1 million invested; the Hudson Bay Company was tiny by comparison with only £32 000 invested in it.

The other risky venture established as a joint stock company was the Bank of England: a combination of several rich men, who provided the necessary capital, created the confidence in its notes which enabled it to survive. As is discussed elsewhere (chapter 2, pages 191–3), it was only the capacity of this bank to secure funds for the government in the crisis years of the 1690s which enabled King William and his regime to survive the war with France. Joint stock companies, as distinct from private partnerships, were a special solution to problems which were still unusual in the seventeenth century. Nevertheless, they were important in the way they allowed a growth area in trade to develop, and in the critical realm of banking.

Though the benefit of a joint stock company for a private investor is that it allows him to spread his risk, another late seventeenth century development helped make such investments into speculations. From the 1660s a lively market in the shares of joint stock companies developed and the profession of stock jobber or or stock broker came into being. By the end of the century, there was a well-developed system based on that of the Amsterdam Bourse, which had been established in 1609. Both the shares of joint stock companies and government bills were the objects of much wild and risky speculation, which made fortunes for some and ruined others. By the mid-eighteenth century at least, the stock exchange was inhabited by two animals still living there today:

A Bear in the language of Change Alley is a person who has agreed to sell any quantity of the public funds more than he is possessed of and often without being possessed of any at all, which, nevertheless, he is obliged to deliver against a certain time: before this time arrives, he is continually going up and down selling . . . whose property he can devour . . . rejoicing in mischief at any misfortune that may bring about the wished-for change or falling the stocks, that he may buy in low and settle his account to advantage.

A bull was:

the name by which the gentlemen of Change Alley choose to call all persons who contract to buy any quantity of government securities, without any intention or ability to pay for it, and who consequently are obliged to sell it again, either at a profit or loss, before the time comes when they have contracted to take it. (Quoted in Wilson, 1971, pages 326–7.)

This form of speculation did not suit investors who wanted security, and alongside the dangerous, but potentially profitable, investment in ordinary shares developed a system of investment in bonds at fixed interest rates. This provided comparative safety for their capital and a regular income, thus encouraging investment, which enabled the company whose bonds were at issue to expand its operations.

It is safe to assume that the growth of banks, the development of better methods of securing loans, the spread of insurance and the emergence of joint stock companies with freely traded shares all assisted in making funds available for economic development. Their total effect must have been to increase the velocity of circulation by making it less likely that funds would lie idle for want of a suitable investment: they could, therefore, have offset to some extent any contraction in the money supply. With the possible exception of developments in mortgage finance, they all tended to channel investments in the direction of trade and industry rather than into the purchase, as distinct from the development, of land. Once more, one finds in the late seventeenth century a series of changes which contributed to the economic revolutions which were to follow.

One of the most significant changes which took place between the mid-sixteenth century and the end of the seventeenth was the decline of the guilds. At the accession of Elizabeth I they were still a potent force, but by 1700, most had become little more than social clubs.

In the Middle Ages guilds had come into existence to control entry into trades, to regulate training, workmanship, hours of work and prices, to ensure the well-being of members, and to see that all received a fair share of the market. Like modern professional associations, they also claimed to represent the interests of the consumer. By the early sixteenth century, there had been significant changes, especially as the trade guilds had come to dominate the craft guilds, whose members actually produced the goods. In addition, there had been a move towards a distinct status hierarchy of guilds, with the sellers of imported goods and the manufacturing employers constituting an élite, while the provincial craft guilds declined into an inferior position.

Within guilds there was a change from the medieval ideal, whereby every apprentice could pass through the graduations of apprentice and journeyman (qualified craftsman who worked for daily wages), to master craftsman (who was self-employed and might employ others); the change was to a situation in which only those apprentices who had good family connections could confidently expect to rise beyond journeyman. Naturally the master craftsmen continued to dominate the guilds and to do so in the interests of the employers (Ramsay, 1972, pages 95–102). Thus many guilds were to experience a tension between the dominant élite and the ordinary members which was to make them much weaker than if members had been united.

The guilds began to lose importance in the late seventeenth century. The main reason was not the internal disunity discussed above, but the economic changes which were taking place. Changing patterns of demand and new technology, as well as a desire to escape guild restrictions, led to an expansion of industry outside the cities in which guild regulations prevailed. As Sir John Clapham wrote, 'Water power had been a solvent of gild-power from the days of the first rural fulling mill' (Wilson, 1971, page 136). The increased use of water power drew industry from the cities to hill country rivers.

By the late sixteenth century the convention developed that a freeman of one trade could transfer his interests to another, thus destroying one of the most important roles of the guilds: protection of their members against competition from people who had not passed through their training and entry procedure. There was a short-lived attempt to return to closer guild regulation as part of the social reaction under Charles I. This was not successful and was an easy subject for ridicule when the Privy Council attempted to settle a demarcation dispute between the makers of felt hats and their rivals in the beaver hat industry by 'forbidding . . . mixed hats as injurious to public morals' (Wilson, 1971, page 101). More significant was Cromwell's decision to open all trades to disbanded parliamentary soldiers.

The new cities and the new industries which grew from the mid-seventeenth century were not subject to guild controls, and the courts refused to extend them into either new technology or new geographical areas. Neither Birmingham nor Manchester was subject to any form of guild regulation, and even in London suburban industries were beyond effective control. By the end of the century guilds and even the London livery companies had become little more than social organisations (Wilson, 1971, page 169; Coleman, 1977, pages 73–4).

Colonisation

Early sixteenth century English exploratory ventures were designed to increase trade, not to colonise or even to convert the pagan. Moreover, they were abortive ventures, intended to circumvent the Spanish and Portuguese monopolies in the Americas and tap instead the wealth of the Far East. When Elizabeth became queen, however, successive attempts to find these passages had failed. Interest was turning back to trade in 'prohibited' areas, such as the Spanish Caribbean and Portuguese Africa and India. The State threw its weight (but not its money) behind such ventures, and contemporary propaganda encouraged them. So Richard Hakluyt the younger, an Elizabethan clergyman and geographer, wrote: 'I conceive great hope that the time approacheth and now is, that we of England may share both with the Spaniard and the Portingale in part of America and other regions as yet undiscovered.' He declared that 'the countries lying north of Florida God hath reserved the same to be reduced unto Christian civility by the English nation'. And this is precisely where all the Elizabethan colonial experiments took place.

Not that these experiments succeeded. In 1583 Sir Humphrey Gilbert explored Newfoundland, claimed it for the Queen, but he left not a single Englishman to colonise it—and in any case he drowned on the way home. Inexperience, lack of resources, and the desire to combine settlement with quick profits: all joined together to thwart early attempts at colonisation. Sir Walter Raleigh's first expedition to found an American colony in 1585 is a classic example. He received a grant of land from the Queen and an Act of Parliament to add weight to her authority. However, the Act revealed the inexperience of members, because it forbade wives on the expedition. Without women, the colony had no chance of survival or growth. Moreover, the 107 settlers and their governors were more interested in gold than farming, hardly the economic basis of a viable colony. Left on Roanoke Island, off Virginia, they whittled away their time waiting for relief convoys. After ten months Francis Drake, fresh from his raid on the Spanish West Indies, transported them home.

Undeterred, Raleigh tried again in 1587; this time with the invaluable experience of his first failure under his belt. He recruited men

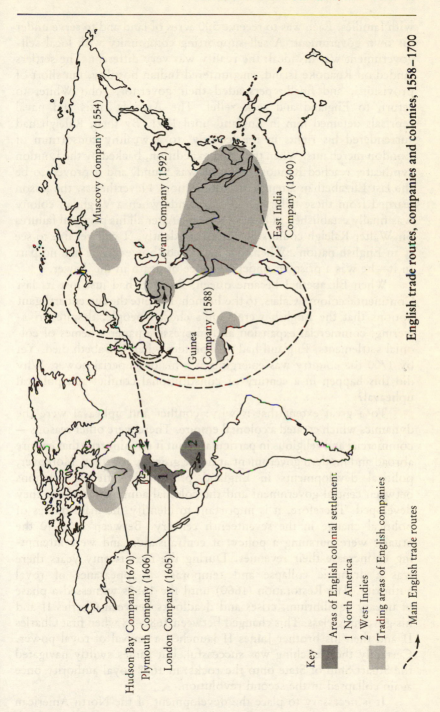

English trade routes, companies and colonies, 1558–1700

Muscovy Company (1554)

Levant Company (1592)

East India Company (1600)

Guinea Company (1588)

Hudson Bay Company (1670)

Plymouth Company (1606)

London Company (1605)

Key

Areas of English colonial settlement
1 North America
2 West Indies

Trading areas of English companies

Main English trade routes

with families. Each was to receive 500 acres of land and to serve under his own government. A self-supporting community with local self-government was his ideal: the reality was very different. The settlers landed on Roanoke Island, encountered Indian hostility, ran short of provisions, and finally persuaded their governor, John White, to return to England and seek relief. The Armada crisis and naval reprisals detained him in England until 1591. By then, Raleigh had surrendered his rights in the 'colony' to a wealthy consortium of London merchants. When the relief expedition, backed by the London syndicate, reached Roanoke, no one was found, and it proved to be the last Elizabethan attempt at colonisation. Nevertheless, the lesson learned from these failures bore dividends when a Virginian colony was finally established in James I's reign. After all his personal failures Sir Walter Raleigh could still write confidently, 'I will yet live to see it an English nation'. When that happened, however, he had no part in it—he was a prisoner under sentence of death in the Tower.

When Elizabeth I became queen, England had just lost its last Continental colony, Calais, to the French. Despite the current arrogant notions that the English were God's chosen people, despite privateering, commercial expansion and impressive paper schemes of colonial settlements, England had no colonies when Elizabeth died. Yet by 1700 the country was emerging as a major imperial power. Why did this happen in a century of constitutional conflict and political upheaval?

To a great extent that *is* why: conflict and upheaval were the dynamics which created a colonial empire. There were other reasons—commercial and religious in particular—but it remains true that empire abroad and modern government at home grew up together. Moreover, political developments in England profoundly affected relations between central government and the colonial administrations as they developed. Therefore, it is important to identify the main phases of political change in the seventeenth century. Between 1603–40 the Stuarts were pursuing a policy of centralisation and were attempting to increase their revenues. During the next twenty years there was a dramatic collapse and temporary disappearance of royal authority. The Restoration (1660) until the 1680s witnessed a phase of uneasy equilibrium, crises and deadlocks between Charles II and his governing class. This changed between 1681–88 when first Charles II and then his brother James II launched a revival of royal power. Certainly the launching was successful, but James swiftly navigated the Stuart Ship of State onto the rocks: in 1688 royal authority once again collapsed in the second revolution.

It is necessary to place the development of the North American colonies in chronological relationship to such changes in the English

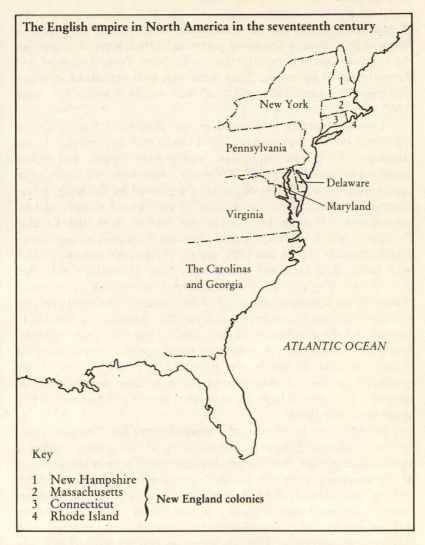

The English empire in North America in the seventeenth century

New York

Pennsylvania

— Delaware

— Maryland

Virginia

The Carolinas
and Georgia

ATLANTIC OCEAN

Key

1 New Hampshire
2 Massachusetts   } **New England colonies**
3 Connecticut
4 Rhode Island

political system. It was appropriate that the first colony was settled, in 1607, on that part of the coast on which Sir Walter Raleigh had concentrated his efforts, and that it should adopt the name of Virginia, originally chosen by him. If Raleigh was no practical organiser, he was at least a man of imagination who divined England's future. Raleigh was executed in 1618, a victim of early Stuart Anglo-Spanish politics. Yet not long afterwards, by the time of the English constitutional crisis of 1640, the New England colonies had been established: New Hampshire, Massachusetts, Rhode Island, Connecticut, all in the north; so too had one of the middle colonies, Maryland. The political disruption in England in the forties and fifties put a temporary halt on the creation of new settlements, but the restoration of Charles II in 1660 was followed by a spate of new royal grants and a fresh wave of migration: the Carolinas and Georgia in the south; New York, Delaware and Pennsylvania to the north. Thus there were two periods of intensive settlement: between 1603 and 1640 and during Charles II's reign (1660–85).

Two instruments were used in the process of founding new colonies. One was the chartered (joint stock) trading company. It was established by private enterprise, with private capital, and it was organised primarily for profit. Although it was organised under royal supervision, with a charter of possession granted by the King, it was generously treated, receiving a grant of very broad powers of self-government. This can be seen in the case of both the London Company, which was empowered to colonise Virginia in accordance with its charters of 1606 and 1609, and the Plymouth Company, which was chartered in 1606 and settled both New Hampshire and other parts of New England. They were permitted to establish governments chosen by the investors, and many of the powers of the royal prerogative were delegated to them, such as military defence, the minting of coinage and the distribution of land. During the early years of settlement, the Crown did not even send royal agents or officials to the colonies in order to watch over its interests. However, the Crown continued to claim ultimate sovereignty over them and, in order to safeguard its rights, it kept the colonies' charters in London where it could scrutinise them.

In 1629 a third company, the Massachusetts Bay Company, also received a charter. However, the founding of this colony marked a significant departure from the previous pattern. The chief stockholders of the company were not simply businessmen mounting a profit-making venture. They did not stand at the quayside, waving off boat-loads of settlers, before returning to London to await a profit from their investment. They too emigrated to Massachusetts, and they took their charter with them. This was an action which Charles I certainly had not intended. Now he would be unable to scrutinise and revise the terms of the charter whenever he wished to do so. As a result of this unexpected action, Massachusetts became, in practice, a self-governing colony which left the Crown impotent and unable to interfere. This must have been particularly galling for Charles I, because its governors were Puritan activists. Far away from the centralising trend of Stuart government, and free from the anti-Puritan, disciplinarian Arminian movement in the Anglican Church, they threw themselves into the virtuous and cheerless task of creating a godly commonwealth. Massachusetts became a dogmatic, intolerant and theocratic community, in which God, not the Crown or Parliament, was sovereign and in which the law was religion, not the Common Law of England.

The elect of Massachusetts created a new orthodoxy which was even harsher than that of Laudianism in England in the 1630s (see chapter 5, pages 285–9). Deviation was not to be tolerated, especially in matters religious. So, in 1636, it expelled a minister, Roger Williams, who believed in religious toleration and the separation of Church and State: anathema to the Puritan elect. Williams retaliated by founding a new colony which gave visible and physical expression to his beliefs: Providence (Rhode Island), which developed as a loose association of towns united by the common bond of hostility to the religious intolerance of New England. In the same year another clergyman, Thomas Hooker, rebelled against the suffocating orthodoxy of Massachusetts. Like a Moses he led his congregation away to search out and settle yet another promised land—and when it was found it was named Connecticut. So colonies proliferated, but they did so out of the reach of royal control and, in the case of Providence and Connecticut, independently, without reference to royal wishes.

In stark contrast was the only other colony founded before the constitutional crisis of 1640 and England's slide into civil war and revolution. The founding of this colony was important for two reasons: that the Crown reasserted its right to grant land to be settled in faraway places, and that this grant became the model for future colonisation of North America. In 1632 a Catholic peer, Lord Baltimore, received a proprietary charter from Charles I for the foundation of the colony of Maryland. This was no grant to a group of profit-making investors, but a gift of land which the proprietor could dispose of as he saw fit. In the process, the King reasserted the Crown's rights in a backward-looking quasi-feudal sense. Baltimore acknowledged Charles as his overlord, owing him loyalty and nominal payments: in this case, two Indian arrows each year. Perhaps Charles was hopeful of finding another Spanish El Dorado, so Baltimore had to surrender to the Crown twenty per cent of all gold and silver found within his lands. The financially straitened early Stuarts may have had such wild dreams but, whatever their motives for inserting clauses of this kind, they and their successors clearly preferred the proprietory grant to the chartered trading company. Charles II made proprietory grants of Delaware and Pennsylvania. He granted the Carolinas and Georgia to a consortium of eight courtiers. And he issued a fourth proprietory charter to his brother James, Duke of York. There was, however, one flaw in this particular grant. The tract of land was already occupied by the Dutch settlement of New Amsterdam. The Duke of York resolved the problem in a straightforward military manner: he conquered it and renamed it New York.

It is clear why the Crown changed its policy towards colonial settlement. The early chartered trading companies were given generous terms and considerable autonomy because the Crown had not yet grasped their considerable economic potential. However, in the 1620s the monarchy was desperate for money to wage war. And in the 1630s Charles was anxious to make ends meet without being forced back into financial dependence on Parliament. However, it was not simply a matter of money. One of Charles I's more consistent ambitions was to centralise political authority in the Crown: not to create an absolutism, but to give the monarch a more effective voice in local, regional and (now) colonial politics and government. The first step toward Caroline centralisation come even before his father's death, in 1624 when he and Buckingham were exercising a growing influence in government: the charter of the London Company was suppressed and Virginia was taken over as a royal possession. A year later Charles was king, whereupon he extended his direct control, declaring not only Virginia, but also the New England colonies 'to be a part of our Royal Empire descended upon us and undoubtedly belonging and appertaining unto us'.

In retrospect we can see Charles' action as a rash one. He was a new king, who needed time to acquaint himself with the problems of government in England. Yet almost at once he took to himself the task of administering territories which were thousands of miles away—a problem which never before had burdened an English government. Added to his inexperience as king, and the novelty of the problem, was the cost: because the Crown assumed the responsibility for defence of the colonies at a time when it was moving into a state of war against Spain and, soon afterwards, France. Moreover, when Charles declared that, in future, he would appoint colonial governors and their councils, he also undertook to pay them—another burden. The most serious, immediate problem was how to translate his bold words into practice. The government had no blueprint, no master-plan of colonial management, from which to work. It had to experiment, and for a decade it did just that, tinkering with various devices such as the Privy Council, the King's Secretary, special commissioners and a body known as the 'Committee for Foreign Plantations'.

This brief and muddled apprenticeship in the management of colonial affairs came to an end in 1634, when all these devices were replaced by a new commission. It was typical of Charles that he appointed, not an expert in colonial matters, but a theological Arminian hardliner to head it: William Laud, Archbishop of Canterbury.

The commission, which included the greatest officers of both Church and State, was granted sweeping powers, not only in Virginia but in the entire North American empire. It was authorised to appoint and dismiss all judges and other royal servants. In particular, as a step in the advancement of royal authority, it was empowered to scrutinise the charter of each colony to see if any of its privileges 'hurtful to us or our Crown . . . have been prejudicially granted.' Behind the sweeping powers of this commission and Laud's chairmanship, stood the ultimate power, Charles I. The direction of his thinking was unmistakeable and it ran upon two rails: the colonies could no longer be ignored as a possible source of royal revenue; and they could not be excluded from the Caroline policy of centralisation, which was also being pursued in England, Scotland and Ireland.

In both respects, the New England colonies, and in particular Massachusetts, were an offence to Charles's concern with royal rights. He must put an end to the virtual independence of Massachusetts, which had been achieved by transferring the company and charter across the Atlantic. Worse still, it had been founded by Puritans, who had migrated not only with a positive enthusiasm and desire to create a new society; they were also in flight from oppression in England. They were not loyal subjects but opponents of the King, and as such they had to be brought to heel. However, there was a danger that Massachusetts might secede and unilaterally deny any connections with the Mother Country. Charles moved to prevent such a novel action, and he did so with a well-tried medieval device: the *quo warranto* commission. The purpose of such a commission was to inquire, literally, by what warrant (right) did a town, a company, or in this case a colony, exercise its powers. A *quo warranto* inquiry, instituted by Charles I, resolved that the privileges of the Massachusetts Bay Company were excessive and so, in 1637, its charter was annulled. Thereupon, Charles I took the government of the colony into his own hands.

However, this early exercise in distant royal control was destined to be brief. The constitutional crisis of 1640 resulted in the collapse of the Crown's authority, both at home and abroad. During the following decade, both King and Parliament were absorbed in the great political issues being fought out on the battlefield and elsewhere in England. No one had the time or energy to trouble about the colonies, which simply and easily reasserted their autonomy: in particular Massachusetts, which reverted to government by its old charter. The troubles in England did not leave the colonies untouched, however. They divided in their allegiance, just as England had done: the New England colonies were for the revolutionary forces, whereas the middle colonies remained royalist, a sentiment reinforced by the influx of *émigré* royalists after the Civil War. Nevertheless, what mattered most was that they were left free to develop as they chose, without interference or attempts to regulate them by English governments. And this state of affairs continued throughout the 1650s when the revolutionary regimes displayed only an intermittent interest in the colonies. Certainly there was no consistent attempt to reassert English control. Oliver Cromwell, in particular, directed his energies to attacks on the Spanish empire in the West Indies (see page 102).

The Restoration of the Stuarts in 1660 not only ended the dreams and regimes of the revolutionaries in England. It also spelt the end of autonomy as the colonists had experienced it for the past twenty years. Once again, as under the early Stuarts, it was the Crown, not Parliament, which provided the dynamic in colonial growth and control. It patronised colonial expansion by the creation of new proprietary colonies, and it took the appropriate steps to assert effective royal control over new and old colonies alike. On paper and in law, the Crown's power was limited. Whereas James I and Charles I had successfully denied Parliament a voice in imperial matters, Charles II had to concede to it a share in authority. But, as in so many other matters, the difference between post-Restoration forms and practices was considerable. In practice, Parliament simply provided Charles with laws which gave him statutory authority and so augmented his power in his dealings with the colonies. In any case, Charles was not swimming against a political tide when he pursued a policy of centralised imperial control. There were powerful vested interests in the country which pressed for, indeed demanded, strong royal control: the merchant communities, especially London, now recognised the benefits of a colonial empire, which provided both a captive market for English goods and a source of commodities which England itself could not produce.

The Crown's motive in asserting imperial control over the colonies is an obvious one. This was made quite clear when, in the very year of his Restoration, Charles II created a Council for Foreign Plantations, which was intended to be the chief vehicle for the centralised management of the empire. The terms of creation certainly refer to the advantages which would accrue to the shipping, trade and industry of England: this was bound to appeal to the powerful economic lobbies spearheaded by London interests. But the crucial point for Charles II was, surely that they 'bring a good access of treasure to our Exchequer for customs and other duties'. Revenue was what Charles wanted, and he pursued it with both determination and flexibility. Between 1660 and 1675 he experimented with a number of councils and committees, all created with the same object in view: to manage the colonies for revenue purposes.

This, then, was a period of experimentation, of apprenticeship in colonial management. However, in 1675 Charles II established the Lords of Trade and Plantations, and when he did so the period of apprenticeship was over. This new committee incorporated all the lessons learned in the last fifteen years. It was a permanent organisation, specialising only in colonial matters, and it was equipped with its own Civil Service department—in other words, its orders and decisions could be implemented by a body of professional bureaucrats.

The Committee of Lords of Trade and Plantations was not, however, the flawless model of efficiency and success that this description implies. It could, and did, display gross incompetence and it was capable of acts of crass stupidity. Nevertheless, it remained relatively efficient by Stuart standards, and it built up a corpus of experience and information on which the later Stuarts were able to capitalise during the royalist counter-revolution of 1681–88. When Charles II defeated his political opponents, the Whigs, in 1680–81 and embarked on the revival of royal authority at home, he now had at hand an instrument for a similar revival in the colonies. And the prime target was Massachusetts. It had acquired such a degree of independence that, for eight years, there had been no recorded communication of any kind between it and Charles II's government in England. Now, albeit briefly, that was to change dramatically. Edward Randolph, flamboyant and enthusiastic in the royalist cause, was despatched to inspect the colonies of New England. As a result of his report, Charles II resorted to the old and trusted royal procedure of *quo warranto* to get his way. His objective in this case was to detect irregularities in the Massachusetts charter. At first, the governors of the colony treated his decision with mirth, and even derision, describing the *quo warranto* proceedings as 'a poor toothless creature'. In this they committed a major error, because in 1684 their charter was suppressed. And that was only the beginning: between 1684 and 1687 the Crown liquidated the charters of six other colonies. At the same time, James II, consciously adopting the model of Louis XIV's Canada, created the new Dominion of New England, which covered the whole of English America from New Hampshire to Delaware. In 1686 Sir Edward Andros, the first governor of the new Dominion, arrived. He was harsh, agressive, and his lavish demonstration of loyalty to the Crown was matched only by the extravagance of his clothing.

Most of the North American colonies were now under direct royal control. But, as in 1640, so in the English Revolution of 1688: it all fell to pieces. Massachusetts led the way by toppling the

Dominion and its Governor, Edward Andros, in a bloodless rebellion. New York, Maryland and other colonies followed its example. In a wave of unilateral actions the colonies restored their old charters. However, there could be no return to the old autonomy. Circumstances had moved against the colonies.

William III did not revert to the Dominion of James II, but he firmly rejected the notion of colonial autonomy. Both King and governing class coveted the potential wealth and the actual customs revenue which came from the colonies. Moreover, the colonies were in an exposed and vulnerable position. As England was almost continuously at war with France for the next twenty-five years, the colonists needed the English army to protect them against French Canada. This basic consideration weakened the colonies' resistance to what followed in the 1690s. Thus in 1693 Massachusetts received a new charter which empowered the Crown to appoint a governor, who was armed with extensive executive powers. The Navigation Act of 1696 regulated colonial economies in order to make them complementary to England, and it controlled their trade in the interest of English mercantile communities. In the same year, William III established the Board of Trade, an aggressive panel which proceeded to supervise the colonies as adjuncts of the English State. Rhode Island and Connecticut remained peculiar exceptions: mini-republics within the empire, electing their own officials and making their own laws. These apart, however, the North American colonies were enmeshed in the administrative network of a growing English empire. The Revolution of 1688–9 may have ended the kind of imperial absolutism epitomised by the governorship of Andros, but it sustained and continued the Stuart ideal of an empire subordinate to the economic interests of England.

The West Indies
As in North America, so in the West Indies: England had no colonies at the end of the sixteenth century. Government and private investors alike preferred to snatch quick returns from raids on Spanish settlements and silver fleets, rather than embark on more costly and riskier colonisation projects which would then have to be defended against the Spaniards. To the Dutch and French, as well as the English, Spain was the great enemy, and to all three countries such attacks had a strategic value: to disrupt and plunder the Spanish traffic in silver, which Philip II used to finance his wars. However, at the turn of the century Spain made peace with France (1598) and England (1604) and signed an eleven years' truce with the new Dutch State (1610). This did not keep her rivals out of the Caribbean, but increasingly they

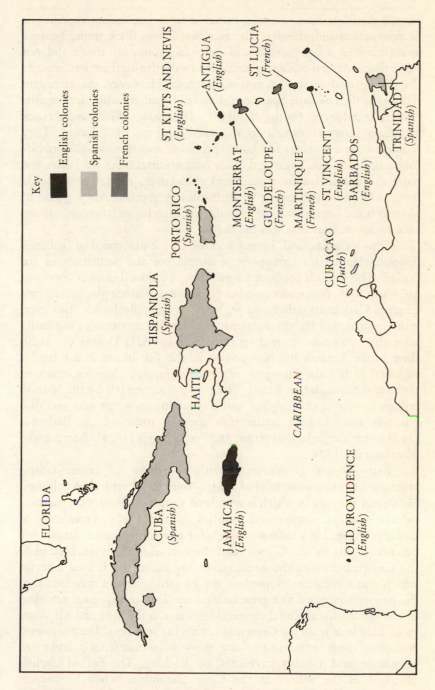

English expansion in the West Indies in the seventeenth century

turned their attention to trade, rather than to marauding expeditions of destruction and plunder. The fact that it was illicit trade, because Spain claimed a commercial and colonial monopoly there, did not deter them. At first trade was conducted with the local settlers, despite the disapproval of the Spanish authorities. However, the attendant risks were high because Spain could and did retaliate with force against trading interlopers. So the thoughts of English, Dutch and French merchant interests turned to the establishment of colonies. They would become markets for home-products and they would provide tobacco, hides, salt, sugar and other commodities from the Indies and from the South American mainland. Moreover, though they would have to be protected against Spanish military reprisals, they would be able to trade openly and freely with the merchants from their home countries—at least that was the theory.

Thus were England. France and the Dutch prompted to challenge Spanish claims to a monopoly of commerce and settlement in the region. The English promoted a number of colonial projects between 1604 and 1624. None succeeded until Thomas Warner planted the first English Caribbean colony on St Kitts. It was the Dutch, however, who spearheaded the drive against the Spanish monopoly, especially after the two countries had resumed war in 1621. During the 1620s they broke Spanish military power in the Caribbean and settled a number of islands. However, they concentrated their expansionist ambitions thereafter on Brazil. The power vacuum left by the Spanish collapse enabled the English and French to move in and establish colonies too. English settlements quickly followed: in Barbados (1624), the Virgin Islands (from 1625 on), Nevis (1628), Antigua and Montserrat (1632).

Early Stuart government, with its drive to centralisation, attempted to exert some kind of control over the West Indian colonies. However, the way in which it was done simply illustrates the faction-ridden, corrupt, competitive politics of the 1620s. Promoters of colonies engaged in a furious struggle for powerful patrons, favourable patents (grants by the Crown) and the exclusion of rivals. Instead of the Crown becoming the direct governing authority, it used a device which was sometimes adopted on the North American mainland too: the proprietary grant to a great nobleman. This arrangement smacked of the old medieval feudal connection between the king and his vassal (who held land from the Crown in return for services). The proprietor appointed the governor of a colony, drew an income from it, and owed allegiance (and possibly payments) to the king. The Earl of Carlisle emerged as the winner in the Court scramble, when he became proprietor of St Kitts, Barbados, Nevis and other islands. But this kind of grant, born out of the faction politics of the Stuart Court, bedevilled the early history of the settlements. The bitter conflicts of Court interests and their opponents were transferred across the Atlantic to the new colonies. It was only the commonsense politics of Lord Willoughby (governor from 1650 to 1652, when a Cromwellian expedition expelled him, and again from 1660 to 1666) which produced some order out of the political friction and feuding.

One other colonial project had important political implications in England. The Providence Island Company was formed in 1629, the very year when Charles I decided to dispense with parliaments for the time being. Its founders included John Pym, the Earl of Warwick and Lord Saye and Sele, all of whom were Puritans and critics of Caroline government. Providence was colonised in the 1630s and its existence enabled members of the Puritan opposition group to maintain contact with each other by meetings as governors of the company. However, the Crown's attitude to their project must have fuelled their discontent. Charles I's foreign policy included friendly relations with Spain. Therefore, he would not protect Providence, which was another breach in the now tattered Spanish monopoly in the Caribbean, and in 1641 the island was recaptured by the Spaniards.

Despite this failure, the other new colonies were attractive to would-be emigrants. J.H. Parry and Philip Sherlock (1981, page 36) estimate that by 1640 the islands of Barbados, St Kitts and Nevis had a combined population of 50 000. On the other hand, they brought no significant economic benefit to England. They practised subsistence farming, and those commodities which they did export—tobacco and cotton—were carried in Dutch vessels. The Dutch were Europe's great carriers, and their supremacy was not challenged until the revolutionary governments of the Commonwealth (1649–54) and Protectorate (1654–60). The reasons for this challenge were mixed: the pressure from English merchant interests; the fact that Barbados and Antigua remained loyal to the Stuarts; and the agreement in official circles that the Dutch supremacy must be challenged everywhere (and not just in the West Indies). The immediate result was the Navigation Ordinance of 1651, which limited trade between England and her colonies to English or colonial ships. This in turn led to war between the two countries (1652–4). The English objective was a simple one, later voiced by one of Charles II's advisers before the second Dutch war: 'What we want is more of the trade the Dutch now have'. It was a naval war in which the English triumphed. Hundreds of Dutch ships were captured, Dutch commerce was temporarily crippled, and, in G.M. Trevelyan's words, 'Grass grew in the streets of Amsterdam'.

Not that the war permanently displaced the Dutch as Europe's leading dealers and carriers. The English did not yet have the merchant shipping to carry out the terms of the Ordinance of 1651. So the Dutch slipped back into their usual role as factors (agents) in the traffic between the West Indies and Europe. In any case, after the conclusion of war with the Dutch, Cromwellian energies were directed against the traditional Spanish enemy. A military expedition was mounted in 1654. Its mission was to seize and settle Spanish colonies, in particular Hispaniola. The attempt on Hispaniola was a fiasco, but the capture of Jamaica was some kind of consolation prize, although it led to full-scale war with Spain in 1657. In these circumstances further designs against the Dutch were shelved, so that when Charles II was restored, his imperial inheritance in the Caribbean was an unimpressive one: a few islands with an unpromising future. There was no rush of migrants to Jamaica, and the Dutch retained their stranglehold on the trade of the other islands. Not that any of them seemed to have much to offer economically anyway.

However, the Restoration ushered in a period of fundamental change, which was the product of a process of interaction. In England, Charles II's government resumed the Stuart policy of more centralised control of the colonies. At the other end, the 'sugar revolution' (see Parry and Sherlock, 1981, chapter V) rapidly made the West Indies financially important to a government forever in search of more cash. Sugar cane was planted in Barbados in the 1640s and after 1650 it became the most important product in all the English possessions. They could not produce enough sugar to meet the growing European demand, but only the Dutch had the skill to refine it, and so their pre-eminence continued. This was reinforced by the labour needs of a sugar economy. At first the English colonies had depended upon indentured labour (men who signed an indenture agreement to work for a master for several years in return for a free passage and the prospect of a grant of land at the end of their service). They were worked hard and treated very harshly. Furthermore, as the population increased, the land available for grants ran out. As a result, men were unwilling to come, and so indentured labour dried up too. However, sugar production was a labour-intensive economy. Where was the labour to come from?

Two sources provided the answer. Neither was voluntary. The West Indies were used as a 'dumping ground' for the outcasts of later Stuart England: vagrants, criminals and political prisoners were condemned to transportation to the Caribbean, where they virtually became white slaves. They were never enough. Secondly, and increasingly important, there were the black slaves who were transported, chiefly by the Dutch, from West Africa. It was this traffic in human misery which revolutionised the West Indian economy. According to Parry and Sherlock the Negro population escalated rapidly in the later seventeenth century—in Jamaica rising from 9500 in 1673 to 74 000 fifty years later—so that, by 1700 'the Europeans had become a small garrison among the slaves' (Parry and Sherlock, 1981, pages 69–70). It was this supply of cheap labour which at long last made the West Indies an important concern to English kings and merchants alike. It explains the dual concern of later Stuart government: to establish a more centralised control over the colonies, and to exclude the Dutch from a share of the profits. The implementation of these policies was not without its problems. Each island accepted allegiance to the Crown, but demanded extensive local autonomy. Their assemblies often resisted and defeated the policies of royal governors. Nor were the Dutch likely to bow out politely and lose a rich source of profit.

However, the Restoration government enjoyed some successes. It appointed the governors and other senior officials, it scrutinised laws passed by the colonial assemblies and vetoed them when it saw fit, and it developed the ideal of a mercantilist commercial system, the seeds of which had been sown by the revolutionary governments of the 1650s. Mercantilism was a nationalist (and now, increasingly, an imperialist) theory of the economy. Originally it had been based upon two misconceptions: first, that wealth equals money or bullion (gold and silver), and second, that there was a fixed volume of wealth in the world and therefore the objective of national policy was to win the biggest possible share of it. By 1660 thinking on the subject had become more sophisticated. The prime concerns of government were protectionist (to protect imperial and native markets, commerce and industry from foreign competitors) and the achievement of a favourable trade balance.

With such thoughts in mind, Charles II's parliaments passed a series of mercantilist Acts. In 1660 the Navigation Act confined trade between England and the colonies to English or colonial vessels. It also listed a number of colonial commodities, including sugar, which could not be sold to Europe direct, but had to be re-exported from England. Three years later, the Staple Act tightened up the system. Goods from anywhere, not just from England, had to travel to the West Indies from English ports. Of course there were compensations for the colonies. Their ships were entitled to be escorted by the King's ships and their goods had a guaranteed market in England. But it all added up to an exclusive 'closed shop' policy which was specifically aimed at the Dutch. The mercantilist policies of the 1660s led to a second and much less successful Anglo-Dutch War (1665–7).

Yet, in the longer term, the Navigation Acts of the 1660s, and the much increased English capacity to enforce them, led to a decline in Dutch control. Important too was the foundation of the Royal

African Company in 1672 (succeeding an earlier company patented by the Crown in 1663). Despite the financial difficulties which plagued the company in the next thirty years, it broke into the Dutch monopoly of the West African slave traffic, established a chain of forts to protect its traders, and carved out a share for the English. The labour supply for the production of sugar was guaranteed. So too was the importance of the West Indies to the finances of the English State and to the prosperity of the English economy. The cost in human suffering was conveniently overlooked.

CHAPTER TWO

The early modern state:
problems of government and shifts of power,
1558–1629

The Crown

The form of government in Tudor and early Stuart England was personal monarchy: that is to say, the authority to govern was vested in the head of a royal dynasty who was, until Mary Tudor, invariably a male and, until Edward VI, always an adult when he succeeded. Its fundamental characteristics were that it was hereditary, dynastic, divinely sanctioned and personal. It was hereditary and dynastic because the crown was always supposed to pass on to the strongest male claimant (that is, usually the eldest son) within the ruling family. This principle was sometimes breached: when, for example, Richard II was deposed (1399), and when Henry Tudor defeated and killed Richard III in battle. Nevertheless, it was a principle which was usually honoured. The monarch was also ruler by divine right. He was God's lieutenant on earth, ultimately answerable only to his Maker, and so to resist him was not only treasonable—it was also sinful. As the Bishop of Winchester thundered from the pulpit during the 1530s, 'the Prince is to be obeyed, yea and to be obeyed without exception'.

Finally, and in practical terms perhaps most important of all, the Tudors and early Stuarts were personal monarchs. Government was *royal* government in a very personal sense. The King had not yet become the head of an impersonal State: civil servants were royal servants not officials of the State, and inhabitants of the Kingdom of England and Wales were subjects of the King rather than citizens of the State. All roads led to the royal Court, where the King was the dynamic, the mainspring of government: he alone had the right to determine policy, to appoint and dismiss ministers, judges and all other royal officials (after 1534, except for 1555–9, this right also applied to the choice of bishops), and to declare war and make peace. Therefore the personality of the monarch determined the quality and style of government. Henry VIII had been a warlike king and a lazy administrator, who preferred to delegate much of his authority to hard-working servants such as Cardinal Wolsey and Thomas Crom-well. Elizabeth, however, was more conscientious. She tried to avoid war and was careful in money matters. Her lightning investigations into the costs of administration kept her officials on their toes (even though much still escaped her watchful eyes). The important point to remember is that each monarch imposed the stamp of his personality on his reign: no less if he was lazy (like James I) or shy and difficult in public (like Charles I), than if vigorous and extrovert (like Elizabeth).

The monarch's personality and attitude to kingship determined the extent to which he or she made use of the powers of the Crown. However, there were limits beyond which he could not go with safety, because the extent of his authority was known and defined. The royal prerogative—the term used to describe those rights which enabled a king to govern—has been the subject of frequent misunderstandings. Yet there is nothing mysterious, or obscure, about it: prerogative power was clearly defined. It acknowledged the monarch's superiority over all others in the realm by protecting him and his possessions against legal action; and it equipped him with the means to protect the realm against rebellion and invasion, to maintain law and order and dispense justice, and to carry on day-to-day government. The King was also commander-in-chief of the armed services. As the fount (source) of justice he could compensate for the shortcomings of the law courts by pardoning those convicted of crimes, by creating new courts which were more accessible, cheaper, and which held out greater promise of justice. He could also exercise a dispensing power: in other words, he could set aside existing laws and their penalties in individual cases. However, Sir Thomas Smith (Elizabeth's secretary) added the qualification that justice and fairness 'requireth a moderation to be had'. The later Stuarts' extravagant use of this particular prerogative on a large scale aroused a widespread resistance and led to its suppression in 1688–9. Other prerogative powers are too diverse to be marshalled under particular headings, such as 'security' and 'order and justice': for example, the minting of money, the right to vary customs duties in the interest of regulating trade, negotiating commercial treaties and so on. The sum total of these individual prerogatives, and indeed their very purpose, was the endowment of the Crown with sufficient authority to govern effectively. And this is precisely what they did: English monarchy was, potentially, very strong monarchy.

However, this strength must not be misinterpreted as unlimited. The individual prerogatives of the Crown were known, defined, limited and under the Common Law of the kingdom. A medieval lawyer, Bracton, summed it all up in the dictum, 'That the King ought not to be under Man, but under God and the Law'. In the mid-sixteenth century another lawyer, William Stanford, said the same thing in another way: that 'Parliament maketh no part of the king's prerogative, but long time before it had [its] being by the order of the common law'. Moreover, certain fundamental powers of government did not form part of the royal prerogative. In particular, taxes could only be levied, and new laws made, with the assent of Parliament, which meant Lords and Commons as well as King.

There was one exception to the defined and limited nature of royal authority. This was an additional reserve of power, known variously as the residual or emergency prerogative. Both terms tell part of the truth, because it was a residue of additional authority which enabled the monarch to take prompt action in an emergency—and to do so without reference to the normal limitations on his freedom of action. Consider a hypothetical case: England is threatened with imminent invasion and the King needs the money to raise and maintain an army. It took six weeks to call a parliament and many months more to collect any tax which it granted. By then the kingdom might be under the 'iron heel' of the aggressor. This was the argument set forth by one of the King's judges, Sir Robert Berkeley, in the notorious Ship Money Case of 1637–8 (see pages 166–7).

Now whether to set the commonwealth free and in safety from the peril of rule and destruction, the King may not, of his own royal authority, *and without common assent in Parliament*, impose a charge [tax or levy] upon his subjects in general .... [I]t is a dangerous tenet [doctrine] ... to hold that the weal public must be exposed to peril of utter ruin ... rather than such a charge as this, which may secure the commonwealth, may be imposed by the King upon the subject, without common consent in Parliament. So that the security of the commonwealth ... must stay [wait] and expect until a Parliament provide for it; in which interim of time it is possible, nay apparently probable ... that all may be, yea, will be brought to a final period of destruction and desolation.

That the Tudors did not use (or abuse?) the emergency prerogative in Charles I's controversial way does not concern us here. The power did exist. It was used to collect ship money from the ports. And it was a sensible, indeed necessary, supplement of flexible, undefined authority which could be brought into play when time was of the essence. Nor was it a novel power introduced by Elizabeth or the early Stuarts. During the 1470s Sir John Fortescue had described English government as *dominium politicum et regale* (power which was both limited and unlimited: that is, the defined prerogative and the emergency prerogative). The reason that the latter provoked such hostility in the 1630s was because it was used to justify the unpopular levy of ship money as a permanent tax on the whole kingdom.

While it is necessary to consider the formal authority of government, the political realities of contemporary England cannot be ignored. After all, there can be a world of difference between theory and practice; between what the law allowed the monarch to do, and what he was actually able to accomplish. Contemporary attitudes certainly bolstered royal authority. Elizabeth's position as Head of State was reinforced by the general recognition of her as the Lord's anointed. A male-dominated Parliament in 1559 might apply its chauvinistic prejudices and make her a lay supreme Governor *over* the Church and not a spiritual Supreme Head *of* the Church: this was in accordance with Biblical injunctions that no woman could occupy an office within the Church, as Henry VIII and Edward VI had done (see chapter 4, page 254). Nevertheless, in practice (and with only the occasional exception, such as Edmund Grindal), she could persuade, cajole and bully the bishops into obedience and acquiescence in her policies. And although the basis of her authority over the Church was statute, not the traditional prerogative sanctioned by the Common Law, she claimed that it was a prerogative power and successfully resisted parliamentary interference in her ecclesiastical authority. Weaker than Henry VIII she might have been, but her control over the Church was greater than that of the pre-Reformation kings. Sir Thomas Smith, writing in the mid-1560s, actually regarded her right to appoint bishops and tax the clergy as part of her prerogative.

In any case, her right to be queen was never called into question, except by a handful of Roman Catholics. No other form of government was contemplated. And her particular right to the crown was increasingly accepted and assumed without question. Not only was she God's lieutenant, her governing class was also raised in the belief that the 'Prince's' service was the highest form of occupation. Nobles and gentry were imbued with habits of obedience. Not only did they accept that the Treason Act of 1352 (making it treasonable to plan or attempt the monarch's death, to make war against him, or to support his enemies) was both desirable and necessary, but during Elizabeth's reign they also attempted to create new defensive barriers around her, in face of the Catholic menace and despite her reluctance to agree to new penal laws against Mary Stuart and the English Catholics. Irritated and frustrated they might become, but members of the two Houses of Parliament persevered in their attempts to protect their Queen, despite herself. It was all summed up by an M.P., Thomas Norton, who was convinced that it was his duty to speak out in the

Queen's defence, and who laboured long in Parliament to care for her person, even though he acknowledged how humble and unfit he was for the task:

Neyther do I altogether allow of the mannerlinesse of that goodfellowes curtesie, that would not unlocke a gate to the kynge, but made the kyng to staye there, while he ranne two miles to fetch a more worshipfull man to open it. And farre more discommendable had such good manner ben, if the kyng had then ben nerely and egrely pursued by an enemye.'

Even her sex was turned to advantage. Remember that the ideal monarch should be adult and male. Edward VI and Mary Tudor had each fallen short on one of these requirements. Furthermore, the first reigning queen, Mary, had confirmed men in their doubts and fears about 'petticoat government'. She had divided the realm, brought it under foreign domination, and filled London with the stench of burning martyrs. Her conduct had encouraged Protestant Englishmen in exile, such as John Ponet and Christopher Goodman, to preach tyrannicide (the justifiable assassination of ungodly rulers). And had not John Knox recently published his 'first trumpet blast' against the 'Monstrous Regiment [government] of Women'. Thus, Elizabeth was burdened with the supposed disadvantages of her sex when she became queen. She was not unaware of the problem when, for example, she castigated forceful male courtiers with the angry truth that they would not have treated her father thus. But she was herself a forceful personality: within days of her succession, the Spanish ambassador was reporting to his master that Elizabeth was 'incomparably more feared than her sister and gives her orders . . . as absolutely as her father did'.

However, Elizabeth also had the political astuteness to convert her sex into an asset. She consciously and deliberately sponsored the cult of 'Gloriana'. She became the 'Virgin Queen', and forced her arrogant self-confident male courtiers into the role of ardent suitors, always pursuing but never conquering her. It was only in the 1590s that the young Earl of Essex ripped away the veil of adulation which surrounded the now ageing, black-toothed and wrinkled Queen, when he bluntly informed her that her 'conditions [policies] were as crooked as her carcass'. Until then, sheer force of personality and conscientiousness, combined with her sexual artifices and artistry, worked to her advantage. It says much for (or rather against) Charles I that in a few short years he managed to destroy the adulation and near king-worship which had characterised the reigns of Henry VIII and Elizabeth.

Even the advancement of Parliament worked to Elizabeth's advantage. Whether or not most people realised it (and it is probable that few did at the time), the major changes of the 1530s made Parliament *omnicompetent*—that is, legally competent to legislate on all aspects of society, spiritual as well as temporal—and statute sovereign—that is, the supreme form of law. Yet this did not, in the short term, result in a shift of power from monarch to Parliament. The later Tudors, and even James I, kept the initiative. So long as they maintained control over the life and business of Parliament, and achieved a sound working relationship with the governing class (which, after all, monopolised the membership of the two Houses), its new power was not independent but simply added to their own. On the other hand, Parliament was becoming increasingly irrelevant to the needs of royal government. From the 1580s and 90s on the Crown was losing interest in legislation. In the last fifteen years of Elizabeth's reign, Parliament could not (or would not) provide adequate and prompt financial war supplies, while James I exposed Parliament's inadequacy when it failed to meet his blunt, realistic demands in 1624 (see chapter 6, page 377). Within this period, Parliament usually co-operated with the Crown and strengthened it. At worst, it fell short of royal expectations because of its inability to provide them with the necessary money, which was becoming the only reason for its continued existence (see chapter 6, pages 372–4).

If we look at the political realities, however, we should recognise that the Crown's power and freedom of action were much less than its constitutional rights indicate. Royal poverty was a basic, unpleasant fact of life which required constant attention and could never be ignored. Poverty is of course, a relative term: it must be related to the expectations, needs, and possibilities of government. The Tudor and early Stuart monarchy had to jettison many desirable policies for lack of money (see chapter 1, pages 75–9). Programmes of poor relief, social justice and education existed only on paper, or the financial burdens were displaced onto the governing class. It was necessary for the State to combat the lawlessness of a turbulent society. How did it defend the realm? How did it enforce royal policies in the countryside? It could not afford a police force, a standing (permanent) army, or a professional country-wide civil service. Instead it had to depend on a governing class of nobles and gentry to combat crime, staff its army and navy and carry out its administrative orders. Government could only operate effectively if there was a general consensus of opinion between the Crown and that class on the objectives of government.

This consensus, however, was not difficult to achieve. Until the 1620s, the monarch and his nobles and gentry were in general agreement: that security, order, the right of the Crown to govern and the socio-political supremacy of the governing class must be maintained. Nevertheless, this also meant that the ruler depended on others for the translation of his policy decisions into practice. It was one thing for Elizabeth and her Council to decree, for example, that Catholics should attend the Anglican Church. But, unless the local nobles and gentlemen enforced this command, it became a dead letter. The practical basis of Tudor government was co-operation and consent. It can be expressed in another way, which seems a contradiction in terms, but which embodies a contemporary political truth: it was local self-government at the King's command. Local, grass-roots administration, in areas where the State impinged upon the lives of people, could only be effective if the local agents of the Crown did their job efficiently and loyally. This set the Crown at a disadvantage. Its local agents—nobles and gentry—were usually unpaid and, if paid, always underpaid. Moreover, they did not depend primarily upon the monarch for their income or future prospects, unless they were numbered among the needy younger sons or the ambitious minority who looked to the Court for wealth and advancement. The majority were propertied men with power-bases of their own: estates, income, social status and influence, and a whole hierarchy of their own servants, allies, kin and clients—dependants who looked to them for benefits and advancement. As G. R. Elton wrote of Henry VIII, probably the most powerful king ever to sit on the English throne, it was still 'the governing class which called the tune'.

Nevertheless, it was the Crown which could arrange the music and orchestrate the performance. For government was a two-way process. If the Crown looked to the governing class for enforcement of its policies, the latter was dependent upon it for social and economic advancement. The Crown was the fount of patronage. It could raise men to exalted office, membership of the noble élite, and wealth. Conversely, it could cast them into a social wilderness, political oblivion and financial bankruptcy. Elizabeth wielded that power when she struck lazy and unjust gentlemen off the list of Justices of the Peace, imprisoned the Earl of Hertford and Sir Walter Raleigh for marrying without her consent, and deprived the Earl of Essex of his chief source of income, the customs duties on the importation of sweet wines. James I was no different when he raised up George Villiers, son of a Leicestershire squire, to the dukedom of Buckingham and the dominant position in government. Charles I persecuted the Earl of Arundel and the Bishop of Lincoln, confirmed Buckingham in his authority and took a prominent critic, Thomas Wentworth, into government in 1628. Men looked to royal government, not only as a divinely ordained institution, but also as the road to power and profit, with the former goal at least as important as the latter. Noblemen and gentry were not simply economic animals. They also respected, revered, and in some cases even worshipped, monarchy as the only conceivable government sanctioned by God.

The Court

Whatever their attitude, these loyal, God-fearing, ambitious men knew that they could only serve their monarch, or make their fortunes, by making their presence felt in the Court. There is a common tendency to regard the Court as a show-place, a kind of Hollywood extravaganza which was solely concerned with pomp, show, colour and expense. This is to misunderstand the very heart of government. Of course, spectacle and pageantry were among the Court's essential features. But we must remember that Tudor government operated before the age of modern communications media. It did adapt itself to such new techniques as became available: the printing press, for example. New Acts of Parliament and proclamations were printed and despatched to county courts, where they were read aloud, or to the leading towns in the counties, where they were pinned up in market places. Nevertheless, communications remained primitive by modern standards. How to inform the public quickly of political developments? How to learn of sudden political (and military) crises? How to justify official actions to a sceptical and even hostile public? Once again the printing press was vital. A classic example of this concerns the use of torture by the Privy Council in order to establish the 'treason' of Catholic missionary priests and Jesuits during Elizabeth's reign. Lord Burghley, with the assistance of Thomas Norton, took it upon himself to justify it in print by pointing out that torture was only used to extract confessions of treason, not heresy, and that the tormenting of Edmund Campion, the great hero-martyr of the Jesuit Order, was not so severe as to prevent him from standing during his trial. (The Council was empowered to use torture, but it seems to have caused public unease, and it certainly provoked Catholic attacks in the 1580s.)

However, the tools of modern government—rapid communications and surveillance techniques—were not available. In their place, the Court served as an important instrument of propaganda. Its purpose was to project the image of the monarch as a powerful, wealthy and godly Prince. Hence the magnificence and ostentation of the Court were not mere personal whims of the monarch, even if they also served to satisfy the ego and personal pleasures of a Henry VIII, an Elizabeth, or a James I. They were designed to create foreign respect for the English monarch and to induce awe and obedience in his subjects. In the summer the Court went on 'progress', travelling mainly around the more populous south of England and lodging with loyal nobles and gentlemen (expensively and sometimes with disastrous effect: two visits by Elizabeth to Horham Hall, for example, resulted in the bankruptcy of the Cutte family). Once again the Court was engaged in a public relations exercise. On these occasions Elizabeth was a superb artiste, excelling as the protector, lover and mother-figure of her people. Like the other Tudors, she learned the art of raising the Crown to a remote, awe-inspiring peak and yet remaining familiar and accessible to subjects of all classes (though, naturally, most of all to her nobles and gentry). Although her Court was, perhaps, the most elaborate and formal in Europe, she retained the common touch. (Probably this was not difficult. For all the pomp and ceremony which surrounded them, the Tudors were coarse and vulgar, always retaining a touch of the 'nouveau'. Elizabeth's oaths and blasphemies were well known, and Henry VIII's new palace, 'Nonsuch,' lacked refinement or good taste.) Godfrey Goodman, who became Bishop of Gloucester late in James I's reign, recalled that, as a breathless young boy in the year of the Armada, he had watched her as she emerged from the Court. The crowd roared its greeting, to which she responded, 'God bless you all my good people'. Goodman recalled how he and his young friends swore 'how we would adventure our lives to do her service'. She used similar artifices, to good purpose, with her parliaments. We may question whether Elizabeth's preference for such devices and techniques, rather than for sound policies, was beneficial to her people. Whatever the answer, there is no doubt that she turned her personal arts into a political skill, and she exploited the Court as a supporting political instrument.

However, the Court, wherever it was, served as much more than an instrument of propaganda. It housed the Queen's Councillors and her chief ministers who lived there in order to be in constant touch with her. This is where vital political decisions were made. It was also the nation's great political arena, where men competed for royal favour. For all competitors, she was the female equivalent of King Midas, who, by the touch of royal favour, could turn their hopes into gold. So the Court became a market place in which royal favour (under Elizabeth, no less than James I and Charles I) became the prerequisite of profit, power and social advancement. The monarch was the source of patronage: royal office, knighthoods and noble titles, grants of Crown lands, pensions, trading benefits, monopolies—all came from the Crown. James was careless about such grants, Charles I left much to his favourite Buckingham during the early years of his reign, but

Elizabeth was much more cautious, economical and even suspicious of such requests. Whatever the monarch's response, the struggle for his (or her) favour had to be fought out at Court. For only there could the ruler's favour be won. And that was the coveted prize which might lead on to great rewards.

The Elizabethan Privy Council

However remote and awesome Elizabeth and her successors might have appeared to their lowlier subjects, they could not govern in isolation. They needed counsel, advice and information, and to this end they surrounded themselves with men who were in touch with the everyday problems of government. They were empowered to communicate with embassies abroad and with Justices of the Peace and other royal officials at home. They also received a constant flow of information, sometimes from paid agents, but more frequently from local officials, ambitious men with an eye to the favour of a great man, well-meaning loyal subjects, and friends, clients and followers of their own class. The surviving papers of Lord Burghley and Sir Francis Walsingham are stuffed with advice and reports on all aspects of government. They were more likely to know what was going on in the kingdom or overseas; much more so than the monarch who moved in the gilded and remote world of the Court. Elizabeth had to rely upon them for information and advice about the harsh realities of the world outside. The fact that some Councillors accompanied the Queen on her summer progress emphasises how necessary was their role in government.

It was not simply a matter of necessity. It had always been commonsense politics to seek the advice of trusted men from the governing class. Indeed the élite expected to be consulted about high policy and the management of the kingdom. For centuries, consultation had been institutionalised in the King's Council, a large amorphous body which between 1536 and 1540 was transformed into the Privy Council, a board of some eighteen to twenty members with its own clerk and records. In Mary's reign it acquired a seal to authenticate its letters and other documents. Although it grew in numbers under Edward VI and Mary Tudor, Elizabeth reverted to the kind of Council which had existed in her father's later years: a small panel of experts, usually (though not necessarily) holding important offices in the central administration and household, and answerable to the monarch for their management of the realm. Indeed it was a very small body, numbering no more than eighteen at the beginning of the reign and shrinking to about a mere dozen towards the end.

Consider the composition of the Council in 1601: Archbishop Whitgift (the only bishop appointed to the Council during the reign), five peers, five knights, a judge and one plain gentleman. Six held offices of State and four were members of Elizabeth's royal household, but Whitgift and the Earl of Shrewsbury occupied no important government posts. Why were *these* men chosen to serve Elizabeth on this exalted board, the very lynch-pin of government? There is a simple answer: they were trusted men. Her household officers, constantly about her person, were always well-represented. Her Lord Chancellor (or in this case Lord Keeper, Sir Thomas Egerton), Lord Treasurer, Admiral and Secretaries were usually included by virtue of the offices which they held. And great peers such as Shrewsbury were appointed because they were politically powerful in the countryside. But, in the last resort, inclusion rested upon the Queen's confidence. This is not surprising, because collectively the Council wielded a formidable power.

That power can be summed up as the three 'a's: advice, administration and adjudication. Just as advice was the Council's most important political function, however, so it is the activity about which we know least. Discussion of matters of high policy was held *in camera* (in secret). The Council's clerk withdrew and no minutes of the debate were kept. Occasionally snippets of information come our way: when, for example, the Privy Council sat on five days from 8 a.m. until 'suppertime', over the negotiations for Elizabeth's marriage to the Duke of Anjou, which had reached a delicate point. But we know nothing of what was said, who was for, who against or why. At this level government was informal, unwritten and secret.

In any case, it was the monarch, not the Council, who took the final decision. Councillors might reach a consensus of opinion, or offer two alternative proposals: in either case Elizabeth was under no obligation, moral or constitutional, to heed their voices. Frequently she did not. She refused to surrender to their pressure, in 1563 and 1566–7, that she should marry or name a successor, even though they enlisted Parliament's support in order to bend her will to theirs. As she grew older, more experienced, more self-confident and obstinate, her inclination to listen to her Council's opinions diminished. Therefore, it is important not to exaggerate the Council's role in policy-making. On the other hand it was not impotent: it forced Elizabeth to act against the French in Scotland in 1559; it pressured her into war with Spain in 1585; and it finally wrung Mary Stuart's execution from a reluctant, vacillating (and eminently sensible) Queen. Always the policy relationship between monarch and Council denoted a subtle interplay of relationships, opinions, pressures and decisions. Councillors figuratively tore their hair as their royal mistress went her own imperious way, keeping her own counsel, rejecting succession petitions with meaningless honeyed words, deferring the Bill against Mary Stuart in 1572 and driving them to frenzied despair as she acted out her love games with foreign suitors. So Burghley lamented, after the farce of 1572, that the fault lay not in 'us that are accounted inward counsellors'. The Council could do no more than advise, and hope that their advice was heeded.

Its second function, however, was not limited by an obstinate royal mistress, nor is our knowledge of it likewise restricted by a lack of information. Elizabeth allowed the Council free rein to administer the realm. What does this mean? Simply everything: the Privy Council's competence (that is, scope of business) was infinite. Nothing came outside its sphere of interest or concern: foreign affairs, finance, law and order, religion, social controls and economic regulation. Everything and anything that happened in the kingdom was corn to be ground at its mill. So it authorised payments and rewards to trusty officials, organised the reception of foreign ambassadors, closed theatres in plague-time, instigated commissions of inquiry, hunted out Catholic recusants and supervised all aspects of local government. Nothing was too trivial, too local, personal or sectional to escape the attention of this body of conscientious, overworked men.

Consider two sample days in the life of the Elizabethan Privy Council. On 10 July 1576 it authorised the release from prison of a northern recusant, John Towneley Esquire, into the custody of a fervent Protestant whereby 'he maybe the better reduced to conformitee'; it dealt with a private complaint against Sir Thomas Wroughton by referring the case to the Earl of Pembroke for a solution, ordered the apprehension of Alexander Parker for 'lewde and contemptuous speches', and demanded Owen Holland's appearance before it; a passport was issued to a Scot travelling home from France, the despatch of money to Ireland was authorised, and the seizure of a merchant's goods in Spain was discussed; the Council heard a complaint by Marmaduke Middleton, 'a pore man', against Lord Rich, approved an appointment to an office in the Church, permitted a merchant to import bowstaves, thanked local officials for preventing the export of grain and examined a gentleman, Henry Carew, who had been ordered to appear before them. Nor was its business then done. It reprimanded Queen's College, Cambridge, for denying a Welshman a fellowship there; it required the Justices of the Peace to punish those who 'pulled downe and burned Sir Thomas Gresham's parke pale [fence]' in Middlesex; and it commanded the J.P.s of Wales to assist Christopher Saxton, appointed by the Queen to survey the principality, 'that he may be accompanied with ii or iii honest men such as do best know the country for the better accomplishement of that service', and that he should be given safe conduct to the next town. It must have been a hungry and thirsty octet of Councillors who withdrew to lunch thankfully after a hard morning's toil: Lord Keeper Bacon, Lord Burghley, the Earls of Sussex and Warwick, Sir Francis Knollys, Sir James Crofts, Sir Francis Walsingham and Sir Walter Mildmay. (The Privy Council usually met in the early morning, but afternoon sessions were not uncommon.)

On 6 August 1581 the personnel had changed: Sir Thomas Bromley (who was Lord Chancellor), Sir Christopher Hatton (who was Vice-Chamberlain) and Bedford and Leicester were present. But so too were old faces: Burghley, Sussex, Crofts and Knollys. As usual they ranged over all aspects of the life of the realm: the private affairs of one recusant and the release of another on bail; a letter to the Bishop of Rochester to reduce an obstinate Kentish Catholic to conformity; the examination of Lord Vaux, whose house had been visited by the notorious Jesuit Edmund Campion; payments to maintain the mail service to Holyhead; an exemption to the wine monopoly at Norwich; the despatch of munitions to Ireland; a summons to a gentleman to appear before it; issues arising out of cases of piracy at Southampton; and a land dispute on the isle of Guernsey. Finally, it issued a harsh rebuke to the Bishop of London, who had ordered schools in his diocese to use a book which the Queen had not authorised and which, moreover, 'containethe no sounde doctrine'.

So the Council maintained a watching brief on the affairs of the realm and provided the dynamic which motivated the State machine into action. Notice, however, how public and private matters were given equal, indiscriminate consideration by the Council, without any apparent order of priority. Private matters, particularly, absorbed an increasing amount of the Council's time, which brings us to its third function: adjudication, a term about which there has been much misunderstanding. The Privy Council was not a law court, nor did it ever act as one. True, its members sat as judges in the Star Chamber, but that was a separate institution (see pages 132–4). Yet the Privy Council still exercised judicial functions. First, it received petitions of complaint which it passed on to the relevant courts for a hearing and decision. Secondly, it referred cases to men of substance (that is, nobles and gentlemen) for a resolution. And, thirdly, it acted as an arbiter in disputes. So, on 20 January 1577, it heard a complex dispute between a doctor of divinity and a gentleman over a deceased man's goods. In its customary manner, it did not proceed to a verdict, but referred the case to be heard in the courts of Exchequer and Chancery. In judicial matters, the Council usually acted as a clearing house, directing cases to the requisite courts. (However, it did order men to prison, which implied a judicial verdict of 'guilty'. Smith, 1972, pages 24–5.)

Nevertheless, this did not deter petitioners, who threatened to swamp the Council with their pleas for justice. Some had genuine grievances: the lesser, the weaker, the poorer who had been victimised by the stronger, wealthier, more influential members of the community. But others were astute enough to realise that the Council would direct their petitions to the courts, thereby enabling them to 'jump' the long queue of suitors waiting for their cases to be heard. Vainly the Privy Council attempted to stem the tide. In 1582 it resolved that only private causes which, in some way, 'concern the preservation of Her Majesty's peace or shall be of some public consequence to touch the government of the realm', should be heard. In 1589 and 1591 it repeated its former order, but still to no avail. The clamour of suitors for the Privy Council's attention undoubtedly interfered with more pressing public business, but, at the same time, it registered its popularity and a public recognition of its ability to get things done (Smith, 1972, pages 22–5).

The Council provided the ultimate test of Tudor government: it was the motivating force in the State, except in high-policy decisions which were the Queen's. It supervised local and central government and generally managed Elizabeth's affairs at a sub-policy level. However, its level of efficiency and effectiveness did not remain the same throughout the reign. During the 1560s it was finding its feet and transforming itself into a small, close-knit administrative board under Cecil and his lieutenants, Knollys and Mildmay. In 1568–72 it met and threw off the challenges of old (Arundel and Norfolk) and new (Leicester) peers. Between 1572 and the end of the 1580s it entered upon its golden age, administering every aspect of the nation's affairs in a way which was the envy of Europe. But between 1589 and 1598 the old, well-tried hands died off: Leicester, Walsingham, Knollys, Mildmay and finally Burghley himself. Their successors, especially Sir Robert Cecil and the Earl of Essex, could not compensate for the losses. During the 1590s the Privy Council struggled to cope with war, bad harvests, social discontent and war-weariness. Worse still, Cecil and Essex split the Council (and Court) with their deadly rivalry. Thus, the consensus politics of Burghley and Leicester were replaced by the divisive factional conflicts of their heirs. And the Council revealed itself to be incapable of coping with the problems which faced it: renewed soaring inflation, economic depression, a recurrent food shortage and war. After a brief glory the Council was in decline.

This is not to suggest, however, that before the 1590s a spirit of unanimity prevailed in the Privy Council. Factions were the essence of the Elizabethan political system, and they were certainly present in the Privy Council. In this respect, the reign falls into two periods: the first under William Cecil and the Earl of Leicester, and then under their heirs, Robert Cecil and the Earl of Essex. Faction politics were about both power and policies, especially during the first thirty years, when the Queen's chief minister Cecil (Burghley) and her favourite (Leicester) struggled for power. Cecil stood for peace, economy and a settled succession, whereas Leicester sought war with Spain and, for his own purposes, preferred the Queen to remain single. On both great issues, the favourite was the ultimate victor, but he was never able to unseat his rival or displace him from his position as Elizabeth's most trusted servant. Nevertheless, their rivalry affected the Privy Council, which divided into two groups behind them. Cecil could usually look to Bacon, Sussex (who hated Leicester: he warned his friends, 'Beware of the gypsy. You know not the beast as well as I do'), Mildmay and Crofts, while Leicester's supporters included Sir Christopher Hatton, his own brother Warwick, and the more ardent Protestants such as Walsingham, Bedford and Knollys. However, neither the leaders nor their factions adopted a rigid, doctrinaire position, as government and opposition do in a modern parliament. More often than not they worked together in the co-operative business of managing the Queen's affairs and administering the realm.

Their successors, however, were not cast in the same mould. Robert Cecil, whom Burghley groomed for power, was more devious, cynical and dishonest than his father. He manoeuvred himself and his friends into the seats of power and slowly but inexorably shut out his rival, Essex. The Earl was himself much to blame. When he insisted that those who were not with him must be against him, he forced Court and Council to divide and range themselves alongside him or his rival. Politics in the 1590s were characterised by rigid divisions, inflexible positions and a ruthless scramble for power—conditions which invaded the Privy Council and rendered it less effective than before.

Patronage, the patron-client system and faction

In the 1590s the Privy Council became a prey to the corruption and divisive politics inherent in the Elizabethan system. That system was structured around three mechanisms: the Crown and its patronage, the patron-client relationship, and faction. The interplay between these mechanisms determined the nature, intensity and thrust of most political activity at all levels: in the counties, the Court, and the Council, where it could influence even major policy decisions. This was particularly true under the early Stuarts, when the emergence of the great favourite (of whom the Earl of Essex was the forerunner) combined personal favour and control of policy in one man, when faction rent Government and Parliament and when, under the easy-going James I, patronage deteriorated from an orderly system to a frantic, undignified, often corrupt, scramble. In this changed climate, the Privy Council's role diminished and its prestige declined. So before examining the early Stuart Council, it is necessary to understand, first, how the Elizabethan political system operated and, secondly, how it changed between 1590 and 1629.

The mechanisms of the political system need to be defined; in particular **patronage**, the **patron-client relationship, faction** and **the favourite**. This brings us back to an old, familiar starting-point: that the State's finances were inadequate. The Crown could not afford to recompense even its greatest servants adequately. Most bureaucrats in central government were underpaid, and most of the men who staffed local government were unpaid. As members of the traditional governing class, they were bred to and indoctrinated in the ideal of service to the Prince as the highest form of occupation. Royal office also gave them prestige and status in the eyes of their fellows. But they were also acquisitive, ambitious men 'on the make', seeking a fortune. The Crown not only appealed to their natural loyalties, but also, through the **patronage** which it dispensed, it held out the tempting bait of financial benefits. For example, according to W.T. MacCaffrey (see Bibliography), Elizabeth had at her disposal 1200 offices 'worth a gentleman's having'. At one end of the scale were the top men: the Lord Chancellor, Lord Treasurer, and Keeper of the Privy Seal; at the other were the local paid agents, such as the stewards of Crown lands, and escheators seeking out feudal dues. In addition, she could grant peerages (titles of nobility: duke, marquess, earl, viscount and baron) and knighthoods, posts in the Church, gifts of Crown land or leases at cheap rents, pensions, and economic benefits, such as monopolies, the right to receive customs duties on specified items, and permission to export normally prohibited goods.

Although the Elizabethan gentry must have numbered 15–20 000 (the largest section of the governing class), it is probable that only a minority actively sought such benefits from the Crown. Even so, according to MacCaffrey, that minority numbered about 2500. There was simply not enough patronage to give every interested party even a small slice of the cake. So there was competition, with men organising themselves to get the biggest possible slice. The mechanism by which they sought to do so was the **patron-client relationship**. This was not simply a device for extracting patronage from the Crown: it reflected the hierarchical nature of Tudor society at the governing class level. Lesser men (clients) attached themselves to greater men (patrons).Clients provided the great man with a visible following, a 'presence', which added to his prestige; they provided his personal court, acted as his political agents and informants, and supported him in his local feuds. The patron, in his turn, distributed among them his personal patronage and worked on their behalf for a share of the offices, titles and other benefits in the Queen's gift. It was a civilianised form of the old feudal connection between lord and vassal, whereby the former had granted land in return for the military service of the latter.

The patron-client relationship in Elizabethan politics was insep-arable from **faction**, which was the mechanism adopted by patrons and clients in their hunt for royal patronage. Factions should not be confused with our modern concept of a party. Modern political parties have some characteristics in common with Elizabethan factions: their ambition for power, status and profit. Parties, however, are divided more obviously by differences in policy and political principle, although these elements were not absent in factions. For example, Leicester stood for war, and Burghley for peace and economy; later, the early Stuart factions were deeply-divided by pro and anti-Spanish sympathies and religion. Nevertheless, it was patronage, rather than policy, which kept factions in existence, and policy was sometimes a factional instrument, designed only to discredit rivals.

The word faction has become a discredited term: it connotes self-interest, an unprincipled group anxious to feather its own nest regard-less of the public interest. This was not necessarily true in the sixteenth century. Rather it was a political reflection of the status competition between great men in the localities. The term does, however, describe a group which operated on the basis of an exclusive self-interest, and there were inherent dangers in this kind of system. The possibility of corruption and subversion of the public interest was always there. However, with great skill, Elizabeth learned to manipulate the system to her own advantage and, at the same time, to minimise its harmful effects.The secret was to deny any one man, favourite or minister, a monopoly in the distribution of patronage. Neither Leicester nor Burghley (nor the two men together) had such a monopoly.

To understand this arrangement requires a knowledge of the workings of the patronage system. At the top was the Queen, the fount of patronage. At the other end were the suitors, the men who sought royal favours. In the middle were the patrons, the 'go-betweens' who had access to the monarch and might be able to extract titles, offices and other benefits. There also evolved a fourth tier, between the patrons and clients (or suitors): the 'contact men' as A. G.R. Smith describes them (see Bibliography). They were the personal servants and secretaries of the patrons, acting as intermediaries, advancing petitions from suitors in return for gratuities. The classic example is Michael Hickes, who was first Burghley's, then Sir Robert Cecil's patronage secretary. As he once informed a grateful client, 'these petty kind of offices [services] . . . are as welcome and acceptable to you as twenty fair angels [an angel was ten shillings] laid in the hands of us poor bribers, here in Court'.

Probably Elizabeth knew few details about individual manoeuvres behind the scenes. However, she was watchful and acquired a sound knowledge of the way the whole system operated. It should be emphasised that 'gifts in return for services' was an accepted practice in a State which could not pay its servants a salary corresponding to their workload and responsibilities. This was recognised when most civil servants were permitted to charge the public for their services, in accordance with a fixed scale of official fees. You would at least raise your eyebrows in surprise if you had to pay a Post Office clerk a personal tip of five cents when you purchased stamps for a letter, but an Elizabethan would have accepted such a transaction as normal practice. Nevertheless, corruption and subversion of the public interest were possibilities inherent in this system, and for most of her reign Elizabeth prevented them from reaching a harmful level. She did this by observing two practices: first, she was watchful and careful, at times to the point of meanness, in her grants of patronage; and second, she distributed patronage through a large number of patrons, not just Burghley and Leicester. There was no way in which one man could monopolise royal patronage and confine it to his faction. Instead it was disseminated through a number of channels and all members of the governing class—except for a handful of Protestant extremists and Catholics—could live in hope of a few pickings.

At least that is true until the 1590s. There then emerged the prototype of the **favourite**, the Earl of Essex. And here we must distinguish between the minister and favourite. A minister was (ideally) a faithful, able servant who performed his official duties to the monarch's satisfaction: it was not necessary that he be liked. Elizabeth disliked Sir Francis Walsingham, for example, but she respected his ability. In contrast, a favourite was personally liked by the Queen (in the case of the Earl of Leicester, perhaps loved). He might receive a 'golden shower' of patronage, but he would not control policy. Herein lies the fundamental distinction which characterised good government: the favourite received gifts, but the minister managed affairs under the Queen. However, in the 1590s change was on the way. Essex demanded a monopoly of patronage and control of policy. In self-defence Elizabeth fell back on Sir Robert Cecil, Burghley's heir, whom he had groomed for office. When she died the 'Cecilian' faction managed both patronage and policy. The old Elizabethan system had already vanished, although this was concealed by Cecil's moderation and readiness to consult others.

Then James I (VI) came south from Scotland. There was no sudden, dramatic change. Cecil had engineered and organised James' peaceful succession, and the new King was extraordinarily grateful. Cecil was confirmed in power, became Earl of Salisbury in 1605 and Lord Treasurer in 1608. During Cecil's supremacy, much that was Elizabethan remained: his father's sense of economy, a willingness to consult other power groups, such as the Howards and James's Scottish friends, and a concern to act with the rest of the Privy Council rather than for Cecil to set himself up as some kind of political monopolist. In other words, he did not take advantage of the unrivalled position which he held at the end of Elizabeth's reign.

In the meantime, the gifts and gratuities flowed in, because he was realistic and sensible enough to take full advantage of the situation. As the most powerful man in government, he was the main target of suitors' petitions for patronage, and the recipient of most perquisites. After the execution of the Earl of Essex in 1601, the flow increased: cash, horses, a barrel of preserved fruit from a captured Portuguese ship, partridges and pheasants, a 'syve of the best cherries', an Irish falcon, bed coverings, a basket of chickens, 'apricoks' and plums, and 'the tincture of pyony water, good against all affections of the heart'. The Earl of Cumberland sent him 'a stag and buck', Sir Samuel Baganall a 'great white dog' which 'is the most furiosest beast that ever I saw', Sir Arthur Capel 'a brace of does and a brace of pheasants' (and from his wife 'three of her cheeses'). Richard Hawkins offered to purchase a captured Spanish ship and smoothed the way with 'a dozen porcelain dishes, the best that I could find'. A clergyman, the Dean of Gloucester, wrote begging Cecil 'to be another patron to me instead of your father, lamenting that 'then I should not lie in the dirt and dust of indignity and disgrace', but remembering to send a 'couple of Worcestershire cheeses, as a present, small in quantity, but in quality excellent'. From Sir John Harington came a flush lavatory of his own design. Sir Robert Cecil's father had once advised him to give his patron gifts which he would often use and so often remember him. Surely this gift would serve!

The stream of gratuities turned to a flood in James's reign. And yet old Elizabethans like Cecil had a sense of proportion: they knew when a gift was too large, excessive. So he wrote to Lord Cromwell that he would be pleased to accept one of the two horses which he had sent him 'but it would be unreasonable to accept them both unless I see some imminent opportunity to requite you'.

Change did not come at once, but it came nonetheless. Cecil was an expert financial administrator, who tried to extract more money from existing sources and, at the same time, to moderate the King's lavish spending. He also made a fortune for himself, and built magnificent Hatfield House out of the proceeds. Above all, he surrounded himself with mediocrities, and groomed no one as his successor, as his father had done with him. When he died in 1612, he left a yawning vacuum. It was filled, not by an expert financier, but by James's pretty homosexual favourites.

Yet even before then, in 1610, Cecil's prestige and influence with the King had slumped, because of the failure of the 'Great Contract'. Indeed the years 1610–12 probably mark the turning point in the reign. Although the Cecilian faction dominated the political scene until 1612, their power ebbed after 1610. Sir Robert, astute politician that he was, had always come to terms with other power groups— Howards, Scots, the royal family, household officers and judges. He syphoned off a modest share of patronage to them, in particular to the Howard family, and James's Scottish hangers-on, while keeping a firm grip on policy (subject to a lazy King's approval). But change was afoot long before he died. Between 1607 and 1611, the dull-witted Robert Carr, first of the handsome young men to whom James seems to have been attracted, was being raised to wealth, title (Earl of Somerset) and political influence. And with him rose his talented lieutenant, Sir Thomas Overbury.

Thus the factional pattern was set for the rest of the period until 1629. Cecil's death set in motion a frantic power scramble between the Howards and the Somerset-Overbury alliance. At first James balanced the factions in government—a last gasp of Elizabethan moderation. But in 1615, scandal broke. Somerset had seduced Frances, the wife of the Earl of Essex (the son of the Elizabethan Earl), secured the annulment of her marriage on the grounds of the Earl's impotence, married her, and then he (or Frances) had murdered the disapproving Overbury with poison. Somerset and his wife were convicted of murder, and the Howards seemed triumphant: the Earls of Northampton, Nottingham and Suffolk ruled all, holding a monopoly of patronage and policy.

However, their tenure of power was brief. Early Stuart factions, after Cecil's death, played for policy as well as patronage, because the slap-dash, idle King was willing to surrender all to the faction of his favour. The Howards, for example, were pro-Spanish and pro-Catholic, as well as up to their elbows in Treasury money. Now, a rival faction emerged. It was Protestant, anti-Spanish, and insistent on government economies; its leaders were the Archbishop of Canterbury, George Abbot, and three earls, Montgomery, Pembroke and Southampton. Policies, however, mattered less than pimping. Once the factions discovered the King's taste for beautiful men, they rushed to satisfy his needs. Willing young men were procured, given facial treatments and mouthwashes, and lavishly dressed. The anti-Spanish faction won, when James's own wife and Archbishop Abbot promoted George Villiers. The King was besotted and Villiers rapidly rose to high office and title—a viscount in 1616, earl in 1617, marquess in 1618 and Duke of Buckingham in 1623. This spelt the end of the Howards' supremacy: Northampton had died in 1614, Nottingham was removed from the Admiralty in 1618 for his incompetence, Suffolk was imprisoned for embezzling from the Treasury. Buckingham was supreme. And James was happily doting on his new love: 'Christ has his John and I have my George', or so the Lord's anointed monarch informed his Council.

Now the full extent of the change could be seen. The distinction between favourite and minister had vanished. By 1623 Buckingham not only enjoyed the King's exclusive personal favour, he also monopolised all patronage, and the King took counsel with him alone. Not that we should underestimate James. When Buckingham and James's heir, Prince Charles, used Parliament to force the King into war, he outwitted them both (see page 377). Nevertheless, Elizabethan government was dead, and the Duke was already organising his future with the impending transfer of power to Charles. He did not go unchallenged, however. The advancement of his family, the extravagance and frivolity of the Court (which he seemed to symbolise), his manipulation of foreign policy in response to personal whims, his monopoly of patronage, his autocratic control of his clients: all contributed to the emergence of a faction which aimed to secure his downfall. Its leaders were the Lord Keeper, John Williams (Bishop of Lincoln), the Lord Treasurer, Lionel Cranfield (whose parliamentary impeachment Buckingham secured in 1624), the Earl of Bristol and, above all, the Earl of Pembroke. The fierce faction battles pervaded the Court, Council, and even Parliament during the early years of Charles I's reign. Early Caroline government, by factions which sacrificed King, Court, and stable government to the immediate needs of personal ambition, was a far cry from the moderation of Burghley and Leicester during the heady champagne years of high Elizabethan government.

The Privy Council, 1603–29

The change of monarch in 1603, and the political developments consequent upon that change, accelerated the decline of the Privy Council. Once again, the change was not immediately apparent, because Robert Cecil provided a vital element of continuity with the Elizabethan system. As we might expect, he reflected the tradition of Burghley rather than that of Buckingham. In other words, although he was less scrupulous and moderate than his father, he was much closer to the great Elizabethan minister than he was to the early Stuart favourite. As Secretary and Treasurer, he kept an exclusive grasp on the business of State, rarely delegating power, grooming no successor and surrounding himself with mediocrities. On the other hand, he was realistic, aware that he must conciliate rivals, consult others and at least make a show of power sharing. Cecil, like his father, worked with the Council, even though (at the same time) he dominated it. He behaved as if he was merely first among equals in the Council, with the result that it remained significant as a body, not merely Cecil's compliant tool. James I emphasised the importance of the Council as a body by leaving matters of State in its hands. So much so, that an ambassador could write home, 'The Council spares the King the trouble of governing . . . and one might say it was the very ears, body, and voice of the King'.

However, as in so many other ways, Cecil's death in 1612 marked a turning point in the history of the Privy Council. Thereafter it rapidly declined in importance, and became a prey to factions which often tore it apart, rendered it incapable of offering responsible advice to the King and reduced it to political impotence. The Howards and the anti-Spanish faction, Lord Ellesmere, Archbishop Abbot and the Earl of Pembroke, warred over fundamentals of policy, religion and the role of Parliament; and in the years after the Howards' fall in 1618 the Council was rent by Buckingham's factional battles with his opponents. In these circumstances, the Council ceased to serve the monarch as an advisory body. Not that it was a source of concern to the King. As early as 1613 the Spanish Ambassador reported that 'the King resolveth all business with [the Viscount Rochester, Robert Carr] alone, both those that pass in Council and many other wherewith he never maketh them acquainted'. Thereafter, the King displayed a preference for taking advice elsewhere. He listened to the Spanish Ambassador, Gondomar, while by 1620 Buckingham had become his chief adviser on foreign policy. By 1622 the Venetian Ambassador was reporting that all important policy matters were determined by the Duke, Prince Charles, and a small cabal of ministers. Four years later he wrote that 'there is no longer any council'. If this was not literally true, certainly it had ceased to exist as an advisory body. Having denied it this crucial function, both James I and Charles I treated it with contempt. Anyone who dared raise a critical voice was dubbed a fool or accused of disloyalty. Silence and dumb approval were the safest courses.

What then did the Privy Council do? Robbed of its advisory role, it absorbed itself in administrative duties, the day-to-day government of the realm. This change is reflected in the membership: more and more civil servants and fewer politicians were appointed. Sir Robert Naunton, Sir Richard Weston and Sir Francis Windebank typify the new kind of bureaucratic Councillor: expert in administrative detail and routine, but unversed in matters of high policy. That was left to the King and his inner circle of favourites.

Even so, the Council could have continued to perform a vital administrative function if it had become a board of expert bureaucrats. But that was not to be: many of the new appointments were courtiers, creatures of faction without wit or talent. Their presence at the Council board spelt out the dominance of a Court faction or favourite and served only to frustrate efficiency with petty Court conflicts. The Council's performance also suffered from the increase in its size. Elizabeth's latter-day Council of a dozen members had doubled within two months. Although James recognised that this was too large and made spasmodic efforts to reduce it, the Council continued to grow: from nineteen to twenty in 1610, to twenty-four in 1615, thirty-one in 1618, thirty-five in 1620–5 and forty in 1630. It is true that rarely more than half attended, but that was also the case with Elizabeth's smaller Council. The fact remains that a large unwieldy Council, staffed with bureaucrats and courtiers, divided by faction, stripped of its policy role, treated disparagingly and used as a scapegoat by the early Stuarts, ceased to be an effective instrument of government.

Central government

For most of Elizabeth's reign, Queen and Council together provided the dynamic force in the State: the former alone (with varying degrees of conciliar influence, as we have seen) initiated policies and the latter authorised their execution. The Council also supervised all aspects of the nation's life. How, then, were the paper decisions of Queen and Council translated into practice, how were they enforced? We can invent an example, in order to demonstrate how the process worked. During the war with Spain in the 1580s, Walsingham began to fret about the lack of an adequate defence and warning system on the south coast. He included the subject in the agenda of matters for discussion at the next Council meeting. It was agreed to advise the Queen that beacons be erected, the existing fortresses be reinforced with additional troops, and that negotiations be set on foot with the Dutch for joint patrols in the English Channel. Elizabeth quibbled about the cost, but saw the necessity and gave her approval. The matter was now in the Council's lap. It authorised letters to the Deputy Lieutenants and J.P.s (for the functions of these officials see pages 146–52) of the coastal shires, instructing them to prepare the beacons and muster the necessary soldiers; it made provision for the payment of the soldiers' wages; it recommended to the Queen a suitable ambassador for negotiations with the Dutch and, when to their relief she agreed, they ordered the drawing up of his diplomatic credentials.

This description of the bureaucratic process by which Tudor/early Stuart government operated should provoke a number of questions: who drafted the letters and the ambassador's credentials and where did the money for the soldiers' wages come from? The questions can be answered briefly: central government. The Council presided over a number of Departments of State which provided the essential bureaucratic tools of documentation, authentication and finance. By documentation is meant the drafting of the necessary letters or documents ordered by the Council; authentication was the means by which it was possible to ensure that a document was a genuine official instruction or advice and not a forgery; and of course all government processes cost money. Departments of State which provided these services were essential to the success of the Council's work—work which was facilitated by the inclusion of departmental heads in the Privy Council.

Nevertheless, it is important to keep the Council's 'back-up services' in their right perspective. We have to forget the modern State, with its detailed supervision of the daily lives of citizens and its civil servants numbered by the tens or even hundreds of thousands. In the entire realm, which had a population roughly the same as present-day New Zealand's—about three million—there were only 1200 bureaucratic posts 'fit for a gentleman'. And many of these were local stewardships of Crown lands and custodianships of castles. Central government consisted of a tiny bureaucracy institutionalised in four departments: Chancery, the Privy Seal Office, the Signet Office and Exchequer.

Chancery was old, formal, and very dignified. It drafted royal grants, treaties, appointments, all the most solemn acts of Tudor government, and it authenticated them by attaching to them the Great Seal. The Privy Seal Office drew up and sent instructions to royal officials, whether at home or abroad, attaching to them its own seal. This was, above all, the office used by the Privy Council to send out its steady stream of orders, instructions, admonitions, reprimands and, more occasionally, letters of praise, thanks and commendation. Thirdly, there was the Signet, held by the secretary and employed by him to authenticate the monarch's more informal and private advices and commands to friends and trusted subordinates. Sometimes a document went through more than one seal office, passing through the hands of the Privy Seal or Signet clerks to the Great Seal. No hard-and-fast rules can be made about Tudor bureaucratic procedure. However, of one thing we can be sure, that all official documents were posted out with one or other of the seals affixed to them.

There remains the Exchequer, an elaborate, cumbersome machine which handled most of the royal revenue. Not all of it, because three other agencies were also involved in financial business: the Court of the Duchy of Lancaster (which administered the lands brought to the Crown by Henry IV in 1399), the royal household, and the Court of Wards (which handled the Queen's feudal revenues). Nevertheless, it is true to say that, in the reigns of Elizabeth, James I and Charles I, the Exchequer was far and away the most important financial institution. It was organised into two sub-departments: the Lower Exchequer ('which received and paid out money') and the Upper Exchequer, which annually audited the accounts. It displayed a particular expertise in the collection of debts and the ferreting-out of dishonest practice by royal officials. And it could render a fairly reliable account of royal income, expenditure, what was owed to the Queen, and what her outstanding debts were.

However, the Exchequer had serious limitations. It was a purely mechanical operation, collecting and spending without seeking new sources of revenue or extracting more from the old. It was slow, understaffed at vital points and overstaffed in others. So, when money was paid in to the Lower Exchequer, three officials carefully recorded the payments and duplicated each other's work. A campaign to reduce their number rumbled on throughout Elizabeth's reign, and it only ended when the ultra-conservative Lord Burghley ruled that none of the offices should be suppressed. It was more important to retain 'jobs for the boys' than to streamline the Exchequer's efficiency. In many ways it was antiquated and out-of-date: for instance, it kept its accounts in Roman numerals. When money was paid in, receipt was recorded with notches on a wooden tally (in appearance rather like a tent peg). The tally was then split in half, one piece being given as a receipt to the sheriff or other official who had paid in the money, the other half being retained for presentation at the annual audit of the accounts. Despite its drawbacks, however, the Exchequer provided the Crown with a solid, conscientious, albeit conservative, unimaginative financial support.

The Common Law courts

This then was 'central government', the apparatus on which Queen and Council depended for the execution of policy decisions and administrative decrees. And yet this was not the sum total of central government. There is a fundamental difference between Tudor/early Stuart and modern government—a difference which is located in the relationship between the executive and judicial branches of the State. Nowadays we understand the distinction: that the **executive** initiates and carries out policies, while the **judiciary** is concerned with justice, punishing the guilty, protecting the innocent and adjudicating between citizens in their private disagreements. Not so in the sixteenth century, when there was no such obvious division of powers and functions within the State. After all, the monarch took a coronation oath, promising to minister justice and maintain law and order. These were prime functions of government, and that fact was reflected in its organisation. Chancery was both a civil service department, concerned with documentation, and a law court. The Privy Council advised and administered, but it also adjudicated. The Exchequer was not only a financial machine, but also a kind of Tudor equivalent of an income tax tribunal. The Lord Chancellor was, at one and the same time, Keeper of the Great Seal, the senior civil servant who administered the 'documentation' department of Chancery, the presiding judge when it sat as a court, and the head of the judicial system under the King. Such examples could be multiplied endlessly.

　　Given this state of affairs, it is legitimate to treat the law courts as an integral part of central government. The local courts will be described in due course, in their appropriate place (the ecclesiastical courts are dealt with in chapter 4, the county courts on pages 147–8). Here we are only concerned with the central courts, all of which were housed in Westminster Palace. Theoretically, their jurisdictional boundaries were clearly defined: the Court of Queen's Bench dealt with criminal cases, when the State prosecuted subjects for breaches of the peace; the Court of Common Pleas, which heard disputes between subjects; and the Exchequer, which heard financial cases, especially concerning money owed to the Crown. However, lawyers were (and are) notoriously greedy. As Dr Thomas Wilson wrote in 1600, Anglesey was the best county in England or Wales 'for there be neither foxes nor lawyers'. Courts tried to encroach on each other's competence and draw cases away from their rivals, in order to make money. Nevertheless, the general lines of demarcation hold true: that the central courts each had one primary area of competence: criminal, civil or financial.

A judicial system can only be effective if justice is accessible to all. But if litigants and suitors had had to journey to Westminster for every case, it would have seriously disadvantaged those in the more distant counties. The expense of travel, the time involved, loss of earnings, impassable roads in winter: any of these could have denied them justice. The problem was resolved by taking the courts to the community. Counties were grouped into circuits. Twice a year, judges from the central courts travelled a circuit in pairs and held **assizes** (sittings or sessions) in each county town. They heard the more serious criminal cases which were outside the competence of the J.P.s, and they dealt with civil suits which were too complex for amateur justices. The twice-yearly visits by the judges of assize were also important as a point of contact between central government and local officials. They brought down instructions from Westminster, inquired into the conduct of the J.P.s, and reported back to the Council.

The prerogative courts

One important qualification must be added to this idealised description of Common Law courts. Pre-Tudor law was failing in its duty, promised in the royal coronation oath, of providing justice to all, and the problem was an ancient one. The central law courts administered **Common Law**, a mixture of custom and case law (that is, verdicts handed down by judges in particular cases). This was in turn supplemented, modified, and even replaced by statute or Acts of Parliament. However, the law had not kept pace with social and economic change. Worse still, the way in which the courts operated often denied justice. They were slow, expensive and dogged with procedural technicalities which could ruin a man's case, no matter the justice of his cause.

As the source of all justice, the monarch had the right and responsibility to remedy the shortcomings of the judicial system, above all by the drastic remedy of creating new courts: these were called prerogative courts because they were the consequence of an exercise of the royal prerogative. The Crown had already done this in the fourteenth century, when authority was delegated to the Lord Chancellor to hear petitions for justice. The Chancellor, sitting in Chancery, dealt with cases for which the Common Law had no remedy, in which the law had not kept pace with economic and social change, or in which the plaintiff (the accuser) had little hope of justice against a powerful opponent. The second of these proved with time to be the most important of Chancery's concerns. In the absence of specific laws, the Chancellor had to apply a mixture of fairness and common sense (equity) to the cases before him. In time the judgements made in Chancery came to form a body of case law or precedents, which bound future Chancellors in their decisions in similar cases. During the sixteenth century, however, they still enjoyed a certain freedom of action and greater flexibility than the Common Law courts—a fact which accounts for Chancery's continued popularity. Perhaps even more important in its record of success was its use of written instead of oral evidence. This ensured a more thoroughgoing examination and a greater possibility of reaching the right verdict.

On its own, however, Chancery could not eliminate all the deficiencies of the courts and the law which they enforced. So the King's Council was gradually drawn into the business of justice. Its right to do so sprang from its ancient authority to hear petititons from aggrieved subjects. Long before the Tudors ruled, it had sat in the Star Chamber (so-called 'either because it is full of windows or because at the first all the roof thereof was decked with images of stars gilded') in Westminster Palace, arbitrating between feuding parties, punishing violent breaches of the law, misconduct by judges, juries and sheriffs in the law courts, and intimidation by overmighty subjects. Thus far, it was just a matter of King's Councillors sitting in Star Chamber and exercising the King's judicial authority.

In Henry VIII's reign, however, the Council in Star Chamber was, in two steps, transformed into a separate law court. First, its power, competence and activity increased dramatically during the vigorous chancellorship of Thomas Wolsey (1515–1529). Sir Thomas Smith gave him the credit when he wrote, in 1563, that 'This court began long before, but took great augmentation and authority at that time that Cardinal Wolsey, archbishop of York, was chancellor of England, who of some was thought to have first devised the court because that he . . . augmented the authority of it, which was at that time marvellous necessary to do . . .'. Then in 1540 it acquired its own clerk and records, and from that date on it was certainly a recognisable court of law. Privy Councillors, headed by the Lord Chancellor, continued to sit in Star Chamber as judges. From now on, however, Privy Council and Star Chamber were separate institutions.

Throughout Elizabeth's reign, and indeed until its abolition in 1641, Star Chamber dealt chiefly with criminal cases. It could not take life or property and usually punished with fines. This did not prevent it from exercising a wide jurisdiction, in particular because it could deal with any case which had provoked or threatened to cause riot. All that a petitioner had to do was to complain that someone had assaulted him, or simply paraded before him in intimidating manner, with others carrying 'weapons invasive and defensive', such as clubs, daggers, swords, halberds and the like, and that was sufficient for Star Chamber to take up the case. Libel, slander, fraud and embezzlement could all be brought into its net, simply by warning that riot would follow if the issue was not heard and resolved. Nor did its jurisdiction end there. It continued to punish misconduct in the law courts as well as breaches of royal proclamations. It was probably the most efficient of all the Tudor courts, even though its decrees (verdicts) often had to be re-issued—a sure sign that they were not being obeyed.

By the end of the reign, Star Chamber was coming under growing criticism from the common lawyers. They resented its popularity and the way in which it drew business away from the Common Law courts. That criticism continued in James I's reign. Yet it remained a popular court, burdened with business from a swarm of suitors who wanted to take advantage of its four special virtues. First, it was less expensive than the Common Law courts. Secondly, whereas judges and jurors in local courts could be harassed and intimidated by local magnates to give verdicts favourable to them, the judges in Star Chamber were the highest men in the realm under the monarch. They sat, not in the area of magnate influence, but at the very heart of power, Westminster. There was no way they could be, or would be, pressured into partial conduct and false verdicts. Thirdly, the court did not invent or apply a new body of law. It enforced Common Law and Acts of Parliament, but it did so with an impartiality and fairness which were not so obvious in the Common Law courts.

Finally, Star Chamber procedure enabled it to hear more cases, and bring them to a conclusion more rapidly, than the ordinary courts. This may be surprising because, like the other courts, it sat only during the law term (a total of sixteen weeks each year), and then only on Wednesdays and Fridays. How could it hope to dispense relatively speedy justice? The answer lies in the way in which it collected the evidence on which it based its verdicts. The Common Law courts took their evidence verbally (orally) in court, during the short law terms. This was a time-consuming process. In contrast, Star Chamber proceeded by the written word.

Consider one imaginary case. John ap Rees and his drunken Welsh confederates had raided the lodgings of Morris Knyvett, threatened him with an array of menacing weapons so that he was 'afraid for his life', and turned him naked from his bed into the street. The bruised body and pride of Morris prompted him to address a written bill of complaint to the Queen, petitioning for justice from the Councillors. Star Chamber accepted his bill, whereby he became the plaintiff (accuser) and John ap Rees the defendant (accused). John was required to produce a written defence and to swear on oath that it was true and accurate. Morris was permitted to read it and write an answer, to which John replied (again on paper). Both plaintiff and defendant could go through the same procedure a third time, but when they did they usually did no more than restate their positions. Star Chamber then ordered the examination, as witnesses, of all those people named in the documents drawn up by Morris and John. Usually this work was performed by J.P.s in the counties where the witnesses lived. They then returned the collected information on paper to Star Chamber.

This, then, was the process, a thorough and rigorous one, even if it left the Councillors with the tedious and unenviable task of sifting through the compound of truth and lies, honest complaint and malicious accusation which went by the name of evidence. However, in this case they finally reached a verdict in Morris' favour. The important point is that this work could be, and had been, done outside the law terms. When Star Chamber met in the next term, it simply handed down its verdict: that John ap Rees was guilty. He was fined £2000 (an enormous sum, which expressed the court's indignation at such wicked violence, but which was later reduced to less than one-tenth of the original amount) and required to keep the peace and refrain from molesting Morris Knyvett in the future.

The Chamber's procedure thus gave it an inestimable advantage: it could sift evidence and determine verdicts throughout the year. Although it was sometimes dissatisfied with the written evidence and held a public oral hearing (like the Common Law courts), more often than not it simply handed down judgements during the law terms. No wonder it achieved a much higher turnover of business. However, its very efficiency has marred its reputation: assembling merely to give judgement has given it the appearance of an arbitrary royal tribunal, which imposed crippling fines on defendants without a careful consideration of the evidence. In fact the reverse was true. It was more thorough, speedier, cheaper, and therefore also more popular, than the Common Law courts, and its popularity survived until the 1630s.

Whereas Star Chamber concerned itself with crime, another prerogative court, the **court of requests**, specialised in civil matters (disputes between subjects). However, like Star Chamber, its powers derived from the King's authority to remedy any shortcomings in the Common Law. It began in an informal way when a number of Councillors were appointed by the King to hear the petititons of poor men, who could not afford the cost of justice in the Common Law courts. Appropriately enough, they were usually headed by the almoner, the royal official responsible for doling out charity to the poor. By the reign of Richard III (1483–5) it had evolved into a formal court and certainly it enjoyed a vigorous existence and wide popularity throughout Elizabeth's reign. This is hardly surprising: it met the needs of a large number of people whose slender purses could not sustain an action at law in defence of their rights. They found in the Court of Requests a very cheap and (at first) an easily accessible tribunal. Moreover, like Star Chamber, it worked ceaselessly, even if its public hearings took place only during the law terms. And when the monarch was on her summer progress, petitions of complaint could be handed to the Councillors who travelled with the Court, or to those who remained behind at Westminster.

However, like all Tudor institutions, there was a wide gulf between the ideal and the reality. The Court became accessible not only to poor men, but also to the monarch's household servants, who, because of their closeness to the King, usually moved to the head of the queue. However, others saw the benefits of getting their cases into the Court of Requests and 'sundry knights, esquires and other rich and wealthy complainants', succeeded in doing so. Eventually the Crown acted to prevent this, decreeing that 'all gentlemen . . . not being his Grace's Household servants attendant upon his person . . . be remitted to the common law . . . considering their suits to be greatly to the hindrance of poor men's causes admitted to sue to the King's grace . . .' (Elton, 1960, page 191). The Elizabethan Court observed this restriction. The Court's competence was also extended to protect the rights of tenants. It was, in consequence, a very popular court, but for this very reason it aroused resistance from the judges of Common Pleas and the lawyers who practised there. The loss of business to Requests meant a loss of fees. So, late in Elizabeth's reign, and increasingly in the early seventeenth century, they challenged the validity of the Court of Requests' verdicts and even its right to exist at all. Yet it continued to operate until the Civil War put an end to it in 1643.

The regional councils

This does not complete the catalogue of such courts, because prerogative justice was dispensed also by the regional councils. Reference to these, however, introduces for the first time another important, even

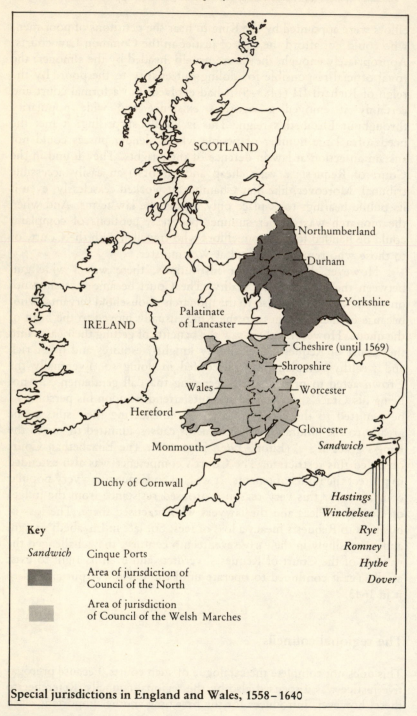

SCOTLAND

IRELAND

Northumberland

Durham

Yorkshire

Palatinate
of Lancaster

Cheshire (until 1569)

Shropshire

Wales

Worcester

Hereford

Gloucester

Monmouth

Sandwich

Duchy of Cornwall

Hastings
Winchelsea
Rye
Romney
Hythe
Dover

Key

Sandwich   Cinque Ports

Area of jurisdiction of
Council of the North

Area of jurisdiction
of Council of the Welsh Marches

Special jurisdictions in England and Wales, 1558–1640

vital, institution in the Tudor/early Stuart structure of government. And it is probable that any attempt to make sense of these prerogative courts (their purpose, their power, where they fit into the contemporary political scheme of things) will fail, unless they are examined as an integral part of the conciliar system. That system was, in its turn, a response to serious, seemingly permanent and, in the past, intractable problems of government.

Although the Tudors ruled over a small kingdom, only the southeast and the Midlands were under stable and effective political control. These were populous, settled areas: they were within striking reach of the government at Westminster and constantly visited by the itinerant Court of the Tudors, up and down the Thames to their riverside palaces, or rambling expensively through the countryside on summer progresses. But what of the more distant regions: the north, Wales, the far west, all of which were outside the normal royal circuit? It was not just a problem of poor communications, although that problem certainly existed, especially in the more difficult terrain of the north and west, and it grew as the ancient road network continued to deteriorate. However, it was much more complicated than that. The distant regions presented a security problem. Scottish 'reivers' (rustlers, abductors, and robbers) constantly crossed the border in part of what was a two-way traffic of crime; Scottish armies occasionally invaded, while their 'auld' alliance with England's traditional foe, France, escalated the threat to what was known as 'the postern gate' (the back-door) of England.

Wales was less of a loophole in the network of national security. Yet had not Henry, the first Tudor, landed and marched unmolested through Wales to defeat and kill Richard III at Bosworth in 1485? Armies might easily land undetected on isolated stretches of its coastline, and the fears, at least, were revived when Spain began to probe Elizabethan England's weaknesses in the west. Ireland and Cornwall were tested in the 1580s, so why not Wales too? The southwest, with its long peninsular coast, posed another security problem. Official concern was justified when Spaniards burned the Cornish village of Mousehole in the 1580s and Moorish slavers descended upon it in the 1630s.

However, while the insecurity of distant areas sometimes caused official consternation, and even threatened the ruling dynasty, this was not the continuous and permanent problem which they posed. That can be expressed in terms of the basic problem which faced all Tudor and early Stuart rulers: how to maintain law and order in a turbulent society, where men were quick to reach for the club and turn the knife. Christopher Marlowe was stabbed to death in a drunken gambling brawl, Ben Jonson cut down a fellow actor, bloody feuds were fought by Knyvetts and de Veres around Elizabeth's Court (Stone, 1965, pages 233–4). Such examples are endless, and yet those cited all occurred in and around London and Westminster, the seat of royal power.

The problem was magnified many times over in the remote areas, which to many officials must have been seen as a standing offence to good government. The Welsh were notoriously ungovernable: 'malefacts and scandalous deeds be so rooted and fixed in the same people that they be not like to cease unless some sharp correction and punishment for redress . . . be provided.' They 'have of long time continued and persevered in perpetration and commission of divers and manifold thefts, murders, rebellions, wilful burning of houses and other abominable malefacts, to the high displeasure of God and disturbance of the public well-being'. The mixture of bureaucratic long-windedness and the cumbersome Tudor way of saying things should not obscure the point which was being laboured. It was summed up by a Tudor bishop, Rowland Lee, who, earlier in the century, was a veritable 'hanging judge' in Wales, handing down savage verdicts and executing scores of malefactors. At the end he sighed in exasperation and admitted that he had found the Welsh thieves and left them in an unchanged condition. A different approach was necessary if the problem was to be permanently resolved.

The same was true of the north, but even more so. There, too, lawlessness was endemic. Elizabeth's government lamented, 'of late years very many of her Majesty's subjects within Cumberland, Northumberland, Westmorland and the bishopric of Durham have been taken, some forth of their own houses and some in travelling by the highway . . . and carried out as prisoners, and kept barbarously and cruelly until they have been redeemed by great ransoms'. The catalogue of woes continued: 'incursions, robberies and burning and spoiling of towns, villages and houses . . . and the inhabitants of divers towns there have been enforced to pay a certain rate of money, corn, cattle or other consideration, commonly there called by the name of black mail' (an early form of protection racket). It was a sorry picture of indiscriminate lawlessness, victimisation and feeble royal authority.

The north and Wales sound very similar. Yet there was a vital difference. In the northern border, or marcher, counties the problem of lawbreaking was compounded and magnified by the presence of formidable noble power. The Crown had customarily delegated marcher management to four great, autonomous families: the Percies, Cliffords, Nevilles (the Earls of Northumberland, Cumberland and Westmorland respectively) and the Barons Dacre. The Percies were supreme in the east, the Cliffords and Nevilles vied for a similar superiority in the west, while the Dacres maintained a turbulent primacy in the central border area. All of them served the Crown in their own fashion, but more often than not they were more concerned to pursue their own feuds, embroil themselves in faction fights, raid across the Scottish border and subvert the King's justice whenever it suited them. Always they conducted themselves in the high, lordly, and vice-regal manner of kings in their own backyards. Always they were aggressive, independent; and they could be disloyal, even treasonable, to the Crown. In brief, they constituted a permanent potential threat to the Tudor dynasty and a challenge to the notion of 'good governance'. Yet what else could the Tudors do but rely upon them and hope for their loyalty? In 1558 Elizabeth needed these families as much as her predecessors had done. She was dependent upon their 'manred' (manpower), their network of social allegiance and their capacity to bear the main financial burden of their wardenships. These were the offices which legitimised the great noble families' management of the borders. So the Percies were usually wardens of the eastern marches, with Cliffords or Nevilles in the west, and the Dacres in the middle marches against Scotland.

Once again, here was the perennial problem: lack of money. How could the Crown maintain national security, impose royal authority, enforce obedience to the law and implement what it conceived to be 'good governance' without a large, expensive, national, salaried and professional civil service? The alternative that presented itself was the regional council. In the past there had been no choice but to lean on the powerful quasi-feudal northern nobility. Now there was an alternative which, if effectively implemented, would threaten the traditional authority of these ancient magnate families. The regional council introduced a new level of administration, with the result that Tudor government became a three-tiered operation: central, regional and local.

Regional councils were not, however, an English innovation, nor were they a sixteenth century novelty. Government by a co-ordinated system of councils had evolved on the Continent during the previous century and was already well-established in contemporary France, Spain, Germany and Sweden. Not that Elizabeth or the earlier Tudors had to look to the Continent for an example, a model. Nor did they introduce councils into the structure of English government. The Tudors were skilful political mechanics, fine-tuners and renovators, but for the most part they simply built on the work of their more creative, imaginative predecessors. In this case the credit for the creation of regional councils must go to the Yorkist kings, Edward IV and Richard III (1461–85).

In the early days, the regional councils were less government agencies than councils responsible for the estates and interests of the Prince of Wales and the Duke of York. This was reflected in their 'Courtly' membership of peers, bishops and great gentlemen. However, there followed a long period of experimentation in which the early Tudors and their ministers, especially Thomas Cromwell, gradually transformed them into genuine instruments of government. In the process, their membership also changed: although the Elizabethan/early Stuart presidents were usually great nobles or gentry (Sir Henry Sidney in Wales, the Earls of Shrewsbury and Huntingdon in the north), the real work was carried out by a nucleus of lawyers and bureaucrats. The regional councils became professional councils. They were given added muscle by the dignity and social authority of a regional magnate who wielded his presidential power by royal commission. And they enjoyed a wide competence to administer daily affairs, to maintain law and order, to dispense prerogative justice, and to supervise the work of local officials.

This last function pin-points their position in the Tudor communications chain. If, on the one hand, sheriffs, J.P.s and other county officers were responsible to them, they were in turn answerable to the Privy Council. Indeed their great advantage was that, while they were supervised from the centre, they were on the spot, able to get the feel of public opinion, transmit information on security matters, and scotch conspiracy and rebellion promptly (although the Council of the North was inept during the northern earls' rebellion in 1569). As members learned from experience of local conditions, they became better equipped than the Privy Council at Westminster to administer societies very different from that of south-east England. They differed in geography, economy and social organisation. Moreover, Wales was Celtic, not Anglo-Saxon, and many Welsh spoke no English. Until the acts of 1536 and 1543, it had its own system of land tenure; it had no representation in Parliament, and it was not even 'shired' (divided into the classic English administrative units of counties or 'shires'). The far north was, in contrast, an Anglo-Saxon frontier land in a more or less constant state of sporadic border warfare against the Celtic Scots. This was not true of Yorkshire to the south, though even here the system of warning bells was a reminder that it was not immune from the depredations of Scottish armies. The north had little choice but to be militaristic. Its sparse population, its often difficult terrain and relatively backward economy, emphasised what a different world it was from Whitehall, Westminster, London and the settled, populous shires which surrounded them.

Similarly with the Percies, Cliffords and other magnate families. Their power derived less from royal offices than from their own socio-economic position as traditional overlords, warrior-leaders, patrons, landlords and patriarchal heads of a conservative community. In their traditions, their priorities, and above all in what they wanted, they were very different from the centralising Tudor/Stuart princes and the calculating bureaucrats of Whitehall whom they supposedly represented and served. For the northern nobles were unambitious; they wanted no more than the *status quo*: perpetuation of their traditional parochial authority as mini-kings and tribal leaders. A centralising Tudor monarchy could not tolerate this, and by 1558 it had already eroded their traditional power-bases. Traditional loyalties snapped as the Crown raised local gentry such as Thomas Wharton and William Eure to noble titles, as it seduced old clients and retainers from noble into royal service, and as it transferred royal offices to its new supporters. The process was aided by inflation, executions for treason, and economic mismanagement by some of the northern nobles. The net result was that Elizabeth inherited a situation in which the tide was running in the Crown's favour. Nevertheless, the old northern peerage remained a formidable political force, diminished in power but by no means broken. In any case, Wales, the Welsh Marches and the north remained remote areas, in which royal authority had been traditionally weak. And even if the security risk (from invasion or noble rebellion) had diminished, the related problems of law-breaking, abuse of office, and contempt for judicial process presented a difficulty of some magnitude. So the regional councils remained crucial to the Crown's ability to fulfil the obligation of good governance.

The councils which Elizabeth inherited had clearly specified functions and powers. The Council of the North, for example, was authorised to administer daily affairs, maintain law and order and render justice. In order to carry out these tasks, it was given appropriate, indeed sweeping, powers, exercised under the supervision of the Privy Council. It dealt with civil cases (between subject and subject) and crimes, including treason and felony (which meant that, unlike the Privy Council and Star Chamber, it could take property and life). Like the Star Chamber it could handle all cases involving or threatening riot—which in the violent north gave it a very wide scope indeed. And, like Chancery, it could exercise equity (fairness) in matters not adequately covered by existing laws, such as fraud, embezzlement and breach of contract. It also enjoyed the Star Chamber's authority to investigate and punish injustices and abuses committed by local magistrates and other royal servants. In brief, the Council of the North was armed with the competence and authority of almost all the Common Law and prerogative courts at Westminster. On paper at least, it was a mighty machine, as was the council in the marches of Wales, which had jurisdiction over the whole of Wales and the adjoining English border counties. It had much in common with its counterpart in the north, because it too exercised the powers and jurisdiction of Star Chamber, Chancery and the Common Law courts—including treason and felony. However, unlike the northern council or any other English institution, it was specifically empowered to use torture.

How effective were the regional councils? It is impossible to measure success or offer a precise answer. However, it does seem that, apart from the northern council's ineffectual performance during the 1569 rebellion, they were successes rather than failures. In particular, they did much to lower the level of violent crime in the respective areas of their jurisdiction. This was achieved partly by their policing and law-enforcement activities, and partly by encouraging men to use lawsuits instead of swords and bills to settle their differences or harm their opponents. The conciliar experiment was particularly successful in the north, where the Scottish Reformation produced a novel friendship between the two countries. National confrontations, wars, invasion and counter-invasion all came to an end. Border warfare diminished to no more than the ingrained habits and traditional pastimes of a militaristic marcher society: kidnapping, robbery with violence, cattle rustling and arson. The power of the Crown's old rivals, the Percies, Dacres and Nevilles, was finally broken in the rebellion of 1569. And thereafter, in the absence of a Scottish or aristocratic military threat, the marcher wardens were reduced from military commanders to mere policemen. The council could concentrate on its more important and continuous administrative and judicial responsibilities.

However, the success of the councils must not be exaggerated. Along with other organs of Tudor Government, their energy and efficiency were progressively sapped by the steady conservative decline of Elizabethan administration. Their very popularity as prerogative courts resulted in a large and growing backlog of cases, which robbed them of their early virtue of producing speedy decisions. Moreover, the councils were frequently divided and even rendered impotent by faction fights—a common characteristic of Tudor government. As usual their members were underpaid. Indeed, at one point £300 a year was supposed to suffice for the president and entire Council of the North—of course, it did not. It is true that this pathetically small sum could be augmented by the classic Tudor 'user pays' principle: in other words, fixed fees for services rendered to members of the public: 12d for cancelling a surety or bond; for every letter 4d; for copies of evidence, 1d for every ten lines, and so on. They were still underpaid, however, and this circumstance combined with natural human greed.

Corrupt practices crept in, took root, and multiplied: for example, prolonging law suits in order to extract further fees, or the misuse of office by councillors like Sir Thomas Throckmorton, Sir William Herbert and Edward Lord Stafford, in pursuit of quarrels and vendettas.

Much depended on the integrity and energy of conciliar presidents. It was no coincidence that the Council of the North reached its zenith under the Earl of Huntingdon's presidency (1572–95). But not all of them matched his devotion. Not long before Elizabeth became queen, her sister, Mary I, inquired of the Earl of Pembroke how he could conduct the affairs of the Council of the Welsh Marches when he continued to reside at Court. She lamented the 'state of disrepair for a want of a President living there' and dismissed him. Pembroke sulked and declined to recommend a successor. Nor was the Council of the North free from such problems. One president, the eighth Earl of Shrewsbury, preferred the comforts of his own home, which was many miles away from the council's headquarters at York. This was doubtless conducive to the good Earl's peace of mind and the comforts of his body; on the other hand, neither efficient presidential management nor fruitful council meetings were likely in the circumstances.

Even energetic and attendant presidents and councils had problems enough to contend with. In particular, they had to combat frequent attempts to wriggle free from conciliar jurisdiction: the city of York had a number of tries, while in 1569 Cheshire actually secured its freedom from the Welsh marcher council. There were also conflicting jurisdictions, which further complicated life. An important example of this occurred earlier, in Henry VIII's reign, leaving a legacy of conflict. In 1536 the Welsh Council was made responsible for civil and criminal jurisdiction; seven years later an Act of Parliament created another series of courts with the same functions throughout Wales. Nor was this the only challenge to the Council's jurisdiction because, in the English border counties, it competed with the Common Law courts for business. Life as a councillor, and especially as a president, was not for the nervous, sensitive or thin-skinned.

Nevertheless, the regional councils can be credited with at least a modest degree of success. They were stabilising institutions, curbing the worst excesses of a turbulent society and bolstering royal authority. However, their very success brought with it new problems. Late in Elizabeth's reign, there was a growing swell of murmur, grudge and complaint, especially in the north where local magistrates were becoming restive. They felt that they could now manage their affairs on their own, without the heavy, official supervisory hand of the Council. Their natural allies were the Common Law judges in Westminster, who resented the loss of business to the relatively cheap and fast conciliar courts. Judges began to issue **writs of prohibition** which denied the competence of the councils in specific cases. It was a sinister portent for the future of regional councils. They had rendered an important service to the stability of the Tudor State and society, but their great days were over by 1603. And the challenge of localism, and of the common lawyers, grew during the period 1603–29. Moreover, the quality of presidents declined after the Earl of Huntingdon in the north (1572–95) and Sir Henry Sidney in Wales (1560–86).

The Tudor and early Stuart regional councils were a vital link in what Penry Williams calls the 'chain of command'. So far as administering the realm was concerned, theirs was a 'middle-man's' role, enforcing Privy Council decrees and instructions, passing back information, and supervising local officials in the grass-roots work of government. They stood between two extremes. At one end of the spectrum were the monarch and the Privy Councillors, resolving matters of great moment in their deep counsels of State. Perhaps a war with Spain, a trade embargo, royal marriage with a Habsburg or a French consort, a new approach to the problems of vagabondage and poverty, an attack on Cadiz or suppression of an Irish rebellion. However, paper resolutions had to be translated into practice through the machinery of local government: only there could manpower, money and materials be mobilised. And this, the other end of the spectrum, was also the level at which most people come into contact with the State: as taxpayers, victims of the vagabondage laws or recipients of poor relief, as criminals or litigants in civil suits, as men pressed for the navy or mustered for service in Ireland.

Local government

Any study of Tudor and early Stuart local government must rest upon four fundamentals, unchanging throughout the period 1558–1629. Local government was staffed, not by a salaried, professional civil service, but by an unpaid (and at the best grossly underpaid) governing class of amateur administrators. Second, the basic administrative unit was the county, within which offices were monopolised by local peers and gentry. Third, local government was a mechanism delicately balanced between central government and local interests. The Crown issued its orders and decrees, but left their enforcement to local peers and gentry, whose monopoly of offices in their home counties was

scrupulously recognised by the monarch, at least until 1629. Fourth, and typically, the Tudors and early Stuarts operated an inherited system of local government without radically restructuring it. The Tudors made only one important innovation: the office of Lord Lieutenant. He became the glittering, aristocratic pinnacle of county administration: usually, though not always, a peer. His office was originally a military one. The Lord Lieutenant was responsible for the organisation and efficiency of a county's military strength, its militia, equipment and arms depot. However, as so often happened in early modern England, he soon shed his original garb and donned new clothes. In practice, he became a local agent of the Court, a gilded figurehead of county society, and patronage adviser to central government. His military functions were soon taken over by his assistants, the Deputy Lieutenants, who were recruited from the gentry.

Below the Lord Lieutenant and his deputies, the old county hierarchy of officials survived intact. The sheriff had once been the all-powerful local officer, but the frequent and dramatic abuse of that authority had resulted in its progressive and drastic diminution. The Tudor/early Stuart sheriff, shorn of power and burdened with responsibility, had an unenviable, tedious, unpopular and personally expensive responsibility. He organised county courts, executed their writs, hosted the judges at each assize, supervised the county gaol, engaged in police work, called out the *posse comitatus* (the sheriff's posse) and conducted parliamentary elections. (See pages 208–10 for a detailed study of the Stuart sheriff's work.) They were all thankless tasks. It is hardly surprising that the Crown chose him to serve only once in his life, and then only for one year.

Long before Elizabeth's reign, some of the sheriff's authority and important functions had been transferred to the Justices of the Peace (J.P.s), who had become the determinant of effective (or lax) local government. They were assisted in turn by Chief Constables, chosen by the Crown and chiefly engaged in the collection of revenues and hunting down recusants, and, at the bottom of the heap, by the petty constables who were elected by their fellows in the village élites. At these lower levels there was considerable laxity and backsliding. In 1585 the Privy Council lamented 'how unready and unperfect many of our chief Constables [are] to yield their [financial] accounts' to the J.P.s. Many had died without rendering an account and payment of monies collected, to the Crown's considerable loss. So in 1597 the Norwich Poor House accounts were seven years in arrears. The petty constables were no better. The town of Wells in Norfolk petitioned a magistrate to remove Robert Jarye. 'We did chuse him for office thinking thereby to have somewhat restrained him from his former unrulynes in gaming and using the ale houses. But rather it doth incourage him to bolster out both his owne loose behavioure and also the ill demeaner of others and therefore think him to be a man utterly unmeet for that office'. In Cromer village nearby, the constables seized property and set up nine alehouses, where unlawful games were practised 'to the ill example of many idle and ill-disposed people'. The Justices of the Peace were instructed 'to examyne that point exactly'.

So we return to the J.P.s, or, to be more precise, members of the Commission of the Peace, as one must always do when surveying Tudor/early Stuart local government. These men, and their quality, honesty and energy, were the keys to good governance. They are also the most important example of the characteristic way in which local government was organised by commission. Panels of peers and gentlemen, judges, lawyers and bishops, were appointed (and dismissed) by the Crown in each county, and their warrant of authority (their written authorisation to act and exercise power in the Queen's name), the form and extent of their power, and their duties and responsibilities were all set down in letters patent (a royal document of grant to which the Queen's privy seal was attached.) Commissions were of various kinds. Some were *ad hoc* commissions, appointed to deal with a specific crisis or problem. In 1559, for example, a salt monopoly granted to a group of merchants in the Norfolk town of Lynn had 'much damnified' Elizabeth's subjects. The monopolists had trebled the price, imprisoned rival salt sellers, bought by one measure and sold by another, and forced buyers to accept a mixture of pure and impure salt, at least if we are to believe the chorus of contemporary complaints. The government's answer was to appoint a special Commission of Inquiry.

More important were the standing (that is, permanent) commissions: for military musters, for sewers (drainage, irrigation, waterways and coastal defences) and the Commission of the Peace. The last of these is also by far the most important, for it appointed the county magistracy—the Justices of the Peace—and it defined their powers and duties. A reading of the terms of the Commission can be very misleading, because they suggest that the J.P.s were simply law officers and judges. It was their duty to: enforce all statutes against crime, take bonds of money as a guarantee of good behaviour, conduct inquiries into a variety of alleged felonies (that is, reported crimes punishable by death), supervise other local officials, and hold regular county courts in order to hear and determine cases. These courts were of two kinds. Every three or four months a body of justices met in **quarter sessions**, where they heard cases on **indictment** (that is, resulting from written accusations laid before them). Whereas these were trials by jury, at the monthly **petty sessions** one or two magistrates, without a jury, could dispense summary justice on minor offences.

Thus far it is quite clear that J.P.s were judicial officers, and, if we did not look beyond the terms of their commission, we might assume that this was the limit of their functions. That would be a serious mistake: they were, in fact, so useful that both Crown and Parliament burdened them with a growing number of duties in local government. By 1600 they were enforcing over 300 Acts of Parliament, many of which were purely administrative. They administered proclamations and acted upon a stream of Privy Council instructions. In fact, they were just as much civil servants as they were law officers and judges—the famous donkeys of Tudor and early Stuart government, unpaid yet weighed down with tiresome and time-consuming duties. Why they did it so willingly seems clear enough: the office became the badge of a select group, the mark of membership of the social élite of one's county. They were reappointed annually, hectored and bullied by the Privy Council, supervised by regional councils, scrutinised by assize judges, and sometimes dropped for laxity or dishonesty—a serious blow to their social status in their county. The gentry, however, clamoured to secure a place on the Commission and, as the Crown yielded under pressure, so the numbers rose. Already in 1565, Sir Thomas Smith was observing that, 'At the first they were but 4, after 8, now they come commonly to 30 or 40 in every shire'. From 1244 in 1553, they multiplied to 2500 in 1640.

The J.P.s were, as one might expect, of variable quality. Many were devoted and industrious, but even these, like all the rest, were amateurs: they needed guidance. Therefore, the Commission in each county included several lawyers who were 'of the quorum' (that is, one of them had to be present at both quarter and petty sessions. Each county court was also served by a Clerk of the Peace, who was someone learned in the law. Yet another trained lawyer was occasionally (but increasingly in the seventeenth century) appointed *custos rotulorum*, or keeper of the Justices' records in the county. These officials provided a professional stiffening to a body of amateurs, whose services were vital to good government.

The Council was well aware of both amateurism and human failings. Lax magistrates drew forth an angry response: 'Although there be many of great integrity and discretion, yet there are many who possess public places and attend only private things'. Disloyalty, too, concerned an anxious Council. A survey of 1564 must have caused alarm when it revealed that only half the kingdom's Justices were 'favourers of true religion and godly orders' and 'favourers of God's

Holy Word'—in other words, reliable in religion. Just under one-third were quaintly described as 'indifferent' or 'neuter'. And eighteen per cent were 'obstinate adversaries of God's Holy Word, hinderers and mislikers'. In Herefordshire Sir Thomas Havard 'by common fame is a daily drunkard, a receiver and maintainer of the enemies of religion. He useth to pray upon a Latin primer full of superstitions. His wife and maiden use beads and to be short he is a mortal enemy to Christian religion'. In the north, three-quarters of the Lancashire Commission were Catholics. The Privy Council was understandably disturbed. After all, its labours were wasted unless proclamations, statutes and conciliar orders were enforced in the countryside, and that in turn depended upon the drive, integrity and loyalty of the Justices.

Nathaniel Bacon is an excellent example of the dedicated magistrate. He lived at Stiffkey in the grain-growing coastal county of Norfolk, and was a trained lawyer and a J.P. from the mid-1570s to 1620 (when he was seventy-three). As he was of the quorum, he frequently attended quarter and petty sessions. He also arbitrated in disputes passed on to him by the central courts and he attempted to settle them without going back to law. So he hammered out an agreement whereby Ralph Dade repaid eight creditors in instalments. He arranged for John Corbie to pay Wighton village 6d a week to maintain his wife, 'a lunatic, who is detained in the hospital'. He also remonstrated with an ill-tempered and violent farmer, a Mr Armiger, who refused to pay tithes in kind (a levy of one-tenth of farm produce which was devoted to the upkeep of the local clergyman) to his vicar. Armiger protected his harvest with armed men, kept a fierce dog which he set on to the vicar's tithe collectors, ploughed up the minister's orchard and emptied the collector's cart. Sometimes on his own initiative, sometimes at the Council's behest, Bacon conducted public investigations. He did so when the notorious Mr Armiger received what he probably deserved from William Howsegre, who 'smyte him with his fist, and pulled him by the hair of his head'. Or when a seventeen year-old youth, Gregory Martin, was found dead, 'his arm in two places wounded and torn, his breast wounded, and his neck broken'. Bacon's patient enquiry finally established that Gregory had been 'negligently' playing around Methwold windmill when he 'was caught by the cogges of the same wheel and so through the force and violence thereof, the mill being then under sail, he then received his mortal wounds'.

Bacon also collected evidence prior to a trial. He took evidence against Agnes Amies on a charge of witchcraft, when her neighbour Elizabeth Mower became 'vexed and troubled in mind and became lame of her body' after a dispute between them. He also examined one

Thirkle's complaint that his wife had been stolen. John Jordan had abducted Thirkle's wife and 'she was kept by him and [he] was in her company and [they] sent for sundry pots of beer'. More complicated was the case of a pregnant girl, Elizabeth Reeve. She named the local vicar, Mr Poynter, as father. He had 'defiled her sundry times' (six or seven she specified) for money, telling her to blame a local wool-worker, Sandar Dove. A friend protested her innocence, but Bacon had his doubts. Under examination, Elizabeth admitted that, not only had Dove enjoyed her body 'in the field among the furze', but she had also surrendered herself to a local gentleman's servant. Yet was the vicar innocent? It seemed not. Bacon discovered that Mr Poynter's marriage had not satisfied his sexual drives. He 'hath dwelt long in this kind of sin', and his past record included convictions for sexual offences, several children by one Alice Whitby, and even a charge of rape. Bacon advised the Council to remove him promptly. As an ardent Protestant and devout churchman he was also concerned to reach to the bottom of the truth when he interrogated two women who had burned Wymondham Village to the ground, because they 'should have pardon from the Pope' and a handsome financial reward.

The picture emerges of a common (not universal) figure: the dedicated J.P., concerned not only with order but also with justice, acting as a kind of honest broker, a citizens' advice bureau and a mediator. Armed with local knowledge, he performed these services to both government and community in a patient and paternalistic manner. Much of his time was also devoted to administrative business, particularly the arduous and unpleasant task of collecting parliamentary taxes, forced loans and (in wartime) ship money from the ports. He had to sift through a flood of petitions for tax exemption and excuses for non-payment. Was Thomas Reed so 'greatly in debt as he dareth very seldom [to] come out of his house'? Should he accept the plea of Thomas Clere who claimed to be much in debt 'by house-keeping and . . . a great charge of children'?

War always made heavier a J.P.'s burden of office. As Bacon lived in a coastal county, he had to compile lists of men pressed into naval service. He was also required to investigate some recent abuses by the impressment commissioners: in particular, that they were pressing an excessive number and then 'discharging some of them for money, to the grievance of the poor men'. He maintained a coastal watch in order to detect secret landings by Jesuits, he hunted down and examined Catholic missionary priests and he presented obstinate recusants for trial (see chapter 4, pages 252–3). He also submitted detailed proposals for improving the machinery for discovering recusants and Catholic children who had not been baptised in the Anglican Church—all part of the unceasing war against Catholicism.

Nevertheless, the bulk of his work continued unabated in peace as in war. As a J.P. he served on most of the important standing commissions in his county, especially those to maintain highways and bridges, and to regulate the export of corn from Norfolk. He was also on the Commission for Sewers which, in a coastal shire, involved much time in financing the renovation of derelict wharves and piers. One case seems to have spawned a bureaucratic monument of paperwork after the Norfolk marshland town of Torrington was flooded by the sea, which broke through its protective earthworks, 'wasted thirty houses, spoiled all the corn upon 1,600 acres, drowned very many of their great cattle and almost all their sheep'. A new bank and stone walls were desperately needed, at an estimated cost of £5000. The Queen would not pay, even though she was the greatest local landowner and so, potentially, the greatest loser. Instead the official proposal was to make the marshland towns foot the bill. And so we enter into a familiar Tudor tale: everyone pleading poverty; everyone wriggling out from their financial obligations; conflicts between different authorities about who should and who could make the necessary decisions. There were wrangles, obstructions and delays as the local towns, J.P.s, Commissioners for Sewers and Privy Council were drawn in, and the matter dragged on from 1600 to 1613. During that time Torrington was twice 'overflowed and drowned' again. There were clear limits to what even dedicated magistrates could achieve. (For Bacon see *Stiffkey Papers*, Camden Society, third series, 26 [1915].)

Indeed it is a wonder that Bacon achieved as much as he did. He inspected prison conditions, assisted in the suppression of Puritan 'prophesyings' (see chapter 4, pages 270–1), despite his own Puritan inclinations, and furnished the Council with elaborate surveys of Norfolk's merchant navy and corn production. The regulation of ale houses occupied much time; licensing 'an ancient man and of good government [responsibility]' to open one, and permitting the dry town of Warham to establish another in order 'to serve our poor with beer from their [poor relief] money'. He closely supervised the strict terms of licences: no children or servants, 'none to tipple in your house above one hour in one day', nor on the Sabbath 'in the time of divine service', nor 'after nine of the clock at night'. No vagabonds were to be admitted. There was to be no dicing or carding, no drunkenness and no home-brew, 'but take your drink from the Brewers'.

However, none of these duties could match the labour involved in administering the Tudor poor relief system. Bacon and other J.P.s supervised the Poor Law Commissioners in the collection of poor rates (that is, payments levied upon the gentry and other local inhabitants), the stocks of materials for setting the poor to work, the establishment of Poor Houses, and the whipping of vagabonds. In only one activity, as a Commissioner of Musters (the county militia), was he ever accused of slackness. However, there seems to have been an official recognition that this was because he was overburdened with other administrative duties, and so he was relieved of the task. Elsewhere, like other conscientious J.P.s, he struggled to cope with a formidable burden of business and with what one of them, William Lambarde, called the 'stacks of statutes on their backs'. Bacon was not a universal type: Shakespeare's Justice Shallow, a stupid, bragging, slothful ass, was a more familiar figure to contemporary theatre audiences. But neither was Bacon unique. Many others, such as Lambarde who wrote a handbook for his fellow magistrates, served with equal vigour, tempered with a sense of justice and even charity. There were always enough Justices in each county to activate official directives from the Council and attend to the minutiae of administration, and, moreover, to do so with at least a modicum of energy, efficiency and success. For poverty-stricken Tudor/early Stuart government, operating on a shoe-string budget, that was a considerable achievement.

The financing of government

This reflection should provoke the question, why was the English State so poor? Other questions should follow: why was its income seldom enough to meet expenses? Why could it not expand its income by extracting more from established sources or finding new ones? And why did not Parliament recognise its poverty and put its finances in order? The financing of government is a prosaic subject, but also a vital one. Money is the sinew of power: without it a State cannot function at all. Without enough it cannot fulfil adequately what it conceives to be its obligations and responsibilities. The simple painful reality of Tudor/early Stuart government is that the State rarely had enough to do this.

Elizabeth inherited an antiquated and obsolete financial machine, which did not effectively tap the agricultural, industrial and commercial wealth of the kingdom. This was only possible by levying taxes on those sources of wealth. However, the Crown had no right to tax at will. Its regular revenues—those which were its hereditary right and did not have to be granted to it by a parliament or any other body— did not, with one exception, include taxes or levies of any sort. Admittedly that exception was an important one: customs duties on a wide range of imports and exports which, by 1600, constituted the largest source of income for the Crown. However, customs had originally been granted to the Crown in perpetuity, and therefore had become an hereditary right. The Queen's other ordinary revenues derived from her various roles as landowner (lease-rents from Crown lands), feudal overlord (feudal dues), head of the judiciary (fees and fines from the law courts), and supreme governor of the Church (first fruits and tenths levied on the clergy). None of these sources bore any relationship to the national wealth, nor were they devices which would enable the government to tap that wealth.

Of course the monarch could turn to Parliament and request assistance in the form of a tax. However, it was a governing class expectation and a constitutional convention (something which by long practice and tacit acceptance had come to have almost the respect accorded to a law) that the Queen should 'live of her own'. In practice, this meant that she should manage on her hereditary revenues and only seek parliamentary assistance in an emergency, which usually meant war. When Elizabeth did so, supplementary revenue was voted in the form of a 'fifteenth and tenth' (a levy on chattels, merchandise, live-stock and other moveables—one-fifteenth in rural and one-tenth in urban areas) and/or a subsidy (a graduated income tax). As so often happened in medieval and early modern English State finances, these taxes had fossilised. The State lacked, because it could not afford, the large professional civil service which could assess the value of move-ables and the income of taxpayers. So it resorted to a 'composition' system, whereby the amount to be levied on each county became fixed and unchanging. During the sixteenth century, inflation resulted in a serious drop in the real value of the yield. Parliament was not unaware of the problem. It tried to compensate for this loss of revenue by voting each time more than one-fifteenth and one-tenth or subsidy. Moreover, until Charles I's reign, it granted to the new monarch tunnage and poundage for life (for Parliament's action in 1625, see chapter 6, page 378). Originally a levy on tuns (large casks) of wine, wool and leather, it had been extended to include other imports and exports. In brief, it was an important supplement to the Crown's hereditary customs revenues.

Despite such parliamentary aids, the Crown remained poor. And its poverty restricted its activities. Educational schemes and social welfare programmes were, for the most part, beyond the modest means of royal government. War was a natural, even necessary, instru-ment of foreign policy; yet neither Elizabeth nor the early Stuarts could afford to fight one without the approval and financial support of the governing class in Parliament. In fact Elizabeth and Charles were to discover that they could not afford to do so even *with* parlia-mentary assistance. If their ordinary revenue was pitifully inadequate for war, then the supplement of parliamentary subsidies was never enough either; it was collected in instalments over several years, and its real value steadily declined with inflation, under-assessment, exemptions and evasions of taxation. Apart from the abortive Great Contract of 1610 (see pages 159–60), no attempt was made to rationalise the State's finances. So the Crown continued in its efforts to make ends meet with an insufficient income, slowly collected, and often a prey to dishonest officials. This was a problem in peacetime. But the demands of war are immediate, urgent, imperious: there were troops to be paid, provisioned and equipped, ships to be built, maintained and repaired. Neither Elizabeth's Privy Council in the 1590s nor Charles I's Duke of Buckingham in the 1620s could satisfy such financial demands.

Yet there was a time in the sixteenth century when the Crown had acquired such a large income, and such a handsome surplus, that its financial independence was assured without the necessity of calling Parliament. That was in the 1530s, when Henry VIII broke with Rome and obtained, in the process, an enormous income from the Church. However, his wars against France and Scotland (1542–6), followed by the extravagance, mismanagement and peculation of Edward VI's noble governors (1547–53) destroyed the Crown's brief spell of financial security and prosperity. Grants and sales of Crown lands by the ruling Edwardian cliques reduced the Crown's annual income by almost twenty per cent (£42 000).

By 1552–3 the State was faced with imminent financial collapse, from which it was rescued only by Mary's government (1553–8). She recognised that the Crown's lands were its most valuable capital asset and promptly stopped the sale of them. She practised stringent economies and streamlined the financial administration in order to make it more efficient and less expensive. Although Mary was at war with France in 1557–8, she paid for it with parliamentary taxes and loans, not by the renewed sale of Crown lands. The achievement of the Marian regime was to steer the State away from financial disaster and to husband the resources left to it after the mismanagement and folly of the years 1542–53. It exploited these surviving resources to make them yield more: feudal dues were searched out more vigorously, rents on Crown lands were increased and customs duties were revised upwards.

Although Mary borrowed heavily to balance her budget in 1557–8, and left Elizabeth to clear the debt, the crucial fact is that she had enabled the State to stage a partial financial recovery. If, in 1558, Elizabeth had been faced with a financial situation which had worsened since 1553, the crisis might have compelled Queen, Council and Parliament to take drastic action. Not just emergency taxes, but something more fundamental, a 'modernisation' of the State's finances, would have been required. This would have tapped the growing wealth of England and it might have given the Crown a large enough income to govern effectively. Instead disaster was averted, and Elizabeth inherited an adequate income (if she pursued inexpensive policies and above all avoided war) and a financial machine which had been made more efficient by the Marian reforms. The need for drastic reform and 'modernisation' was less urgent; it could be deferred. And it was, again and again, until civil war, revolution and large military budgets forced such changes.

In the meantime, the conservative Queen preferred to muddle through, avoiding change, and relying instead upon economy, caution and efficiency to make ends meet. At first her government enjoyed some success. Her Lord Treasurer, the Marquess of Winchester (1558–72), called in the coinage and re-issued it with a higher silver content. This reduced the volume of money in circulation and was designed to have a deflationary effect. Moreover, for twenty-seven years (until 1585) Elizabeth avoided war. By then two Lord Treasurers, Winchester and Lord Burghley (1572–98), had built up a reserve of cash equal to more than one year's royal revenue.

Despite these successes, however, Elizabeth's reign marked a further deterioration in the Crown's financial position. Already, in the 1560s, she was selling Crown lands to pay her sister's debts, and even in peacetime she had to apply to Parliament for assistance: in 1563, 1566 and 1571. Thereafter there were, in her reign, two turning points which accelerated the financial decline. One occurred in 1572, when Lord Burghley (William Cecil) became Lord Treasurer. He, like his royal mistress, was a conservative. Under his management, the Exchequer, the State's chief financial organ, steadily declined in efficiency and vigour. He displayed no imagination in searching out new sources of revenue, and he was cautious in his exploitation of existing ones. Certainly he had his successes. Increases in rents on Crown lands meant that, in 1600, the income from royal estates was running at the same level, £60–70 000, as in the 1550s, though the real value was much less because of inflation. The customs rates were raised twice, in 1583 and 1590. Furthermore, the Crown introduced some **impositions**, which were new duties imposed on previously untaxed commodities. Their legality was doubtful, but financial need in war overcame scruples about what was legal and what was not; and in any case the Crown's action was not challenged. On the other hand, Burghley shrank from a bold and adventurous campaign to improve the yield from feudal dues, because they were unpopular and he was afraid of stirring up criticism and opposition. His son Robert, who succeeded him in 1598, had no such qualms and within five years he had trebled the income from this source.

However, the steady rise in royal revenue, resulting from these increases, at no time kept pace with inflation. Then in 1585 occurred the second turning point in Elizabethan financial history, the outbreak of war with Spain. Within two years, the Treasury reserves had been spent and the long war (1585–1604) threatened to turn the financial decline into a collapse. Parliaments were regularly called to assist the war effort: in 1587, 1589, 1593, 1597 and 1601. Each one voted subsidies to be collected in annual instalments, and as soon as the last payment reached the Treasury, a new Parliament was summoned. Annual taxation had become a painful fact for the governing class.

On the other hand, the yield from parliamentary taxes was unrealistically small and inadequate in wartime. The tenths and fifteenths, based on the values of 1334, produced only £30 000 instead of the original £100 000. The subsidy, theoretically four shillings in the pound on annual rent from land, should have yielded a similar amount, but less than £80 000 was collected and the total was still falling. Without a professional civil service, the Crown could not investigate incomes. Gentry swore on oath that their declared income was the truth, while nobles, as men of honour, simply made a declaration without an oath. The result was widespread evasion. The average income (as declared by the nobility) fell dramatically between 1547 and the 1580s, despite inflation. Burghley himself, Lord Treasurer and custodian of the State's finances, declared his income (for tax purposes) at only one-twentieth of its real value. Even so his was a modest assessment in relation to hundreds of others. An annual income of £20 was a necessary qualification for the office of J.P., but not one magistrate was registered at that level for tax purposes. Sir Walter Raleigh bluntly told the House of Commons that the incomes recorded against their names in the subsidy book represented 'not the hundredth part of our wealth'. This was the price which the Queen had to pay in return for the unpaid or underpaid services which the nobles and gentry performed for the State: that their tax burden should remain a light one.

However, this did not help the impoverished Elizabethan State which was financially unequipped to fight a protracted war. For seventeen years it tottered on, plunging deeper into debt, despite renewed sales of Crown lands and savage economies. Patronage was reduced and the cost of the Court, despite inflation, was only £4000 a year more than the £41 000 it had been fifty years earlier. Elizabeth was financing war on several fronts. In 1601 her income (almost one-third of which derived from Parliament) was £374 000. But £320 000 of that was swallowed up in the campaign against Irish rebels: the costs of war alone consumed 99.5 per cent of the year's revenue, and her final deficit for 1601 was over £60 000.

When the last Tudor died, a serious dilemma faced the State: how to fund itself so that it could fulfil its duties and functions effectively. Both the Crown and the governing class chose to ignore the urgent need to provide an adequate revenue: Elizabeth knew that this would involve public scrutiny of her finances, and she preferred government by secrecy; the governing class knew that it would have to foot the bill for financial reform and extra money. So they all carried on in the same old way, tinkering with an obsolete financial machine and hoping that the problems would go away. But they did not. James I was soon uncomfortably aware of one aspect of the problem: that an antiquated system of funding could no longer provide enough, even in peacetime. And his son, Charles I, experienced the problem in acute and dramatic form: the early Stuart State could not finance a war until the financial system was modernised.

After his poverty in Scotland, James thought that he had inherited a treasure house when he came south to Westminster in 1603. He smacked his lips in anticipation, hoping 'to enjoy the fruits at my pleasure, in the time of their greatest maturity'. In one sense James was right. In contrast to Scotland, England was a wealthy country— but the Crown was not. Over £60 000 awaited him in the Exchequer, and £355 000 was still due from parliamentary subsidies. But the former looked meagre alongside the current debt of almost half a million, while the latter was already earmarked for war in Ireland and the Low Countries. James was not unaware of the problem of debt, or that its chief cause was war. The average annual expenditure of Elizabethan government spelt that out: £190 000 in the last years of peace (1580–6), £380 000 in the first years of war (1587–90), rising to £504 000 in 1600–2. The simple short-term answer was to stop the war, which was done in 1604, with dramatic financial consequences. The military budget of £277 000 in 1603–4 shrank to a mere £75 000 three years later. This reflected a financial motive in the King's foreign policy in his early years: that a pacific policy would mean fewer requests for parliamentary assistance.

However, despite the enormous savings achieved by the end of the Irish rebellion and peace with Spain, James's financial position did not improve. In 1606 his annual deficit was £50 000 and his current debt was £550 000, figures which two years later had grown to £80 000 and £597 000 respectively. Inflation is not an adequate explanation for this worsening situation, because by then an increasing royal income was more than keeping pace with it. Court extravagance seems a likelier answer, although this was a general condition of western European courts at the time, rather than a singular weakness of James I. In any case, his expectation was that he was a wealthy King, and his Court expected him to demonstrate that this was so. Nevertheless, his personal extravagances troubled both Robert Cecil, Earl of Salisbury, who was Lord Treasurer and a financial reformer (1603–11), and Lionel Cranfield, Earl of Middlesex and a champion of economic retrenchment (1621–23). This is hardly surprising. The sum of £37 000 spent on jewels in 1608 might be regarded as a form of savings, and, unlike Elizabeth, he had to provide separate palaces and households for Queen Anne (his wife) and his sons Henry and Charles. However, less excusable was the way in which the running costs of his own chamber—his private household—rose relentlessly: from £14 000 in 1600, to £20 000 in 1607 and £31 000 in 1622.

James compounded the problem by his lavish gifts to courtiers. When he casually promised Robert Carr a present of £20 000, Robert Cecil had coinage to that value stacked in an ante-chamber, through which the King had to pass. The wide-eyed James demanded an explanation from Cecil for the presence of this golden mountain, then promptly cancelled the grant. It has been suggested that James thought in terms of Scottish pounds which were almost worthless, but it is hard to believe that the canny Scot learned nothing about exchange rates in a twenty-two-year reign. The simple fact is that he was habitually extravagant. In spite of large savings on foreign policy and the army, and with a navy rotting through sheer neglect, James could not balance income and expenditure, except briefly late in Salisbury's life, and again at the peak of Cranfield's career. Thomas Wentworth expressed a common feeling when he asked the Commons, 'What purpose is it for us to draw a silver stream out of the country into the royal cistern if it shall daily run out thence by private cocks?'

The significance of royal extravagance is heightened by the fact that James's government, unlike Elizabeth's, was fertile in seeking out new sources of revenue. Its greatest success was in the exploitation of customs duties. The professed purpose of customs was to regulate trade, not to raise money for the Crown: whatever the Crown received was incidental to that purpose. In practice, of course, it was vitally important to the funding of government. However, it was questionable whether the King could increase the existing rates at which customs duties were levied or impose them on new commodities. Moreover, their yield could never be estimated in advance. As they depended on fluctuations in trade (that is, the volume and value of goods imported and exported), they varied considerably from year to year. However, these disadvantages could be overcome. The law courts upheld the King's right to impose and vary rates of customs duties at will. This right was tested in Bate's Case in 1606. Bate was a merchant who refused to pay the Crown's increased duty on currants. The judges decided in favour of the King: 'No exportation or importation can be but at the King's ports. They are the gates of the King, and he hath absolute power by them to include or exclude whom he shall please'. On the basis of this judgement, James issued a new book of customs rates (impositions) in 1608. It added £70 000 annually to his income from this source.

Similarly, it was possible to avoid the effects of trade fluctuations on royal income by 'farming out' the customs. In other words, a City financier or a syndicate of financiers would pay a fixed annual rent to the Crown for the right to collect the duties; they retained any profit over and above the amount of the rent. This practice developed late in Elizabeth's reign and by 1605 most customs were farmed out to a single syndicate for a rent of £41 000. As trade boomed after the peace with Spain, so the Crown regularly increased the rent, which by 1609 stood at £90 000. There were obvious advantages in this 'farming' system for a State which lacked a nationwide professional corps of civil servants. It provided a guaranteed annual income regardless of the state of trade. In contrast, the 'farmers' might reap a big profit or suffer heavy losses: in 1615 they collected about £200 000, but only £30 000 in the following year. Despite this, however, the customs farmers were growing richer, while the Crown received only its annual right. 'Impositions' and 'farming' did, however, provide a much larger and more certain income from customs than in the previous century.

If customs duties were increasingly important, Crown lands were quite the reverse. They were the monarch's most readily saleable asset, from which it was easy to raise large sums of cash immediately. Elizabeth and Charles I in war, and James I in peace, spent their landed capital as income. And as they did, the return from Crown rents diminished: from £60 000 in 1600, to £25 000 in 1625. In contrast, that third ancient prop of royal finances, feudal dues, was re-invigorated during Salisbury's term as Treasurer. However, the financial benefits from this source were offset by their political disadvantages. Feudal dues were burdensome. They were capricious in that their payment depended upon the 'accident' of death and when it occurred—so some families escaped and others suffered. Their enforcement required a constant inquisitorial watch to discover who had died and what dues were owed. And, as they fell upon most landed families, they were particularly resented by members of the Houses of Lords and Commons.

Both James and Salisbury recognised the financial and political advantage to be gained if feudal dues were replaced by a permanent parliamentary grant. Between 1604 and 1610, there were intermittent negotiations with the Commons to that end. The climax was reached in 1610, when Salisbury was in charge of the 'Great Contract' negotiations between King and Parliament; but the attempt failed. There has been some debate and disagreement on the reasons for failure and who was responsible. However, the finger points at the King, who continually raised the minimum annual compensation which he expected in return for the surrender of feudal dues. Perhaps he was just greedy. Perhaps he expected (or even wanted) the negotiations to fail. Whatever his motive, they did fail. Thereafter, feudal dues caused growing irritation, partly because they were enforced more rigorously, but also because they were now diverted to reward favourites, rather than employed to meet the costs of government.

The other financial devices used to increase Stuart revenues were also harmful, politically or financially:

1 The sale of titles caused offence to old families, and in any case most of the profits went to courtiers who procured titles for suitors in return for cash payments.

2 Loans did have the virtue of providing quick money, but interest rates were high.

3 Monopolies, which were a long-established form of protection for inventors and for new companies which needed a guaranteed market free from intense competition. No one would have questioned their necessity when they were used in these ways. However, in the 1590s they became a political issue, because Elizabeth misused the Crown's power to grant monopolies for financial purposes.

Elizabeth's stratagem was to sell some to raise money, and she created others as a means of rewarding courtiers. After all, it cost her nothing to grant monopolies for the licensing of taverns or the manufacture of glass, and one must sympathise with her dilemma in wartime. This was one way of compensating for the drastic reduction in patronage forced upon her by war. However, it could cost the public dear: monopolists tended to force up prices and sell inferior products. In 1597 Parliament grumbled but Elizabeth took no notice. She paid the penalty when Parliament reassembled in 1601. The earlier rumblings were now transformed into an open attack on the monopolists and a lengthy debate in which the Crown's power to grant such monopolies was questioned. Belatedly, albeit successfully, Elizabeth promised that harmful monopolies would be examined by the courts. This prompt move forestalled a Bill on the subject, but the episode was a register of widespread discontent.

In James I's reign, that warning went unheeded and monopolies continued to be granted. Those which were the particular object of complaint were war supplies, luxury articles, and especially grants to favoured courtiers in return for money: for example, the manufacture of glass, paper, starch and iron. The growing chorus of discontent burst forth into furious song in the Parliament of 1621. The prime targets were courtiers' monopolies which harmed trade, pushed up prices or produced excessive profits. A Bill, which was introduced into this Parliament, finally became law in 1624. It permitted patents for new inventions and certain industrial monopolies, such as alum and gunpowder. It also recognised the rights of trading companies and manufacturing guilds. However, all other monopolies were banned.

The financing of government was a source of irritation throughout James I's reign. Despite the search for new sources, and the exploitation of old ones, the methods of financing the State remained much as they had been a hundred years earlier. There were only two changes, but these were major shifts in attitude. One was the growing discontent provoked by impositions, the failure of the Great Contract, monopolies, and repeated requests for parliamentary aid in peacetime, in order to provision an extravagant Court. The other was the growing conviction in official circles that Parliament was not making adequate provision for the King's needs. The success of impositions taught the early Stuarts that extra-parliamentary revenues could be much more lucrative (and quicker to come in) than a subsidy. The monarchy had broken free from the convention that new levies on subjects required parliamentary consent. The stage was now set for Charles I's wars (1625–9), which brought to a head parliamentary irritation on the one hand, and the new attitude of government on the other.

Charles's wars were a political, military and financial blunder of the worst kind. To take on Spain and France, the two greatest military powers in Europe, and at the same time, was an inexcusable folly. There was not enough money, nor could the amateur county administrations cope with the demands placed upon them for manpower, equipment and financial aid. The conflict could not even be justified. Unlike Elizabeth's unavoidable defensive war of the late 1580s and 1590s, these were offensive wars. They were irrelevant to the needs of the governing class, and consequently they stirred up no enthusiasm in their support.

However, it would be wrong to suppose that King and governing class were on a collision course from the beginning of the reign. This has been assumed because, whereas the Tudors and James I received tunnage and poundage (additional customs duties) for life, Charles I did not. Conrad Russell has shown that this was not a provocative gesture or act of blackmail by Parliament, but a 'disastrous muddle'. Concerned members wanted a Bill which granted the King tunnage and poundage *and* impositions by authority of Parliament. It would have given the King a larger guaranteed income, but the Bill would have taken too long to draft in that session: the plague was abroad and members wanted to get away. So a temporary Bill was passed, granting tunnage and poundage for one year only. The Lords, doubtless disturbed by this novelty, let the Bill rest after only one reading. Charles proceeded to collect tunnage and poundage without parliamentary consent, and the merchants were willing to pay it.

However, during the next four years the Crown became increasingly disillusioned with Parliament's unwillingness or incapacity to fill the war-chest with money. The Elizabethan war parliaments had supported the Crown with two, and even three, subsidies, to be collected in instalments over three or four years. When James I agreed to fight Spain in 1624, he bluntly told Parliament that, if it wanted war, then it must foot the bill. He demanded five subsidies and ten fifteenths before he embarked on war. The response was an astonished silence. He 'struck a great amazement. [T]here was not heard so much as one "God save the King", who put off his hat to them and went his way'. Such an enormous grant was out of the question. Yet without it, England could not wage a war.

Charles rapidly learned the political lessons taught by his shrewd father. A war with, or without, traditional hereditary revenues and parliamentary grants was not financially possible. But one financed by a realistic number of subsidies *and* lucrative extra-parliamentary levies (such as impositions and the forced loan of 1627) might be. Once again Parliament failed to vote what the Crown required: a mere two subsidies in 1625, none in 1626 and 1629, and five in 1628 (after Charles's assent to the Petition of Right). Official opinion was hardening to the view that a search for extraparliamentary revenues was worth the labour, whereas requests to Parliament for grants were not. When, in 1629, the King decided to dispense with that institution for the time being, he and his advisers had the example of impositions and forced loans before them. Now they were mentally conditioned to experiment with a non-parliamentary system of financing government.

The Crown and the judges

The Crown's increasing disillusionment with Parliament cannot be separated from its relations with the Common Law judges. In order to bolster their incomes to meet a soaring expenditure, both James I and Charles I explored new sources of revenue or revived old ones. Most of them were unpopular, all of them were extra-parliamentary (that is, they were not authorised by Parliament) and so of doubtful legality. Some of them were actually challenged by victims of royal exactions, by critics of the Crown's new approach to financial problems, and by lawyers and M.P.s who questioned their lawfulness and upheld Parliament's sole right to assent to taxes. The early Stuarts, in response, had recourse to the Common Law courts in order to secure verdicts favourable to them. Therefore, as Parliament continually demonstrated its inability (or unwillingness) to solve the Crown's seemingly perpetual problem of too little cash, an alternative solution became more and more attractive to the hardpressed Stuart government.

It matters little whether we believe that James I and Charles I brought their financial problems on themselves: that James sabotaged the Great Contract in 1610, while he poured out money on an expensive, wasteful, over-indulgent Court and extravagant favourites; or that Charles I embarked on futile wars, maintained a cultivated Court (more dignified than his father's but even more costly), and continued to pander to the whims of his spendthrift favourite Buckingham. The point is that they needed money to clear their debts and balance their books. In these pressing circumstances the Common Law courts promised a financial solution which Parliament had failed to bestow.

The technique adopted by early Stuart government was to introduce a new levy or revive an old one, wait until it was challenged in the law courts, or provoke a test case there, and finally secure a favourable decision from the judges. Despite the claim of members of the Lords and Commons that such new levies could be imposed only with Parliament's consent, a successful judicial verdict gave the Crown's actions the full backing of the force and sanctity of the Common Law. This persuaded many to pay up. Moreover, practical considerations worked in favour of the Crown. The merchant communities, especially London, benefited handsomely from their alliance with a State which often lacked ready cash and always lacked a large professional civil service. They purchased Crown lands at profitable rates; they received rich returns as tax farmers, secured lucrative monopolies and lent money at high interest rates. Once the Common Law had given its blessing to a new royal levy, merchants usually coughed up the extra charges without murmur or grudge, rather than jeopardise their lucrative relations with a needy monarch. They had too much at stake, too much to lose.

However, this practical, natural response depended on the Common Law's recognition that the King was within his rights in imposing a novel levy or re-activating an old one. Consequently, the judges became of crucial financial and political importance to the Crown in the early seventeenth century. The novelty of this development must not be exaggerated. After all, judges were royal servants. They were appointed by the monarch, held office during his pleasure and could at any time be dismissed by him. This applied equally to the Lord Chancellor, supervising officer of the judicial system under the Crown, and the judges of King's (Queen's) Bench, Common Pleas, and Exchequer. Elizabeth did not drag the judges into politics in the way that her Stuart successors did, but that was because she rarely explored and exploited fresh ways of increasing the State's revenues as they chose to do. And when she did, by the introduction of impositions (see page 155), her action did not provoke vocal criticism or challenge in the courts. Perhaps her needs, when she was engaged in an expensive defensive war against Spain, were regarded as justification enough.

On the other hand, her lavish misuse of harmful monopolies did come under fire in the parliaments of 1597 and 1601. And here we should take note of Elizabeth's response. When she was driven into a corner by a parliamentary demand for redress, she swept away all indignation by a message to the Commons. The message announced that a number of monopolies:

should be presently [immediately] repealed, some suspended, and none put in execution but such as should first have a trial according to the law for the good of her people.

There followed promptly a proclamation which empowered anyone harmed by monopolies to seek remedy in the law courts. At the same time Sir Robert Cecil reminded the Commons that 'the Queen means not to be swept out of her prerogative'. In other words, there was a compromise: Elizabeth's prerogative survived intact, but she surrendered to governing class agitation on the particular question of monopolies.

Elizabeth thus satisfied immediate concern by cancelling or suspending the most harmful patents, or grants, of monopolies. More important, in this context, was her decision that future grants had to be tested in the law courts and that the victims of existing monopolies could seek redress there. Would they receive justice or would the judges defend the Queen's right to make such grants, by approving all those placed before them, and by rejecting suitors' complaints against existing monopolists? Or to ask another related question: as the Common Law enjoyed great respect in a legalistic society, and as the judges were Elizabeth's servants, was this her way of neutralising a threat to her right to grant monopolies? The Queen was certainly capable of treating the judiciary in a high-handed manner. During a bloody feud between the Earl of Oxford (who had seduced Anne Vavasour) and Thomas Knyvett (Anne's guardian), Knyvett killed one of the Earl's followers. He persuaded Elizabeth to have the case heard *in camera* (in secret), when he would plead self-defence and be acquitted. Although the Lord Chancellor refused, he was ordered to do as he was told. Did Elizabeth also expect the judges to toe the line in the matter of monopolies? She had little time left—she died sixteen months later—but Conrad Russell hints that little had changed: 'Though the situation was saved, the underlying strains which had produced the monopolies were still there, and were to produce more monopolies in the next reign (Russell, 1971, page 251; Stone, 1965, pages 233–4).

James I and his son were more fertile in money-raising devices. They did not confine themselves to monopolies (which increased rapidly in number, resulted in widespread complaint, parliamentary impeachments and, finally, a new law in 1624). James also imposed a new duty on currants which a merchant, Bate, refused to pay on the grounds that it had not been approved by Parliament. The result, in 1606, was a court case which tested the validity of the King's right to impose customs duties. The judges were faced with a problem which would recur. On the one hand, it was the King's undoubted right to impose new duties, and to raise or lower old ones, in order to regulate trade and manage foreign policy—these were both numbered amongst his prerogatives. On the other hand, he had no such right to impose taxation without parliamentary consent. As the judges were only judges of the law and of a person's actions, they could not determine the King's *motive*. They had to assume that his action was, as he claimed, prompted by trade or foreign policy considerations, and so they gave judgement in his favour. The judgement begged all kinds of constitutional questions: what would happen if an untrustworthy king ruled? If the king's word was sufficient, could he use it to break other parliamentary limitations on him? Did this mean that laws were subject to the overriding priority of the king's motives? These were questions which would be discussed again and again in the forty years after Elizabeth's death, and with increasing intensity and urgency.

At the time, no immediate constitutional crisis occurred. However, in 1608 the judgement in Bate's Case proved to be a godsend to the new Lord Treasurer, Robert Cecil, Earl of Salisbury. He acted on the precedent which it provided to issue a new book of rates (increased duties) and imposed customs on previously untaxed commodities (impositions). This brought £70 000 a year into the

King's coffers, but it also provoked a rumbling parliamentary discontent from 1610 through to 1629. The financial rewards were substantial during Charles I's personal rule—over £200 000 annually—but the political cost was probably even greater.

In 1627 the Crown turned once again to the judges for an endorsement of its actions in law. Parliament had voted nothing in the previous year, but wars ate up money inexorably and Charles was desperate. He resorted to a forced loan instead. This was a tax rather than a loan. It was not voluntary but compulsory and, although repayment—without interest—was promised in official letters with the Privy Seal attached, reimbursement was not always forthcoming. It was an unpopular device. In 1525 one such 'loan' was so violently resisted that it had to be given up; a few years later Henry VIII secured the parliamentary cancellation of his debts, in particular the money due to the victims of a forced loan; in 1557 Mary did not even bother to include a promise to repay the capital. No wonder there were increasing signs of resistance when Elizabeth imposed them, and they were particularly unpopular when imposed by Charles to finance pointless wars. Moreover, they sharpened the constitutional issues provoked by Bate's Case. Five knights were imprisoned for refusing to pay on demand. Instead they retaliated by applying for a writ of habeas corpus. They were not, at this point, contesting the King's right to tax, but his right to imprison without cause shown, because habeas corpus required them to be charged with a specific offence or to be released. The judges' response was that they had been imprisoned by the King's 'special command' which was deemed sufficient without public justification. The issues rehearsed by Bate's Case were raised again: was the King limited by law, in particular Magna Carta, which forbade imprisonment without just cause? Was the King free to set aside the known law for motives known only to him? If Charles I could do this, what would happen in the case of a king who could not be trusted? Once again the judges were conditioned by their role as royal servants and by the limitations of their office. They were there to serve their master and to decide matters of the law, not to judge Charles I's motives. Nor were they prepared to question the notion of an emergency prerogative which was designed to enable the King to act with despatch in times of crisis, notably war and rebellion. So they decided for Charles I.

The issue would come into sharper focus in 1637 when the King decided to make a test case of John Hampden's refusal to pay ship money. Once again Charles claimed that his right to act in an emergency took precedence over the normal constitutional requirement that taxes must be voted by Parliament. In the Court of King's Bench

Sir Robert Berkeley lent judicial support to the royal claim (see page 107)—even though the King won only by the narrow margin of seven judges to five and so suffered a moral defeat at the very moment of a legal victory.

The role of the judges in the early seventeenth century became a politically important one, and their loyalty became crucial to the Crown in its hunt for more money. Not that their political significance was confined to financial matters. Sir Edward Coke, first as Chief Justice of Common Pleas (1606–13) and then as Chief Justice of King's Bench (1613–16), was consulted by the King on matters of prerogative. An unpleasant, ambitious social climber, who combined an aggressive bullying manner in court with a servile obsequiousness towards his social superiors and patrons, he was nonetheless a lawyer of immense learning. He upheld the sanctity and supremacy of the Common Law, and he believed that government should conform its actions to an ancient constitution. He was either a bad historian, or a dishonest one, when he insisted that Parliament had always existed— or at least that it had since Roman England. His firm convictions caused him to clash with the King on a series of issues: on impositions, on the power of proclamations, and on the King's right to consult the judges individually in cases which touched his interests. Coke's refusal to stay proceedings in one case which concerned James was the last straw. His bold, inflexible defence of the Common Law against encroachments of the prerogative may contrast strangely with the obsequiousness of his conduct in the faction scramble at Court. But, together with the opposition of his arch-rival Francis Bacon, it resulted in his dismissal in 1616.

Judges were expected to do as they were told. So when Randolph Crewe, Chief Justice of King's Bench, denied the legality of forced loans, he was promptly dismissed. However, most of the judges acted as royal servants, or at least their verdicts coincided with royal wishes. As the Crown's confidence in Parliament as a source of revenue shrank, it looked increasingly to the judges to endorse its extraparliamentary devices. Therefore, the judges were forced to reach judicial verdicts which also had wide political and constitutional implications. It made life uncomfortable for them, but it was yet another reason why, in 1629, Charles I could contemplate governing without recourse to Parliament.

CHAPTER THREE

The early modern state:
problems of government and shifts of power,
1629–1700

The period between 1629 and 1700 produced a number of new difficulties and important changes in the three continuing problems of government: finance, Crown-governing class relations, and the interaction of central and local government. All three were to be affected by the significant changes which were taking place in the economy, by the Civil War and the conflicts which preceded it, and by the foreign wars in the second half of the century.

Charles I's finances 1629–42

The problems of government finance faced by Charles I when he dismissed his third parliament in 1629 were similar to those which had bedevilled his predecessors. There was a perennial tendency for expenditure to exceed revenue, a state of affairs which was, of course, vastly exaggerated by war. Ultimately, the only solution was to close the gap, either by reducing expenditure, increasing revenue, or both. As England was, by the standards of Continental European countries, a lightly taxed country with a relatively cheap system of administration, it was clear that the greatest part of the gap between revenue and expenditure would have to be closed by increasing revenue.

Reduction of government revenue was, of course, popular with the country, with those who paid the taxes, but did not perceive any benefits commensurate with their expenditure. It also had its supporters in the Council, where the sloth and extravagance believed to exist in government departments were attacked as 'Lady Mora' (the reformers' code name for these vices). A number of attempts were made to reduce expenditure. Between 1627 and 1629 the household, wardrobe, ordnance and armoury had come under investigation. In 1627 there had been an inquiry into fees taken by government officers, inquiries which were carried on again with greater vigour by the Treasury Commissioners in 1635. In 1637–8 another effort was made to reduce costs in the household, an institution which absorbed forty per cent of government expenditure during the 1630s. The success of these policies of retrenchment was small. Expenditure was cut little and often in petty and undignified ways, such as the decision by the King and William Laud (Archbishop of Canterbury and a leading member of the Privy Council) that the royal household would dispense with breakfast. At best, the King obtained some improvement in value for money.

The political consequences of the proposals for reform and economies were two-fold. There might have been some slight political gain in reducing the cost of government, but this gain was too small to be of practical benefit and the symbolism was lost owing to the extremely hostile reaction of the country to the concurrent revenue-raising activities. On the other hand, reduction in government expenditure disappointed many who had expected royal generosity. On balance, it is probable that the political consequences of expenditure cuts were more harmful than not.

Charles I faced a substantial deficit between his ordinary revenues and expenditure throughout the 1630s. The regular Crown revenues were approximately £570 000 a year in the late 1620s, and about £50 000 higher in the early 1630s. This was estimated by Dietz, one of the leading authorities on the financial problems of the period, to be about £20 000 a year less than the King's minimum expenditure and provision had to be made to meet a debt of £100 000.

Charles was faced with a number of advantages and disadvantages in his attempt to balance his budget without recourse to Parliament. Though he might dispense with Parliament, he could not dispense with the services of the parliamentary classes. Englishmen of all social levels were notably averse to taxation. The Venetian Ambassador believed that Charles refrained from imposing an excise because he knew his lack of a professional army made it impossible to enforce. In the short term, economic factors were against him too, as the late 1620s and early 1630s were a time of trade depression and a declining tax base.

The outlook for the King did have many favourable aspects, however. The long-term economic trends were very positive: the great inflation slowed markedly, perhaps stopped, from the 1620s. Secondly, there was pronounced long-term economic growth. Agricultural output and income were rising and trade was to expand again after the early 1630s. Thirdly, from 1630 until the Scottish war, England was at peace. Though the debts incurred in previous wars still had to be serviced, at least they were not increasing. Fourthly, the constitutional situation, although allowing the Crown much less freedom than the Continental monarchs enjoyed, did offer considerable room for increasing revenues. In particular, Bate's Case of 1606 allowed the King to raise customs duties and to impose them on goods not taxed earlier, on condition that he stated that his intention was to regulate trade, not to raise revenue. Finally, there were a number of archaic financial devices which were generally regarded as obsolete, but which were legal and, it was believed, could raise significant revenue.

There were, of course, many difficulties in devising an appropriate taxation policy. In order to raise maximum revenues while harming the economy as little as possible, any government will usually strive to impose taxes which are broadly based (that is, which raise revenue from as many different people and economic activities as possible), which are pitched at a level where they do not prevent growth, which draw on expanding rather than contracting areas of the economy, and which impose proportionately heavier burdens on the rich than the poor. Politically, a government must also avoid offending powerful interests by giving the impression that they are excessively or unfairly taxed.

In early seventeenth century England the land was, without doubt, the most productive and easily assessed section of the economy. The land owners were not, however, the group with the greatest amount of ready money, and they had the greatest political power. There was, therefore, a tendency to impose heavier burdens on the mercantile community, whose greater liquidity (that is, much of their wealth was in cash or easily realised assets, rather than in fixed capital such as land) and lesser political power made them easier to tax.

As a beginning, the traditional revenues were collected more efficiently and more ruthlessly: in particular, the yield of the profits of the mint increased four-fold and that of the Court of Wards by fifty per cent between the first and second half of the 1630s. Secondly, and with a far greater return, the role of customs duties was increased and, as the so-called New Impositions, they were imposed on a much wider range of commodities. The result was a rise in total customs revenue from an annual average of £262 000 in 1631–5 to nearly £450 000 in 1636–41. The political cost was not only widespread disaffection in the business community, but also antagonism among the gentry because the New Impositions were an unparliamentary tax which could make the King independent of Parliament. The social cost (that is, the financial burden imposed upon the poor) is not easy to assess precisely, but it was probably not high, as most of the duties were on luxury or near luxury items affecting only the rich. The rise in revenue from wardships was particularly resented by the land-owning classes, owing to its erratic incidence as a form of death duty and the scope it gave for abuse by the person granted custody of the ward.

As these measures did not produce a sufficient increase in revenue, Charles turned to, 'Projects of many kinds, many ridiculous, many scandalous, all very grievous, the envy and reproach of which came to the King, the profit to other men' (the Earl of Clarendon in *History of the Rebellion and Civil Wars in England*; see page 400). The first of these was the return to monopolies. In 1624 they had been banned by statute (see pages 164–5) but Charles took advantage of a loophole in the law to grant monopolies to companies rather than individuals. In the way the King used them, monopolies were a rudimentary form of the excise and they aroused opposition on the grounds of increased cost to the consumer. Soap was the most important, for which monopoly the monopolists paid £4 a ton royalty to the Crown, producing the not inconsiderable annual sum of £29 000 between 1636–41. The role of Roman Catholic investors in this monopoly inflamed religious prejudice as well as economic grievances. Protests against the quality of the 'Popish soap' were not stilled by the unanimous decision of a panel of peeresses and laundry-maids that it washed whiter than its unlicensed rivals (Russell, 1971, page 317).

In addition to these long-term expedients, Charles turned to fiscal feudalism as a means of raising sums of money, usually on a 'once only' basis. The first feudal revival was the imposition of fines on all gentlemen possessed of £40 a year or more who, not being knights already, had failed to attend Charles's coronation for their investiture. By the 1630s there were few knights with an annual income very much less than £1000, and the fines in distraint of knight-hood were nothing other than a tax on the gentry and even the wealthier yeomen. This device raised about £174 000 over five years. The King also gave employment to a number of historians who searched the records of 300 years earlier to determine the extent of royal forests in the time of Edward I. All who had cultivated land, constructed buildings or cut trees within the boundaries of the old forests were to be fined. Like the knighthood compositions, these fines aroused great resentment among the landed classes. Total returns from extraordinary royal income, 1631–5, averaged a little under £100 000 a year: slightly less than the yield of two subsidies, but even when coupled with the rising ordinary revenue it was insufficient, mainly owing to war debts. Charles was forced to continue selling Crown lands until 1635 and he became dangerously dependent on his ability to refinance his debts as they fell due.

After 1635 the situation improved somewhat and increased expenditure was offset by rising revenue. The average annual ordinary revenue rose from approximately £620 000 from 1631–5 to nearly £900 000 from 1636–41. Total revenue, including the proceeds of selling Crown lands, was between £100 000 and £200 000 a year higher. Charles was not, however, able to balance his budget without borrowing and anticipating revenues and it was impossible to build up reserves. Nevertheless, he had reached a position which could have been sustained for a very long time if the country had remained at peace.

One special device was more important politically than all the rest, but, as the funds were raised for a special purpose rather than for general revenue, it requires separate treatment. In 1634 a combination of Continental war, attacks on English shipping, and piracy and raids by Moslem slave-takers on south-west England combined to persuade the Council that a much larger fleet was necessary. Funds were to be raised by using the King's prerogative power to declare that a naval emergency existed and to call upon the ports and coastal areas to provide ships. Then, on grounds of fairness, the burden was to be extended inland, thus turning a coastal levy into a national rate (see pages 212–14).

Though Charles had achieved solvency in peacetime by the late 1630s, he had no financial reserves adequate for war. English Kings rarely did, and they had to depend on loans and parliamentary grants. When the Scottish wars broke out in 1639 and 1640, the political cost of the King's policies in both financial and other matters was revealed. In the short term, Charles's financial machinery was capable of finding the funds necessary to put his armies in the field. In 1639 £185 000 was provided of the £200 000 demanded for the army; in 1640, £570 000 of £600 000. The extra money was raised by contributions from nobles and the City, by sale of the East India Company's spices, a contribution from the privy purse (that is, the King's private revenues), extra income from the Court of Wards, more rigorous collection of recusancy fines and additional customs duties.

In the longer run, however, it was the financial problem posed by the victorious Scots' demand for £850 a day to pay for their military expenses, while occupying Northumberland and Durham until a settlement was reached, which led to the collapse of personal rule. Faced with the need for this vast sum of money, Charles turned to the City: it would lend only if the loan was guaranteed by Parliament. Though the reluctance of the City to lend to the King in 1640 was in part political, it also reflected a long-term decline in the willingness of the business community to see a loan to the King as a safe investment. Charles's approach to borrowing had been no more creative than his attempts to increase his revenue. With the exception of the mid-1630s, heavy royal borrowing had been a fact of economic and political life. The size of royal borrowing requirements, especially during the wars of the 1620s and again at the time of the Scottish wars, provided an incentive to modernise borrowing and establish a long-term national debt. No such steps were taken and the reign of Charles I saw a steady decline in the royal credit rating.

The cost of the wars against France and Spain in the 1620s induced the government to impose forced loans in 1625 and 1627, to pawn the Crown Jewels in Amsterdam in 1626, and to engage in heavy borrowing from individuals within England, many of whom were government officials or businessmen with government contracts. This last group was willing to lend in return for privileges. Apart from the Amsterdam loan, for which security was provided in a humiliating way, most funds could be raised only by compulsion or the grant of privileges. During the late 1620s, it became progressively harder for the Crown to borrow on normal commercial terms. The King became dependent on the credit of the great financiers such as Burlamachi, Russell, Hicks, Cockayne and van Lore, who re-lent to him at higher interest rates money which they themselves had borrowed.

In the early 1630s the end of the war reduced demands for loan finance, but the royal credit showed little recovery. In these years, the Crown had less need for the services of the great financiers and was able to borrow sufficient funds from the customs farmers and privileged corporations such as the holders of the soap monopoly. The most important was the customs farmer, Sir Paul Pindar, who lent the King over £85 000 in 1638–9. Dependence on this narrow group, who provided the King with loan funds in return for financial privileges, created a circle of men with a large vested interest in loyalty to Charles.

In 1639 the Scottish war revived the need for heavy borrowing: the King planned a loan of £300 000. Courtiers, customs farmers and contractors lent him £232 000; people without a vested interest in preserving the regime did not lend. Thus, by 1640 the resources of the Court group were exhausted and Charles was forced to turn to the City. Its reluctance to lend, unless the loan had the backing of Parliament, foreshadowed a future age when the credit of Parliament as well as that of the King protected any loan and opened up vast new possibilities for government finance.

As we have seen, in the 1630s Charles had succeeded in making significant increases in revenue. It is true that some of his financial devices, such as knighthood compositions and fines for encroaching on royal forests, were only temporary sources, but the more efficient administration of royal lands and the Court of Wards, together with the increase in customs duties, was bringing in a revenue approximately fifty per cent higher than in the early years of the decade. As the rate of inflation had fallen, most of this was clear gain. However, despite the large increase in revenue and the attempt to reduce expenditure, Charles did not succeed in living within his income except, perhaps, for two or three years in the early 1630s. It is clear that he had only eased rather than solved the problem of financing royal government.

Charles had only limited success in restructuring the financial system. The New Impositions (including his additions to them, sometimes known as the New New Impositions) certainly produced more revenue from expanded overseas trade, and this was his most notable financial success. The use of monopolies as a form of excise was a limited and less successful attempt to raise funds from internal manufacture and trade. The greatest omission, however, was the failure to tax, regularly, systematically and fairly, landed wealth. Ship money did, of course, draw on this source, but the ordinary revenues benefited significantly only from the royal lands and from the Court of Wards. The £75 000 a year the latter produced was a trifling proportion of landed incomes and raised in such a way that it placed an unfair and erratic burden on families whose estate passed to a minor heir. Only if some form of land tax had been devised could Charles have raised revenue effectively from the major sector of the economy.

In the final analysis, it is by its political consequences that the financial policy of Charles I must be judged. The political and constitutional situation imposed severe limitations on his freedom of manoeuvre. His failure to impose any form of land tax surely related to his inability to do so with any shadow of legality and his knowledge that such a direct assault on the pockets and principles of the landed class was unenforceable. Charles's methods of raising revenue without recourse to Parliament aroused much resentment: despite early successes in collection, political opposition led to the collapse of ship money. Charles I's financial policies were certainly not the only cause of opposition—religion, foreign policy and relations with local government played an equally important role—but it was his inability to finance his government after setbacks in the second Scottish war which made him dependent on the Long Parliament. Charles had not succeeded in modernising his finances. On the contrary, he had attempted to turn back the clock in an attempt to squeeze more revenue from an unwilling public. Reforms capable of financing the State on a Continental scale still lay in the future.

The Civil War

During the Civil War, both sides were faced by unprecedented demands for money. At the same time, war disrupted the economy and weakened the tax base. Furthermore, the distaste of enemies and neutrals for taxes designed to support a war effort which they opposed, or simply wished to avoid, may have created difficulties in the collection of taxes. On the other hand, both sides could play a trump card denied Charles in the 1630s—they could use their armies to enforce taxation in the areas under their control.

Parliament's first financial device during the Civil War was the Propositions. A committee was set up in Haberdashers' Hall on 26 November 1642 to raise loans secured by the public faith. These loans carried eight per cent interest and were to be repaid after the war. Probably because of the lack of any tangible security, this device was an embarrassing failure in most areas. The Haberdashers' Hall Committee was then empowered to use compulsion. It demanded the so-called fifth and twentieth part, one-fifth of the annual income from land and one-twentieth of the capital value of non-landed property. Though more successful than the Propositions, it was still a quite inadequate source of war revenue.

In February 1643, the weekly (later monthly) Assessment was inaugurated. This tax was raised in various ways, sometimes based on the traditional methods of levying subsidies, but these nearly always proved to be inadequate and a system similar to that used for collecting ship money was adopted. By the end of the Civil War, Parliament was raising £600 000 a year from the Assessment (Russell, 1971, page 351). The amounts raised were much greater than at any time in the past and there were many complaints that the Assessment was bankrupting the country. This was, however, a much lower proportion of national income than is taken by normal peacetime income tax in most countries today. It has been calculated that the Assessment amounted to two shillings in the pound in Buckinghamshire (ten per cent) and two shillings and sixpence in the pound in Kent (12.5 per cent). It did, however, bring within the taxation system everybody except the very poor.

Sequestrations were important sources of revenue in counties which had difficulty in raising the required funds by the monthly Assessment. Sequestration involved taking over control and administration of royalists' property. The profits became part of county funds. The excise, modelled on Dutch precedents, was introduced by John Pym in 1643. It was an indirect tax charged on a very wide range of basic commodities, including, in theory at least, home-brewed beer. It was, needless to say, extremely unpopular and the difficulties of collection were so great that it does not appear to have operated with efficiency anywhere outside London until after the Civil War. In 1646, it raised the very useful sum of £300 000 a year. Customs duties were collected, where possible, by both sides, but the interruption to foreign trade caused by the war reduced their importance.

The central control of finance was, of course, retained by Parliament itself. Executive government lay with the Committee of Safety, which became the Committee of Both Kingdoms after the Scottish Alliance of 1644. These committees acted as a war cabinet, planning strategy with the advice of the commanders and making recommendations to Parliament about taxation and the organisation of the war effort.

On the royalist side, central direction was exercised by the Council of War which replaced the Privy Council. It imposed a system of taxation similar to that of Parliament. The 'Contribution' was the royalist land tax, equivalent to the parliamentarian Assessment and the main source of funds. Voluntary donations and loans from the King's wealthy supporters were probably more important than were the equivalent grants to Parliament. The royalists seem to have made less use of sequestration of enemy estates and the excise than did their opponents. (As royalist fund raising was, in practice, rather more decentralised than that of the parliamentarians, fuller details are given in the section on local government, pages 221–2).

The relative wealth of the heartlands of parliamentary support compared with those of the King is not easy to assess. Conventionally, it has been said that the war was one of the poorer and royalist north and west against the wealthier and parliamentarian south and east. There is some truth in this, because Parliament controlled London, the main source of ready money and the centre of international trade. However, it must be remembered that the ability to produce the goods required in war was just as important as money, and in this respect the advantage of Parliament was less pronounced. Areas controlled by it for most of the war were generally more populous, but this advantage does not appear to have been critical. Parliament ruled the important iron-making (and therefore weapon-producing) areas of Kent and Sussex, but for most of the war this was offset by the King's ability to draw on the expanding metal industries of the Forest of Dean and the Midlands. Parliament probably had an advantage in money and material resources, but whether this was decisive in the Civil War is questionable. Both sides had difficulty in mobilising material resources for war, and shortages of men, money and munitions were to be serious problems. Nor is it clear that financial management was superior on the parliamentarian side. Indeed, most historians believe that the royalists succeeded in imposing taxes which mobilised a higher proportion of wealth in the territories under their control than did Parliament.

The Civil War forced a hasty revision of traditional financial methods, but there was little modernisation. True, a vastly greater sum was raised in taxation than ever before, but the methods of collection usually had more in common with pre-war practice that with the techniques of William III's day. The excise was an exception, but it appears to have had limited success during the war itself. In any case, the war ended with Parliament heavily in debt.

The coming of peace was not followed by a return to pre-war levels of taxation. The years 1647–9 were marked by soaring prices, unemployment and a severe economic depression. The economic situation contributed to problems in disbanding the army. In March 1647 the pay of the 'foot' was eighteen weeks in arrears, and that of the cavalry, forty-three weeks. Total arrears amounted to £331 000 (Russell, 1971, page 378). As the soldiers refused to disband until they were paid, there was a continuing liability to a high wage bill and the arrears continued to accumulate.

Finance in the Commonwealth and Protectorate

During the Commonwealth and Protectorate, taxation continued at a higher level than before the Civil War. The burden constituted a greater proportion of national income than it was to do in any but a few wartime years after 1688. G.E. Aylmer has estimated the State's average annual total revenue, excluding capital transactions such as the sale of land, at around £1.7 million in 1649–54, and around £1.55 million in 1655–9. The Assessment, which was on land, raised an annual average of almost £862 000 in 1647–60, the customs about £362 000 in 1652–7, and the excise £395 000 in 1650–60. Of the remaining revenues, rents from royalist estates and capital sums of money known as Compositions, paid by former royalists to regain control of their properties, raised an average of almost £153 000 per annum in 1643–55. Comparison with pre-war taxation shows that these were unprecedently large sums. According to Professor Aylmer, 'At its maximum (£120 000 a month) the Assessment was running at the rate of something like eighteen pre-war parliamentary subsidies a year!' The financial situation inherited by Interregnum governments called for peace, drastic economy, efficient economic management and sufficient taxation to maintain a surplus for repayment of debts (G.E. Aylmer, *The State's Servants: The Civil Service of the English Republic, 1649–1660*. London, 1973, pages 320–1).

In the event, few of the desirable preconditions for recovery of the State's finances could be met. The cost of the army could not be reduced much without exposing the government to increased attacks from both English and foreign enemies. In any case, the army would not disband until it was paid. Furthermore, the Dutch war of 1652–3 and the Spanish war of 1655 provided an obvious justification for continued military expenditure. Despite the unprecedentedly high annual income, it was impossible to make ends meet. In the late 1650s, the army was costing over £1 million a year, the navy nearly £800 000. There was an annual deficit of £230 000 (Russell, 1971, page 394). Needless to say, the high taxation and heavy expenditure were unpopular. The financial arrangements were one of the thorniest problems in each of the Interregnum constitutional experiments and the Protectorate parliaments showed the same reluctance to vote the taxes demanded by the executive as had the early Stuart parliaments. However, the most significant financial failure of the Interregnum governments was their inability to establish a soundly based method of long-term borrowing. This meant a dangerous dependence on taxation to provide funds for an emergency, and there were under Cromwell, just as under Charles I, political risks in large increases in taxation.

At the end of the Civil War, the Long Parliament could borrow only by 'doubling': that is, by granting confiscated royal or church lands to creditors who would lend a further sum. After 1654 the government could hardly borrow at all. In 1659 the expenses of the Spanish war brought about a financial crisis similar to that experienced by Charles I when the Scottish invasion overstrained his credit in 1640. The persistent gap between revenue and expenditure and the difficulty of borrowing forced the government to raise as much money as possible from the former royalists. Sequestration of suspected royalist plotters, harsh composition terms, and the decimation tax, which took one-tenth of known royalists' income to pay for the militia, all combined to keep alive old hatreds: permanent settlement was made more difficult.

There was a reluctance to lend because of the failure of the State to repay earlier debts. Wealthy City men lacked faith in the ability of the Protectorate to survive and did not wish to risk the repudiation of the money owed to them if Charles II returned. In the failure of the Protectorate to establish a sound credit rating was one of the most important reasons for its collapse.

The Restoration and finance

Despite the serious problems faced at the Restoration and during the reign of Charles II, many significant advances were made in financial management. These included the techniques of collecting money, public borrowing and control of expenditure. Tax gathering became more efficient, expecially when 'farming' in most branches of the revenue was replaced by direct collection. There was a major improvement in borrowing methods, which paved the way for the rapid modernisation which took place after the Revolution. Though never able to curb Charles II's extravagance, the new and strict Treasury control over expenditure enabled it to supervise all government departments. The introduction of 'appropriation of supply' by Parliament in some of the direct taxes voted during the 1670s prevented even the King from diverting funds from their intended purpose.

The actual weight of taxation, though lighter for most of Charles II's reign than it had been during the Civil War and Interregnum, or than it was to be during King William's wars of the 1690s, was very heavy compared with that imposed before 1642. What is more, the burden was imposed and collected without the aid of a large standing army. The tax system of the Restoration was able to provide supply adequate for a more highly developed English State, and one which was playing an important role both in European affairs and colonial expansion.

The general principle upon which Restoration finance was based was that the King should have sufficient money for ordinary expenses and that he should turn to Parliament only in emergencies—an old principle continued. It was thought that, apart from Crown estates, the ordinary revenue should derive from non-landed property, while extraordinary finance should be met by direct taxes, mainly on land. For the most part, these principles were observed throughout the reign of Charles II. Ordinary revenue came mainly from customs duties and the excise (taxes on consumption) which spread the burden of taxation widely across the community. The hearth tax (on fireplaces) was a tax on property, but it can scarcely be regarded as a land tax as it was paid in most cases by the tenant rather than the landlord. The direct taxes— subsidy, Assessment and poll tax—all raised revenue from the incomes of wealthier people, especially from landowners. They were imposed for limited periods by Parliament and did not become part of the regular revenue.

The financial situation in 1660 presented great problems and opportunities. The problems of massive debt, resistance to high taxation, a stagnant economy and strained credit were counterbalanced by the opportunity to learn, not only from Charles I and the English regimes of the past decade, but from the best ideas in Europe. The possibility was there to tax the country's wealth more effectively, to improve assessment and collection, to restrain spending, to establish a sound basis for borrowing and to organise finances on the basis of continual co-operation between Crown and Parliament.

The first year of the reign saw only partial solutions to the problems and a reluctance to take advantage of the opportunities. Over the twenty-five years of Charles II's reign, however, significant steps were taken to improve the State's financing in ways which have more in common with our own day than those of the Middle Ages. Real 'modernisation' did not take place until after 1688, but the foundations were laid in the reign of Charles II.

Once restoration had been decided upon, it was necessary to made a financial settlement. Most pressing was the need to clear debts and disband the Protectorate's military forces. To keep the army intact would be financially crippling and it would be politically dangerous. As long as it remained in being, Cromwell's army would have been as capable of removing Charles II as it had been of restoring him. Total military and naval expense amounted to £1 200 000 a year. Before the forces could be disbanded, however, their arrears of wages had to be met and these amounted to £750 000. Parliament provided an extraordinary grant of about £800 000 by imposing a poll tax and a heavy assessment on land. Priority was given to disbanding the army and this was complete by February 1661, leaving the King with debts of £637 000. Charles was also saddled with the debts of the Interregnum Government, of his father and of his own exile. Parliament did little to help: some was paid off from arrears in the Commonwealth excise, but debts of £300 000 from the 1650s were quietly repudiated. Of the £530 000 in debts left by his father, Charles II ultimately paid nearly £400 000 and he paid £105 000 towards the unknown total of debts he himself had incurred. The inadequate provision for paying off his inherited debts contributed significantly to his later financial problems.

The attempt to provide a permanent financial settlement for the restored monarchy was based on the medieval idea that 'the King should live of his own'. It is clear that the Convention (the irregularly summoned Parliament which restored Charles II, see page 439) continued to see Parliament only as an occasional part of the constitution, rather than as a regular assembly ultimately controlling government. In providing the King with sufficient revenue to support the normal expenses of government, the Convention was, of course, removing the most effective guarantee that Parliament would be summoned. The settlement was based on the calculation that the King needed £1 200 000 per annum to meet his normal expenses, and he was granted a combination of additional customs duties and excise payments to supplement the traditional revenue (including £100 000 compensation for the abolition of feudal dues). There was, however, a serious overestimate in the amount which would be raised by the taxes imposed and it became clear in 1661 that the revenue would fall at least £300 000 short. The hearth tax was voted to make up the deficiency, although it did not do so. It imposed a tax of one shilling per annum on all stoves, ovens or fire places. This was the last addition to the permanent revenue. The first decade of Charles II's reign was one of serious financial difficulty for the Crown. Part of the difficulty sprang from the state of the economy, which had been seriously harmed by the uncertain political situation of the Interregnum. The brief recovery of 1660 was cut short by a poor harvest, the heavy taxation imposed to pay off the army and the poor condition of the coinage. Recoinage, improved harvests and much reduced taxation helped produce two years of economic growth: this was, unfortunately, ended by a series of meagre harvests, the Second Dutch War of 1665–7, the Great Plague of London (1665) and the Great Fire of London (1666).

The 1670s, however, made it easier to raise revenue. There was a period of steady economic growth and thus an increase in tax returns, which was further aided by an improvement in revenue-raising techniques. The boom of the 1670s continued into the 1680s. It provided both Charles II in his later years and James II with sufficient funds from the permanent revenue to make them almost independent of Parliament.

The King's permanent revenue, depending so much on customs duties and the excise, was liable to fall far below expectations when trade was depressed. Throughout the 1660s, the yield fluctuated with economic conditions, but remained well below the expected £1 200 000. The lack of sufficient permanent revenue had at least two important consequences. Firstly, it made the government dependent on parliamentary grants and, secondly, it forced a major reform of administration in both tax gathering and spending. Nevertheless, Charles II was very successful in his requests for additional funds during the 1660s. Parliament made grants to meet special needs. The additional funds voted by Parliament were raised by direct taxation. (A direct tax is one paid by a person in proportion to his or her income or presumed means; an indirect tax is one imposed on a commodity or activity without regard to the means of the payer.) Of these, the most important were the subsidy and the Assessment. They were taxes on all forms of income, both landed and non-landed. In practice, both concentrated disproportionately on taxing incomes from land, which was the form of wealth most difficult to conceal. The subsidy was the older and less unpopular form of taxation. The problem of gaining honest valuations and bringing non-landed property within the tax collector's net had seriously reduced returns from this tax in the early seventeenth century. The yield of Charles II's subsidies, too, was to fall well below expectations.

In contrast, the Assessment provided a fixed yield. A lump sum was decided upon and apportioned between the various counties and corporate towns. County or city assessors then subdivided the burden further until, finally, the sums to be paid by individuals were fixed. The Assessment was a much more satisfactory tax for the government than the uncertain subsidy. However, it was very unpopular, both because it was difficult to avoid and because it was associated with the governments of the Civil War and Interregnum.

The attempt to strike a fair balance between taxing income from land, from business activities and from salaries presented even more difficulties. There was little accurate information about the proportion of national wealth each represented and, in any case, non-landed income was easy to conceal. To compound these problems, tax assessors were not allowed by law to make the payers swear on oath when they declared their income or to impose any rigorous investigation into doubtful returns. They were, furthermore, often hampered by local officials who favoured their friends and relations at the expense of both the revenue and other tax payers. Needless to say, numerous efforts were made in a Parliament dominated by land owners to shift taxation to non-landed wealth. This was probably done most effectively in the poll taxes, as these were designed to tax people who were paying little or nothing in subsidies or Assessments (for example, in 1667 and 1678 when the poll-tax burden fell on the incomes of civil servants, doctors, lawyers and other professional men).

In the 1670s there was less incentive to reform direct taxes. Economic growth, and less money spent on war, reduced the gap between ordinary revenue and the King's expenditure. Some direct taxes were imposed (such as the Assessments of 1673, 1677, 1678 and 1680). All of these were collected more and more efficiently and produced almost exactly their estimated yield.

The heavy taxation of the 1660s was almost more than the economy could bear. Rents fell, land values were depressed and many tenancies were surrendered. The evident strain on landed incomes convinced landowners that the rest of the community was escaping its fair share. However, the estimates of national wealth made in 1671 do not support this view. All lands and tenements were valued at £240 million, eighty-five per cent of the capital in the country. It was intended that income from land should provide only seventy-nine per cent of the return from the subsidy. The problem was the overall weight of national taxation in a period of economic recession, not the fact that it fell most heavily on the nation's largest source of wealth.

Nevertheless, it was not upon the direct taxes imposed from time to time by Parliament that the government depended for its regular finance, but upon the indirect taxes. These consisted chiefly of customs duties, the excise and hearth tax. At the Restoration (as before), customs duties were imposed on foreign trade, usually on imports and occasionally on exports as well. The intention of customs duties can be either to raise revenue or to regulate trade (for example, by imposing stiff tariffs on imported foreign goods in order to protect local industries, or to harm economic competitors and political enemies). At first, with the Tunnage and Poundage and Navigation Act of 1660, the emphasis was on the latter. However, during the 1660s, the financial pressures to which the government was subjected created a demand for higher customs duties, and there was a continuing debate over whether customs should be imposed mainly to raise revenue or to encourage a favourable balance of trade.

In contrast to customs duties on foreign goods, which were ancient levies, the excise was only seventeen years old in 1660. It was highly unpopular; its origins were variously attributed to the Dutch and the Devil. Its opponents charged that it raised the cost of living, especially when imposed on necessary items consumed by the poor, and that its enforcement required a body of officials with inquisitorial powers which constituted a threat to the privacy and liberty of Englishmen. Furthermore, its association with the revolutionary regimes of the Interregnum completed its damnation in the eyes of many loyalists. Not surprisingly, both the Convention and the Cavalier Parliament wanted to abolish the excise. Its retention was grudgingly conceded by the Convention because of the absence of any feasible alternative method of making up the permanent revenue. Its temporary continuance to meet the extraordinary expenses of the Restoration aroused little controversy. Its acceptance as a long-term device sprang from the need to replace the feudal revenue lost by the King's agreement not to revive the Courts of Wards and Liveries which had been abolished in 1645.

The excise was imposed not only on alcoholic beverages, but on coffee, chocolate, sherbet and tea. Despite the wide application of the excise to all types of drink which were sold commercially, English beer, ale, cider and perry (a cider-like beverage made from pears) provided over ninety per cent of excise revenue from liquor between 1661–1688. Attempts by the government to persuade Parliament to increase these duties, or the range of goods on which the excise was charged, met with little success, especially when some M.P.s came to fear the independence from Parliament which additional funds from the excise could give the King.

The third of the great indirect taxes was the hearth tax—a levy of two shillings per year on each fire hearth or stove. It was enacted in 1662 to make up for a deficiency in the permanent revenue. Based on Dutch and French precedents, it was sponsored into the Commons by a minor member of the Court party, Sir Courtney Poole, known thereafter as 'Sir Chimney Poole'. It was not a popular tax and its passage through Parliament took place under government pressure and, again, in the absence of any more palatable alternative. It was resented because it was a tax on a necessity, which would have to be paid by all except the very poor. In 1666, the House of Commons attempted to abolish the hearth tax and offered to raise £200 000 for eight years as compensation. However, the size of the debt which had been secured against the hearth tax, and the difficulty in finding any alternative source of revenue prevented abolition before 1688. The repealing Act referred to to it as a 'great oppression of the poorer sort' and a 'badge of slavery upon the whole people'.

The remaining parts of the permanent revenue were individually small, but collectively they produced £825 000 in the reign of Charles II: from the surviving Crown lands, first fruits and tenths, fees for wine licences, profits from the Post Office and a duty on law suits.

In order to raise more revenue from any tax at existing rates, it was necessary to ensure that the duties were strictly enforced and collected with the minimum administrative expenses. Efficiency improved in all the main branches of Charles II's revenue. One of the most significant advances was the substitution of direct collection of the permanent revenues for farming: customs farming ended on Michaelmas 1671. Direct collection of the excise commenced in 1683, and of the hearth tax in 1684. The result was increased efficiency and a dramatic increase in net returns. Yet tax farming had at least two major advantages for a seventeenth century government. It saved it from having to recruit and pay a large body of officials to collect taxes and it smoothed the flow of government revenue. The tax farmers had to pay their rent in regular instalments, regardless of fluctuations in collection. The tax farmers were, furthermore, a good source of loan finance. Indeed, their role as lenders was so important that the Earl of Danby, Charles II's chief minister in the 1670s, was convinced that the government could not do without them. Customs farming was abandoned in 1671, not because the government was convinced of the superiority of direct collection, but because of a dispute with the new customs farmers. Instead, the government appointed a Customs Commission with six members, supervising a hierarchy of officials whose organisation was copied from that of the customs farmers. It is safe to say that only the revolution of borrowing techniques initiated under Charles II, and developed under William and Mary, made it certain that governments would not be forced to return to tax farming.

The excise was a much more difficult tax to collect than customs, both because of opposition to it and the administrative problems associated with collecting small sums of money from all over the country. From the Restoration to 1683, there were frequent and varied experiments in both direct collection and farming, and their relative merits were hotly debated. However, by the 1680s the superiority of direct collection had become clear and farming was finally abandoned. A royal Excise Commission was established whose management techniques were remarkably modern. Salaries were raised to attract better men to the service, all promotion was to be by merit, officers were not to serve in their own locality and were to move at frequent intervals. Insurance and superannuation schemes were introduced.

The administration of the hearth tax followed a similar path to that of the excise. There were the same alternations of farming and direct collection, both methods hampered by widespread opposition to this unpopular tax. The final abandonment of farming came in 1684, after it was revealed that only three-quarters of the money gathered by the farmers was reaching the Treasury. In the hearth tax, as in the customs and excise, direct collection had led to a vast improvement in efficiency and net yield.

The direct taxes, being occasional in nature, had a less elaborate system of collection. When it voted a direct tax, Parliament appointed commissioners from among its own members and the leading inhabitants of an area. These subdivided the territory and appointed local assessors, who fixed the amount to be paid by individuals. From 1671 there was greater strictness in enforcing prompt payment. The amateur officials of the earlier taxes were supplemented after 1670 by government officers responsible to the Treasury. Collection became speedier and the gap between anticipated revenue and actual returns declined to negligible proportions. By the end of Charles II's reign, the efficient collection of taxes constituted a major step towards modernisation.

The improvements in revenue collection techniques were accompanied by attempts to modernise borrowing, which though not altogether successful under Charles II, prepared the way for the revolution in public borrowing of the 1690s. Before 1665, the main methods of raising finance were loans, advances and tallies. The first involved a cash payment either to the Exchequer or to a particular department. There was no guarantee of repayment on a certain date or in any particular order. Advances were payments of a tax made early in return for a discount. They could be made either by individuals or by the tax farmers. Tallies were hazel-wood sticks with notches cut in them to represent a particular sum of money. This could be a loan paid into the Exchequer or a debt owed by the Crown for goods or services. The tally was exchanged for cash, including interest, when the funds were available. In 1665, however, a way was sought to raise money directly from the public by offering guaranteed repayment, free from government interference. This system of borrowing, made on the security of the permanent revenue, met with a certain amount of success and led to the government raising further credit in the same way in 1667–68. Provided only that the moneyed men remained willing to lend, and that there was sufficient revenue to pay the interest on the existing debt, a large expansion of government credit was possible. Expansion could not, however, be limitless.

In 1672 the government found that it could not repay existing debt out of either revenue or new borrowings. The result was the famous 'Stop on the Exchequer' by which the government suspended the repayment of all loans secured on the ordinary revenue. The result was to drive into bankruptcy several of the government's chief creditors and to make obtaining credit even more difficult. Interest was, however, paid on the frozen debt. Short-term loans had been effectively converted into long-term, indeed virtually permanent, ones.

The twin developments in revenue collection and borrowing were matched by the growth of Treasury control over expenditure. In 1667 the King, acting on the advice of the Duke of York, decided to replace the recently deceased Lord Treasurer Southampton with a Commission rather than a single Lord Treasurer. This procedure was by no means novel. However, the type of men appointed to the Commission were quite unlike the aristocratic commissioners of the past. Sir Thomas Clifford, Sir William Coventry and Sir John Duncombe were the dominating figures. However, two peers, Lord Ashley and the Duke of Albemarle, were added as a gesture to Lord Chancellor Clarendon, who believed that Treasury matters should be handled by peers and wealthy gentlemen. The three 'rougher hands' (that is, professional civil servants rather than landed gentlemen) and their equally businesslike secretary, Sir George Downing, established the system of Treasury administration and control which lasted virtually unchanged until the nineteenth century and provides the basis of financial control to this day. The main changes lay in the strengthening of Treasury power over other agencies of government and the improvement of book-keeping methods.

The combined effect of Treasury control, the transformation of revenue collection and the development of new borrowing techniques was a major step forward in overall financial control. Indeed, some historians see the Restoration period as the critical one in the modernisation of English finances. The one major failure of the Restoration era was the inability to check the extravagance of Charles II. Historians have long debated the question of his financial problems and growing indebtedness. Some have seen the problem as one of inadequate financing by Parliament, others of Charles's personal extravagance and secret expenditure on his many mistresses and his illegitimate children. Chandaman has argued convincingly that the latter was the main problem. His study of the Treasury records has shown that, with the exception of the years 1664–70, Charles's total revenue for ordinary purposes reached the £1 200 000 his government had deemed necessary in 1660 and which it continued to regard as sufficient throughout the reign. Extraordinary expenses, such as those of war, were met by parliamentary or other special revenues.

The changing financial fortunes of Charles II had important political consequences. In the 1660s the dependence of the King on parliamentary grants to supplement his permanent revenue strengthened parliamentary power over the executive. The conflict in Parliament between those who were willing to grant additional money and those who were not, played a very important role in the development of the party system. On the other hand, the rapid growth of the permanent revenue in the buoyant economic conditions of the 1670s and 80s made possible a revival of kingly power at the expense of Parliament. It is hardly likely that Charles could have kept intact, throughout the Exclusion Crisis, his brother's claim to ascend the throne without limitations if he had been as dependent on additional parliamentary supply as he had been in the 1660s.

James II

The reign of James II may be viewed, in terms of financial and administrative developments, as an appendage to that of his brother. There were no major changes in financial principles or practices. James was the last English king to be granted a permanent revenue. Many members of Parliament were unhappy about this extension of medievalism, but the majority caved in under pressure from the King. At James's accession in 1685, Parliament voted extraordinary supply to pay off Charles's debts, strengthen the armed forces and pay the costs of suppressing Monmouth's rebellion. The permanent revenues granted to James were identical to those possessed by Charles. There was certainly no intention by the loyalist majority in Parliament to provide James with such generous supply that he could rule without their services.

Parliament's mistake was to ignore the consequences of expanding trade and direct collection. The taxes of the permanent revenue, and those imposed temporarily for the purposes outlined above, produced far more than was anticipated. James's receipts from the ordinary revenue averaged about £1 600 000 per annum 1685–88 and his total annual income was about £2 000 000. This large revenue enabled James to meet all the normal expenses of government. In addition, he maintained military forces costing £300 000. He did this independently of Parliament, while following policies of which the vast majority of his subjects disapproved. It is scarcely surprising that no other English monarch was to be granted a permanent revenue.

Finance under William and Mary

Having learned from experience under his predecessors, Parliament did not grant any permanent revenues to William III. (The years 1688 to 1694 were unique in that William and Mary ruled as joint sovereigns. However, all executive power was invested in William, who ruled, for most practical purposes, as if he was sole king regnant and Mary merely his consort. The shorthand of referring to William alone, rather than to the joint monarchs, is not twentieth century male chauvinism but a reflection of seventeenth century realities.) William voluntarily agreed to give up the hated hearth tax, but he bitterly resented the lack of trust shown in Parliament's determination to keep him permanently dependent on its grants.

The accession of William committed England not only to the normal costs of government, but to the unprecedented burden of a long war against France; indeed, a war of national survival. During the nine years of this war, England so refined its system of financial management that its economy emerged in far better shape than that of either Holland or France. The administrative basis for the successful financing of this war had been laid under Charles II. The customs and excise, under continued direct collection, were the mainstay of indirect taxation. Additional indirect taxes, such as the window tax of 1696, were unpopular and relatively ineffective.

The demands of war finance forced a greater and greater dependence on direct taxation. Poll taxes were imposed in 1689 and 1698. Like their Restoration antecedents, these taxes imposed a graduated tax according to rank or profession on all those who were not in receipt of parish relief. A tax, usually of one shilling in the pound (five per cent) was levied on pensions and the salaries of government officials. By far the most important direct tax was the land tax. This was levied on either the assessment or the subsidy principle and it ranged between one and four shillings in the pound (five to twenty per cent). Together with customs and excise, it provided the basis of government finance. Between 1688 and 1702 total revenue for the fourteen years amounted to 58.7 million pounds—19.1 million from land tax, 13.3 million from customs, 13.6 million from the excise, 2.6 million from poll taxes, 10 million from all other taxes. The biggest items of expenditure were £19.9 million spent on the navy, 22 million on the army, 3 million on the ordnance and 8.9 million on the civil list; 4.4 million was assigned to cover other expenses (Wilson, 1971, page 217).

Despite the success of William III in raising unprecedented amounts in taxation, the most far-reaching financial innovation of his reign was the development of borrowing techniques. Borrowing, it is believed, allowed about one-third more to be spent on the war than would otherwise have been possible. The additional troops or ships made possible by the extra expenditure were critical in a number of actions. To have raised the additional funds by taxation was neither economically nor socially possible.

The heavy borrowing of William III's reign was of three types: long term, short term and speculative. All showed a considerable advance on previous methods. In order for a government to gain long-term loans, it must be able to offer sufficient security to the lenders. (Remember the Interregnum government's capacity to borrow was severely impaired by fears that a return to monarchy would lead to a repudiation of commonwealth debt.) It must also offer attractive interest rates, and provide an opportunity for the investor to withdraw the sum which he has lent before it is due for repayment, or to sell the rights to interest and capital to another person. An alternative form of long-term loan is one in which the capital is never repaid and the interest is perpetual. Many seventeenth century investors seemed to prefer a speculative loan which appealed to gambling instincts by offering some form of lottery or annuity in place of a conventional loan.

The first long-term loan was the so-called 'Million Loan' or 'tontine' of 1694. (The name 'tontine' is derived from the Italian financier, Lorenzo Tonti, who invented the scheme. He was adviser to Cardinal Mazarin, the *de facto* ruler of France in the mid-seventeenth century. It was commonly used by both the French and the Dutch). This loan, floated in 1693–4, raised £108 100. The investors were to receive ten per cent interest until 1700. In 1700 total interest was reduced to seven per cent, but it was to be divided among a diminishing number of survivors. The last beneficiary died in 1783, drawing £1000 a year on an original investment of £100 (Wilson, 1971, page 218).

Both the tontine and the more straightforward annuities had the benefit of parliamentary authorisation and assignment of revenue to meet the payments. They offered a high return on capital invested, and the tontine appealed to gambling instincts. For the investor who wished to provide for his heirs, they both had the disadvantage that the capital investment was lost at his death. This was, of course, an advantage to the government which did not have to repay the capital. A further means of raising long-term finance appealed even more to the gambler. This was the Million Lottery of 1694. Tickets cost £10 each and winners received returns ranging from £1000 to £1 for sixteen years, after which all payments ceased. Once more, the investor's capital was lost. The State lotteries remained an important financial device until 1826.

The scope for long-term borrowing was obviously greater if provision could be made for eventual return of capital. The major conventional long-term loan of William III's reign was that raised by the Tunnage Act of 1694. Under this Act, additional customs duties were imposed to pay interest of eight per cent on a loan of £1 200 000. The capital could be repaid on one year's notice after 1706. The Tunnage Act, however has much more significance than as a mere device to raise a loan. Subscribers to the loan were to be incorporated as the Bank of England (this was the foundation of that institution). The capital was raised within ten days and supplemented by a further £300 000 raised by the sale of annuities for one, two or three lives at fourteen per cent, twelve per cent and ten per cent respectively. (An annuity for one life is paid until the named person dies, for two lives until two named people die and so on. Those named may or may not not be the recipients of the annuity.) In the late 1690s there was considerable difficulty in raising long-term finance. An attempt to raise £1 400 000 by lottery in 1697 brought in only £17 000 and a Land Bank scheme of 1696 was a total failure. On the other hand, the government was able to raise £2 000 000 on the security of additional excise duties by offering to incorporate subscribers into a New East India Company. Although, the long-term borrowing schemes of the 1690s played a useful role in financing the war, their immediate importance must not be over-rated: they raised only £8 000 000 compared with £32 000 000 by short-term loans. However, it was during these years, the reign of William III, that the framework for government borrowing until the nineteenth century was established.

The much greater volume of short-term loans was a serious problem. Attempts to put loan management on a sound footing were critical to the war effort and the survival of the post-Revolution regime. As was the case under Charles II and James II, the main short-term debts were contracted by anticipating revenue. The men who operated the direct collection of customs and excise, for example, made large loans. Under direct collection, the customs and excise departments were administered by men known as the cashiers, who were wealthy businessmen rather than professional civil servants and often former revenue farmers. They lent the government money which they would then receive in taxation. Similarly businessmen who sold goods to the government had to accept payment in tallies rather than in cash. For example, a manufacturer who sold the navy £1000 worth of cannon balls would receive tallies with a face value of £1000. When the Navy Department had the cash, he was able to return them for money. The government had to pay interest on the sums secured by tallies in this way, and the rate rose as the demands of war created an ever-greater delay in repayment.

In 1696–7 a financial crisis created a real risk of bankruptcy, military defeat and the return of James II. According to Dickson the crisis had four main causes. Firstly, the amount raised by short-term borrowing was too large—a longer term for repayment was needed. Secondly, the new taxes on which the loans were secured were imposed for too short a period. Taxes often expired before the loans secured on them had been repaid. Thirdly, there were too many loans raised on too many taxes. Fewer and larger loans borrowed on the security of more productive taxes would have been preferable. Fourthly, the yield of the new taxes was usually overestimated and the loans raised on them were, therefore, too large (P. Dickson, *The Financial Revolution in England: A Study in the Development of Public Credit 1688–1756*, London, 1967).

The fact that the government could not pay its creditors in 1697 made it virtually impossible to borrow more until better security could be given. Drastic action was needed and drastic action was taken. On 1 April 1697 an Act was passed imposing additional taxes and extending the term of existing ones, to provide funds where the tax providing revenue for a particular loan had proved insufficient. Secondly, the Bank of England was empowered to buy an unlimited number of existing government tallies. It acquired over £800 000 worth—one-seventh of the total outstanding. These two measures restored some confidence in government short-term loans. Another device to place short-term finance on a more regular basis, Exchequer bills, was introduced in 1696. They were issued in return for cash or used in payment. They could be transferred freely from hand to hand like banknotes. Nearly £2 700 000 were issued in 1697, a very useful amount in a time of financial crisis.

By 1700 the financial resources of the State were of a different order of magnitude from those of 1640, 1660, or any of the years between. The machinery of revenue collection had been improved out of all recognition and the abolition of revenue farming meant that all the yield from a tax except the bare cost of collection was available to the State. From 1688, all revenues were granted by Parliament, their imposition or renewal was open to debate and, in the last analysis, they received the consent of the political nation. The establishment of strict Treasury control helped regulate spending and reduce extravagance and inefficiency in the spending departments. The placing of all government borrowing under the security of Parliament made considerably more funds available, since the State debt was then secured on the credit of the nation, not the 'breath of one man's nostrils'. The introduction of long-term borrowing, the so-called National Debt, the creation and use of the Bank of England and the closer regulation of short-term credit in the form of Exchequer bills, had created a system governments could use to find the credit required in emergences such as war. The financial system created between 1660 and 1700 not only paid for the war of national survival in the 1690s, but provided for the expansion of the British Empire in the eighteenth century.

By 1700, the English financial system was arguably the best in the world, superior to those of Continental Europe to which Englishmen had traditionally looked for inspiration. In the 1690s, the English State came of age. It was able to raise and disburse funds in a manner unprecedented in England, and which matched, in proportion to gross national product, the State spending of Continental powers, without the same harmful social and economic effects. Unlike the Dutch and French system, it collected the golden eggs without killing the goose.

Central and local government

England between 1558 and 1640 has been referred to as a federation of counties, and its system of government as 'self-government at the King's command' (A.M. Everitt, 'Social Mobility in Early Modern England', *Past and Present*, 33, page 59). At one time, historians tended to assume that all politically articulate Englishmen were self-conscious members of a national political society. Recent historical writing has revealed that the majority of sixteenth and seventeenth century Englishmen thought of themselves first and foremost as members of a county or town, the local unit of administration and social life which constituted their 'country'.

The political and administrative importance of the counties was closely associated with their role as social units. Kent is an excellent example of a county which was almost self-contained. In 1640, seventy-five per cent of the Kentish gentry had been settled in the county since the fourteenth century. Two-thirds of the entire gentry

194 Revolution, Reaction and the Triumph of Conservatism

and four-fifths of the lesser gentry married within the county. Some other counties showed very similar patterns of ancient families and marriage within the county. Cheshire had 'one of the most stable ruling élites of any county in England' and, like Kent, two-thirds of the marriages of its gentry were within the county. A similar situation existed in Norfolk and Suffolk. In the other counties of East Anglia and in the Midlands, however, the proportion of new gentry and the number of marriage alliances with gentle families in other counties was higher than in Kent or Cheshire, but there was still a nucleus of long-established families, and ties to the local community, though perhaps weaker than in Kent, were still strong.

The gentry of each county can be divided broadly into two categories: the 'county gentry', whose estates spread over several parishes and might be scattered all over the county, and the 'parish gentry' who frequently owned only one manor and whose estate was usually found in a single parish. The county gentry were, naturally, wealthier on the whole than the parish gentry and it was these men with their widespread interests who took the lead in county government. The minor or 'parish' gentry were rarely found in any major county offices: they were monopolised by a narrow élite of wealthy and long-established families. As in all else, there was considerable variation from county to county in the size and power of the inner core of magnates, but information from a few counties will reveal some of the patterns. In Elizabethan Norfolk, there were at least 424 gentlemen, including 130 knights and esquires, but only fourteen families in 1558 and about a dozen in the late 1570s belonged to the established magnate class. In Caroline Cheshire there were at least 424 gentlemen, but sixty-five to seventy families constituted a distinctive group with a status superior to the rest. Within this group, the twenty-five families descended from the 'chiefest gentlemen' in Cheshire in the 1540s constituted an inner élite. In Kent, where there were between 800 and 1000 gentlemen, 170 families appear to have been of higher prestige than most of the rest and between twenty and thirty families were the real leaders of Kentish society. Barnes regards twenty-five Somerset families as of magnate status and a further seventy-five as of magisterial rank (that is, from one of those families whose members were eligible to serve as Justices of the Peace) in a county with about the same number of gentlemen as in Kent.

Though the magnates, and those of the county gentry who could win their favour, held the most prestigious offices in the county, at least their more affluent social inferiors were not powerless. The lesser gentry, the yeomen, other prosperous farmers and the businessmen of the towns had an important role to play in local politics and administration. This group may be associated with the gentlemen of magisterial rank as the 'country', the political nation of the county community. Men below the magisterial class filled the positions of grand juryman, hundred constable (chief constable for the subdivision of a county known as a hundred), member of special commissions, taxation assessor and voter in parliamentary elections.

County government was not the preserve of any one class: participation was shared widely among all men, except the very poor. The system was, nevertheless, paternalistic. Within the county, the greatest amount of power lay with the upper gentry who filled the posts of Justice of the Peace, sheriff, Deputy Lieutenant and acted as members of various commissions. These were members of the landowning class and they had tremendous influence by virtue of the fact that they controlled the land. In a hierarchical society they were the natural leaders, the patriarchs in a patriarchy. By their education, their visits to London, their participation in national politics, these men linked the community of the county with the wider community of England. There were, of course, limits to their authority. The Council, Star Chamber and the judges of assize punished abuse of power and forced slothful gentlemen to act.

The restrictions on the squirearchy imposed by the government are obvious, yet those exercised by the yeomen and lesser gentlemen had a certain importance too. Much administrative and judicial work could be performed only with the aid of a jury—even the power to bind over to good behaviour, the authority which gave a magistrate the greatest degree of control over his neighbours, was checked by the requirement that a jury decide whether this bond had been broken.

The Crown could easily remove from county office those gentlemen who were disobedient, obstructive or inefficient. Fear of this disgrace was an effective weapon against dissent by individuals and it was a sanction which was frequently used. However, the power of the Crown to effect policies which were opposed by the majority of the magisterial class was limited by the knowledge that dismissal of any substantial number of county officers would only weaken the authority of the remainder. Provided that provincial governors remained united in opposition to a particular policy of the government, that policy could never succeed.

The period of this study is 142 years and it is scarcely to be expected that the relationship between central and local government remained unchanged for nearly a century and a half. It did not. Until the 1630s there was a comparatively stable balance of power between central and local government. Despite inevitable conflicts over particular policies, local government was prepared to accept direction from above and a degree of supervision in return for the significant degree of autonomy it enjoyed. In return, the Crown was generally willing to allow discretion in the details of local administration, provided there was no open opposition to its policies.

In the 1630s, Charles I's policies of 'Thorough' involved an attempt at centralisation. The resentment that they produced was an important reason for the failure of his government and the outbreak of the Civil War. In 1640–1 the machinery by which the King had enforced his centralising policies was swept away. During the Civil War, it was, paradoxically, Parliament which attempted to impose centralisation, but on both sides there was a continued tension between the demands of the national leadership and the desires of the provinces. In the 1650s, a centralising Government aroused the same sort of opposition as had that of Charles I and it was probably its failure to re-establish a viable relationship with county leaders which led to the ultimate fall of the Cromwellian regime. In 1660 the Restoration government allowed a very large measure of local autonomy and left the county magnates virtually unchallenged rulers in their shires. An attempt to reverse this policy in the 1680s was instrumental in bringing about the Revolution of 1688. The relationship between central and local government is one of the key issues in the history of this period.

The central direction of government came primarily from the Privy Council. Its decisions inevitably involved dependence on county officers. Contact with the county could be made either by letter to the officials concerned or by means of directions issued through the judges of assize. Such orders from the Privy Council might implement national policy or criticise local administration. Military requirements, poor relief and taxation produced the greatest number of directives to the counties. From time to time, the Council intervened in the routine administration of county affairs. A selection of Worcestershire examples will illustrate this: in 1615 it investigated a claim that the sheriff had seized goods worth £600 to pay a debt of £460; in 1619 it heard the case of a clergyman said to have called on God to turn the King from his wickedness, and it had to enforce the payment of maimed soldiers' pensions on at least three occasions. Other cases included unlawful arrest, riot, plague relief and a false charge that a gentleman had infected his nieces with the 'French pox'. In short, every aspect of county administration was subject to the over-sight of the Privy Council.

The Privy Council was not a court and it could not impose fines or corporal punishment. However, people who refused to submit to its decisions could be imprisoned indefinitely for contempt. Even the power to summon was an important sanction as those called before it might be kept waiting for months.

While the Council itself dealt with cases of neglect, inefficiency and simple disobedience, the Court of Star Chamber was concerned with positive wrongdoing. It is important to realise that the Star Chamber was not an instrument of royal tyranny. This was a myth created in the late 1630s by the opponents of Charles I, from a small number of political decisions. A few of these cases involved deliberate resistance to proclamations, others a support of the church courts and the enforcement of Laudian religious ceremonies. The cases for which Star Chamber became notorious were the small number—only nineteen of 236 known sentences—in which corporal punishment was ordered. There can be no doubt that the atrocity stories, like that of Sir William Wiseman who had been twice flogged, pilloried and had his ears cut off and his nose split, as well as being fined and imprisoned, contributed to the fall of Star Chamber. Of more importance, however, was the way in which it had humiliated men of the ruling class in the enforcement of unpopular political, social and religious policies. Parliament was very willing to sweep away a court which, in a few short years, had gained a reputation as an instrument of royal tyranny.

The regional councils
The policies of the central government were enforced by the two regional councils, the Council of the Marches of Wales and the Council of the North. Though both these councils had a very wide range of both administrative duties and judicial powers, they did not have any independent role in policy-making. Their function was simply to provide closer administration and supervision of the county authorities in parts of the country which were both far from Westminster and regarded as turbulent.

The Council of Wales was originally an important administrative body responsible for the regulation of almost every aspect of life within Wales and the marches , but it had assumed a primarily judicial role in the seventeenth century. The work of the Council was concentrated in the hands of professional courtiers and lawyers. Regional magnates had only an ornamental role. Its judicial powers included both civil and criminal Common Law cases as well as a wide Star Chamber jurisdiction. It was a very active court, hearing approximately 1200 cases per annum in the reign of Charles I. Of these, approximately two-thirds were civil cases and one-third criminal. To get through this volume of work in its short legal terms, the Council had to hear approximately twenty cases a day, a number which was probably too great for consistent justice to be done. Despite this reservation, it fulfilled a useful role in hearing civil suits. In its exercise of criminal jurisdiction, however, it was open to a great deal of criticism. It was charged with excessive willingness to convict, as the salaries of the judges were drawn from the proceeds of fines inflicted, and with allowing too much scope to common informers. It was said to be more interested in the collection of fees than in justice.

The greatest number of cases heard by the Council involved sexual offences—adultery, fornication and incest. The charges were usually brought by common informers, some of whom were accused of combing the records of the ecclesiastical courts, thus ensuring the double prosecution of those already convicted there. The second most important category for which offenders were fined was acts of violence—riot, affray, riotous assembly and forcible entry. Third, was contempt of court and fourth, fraud and forgery. Attempts were made to prevent abuse of power by county officials. As part of its Star Chamber jurisdiction, the Council imposed a fine of £100 on a J.P. who had wrongfully put a tailor in the stocks and had him whipped.

A study of the Council's records shows that some of the criticisms were unjustified. It has been discovered that the Council convicted only thirty per cent of those brought before it, and that it awarded costs to seventy per cent of those acquitted, something which shows it did not encourage informers and malicious prosecutions in order to increase its fees. It also imposed moderate fines and often reduced them. On the other hand, there is ample evidence that the Council depended on the fines and costs involved in sexual offences to pay its way. It is quite clear that court procedure was designed to maximise the income of its officials, the number of whom increased rapidly during the early seventeenth century.

Partly because of the abuses outlined above, the Council became increasingly unpopular and a number of attempts were made to curtail its powers and remove the English shires from its jurisdiction. The local gentry of the four shires campaigned for exemption from its authority for two main reasons: it was regarded as parasitic and, more importantly, it represented a measure of centralisation of authority which was resented by them. In the Long Parliament it was attacked as part of the campaign against Star Chamber. Its demoralised members could not put up a strong defence and Parliament took away its criminal jurisdiction and exempted the four shires. Its remaining civil jurisdiction fell into disuse and it was very surprising that this aspect of the once mighty Council was restored in 1660. The Council of Wales was abolished, finally, in 1689 (Elton, 1960, pages 195–213; Kenyon, 1969, pages 192–224).

The Council of the North

Unfortunately, there is much less detailed information about the cases heard in the Council of the North. No worthwhile comparison can be made of the way in which the two councils exercised their judicial functions. Under Sir Thomas Wentworth's presidency, the Council aroused great resentment in the North. There was an acute dislike of any institution which curtailed local autonomy. Secondly, the Council was required to enforce the unpopular and unparliamentary taxes of the Personal Rule. Moreover, Wentworth was a Yorkshireman who abused his position in factional squabbles. The antagonism this aroused was so great that the authority of the Council could be preserved only by the imposition of heavy penalties on several leading Yorkshire landowners.

In the late 1630s the common lawyers grew to resent the Council as a competitor with the Common Law courts and they attacked it in the same way that they attacked the other conciliar courts. Nevertheless, the Council was not dissolved by the Long Parliament: it simply fell into disuse at the outbreak of the Civil War and it was never revived (Smith, 1972, page 47).

The judges and local government

It was as assize judges that members of the judiciary made a regular and significant impact on provincial England. The assizes were the most important events in the provincial calendar. In the first place, they had great social importance as occasions when the gentry and freeholders of the county met each other and the judges. Their significance is shown by the prominence given to an announcement of impending assizes in contemporary newspapers. The way in which the lesser gentry and wealthier farmers joined with their social superiors to make administrative decisions made the assizes, like quarter sessions, remarkably democratic assemblies.

Secondly, they had a very real political importance. The justices of assize were very important links between central and local government. According to Lord Keeper Francis Bacon's Star Chamber address in 1617, the judges were not only administrators of justice, but also men who:

carry the two glasses or mirrors of the State. For it is your duty in these your visitations to represent to the people the graces and care of the king; and again, upon your return, to present to the king the distastes and griefs of the people.

Judges acted as legal advisers to the J.P.s and supervised their administrative duties. J.P.s often passed the responsibility for a difficult administrative decision to the judges, and they were occasionally fined by the judges for errors committed in their official duties.

The structure of county government

Within the county, government was in the hands of a triarchy of officials: the Lord Lieutenant (and his deputies), the sheriff and the Justices of the Peace. Of all the offices in the county, that of the Lord Lieutenant was the most prestigious. Owing to the high social status and national preoccupations of most of the Lords Lieutenant, much of their work had to be delegated. The office of Deputy Lieutenant was first created in 1559 and most counties had deputies by 1569. Six per county was usual during the reign of Charles I. The Deputy Lieutenants were an élite within the broader élite of the magisterial class. For example, in early Stuart Cheshire all the Deputy Lieutenants, but only a third of the J.P.s, were drawn from the twenty to twenty-five families which constituted the core group of the county governors. Under the early Stuarts, Worcestershire Deputy Lieutenants had an average annual income of £1121 compared with £795 for J.P.s, and all were men of high social rank and ancient family.

Justices of the Peace were by far the largest group in the triarchy. As G.M. Trevelyan said, they were the 'most influential class of men in England', or in the words of a contemporary writer, Sir Thomas Smith, 'Justices of the peace are those in whom . . . the Prince putteth especial trust' (G.M. Trevelyan, *English Social History*, London, 1941, page 171; Sir Thomas Smith, *De Republica Anglorum*, 1583). They were appointed by a Commission issued for each of the counties, for each of the three Ridings (administrative divisions) of Yorkshire, and for those corporate towns whose charter entitled them to their own magistrates. The Commission was issued by the Lord Chancellor, who acted on the advice of the presidents of the Councils of the North and of Wales, the judges of assize, the bishops, the Lords Lieutenants and the local magnates (for details of the Commission, see pages 147–8).

The Justices of the Peace constituted a social as well as an administrative élite: in every county they were men of high standing. Though a few were merchants, lawyers or clergymen, the vast majority were drawn from among the landed gentry. Stuart J.P.s were also nearly always men of wealth, although there was a considerable variation from county to county. During the reign of Charles I, the mean income of Worcestershire esquires was £325 a year, compared with nearly £650 for county magistrates. By and large, J.P.s were more likely to be members of families long settled in their county, rather than newcomers. Their standard of education, or at least the proportion of them which had been to university or an Inn of Court, was higher than that for the gentry as a whole and it rose steadily until 1642. In 1562 only forty-nine of the 143 gentlemen who made up the working part of the six jurisdictions studied by Gleason had been enrolled at either a university or an Inn of Court (J. Gleason *The Justices of the Peace in England, 1558–1640*, Oxford, 1969). In 1584 it was 110 of 246, in 1608 it was 220 of 311, in 1626 it was 207 of 265, in 1636 it was 224 of 266. Of the 114 men who served on the working part of the Worcestershire Commission between 1603 and 1641, forty-eight per cent had been to a university, forty-six per cent had studied at one of the Inns of Court and twenty-six per cent had been educated at both. The heads of about half the gentry families in Worcestershire in the 1630s had gained some form of higher education. It is clear, then, that the Justices of the Peace constituted an economic, social and educational élite in each county.

The sheriff had once been the principal officer of the King in every county, but by the time of Elizabeth he had lost his medieval pre-eminence (see page 146). Though the office was regarded as something of a burden to be inflicted on the heads of families newly established in a county, there is no doubt that magnates of the first rank continued to be appointed. Nearly all sheriffs were J.P.s at the time of their appointment.

The functions of the county governors
The Deputy Lieutenants, the Justices of the Peace and the sheriff all had their defined role to play in county administration. Though their activities frequently overlapped, it is appropriate to examine the special responsibilities of each.

The Deputy Lieutenant
The tasks of the Deputy Lieutenancy can be divided into three: organising the county militia, co-operating in the levying of men for service in expeditionary forces, and taking special responsibility for duties appertaining to all J.P.s Throughout the whole period 1558–1640, a time of international tension and numerous wars, England's main land defence against invasion was a force of amateur soldiers. During the Civil War and Interregnum the large regular forces in existence reduced the importance of the militia, but it was never negligible and played an important part in the defeat of the Scottish invasion of 1651. For most of Charles II's reign, it was once more the main bastion of home defence, though under both James II and William III it was overshadowed by the regular army. During the period in which the militia constituted England's main land force, England was faced by

enemies and potential enemies whose armies were professionals, armed with the latest weapons, trained and experienced in the most modern techniques. In England, attempts to meet the challenge of these veterans were beset by problems of unwillingness, lack of serious purpose, inadequate finance, an uncertain legal situation and, above all else, by the dependence of central government on county gentry to enforce policies for which neither they nor their neighbours felt any enthusiasm. The concentration of political power in the hands of the class of men who had to pay for the militia provided a serious obstacle to improved efficiency.

Indeed, the problems of military organisation reflected the difficult relationship between central and local government. Policies seen as essential by the central government were often unrealistic and frequently foundered in a mire of localism and parsimony. Yet to say this and no more is to paint an unjustifiable picture of gloom. Despite all obstacles, much was achieved. The Elizabethan trained bands constituted a formidable obstacle to Spanish conquest in the 1580s and 90s; those of Charles I may not have been a 'perfect militia', but it was the struggle between King and Parliament for control over them which sparked off the Civil War.

The trained bands, or militia, were a product of the greater professionalism of soldiers in the sixteenth century and the ever-increasing cost and complexity of their weapons. The ancestors of the Tudor and Stuart local defence forces were the Anglo-Saxon *fyrd* and the medieval *posse comitatus*, both consisting of all able-bodied men between sixteen and sixty, the longest draft liability in history. An Act passed in 1558, immediately before the accession of Elizabeth, provided a statutory basis for the military obligations of her reign. It was, however, repealed in 1604, leaving Common Law and prerogative as the bases of military obligations until the Interregnum.

By the mid-sixteenth century most military experts agreed that it was better to arm a proportion of each county's manpower with the latest equipment and train them in its use than to expect the *posse comitatus* to turn out with 'country weapons' and fight 'pell mell'. In this idea lay the origins of the militia or trained bands. The most important obligation of those commanding the county forces was to select men for service, ensure that they had adequate arms and train them in their use. Except in an emergency, these troops were to be retained for local defence. Members of the trained bands were exempt from conscription into expeditionary forces. Ideally, trained bandsmen were young, fit and well-off enough financially to buy their own weapons. These relatively wealthy men, it was thought, would be politically reliable if called out against rebels or rioters. The trained bands of each county consisted of infantry, pioneers and the 'horse'. The first were a mixture of 'shot' and pikemen until the late seventeenth century, when the bayonet was adopted. Under Elizabeth, indeed until the 1620s, the 'shot' included archers as well as those carrying firearms. The pioneers were the men responsible for trench digging, road repair and other low-status activities. The 'horse', made up almost entirely of gentlemen, had the greatest prestige, but reports to the Privy Council indicate that it was the hardest to discipline.

Training consisted of an annual muster for all county forces, usually held in early summer between seed-time and harvest, and a series of training days held by the local companies. The effectiveness of the training varied from time to time and place to place. There can be little doubt that the militia reached its peak of efficiency at the time of the Spanish Armada. Its readiness declined during the 1590s and then slumped completely during the first ten years of James I's reign. Attempts to revive an effective militia during the rest of his reign achieved only limited success. Charles I set himself a very difficult task when he established the objective of a 'Perfect Militia'.

The success of Charles I's programme of military reform is a matter for considerable controversy among historians. In his study of Somerset, Barnes paints a gloomy picture of incompetent amateurs, reluctantly playing soldiers with obsolete weapons, under the command of faction-ridden and inept officers as a preliminary to feasting and drinking, once the perfunctory military exercises were completed (T.G. Barnes, *Somerset 1625–1640: A County's Government During the 'Personal Rule'*, Harvard, 1961, pages 98–123, 244–280). Barnes's interpretation is probably too harsh if applied to England as a whole. Historians such as Boynton and Fletcher have studied other parts of England and have arrived at more favourable conclusions. Fletcher considers Charles's plans too ambitious, but he concedes that there were significant improvements in the Sussex trained bands (A. Fletcher, *A County Community in Peace and War: Sussex 1600–1660*, London, 1975, pages 201–2). The most comprehensive general work on the trained bands is, Boynton's *Elizabethan Militia, 1558–1638* (Newton Abbot, 1967). Boynton's interpretation of the efficiency of the trained bands is much more favourable than that of Barnes or Fletcher, possibly because he has made considerable use of documents relating to Hampshire, a county regarded as particularly liable to invasion owing to the attraction of the Isle of Wight and its sheltered anchorages.

The failure of the English forces to defeat the Scots in the two 'bishops' wars' in 1639 and 1640 is often seen as proof that training had been a farce, an exercise in drinking rather than drill. This would be an unfair conclusion. The war in the north was unpopular: many Englishmen regarded the Scots not as enemy invaders, but as allies against hated religious and governmental innovations. In any case, Charles allowed members of the trained bands to send substitutes. As a result, trained men were a minority in the King's army. As Gilbert Burnet wrote in 1677, allowing substitutes meant that 'of the 5000 there were not 200 that could fire a Musket . . . not so much as the Serjeants and Corporals were trained'.

In the Civil War it was trained band weapons and, to some extent, trained band members which provided the nucleus of the field armies. Some militia units served intact, the most spectacular example being the London trained bands, which prevented an early and royalist end to the Civil War by stopping the King's army at Turnham Green. There can be no doubt that the English militia of the 1630s was far from 'exact' or 'perfect'. In attempting to make rapid and drastic improvements, the King had revealed the limits of his power. Nevertheless, the trained bands constituted a worthwhile military force and one which had been improved as a result of his efforts.

The main factor limiting the willingness of the county gentry to conform to Charles's plans for military reform was expense. In 1612 it cost £3.4s.5d to equip a light horseman, £4.7s.4d for a lancer, and about £1.9s.8d for a pikeman. These were substantial sums for almost anyone below the rank of gentleman and it is not surprising that the muster master (a professional soldier associated with the trained bands) was unable to recruit enough young men who could afford to buy their own weapons. In addition to the capital cost of providing arms, there were the regular expenses of maintenance, wages, food and accommodation for soldiers in training, the cost of powder and shot, the provision of so-called 'maimed soldiers' pensions and the salary for the muster master.

Funds to meet these charges were raised by the Deputy Lieutenants who imposed taxes based on the subsidy assessment. It was charged that military taxes were a heavier burden on a county than any other taxes, that they were as expensive as several subsidies. A study of a single county suggests that military rates constituted two-thirds of regular taxation in the period 1629–1642. However, these direct military rates paid to the county were only part of the total cost. Expenses met at the parish level were approximately four times as high. Total public expenses on the Worcestershire trained bands were equal to approximately one-third of the 1635 ship money demand or about the same as a single subsidy. This does not, however, take into account the expenses faced by more prosperous inhabitants who had to buy and maintain arms. Complaints about expenditure on the trained bands were not dramatically exaggerated.

A further military cost was that of providing coat and conduct money for men enlisted in expeditionary forces. Providing uniforms cost about £1 per man in 1640 and each county had to pay its levies at a rate of 8d per day per man from the time of enlistment until they embarked. Billeting was another expense met by counties. All these sums were repayable by the Exchequer, but this took a considerable time.

One important duty of the Deputy Lieutenants was to raise troops for expeditionary forces. During the reign of Elizabeth, soldiers were sent in large numbers to Ireland as well as to the Netherlands, France and Spain. In all, over 106 000 men were sent abroad; as many as 12 600 in the single year, 1601. During the mid-1620s, 12 000 troops were raised for Count Mansfeld's expedition to the Palatinate (1624), 10 000 for Charles I's attack on Cadiz in 1625, an initial 6000 for the defence of Rhé two years later. Between 1585 and 1602, Elizabeth levied approximately 5000 men a year. Between the years 1624 and 1627 the annual average was twice as high.

Men could not be raised on the scale required in the late Elizabethan period or in the 1620s without recourse to impressment. When the Deputy Lieutenants received an impressment order, they divided the county total among the various parishes in proportion to population and ordered the constables to produce the number for which the parish was responsible. Writers are virtually unanimous in condemning the quality of pressed men. Sir Jacob Astley stated that the conscripts he was to command in the Second Bishops' War were 'all the arch-knaves of this Kingdom'.

The reason for the generally low quality of conscripts is fully discussed by Stearns. In the first place, the general attitude was that the best young men should not be sent abroad to be slaughtered or die of disease. The attitude of the Council was ambivalent: though frequently ordering that men should be 'able and fit for service', the way in which its members shared contemporary attitudes is summed up by the instruction that Deputy Lieutenants press 'unnecessarye persons that want not employment and live lewdly or unprofitably'. The second reason is influence and corruption. The strong young men desired by the army officers were often the sons or servants of men of substance in the village community, people the constable could ill afford to offend. Many would have enlisted into the trained bands in order to avoid professional service. Where influence was not strong enough to avoid the draft, bribery was often employed. Constables, conductors, officers and even the Deputy Lieutenents themselves were regularly charged with corruption, apparently with justification. In 1597 the Worcestershire town of Bewdley used public money to buy the release of its citizens from military service.

It is apparent that military administration depended far more on directives from the Council than did any other aspect of county government. Except in times of conspicuous emergency, it was unpopular. The history of military administration is a catalogue of conciliar demands for improved efficiency, better arms and more men being met by complaints that neither money nor manpower was available. It was rare, however, for grumbles about military service to become full-blown political and constitutional grievances. Virtually the only time this happened on a large scale was in 1628 when compulsory billeting and the imposition of martial law on civilians were condemned by the Petition of Right.

In general, there was little open opposition to military taxation or impressment. Despite grumbles, unwillingness never reached anything resembling ship money proportions. There is no certain explanation for this, but there are a number of possible reasons. In the first place, it was the Deputy Lieutenants, the most senior gentlemen in the county, who fixed and administered military taxes. Secondly, money spent on the trained bands resulted in improved weaponry, increased numbers and more training: the results were apparent in the locality. Ship money may have improved the fleet, but the fleet was far away. Thirdly, there was no doubt about the Common Law obligation to defend the realm or the King's prerogative to organise that defence. It may be significant that it was the relatively new position of muster master which aroused the greatest antagonism. The precedent for his existence was not of long enough duration for his payment to be regarded as warranted when ordered by the force of prerogative alone.

During the Civil War, trained band weapons were taken over by the field armies in most provincial areas. Some units served with the field armies, though the only ones to do this on a large scale were the London trained bands who served with the parliamentarian army which halted the King at Turnham Green and remained a formidable force throughout the Civil War. Between 1646 and 1649, the rival factions in Parliament struggled to gain control of the militia and the professional army was determined to ensure that it did not fall into the hands of hostile commanders. In the Interregnum the local militias were re-established and, as mentioned above, they played a useful role during the Scottish invasion of 1651. Forces from the militia were active in the battle of Worcester. The country gentry naturally stressed the advantages of a militia against those of a standing army during these years, but it is obvious that the amateur forces were totally overshadowed by Cromwell's professionals until after the Restoration.

In 1661 the Militia Act restored full control of all the armed forces to the Crown and re-established the militia on something like its pre-Civil War footing. Once more the Deputy Lieutenants were to impose rates to pay for local forces and conduct an annual muster of four days as well as four training musters lasting not more than two days. Under Charles II these forces were England's main defence against both rebellion and foreign enemies. (Charles II also had a small and dubiously legal standing army, never more than 7000 strong, much of which was abroad.) In 1661–2 part of the militia was mustered and placed within walled towns, as the Government feared a rising by dissenters and republicans. In the Dutch wars the militia was regularly called out to repair forts, to dig trenches and to patrol the coasts. In 1666 militia forces were concentrated at Maidenhead, St Albans and Northampton to meet the anticipated Dutch invasion.

Throughout the 1670s and early 1680s the role of the militia was largely political. It was called out to 'maintain order' at elections, something which gave the candidates favoured by the Government a considerable advantage. During these years, the Lord Lieutenant was the principal agent of the government in each county and he appointed officers and exercised police duties in a highly political manner. The militia was to become an instrument in the conflict between Whig and Tory.

The only significant military engagement in which post-Restoration militiamen were engaged was the battle of Sedgemoor in 1685. Despite the way in which their officers had been selected on the basis of their Tory credentials, the rank and file showed strong sympathies for Monmouth and were such reluctant fighters against him that it was feared some would go over to the other side. It was the regular regiment returned from garrison duty in Tangier which did the effective fighting. Partly as a result of this experience, James II concentrated on building up the regular forces.

Under William III the militia continued as a significant force for home defence, but it was naturally overshadowed by the very large regular forces raised in the Nine Years War. Perhaps it can be seen as yet one more example of the way in which the English State expanded and modernised its functions after the Revolution that the local forces gave way to mass armies raised by central government as the main defenders of the realm.

The Justice of the Peace

The most important officials in counties were the Justices of the Peace. They possessed an enormous range of administrative, police and judicial powers. Indeed it may be said that the J.P.s were concerned with every aspect of local government. It was on their co-operation and efficiency that successful administration of each county depended and, finally, the successful management of England. (For a detailed study of their functions, see pages 147–52.)

The sheriff

The sheriff had judicial, police, military, revenue collecting and political responsibilities. In most of these areas, however, many of the powers he had once held were shared with other officers by the mid-sixteenth century or had been transferred to them absolutely (see page 146). By then, he had a far more important role as the administrator for other courts than as an independent judicial officer. After each court session, he supervised the hangings, whippings and brandings which had been ordered and levied fines. One expensive and some-times dangerous responsibility was the transfer of prisoners to West-minster or other counties. In 1609 the sheriff of Worcester had to hire four guards to conduct a notorious horse stealer from London to Worcester. His task was probably not as difficult as that of the sheriff in 1640 who claimed from the government the cost of conveying Richard Tack 'being a notorious theife who had the name to blowe open any lock and comitted twelve burglaries and broake three prysons in vii weekes space from Sturbridg where the Sheriffe of Staff[ordshire] delivered him to the Gaole of Wigorn [Worcester] to receive his trial'.

Sheriff's records also reveal the labour and cost of executions. In 1608 the removal of the assizes to Kidderminster required the purchase of 'Timber to erect the gallows, there being none before, xxs, carriage & erection 26/8d.' In 1640 the disorderly behaviour of soldiers drafted to fight in the Scottish war is revealed by the claim for 'timber to make a newe tree for execucon the souldyers having cutt downe the old one and burned the same 27/-'.

Executions more gruesome than ordinary hanging were carried out from time to time. In 1619 the sheriff of Worcester's accounts include the costs:

for burninge Mary Perkins the wyfe of Thomas Perkins convicted for poyson-inge hir former husband for faggots xviiis for pitch and gunpowder vis for makinge the poste lynkes of Iron and staples vis viiid for Strawe iiis for six men's wages that made and attended the fier xvis.

In 1632 the cost is recorded of 'pressing to deathe one Turner a prisoner who refused his legall tryall', but probably the most grue-some type of execution which the sheriff was ever called upon to organise was a hanging, drawing and quartering for treason. Several prisoners implicated in the Gunpowder Plot were executed in this way early in 1606. Among the other details recorded in the sheriff's accounts is the cost of four shillings and eight pence 'for faggotts to burne their Bowells' and one pound seven shillings for 'carryinge of the quarters of the prysoners executed to the sev[er]all markett Townes and settinge them upp as was appointed by the Comissioners'. The executioner was paid two pounds.

Among the most burdensome duties of the sheriff was collection of the traditional royal revenues, such as the rent on Crown lands, debts owed to the King and legal fines. Revenue collection did not give the sheriff power or prestige. It was a burdensome task which had to be performed by deputies, who were often unreliable and who could leave the sheriff personally liable for their incompetence or dishonesty.

One of the most important powers of the medieval sheriff had been control over the military forces. It was he and he alone who had the power to call out the *posse comitatus*. The creation of the lieutenancy and the trained bands took away much of the sheriff's military authority. It did not, however, lapse completely. In 1605 the small-scale Catholic rising in the Midlands which was associated with the Gunpowder Plot led to the mustering of the Worcestershire *posse comitatus*. Forces acting in the sheriff's name pursued the rebels across the county border and overwhelmed them at Holbeche House in Staffordshire. This was probably the last time the sheriff assumed primary responsibility for suppressing a rebellion, a situation that may have resulted from the neglect of the trained bands at the beginning of James I's reign. The Norfolk riot of 1607, the Wiltshire agricultural disturbances of 1631 and the 1632 anti-enclosure riots in Worcestershire were all regarded as the responsibility of the Deputy Lieutenants and the trained bands.

If the power of the sheriff had been reduced in many respects, there was still one area in which he retained full responsibility. He was the officer responsible for conducting county elections to Parliament. This was one task which he always performed in person. The normal method of voting was by acclamation, with the electors shouting the name of the preferred candidate until the sheriff, assisted by at least two officials, decided which two candidates had the greatest support. Should he be unable to decide, he normally 'divided' the electors, instructing them to form groups for easy counting. Failing a decision from a division, the sheriff was to adopt the time-consuming method of polling the voters by summoning each to declare his vote individually. It is obvious that this method offered the sheriff many opportunities for favouring his friends. Voting by acclamation or even by division made possible a wrongful declaration. Sheriffs convicted of malpractice could be fined £100, but as the election result could not be reversed, this was little deterrent to a wealthy man whose fine, in any case, might be paid by those he had favoured. The responsibility for conducting elections left the sheriff with very real power.

The sheriff was thus still an important figure in county government. His authority was shared with the J.P.s and Deputy Lieutenants and restricted by imperfect control of his subordinates, but he still had power to enforce his own wishes and thwart those of others. Though less powerful than the collective authority of J.P.s and the Deputy Lieutenants, he had more influence than any one of them. He remained the principal individual officer in the shire.

Other county officials

As well as the county magnates of the triarchy, the wealthy farmers of the grand jury and husbandmen who held parochial office, there was an important middle-class element in county government. Officials falling into this category relied on office-holding for a livelihood. The professional officers who held the greatest power and prestige were the coroners, escheators and feodaries. Coroners had been appointed for the first time in the Middle Ages to limit the power of the sheriff, but they had become less important as J.P.s took over more and more of their duties. In the sixteenth and seventeenth centuries their main function was the holding of inquisitions into the causes of sudden deaths. Their findings had considerable importance as they could result in murder charges being laid; their verdict that a deceased was a suicide would result in the forfeiture to the Crown of all his possessions except land and any instrument found to have caused death was seized as a 'deodand' (an object forfeit to the Crown as the cause of death of a person). Feodaries and escheators were crown revenue officers who played only a minor and specialised role in the county.

Local government after the Restoration

The working of local government after the Restoration revealed the continuation of trends apparent before the Civil War. The amount of administrative business carried out at quarter sessions increased tremendously in the half-century after 1660. Clark claims that it doubled in Kent between 1660 and 1720. Certainly Kent resorted to eight meetings of quarter sessions rather than the customary four implied in the name and, like the rest of England, made an ever increasing use of petty sessions in which the J.P.s made administrative decisions and heard minor cases. The Restoration was to see one diminution of the powers of J.P.s: capital offences were increasingly left to the discretion of the judges at assizes.

The basic machinery of county government, however, operated in much the same way as it had before the Civil War and the problems of county government showed no dramatic change. There was an increase in poverty which resulted in the displacement of villagers into the industrial areas. The response of the class-conscious magnates who dominated the House of Commons was repressive legislation, such as the 1662 Act of Settlement, which made it possible for any landless person to be sent back to the parish of his birth, even if he was settled in another parish and had work there. On the other hand, the problem of endemic poverty produced an acceptance of the need for regular poor rates in virtually every part of the country.

The machinery of local government, both at county and parish level, showed increasing rationalisation and professionalism. Though the process was not complete until well into the eighteenth century, there was an increased use by the counties of salaried experts, such as the County Treasurer, Master of the House of Correction, surveyors of bridges and highways. (For changes in Poor Law administration, see chapter 1, pages 79–80.)

Conflict and co-operation

The government of provincial England required the co-operation of all classes: lazy or defiant officials could be dismissed or punished. However, general inertia imposed limits on the extent to which the will of the Privy Council could be exercised in the provinces. Widespread opposition could make the implementation of policy virtually impossible. The issue of the Book of Orders showed that the Council could impose somewhat higher standards of administrative efficiency in matters which were largely non-controversial. In contrast, the attempt to convert ship money into a regular national tax revealed the limitations imposed by the opposition of those who exercised political and administrative power at the local level.

The Book of Orders

The issue of the Book of Orders was a response to the combination of harvest failure and recession in the cloth industry which produced widespread suffering, notable for its severity even in the economically unstable years of 1629–42. The particular steps taken to meet the problems were influenced by the vigour and determination of Charles I and the genuine concern for the poor felt by Archbishop Laud. In January 1631, a copy of the Book of Orders was issued to each county and corporate town in England. The Orders instructed the J.P.s to check the performances of high constables, petty constables, churchwardens and overseers of the poor. The J.P.s were to send a certificate of their actions to the sheriff who was to give it to the judge of assize.

The directions, which laid out in detail the matters which were to receive attention, stressed most aspects of the J.P.'s administrative duties. They were to supervise the provision of work to prevent vagrancy, the keeping of Courts Leet (manorial courts dealing with breaches of local custom), the apprenticing of youths, the enforcement of the Statute of Artificers, the payment of weekly poor relief by individual parishes or groups of parishes, the selection of constables, the keeping of watch and ward (police patrols at night), the punishment of tipplers, the building of Houses of Correction adjoining the common gaols, the enforcement of laws prohibiting rogues from sleeping in barns or outhouses, and the repair of the highways.

The short-term effect of the Book of Orders was marked. Justices were startled into renewed efforts. Certificates were forwarded as instructed. There is ample evidence to show the rapid erection of Houses of Correction, the vigorous enforcement of the vagrancy laws and renewed efforts to repair roads and bridges. Though no mention of the criminal law was made in the book, there is some evidence of greater harshness. In Worcestershire, bail seems to have been granted less freely and in Essex there was a marked rise in the number of capital sentences passed. As time went on, however, the administrative machinery showed a slackening of enthusiasm and efficiency.

The extent to which the initial improvements in administration were maintained is uncertain. There appear to have been variations from county to county. In Somerset and Worcestershire, the administrative innovations of 1631 appear to have become standard procedures by the end of the decade. In Kent and Sussex, they were probably less lasting. It is significant, however, that there was no open opposition to the Book of Orders. It did not cut across the interests of the county magnates who were, in any case, well aware of the gravity of the crisis faced in 1631. To enforce the Book of Orders was well within the powers of the government.

Ship money
The Book of Orders was at least a relative success, as its provisions reflected the common interests of the Council and the provincial élites. However, the Council's next venture, ship money, brought conflict between the desires of the central government and the magisterial class. Precedents before 1634 showed quite clearly that the Crown had the power to demand either ships, or money to hire ships, and men from

the maritime areas. However, these demands had always been of short duration and at a time when there was an emergency recognised by all. Despite this, ship levies and ship money demands had been unpopular and there had been little, if any, success, in extending liability to inland areas. In consequence, there can be little surprise that Charles's ambitious scheme to improve the permanent fleet by the use of his prerogative should have been opposed.

The first ship money writ was issued in 1634. It was justified by reference to the Continental war and the coastal raids by Moslem pirates, and was therefore imposed only on maritime counties. The amount was small, less than a quarter of that demanded in any of the later writs except 1638 and there was no suggestion of permanence. There were no more grumbles than attended the collection of any tax and the money was paid.

In 1635 a new ship money writ made it clear that Charles had in mind a method of financing the fleet which was permanent, more expensive to the taxpayer, radical in its methods of collection and imposed by a novel exercise of prerogative. When it became apparent that ship money was intended to be a permanent tax, opposition became stronger with the issue of each writ. Despite this, it was not at first apparent that ship money was a failure. Opposition varied from one part of the country to another and was probably strongest in Somerset, where there was significant dissent from 1635. As a purely revenue-raising measure, ship money displayed considerable success until 1639.

The failure of ship money was not, until the end, financial. It was political. Opposition passed through three stages. In 1635 and 1636, attempts to circumvent the payment of ship money rarely involved open refusal. Apparently reasonable queries and objections in detail caused the hapless sheriffs a great deal of work and delayed the collection of money. Hundreds complained that their assessments were unfair in relation to those of other hundreds. Corporate towns complained that their rating was excessive in comparison with that of the surrounding countryside, and county officials argued that the towns should pay a greater share. Tenants tried to place the burden on landlords and landlords on tenants. Many of the objections were undoubtedly motivated merely by the desire to pay less tax, rather than by any objections to the principle of ship money. In the end most of the money demanded in the 1636 writ was paid.

In 1637, the year of Hampden's Case, there was widespread refusal to pay. Opposition grew in 1638. In 1639 it reached its final stage. Attempts to distrain (seize by a legal warrant known as a distress) goods to meet unpaid assessments were met with law suits against sheriffs' officers when they took the property of gentlemen, and by actual physical violence when they acted against the goods of ordinary farmers. Resistance became so intense that constables and sheriffs' officers were preferring imprisonment to continued collection of the tax. By 1639 refusal to pay was widespread and found in all classes, appearing earlier and more forcefully among the farmers and townsmen than among the gentry. Ship money brought many men within the scope of a national tax for the first time and it probably hit them more heavily than it did the gentry. By 1639, however, they were joined in opposition by the magnates of most counties. Little ship money was collected in 1640.

There can be little doubt that ship money would have aroused considerable resentment even if it had been voted by Parliament, but the fact that it was imposed by prerogative alone gave reluctant payers a constitutional as well as a financial objection. The political consequence of ship money was to turn the county leaders against a device which was causing so much disharmony. It inclined many of them to accept that ship money was part of a conspiracy to create a Continental-style absolute monarchy. The influence of this belief was apparent in the elections to both the Short and Long Parliaments in 1640.

Local communities and the approach of war

By 1640 the King had lost control of local government. He could no longer collect ship money, he could not raise a loyal and efficient force to fight the Scots, his religious policies were arousing widespread opposition and the City of London would not lend him money. Given this combination of circumstances, and lacking the means to impose his will by force, Charles I had no choice but to summon Parliament. In the two elections of 1640, opponents of royal policies won an overwhelming majority. A very important reason for these election results was to be found in the way Charles had offended the local communities.

With the backing of provincial England, the first session of the Long Parliament set about reversing the novel elements of the personal rule. They swept away the whole structure of conciliar government. Without the Star Chamber and with only the remnants of the regional councils, the central government would be unable to maintain close supervision over provincial England. It seemed that the uneasy balance between the capital and the counties had swung very strongly towards greater autonomy for the latter. Unfortunately for the locally minded country gentlemen, the Civil War was to cut across their vision of traditional ways unrestricted by dictates from Westminster. For the next twenty years, the determination of the country gentlemen to regain the situation they believed they had attained in 1640 was to stand in the way of any permanent settlement (Morrill, 1976, pages 14–31).

It is certainly incorrect to assume that the Court and Country parties corresponded to royalists and parliamentarians in the Civil War. As national events swept Parliament towards a constitutionally more aggressive role and the country towards Civil War, the provincial united front broke, and the local communities split. As Lucy Hutchinson, the wife and biographer of a parliamentarian army officer, said, 'every County had more or lesse the civill warre within itself'. In the past, historians have tended to assume that the conflict in local communities was one between two parties, royalist and parliamentarian. Local historians of the 1960s and 1970s have revised this picture to one of three parties, the third and largest being that of the localists who wished to avoid any part in the Civil War. As war approached, King and Parliament were recipients of numerous petitions desiring peace, reconciliation and the ancient constitution. The small number which made strong statements in favour of any of the parties at Westminster usually reflected the influence of agents sent from the capital.

Throughout the country, leaders took more concrete steps towards the preservation of peace with a series of neutrality pacts—attempts were made to maintain local neutrality in at least twenty-two counties and in many boroughs. Counties with particularly strong neutralist movements included Cheshire, Staffordshire, Shropshire, Lincolnshire, Yorkshire, Cornwall, Devon and Wiltshire. Some attempts at neutralism were made even in the supposed parliamentarian stronghold of East Anglia. Both Everitt and Morrill place great stress on neutralism as the normal response of the county community. However, they may have overstated their case. Everitt's major study is about Kent and Morrill's about Cheshire, both counties in which the gentry were particularly close social communities. In many counties of the West Midlands, the greater gentry did not form such a cohesive group and may have been more nationally minded. While neutralism was a powerful force in all parts of the country, it is quite clear that its strength varied from place to place. In this, as in everything else, the counties of England displayed their individuality.

Parliamentary local government
Once the Civil War had broken out, both sides had to establish a relationship between the central authority and the provincial communities and face the conflict between the localism of county leaders and the centralising demands of military necessity. On the outbreak of the

war, there was a need for men, for munitions, uniforms, food and horses, for vaster sums of money than anyone had imagined to pay the soldiers and buy their requirements, and to maintain security in the areas which they controlled.

In areas controlled by Parliament, a system of county committees was quickly established, but there was a very large amount of local variation in their organisation. The committees were responsible for virtually everything relating to the war. They raised funds and levied men for the field armies. They maintained local security by arresting the opponents of Parliament and recruiting local forces. They were responsible for meeting at least monthly to receive and disseminate ordinances from Parliament. In addition, they had oversight of the courts and the appointment of J.P.s. Probably the most important function of the county committees was the raising of funds, both for local needs and for Westminster.

The military responsibilities of the committees seem to have been carried out with reasonable efficiency. Local forces were raised and strongpoints garrisoned. There was little difficulty in filling local companies, but much more in recruiting for the field armies. By the middle of the war, conscription had been adopted in many areas. In counties where a parliamentary field army was present, there were obvious difficulties in the relationship between the military commander and the county committee, but in this respect there seems to have been a more satisfactory arrangement than there was in royalist areas.

The presence of a field army meant that accommodation had to be found for the soldiers and food for both them and their horses. It was nearly always necessary to resort to one of the most resented expedients of the Civil War: billeting and free quarter. Ready money to pay for accommodation was rarely available and those who had soldiers compulsorily intruded into their homes were paid only with vouchers. There were many complaints about theft and misconduct by billeted troops. Though the organised plundering for which royalist troops were noted was comparatively rare among the parliamentarian armies, it was a sufficiently serious problem for trial by martial law to be introduced for such offences in 1644 (Morrill, 1976, pages 86–8).

The overall success of the county committees depended very much on their composition and the stability of their membership. In the majority of counties, members were drawn mainly from the pre-war élite until the formation of the Commonwealth in 1649. During the Civil War, committees were generally able to operate with efficiency and without arousing undue resentment, at least among parliamentary sympathisers. The other critical factor in the effectiveness of the county committee was the role played by county M.P.s. In Sussex there was a core of M.P.s who shuttled backwards and forwards keeping open the lines of communication between Parliament and county committee. On the other hand, counties under parliamentarian control which had royalist or ineffective M.P.s were often resentful of committee rule.

In some counties the committees displayed a trend towards lower social status. At first they included men of pre-war magisterial rank supplemented by a comparatively small number of parish gentry. As time went on, many counties became dominated by a man who was not a pre-war magnate, assisted by a core of committee members who had not been of magisterial rank. Sir Anthony Weldon in Kent, Sir William Brereton in Cheshire and John Pyne in Somerset became the most hated men in their counties. They alienated the leading gentry and, as more and more of them refused to serve, the social status of the county committee fell. With the lowering of social status came an increased dependence on central government. They did not have the local connections, nor did they command sufficient deference, to rule by their own authority.

Paradoxically, those counties which were to rebel against Parliament in the second Civil War were those in which the county committees had been the most acquiescent in implementing its will. It was in these counties that the committees came to be dominated by social nonentities—parish gentry, yeoman, townsmen, with perhaps an occasional member of the magisterial class. On the other hand, counties with a stable county committee, led by men who had dominated pre-war society and government, tended to adapt the orders of Parliament to suit local conditions and accustomed ways. It was this second group of counties which remained loyal. Only where Parliament was able to obtain the support and loyalty of the traditional ruling class was its power secure.

It was quite obvious during the Civil War that the county was too small a unit to support a field army and that full centralisation was neither politically nor administratively desirable. As early as December 1642, a series of regional associations was formed, usually at the instigation of Parliament. Many of those suggested in 1642 and 1643 were geographically absurd and they disappeared before they became operational. By far the most important of the regional authorities was the Eastern Association. Its success has usually been explained by social unity and Puritanism in the area. These factors, it has been believed, broadened the social horizons of East Anglian gentlemen to the region, rather the county, and provided a religious dynamic to their co-operation. Clive Holmes has demonstrated that the traditional view of the Eastern Association must be modified. He found that the social structure of East Anglia was diverse. There were few social ties between the gentry of other than adjoining counties. The influence of Puritanism varied from one part of the region to another and localist feeling was just as strong as it was in other parts of the country. (Holmes, *The Eastern Association*, London, 1974, pages 1–2.)

The Eastern Association was successful because it possessed the essential feature which the other regional associations lacked—strong backing from Parliament and an administrative structure which provided the general of the Association with adequate funds and clear-cut authority over the constituent counties. The reason for this grant of power to the Eastern Association and its general, the Earl of Manchester, lay in the factional politics of Westminster. In 1643 both the middle group and the radicals in Parliament were highly dissatisfied with the performance of the Earl of Essex. They hoped to strengthen Manchester's army and, if possible, appoint him as Essex's replacement. The power granted to Manchester was widely resented by the East Anglian gentry, most of whom wanted the forces of the Association to be used for local defence rather than the national war effort. Nevertheless, they obeyed the central commands, something which reveals that there were limits to the localism of the gentry.

Through the county committees and the M.P.s acting as links between Westminster and the counties, Parliament was able to establish a reasonably effective method of governing the provinces. It was able to impose a much more arbitrary and centralised system than anything the King had ever dreamed of and it was able to raise taxation to unprecedented heights. Though the administrative efficiency of the committees varied from one part of the country to another, it was as high as that of any other body which had been charged with responsibilities in local government. Their great weakness was their dependence on the support of the greater gentry. Where the committees were dominated by men from outside this class, the result was resistance to parliamentary rule.

Royalist local government

The royalists were faced with many of the same problems as those which beset their enemies, but they did have other advantages and disadvantages. On the credit side, the royalists were headed by one accepted leader, the King; they could appeal to traditional loyalties, they were supported by the majority of the peerage, and they kept control of many of the established financial and administrative institutions. Chancery, Exchequer and the Court of Wards all moved from Westminster to Oxford with their civil servants and records. On the debit side, the King had lost control of the traditional political capital, Westminster, and the financial capital, the City of London, as well as the wealthier southern and eastern areas of the country.

There was also a further factor, one which was a considerable advantage in the short term, but which might have cost Charles the war in the end—he could call on his German nephews, Prince Rupert and Prince Maurice, men brought up in the holocaust of the Thirty Years War, to command his armies. The two princes and the experienced professional officers they brought with them were able to inject into the royalist armies at the outset of the war a practical and realistic spirit which they could never have obtained from recently commissioned and amateur country gentlemen. In the long run, the influence of the German professionals was disastrous. Their effect on loyalty in royalist counties can be compared to that of low-born county committeemen in parliamentarian counties. By their introduction of the brutal military codes of Continental warfare, by their contempt for civilian and constitutional authority, and by the way they ignored provincial sensitivities, these men lost the King so much support that it may have caused his defeat.

From 1642–6 the central organ of royalist war planning and administration was the Council of War. It consisted of some of the Privy Councillors and those senior military commanders who were in Oxford. The Council of War sent instructions to the royalist armies throughout the country and to the civilian authorities in the counties. It was not, however, an effective instrument which can be compared with the parliamentarian Committee of Both Kingdoms. Its power was weakened by the way in which the King made strategic decisions on the basis of private interviews, by factionalism and by the King's restriction on the area of its authority in the later stages of the Civil War. Failure to establish strong and centralised control contributed to the royalist defeat.

The other important body at the centre of royalist government was the Oxford Parliament. When war broke out, approximately half the Lords and a third of the Commons joined the King at Oxford. In 1644, ennobled generals reinforced the Lords and new M.P.s were elected to replace sitting members who had sided with the Westminster Parliament. It voted the King the excise, but it expressed the moderate constitutionalism of the country gentlemen rather than the cavalier attitudes of the professional soldiers. Little is known about the details of its work as its records were deliberately destroyed by its officers before Oxford fell to the parliamentarian general, Sir Thomas Fairfax, in 1646. The destruction of records by royalists, who feared that they would be incriminated if the documents fell into the hands of the victorious parliamentarians, means that there is far less evidence about royalist government during the Civil War than there is about the activities of its enemies.

In royalist-controlled counties, the pre-war machinery of government was maintained as far as possible. Assizes were held, at least in the early stages of the war, and quarter sessions became a very important part of county government. In some respects the Civil War enhanced their role. The assembled J.P.s, gentlemen and freeholders often acted as a local parliament, passing resolutions affecting the whole county in a way that was rare before the Civil War. It is, perhaps, not too fanciful to see the Committee of Safety (see below) as the county equivalent of the King's Council of War and quarter sessions as the county version of the Oxford Parliament. The Committee of Safety was the royalist equivalent of the county committee. It was created by extending the powers of the Commissioners of Array in 1643. The Commissioners had been appointed to take control of the militia and raise forces for the King at the outbreak of the war. The Worcestershire Committee of Safety was ordered to meet, consult garrison commanders about county defence, to levy rates for the support of the garrisons, to borrow money, plate, arms and ammunition. They were to meet in the city of Worcester and 'to take notes and Remembrances of your Councils and consultations in writing from time to time'. In Worcestershire, the Commissioners of Array and the members of the Committee of Safety numbered between twenty-three and twenty-seven and they were, for the most part, pre-war magistrates. Though the evidence is not as complete as it is for parliamentary county committees, there does not appear to have been any of the decline in social status which occurred during the war in many counties controlled by Parliament.

The minute book and the diary of Henry Townshend, one of the Commissioners of Array and a member of the Committee of Safety, show regular attendance at meetings, numbers present being about the same as the number of J.P.s who attended quarter sessions, and the conscientious exercise of duties. The Committee of Safety ordered the collection of assessments, settled rating disputes, enforced collection by sending a troop of horse to recalcitrant parishes, arrested those suspected as security risks and engaged in correspondence with Prince Rupert when they believed the county was threatened by a parliamentarian army. The Committee of Safety was also responsible for levying men for both local military service and for the field armies. There was little difficulty in filling the local units, but by 1645 men were being conscripted to the field armies.

As in the parliamentarian areas, the royalist committees were responsible for raising funds for local defence and for the central organisation. Royalist fund raising had many similarities with that of their enemies. It included loans, regular taxation on a weekly or monthly basis, sequestration and the excise. In royalist areas, loans appear to have been more important and more successful than were funds advanced to Parliament on the Propositions. One Worcestershire gentleman advanced £7000 to the King and the county as a whole lent more than £31 000 between December 1642 and May 1643.

The regular tax imposed in the royalist counties was known as the Contribution. The amount and method of collection was assented to either by the grand jury at quarter sessions or by a special meeting of gentlemen and freeholders. The amounts levied in royalist counties were high. Henry Townshend had paid only eight shillings in a single subsidy and £4 for ship money. He paid £2.15s.4d. monthly or £33.4s.0d. per annum towards the Contribution. This was not, however, a crippling amount by present-day standards of taxation as it amounted to only 16.6 per cent of his pre-war income. Nevertheless, the Contribution was difficult to collect in full. It was impossible to find the full amount in money, and contributions of produce were accepted in lieu of cash. Despite this, the Contribution payments were usually in arrears.

Sequestration (that is, seizure of revenue from the estates of opponents) was not, it seems, exploited as effectively in royalist as in parliamentarian counties. By October 1643, less than £500 had been raised from sequestration in Worcestershire and a little over half that in Gloucestershire and Warwickshire. As in parliamentarian counties, the excise was much resented and difficult to collect. Though there are no detailed figures known, it does not appear to have made a significant contribution to royalist finances.

Had the Contribution money been raised in full, there would have been ample funds to pay the county forces and still leave a surplus for other purposes. Money raised from all other sources could have been available for the support of the field armies. The maximum recorded Contribution was only two-thirds of the amount demanded and the pay of the troops rapidly fell into arrears. There were two consequences of this. The first was the taking of 'free quarter' (lodging) on the voucher system. Somerset people, at least, accepted that they had to tolerate free quarter 'soberly taken', but royalist troops gained an unsavoury reputation as disorderly, drunken, thieving and dangerous guests. The second consequence was collection of arrears by troops. It was the policy of the Council of War that parishes which failed to pay their Contribution should have a troop of horse quartered on them and it was the practice of the Worcestershire Committee, at least in early 1643, to charge double rates on those parishes which fell into arrears.

All this was bad enough for the countrymen. What was much worse was organised plunder. Plunder is not to be confused with looting by individual soldiers. It was organised by officers and it consisted of the seizure and destruction of goods in parishes which had not paid their Contribution, or had in any other way earned their displeasure. This was normal practice in Germany and many of the professional soldiers considered the methods which could be used legally to collect arrears overly squeamish. Prince Rupert himself gained the nickname 'Prince Robber, Duke of Plunderland' from the way he followed German practices. An example of a threat of plunder is that made by the notorious Colonel Bard, criticised by the royalist writer, Clarendon, as one who 'exercised an illimited tyranny over the whole country'.

Know you that unless you bring unto me . . . the monthly contribution for six months, you are to expect an unsanctified troop of horse among you, from whom if you hide yourselves they shall fire your houses without mercy, hang up your bodies wherever they find them, and scare your ghosts.

As the King seemed unable to make his senior commanders maintain discipline, there were various responses from the county community. Earlier in the war there had been much opposition to the trial by court martial of soldiers accused of Common Law offences, on the grounds that this would be a breach of personal liberty. As the problems of looting and plunder grew worse, the grounds for objecting to trials by military courts were that they did not result in the conviction of looters and plunderers. The Committee of Safety tried to force the trial of persons charged with these offences at quarter sessions. In Somerset some villages tried armed resistance to plundering, but after initial success, they were defeated when the plunder party called up reinforcements. In Wiltshire it was proposed that the county appoint a provost marshal and raise a troop of horse to protect the county against 'friendly troops'.

Perhaps the most sweeping response by the local communities to the problem of arbitrary military commands from the senior officers, plundering by local military officers and bad behaviour by individual soldiers was the creation of the West Midland Association of Worcestershire, Shropshire, Herefordshire and Monmouthshire at the beginning of 1645. It was quite explicit in attributing the need for such an association to the poor discipline of the royalist troops as well as to the threat posed by the enemy. The association offered to mobilise the *posse comitatus* and place it under local officers in return for exemption from free quarter, total control over the collection of the Contribution, the power to muster the royal garrisons they financed (in order to see that the officers had the number of men paid for), and the power to try any military offenders at Common Law. The Western Association was, therefore, quite different in its intention from the parliamentarian Eastern Association. Perhaps it was not very different from the type of association the gentlemen of the eastern counties would have created if they had been left to themselves. Royalist methods of local government were, at least in intention, more traditional and more scrupulous of the politically articulate classes than were those of their opponents. However, just as the arbitrary demands of the Committee of Both Kingdoms led to an alienation of the traditional county governors in many parliamentarian counties, the German code of military conduct followed by the professional soldiers led to mutual antagonism between them and the county magnates. Sir John Mennes expressed the professional soldiers' contempt for civilian authority when he wrote of his relationship with the Commissioners of Array in Staffordshire:

For my part I cann doe his Matie noe service heere at all being made useless by the insulting people whoe now tell us thire power & if 3 of the commissioners of aray may question the best of us, from wch power good lord deliver me & and rather send me home from Cunstable to Cunstable to the parish I was born in.

Certainly this was not the way the country gentlemen perceived the situation. Henry Townshend blamed the loss of the war on the alienation of the country by ill-disciplined soldiers and the seizure of civilian authority by the officers. He believed that the frustrations of the Worcestershire Committee of Safety at the loss of their powers led to lax attendance and all the work being left to five members in the latter stages of the war. The work of the committeemen had made royalist victory possible; the failure of the King to adhere to the moderate constitutionalism he claimed to uphold, and his inability to impose discipline on the army, had cost him local support and, eventually, the war.

If the response of the gentry was to withdraw from any participation in county government or to form regional associations strong enough to protect local interests, that of the lower ranks of the 'country' was to be found in the armed neutrality of the clubmen. The clubman movement began in the West Midlands in early 1645 and quickly spread throughout the royalist areas of south-western England and Wales. The clubman associations all claimed large membership, that of Wiltshire and Dorset informing both sides that it could raise 20 000 men. What the clubmen had in common is that they were members of a peasant movement which owed nothing in its origins to the leadership of the gentry. In this it was as radical as the Levellers. The movement sprang from a reaction by the lower ranks of the 'country' against the abuses of wartime rule, and their desire for peace. It is significant that in royalist-dominated areas the specific grievance which was most commonly expressed was once more misconduct by soldiers '. . . threatening to fire our houses, endeavouring to ravish our wives and daughters, and menacing our persons.'

In the end the club movement, though not the club sentiments, were swept away by force in any areas where they attempted to use their numbers to stand in the way of the army which dominated their locality. Poorly armed and untrained men had no chance against much smaller numbers of soldiers experienced in years of civil war. Perhaps the defeat of the clubmen was as indicative of what was to come as the failure of all negotiations between King and Parliament. The war could not be ended by an appeal to old values and traditional ways. The issues had changed and the leadership in Westminster and Oxford had become more extreme. Peace could come only out of victory, and victory, whoever won, would profoundly change the face of traditional England (Morrill, 1976, pages 98–111).

Localist opposition and the second Civil War

1646 brought victory, but it did not bring peace. The radical minority in Parliament was being pushed to ever more sweeping changes by the victorious army. The radicalism and the revolutionary sentiments which had increasing influence at the centre were supported by a tiny minority in the provinces. The majority in the provincial communities wanted an end to war, to high taxation, to arbitrary rule and to a large army. They wanted a moderate settlement to the issues which divided King and Parliament. They had never moved from their preference for the traditional ways.

As the negotiations between King and Parliament dragged on, discipline in the army began to break down. One result was local mutinies and the outbreak of indiscipline of the type which had been much more prevalent in the King's armies during the Civil War. At the national level, the disaffection of the army seemed to be pushing Parliament towards greater and greater radicalism. Faced with hated centralisation and the rule of men from outside the circle of pre-war magistrates, many of the moderates, in counties which had been predominantly parliamentarian during the Civil War, came to the conclusion that only armed rebellion against the radical minority who had usurped power could bring the return to traditional ways which they so ardently desired. There was a wave of petitions calling for a quick and moderate solution to the constitutional deadlock and disbandment of the army. In their frustration, the moderate gentry of Kent, South Wales and, on a much smaller scale, some other parts of England rose against Parliament in April 1648. The expected aid from the Scots did not come until too late and the risings were suppressed. Gentry constitutionalism had been suppressed by the power of the sword.

Cromwell and the counties

Cromwell's victory in the second Civil War was quickly followed by Pride's Purge, the execution of the King and the rule of the Rump (see chapter 7, pages 420–1). England was now ruled by the power of a victorious army and the small and unrepresentative portion of Parliament which agreed with its policies.

The new rulers of England were faced with a problem to which they were never to find a fully satisfactory solution. The majority of the political nation found their policies anathema. The new regime claimed to have fought for liberty, but it ruled by force. However, it could not perpetuate the new order without the consent of the traditional ruling class. It could not get that consent without so modifying the policies for which it stood that it would alienate the armed minority which kept them in power.

The whole period of the Interregnum, from 1649 to 1660, is marked by the uneasy alternation between experiments in radical centralisation and cautious movements towards gentry rule. After Pride's Purge and the execution of the King, the Government instituted a large measure of centralisation and transfer of power from the traditional county rulers. This process was carried further at the time of 'Barebone's Parliament' (see chapter 7, pages 427–9). The Protectorate was a break with the more extreme forms of radicalism and a partially successful attempt to reconcile the gentry to the republic. The failure of the first Protectorate Parliament induced Cromwell to abandon reconciliation and follow the policies of Puritan repression advocated by Generals Lambert and Desborough. The result was the enforcement of centralised rule by the major-generals in 1655. Despairing of the success of this policy, Cromwell abolished the major-generals and turned once more to a policy of co-operation with the county gentry. Many were reconciled to his rule. His death in 1658 removed a personal barrier which had prevented some of his enemies from accepting the regime. On the other hand, the absence of his political skill paved the way for a breakdown in the alliance which had kept him in power and the restoration of Charles II as the only alternative to anarchy.

The revolution was followed by a recasting of the county committees. Their power to control sequestrations was transferred to sub-commissioners of sequestrations who were appointed by and responsible to Whitehall. In place of the old committees were appointed new bodies to control the militia and taxation, committees which had nothing like the far-reaching powers of their predecessors. Attempts were made to transfer more power to the traditional machinery of government by stressing the role of the J.P.s and quarter sessions. Reaction to the revolution and the new methods of county government established by the Rump varied throughout the country. However, the general trend was for a further group of the greater gentry to withdraw from participation in county government. The Rump was anxious to reconcile the gentry. It purged only public opponents from either the Commission of the Peace or the new county committees. Uncommitted gentlemen were allowed a surprisingly long time before they were dismissed if they failed to take the Engagement (an oath to be 'true and faithful to the commonwealth'). The Rump was willing to appoint J.P.s who were insufficiently committed to the regime to accept the more political role as members of the committees.

The dismissal of the Rump and the calling of Barebone's Parliament seems to have made little difference to the structure or the personnel of county and borough government, except for some purging of the Commissions of the Peace in North Wales and a few English counties (Underdown in Aylmer, 1972, page 170).

The whole issue of county government was open for review when the Protectorate was declared in 1654. Cromwell was faced with the alternatives of radical centralisation or conciliation. His first moves were conciliatory. J.P.s and other officials were confirmed in office, the Engagement was abolished and replaced by an oath of loyalty to the Protector, oppressive local rulers like Weldon's replacement in Kent, Sir Michael Livesey, lost influence. The new church system based on the 'tryers ' and 'ejectors' gave the gentry a great deal of power. They were allowed to run their counties and lead their own lives in a way that had not been possible since the Civil War. The result was a significant degree of reconciliation. Political Presbyterians who had been excluded or had voluntarily withdrawn from local government during the Commonwealth began to return. The social status of the magisterial bench showed a significant rise. Worcester-shire magistrates appointed in 1654 had an average income of £478, twice as high as in 1652. There was no corresponding rise in the average incomes of committeemen, which suggests a lack of full political commitment by the men from prominent families who were drifting back into the Commission of the Peace.

In 1655 Penruddock's rebellion in favour of the King and Cromwell's inability to reach agreement with the first Protectorate Parliament persuaded him to resort to military government. England was divided into eleven districts, each of which was headed by a major-general. The original task of the major-generals was to organise a citizen militia as a protection against further royalist plots and to impose a decimation tax (that is, one-tenth of income) on known royalists to pay for it. However, a vast number of additional tasks were placed on them until they became the supervisors of virtually every aspect of local government. They quickly gained a reputation as oppressors of royalist and neutral gentlemen and as strong advocates of Puritan measures of moral reform in local government. They rapidly became the most unpopular men in England, though the precise relationship between a major-general and his region was determined very much by his character and its own.

The rule of the major-generals alienated the moderate gentry and reversed the trend towards the return of the traditional families to active participation in county government. While there does not appear to have been any drastic purge of the Commission of the Peace or county committee membership in 1655 and 1656, the social status of J.P.s and committeemen fell once more. In Kent there were virtually no members of greater gentry families taking an active part in county government. The way in which the major-generals and the policy of Puritan authoritarianism had alienated the country strengthened the conservative civilian advisers such as St John. He was advising Cromwell to attempt again the establishment of a more traditional type of government which would be acceptable to far more of the old ruling class. Events in the provinces played an important part in persuading Cromwell to accept the Humble Petition and Advice in nearly every respect except the kingship.

Though it is probably true, as Underdown claims, that the experience of the major-generals made it more difficult for this new attempt at reconciliation with the county magnates to succeed, it did result in a marked rise in the social status of the committeemen and J.P.s in most counties. Radical supporters of Puritan authoritarianism were purged from the Commissions of the Peace in 1657 and members of the traditional ruling families appointed. Worcestershire evidence about incomes may, once more, be indicative of a more general trend. The county committeemen of 1654 had an average income of £318. Those of 1657 averaged nearly £442 (Underdown in Aylmer, 1972, pages 176–7).

Reconciliation was far from complete. In Kent, for example, only a small number of the old governors returned to office. However, there was an unmistakable drift towards unity among the gentry and an acceptance of an increasingly conservative Cromwellian regime. The death of Oliver Cromwell in September 1658 removed one barrier to acceptance by the conservative gentry of the regime he had created. The person of Oliver Cromwell, however much he tried to heal the old wounds and return to something like the traditional constitution, could only be a barrier to gentlemen who saw him still as their civil war enemy, revolutionary and regicide. On the other hand, it left as Protector his amiable, well-meaning and politically inept son, Richard. He was not the man to negotiate the precarious path to settlement among the warring factions, which even his father's strong hand had been hard pressed to keep in check. The complex negotiations which led to the fall of the Protectorate, the recall of the Rump, royalist rebellions and ultimate restoration belong to another section of this work, but there was a close relationship between the negotiations and the swift political changes at the centre, and events in the provinces.

An attempt by the hard core of disaffected royalists to restore the King by force was led by the Cheshire knight, Sir George Booth, in August 1659. Booth's rebellion had its supporters throughout the rest of England, though in Kent and in Worcestershire they seem to have been drawn from the cavaliers rather than the moderates. The principals in the rebellion were not harshly treated, but rigid security precautions were taken. At least in Worcestershire, the county committee was purged of several men from prominent local families, presumably on suspicion of sympathy with Booth's rebellion. The repressive measures taken after the rebellion drove more and more of the moderate gentry to the conclusion that only restoration of the King could return them to their traditional place in county government and check the centralising power of a militaristic nation state. Events in the centre made possible the calling of the Convention Parliament, but the election of former royalists and Presbyterians who had converted to restoration left no doubt about opinion in the country. An attempt was made to stabilise the provinces by appointing new county committees with a much higher proportion of members drawn from the traditional ruling families in January 1660. These committeemen were among those who declared for the King.

The Restoration brought back not only King, Parliament and Anglican Church, but also rule of the provinces by the gentry. The first post-Restoration Commissions of the Peace were virtually lists of the greater gentry of each shire. Royalists, Presbyterians and revolutionaries—they were all included. Only the tiny minority of county leaders who were ideologically committed to republicanism were left out. The old county community had been united.

The Crown and the counties 1660–1700

In 1660 the greater gentry were returned to their accustomed places in county government, but the clock could no more be turned back to 1640 in local government than it could be at Westminster. In 1660 the gentry lost their rivals in county administration. The coercive machinery of Star Chamber and punitive Council was swept away, leaving the Crown without any effective means of intervening in the day to day affairs of the shires. They consolidated their power over their social inferiors who were not only excluded from the bench for the next half century, but replaced on the grand juries by the foremost gentlemen of the shire. The authority of the county gentry over the boroughs was extended by appointing county magnates to the commissions which purged the corporations of dissenters from 1661 to 1664. The weakened episcopacy and less confident hierarchy of church courts wished to preserve their alliance with the county gentry, not challenge it by trying to gain the upper hand as Laud had done, and they allowed the gentry extensive power over their local church. In local government, the twenty years which followed the Restoration was the golden age of the gentry.

The increased confidence and class-consciousness of the magnates, as well as the increased problem of poverty, was responsible for the passage and enforcement of repressive legislation such as the 1662 Act of Settlement (see page 211). Perhaps the Game Act of 1671 and its enforcement by the landowning magistrates, whose sporting rights it protected, was an even narrower and more blatant use of the law in the interests of the resurgent landed magnates, in that it took away the hunting rights of farmers and minor gentlemen, even on their own land.

A partial exception to what has been written above, and one which signified the revival of the power of the peerage, was the enhanced importance of the Lord Lieutenant. Before the Civil War, Lords Lieutenant were regional officers who often had a shadowy connection with the counties and the Deputy Lieutenants under their nominal jurisdiction. After the Restoration, every county had its Lord Lieutenant and he was the linchpin of local government. Together with his deputies and the members of the magisterial quorum, the Lord Lieutenant often dominated his locality in both local government and in parliamentary elections (Kenyon, 1969, pages 494–5).

There is no doubt, however, that the relations between central and local government were of a quite different nature after the Restoration. No longer did attempts by central government to enforce its will in local administration create the issues—to a very large measure, the Crown had handed the counties over to the gentry. The main areas of conflict between central government and the county leaders involved national matters and the power of their class. The local affairs and traditional rivalries remained important, but the main source of conflict among the gentry was increasingly their attitudes to events at Westminster and, in particular, their identification with party. Struggles for local office were frequently submerged in national politics. (It is for this reason that the section on central-local government relations after 1660 is so short. Much material which could be handled here is more appropriately discussed as part of the development of Parliament.)

Perhaps the most important characteristic of the Restoration was its dominance by the relationship between the Crown and the recently re-united ruling class, made up mainly of landowners. Parliament, especially the House of Commons, was the forum for this class. To the landowners it was not just the continued existence of Parliament which was important, but its continuation under their domination. Parliament had to be independent of both overt manipulation by the Crown and of any significant influx of members from outside the ruling class. Much Restoration history can be explained in light of the landed gentry's determination to retain the power to which their class had been restored in 1660.

The attitudes of the King, Parliament, the gentry and their social inferiors had all been conditioned by the Civil War and Interregnum. All feared the outbreak of a further civil war. The gentry did not wish to risk either the agonies of war itself or a renewed eclipse of their power by the armed forces and by the bourgeois administrators which such a war would bring to the fore. Charles, to repeat two well-worn clichés, 'did not want to go on his travels again', and he 'never forgot that he had a joint in his neck'. Had it not been for wartime memories, it is quite possible that a full-scale civil war would have broken out on at least three occasions: in 1681 during the Exclusion Crisis (see chapter 7, pages 456–62), in 1685 with Monmouth's rebellion, and at the time of William's invasion in 1688. On the first two occasions, it was the opposition gentry who backed down; on the last, the King and his dwindling number of supporters (Jones, 1978, page 1).

The landowning class was seldom completely united, but there was a broad central group which shifted its political stance in reaction to perceived threats to gentry power. The royalist reaction to the Exclusion Crisis was made possible, in large measure, because the country gentlemen saw Whig mobilisation of town dwellers and yeomen into political activity independent of their landlords and patrons as more threatening to gentry power than a Catholic king. The reaction of the Tory gentlemen misled James II into thinking that they were committed to the ultra-royalist rhetoric of the more extreme Anglican clergymen. His downfall came because he did not realise that their loyalty was conditional on his furthering their interests and protecting their church.

Between 1660 and 1678, Charles II's policies showed a fluctuation between dependence on the Anglican ruling class, and an attempt to broaden the basis of support by including dissenters and Catholics. During this period, however, royal policies and opposition to them had only limited influence on local government. Though openly hostile Justices of the Peace might be dismissed, the bench was not consistently packed on party lines and the duration of the Cavalier Parliament limited the opportunities for divisions in the local communities becoming apparent in electoral contests.

All this was to change after 1678. The dissolution of the Cavalier Parliament and the heat generated by the Exclusion Crisis were to see local communities as riven by party divisions as was Parliament itself. From that time onwards, every appointment to local office, every election, and even the constitutions under which the boroughs were governed, reflected national politics. It was, however, a two-way process. In the localities, attitudes to national issues were coloured by local conflicts and personalities. As discussed in chapter 7, the elections to the Exclusion parliaments, especially the second and third, were dominated by that single issue. Indeed, it was the way in which exclusionists ignored local conventions in their determination to elect the candidates they wanted which helped create the reaction against their movement. Boroughs refused to elect the candidates nominated by the neighbouring magnates they normally followed, and tenants ignored the advice of their landlords. The Exclusion Movement, as it operated at the local level, marked a declaration of independence by the middle classes against their social superiors. Faced with this threat, the Anglican gentry increasingly turned Tory and anti-Exclusionist. Once Exclusion had been defeated, the King and the Tories co-operated in seeking revenge on the Whigs who had challenged the pre-rogatives of the first and the local supremacy of the latter. Whereas there had usually been resistance to any attempts by kings to interfere in the localities for political purposes, this time the Tories welcomed it.

In the early 1680s, men who had favoured Exclusion were dismissed from Commissions of the Peace. Care was taken to appoint Tory sheriffs as they would select Tory juries for political trials. The Earl of Shaftesbury owed his life to the fact that the sheriff of London was still a Whig at the time he was tried for treason. A Whig jury threw out the charge. With the active co-operation of the Tories, Charles remodelled borough corporations to ensure that they would elect Tories to Parliament and to positions in local government. His most significant victory was the surrender of London's charter. After this, there was little resistance from other boroughs.

The aftermath of the Exclusion Crisis reinforced the alliance between the Crown and the gentry, but the Catholicising policies of James II were to see it broken. Between 1686 and April 1687, James determined to dismiss all officials in local and central government who would not accept his policies. His campaign had two phases: the packing of Parliament and the appointment to local government positions of those who would collaborate. His purge of local government involved both boroughs and counties. Between November 1687 and March 1688, 1200 municipal officers were dismissed, a further 255 between August 1688 and the Revolution. Many of those appointed to take their place were not supporters of James II's national policies, but townsmen with a purely local consciousness who welcomed the ejection of the Tory gentlemen and their dupes.

In the counties, the only replacements for dismissed Anglican gentlemen were Catholics and dissenters. By early 1687, 290 Catholic J.P.s had been appointed. Between February and April 1688, 709 new J.P.s were added to the Commission. Of these, ninety-nine were Catholics and most of the rest dissenters. By the Revolution, nearly a quarter of all J.P.s were Catholics. A large, though uncertain, proportion of the rest were dissenters. By assaulting the power of the Anglican gentry in both central and local government, James succeeded in reuniting most Whigs with most Tories. By his attempt to deprive the gentry of what most saw as their birthright, James added a very powerful reason to support the Revolution.

William came to the throne determined to be the King of the nation rather than the King of a party. Although he was naturally authoritarian, he was unable to ignore the claims of the gentry to rule their local community, nor could he ignore party. In the 1690s, appointments to local office were recognised as party appointments. William sometimes signalled his preferences in parliamentary elections by his dismissals and appointments to the lieutenancy and the bench before elections, though more usually he carried out remodelling after a change of government.

By 1700, local government was affected by two conflicting tendencies when compared with the situation in 1558. In its day to day administration it was much less regulated by the central government, yet in appointments to positions within it, it was dominated by considerations of party and national politics. Both reflected changes in society. The Restoration had ensured the dominance of the landed classes in their localities; it had also made them part of a wider gentry community.

Summary

In the 1630s King Charles and his government had adopted a policy of centralisation and alienated most of the traditional ruling class. By his failure to call Parliament, he cut away one of the main ways in which they could influence national affairs. The Book of Orders attempted to impose national uniformity and a higher standard of efficiency in local government. Plans for a 'Perfect Militia' and for a powerful fleet involved time, effort, expense and acceptance of an extended exercise of prerogative. Laud's plans for greater uniformity in religion meant the imposition of doctrines and outward ceremonial which offended not only Puritans but the the vast majority of English Protestants. By 1640 the county governors, followed and sometimes led by their social inferiors, had turned against 'Thorough'. The solidity of their opposition is demonstrated by the ease with which the first session of the Long Parliament reversed the decisions made during the period of personal rule and destroyed the institutional base which had made it possible.

The destruction of centralisation and innovation satisfied a large part of the political nation. As the minority in Parliament moved towards constitutional changes which would take from the King powers which were traditionally his, the solidity of the ruling class broke. During the Civil War, the bulk of the royalists and parliamentarians were moderates, men who had more in common with the neutrals than with the tiny minority of extremists on either side. The first Civil War was fought to determine the distribution of power within something like the traditional constitution: indeed, to settle by force of arms what the traditional constitution was. Though the original leaders had not intended even the mildest of social revolutions, the events of the war produced new ideas and created new power bases. In the counties, especially the parliamentarian ones, the traditional ruling class was progressively displaced by new men of lower social rank who were prepared to put the nation state and an ideological cause before local and personal loyalties. (For example, Colonel Brian Hewson, a cobbler's son, Major-General Berry, a former ironworker, and Praise-God Barbon, a leather seller, by a corruption of whose name a parliament is known.) As these men gained more authority, the gulf between the formal power conferred by the central government and the informal influence exercised on the basis of wealth, family and traditional deference became wider.

The second Civil War and the execution of the King occurred because Charles was unwilling to agree to terms which would have gained him the overwhelming support of the traditional ruling class, and because the moderate gentry constitutionalists were unable to deal effectively with the new centre of power which had arisen, the army. Originally the instrument of Parliament, the army had become a political power in its own right. Indeed, it can be considered, to some extent at least, as being two powers: the grandees (the senior officers), on the one hand, and lower ranking officers and men on the other. While the war had strengthened the conservatism of the majority of civilians, a minority of religious radicals in the towns excepted, it had encouraged the growth of political views so radical as to have been unthinkable at the beginning of the Civil War. In 1648 a section of the old ruling class which had been mildly parliamentarian in the first Civil War rose against the arbitrary rule of the new men. They were crushed and the real revolution took place at Pride's Purge and the execution of the King.

In 1649 a social as well as a political revolution was confirmed. For the next eleven years, only a minority of the old ruling class of peers and wealthy gentlemen were to hold formal authority. A minority, a tiny minority, of the men who had traditionally ruled England accepted the changes. They remained in power joined by minor gentlemen, yeomen, tradesmen and those who owed their advancement to success in the army. These men held power, but they did not hold it by consent. The traditional ruling class still held their accustomed informal authority. The new regime could perpetuate its power in one of two ways. It could crush the peerage and gentry in a drastic social revolution or it could so moderate its policies that they became acceptable to the traditional ruling class. There was no 'red terror' and no very significant transfer of wealth from the old rulers. The Protectorate provided a conservative reaction sufficient to attract some of the gentry into accepting the new regime, but Cromwell's personality was too ambivalent, his dependence on the army too great and his time too short for full reconciliation to take place.

Oliver Cromwell's death was followed by a flurry of experiments designed to create a stable government. The result was increasing confusion and a rapid growth in the belief that settled government could return only with Charles II.

The reunion of the county communities which had taken place in 1660 lasted for less than ten years. From the late 1660s, events in national politics were arousing something similar to the Court *v.*

country split of the 1630s. The national issues which produced this division concerned foreign policy, religion and the succession, not matters which affected the relationship of local authority to central government very directly (except, perhaps, in the way the religious disabilities imposed on dissenters excluded many of the natural participants in borough government). At the county level the greater degree of political sophistication gained by the gentry since the days of the Civil War was shown by the way most counties developed strong factions, each led by a peer or powerful landed magnate. In the late 1660s and early 1670s, national politics were splitting the county communities once more. This time, however, it was the relationship between the gentlemen of the counties and the factions in Parliament which was important.

In the late 1660s and early 1670s the Court-country split seems to have reopened old wounds. Supporters of the country party were drawn disproportionately from the areas which had been radical in the Civil War, while the Court party was dominated by placemen (those who held paid government office) and former cavaliers. By 1680, the gentry were clearly divided into Whigs and Tories.

So bitter were the political divisions at the time of the Exclusion Crisis and Monmouth's rebellion that it is probable that only the memory of the Civil War prevented a recurrence. The attempts of Charles II from 1680 to 1683, and by James II from 1686 to 1688, to regain control over local government by massive dismissals from the Commission of the Peace, and by questioning the charters of the self-governing boroughs, produced some short-term political gains: for example, in the Parliament of 1685. In the long run, however, these tactics showed how dependent the Crown was on the co-operation of the traditional leaders in the counties. The increased disillusionment of the Anglican gentry with the Catholicising policies of James II and the further purges of their number did not in itself produce the 1688 Revolution, but it created the atmosphere in which even men who had been fervent 'Church and King' Tories were willing to accept, however reluctantly, the armed displacement of their sovereign. The threat to the rule of the gentry in their counties played a very important role in reuniting the county communities against James II. In the early 1680s, fear of Civil War had, in the end, induced the opposition to back down. In 1688 the King's religious policies and his threat to the traditional ruling class in the counties had changed the balance so far that this time it was the conservatives who yielded in order to keep the peace.

After 1688 splits reappeared among the gentry, but they were, for the most part, related to the pursuance of national politics in Parliament. By and large the gentry were to be left in charge of their counties for the next hundred and fifty years, though the role of the peerage was to increase in the eighteenth century. Paradoxically, the greater gentry and the peerage tended to withdraw from direct participation in local government almost as soon as their unchallenged power had been recognised. Even before 1700, and certainly afterwards, the peerage and the untitled magnates put aside their preoccupation with county affairs and busied themselves in London social life, Continental touring or national politics. The magnates cut themselves off from their roots and participated in a national society, leading the way into a world which was increasingly stratified on class lines rather than divided vertically into a mosaic of local communities.

The judiciary 1642–1660

During the Civil War and Interregnum, there was no major change in the judicial system, except that imposed during hostilities. Criminal and civil justice was carried out much as before, except that it was usually possible for only a single judge to go on assize circuit and assizes were often not held during the Civil War. Most judges were willing to accept a subordinate political role. During the war itself, the judges who had remained at Westminster did their best to assist the parliamentarian cause; those whose activities were based on Oxford did all in their power to aid the King. (For the judges, 1640–2, see chapter 7, page 393.)

Members of the judiciary found it difficult to accept the legality of the execution of the King: six refused to accept new patents in 1649. The judges appointed to take their places saw it as part of their duty to encourage acceptance of the new regime. During the periods when the government was unpopular, the judges of assize often had to be escorted by armed soldiers. Later in the Interregnum, relations between the judiciary and the government deteriorated. When the major-generals were appointed in 1655, several judges resigned in protest and two were dismissed for disobedience. After the death of Oliver Cromwell, there was considerable difficulty in finding well-qualified lawyers who were loyal to the regime and willing to serve. From 1658 the judges had joined the drift towards restoration.

The judiciary 1660–1700

The Restoration brought back the system of Common Law much as it had been before the Civil War: Latin, Norman-French and all. A few of the minor Interregnum reforms were retained. In all, it represented a victory for the conservatism of the common lawyers and an advance for their professional interests over those of the civil lawyers. The prerogative courts were not revived and jurisdiction over wills was transferred from the ecclesiastical courts to Chancery. The surviving civil law courts, the Court of Admiralty and the ecclesiastical courts, lost both jurisdiction and status to the Common Law courts. Common lawyers increasingly dominated the courts of equity which, in any case, adopted a fixed procedure along Common Law lines (Hill, 1974, pages 225–7).

The Restoration left the procedure of the law courts unchanged, though certain alterations were to be made during the reign of Charles II. A continuing defect not remedied until after the Revolution was the inability of persons accused of felony or treason to make use of counsel, except on points of law, or to call witnesses on oath. Neither were they allowed a copy of the indictment before the case commenced: it was merely read to them in court. If, however, a technical flaw could be found, the case was dismissed.

Judges after the Restoration showed a greater tendency to interpret the law harshly and to the disadvantage of the defendant. Algernon Sydney, for example, was convicted and executed for treason in 1683 on the basis of opinions expressed in an unpublished manuscript. In 1688 apprentices who had rioted and attacked brothels were convicted on the grounds that assuming the King's duty of suppressing an evil was treason. Judges also seem to have shown greater severity in dealing with offences against property, censorship and the game laws, and they were often accused of putting pressure on juries, bullying witnesses and demanding excessive bail (Carter in Jones, 1979, pages 82–3).

There were, however, positive changes as well. The courts became increasingly willing to provide redress against wrongful acts by royal officials. In 1679 one of the most important safeguards of freedom was enacted with the passage of the Habeas Corpus Act. Under its terms no one could be imprisoned by mere administrative order, but only when charged with a specific offence known to law, and only until his or her case could be heard in court. Even in Parliament there were many who believed that administrative arrest was essential to the security of the State, and the story may be true that the Bill passed the Lords only because the teller jokingly counted a fat lord as ten.

Even at the Restoration, the jury's independent role to decide the facts of a case was not fully established. Under Elizabeth, the judges' right to threaten juries in order to get the verdict they wanted was accepted and, in the rare cases where this approach failed, they could be summoned before Star Chamber. After the abolition of Star

Chamber in 1640, the judges took it upon themselves to punish intractable juries. In 1665 Chief Justice Hyde told a split jury, 'You must go out and agree. And as for you that say you cannot in conscience find him guilty, if you say so again without giving reason for it, I shall take order with you'. In 1667 Chief Justice Kelying was called to the bar of the House of Commons to explain why he had imprisoned a jury which had refused to bring in the verdict he wanted. The House condemned his action, though owing to the special circumstances of the case they let the matter rest. The resolution of the House was reinforced by King's Bench. In 1670 Lord Chief Justice Vaughan declared in Bushell's Case that jurors could not be punished for bringing verdicts against the wishes of the judge, unless there was evidence of criminal collusion. However, old habits died hard and in 1687 Justice Holloway could refer quite openly to his 'menacing and threatening' a jury to obtain an acquittal.

The tenure by which judges held their office was one of the critical issues of the period. During his earlier years, Charles appointed judges during good behaviour (*quamdiu se bene gesserint*), thereafter during pleasure (*durante beneplacito regis*). The first allowed him to dismiss judges only for a specific offence—though he could suspend them at will—while the second tenure gave him freedom to appoint and dismiss without having to show any reason. In fact judges were dismissed only when there were strong political reasons for so doing, and in these circumstances suspension could be just as effective. It is claimed by many historians that the quality of judges declined after their tenure became subject to political interference. The first judge to lose his office for a political reason was Justice Ellis in 1676. Charles II removed eleven judges between 1676 and 1682, James II twelve in the four years of his reign. It was not only the King judges had to fear, but Parliament as well. Chief Justice Scroggs was impeached for summing up in favour of Sir George Wakeman, one of the last to be charged by Oates and Bedloe with complicity in the Popish Plot. His conduct and that of Judge Weston in other political cases was called to account in Parliament. In 1679 Charles's dismissal of four judges was probably an attempt to placate Parliament. Fear of Parliament may have outweighed fear of the King in the decision of some judges to acquit the seven bishops in 1688.

There is no doubt, however, that royal power over the judiciary was responsible for many of its unpopular decisions. The bullying of witnesses and intimidation of juries in political trials reflected the belief that it was the judge's duty to get a conviction in such cases. Atrocious cruelty and vindictiveness was shown by Lord Chief Justice Jeffreys in the Bloody Assizes which tried those who had joined Monmouth's rebellion. Perhaps 300 were executed, 800 were transported and large numbers were sentenced to be flogged through every market town of a county, a punishment which could mean death by torture. His most notorious single case at that time was his extreme pressure to obtain the conviction of Lady Lisle (the seventy-year-old widow of John Lisle, who had been a member of the High Court of Justice which had tried Charles I) for harbouring a rebel after the battle of Sedgemoor. Though there was little evidence that she knew the man was a rebel, he managed to obtain a conviction and sentenced her to death by burning.

One of the most important constitutional cases was Godden *v.* Hales in 1686, in which the legality of royal dispensations for Catholics to be granted military commissions was asserted. However, James was able to obtain the verdict only by dismissing four judges, including the Chief Baron of the Exchequer and the Chief Justice of the Common Pleas. It was now possible for James to nullify the Test Act by issuing dispensations. Two Catholic judges were appointed: Christopher Milton and Richard Allibone. The latter openly attended mass when on assize circuit in Lancashire and went out of his way to dismiss Protestants from the Commission of the Peace. As a result of such activities, there was a considerable loss of respect for the judges.

Despite James's evident willingness to dismiss judges who did not rule as he wished, at least some were willing to risk his displeasure in other cases. The creation of a standing army without statutory authorisation had raised the question of discipline, in particular the punishment of deserters. In 1687 Sir John Holt, the Recorder of London, had refused to convict a deserter, and Lord Chief Justice Herbert and Sir Francis Wythens refused to order that a deserter condemned at Reading assizes should be shot before his regiment at Plymouth. Wythens was dismissed and Herbert was forced to change places with Sir Robert Wright, Chief Justice of Common Pleas.

The last major constitutional case of James II's reign was that of the seven bishops in 1688. The Archbishop of Canterbury had presented a petition to the King asking him to withdraw the order requiring the clergy to read the Declaration of Indulgence on two successive Sundays. The seven bishops (as signatories) were charged with seditious libel when their petition was published. Lord Chief Justice Wright was assisted by two colleagues in this case. They allowed a full discussion of the suspending power, even though it was not strictly relevant to the charges brought against the bishops and two judges, Sir Richard Holloway and Sir John Powell, summed up in favour of acquittal. The jury followed their recommendation. The two judges were dismissed, but the King had lost a major legal battle (Kenyon, 1969, page 424).

In the last few months of his reign, James dismissed more judges he regarded as politically unreliable and appointed Catholics in their place. It was said that he would 'continue none but those who will help him maintain his prerogative'. The Catholic judge, Allibone, obviously lived up to James's expectations when he made his charge (speech) to the grand jury at Croydon assizes. He told them that 'If the king had been Turk or Jew, it had been all one, for the subject ought to obey'. After the Revolution of 1688, Parliament turned on the judges as collaborators with the previous regime. In the Commons, Sir Richard Temple said, 'How has Westminster Hall been tutored, judges packed for purposes . . . so that Westminster Hall was become an instrument of Slavery and Popery, ordinary justice destroyed . . . in that little and short time of the late King James's reign!' It was seriously proposed that at least two judges should be hanged. However, many members recognised the intolerable pressure to which the judges had been exposed. One said of the judges' support of the dispensing power in 1686, 'Some did it out of weakness, others out of fear, and not out of the dictates of their judgement'. Though they escaped hanging, not one was reappointed to office.

Under William, the judges continued to have a political role. They were still summoned to Whitehall to receive instructions about their conduct while on assize circuit. They were expected to take note of the party composition of the magisterial bench and to resolve differences between Whig and Tory magistrates. There were, however, no major political trials in this reign in which the King or Parliament put pressure on the judiciary to bring in a particular verdict. William was careful not to interfere in the ordinary course of justice and he did not dismiss judges for political reasons. Nevertheless, he vetoed a Bill early in his reign to make the tenure of all judges *durante se bene gesserint* (during good behaviour). It was the Act of Settlement which gave the judges their greatest measure of independence. All were to be appointed during good behaviour and dismissed only if both Houses of Parliament resolved that they had broken their oath of office. This is still the situation in 1984.

By 1700 England had a much more independent judiciary than in 1559. The judges were no longer dismissed for political reasons. Juries might still be subject to judicial browbeating, but they could not be punished for their verdict. The writ of habeas corpus prevented administrative imprisonment. England was well along the road towards a modern judicial system.

CHAPTER FOUR

Religion: the Anglican Church, its condition, critics and enemies, 1558–1629

Uniformity

Uniformity in religion was the common principle operating in sixteenth century Europe. It was generally held that two religions could not exist side by side in a society without friction, bloodshed and even civil war. As the century progressed, events seemed to bear this out: in the long religious wars in Germany, which ended in the Peace of Augsburg in 1555; in the French civil wars; and in the Dutch rebellion against Spanish Catholic government. Rulers responded to this by insisting on a strict uniformity, backed by bloody reprisals against obstinate heretics: Philip of Spain in the Low Countries, Mary Tudor in England, Calvin in Geneva, and the massacre of St Bartholomew's in Catherine de Medici's France.

This action was understandable. Heretical movements not only posed a threat to social order, but in turn threatened the security of the State and the ruling dynasty. Kings such as Henry VIII and Gustavus Vasa (Sweden) and some of the north German princes may have been influenced in their rejection of Roman Catholicism, or their conversion to Protestantism, by the prospect of seizing Church property. But they, no less than Roman Catholic governments, were also motivated by a concern for order and especially religious conviction. They were the Lord's anointed and His lieutenants who had been entrusted with the spiritual welfare of their subjects' souls. Those who rejected the faith were ungodly. They had to be brought to conformity, not only to save their souls but also as an example to others. The only difference between Protestant and Catholic rulers is that they had a different conception of 'the faith': to Philip II, God was a Roman Catholic, to Henry VIII he was Catholic (and probably English), and to many German princes he was a Lutheran. In practice this meant that the monarch determined the faith and his subjects were expected to obey. Deviation was not permissible. It was in this near-universal climate of uniformity that Elizabeth became queen.

Comprehension and toleration

Much has been written about Elizabeth's liberalism in religion. In particular, she supposedly represented what became, over the centuries, the classic Anglican *via media* tradition. In other words, the Church eventually became a middle-of-the-road institution which included within it a wide range of religious opinions and a diversity of doctrine, and which tolerated protest, dissent and a broad spectrum of theological positions. It is often taken for granted that Elizabeth preferred comprehension (a Church embracing as many opinions as was politically sensible and possible). It is often assumed that she was inclined to be tolerant, requiring only outward conformity: a public acceptance of uniformity, which was best demonstrated by regular attendance at the local Anglican parish church. Did she not say that she would not 'make windows into men's souls', by which she meant that she would not apply the kind of religious test which exposed the secrets of their consciences? To be precise she would not compel her subjects to take communion, because Catholics, believing in the sacrificial nature of the mass, could not take part in a ritual which denied that the bread and wine were transformed into the flesh and blood of Christ. Undoubtedly there is some truth in all of these assertions and assumptions, and to that extent she was an unusual figure in sixteenth century Europe. Yet this picture is not an entirely accurate one. It derives from three traditions. One is the Protestant interpretation which casts Elizabeth in the role of godly heroine—and as Protestantism eventually carried the day in England, it is that version which has survived to the present day. Secondly there is the nationalist tradition which represents the Queen as the saviour of an independent English State and Church against the Spanish threat. Finally, there is the Gloriana cult. This is best represented by A.L. Rowse and Sir John Neale, who mirror the adulation of many of her contemporaries in their lavish and often uncritical praise of her.

We need to stand back and examine Elizabeth's performance in a cool, dispassionate way. She must be judged by her actions rather than by her public pronouncements and the opinions of ardent Protestants and royalists. Some conclusions we can draw easily enough. Like her father she viewed matters of Church and religion politically rather than theologically. She was secular and treated the Church as an arm of the State. The result was that Elizabeth, the supreme governor, frequently abused and misused it in her own interests, rather than protecting it. The Church provided the Queen with her only professional nationwide civil service. It was a source of revenue (taxation), while its property provided cheap rewards to royal servants. It made available a propaganda platform, through sermons and homilies of obedience delivered from the pulpit. Indeed the new Church became one of the chief pillars of the State. However, we must not fall into the common error of studying the Church as if it was no more than a department of State. No matter how important were the benefits which it brought to the monarchy, its prime functions and purpose were spiritual not temporal: to save souls, guide them through this life and prepare them for the next; to supervise the moral and spiritual welfare of the people; and to discipline and punish offences against the established religion and moral code.

Not that the Church stood apart from the secular world. It was an important property owner. It collected tithes (ten per cent levies on the laity for the upkeep of the clergy), it registered wills, and Church courts often dealt with property matters. Moreover, the Church could not have stood aloof from the secular world, even if it had wished to. Most bishops were J.Ps, and all of them, whether magistrates or not, received a stream of instructions and requests for information from the Privy Council. For example, in 1564 they were required to survey the religious opinions of J.Ps, and in the 1570s they were ordered to suppress the Puritan prophesyings. Some of the bishops were consulted by the Queen on religious matters of political significance, although only one, Whitgift, was appointed to the Privy Council. Above all, the discovery and punishment of heresy and recusancy were collaborative exercises between lay and ecclesiastical officials: bishops, sheriffs, Justices of the Peace and judges in the ecclesiastical courts. Nevertheless, we must not lose sight of the fact that these activities had spiritual as well as political objectives, and that the Church existed to serve spiritual ends.

It is conventional to begin the religious history of Elizabethan and Stuart England with an account and explanation of the Elizabethan Settlement of 1559. And to follow it with a history which, particularly in Elizabeth's reign, concentrates its attention on the right and left wing challenges to the new Church—the Roman Catholics and the Puritans. In three respects, however, the present study departs from the common format. The account of the religious settlement is preceded by, first, a brief selective survey of the recent literature on Tudor/early Stuart religion and, second, an attempt to define the three terms which are crucial to an understanding of this subject: Anglican, Puritan and Roman Catholic. Thirdly, more attention than is usual will be given to the Anglican Church itself: its structure, organisation and operation, its theology and spiritual standards, and its relations with the State. It would make little sense to study the governments of President Reagan, Mrs Thatcher and Mr Muldoon by focussing attention on their critics and opponents. It is equally pointless to study organised religion in early modern England through the activities of Puritans and Roman Catholics (with the exception of the years 1640–60). After all, organised religion was the legal monopoly of the Anglican Church. Furthermore, it is impossible to understand Puritan or Catholic challenges unless we have a knowledge of the institution which they were challenging.

Bibliography

The point was made in the Introduction, but should be repeated here, that the varying length of chapters in this volume is no register of the relative importance of particular themes. It has been assumed that no one theme is more important that any other. However, some are more adequately served than others by the existing literature. This is particularly true of the history of religion and the Church. It applies not only to the dissenting Puritan and Catholic movements, but, as a result of a recent spate of works, to the Anglican Church as well. As it is not the specific purpose of this book to be comprehensive, the reader is directed (where relevant) to recent publications (usually paperbacks) which are, in most cases, cheap enough to be realistic purchases by schools and which are still available in print. One or two essential items, however, are expensive but unavoidable (for example, P. Collinson's, *The Elizabethan Puritan Movement*) or exist, as yet, only in article form. The prime purpose of this chapter is to create a framework of reference, and to provide a springboard from which the reader can plunge with confidence into the more specialised literature on religion and the Church.

The starting point must be the Anglican Church. The new litera-ture of the last ten to fifteen years denotes a healthy re-thinking about priorities in the study of early modern religion. In the past much attention has been given to the 1559 settlement which established the new Church, but little to the way in which the Church thereafter evolved. Instead it was examined from the viewpoint of its critics and those who sought to overturn it. Little was known about the efforts of bishops to give substance to the Acts of 1559, or how they related to the Queen and Council; even less how they administered the new Church. The ecclesiastical courts, the pastoral function (spiritual guid-ance) of the clergy, the state of religion in the parishes, the education of the ministry: few of these areas were studied for their own sake, but only as targets for the critics of the Church.

A colourful contemporary example of this approach is the oft-cited Puritan survey of the Anglican ministry during the 1580s. It was both scurrilous and amusing: about clergymen who could not recite the articles or give an account of their faith, either in Latin or English; about one clergyman known to his parishioners as the vicar of Hell; another who had sired several bastards in the course of his parish duties; yet another who was taken in bed with a woman and swore never to preach against adultery 'which promise he hath hitherto kept'; and a fourth who drifted from job to job, became a minstrel and, as a last resort, took refuge in the ministry. We are inclined to remember such tales, which are part of a tradition stretching from Chaucer to the more sensational tabloid newspapers of today. However, we may forget that they were written in an anti-clerical society, by men who were attempting to change the Church. It was a skilful propaganda exercise, throwing mud in the knowledge that some would stick. However, recounting such a propagandist exercise is no substitute for an unbiased examination of the facts, and this was lacking until the end of the 1960s. (There are notable exceptions. See C. Hill, *Economic Problems of the Church from Archbishop Whitgift to the Long Parliament*, London, 1956.)

Claire Cross led the way with *The Royal Supremacy in the Elizabethan Church* in 1969 and other books and articles since then, the latest being 'Churchmen and the Royal Supremacy' in *Church and Society* in England (see the Bibliography for details of this and other works mentioned in this section). These, however, were still partly concerned with the heady stuff of high politics: in other words, relations between Crown and bishops. Ralph Houlbrooke has added a new dimension to the bishops' role in his essay on the pastoral work of the episcopate (bench of bishops), also in *Church and Society*. But what was sorely lacking was a study of the Church at the lower level: the parochial clergy, the local ecclesiastical courts and parish churches. This is the level at which the Church impinged on the life of society and its members. And the lack is rapidly being rectified, especially in the two collections of essays, *Church and Society* and *Continuity and Change* (see the Bibliography). Gradually we are becoming equipped with a literature which will enable us to evaluate the Church in its own right, rather than as the butt of witty, cynical and even malicious critics and opponents.

Puritanism and Puritans

Of course, opposition and criticism cannot be ignored. One dissenting stream, Puritanism, provided a necessary dynamic for improvement and change in Elizabethan society, religion and morals. The other,

Roman Catholicism, appeared to threaten the very existence of the Elizabethan Nation-State and national Church. The former may seem to be the more difficult to identify and define. After all, *Roman* Catholics, by very definition, stood outside the Church and owed their allegiance to a foreign authority, the Pope. However, appearances are deceptive. As we shall see, even contemporaries could only guess that particular men were 'suspect' in religion. Protestants could not always be sure that they were actually 'obstinate adversaries and hinderers of God's Holy Word' (that is, papists). Nevertheless, it is true that 'Puritanism' and 'Puritans' usually cause many more problems for students. How to describe Puritanism? How to identify Puritans? The questions are best considered separately before they are related, as inevitably they must be: after all, how could Puritanism exist without the exponents of its ethos, its spirit?

Puritanism presents a particular problem because, unlike Roman Catholicism, it was not an organised religion. At its broadest it must be described in less precise terms. It was a spiritual, moralistic attitude to contemporary problems in society, government, the Church, and everyday life. That attitude did not necessarily lead on to political activism, attempts to reconstruct the world-order and to impose godly behaviour on one's fellow men. In its mildest form it was a matter for the individual, a desire to raise personal standards and live the virtuous life: reading the Scriptures, praying, practising abstinence, attending church, and caring for the poor. Lady Margaret Hoby was a classic example, passing her days in prayer, reading the Bible and annotating it, meditating, talking religion with her chaplain and being a dutiful wife. She kept a diary of her daily round, which most of us today would regard as an exercise in martyrdom or boredom. However, she was a pure spirit, seeking only to raise her own standards and not wishing to impose them on others. William Perkins, as a man and one of the ministry, was obviously in a position to exert more influence than Lady Hoby. He was a noted preacher, a formative influence on Puritan thought, and he might have risen high in the Church. Instead he preferred to write, preach and quietly minister to the flock of his parish. We make a fundamental mistake if we imagine that Puritanism was a kind of party political creed or that, even more misleading, it had a political programme.

Puritanism was part of the spiritual, intellectual and moral climate of the age. It touched most people in varying degrees. The Elizabethan Church had emerged after thirty years of bewildering change, during which the State had required clergy and laity to reject the Pope, abjure Catholicism, adopt an advanced form of Continental Protestantism, receive back the mass and Papal authority, and then give them both up again. By 1559 most members of the clergy and laity were used to drilling on a religious parade-ground: left turn, right turn and turn-about again. The Church had been plundered in the name of pure religion. Little attention had been given to the education, income and moral standards of the clergy. Each time the State imposed a new order of worship, everyone was expected to say 'Amen'. No wonder that, in 1559, apathy and cynical disobedience had become ingrained habits. Puritanism was a backlash against this state of affairs: against secularism, moral backsliding and the politicians' manipulation of Reformation for their own ends.

However, Puritanism can be defined in a narrower, more precise sense than this. Theologically it was Calvinist and it rested four-square upon the doctrine of predestination (that Man could not work for his own salvation, because God had pre-ordained who was to be damned and who was to be saved—the bestowal of grace in an arbitrary manner). Yet this did not mark off Puritans from the rest of the Anglican Church. Archbishops Parker and Whitgift (and Abbot) were no less Calvinist than such ardent Puritans as John Field, Thomas Cartwright, Thomas Wilcox and John Pym. Puritanism was anti-papal, anti-Catholic and anti-Spanish. But so too were the great majority of the governing class. Indeed so were most of the Privy Council (for example, Burghley, Walsingham, Knollys, Mildmay and Leicester) and the bishops. Elizabeth was the important exception. Her doctrinal position remains obscure. On the other hand, her refusal to make even modest concessions to reform (such as the abolition of the surplice, or at least a dispensation freeing the clergy from the necessity of wearing it), her opposition to the prophesyings, the classical movement and separatism (see below) reveal an anti-Puritan temper.

For this very reason, however, Elizabeth may be crucial to an understanding of Puritanism. She worked for political stability: this required at least an outward conformity, an insistence on no public deviation from the official line. The Church became an instrument of political stability. The Church also became a branch of the civil service. Its pulpits were designed to instil obedience, not to be a springboard of protest about a 'half-reformed' Church. Public protests about the state of religion were, by implication, criticisms of Elizabeth's stewardship of the Church—they might lead on to questions about the way she managed the State. So Elizabeth was ultra-sensitive to demands of almost any kind, whether they were for reforms in 'matters indifferent' (which may seem trivial to us) such as vestments, images, candles, pictures, points of ceremony and other Catholic remnants, or whether they were attacks on matters fundamental, with political implications: the abolition of the office of bishop and even that of supreme governor. These were among the demands of many whom we can call Puritans. Once again, however, it does not resolve the problem at hand: what was Puritanism? The answer may be found in more subtle theological positions than those which have been discussed so far. Patrick McGrath's, *Papists and Puritans under Elizabeth I* (1967, pages 32–41) is useful here, but he still employs 'Anglican' and 'Puritan' as distinct categories: when, for instance, he discusses the fallen nature of 'Man', or the role of preaching and the sacraments. For example: 'the "puritan" believed that fallen human nature was totally evil, and that all men's faculties were affected, including his reason', whereas the 'Anglican', 'assigned to human reason an important role in deciding the way in which men should behave in this life'. Admittedly, at this point in his book McGrath is describing the views of J.F. New in *Anglican and Puritan. The Basis of their Opposition 1558–1640*, London, 1964; but he persists thereafter in referring to Anglicans and Puritans as distinct and even separate groups

The important point to remember is that the Anglican Church was a broad-spectrum Church which embraced Puritanism. From its very inception, it encompassed a wide range of opinions and, Presbyterians and Separatists apart, differences were not fundamental, but rather a matter of degree. There was a general acceptance of predestination, and no one denied the importance of the Bible, although there was some disagreement as to how important it was. To the ardent Puritans of the Anglican left it was the *only* authority: 'The Bible only is the religion of Protestants'. Anglicans of the centre and right, however, recognised the importance of man-made institutions too (for example, the supreme governor and the bishops). Unlike the hard-line Puritans they distinguished between *adiaphora* (things which were not essential or fundamental: matters indifferent, which reason and the government of the Church could resolve) and the fundamentals on which the Bible alone was the authority. Nevertheless, on such matters it is often difficult, even impossible, to distinguish most Puritans from the rest of the Anglican community.

Puritanism was an ethos which pervaded society and touched most people, except the Roman Catholics and the Queen. If this is still too vague, we can be more specific and identify two main streams of Puritanism. One was **passive**, concerned with self-improvement. The other was **activist**, desirous of change and willing to impose it on others. However, until the 1630s there is one binding and common denominator between the passive and the active. They were all members of the Anglican Church (with one insignificant exception— the Separatists—who will be considered later). The passive Puritans—

the Lady Hoby type—have already been considered. Now is the time to identify and examine the characteristics of the activists.

The great majority of the activists were moderate men. They did not question the fundamentals of the new Church: the royal governorship, the survival of the Catholic office of bishop, the prayer book and the thirty-nine articles. Their prime concern was with the moral condition of society, the standards of the clergy, insufficient preaching, and with *adiaphora* and the order of worship. They fretted about the use of candles and altar cloths in the Queen's chapel, the use of the wedding ring, the wearing of vestments, and so on. This did not strike at the heart of the new Church but questioned rather the survival of Roman Catholic practices. Above all, they were concerned to cleanse the Church of ancient abuses such as simony (the buying and selling of ecclesiastical offices) absenteeism and pluralism (the possession of more than one living, which, like absence from a parish, did not make for regular services). Elizabeth, as always, overreacted to such criticisms. The 'vestiarian controversy', provoked by the refusal of some clergy to wear the 'signes of popyshy priesthode', resulted in her instruction to Archbishop Parker in 1565 to enforce uniformity of dress. As usual, the Queen was the author of such unpopular orders, and her bishops bore the brunt of criticism. The important point to remember is that dissenting clergymen obeyed or suffered the consequences, without leaving the Church. They remained Anglicans.

A new, second generation of activist Puritans, the Presbyterians, threw down the gauntlet in a more serious challenge to the new Church. In 1572 they questioned the prayer book (the order of worship) and the office of bishop. Fertile in ideas, they challenged the established Church in Parliament, in the dioceses and at the grassroots—the parishes. Elizabeth broke them. But at no time did they move outside the Church, transform themselves into a revolutionary body and plan to overthrow the institution from without. When James I denied many of their aspirations at the Hampton Court conference in 1604, their response was much the same. They retreated into nonresistance, meditation and the improvement of their personal lives. It was not until Charles I's policies in the late 1620s and 1630s that they began to secede from the Church. Until then they remained Anglican reformers, anxious to transform the Church and society from within. But during the years of the Personal Rule they became something different, a potentially revolutionary movement which organised itself to overthrow a much-hated institution. The fundamental lesson to be learned from this is that Elizabethan, Jacobean and even early Caroline activist Puritans were Anglican reformers and very different creatures from the Puritan revolutionaries of the 1640s. In such a short time, between 1629 and 1640, the politico-religious geography of England was redrawn, for reasons which will be considered later (see pages 281–93).

There is one exception, a minor one, but possibly a portent of things to come. The Separatists were Puritans who rejected the idea of reforms from within and who proposed instead to secede and set up their own Churches. The idea had been mooted in the 1560s and 70s, but it was not until the 1580s that the movement came to fruition. Its early leaders were Robert Browne and Robert Harrison, though the former eventually submitted to the Anglican establishment (1591) and the latter died in 1585. The Separatists had a chequered career. They were persecuted by the authorities and attacked by the rest of the Puritans. The new leaders, Henry Barrow, John Greenwood and John Penry were imprisoned and executed. An Act of Parliament of 1593 finally offered the community the options of conformity or exile. They chose the latter and ended up in Amsterdam in the Dutch republic.

The Separatists were a common target for the hostility of both the government and Puritans. The reasons are not hard to find. Separatism fundamentally challenged the official belief that only one organised Church could exist in one society. It was also contrary to the conviction of Elizabethan and early Stuart Puritans that reform must come through the Anglican Church and, moreover, that it must come with the approval of the monarch. 'Tarrying for the magistrate'—waiting until Elizabeth or James I came round to their point of view—was their watchword. Of course they laboured, through instruction, persuasion, even pressure tactics, to persuade the ruler of the error of his or her ways. But they did so within the framework of the established Church and they regarded secession from it as politically dangerous, even a step towards anarchy. Fears were heightened by the radical opinions of such Separatists as Harrison and Barrow. They attacked the bishops with a barrage of malicious insults in print, and they claimed authority in religion for each congregation alone. This constituted an attack on the entire structure of Church government. It was also a rejection of the disciplined Church as envisaged by the Presbyterians. It is no surprise that they were cast into the wilderness and condemned by everyone else (McGrath, *Papists and Puritans*, chapter 2 and pages 303–11).

Roman Catholicism and Catholics

It has already been suggested that because Roman Catholicism was a separate religion and opposed to the Anglican Church, Catholics should have been easy to identify. In practice this was not the case: the paradox needs to be explained. However, any explanation is complicated by the fact that the religious situation in Elizabethan and early Stuart England was not static. When Mary I died, the English Church was part of the universal Catholic Church, which acknowledged the supremacy of the Pope. Everyone was bound in law to attend mass, reject Protestant heresy and accept the authority of the Bishop of Rome. There is abundant evidence that, even in Mary's reign, many defied the law and remained obstinately Protestant. So, between November 1558 and the enactment of the Elizabethan Settlement nearly six months later, the country was in a state of flux. The government had no way of knowing how many remained Catholic at heart, and what proportion would accept a Protestant Church.

On paper the Elizabethan Settlement should have clarified the situation. It required everyone to recognise the Queen as supreme governor and to worship according to the Book of Common Prayer. However, human responses are never as neat and tidy as the paper schemes of bureaucrats and politicians. Catholics responded in a variety of ways, which were determined as much by their social position, local and national loyalties, ambition and self interest, as by their courage and conviction. Some remained rigid and unalterable in their opinions about the mass and loyal to the papacy. Only a few of them fled abroad during Elizabeth's reign, but their importance cannot be measured in numbers. They included distinguished scholars, many of whom were also men of great courage: William Allen, Nicholas Sander(s), Thomas Stapleton, Laurence Vaux, Edmund Campion and Robert Parsons were the most prominent. They were not only a great loss to a newly established Church which needed men of such calibre, but also a major threat to it. And to the Elizabethan State as well. Allen's seminary at Douai trained the missionary priests who infiltrated England in the 1570s and 80s. Sander engaged in a polemical pamphlet war with the English government. Stapleton was a controversial propagandist. Vaux, Campion and Parsons were members of the Jesuit mission who, from 1580 on, attempted with some success to halt the declining numbers of Catholics and win converts to the old faith. These men were naturally feared by the Elizabethan authorities, especially as some of them supported a Spanish invasion of England.

Nevertheless, the exiles were relatively few in number. The common response of English Catholics normally involved a compromise, between conscience and conviction on the one hand, and convenience and national loyalty on the other. This was expressed in several ways and largely depended on the priorities of individuals. Each one had to wrestle with two problems: one concerned doctrine; the other, supremacy. The doctrinal problem was clear-cut. Although there has been considerable debate over the precise meaning of the wording of the communion service in the 1559 Prayer Book, the mass—the very centrepiece of Catholic worship—was undoubtedly prohibited. How to respond to this? There were two alternatives. Some defiantly practised recusancy (non-attendance at their Anglican parish church on Sundays), which incurred a fine of 12d per offence. But many did attend in order to evade the financial penalties. This involved an important and recurring compromise: they continued to regard the Roman Catholic Church as the one true Church; but they went through the motions of an Anglican service. Some afterwards 'cleansed' themselves by attending secret mass.

Papal supremacy was a more complicated issue. As events were to prove, the majority of even die-hard Catholics placed their loyalty to the Queen and to England above their political allegiance to the papacy. Even for them, however, this must have involved battles with conscience and often agonising soul-searching. At first it was probably a less acute problem than the weekly one of whether to attend the local church or not. Then, in 1570, the papal bull (decree) *Regnans in Excelsis* was issued by Pope Pius V (1566–72). It condemned Elizabeth as an usurper, heretic and schismatic and excommunicated her. It deprived her of 'her pretended title' to the Crown, absolved her subjects from their oath of allegiance to her, and called upon them not to obey her orders or laws. One might assume that this placed the English Catholics in a painful dilemma: whether to obey their spiritual father or remain loyal to their Queen. In fact, for some time the dilemma was more apparent than real. No Catholic power was ready to enforce the bull in 1570, or in the years following. Moreover, English Catholics were able to distinguish between the spiritual supremacy of the Pope and his much more questionable authority to depose monarchs. Most of them remained loyal to Elizabeth. The papal attitude to the heretic Queen did not change. Nor, perhaps, was the papacy willing to recognise that most English Catholics were English rather than Catholic. It preferred to assume that they lacked the strength to enforce the bull of 1570 by deposing Elizabeth. So in 1580 Gregory XIII excused them for their inactivity until it could be enforced, presumably with the backing of a foreign power.

Not that this was much comfort to the English Catholics. The bull of 1570 had produced a sharp official response in the Treasons Act of the following year (see pages 262–3). Life for them was made increasingly difficult, their economic resources were eroded and their loyalties were tested as the crisis mounted: with the papal expedition to Ireland in 1579–81, the Ridolfi, Throckmorton and Babington plots (1571, 1583, 1586), the Catholic threat from Scotland (1581–3), the arrival of the secular priests in the 1570s and the Jesuits in the 1580s, and finally the Spanish armadas of the 1580s and 1590s. Of all the Acts which a frightened government and governing class enacted in Parliament, the one which concerns us most here is the Recusancy Act of 1581 which raised the fine for non-attendance at church to a monthly rate of £20. This must have sorted out the compromisers from the men of conviction, because the penalty was such a savage one. Even then the government confined itself to the outward show of conformity—attendance at church. It did not apply the ultimate test of conscience, the act of receiving communion. The Anglican communion service differed fundamentally from the mass. To have imposed this test of conscience on Catholics would have been politically explosive and dangerous to the government; instead, it bled them of money and, in the process, persuaded many to conform as the only alternative to bankruptcy.

The interplay of Elizabethan politics, Catholic responses in England, and the conduct of foreign powers was to produce a number of Catholic 'types'. The most extreme (or dedicated) was the exile: a mixture of clergy (like William Allen), gentry (like Sir Francis Englefield), renegade peers (like the Earl of Westmorland) and adventurers (like Sir Thomas Stukeley). Of those who remained, the most obstinate and easily identifiable were the recusants. However, their refusal to attend church was a matter of conscience and in most cases that conscience was able to live comfortably alongside political allegiance to Queen and country. There were, of course, those who conspired to enthrone Mary Stuart or carry out the terms of the 1570 bull, but they were not representative of the English Catholic community. More typical were the protestations of loyalty by men as diverse as Edmund Campion (at his trial in 1581) and prominent gentry, as the Armada crisis approached in 1588.

In any case, the majority of English Catholics did not fall into any of these categories. It should be added that it is difficult to draw hard-and-fast lines between groups within the Catholic community, let alone separate Catholics from Anglicans. This is because their dilemma was both political and theological. Some upheld papal supremacy but compromised on worship in an Anglican church, and vice versa. In the midst of all this confusion, however, it is possible to discern two streams of opinion: the **schismatics**, those who remained loyal to the Queen, regardless of the 1570 bull, but who might still be recusants; and the **church papists**, who attended church despite their private convictions. The church papists have been the most difficult to identify, both to contemporaries and historians. Some we can detect. They chattered during the service, ostentatiously pretended to fall asleep, or coughed and spat during the sermon. Others conducted themselves modestly, then went home and were privately absolved (pardoned) by a Catholic priest. As the Elizabethan recusancy laws did not extend to women and children, it was sufficient for the male head of the family to put in regular appearances at the parish church. So the rest of the family could continue to practise their religion unhindered and without penalties. In such circumstances, how could any upright, God-fearing Anglican be sure that his neighbours were of similar opinion and not a nest of papist vipers?

The Elizabethan Settlement, 1559

It is time to return to the beginning again and raise the curtain on the opening act of Elizabethan/early Stuart religious history. Immediately we come up against Sir John Neale's classic account of how the new Church was created. It is a persuasive and well-documented account. In particular, he is right in identifying it as a parliamentary settlement. The Acts of Uniformity (which enacted the order of worship) and of Supremacy (which created the royal governorship) were passed 'by the authority of Parliament'—the words are there in the Acts. To Neale, the Settlement had three important characteristics:

1 It was enacted by Parliament, which therefore could claim the right to future interference in the management of the Church. In contrast Henry VIII's Parliament had simply acknowledged him as supreme head of the Church. It was a God-given right, and Parliament's only contribution was to equip him with teeth: laws for the punishment of dissenters, opponents and heretics.

2 Henry VIII and Edward VI had been supreme heads of the Church, with the power to discipline, exterminate heresies and even pronounce on matters of doctrine. They were spiritual figures. However, a parliament of men in 1559 heeded the words of St Paul, that a woman could exercise no spiritual office in the Church. Instead, Elizabeth was made supreme governor. She remained a lay 'supervisor' who managed the Church through her bishops. They alone could perform the spiritual functions of a Henry VIII. Formidable figure that she was, Elizabeth could and did bully and command her bishops to act in accordance with her wishes. However, if an obstinate prelate defied her, she could punish him, but she could not act instead of him. In 1576 Archbishop Grindal refused to obey her order to suppress prophesyings: these were meetings of the clergy, who debated Scriptural texts and heard trial sermons. To Grindal, they were an instrument for the improvement of the clergy; to Elizabeth they were Puritan propaganda platforms. He was no doctrinaire radical, just an

archbishop concerned with the state of religion. He was also a tactless Tudor male, lecturing a woman who happened to be Queen. She responded vigorously. In 1577 Grindal was suspended from his spiritual jurisdiction. For six years, until his death in 1583, the Church remained without an effective episcopal head. In the meantime, the Queen could not assume his powers. Instead, in 1577 she had to order the bishops to suppress prophesyings. The 'Grindal affair' is a prime example of the institutional weakness of a woman in a male-dominated world.

3 According to Neale, the Elizabethan Settlement was the outcome of a political tug-of-war between an obstinate conservative Queen and the more radical elements in her first Parliament. At Mary's funeral, Bishop White of Winchester warned that 'the wolves' were 'coming out of Geneva and other places of Germany'. He meant the Protestant exiles who had fled abroad to escape the Marian persecution. In fact, few returned in time for Elizabeth's first Parliament. Nevertheless, Neale identifies a formidable radical minority in the Commons which compelled the Queen to accept a more radical order Of worship than she desired. However, the work of Norman Jones (*Faith by Statute. Parliament and the Settlement of Religion, 1559*, London, 1982) has drastically modified Neale's interpretation. Puritanism was not a potent force. Resistance to the government's programme came from the Catholic bishops and a few Catholic peers in the House of Lords. Secondly, Elizabeth obtained more or less what she wanted from the religious settlement. The Queen, like all successful politicians, regarded politics as the art of the possible, and she obtained about as much as she could have reasonably hoped for—she was in a weaker position than her father. However, both the order of worship and the thirty-nine articles (ratified by convocation in 1563) were moderate, ambiguous, and certainly not designed to satisfy the aspirations of the more ardent Protestants. They bear the stamp of the Queen's own uncommitted theological position.

The new Anglican Church, 1559–1603

Government of the new Church was to be in the hands of a woman who was supreme governor and could not exercise spiritual authority herself, but had to direct it through the bishops. Episcopacy was the characteristic feature of Church government. The pressing question was, who were to be the bishops? With one exception, Anthony Kitchin of Llandaff, the surviving Marian bishops refused to participate and were deprived. Elizabeth had no choice but to recruit men of Puritan persuasion. Some had been exiles, but whatever their past track record and their suitability for the job, their task was not an enviable one. They had to cope with a spiritually demoralised society which, for thirty years, had been bombarded with more brands of religion than we are with washing powders. They had to contend with apathy, indifference, cynicism and criticism among both clergy and laity. Even worse was the hostility of a substantial Catholic minority and the menacing disapproval of Catholic Europe.

Moreover, thirty years of Reformation had eroded the bishops' status and stripped them of much of their capital and income. They no longer had the revenue to subsidise the meagre incomes of many parish clergy, to ensure adequate ecclesiastical administration in their dioceses, and to finance the new Church's missionary role. It must not be assumed that all of the new bishops were heroic figures, fighting against great odds to improve the condition of the Church. Some certainly were: for example, Matthew Parker, in 1559, warned the Queen against the retention of images in churches, and Grindal, in 1576, lectured her to leave matters spiritual to the bishops. On the other hand, Bishop Cheyney of Gloucester got himself into hot water for holding Lutheran opinions in a Calvinist Church, and Archbishop Sandys and others were accused of feathering their families' nests with livings and cheap leases of ecclesiastical property. Contemporaries, like the modern press, were much more interested in tales of greed, ambition, laxity and corruption than in the daily administrative grind of conscientious bishops. Yet, as Ralph Houlbrooke has demonstrated, here was a bench of bishops who, for the first time in English history, spent most of their time in their dioceses and, in the process, did much to put the new Church on its feet.

It is true that, as the first generation of bishops died out, their successors were more conservative. Elizabeth saw to that. Second-generation prelates such as Whitgift and Bancroft were anti-Puritan and (especially Bancroft) more inclined to regard the office of bishop as divinely ordained than as one of convenience (which upset the Puritans). That does not mean that they were less conscientious, dedicated or hard-working. All of the Elizabethan bishops were faced with a formidable challenge: no less than the building of a new Church. It was a mongrel, combining features of all the experiments of the previous thirty years: a royal headship, a Calvinist theology, government by the Catholic office of bishop, and surviving Catholic ritual and ceremony. Out of this uncomfortable compromise the bishops had to mould an institution and religion which would win the attachment and loyalty of English society. They had to make it strong and unified enough to resist the Catholic challenge and even win converts from the Catholic ranks.

The bishops attempted to achieve much in the most unfavourable circumstances. They were not only the common target of both Puritans and Catholics; they were also the frequent victims of a secular political establishment, above all of the predator Queen. In 1559 Elizabeth secured an Act of Parliament empowering her to exchange 'properties' with the bishops—and when she did so the exchange was always to her advantage, because she received estates in return for tithes which were always difficult and unpopular to collect. She was a demanding and unsystematic royal mistress. Her Council imposed a wide range of administrative duties on the bishops. She harried them to execute her policies, particularly against activist Puritans, yet frequently, once she had issued her orders (as in the vestiarian controversy) she would not lend them the public support of royal authority. The bishops were left to fend for themselves and they were exposed to all the slings and arrows of those who disapproved of their actions. (For recent studies of the Elizabethan bishops, see Cross and Houlbrooke in F. Heal and R. O'Day (editors), 1977.)

Royal exactions on the Church simply magnified its financial problems. They did not cause them. This was especially true of the parish clergy, whose income was derived from two sources: **tithes**, levied on the laity, and the **glebe**—the land attached to the minister's benefice, or living. The income from these sources varied enormously from one place to another, but even in pre-Reformation England no more than thirty-three per cent of the parish clergy could afford to carry out their duties efficiently and still maintain a reasonable standard of living.

From the 1530s on, two processes worsened their financial condition. One, inflation, eroded their real income. The other was a direct consequence of the Reformation. Before the 1530s, the **advowson** (the right to appoint clergy to livings and to receive tithes) was in the hands of a number of agencies: the Crown; nobles, gentry, merchants and other laymen; bishops and monastic houses. When the monasteries were dissolved in the 1530s (and the chantries in 1547) many advowsons passed to the Crown, which in turn sold them or gave them away. The impropriators (lay owners of benefices) frequently pocketed most of the income from tithes and left the incumbents (occupants of benefices) with a meagre and inadequate income. Beset with pressures from the Crown, the laity and inflation, the clergy were still expected to carry out their old traditional functions, build a new Church, and perform a missionary role persuading non-believers, the doubtful, and the hostile Catholics to enter its ranks. Despite such pressures, demands and depleted resources, and their own personal shortcomings, the Elizabethan bishops did achieve a great deal. By the end of the reign, Richard Hooker had crowned their efforts by writing a kind of philosophical justification for the existence of a Church governed by royal authority through the old office of bishop (*The Laws of Ecclesiastical Polity*). For the economic condition of the clergy see C. Hill, *Economic Problems of the Church from Archbishop Whitgift to the Long Parliament*, London, 1956 and Heal in F. Heal and R. O'Day, 1977, pages 99–118.

The bishops, like generals in a military campaign, oversaw the general execution of ecclesiastical policy. But they depended on their front-line troops—their diocesan machinery and their parish clergy—for the detailed enforcement of that policy, as well as daily administration and the fulfilment of the Church's pastoral (spiritual) function. Their chief weapon was an elaborate system of over 250 Church courts, which were organised into a hierarchy: the archbishops', below them the bishops' and at bottom the archdeacons' courts. They exercised a wide jurisdiction over laity and clergy in matters of wills, marriage and morals. On paper they wielded great influence, but in practice they were paper tigers. They had overlapping jurisdictions which led to conflicts. They were plagued with dishonest practices, corrupt officials, too much business and yet no effective means of enforcing their decisions, a declining prestige and the hostility of an anti-clerical laity. They could punish offenders with excommunication, but this no longer made the blood in the veins of the convicted run cold; it just provoked annoyance and resentment.

The ineffectiveness of the courts spiritual was to some extent offset by the Crown's appointment of ecclesiastical commissions. The most famous of these was the Court of High Commission. It was afflicted with the usual weaknesses—incompetence, corruption and faction politics—but it also had much more muscle than the ordinary Church courts. In particular, it could impose harsher penalties than excommunication, such as fines and imprisonment. It had other advantages too: it worked fast and often dispensed justice in a summary fashion, and the fact that it included laymen neutralised much of the anti-clerical hostility to the Church courts. It proved to be one of the Crown's most effective front-line weapons against both obstinate Puritans and recusant Catholics.

Society in every age seems to need its scapegoats. Today they include bureaucrats and M.P.s. In the sixteenth century a popular butt was the legal profession, waxing rich on property disputes and the misfortunes of clients. But the particular target for satire, abuse and malice was the Church. Puritan surveys in the 1580s pilloried (with exaggeration and even vicious libel) the unqualified, uneducated, money-grubbing, immoral clergy. The secret, Puritan, Marprelate

Press taunted and mocked the bishops. We must, of course, treat Puritan polemics and propaganda with caution. Some of the descriptions and tales are witty, salacious and great fun. When scandals are published some of the public will believe them, and even more will enjoy them: this is one of the secrets of skilful propaganda well learned by the Puritans.

On the other hand, it was true that the Reformation had not dramatically raised the qualifications and quality of the clergy. Many lacked the education or income to carry out their spiritual duties effectively. Favoured clergymen still acquired more than one living apiece. Indolent ministers did not bother to attend to their duties or they delegated them to underpaid deputies. Such abuses were the subject of running criticism from reforming Anglicans. The first archbishop of Henry VIII's new national Church, Thomas Cranmer, wrote that he might just as well give a benefice to his sister as to an absentee vicar or his substitute. Thomas Norton, a loyalist Puritan, wished that those guilty of absenteeism, pluralism and simony were consigned to hell. However, critics like Norton remained within the Church. During Elizabeth's reign, not only the bishops, but also conscientious parish clergy, pious laymen and even harsh critics had a common interest: to create a new Church with a tradition of its own.

The Catholics

The chronology of Elizabethan Catholicism need only be summarised here, because there are already in print a number of sound, accessible studies (for example, P. McGrath's *Papists and Puritans under Elizabeth I*, and standard accounts in text books on Tudor England, such as those by G.R. Elton, J. Hurstfield and S.T. Bindoff; see the Bibliography). The inevitable starting point must be the Elizabethan Settlement of 1559. The Acts of Supremacy and Uniformity required recognition of the royal governorship, renunciation of all foreign spiritual authorities (this was aimed at the Pope) and worship according to the Prayer Book. This placed all Roman Catholics in an acute, even agonising dilemma: whether to obey statute or adhere to the Pope and the mass. During the next decade, many opted for the national Church. They were probably encouraged to this decision by two seemingly contradictory circumstances. One was the penalties in the 1559 Acts, which hung like a sword over their heads. The other was their lax enforcement in practice. This is often attributed to the Queen's studied moderation and her refusal to harrass the Catholics and so push them into opposition and even treason. However, there is little evidence that the Privy Council was troubled by the presence of a sizeable Roman Catholic minority during the 1560s. It was not until the crisis of 1569–72 that the government changed its attitude. The flight of Mary Stuart to England, the rebellion of the northern earls (1569), the papal excommunication of Elizabeth (1570) and the Ridolfi plot (1571–2) frightened both the Council and the governing class into action. The fear that the English Catholic community was a subversive force, working on behalf of an international Catholic conspiracy, dated from this crisis.

That fear was strengthened by events in the 1570s and it is easy to understand why. In 1574 the first missionary priests, trained in the Douai seminary (which the English exile, William Allen, had established five years before), landed in England. By 1580 about 100 had slipped secretly into the country. Their task was religious, rather than political: not to incite rebellion but to stiffen the faith of surviving Catholics and to reconcile Anglicans to the Catholic Church. Although they wrote back to Douai and Rome exaggerated accounts of their success, there is no doubt that they put a brake on the decline in numbers. They persuaded many church papists not to compromise. They even secured a number of converts. Official hopes that the Catholic community, cut off from Catholic Europe and neglected by the papacy, would die a natural death from spiritual starvation was itself now dead.

Unfortunately for the English Catholics, this process coincided with some other, sinister, political developments. The papacy and Spain sponsored military expeditions to Ireland which was, as always, England's Achilles' heel. One, under the eccentric leadership of a quixotic English exile, Sir Thomas Stukeley, went astray and ended in destruction in a crusade against the North African Moors in 1578. But another, under James Fitzmaurice Fitzgerald, raised rebellion in Munster in 1579–81. It enabled Elizabeth's government to argue that to be a Catholic was to be a traitor. What else was adherence to a papacy which had excommunicated Elizabeth in the bull of 1570 and which had since sought to implement that document. This was no mere cynical exercise by the Privy Council: it felt that England was under siege, especially when the Jesuit Mission began in 1580. The Jesuits were there to reinforce the efforts of the secular priests. Their objective was spiritual and they were expressly forbidden to engage in politics. Most of them—such choice spirits as Edmund Campion, Robert Southwell and Henry Garnet—observed these orders. But one of them, Robert Parsons, used political action to achieve the spiritual ends of the Mission. The government and governing class feared and hated him as a political subversive, and his reputation tainted the other Jesuits and the entire Catholic community with treasonable intent.

In the early 1580s the Council's fears were heightened by events at home and abroad: the exposure of more Catholic conspiracies (for example, Throckmorton and Babington), Mary Stuart's involvement (which led to her execution in 1587), and the assassination of a Protestant hero, the Dutch rebel leader William of Orange. Moreover, the Catholic forces in Europe were moving against Elizabeth. Philip II's acquisition of Portugal (1580) and its navy made it possible for him to contemplate an invasion of England. Mary Stuart's death provided him with the justification for it. New laws, economic sanctions, supervision and searches, prison and executions characterised the government's treatment of Catholics in the 1580s. Yet the great majority of them remained loyal, even during Armada year. It brought them no dramatic relief, but in the 1590s both sides were inconsistent and equivocal in their conduct. The Catholic community was rent by divisions: native Catholics against the exiles, the secular clergy against the Jesuits, and a clash of opinions over Elizabeth's successor. The government was no more consistent in its actions and attitudes. Some Catholics were mulcted for the full recusancy fine of £20 a month; others got off scot-free; while more were allowed to compound (make individual agreements with the government whereby they paid, not in full, but what they could afford). Conciliar action was a mixture of strict law enforcement and laxity. It was a matter of select victimisation rather than a campaign directed against the entire Catholic community.

This inconsistency was magnified by two other factors. One was the intrusion of external threats: further armadas sent by Philip II in 1596 and 1597, the progress of the civil wars in France and the Dutch rebellion against Spanish rule, and the Irish rebellion which, in 1601, was reinforced by 3000 Spanish soldiers. Each crisis encouraged repressive measures against the English Catholics. The other factor was the Queen. She remained a moderating influence who could overrule the anti-Catholic diehards in her Council, although she would not tolerate political disloyalty. At one point in the 1590s she even contemplated a limited measure of toleration. It did not come about. At the end of the reign the Catholic community was divided, demoralised and economically eroded. It looked for a better day with the accession of James VI of Scotland.

These are the bare facts of the history of an increasingly nervous, even frightened, government and an increasingly repressed minority. It is a history of interaction between the two: this is the only meaningful approach to the 'Catholic problem'. The Catholics constituted a problem to a security-conscious government. However, to be a Catholic was also a problem: whether to become an Anglican or to remain in the old faith, whether to compromise (as the church papists did), whether to put Queen or Pope first, how to respond to the seminary priests and the Jesuit Mission. For many the soul-searching was endless. The important point to remember is that the role of Catholicism can only be understood if it is studied from two points of view: that of the government and that of the Catholics themselves.

The most important practical expression of official concern is to be found in the Elizabethan penal laws, which were the product of Council-governing class collaboration. The Queen signed them into law, but if she had been of one mind with her advisers and her parliaments, the penal code would have been harsher and it would probably have included a test of conscience. Instead, she acted as a constant brake upon Protestant 'paranoia'. Nevertheless, the mounting crisis of the 1570s and 80s strengthened the hand of those who advocated harsher penalties. Gradually Elizabeth was forced to recognise the need for deterrent and punitive laws. Certainly, enough were passed to make life difficult and costly for devout Catholics and impossible for some.

The first statutory penalties were written into the Elizabethan Settlement. All officials in Church and State were required to take an oath acknowledging the Queen as supreme governor (a provision extended in 1563 to the professions as well). The penalty for refusal was loss of office. Punishments for refusal to use and observe the order of worship set forth in the Prayer Book were more severe, ranging from six months to life imprisonment. Non-attendance at church on Sundays incurred a shilling fine for each offence. Those who uttered or wrote criticisms of the Prayer Book were also liable to fines. The penal clauses of the 1559 Settlement were designed only to achieve outward conformity and political obedience. In no way did they represent a repressive policy. Perhaps the government hoped that in time English Catholicism, without leadership or guidance, would simply wither and die. If so, official optimism was justified by events in the 1560s. The papacy gave no direction or support and many Catholics entered the new Church. Numbers dwindled. The government's connivance at quiet and private Catholic worship actually assisted the process: a repressive policy would have antagonised them and made them obstinate in their faith. And so they were left, for the most part free and unmolested, to make their personal decisions about conversion.

The crisis of 1569–72 dramatically altered the situation. The Parliament of 1571 responded to the excommunication of Elizabeth with a new treason law. It became a treasonable offence to introduce papal bulls into England, to receive copies, or to call the Queen a heretic, schismatic (one who has caused division in the Church by seceding from it) or usurper, all of which the bull of 1570 had done. This Act was concerned to protect the Queen and State and so, thus far, it did not depart from previous official policy. However, in one important respect it did. It punished those who imported crucifixes, rosary beads and the other items of what the Council called 'superstitious gear', essential to Catholic worship and life. It marked the initial step in the campaign finally to stifle the practice of the old religion.

In the same Parliament, the Fugitives Act carried this policy a step further. It commanded all emigrants to return to England within six months on pain of forfeiting their property. The immediate reason for this Act may have been the flight of the northern rebels. However, it also had a long-term objective: to put a stop to the exodus of gentlemen, students and scholars, many of whom in the 1560s and 70s went as recruits to Douai and Rome. The Act was also intended to coerce many of them into returning. If successful it would have broken up the communities abroad and helped to seal off the English Catholics from the Continent.

The Act proved to be ineffective, however, and the Privy Council's worst fears were realised with the coming of the missionary priests and Jesuits. The government now responded with punitive measures in pursuit of two objectives: to destroy both the English Catholic community and the missionaries who gave it spiritual succour. The opening blow was the 1581 Act 'to retain the Queen's Majesty's subjects in their true obedience'. It denounced the missionaries as traitors, penalised (with imprisonment) those who sheltered and concealed them and made reconciliation to Rome a treason. The Act also attacked the Catholic community with spiritual and economic weapons. It imposed fines and a year in gaol for attending mass and of course it inflicted that notorious monthly fine of £20 for recusancy. The government pursued these twin objectives for the rest of the reign, and later Acts simply built on the 1581 statute. In 1585 the target was the missionaries, who were now automatically guilty of treason if they did not leave England within forty days. The terms of the Fugitive Act were repeated, and those who aided and abetted the missionaries could be executed as felons. This Act, and the remaining penal legislation of the reign (1587 and 1593), was also designed to supervise the Catholics more closely, make life intolerable and so coerce them into surrender. The legislation provided for more stringent regulations for J.Ps, more efficient machinery for the administration of recusancy fines, and more restrictions on the lives of

Catholics (for example, their movements were restricted to within five miles of their homes). Elizabethan government was armed with a formidable battery of weapons against the Catholic 'threat'.

How effective were the penal laws in practice? There was, as always in Tudor and Stuart England, a wide gulf between laws enacted in Parliament and their effective enforcement. The hierarchical structure of society, with its built-in patron-client relationships and faction politics, protected some but victimised others. Catholic magistrates, in Catholic countries such as Lancashire, connived at the worship of their co-religionists. Some J.P.s were lazy and would not activate themselves to hunt down missionaries, search out recusants and secret masses, interrogate suspects and remain eternally vigilant. On the other hand, ardent Protestant Justices had the power and capacity to make the lot of local Catholics a miserable one. County rivalries often sharpened hostility. In Cornwall, the Arundells and Tregians (related by marriage), together with the Tremaynes, formed the nucleus of the Catholic community there. Sir Richard Grenville, thwarted in his attempt to contract a marriage alliance with the Tregians, wreaked his revenge during his year as sheriff in 1576. He caught the Arundells for recusancy. He also discovered a missionary priest in the Tregian household and so accomplished the ruin of the family. The persecution of Cornish Catholics in the following years was the simple consequence of Grenville's vindictiveness. Everywhere we look, the picture is the same: infinite variety in the enforcement and impact of penal laws.

Local conditions were not the only reason for such variations. Only the wealthier Catholic recusants could have survived the crippling burdens imposed by the 1581 Act. However, as we have seen, the law was tempered by the practice of composition. In 1584 and 1587 the government imposed emergency levies for the defence of the realm. The Catholics paid up promptly and in full. In return for their loyalty they were given the option of compounding. Several hundred immediately took advantage of the arrangement. For one gentlemen, Thomas Throckmorton, it meant an annual payment of £100 out of his income of £666. Nevertheless, recusancy fines continuously eroded the wealth of the Catholic community and steadily nudged many of its members towards poverty and bankruptcy. Sir Thomas Tresham is a classic example. He was a progressive, improving farmer and a commercial landlord. But he was in and out of prison and burdened with recusancy fines, mounting debts and seizures of land in the 1580s and 1590s. It is no surprise that the financially desperate Tresham family was deeply implicated in the Gunpowder Plot in James I's reign.

Recusancy fines were not the only rods with which to beat and bloody the backs of the Catholics. They were also debarred from entering royal service or the professions, so that an important avenue to lucrative employment was cut off. There were also the restraints, such as those on freedom of movement, which could make it difficult to lead a normal life. To this must be added the various forms of official harrassment, such as searches, interrogation (sometimes under torture) and imprisonment. More subtle were the social pressures and the isolation of the Catholic community within a predominantly Protestant governing class. The lines were not always clearly drawn between Catholic and Anglican—witness Grenville's attempt to marry into the Tregian family—but gentlemen were expected to assume their share of social responsibility and take their turn in the more arduous and unrewarding county offices, especially as sheriff, but also as J.P.s Their obstinate attachment to their religion increasingly excluded Catholics from office as the reign wore on, and so the burden fell on the Anglican gentry alone. Governing class hostility was not simply an ideological one. It was also a resentment of the way in which the Catholics had reneged on their duties as gentlemen and members of the governing class.

However, it is not enough to study the Elizabethan Catholics from the official position. History should not be exclusively concerned with the mainstream and majority of a society. In any case, the Catholic minority was, at least in the early years, a formidable minority. It had extensive connections in the governing class, with the exiles, the colleges at Douai and Rome, the papacy, Spain and the French Catholic faction. Moreover, some of them sympathised with the bull of 1570, the aspirations of Mary Stuart, and the Spanish Grand Design against England. A few were prepared to translate their sympathies into treasonable acts. Although events were to prove the loyalty of the overwhelming majority, the Privy Council could not know that. It had no way of gauging their loyalty. Indeed, it did not even have an accurate notion of how large (numerically) the Catholic problem was. Hence its increasingly repressive policy towards them: a policy born out of fear, ignorance, insecurity and ideological hostility. Yet, despite every penal measure devised by the government, the Catholic community endured and survived. An examination of its size, nature and distribution may help us to understand why.

Within ten years of the 1559 Settlement, only a hard core of devout and conscientious Catholics remained firm in their faith. By then a mere handful of counties contained a sizeable Catholic community: Lancashire, the far northern counties, Yorkshire and Herefordshire. They were strong in Midlands counties, such as

Worcestershire, but here they were confronted by even stronger Prot-estant power groups. In the rest of the country they survived in small pockets or as isolated families. Wherever they were found, however, an impressive number of them were gentry. In the early years of the reign, at least, they were prominent in local government too.

This means that their importance cannot be measured in mere numbers. In 1564 the Privy Council ordered a survey of the religious opinions of J.P.s. It revealed just what we might expect: that the Cath-olics were strongest in the marcher counties, the north and the west. The Bishop of Carlisle lamented that, in Cumberland, many were 'to be admonished in religion and very unfit for that office'. Westmor-land, Lancashire and Cheshire contained many who were 'evil and not meet' (to continue in office). In Hereford, Thomas Havard's entire family was infected: his wife and daughters used rosary beads and other 'superstitious gear' and he was a 'mortal enemy to true religion'. As the reports flooded in, the Privy Council could draw its own grim conclusions. Out of the 852 magistrates named in this survey, 431 (fifty-one per cent) were 'favourable' to the new Church, but 264 (thirty-one per cent) were 'indifferent' ('neuter') and 157 (eighteen per cent) were 'adversaries' or 'hinderers of God's Holy Word'. In the far north-west, sixty-three per cent were Catholic, in Lancashire fifty-three per cent and Herefordshire forty-two per cent. As the survey moved to the south-east, the proportion dropped dramatically: so in Worcestershire it was thirty-five per cent, but in Surrey (just south of London) none were recorded. Yet even in the south-east it was not absent: the governors of some Sussex towns were 'notorious obstinate adversaries'. The presence of so many Catholics in the governing élite naturally caused unease in the Privy Council.

After 1569 the number of Catholic J.P.s dwindled. The power structure of the Catholic Earls of Northumberland and Westmorland was broken. Nevertheless, many of the peerage still adhered firmly to the old faith; others were schismatics, while even such regional magnates as Derby and Shrewsbury were suspected of Catholic sympathies. The Council's insecurity was understandable and its fears were fed by ignorance. It did not know how large or socially influ-ential was the Catholic community. A 1582 census recorded nearly 2000 recusants—with their families perhaps 8000. However, concealed recusants and schismatics must have dramatically inflated this total. Fear, insecurity and a Protestant backlash combined to produce the harsh penal laws and repressive actions of the 1580s and 90s.

Why then did the Catholic community survive? Above all, be-cause it had a powerful leadership within the governing class. Catholic peers and gentry could provide an umbrella of protection for their co-religionists of humbler status and income. The fundamental social characteristic of English Catholicism was that it was **seigneurial**. In other words, it was focussed on the households of peers and gentry in the countryside. They provided the refuges for missionary priests and Jesuits. They established travelling circuits which enabled the missionaries to move in relative safety from house to house, ministering to the spiritual needs of the local faithful, whether gentry, yeomen, tenant farmers, labourers or servants.

As in Puritanism, so in the Catholic community: women played a vital part. To some extent this was a consequence of the anti-recusancy laws, which penalised men, but did not extend to women. Wives could stay at home on Sundays and raise their children in the Catholic faith. However there is more to it than that. The real dynamic in many Catholic households was provided by the women: the Countess of Arundel in Sussex, Lady Stonor in Oxfordshire, Lady Vaux in Northamptonshire, and Dorothy Lawson in the far north. The élitist leadership of Catholicism, its seigneurial organisation, the role of women and the ideological loyalty of the faithful: all combined to ensure the survival of a Catholic community into the next century and a new dynasty.

The Puritans

Puritanism in the 1560s was dominated by men of the 'first generation'. As many as 800 Englishmen had fled abroad during Mary Tudor's reign: merchants, lawyers, gentlemen and Edwardian bishops, such as John Ponet and Miles Coverdale. These men had imbibed radical Continental Protestantism, especially those who passed their years of exile in Calvin's Geneva. Three of them—Ponet, Christopher Goodman, and the Scot John Knox—had preached resistance to the ungodly Prince, Catholic in this case. They had even justified tyrannicide (assassination of a tyrant). However, when the exiles returned, most of them proved to be moderate in religion. They, and other Puritans, accepted the newly established Church, the office of bishop and the fundamentals of the new faith. Some, such as Robert Horne, John Scory, Edwin Sandys and Edmund Grindal, became bishops; while John Jewel's *Apology of the Church of England* was the first notable defence of the new Church. Émigré Puritans (for example, Laurence Humphrey, William Whittingham, Thomas Sampson and Thomas Lever) were appointed deans, archdeacons and heads of university colleges. Although they regarded the new Church as but 'halfly reformed', they would continue the work of reform from within, as Anglicans.

Most of the early Puritans' criticisms were confined to the life of the Church, the quality of the clergy and 'matters indifferent'. So they wrote to their co-religionists in the Reformed Churches of Frankfurt, Strasburg and Geneva, twittering furiously about the Queen's use of candles, images and altar cloths in the chapel royal. Insofar as they sought changes to the Prayer Book (as in the convocation of 1563) they were concerned with practices which smacked of popery, such as kneeling at communion, using the sign of the cross, the survival of saints' days in the Church's calendar and the wearing of special vestments by the clergy. The question of vestments was to become the most serious issue in the Anglican Church in the 1560s. It typified the priorities of first generation Puritans—men who ranged across the broad spectrum of the Anglican Church, from exiles like Sampson and Whittingham, to politicians like William Cecil and many of the bishops. What is known as the 'vestiarian controversy' had its roots in the Puritan clergy's objection to the surplice as a popish remnant. A number of bishops, including Grindal (London), Thomas Bentham (Coventry and Lichfield) and John Parkhurst (Norwich), were lax, sympathetic and even indulgent towards the objectors. However, the government was not. Collinson (1971, pages 69–70) is uncertain whether the true author of the official campaign against nonconformity in clerical dress was Elizabeth, William Cecil or Archbishop Matthew Parker of Canterbury. Certainly it was Elizabeth's letter to Parker in January 1565 which set the State machine in motion, and the end product was the Archbishop's *Advertisements* in the following year. These insisted on the continued use of the surplice.

The bishops were trapped in what was to become a common dilemma. They were men of God with the duty to propagate His Word and to advance the cause of religion. But they were also servants of the Queen who was supreme governor. Elizabeth always manifested herself more positively than God and the bishops acknowledged her authority over the Church, especially in points of ritual and other adiaphora. The episcopal response, however, was not an entirely unmixed one. Parkhurst and one or two others did not rigorously enforce the *Advertisements*, but other Puritan bishops, such as Grindal and Jewel, did. Some clergy were suspended, others were deprived. It was a messy, muddled affair, from which few of those involved emerged with credit. Elizabeth did not publicly support the *Advertisements*, leaving Parker to bear the brunt of Puritan criticism. On the other side, Henry Bullinger of Zurich, regarded by many English Puritans as their spiritual guide, deserted them. He recommended that they conform in 'matters indifferent'.

In the short term the authorities won. The obstinate nonconformists were deprived and the rest conformed. It did not alter their essential loyalty to the Anglican Church. There was no polarisation into two opposing forces, the Establishment on the one hand and Puritanism on the other. Quite the reverse. Puritanism, or a sympathy with its aims, was widespread in the Council, episcopate, and governing class. That was given clear expression in the so-called religious campaigns in the parliaments of 1566 and 1571 (see chapter 6). The ultimate obstacle, however, was the Queen, and Parker and some of the bishops obeyed her and insisted on conformity. Neither of these facts alienated the first-generation Puritans.

However, there was emerging a second generation of Puritans. They were younger, more radical, disillusioned by the events of the 1560s, and bent on reforms which extended beyond the adiaphora to the fundamentals of the Anglican Church. Their elders might lament the conservatism of their Queen, the laxity of some bishops, and the fossilised Catholicism still embedded in the Prayer Book and the thirty-nine articles, yet they did not question fundamentals. The new generation did. They shifted the ground of their attack to the episcopate. The early Elizabethan bishops generally held that their offices were not divinely ordained by God, but rather a matter of convenience. They were, at times, personally criticised for moral backsliding or for punishing those who would not conform or wear the surplice, but this did not amount to an attack on the office.

In 1572 all that changed. The lead had been given two years previously in a course of lectures delivered by Thomas Cartwright, a divinity professor at Cambridge. He took as his theme the primitive Church which had been administered, not by superior bishops, but by an equality of ministers, each of whom was elected by his congregation. This was Presbyterianism. Although Cartwright was deprived of his professorship, his lectures were a battle-cry for the new generation. By mid-1572 their leaders had despaired of both the first-generation Puritans and the bishops. Two of them, John Field and Thomas Wilcox, produced the *Admonition to the Parliament*, which appeared during the 1572 session. It signalled both a breakaway from their more conservative elders and a full-scale attack on the bishops, not as men but as occupants of a Catholic office. It went further and condemned the Prayer Book as 'an unperfect book, culled and picked out of that popish dunghill, the mass book'. And it proceeded, in brilliant and savage fashion, to turn 'matters indifferent' into 'matters of great moment', in particular, the lack of preaching and the wearing of surplices.

The Admonition was not merely negative and destructive. It advocated a Church with a godly discipline, based upon ministers elected by their congregations. Not a Church governed by an élite of bishops, but with a collective management operating from the grass-roots. This was a revolutionary proposal, even if it was advocated by men who remained Anglicans and sought to change the existing order from within. Yet its importance should not be exaggerated. Field and Wilcox went to prison and the older generation of Puritans disowned them and their work. So Thomas Norton wrote, 'Surely the [Admonition] was fond [foolish], and with much unreasonableness and unseasonableness hath hindered much good and done much harm'. Most Puritans continued to entertain more moderate aims related to the life and standards of the Church.

It would be wrong to see in these events some kind of irreconcilable conflict, even if the gap between the Establishment and the Field-Wilcox brand of Puritanism was much greater than the divisions had been in the 1560s. Field and company remained Anglicans and, according to their lights, loyal subjects. Furthermore, the divisions were blurred and muddied by the lattice-work of connections within the governing class. Puritan activists found powerful patrons of similar opinions or sympathies. They sought and received protection and promotion from regional magnates, such as Leicester and Huntingdon in the Midlands and Bedford in the west. It was this 'social basis' of Puritanism which enabled it to survive the official campaigns against it in the 1580s and 90s and in the 1630s.

When the radical Puritans' Admonition effected no changes, they displayed a typical tenacity and did not give up. They continued to work for change within the Church. And with consummate skill they chose the time and occasion to infiltrate the 'prophesyings' (exercises for religious instruction) in order to convert them to their own purposes. The purpose of the prophesyings was a commendable one: to improve the quality of the clergy. In various parts of the country, ministers met to pray, hear and analyse sermons, and engage in mutual examination and criticism of each other's theological positions and moral lapses. In origin they were harmless enough, indeed useful, and they enjoyed the encouragement of most bishops. However, by the mid-1570s the radical Puritans had assumed an important, sometimes decisive, role in them. Elizabeth saw them as a 'Wooden Horse of Troy', designed to plant Presbyterianism within the Anglican Church. Therefore, in 1574 she ordered Archbishop Parker to suppress them.

However, he died a year later and it was left to his successor, Grindal, to resolve a basic conflict of loyalties: to improve the condition of the Church or to serve the Queen. Grindal was a Puritan, in the broad sense that he was a reforming Anglican. As Archbishop of Canterbury he now had the power and opportunity to create a more proficient and godly ministry. Unfortunately, he was appointed at a time when prophesyings were brewing in the pot and just about to bubble over— or at least that was the Queen's fear. In 1576 she instructed him to suppress them: with rare courage he wrote to her in December, emphasising the importance of preaching (which the Queen disliked) and defending the prophesyings. He warned her of the need to equip the Church to combat Catholicism, and he advised her to leave decisions in religion to the bishops, just as she referred to the judges all matters of law.

Grindal's letter was a grand gesture—a bold defiance which all of us might admire. But it was also tactless and stupid. Elizabeth viewed prophesyings as platforms on which the radicals could air their views and subvert the Church. She was prompt to act. In 1577 she sent direct orders to the bishops to suppress the exercises and she suspended Grindal from his spiritual functions. However, there were limits to what she could do. As supreme governor she could not make decisions on matters spiritual, but could only direct her bishops to do so. (In practice, Elizabeth often made the decisions, but they were ineffective unless the bishops carried them out.) In the parishes, sympathetic patrons who held the advowsons could dilute the effect of royal orders and offer some protection to Puritan ministers. In any case, the bishops' response to the Queen's orders was a mixed one: some acted enthusiastically, but others were lukewarm, indifferent or downright unsympathetic. Nevertheless, the Queen's prompt action scotched, if it did not kill, the prophesying movement. Meanwhile, she remained without an effective Archbishop of Canterbury, while Grindal remained without spiritual authority, old and going blind, until he died in 1583. She made no mistake with his successor, John Whitgift.

The new Archbishop could not have been appointed at a more opportune moment. The Presbyterian Puritans remained fertile in ideas and they were becoming more organised. In the late 1570s and early 80s, like-minded clergy began to meet in groups or **classes** to discuss matters of common interest and especially to criticise the Prayer Book. They varied considerably in their size, the frequency of their meetings, the number of the parishes which they embraced, and especially in their organisation and objectives. At their most developed they virtually set up local Presbyterian churches. Some of them were local gatherings, as in Dedham, Essex, which held monthly meetings between 1582 and 1587. Dedham is the most famous of the local classes, but only because its record of business has survived. Others were geographically larger units, such as the regional conference held in Suffolk in 1582. The classical movement (as it is called) was not a systematically organised national organisation. Instead it sprang up here and there, where there were enthusiastic Presbyterian ministers and sympathetic patrons with advowsons. In London, however, John Field and his supporters provided a dynamic which attempted to weld together the local cells into a national organisation and decide on a common policy. Undoubtedly the long-term objective was to create a hierarchy of national and provincial synods recruited from local classes (or party cells). In the course of time, it would take over the Church and transform it into a Presbyterian institution. However, if its intention was revolutionary, its methods were not. It worked from within, and it rested on discipline, persuasion and example, not on public opposition or force.

Nevertheless, the classical movement was a serious threat to the Established Church. Elizabeth knew what she was doing when she appointed Whitgift to succeed Grindal. The new Archbishop was not just an authoritarian. He was aware of the abuses and shortcomings which made the Church a target for attack by the Puritans, and he strove to improve the standards of the clergy. However, uniformity remained his first priority. He enforced Parker's *Advertisements* on clerical dress. Then, in 1583, he promulgated his articles, a three-pronged fork on which to spike the Presbyterians. Every minister was required to swear a triple oath recognising and accepting first, the royal supremacy, second, the Prayer Book (including the ordination of bishops) and third, the thirty-nine articles. As usual, it was one thing to put orders on paper in the sixteenth century, but quite another matter to enforce them effectively. Perhaps Whitgift realised that he needed more muscle than the existing Church courts provided. That may explain why, in 1583, he was appointed president of a new Court of High Commission which proceeded to apply the triple oath.

Powerful interests opposed Whitgift: Puritan Councillors, especially Burghley, Leicester, Walsingham and Knollys, patrons whose appointees were hauled before the High Commission, and common lawyers who resented the dramatic expansion of ecclesiastical jurisdiction. The hostility rippled over into the parliaments of 1584–5, 1586–7, 1589 and 1593. At first there were positive attempts (albeit by only a handful of members) to introduce a Presbyterian order of worship. By 1593 this had shrunk to negative protests against Whitgift's methods of achieving conformity—a sign that the Archbishop

was winning. There were several reasons for his success
1 The relentless way he pursued his campaign, despite the hostility of most prominent laymen.
2 The Presbyterians did not put up a united, concerted resistance. They compromised, conformed or withdrew into a frustrated retirement.
3 Events overtook them. Field, their great organiser, and the Earl of Leicester, their great patron, died at the end of the 1580s.

In any case, Presbyterian activities played into Whitgift's hands. The notorious Marprelate tracts first appeared on the streets in 1588. Produced by an underground Puritan Press—another example of the power of print—they pilloried the bishops. They were scandalous, amusing and commanded a wide audience. However, they were ultimately counter-productive. Many of the more conservative Puritans were shocked. More serious, Burghley, who had always been sympathetic to Puritan aspirations, became hostile. An unauthorised underground Press was a danger to the State's security, whether it was Catholic or Puritan. The government tenaciously hunted it down and, in the process, inaugurated a period of savage reprisals. John Penry, who was deeply implicated in the production of the Marprelate tracts, was arrested in 1593 and executed; so were the Separatists' leaders, Henry Barrow and John Greenwood. John Udall, a Marprelate suspect, died in prison. Whitgift's grinding anti-Puritan campaign, backed by the Queen and Richard Bancroft, the uncompromising Bishop of London, destroyed Presbyterian aspirations. A serious threat had been averted, without leading to a Puritan secession, and so the unity of the Church was maintained. More serious for the future was Bancroft's stand on episcopacy (government of the Church by bishops). He did not regard the office as one of convenience, as the early Elizabethan bishops had done. Instead his arguments implied, not only that it was God-given, but even that it was the only form of Church government acceptable to God. With Bancroft we are only one short step away from Archbishop Laud in the 1630s.

By the end of the reign, the Puritans had been reduced to a state of quiescence. Many had opted for the quiet life. Earlier rebel leaders had died, retired or ended on the scaffold. Puritanism had become politically inactive. However, its influence remained widespread. Many gentry, merchants and ministers remained dissatisfied with the condition of the Church. They still feared the Catholic menace. They desired the moral regeneration of society. When Elizabeth died, they looked northwards to her successor who might satisfy their aspirations.

Catholicism under the early Stuarts

James I was not just a new king; he heralded a new dynasty. He was also, to some extent, an unknown quantity. This should not be exaggerated. His record as King of Scotland was well known in informed circles: in particular that, although Scotland had an established Presbyterian Church, he had successfully imposed bishops upon it. His reputed dislike of the strict Presbyterians, who were the most vehement enemies of Pope and mass, must have given fresh heart to the Catholics. They hoped for a better deal from James than they had received from Elizabeth, and to some extent these hopes were justified. He made peace with Catholic Spain in 1604. Moreover, there were early signs that he was prepared to bargain a relaxation of the recusancy laws in return for political loyalty. On the other hand, only time and first-hand experience of the new King would teach his subjects, Catholics included, that he was lazy, cynical and anxious for the quiet life. He was prepared to compromise, follow the line of least resistance and even give way when trouble threatened. So in 1605 he surrendered to pressure from the Anglicans and re-imposed the Elizabethan recusancy laws.

The Catholics' early hopes evaporated, to be replaced by frustration and anger. A group of Catholic gentry, among them members of the Catesby, Digby and Tresham families, resorted to the most comprehensive treason in early modern English history: not only to kill the King, but also most of the royal family, the peerage, the bishops and nearly 500 gentlemen and burgesses. Their motives were mixed. The Treshams in particular had suffered heavily from recusancy fines in the 1580s and 1590s. However, political ambition, loyalty to the papacy and ideological hard-line Catholicism were also important. The failure of the plot not only destroyed the conspirators but harmed the entire Catholic community. King and governing class were frightened and angered. The Protestant backlash produced fresh penal legislation in the parliament of 1606.

Most public Acts commenced with a preamble or introduction which explained why they were necessary. The new Act of 1606 was no exception and its preamble did not mince words:

His Majesty's subjects that adhere in their hearts to the popish religion by the infection drawn from thence . . . are so far perverted in . . . their loyalty . . . unto the King's majesty, and the crown of England, as they are ready to . . . execute any treasonous conspiracies and practices, as evidently appears by that more than barbarous and horrible attempt to have blown up with gunpowder the King [royal family and parliament] tending to the utter subversion of the whole State.

The terms of the new law were bound to make life more difficult for the whole Catholic community. In the past, penal legislation had been directed against its more obstinate members, the recusants. Now, however, the net was cast wider to catch the compromisers, the church papists. They did not take communion, but they attended Anglican services and swore the oath of allegiance to the Crown. Communion was the test of conscience which Elizabeth had always resisted applying. The Act of 1606 now applied that test, when it required everyone to take communion at least once a year. A new oath of allegiance recognised James as King and rejected the Pope's authority to excommunicate monarchs. Once again, the English Catholics were caught in a dilemma, just as they had been in 1570. Some found a way out in the Jesuit doctrine of mental reservation, whereby they took the oath without intending to observe it, but many devout Catholics could not accept such an expedient solution. The law of 1606 imposed insoluble tests of loyalty and conscience on many in the Catholic community.

When Parliament reassembled in 1610, the Protestant backlash had not run its course. Women had played a crucial part in the survival of Elizabethan Catholicism: in organising priest circuits, sheltering and provisioning the missionaries, and raising their children in the old faith. This state of affairs was only made possible by the exemption of women from most of the penal laws. In 1610, however, they too had to resolve the conflict of loyalties, because they were required to swear the new oath of allegiance to the King. If the Jacobean Acts had been strictly and consistently enforced they might have spelt the death of the Catholic community. But 'consistency' was not a word in the King's vocabulary. As the panic subsided after the Gunpowder Plot, so did James's fear and hostility. His natural laziness, lenience and preference for the quiet life took over. Sometimes the penal laws were enforced by royal command, especially when a parliament was due to meet and James, anxious for money, wished to parade his Protestant loyalties to an anti-Catholic assembly. At other times they were relaxed.

The situation was complicated by contemporary political realities. If James had ruled a twentieth century totalitarian State with modern communications, an efficient propaganda machine and a secret police, he could have guaranteed that his orders would have been carried out to the letter in the localities. But he was only the limited monarch of a ramshackle State, in which local government was the monopoly of a largely unpaid governing class. The King's representatives in the countryside were men of substance who did not depend on a professional career in government in order to make their fortunes. When they received royal instructions, they did not carry them out slavishly and without question. They took into account their own prejudices and economic priorities, the interests of their kin and neighbours and, especially, their own positions in religion. Ardent Protestant magistrates, for example, tended to ignore royal commands to relax the penal laws. Therefore, the strict enforcement or moderation of these laws depended less on the King than on local conditions. Where the Catholic gentry were thick on the ground, as in Lancashire, they could be a dead letter. But in Protestant localities, zealous magistrates enforced them regardless of the Crown's wishes, and they were able to make life miserable for their Catholic neighbours.

Nevertheless, J.P.s could not ignore or defy royal authority openly and persistently without fear of reprisals. It would have mattered less if everything had depended on the inconsistency of the King. However, there were other powerful forces at work at the centre, especially between 1614–15 and 1623: the Spanish Ambassador, Count Gondomar; the Catholic politics of the Duke of Buckingham's family faction; and those, including Gondomar and the King's favourite, who were promoting the projected marriage between Prince Charles and the Spanish Infanta. To some extent, these forces combined to override the fits and starts of James's policies and to afford some protection to the Catholic community.

If this was true of the first Stuart's reign, it should have been even more pronounced under Charles I. When he married Henrietta Maria, who was French and a Roman Catholic, he guaranteed in a secret clause of the marriage treaty 'to all his Roman Catholic subjects the greatest freedom and privilege in whatever concerns their religion [and that they] be unmolested . . .'. Theoretically, the Catholics secured complete protection from the penal laws in the exercise of their religion. Even wars against France and Spain did not alter the official position. Yet, paradoxically, the English Catholics were more exposed and vulnerable than they had been under James. The escalating tension between King and Parliament in the years 1625–9, Henrietta Maria's open Catholic worship at Court and the fashionable conversion of courtiers to the old faith had an impact on the local élites. They were weighed down with the administrative and financial burdens imposed by a government at war. Moreover, it was a war which seemed irrelevant and certainly lacked enthusiastic support. They were also troubled by recent religious developments. Their response, especially if they were zealous Protestants and J.P.s, was to step up persecution of the Catholics in their own localities. That was their answer to Court Catholicism and to a King who had embraced Arminianism, which many saw as the first step back to Rome.

The Anglican Church: the Arminian revolutionaries and the Puritan response

It is impossible to separate the condition of the Anglican Church and the history of Puritanism in the early seventeenth century. This is because of the emergence and rise of Arminianism. It was a revolutionary movement: not only was it bent on the destruction of Puritanism, but it also challenged the theological fundamentals of the Anglican Church. It was a novelty which threatened to demolish the essential religious stability which had existed in Elizabeth's reign. It may seem strange to talk of Elizabethan stability when so much of this chapter has been devoted to Puritan criticism and nonconformity. However, it has been repeatedly stressed that tension and conflict between conformers and Puritan reformers neither threatened nor resulted in a divorce between them. Even the Presbyterians worked for change within the Church and displayed no desire to secede. The reason for this is that there was no fundamental theological division between the bishops and those Puritans who criticised their conduct and even condemned the office which they held. They were all Calvinists. They all accepted, without question, predestination which was the central doctrine of Calvinism. It was a bond which, in the last resort, took priority over other issues, such as the importance of preaching, the authority of the Bible, the importance of the sacraments, and even whether the office of bishop was divinely ordained or merely a matter of convenience.

An understanding of predestination is the necessary starting point for a meaningful study of Arminianism. It was by no means the only point of conflict between Arminians and their opponents, but it was the first and it remained the most important. According to the doctrine of predestination, God arbitrarily determines who is to be saved, the elect, and who is to be consigned to hell, the reprobate: Man cannot work for his own salvation. The eternal fate of all human beings is pre-ordained by the arbitrary will of God. Nicholas Tyacke has demonstrated that Elizabethan and Jacobean society was bound together by a near-universal acceptance (Catholics excepted) of this doctrine. (Tyacke's essay on 'Puritanism, Arminianism and Counter-Revolution' in Russell, 1973, might be described as 'compulsory' reading on this subject. Brief as it is, it remains the authoritative study.) When Whitgift attacked nonconformists and when Puritan critics demanded reform, their conduct was tempered by the fact that they remained Calvinist co-religionists.

Arminianism was a new, divisive force in the Anglican Church. Its name derived from a Dutch theologian, Arminius, who challenged predestination. He rejected the doctrine that salvation depended upon the arbitrary will of God. Instead he projected the image of a loving God, who offered 'universal grace'—the possibility of salvation for everyone—and held that all men could save themselves by the exercise of free will. Tyacke writes, 'It is difficult for us to grasp how great a revolution this involved for a society as steeped in Calvinist theology as was England before the Civil War' (Tyacke in Russell, 1973, page 119). Not only did Arminius reject arbitrary grace, he also upheld free will, which was a Catholic doctrine. So his adherents in England were not simply anti-Calvinist: to most Protestants they also appeared to be pro-Catholic. On both counts they offended and frightened not only the Puritans, but also most of the governing class, whose ever-present spectre was popery. Church unity, resting upon a common acceptance of Calvinist doctrine, was fractured. Whereas the doctrine of predestination had been a bond, it now became the most important cause of division. More important, it reactivated the quiescent Puritanism of the early seventeenth century into a political opposition to the Establishment.

However, the Puritans were not the revolutionaries. That label belongs to the Arminians. They introduced a revolutionary theology into a Calvinist context. This might have had a temporary and less serious political effect if they had failed to win control of the Crown and so of the episcopate. In the early years of Charles I's reign, however, they did succeed in this, but only after a Jacobean confusion which was characteristic of James I's reign. With his hand at the tiller, the ship of State veered and tacked erratically, avoiding turbulent seas, reefs and shoals in the search for a haven of political calm. Certainly, at the beginning of James's reign Puritan hopes were high. The King was a Calvinist predestinarian. He was sympathetic to reforming Calvinist (that is, Puritan) aspirations. This was confirmed by his response to the reformers' Millenary Petition, which was presented to him in 1603. Its name derives from the claim that 1000 ministers had endorsed it with their signatures. In fact, it is not known how many had signed it, but it is probable that the number was much less. Whatever the figure was, it still expressed the views of an important body of opinion within the Church. The contents of the petition amount to a charter for moderate Puritanism. It was concerned with 'matters indifferent', age-old abuses such as absenteeism and pluralism, sabbatarianism (the strict observance of Sunday as a day of rest and prayer), a trained preaching ministry, religious uniformity and anti-Catholic measures (see McGrath, *Papists and Puritans*, pages 339–44).

James was in a generous mood. He agreed to discuss the terms of the petition at a conference called at Hampton Court in 1604, where he swept aside the protests of anti-Puritan bishops such as Whitgift and Bancroft. When the conference assembled, the King emphasised religious uniformity and his opposition to any innovation in doctrine or Church government. However, he was prepared to consider anti-Catholic measures and proposals for the reform of abuses. It is true that, when John Reynold, a Puritan divine, made a reference to Presbyterianism, James exploded in anger. It was then that he spluttered forth such pithy sayings as, 'No bishop, no king', that a Scottish presbytery (assembly) 'agreeth as well with a monarchy as God and the devil', and that 'I shall make them conform themselves, or I will harry them out of the land'. And in the early years of his reign he did deprive some Puritan clergy of their livings because of their nonconformity. However, we do need to keep James's anti-Puritan opinions and policies in perspective. His own Scottish experience had taught him to hate Presbyterianism, but he did sympathise with some of the reforms proposed at Hampton Court and he acted on them (McGrath, *Papists and Puritans*, pages 347–53). He was receptive to ideas of improvement and the reform of abuses, but the safety of the State came first. The appointment of Bancroft to succeed Whitgift as Archbishop of Canterbury may confirm us in the belief that James hated Puritanism. Bancroft's mind was besieged and assailed by the phantom forces of Puritan opposition. He had been the archpriest of Elizabethan anti-Puritan activity. He was also the direct ancestor of Charles I's archbishop, William Laud, as he moved towards the position that the office of bishop was divinely ordained. Was James, who promoted Bancroft, the first royal Arminian?

The answer must be a resounding 'no'. He was inconstant and fickle in religion, as in all things. Yet there was some consistency in his actions. State security came first. Therefore, the Gunpowder Plot in 1605 heralded a period in which anti-Catholic reprisals superseded all other religious considerations as the first official priority—hence the legislation of 1606 and 1610 (see pages 274–5). George Abbot's promotion to Canterbury in 1611, in succession to Bancroft, and Toby Matthews' to York in 1606 underwrote the more anti-Catholic and less anti-Puritan drift of the government. Both men were tolerant of nonconformity and active against popery. New appointments such as these, a declining persecution of Puritan preachers and lecturers, the promotion of Puritans (including John Preston to a royal chaplaincy): all of these developments indicated that the Establishment and its Puritan critics could be accomodated still within the existing Church. This was especially true when a Calvinist King presided over a bench of bishops who were, for the most part, of the same persuasion.

Such a state of affairs could only last as long as the superior demands of diplomacy and foreign policy did not conflict with the defence of Calvinism and persecution of Catholicism at home. Over about a decade (1614–15 until 1623) such a shift of direction occurred. It was partly the consequence of a change in the power structure at Court. The two catalysts of change were the Spanish Ambassador, Gondomar, and the new favourite, Buckingham. Gondomar exerted a powerful influence at Court and with the King. He used it to work for the protection of English Catholics and the preservation of Spanish interests (with such success that Sir Walter Raleigh was executed in 1618 for infringing the Spanish monopoly in the Central Americas). He also promoted the proposed Anglo-Spanish marriage alliance between Charles and the Spanish Infanta: for years he kept alive the project and royal expectations that it would eventually come to pass. By 1618 it had become a matter of the utmost political importance to Gondomar and his royal master, Philip III. In that year Spain was drawn into the first of what became a series of related conflicts, known collectively as the Thirty Years' War. Within twelve months, Spanish troops were invading the territory of Frederick Palsgrave, a German prince who was also James I's son-in-law. It was Gondomar's task to neutralise England, or at least to minimise its intervention on Frederick's behalf, by continuing to dangle the tempting bait of a marriage alliance before the English King. His efforts were crowned with success. Both James and Prince Charles swallowed the bait.

Buckingham's role was more ambiguous. If he was no statesman, at least he had acquired a considerable skill in the manipulative politics of the Court. Gradually he transferred his attentions from the aging monarch to his heir. At the same time, he rode several 'horses' at once, supporting the Spanish Match (which would have required concessions and even toleration for the English Catholics), remaining on friendly terms with the Calvinist Archbishop Abbot, patronising that prominent Puritan John Preston, and taking into service the arch-Arminian William Laud. Buckingham's opportunism, Gondomar's influence and the changing fortunes of faction politics at Court each contributed to a confusing picture of official attitudes to religion in late Jacobean England. So too did James. At the very time when negotiations for a Spanish marriage were under way, James came out firmly in support of the Dutch Calvinists in their power struggle with the Arminians (who were much nearer the Catholic position in their theology).

Despite the apparent confusion in religious politics at this time, and although James seemed to confirm his strict Calvinism, it was in these years that an Arminian party emerged. Bancroft had pointed the way with his anti-Puritan inquisition and his views on the origins of episcopacy. His immediate heirs were the handful of bishops who, in the middle and later Jacobean years, began to disseminate Arminian views: Richard Neile (Rochester, 1608–10; Coventry and Lichfield,

1610–14; Lincoln, 1614–17; Durham, 1617–28), Lancelot Andrewes (Chichester, 1605–9; Ely, 1609–18; Winchester, 1618–26), John Buckeridge (Rochester, 1610–28; Ely, 1628–31) and John Overall (Coventry, 1614–18; Norwich, 1618–19). In the background, a client first of Neile and then of Buckingham, hovered William Laud.

Theirs was a two-pronged attack: to give their opinions a public airing in order to win converts, and to capture the King. The latter was the essential element. Without royal sponsorship, or at least a sympathetic ear, the Arminians could make little headway. As Tyacke has shown, within the confines of their dioceses the Arminian bishops were able to emphasise the sacraments at the expense of preaching. This was important to their cause. Preaching on the Scriptures confirmed the importance of the Bible as the tabernacle of all truth— a characteristic Calvinist position. Against this, the Arminians stressed the importance of the sacraments (especially communion) which, together with repentance, offered a chance of salvation to all men, or at least so the Arminians believed. This was a direct challenge to predestinarian Calvinism.

However, the Arminians could not hope to advance their cause significantly without the King. There are signs that in the closing years of the reign they were achieving some degree of success. In 1624 Richard Montague, one of the Arminian party, published an attack on both Catholicism and the Calvinist doctrine of predestination. Its appearance was due to Bishop Neile, who smuggled it past the existing machinery of censorship. Thus the Arminians were able to reach out to a wider market. When Parliament and Archbishop Abbot protested, the King would do no more than ask Montague to clarify his views. Whether or not James was becoming more sympathetic to the Arminian position mattered little, because time was overtaking him: he died in 1625. Nevertheless, the last two years of the reign were vital to the rise of Arminianism. The abortive, romantic and politically fatuous 'embassy' of Charles and Buckingham to Madrid put an end to the Anglo-Spanish marriage negotiations. In 1624 the Prince and his favourite were hot for war with Spain. So too was a Protestant crusading Parliament. Buckingham was, momentarily, the darling of anti-Catholic, anti-Spanish Puritanism and he responded by cultivating closer relations with prominent Puritans such as John Preston. Even at the end of the reign, Arminianism had made no substantial advance and the essential unity of the Anglican Church remained intact.

Within four years that unity was destroyed. From the beginning of his reign, Charles I displayed an uncompromising Arminianism. He immediately cast the mantle of his protection over Richard Montague. He promoted Arminian bishops to wealthier and more influential sees:

Buckeridge was raised from Rochester to Ely in 1628, and Neile from Durham to Winchester in the same year. Vacancies were filled with Arminian candidates: Richard Montague was elevated to Chichester in 1628, and, most important of all, William Laud moved rapidly up from St Davids to Bath and Wells (1626–8) and London (1628–33). As early as 1626 Laud had been promised Canterbury at the next vacancy. The Arminian King and his Arminian bishops were in the driving seat. The Duke of Buckingham, opportunist that he was, went along for the ride.

It was Charles's fatal mistake to become the sponsor and protector of one religious party. Instead of adopting the role of a neutral or an umpire between warring religious factions, he became the partisan of the Arminian movement. Furthermore, it was a movement with a revolutionary theology which threatened much that was dear to the governing class. Its intensifying anti-Puritanism, culminating in the persecution of Puritans in the 1630s, transformed Protestant nonconformists into martyr-hero figures who suffered in defence of the traditional Church.

This might have been less serious if religion had not been linked with political discontent, but that was not possible in the seventeenth century. No issue was a straightforward conflict between the government and its opponents. Court, Council, bureaucracy and Parliament were but the institutional faces of a political system which was structured around the patron-client relationship and factions. In the past, faction politics in these institutions had tended to cut across religious divisions. Between 1625 and 1629, however, the emergence of Arminianism under royal patronage produced political alignments which increasingly coincided with religious loyalties.

Nevertheless, these divisions would not have become so clear-cut if Charles I had not adopted a rigid, inflexible stand on political issues too: on the protection of Buckingham, on expensive wars which seemed to serve no useful purpose, on extra-parliamentary taxation, and on challenges to the royal prerogative. In the rising political temperature of the late 1620s, when these issues were creating political conflict, Charles's partisan backing of the Arminians was potentially explosive. In the minds of many a noble and gentleman, everything seemed to tie together neatly. Charles I's French wife was a Catholic and there were justifiable suspicions that, when he married her, he had made a secret promise of toleration to her co-religionists. There could be no doubt about the open practice of her religion at Court. These fears and facts fed the anti-Catholic paranoia of the Protestant governing class. The Arminians, with their belief in free will and the divine origins of episcopacy, were half-way back to Catholicism;

Charles I was their patron. Protestants—not just Puritans—smelt a grand conspiracy.

Nor did the Arminians damp down governing class fears with their pronouncements about the absolute nature of royal authority. For his part, the King upheld the divine origins of the office of bishop. There was no organised drive to impose Arminian beliefs on the kingdom. However, they certainly acted on their common anti-Puritan prejudices. This was not to reach a climax until the Laudian campaign of the 1630s, but in the meantime it halted the advancement of men like John Preston, and it destroyed the essential unity of the Church, which a common Calvinism had provided. This was, in turn, aggravated by the mutual hostility of King and bishops towards the powerful role of the laity in the Church, in particular to its extensive control of ecclesiastical appointments, property and tithes. To do justice to Charles, it should be recognised that he was concerned with problems which were real, acute and harmful to the Church. Lay patrons often pocketed the tithes or diverted them to the maintenance of Puritan preachers or lecturers. Again it was not until the 1630s that Laud's campaign to resume control of tithes achieved its greatest momentum. But once again the country was treated to the spectacle of a Crown and episcopate politically allied and pursuing policies which were harmful, not only to the Puritans, but to the laity in general.

By 1629 the old and essential Calvinist unity of the Church had already been thrown into disarray by the emergence of Arminianism. There existed in many minds the ghastly image of an alliance between Absolutism and Arminianism (in other words, between divine right absolute monarchy and a divinely ordained episcopate). The fact that such fears were much exaggerated is less important than the political consequences of such fears. After all, what matters is how men respond to fear and insecurity, not whether their fears are well-founded and so justified. These fears were certainly heightened between 1625 and 1629 by the doctrines of Arminianism. Its emphasis on the renewal of God's grace through the sacraments was given visible effect in the revival of the altar in place of the communion table, and the move to beautify the Church with images and pictures—the trappings of Catholicism according to English Protestants. 'Popery' was, and remained, the classic bogeyman of the governing class. It was but a short step for fevered imaginations to see in current developments the existence of a plot to impose on England an absolute monarchy and the Roman Catholic Church.

These developments occurred in years of unwanted wars, which imposed unprecedented demands on local government, and which drove Charles to arbitrary actions—extra-parliamentary taxation, arbitrary imprisonment, compulsory billeting, the use of martial law and so on. The various causes of discontent were voiced with increasing volume in each parliament. Furthermore, concern about religious developments and political discontent fused together. Nowhere is this more clearly expressed than in the three resolutions of the House of Commons in 1629. Two of them declared that those who 'shall counsel or advise the taking and levying of the subsidies of Tunnage and Poundage, not being granted by Parliament', and anyone who paid them, were enemies of the kingdom. These two resolutions were a commentary on the arbitrary acts of Caroline government. The third resolution pronounced that innovators in religion, or anyone who shall 'seek to extend or introduce Popery or Arminianism', were likewise to be 'reputed' capital enemies. The three resolutions were a symbolic union of political and religious discontent over developments which, in a short space of time, had created distrust of the King's intentions and disunity within the Anglican Church.

CHAPTER FIVE

Religion: conformity, comprehension or toleration, 1629–1700

William Laud

Earlier views of the period in which William Laud dominated the English church see it as one in which the Puritan movement, which had been rising steadily ever since the days of the Elizabethan Reformation, gained the strength and confidence to challenge the Anglican hierarchy. William Haller, writing in 1938, saw a progressive intensification of the Puritan challenge. Archbishop Laud was depicted as a man on the defensive, an archbishop, like Abbot, Bancroft and their Elizabethan predecessors, struggling to preserve the 1559 Settlement. Haller's analysis neatly parallels older historiography about Parliament, particularly, perhaps, the work of Notestein who saw the politics of the same period dominated by the progressively extended claims of the House of Commons. It was, therefore, the ecclesiastical corollary of the Whig political interpretation. As discussed in the previous chapter, it is Laud and his followers who are seen as the revolutionaries by most historians today (W. Haller, *The Rise of Puritanism*, New York, 1938).

When Laud became archbishop, the Church had solved some of the problems which it had faced at Elizabeth's accession—the clergy were much more literate, for example—but many of the old weaknesses remained. The finances of the Church were still inadequate. Laymen and the clergy alike had appropriated Church property to their own advantage, a habit in which the Crown had set a notoriously bad example. Many tithes were impropriated to laymen, or concentrated in the hands of university colleges, cathedrals and a handful of wealthy clerics, while the parishes they were intended to support could not pay an adequate stipend and may have had to share the services of a pluralist. The curates and many of the vicars were paid very poorly. The care of buildings had been neglected. One clergyman had melted down and sold the lead from the roof of his church. Other churches had been damaged by the pious vandalism of those who objected to stained glass windows, organs, statues and carved wood.

The medieval stone altar had been removed from most churches and the wooden table which had replaced it was often left in the body of the church, where it became a convenient repository for hats and umbrellas. As Laud himself said, 'Tis superstition nowadays for any man to come with more reverence into a church than a tinker and his bitch to come into an alehouse'. The ills of the Church were blamed on the excessive powers which laymen had assumed over it. Parliament, J.P.s, lay patrons and parish officers were all condemned in a reaction against the vastly increased role of the laity since the Reformation.

Laud's basic solution to the problem was to establish an authoritarian and efficient central control over the Church with the reins firmly in the hands of the bishops. He began very rapidly after his elevation to Canterbury. One year later, in 1634, he commenced a series of metropolitan visitations, thus reviving a practice which had been in disuse for 150 years. During each visitation, the authority of the diocesan bishop was suspended while the Archbishop and his officials investigated, reformed and punished. Anger was aroused by the insistence that all clergymen conform to the ceremonial requirements of the Prayer Book. No longer were conscientious scruples or local customs to be tolerated.

As part of his campaign to improve what he regarded as decency and order in churches, and as a step towards re-establishing the 'beauty of holiness' which he believed had been lost at the Reformation, Laud ordered that the communion table should be set altar-fashion in the east end of the church and railed in. This is, of course, the modern Anglican practice, but it was the exception rather than the rule in the 1630s and it may, in fact, have been illegal. The Book of Common Prayer ordered that the table be kept in the east end of the church and brought down into the main body when communion was administered. Indeed, when the small parish church of St Gregorys, near St Pauls in London, appealed to the ecclesiastical courts, the case came at last before the highest court of appeal in the Province of Canterbury, the Court of the Arches. The Dean (judge) ruled that Laud's instruction was contrary to Queen Elizabeth's injunction of 1559. Laud dismissed him and obtained a favourable order from the Privy Council. In church matters, as in secular ones, judges who gave verdicts unfavourable to the government were liable to be dismissed.

The dispute over the altar may appear to be trivial, but there were at least two major issues at stake. The first was the religious symbolism of railing-in the altar. Indeed, the name 'altar' itself was significant and to this day there are some Low Church Anglicans who insist on the term 'communion table'. An altar is a place at which a sacrifice takes place. Thus, use of the word may be interpreted as acceptance of the sacrifice of the mass. Railing-in the altar and setting aside an area into which only the minister would enter could be seen as creating a specially holy area from which laymen were to be excluded. Criticisms were put forward in an anonymous pamphlet, *The Holy Table, Name and Thing*, written by Bishop Williams of Lincoln. Laud denied that his order had any theological significance, saying that the altar rails were intended merely to 'prevent dogs from pissing on them or worse'. Less cautious supporters of the change publicly gloried in its sacramental implications and thus strengthened opposition to the change.

The second issue was one of authority. Could the Archbishop override the Elizabethan injunction, the Court of the Arches and the custom of the majority of churches? Many ministers and laymen were determined that he should not. The accompanying order that laymen should go up to the altar rails to receive communion provided them with an opportunity. Laud would be faced not only by the disobedience of vicars and churchwardens, but also by the defiance of whole congregations. Demands that people bow to the altar or at the name of Jesus were similarly resisted. In addition, the removal of family pews to make space for the new altars was often necessary, something which upset the social hierarchy and earned the enmity of those gentlemen whose ancestral rights had been overthrown.

Laud was not to be diverted by opposition. What he could not gain by consent, he believed he could get by compulsion. A reissuing of the Book of Sports (outlining what recreations were lawful after Sunday service) cut across the sabbatarianism which was no longer confined to Puritans, but which was widely accepted throughout the Church. The instructions that churches buy organs offended those who regarded them as popish or even the 'devil's whistles', as well as imposing an unwelcome expense. Laud imposed other costs on often reluctant laymen by insisting that buildings be repaired or rebuilt and, in particular, by his scheme to rebuild St Pauls.

He was unwilling to tolerate any criticism: Bishop Williams, for example, was charged with a string of minor offences and eventually suspended, fined and imprisoned. Lord Chief Justice Richardson was called before the Council for ordering restrictions on Church ales (regular events at which drinks were sold to raise money). The drunkenness which often resulted was regarded as a genuine social evil by many who did not regard themselves as Puritans. Richardson 'received such a rattle' from Laud 'that he came out blubbering and complaining that he had almost been choked with a pair of lawn sleeves'. Even people who shared many of Laud's objectives were dealt with harshly if they did not conform in every respect. The Feoffees for Impropriations provide the most notable example. This organisation was established about 1625 to buy impropriated tithes (that is, tithes owned by laymen) and return them to the purpose for which they were originally intended. The stipends of parish clergy were supplemented and lecturers paid from these funds. Laud objected to the activities of the Feoffees on two grounds: firstly, they confined their aid to Puritans (that is, non-Laudians) and, secondly, the very existence of the Feoffees represented an exercise of lay power in the Church. The Feoffees, who included the Lord Mayor of London, were suppressed and all their assets were confiscated.

Laud attempted to solve the economic problems of the Church in a more direct manner. The collection of tithes was made stricter and efforts were made in London to ensure that those charged on rents were increased to take inflation into account. Lay impropriators were required to pay part of the tithes they gathered to augment the stipend of the vicar. (A vicar was a beneficed clergyman receiving only the lesser tithes, which did not include those on grain. Rectors received the greater tithes as well and usually had a much better living.) Waste by clergymen themselves was limited by stopping bishops and deans from letting out lands at low rentals to members of their own families or by taking high entry fines (capital sums paid at the commencement of a lease) in return for a long lease at a low rental, a tactic which increased the revenues of the present holder of the office, but impoverished his successor. It was forbidden to lease Church land for more than twelve years, a term which ensured a regular review of rents and, the landed class feared, made those who held them very dependent on the goodwill of the clergy. In Scotland, Laud alienated the nobility and greater gentry by making compulsory acquisition for the Church of all tithes impropriated since 1542. Though compensation was paid, owners considered the amount insufficient.

As mentioned above, Laud attempted to increase tithes on urban property using London as a test case. Legally, tithes were payable on all rents, but they were often evaded by the signing of false leases at rates well below the true value, by subletting and by a wide range of semi-legal tax avoidance measures. Even Laud realised that it would not be possible to suddenly raise London tithes from the £6500 paid in 1636 to the £148 000 estimated to be the true amount owed. Laud ordered London tithes increased to £10 600 in 1638. This was bitterly resented. Ministers were jostled and insulted in the street and jeering calls of 'Two and ninepence' were hurled after them. The legality of Laud's order was challenged in the courts and the dispute with the City was still unsettled when the Long Parliament met. Not unexpectedly, it ruled against the increased tithes. A similar dispute in Norwich was settled by the King's order that a tithe of two shillings in the pound (ten per cent) be paid on all rents. This order was reversed by the Long Parliament in 1641.

Laud met all opposition by repression. The Court of the High Commission was used to suspend, deprive and imprison dissident, immoral or incompetent clergymen. Though only five per cent of the cases heard there were instigated by the Commissioners against non-conforming clergymen or sectaries, they were as well publicised as the similarly small number of political cases in Star Chamber, and they created the same unfavourable impression. Unpopularity was intensified by the use of the High Commission to back up the ineffective sanctions of ecclesiastical courts against matrimonial and moral offenders. Sir Giles Allington was successfully prosecuted for incest and Viscountess Purbeck for adultery. The private lives of the peers and wealthy gentlemen were no longer exempt from the law of the Church. This aroused the antagonism of the landed class. Clarendon complained that:

Persons of honour and great quality ... were every day cited into the High Commission, upon the fame of their incontinence, or other scandal in their lives ... and ... the shame (which they called an insolent triumph upon their degrees and quality) and levelling them with the common people was never forgotten . . .. (Quoted in Ashton, 1978, page 119.)

Secular opponents of the Laudian Church were usually tried in Star Chamber. When these or other political offenders appeared before the court, Laud prided himself on voting for the heaviest penalty which had been proposed. In particular, he was associated with the brutal physical punishment of Burton, Bastwick and Prynne in 1637. When convicted of libelling bishops, all were sentenced to stand in the pillory, to have their ears cropped and to be perpetually imprisoned. Brutality was an accepted part of the criminal code—assizes were regularly followed by hangings, brandings and floggings—but its exercise on representatives of the three learned professions, a clergyman, a doctor and a lawyer, for a political offence created shock. Many gentlemen must have been impressed by Prynne's words from the pillory, 'You see, they spare none of what society or calling soever. None are exempted that cross their own ends. Gentlemen, look to yourselves. You know not whose turn may be next.' (Quoted in Lockyer, 1976, page 256.)

By the late 1630s, Laud's methods and his religious policies were bitterly resented by many who would not have been considered

Puritans in the mid-1620s. The reasons for the increasingly bitter opposition to Laud include objections to his personality and authoritarian style of leadership, snobbish resentment at his low birth, fear that changes in the Church were designed to assist more centralised and less parliamentary government in the State, and the almost universal belief among non-Laudians that his innovations in doctrine and liturgy were steps towards Roman Catholicism. One must recall that for most Englishmen of the 1630s the Roman Catholic Church was held in as much hatred and fear as was the Communist Party in the United States during the McCarthy era. It was an alien ideology associated with political repression and dictatorship in the countries where it prevailed, it provided a justification for the attacks of national enemies, and it was the creed of subversives at home: men taught that no lie, no crime, no act of violence was too vile if it could ensure victory. To the devout Protestant there was a further objection to Catholicism—by enticing people into false religion, it led them irrevocably to hell.

Hatred of Catholicism was kept alive in a number of ways. One of the most important was the repeated publication of the 'Book of Martyrs' (John Foxe's *Acts and Monuments of the Christian Reformation*), a record of the suffering of Protestants during the reign of Queen Mary in the 1550s. It appears to have been the most frequently owned book after the Bible and perhaps the Book of Common Prayer. Secondly, there were regular reports of the persecution of Continental Protestants by Catholic monarchs. (Perhaps it should be noted that the execution of Catholic priests by English monarchs provided convenient atrocity propaganda for the other side.) The wars of religion in France and, more recently, the Thirty Years' War provided plenty of ammunition for those who wished to depict Catholics as the enemy. Thirdly, the danger of Catholic fifth columnists was stressed by reference to the plots against Elizabeth and, especially, by the memory of the Gunpowder Plot, kept alive by the annual 'Pope burnings' on the fifth of November.

The importance of Foxe's book was greater than is often realised. Foxe applied the Book of Revelation to the Christian era and concluded that the history of the Church could be divided into five periods. The first 300 years were a period of purity and persecution by the Roman emperors; the second, the time of dominance by Christian emperors from Constantine until 600 A.D.; the third, from 600 until the Norman Conquest. In this third period, the Church suffered from the growing influence of the papacy. The fourth period was marked by papal supremacy and was therefore the reign of the Antichrist. Satan was let loose when the Pope took over the powers of the Christian Emperor. For Foxe, the counterblast of Christ against Antichrist came with the Reformation. Once more, at least in England, a Christian Emperor, a second Constantine, ruled the Church. The Marian persecutions were the reply of Antichrist to the Christian counter-offensive: their victims were saints and fallen soldiers in the war between good and evil. Not only were they, as individuals, members of the Elect, but they were heroes of England, the Elect Nation, destined to lead Christendom to perfection in preparation for the Second Coming of Christ and His personal rule on Earth.

To people reared in the tradition of Foxe, Laudianism was an apostasy from God's will and national destiny. Every country has a national ideology or myth which is believed to give its history meaning. For example, Russians see their history as a vindication of the Communist Revolution; Americans view the history of their nation as a justification of political democracy and free enterprise; nineteenth century Englishmen emphasised the development of parliamentary institutions as England's greatest achievement and example to the world. Their forefathers in the century after the Reformation believed that England's role was theological. England was the Elect nation which under the revived Christian Emperor would lead the way to the overthrow of Antichrist (the Pope), the defeat of the Turks and to Christ's personal rule on Earth.

The probably apocryphal story that Laud referred to the Marian martyrs as 'brainsick and fanatical fellows' was used, like Dean Cosin of Peterborough's reference to the Reformation as the 'Deformation' and Richard Montague's reduction of the differences between the Church of England and the Church of Rome to three, as evidence that the Anglican Church had repudiated its divine mission, even that it had joined the ranks of Antichrist. One extreme view was that of Lady Eleanor Douglas who saw Archbishop Laud as the beast from the bottomless pit; another was that of the leading New England Puritan, John Cotton, who described Anglicanism as the Kingdom of the Beast. Inevitably, Charles I's defence of Laudianism marked him out as a renegade from his role as the Christian Emperor of the Foxian tradition.

Laud and the Arminians were seen as people leading the Anglican Church either directly back to Rome or along the same path of tyranny, priestly domination and idolatry. The first charge was certainly wrong, though the second can only be a matter of opinion. Laudian changes gave the appearance of a return to popery and deceived even the Pope, who offered Laud a cardinal's hat when he should achieve reunification of the Church of England with Rome.

Laud refused to make any such attempt until 'Rome be other than it is'. He had, in fact, first made his name as a theologian for the strong anti-Roman Catholic case he had made in debates.

However, the ordinary man could not help but notice that the apparent Catholic tendencies of Laudian worship were accompanied by the King's choice of Catholic ministers and friends: Lord Treasurer Portland died a Catholic in 1634; Lord Cottington, a leading Privy Councillor, announced his conversion in 1636; the Bishop of Gloucester retained his see despite his request to keep in his house an Italian priest to celebrate mass; and principal Secretary of State Sir Francis Windebank was rumoured to be a convert. The King received and befriended George Con, the first papal diplomat in England since the Reformation, and there were a large number of conversions to Catholicism among the Queen's circle of friends. Though Laud opposed these conversions and the Catholic influence at Court, this was little known by his Protestant enemies.

The identification of Laudianism with the bogeyman version of Catholicism accepted by most Englishmen was easy to make. Like Catholics in absolutist Continental countries, they exalted royal power and insisted that monarchy was a divine institution which had to be passively obeyed. Their stress on the continuity of the Anglican Church with the pre-Reformation Catholic Church in England downgraded the Reformation and emphasised the institutional links with Catholicism. Belief in the essential role of bishops consecrated in the apostolic succession was little removed from Roman Catholic theology. (The apostolic succession refers to the belief that the Twelve Apostles were the first bishops. They consecrated replacement and additional bishops by the laying on of hands, who in their turn continued their order in the same way. Only bishops whose consecration could be traced back to the Apostles are regarded as true bishops.) In denying predestination and asserting that salvation was a matter of free will, the Laudians appeared to be taking the Roman Catholic side in what many Protestants saw as the essential issue of the Reformation. The consequences of the reintroduction of free will doctrines into England included an emphasis on the importance of the sacraments, the introduction of much more ritual and an emphasis on the role of the priest in spiritual and temporal matters. All were evidence, as far as many Protestants were concerned, that the Laudian Church differed little from that of Rome.

With Laud so firmly in control, there was little his opponents could do until the calling of the Short Parliament, an event made necessary by a rebellion provoked by the introduction of Laudian religious practices into Scotland (see chapter 7, page 390). In this

Parliament the floodtide of resentment burst the banks of repression. Members protested at the new ceremonies, condemned the revival of ornaments and attacked the Church courts for suspending ministers who refused to conform. The appointment of the extreme High Churchman, Manwaring, to the Welsh bishopric of St Davids was condemned and Bishop Hall of Exeter was attacked for his book *Episcopacy by Divine Right Asserted*. Hall was forced to apologise to the Lords for saying that the Puritan Lord Saye and Sele 'savoured of a Scots Covenanter'.

Instead of taking the depth of feeling revealed in the parliamentary debates as a signal to follow less provocative policies, Laud and his followers continued on a course bound to arouse even more antagonism. Convocation voted six subsidies to the King, even though Parliament refused, thus symbolising the alliance of the Crown and the Church in opposition to Parliament. Despite the convention that the Convocation of Canterbury should sit only at the same time as Parliament, it remained in session after the dissolution at Westminster. It proceeded to draw up seventeen canons (Church laws) of a highly contentious nature. The first placed great stress on the divine right of kings and declared that to resist royal power by force upon any pretext whatsoever was an offence warranting eternal damnation. Other canons reinforced Laud's orders on the position of the altar and on bowing. The most resented canon was the sixth, which required all clergymen and most other professional people to swear an oath that they would never consent 'to alter the government of this Church by archbishops, bishops, deans, and archdeacons, etc'. The 'etcetera oath', as it was known, was seen as a way of forcing those who took it to accept an increased Roman Catholic influence, which would probably culminate in the rule over the English Church of the Pope himself. So great was the opposition, that the oath was abandoned when the defeat of the King's army by the Scots made it necessary to call another parliament.

When the Long Parliament met, opposition to Laud and his policies had intensified. Nearly all speakers attacked both the specific innovations, especially the canons of 1640, and what they saw as abuse of power by the bishops. Many spoke of reducing their powers and returning to 'primitive episcopacy' with good bishops who did not meddle in politics. The early months of the Long Parliament were a time of fear and panic, and in the unhealthy atmosphere opinions changed rapidly, something encouraged by the cessation of censorship. In December 1641 Laud was imprisoned and a debate was begun over the future of the Church. He had already realised that he had over-reached his power and he had offered to ask the King to withdraw the canons. Parliament was no longer willing to accept such withdrawal. It was determined to assert its power over the Church. Petitions were received calling for radical changes. The Ministers'Petition and Remonstrance signed by 700 clergymen called for big reductions in the power of bishops. Much more sweeping was the 'root and branch' petition, said to have been signed by 15 000 Londoners, which called for the total abolition of bishops. Under the influence of radical M.P.s, similar petitions were circulated in the counties.

At first the temper of the House of Commons was moderate and reformist, something which almost certainly reflected the basically Anglican, but anti-Laudian, feelings of most of the country. Various schemes to modify episcopacy were considered. One was devised by Archbishop Ussher of the Irish archdiocese of Armagh, the man who is better known for his calculation that the world was created in 4004 B.C. Ussher proposed that dioceses be divided into rural deaneries, in each of which there would be monthly meetings or synods to guide the dean. In the diocese, the bishop would share power with synods meeting every six months. Most other plans involved some form of power-sharing by the bishops, perhaps with ministers appointed by Parliament.

In 1641 the majority in both Houses was anti-Laudian, although there was no agreement on any long-term restructuring of the Church. In consequence, it was possible to pass measures condemning ornaments, ritual changes and the railing-in of the altar, excluding the bishops from judicial office, abolishing the Court of the High Commission and removing the power of other ecclesiastical courts to impose fines or prison sentences. The nearest Parliament came to agreeing on Church government, however, was the recommendation of a committee that the powers of bishops be placed in the hands of lay commissioners appointed by Parliament until such time as a permanent settlement should be devised.

As the first session of the Long Parliament approached its end, it was apparent that many who had been opposed to royal policies when proceedings began, now felt that the King had made enough concessions in both Church and civil government. Charles set out to gain the active support of these moderates by making concessions, one of them being his appointment of non-Laudians to important positions in the Church. The most notable was the promotion of John Williams, Laud's greatest critic among the bishops, to the archbishopric of York. It was too late, however, and in any case, Williams proved as strenuous a defender of bishops' rights as did Laud. Early in 1642 Charles was forced to agree to a Bill expelling bishops from the House of

Lords. In one of the Nineteen Propositions presented to the King in June was a demand for reform in the Church 'as both Houses of Parliament shall advise'. The King rejected the Nineteen Propositions and war broke out three months later.

The Civil War cannot be seen as a religious war in the sense that religion was its main cause, but there is no doubt that conflict in the Church played an important part. Laud's policies intensified the fear of Catholicism and belief in its association with absolutism: many Protestants regarded them as a negation of true religion. In addition, Laud's administrative solutions to problems in the Church hit laymen in the pocket. The reaction to Laudianism was the revival of an active Puritanism, virtually dormant for fifty years, but now determined to replace both bishops and the Book of Common Prayer. No longer can this be seen as a logical and continuous development of events since the Elizabethan Settlement. By moving too far and too fast, Laud and his followers reversed the decline of Puritanism and played an important part in provoking the Civil War.

Religious ideas in the Civil War

During the Civil War, the religious situation was simple on the royalist side. Anglicanism remained the established religion in all royalist-controlled areas and feeling against other Protestants was strong, owing to their association with the enemy. Indeed, there was such a revulsion in the royalist army against anything which smacked of Puritanism that its seeming anti-religious bias turned many pious but hitherto non-political men to the side of Parliament. As Richard Baxter wrote, the allegiance of many was affected by hearing 'men swear for the King but pray for Parliament'. Another counter-productive act was the King's suspension of the penal laws against Catholics and his willingness to have them fight on his side. The number of Catholics in the Marquis of Newcastle's army and revelations from captured letters that the King was negotiating to bring in Irish and French Catholic troops confirmed the fears of popery which had been such a potent cause of opposition to him in the 1630s. Despite this, Charles remained a loyal and, indeed, a stubborn Anglican. He might have saved his throne and his head if he had been willing to compromise on religion. In the negotiations at Oxford, at Uxbridge and over the Newcastle Propositions the religious issue played a major part in their failure.

On the parliamentarian side, the situation was more complex. Though there had been a virtually unanimous rejection of Laudianism in 1642, there was no agreement on what was to take its place. Despite the rise of so-called Puritanism in opposition to Laud, and the anti-episcopal sentiments among London apprentices, local studies suggest that the majority of the nation were still Anglican. However, the Anglican cause suffered on the parliamentarian side by its association with armed royalism, and there can be no doubt that those who were most committed to Anglicanism were on the side of the King. Among the most powerful groups on the side of Parliament, the religious options did not include Anglicanism. There were, however, important decisions to be made and, with the exception that Anglicanism seemed to be excluded, the options were little different from those in 1558—comprehension, toleration or repression. The first decision concerned the existence of a national Church. If there was to be one, should it be rigidly uniform or should local customs and personal preferences be allowed to create a diversity of practice? Should people be allowed to opt out of the national Church? If so, should there be any limits to toleration and should the State have a coercive role in religious affairs? Should the ultimate power in the Church lie with the lay authorities, as the Erastians wanted, or should it be held by the clergy? In addition to these fundamental issues were practical considerations: how should the Church (or Churches) be financed, how should the ministers be selected, who should appoint them and supervise their work? How much power over the moral conduct of laymen should the Church have? All these issues were to be faced yet again during the Civil War and Interregnum.

In the earlier stages of the Civil War, religious differences between various groups in Parliament did not create major issues. Two important objectives had been attained before the war started. The Bill of February 1641 suppressed Arminian innovations and the bishops were excluded from the House of Lords in the same year. In 1642 nothing involving the Church was done except the appointment of the Committee for Plundered Ministers: it had the task of finding employment for clergymen favourable to Parliament whose parishes and source of income lay under royalist control. It was also empowered to encourage preaching and to eject 'popish' or pro-royalist clergymen. Differences over religion within the parliamentarian side did not become a significant issue until the Scots entered the war in 1643. In order to gain Scottish aid, without which they feared they would lose the Civil War, the English parliamentarians agreed to establish the Westminster Assembly to advise on Church matters. The Scots had insisted on religion being included in the treaty terms. The Scottish minister, Robert Baillie, said, 'The English were for a civil league, we for a religious covenant.' The Scots wanted the English to adopt something very like their own brand of Presbyterianism, both because many of them believed it was the only form of Church government acceptable to God, and because they saw it as a barrier to England establishing a form of religion which would threaten Scotland. An English Presbyterian settlement would prevent either the resurgence of Laudianism or a victory of the sects.

At the insistence of the Scots, the English signed the Solemn League and Covenant to reform religion in all three kingdoms 'according to the Word of God and the example of the best reformed churches'. The Westminster Assembly was to advise on how this was to be done. One hundred and twenty English ministers were appointed, with thirty laymen and ten Scots commissioners. Only half the English nominees sat. All those committed to the pre-war Anglican system refused to attend, leaving a large majority of Presbyterians. There were, however, ten prominent Independents, determined to put their case as strongly as possible. The Westminster Assembly was set the task of advising on Church government and writing a Directory of Public Worship to replace the Book of Common Prayer. However, every point was debated at great length and two years later the task was still incomplete.

Long before the Assembly had made its recommendations, the basic assumption that all would have to conform to a national Church was challenged. In January 1644, five Independent ministers published *An Apologetical Narration* asking for freedom of worship. Despite, or perhaps because of, the furious Presbyterian response, Roger Williams produced *The Bloody Tenet of Persecution*. Williams had tried to put into practice the ideal of toleration in the settlement he had founded at Providence, Rhode Island, and he was in England on colonial business when be became embroiled in the dispute.

There was also a group of Erastians who did not particularly mind which method of Church organisation was adopted, as long as Parliament remained supreme in religious matters and no power of persecution was given to ministers. They joined with the Independents in the Commons to pass the Accommodation Order. It established a parliamentary committee on religion to 'endeavour the finding out some way how far tender consciences, who cannot in all things submit to the common rule which shall be established, may be born with public peace . . .'. However, the capture of Newcastle from the King by the Scots strengthened the Presbyterian hand in England and the Order was withdrawn. Parliament asked the Westminster Assembly to hasten its proceedings.

This success of the Scots did not lead to the introduction of full-blown Scottish Presbyterianism in England, mainly because of the rise of Independent influence in the parliamentary armies. Especially in the New Model Army and its predecessor, the Army of the Eastern Association, Independency was strong. Oliver Cromwell, the future Lord Protector, put up a strong defence of religious toleration in the army against his commander-in-chief, the Earl of Manchester, who had wished to dismiss an officer believed to be an Anabaptist. The Scots and the English Presbyterians almost impeached Cromwell for his stand, but from that time onwards the demands of the army that religious toleration be allowed were a very important factor in all negotiations to end the war.

In 1645 a royalist rising in Scotland was suppressed only with difficulty and it weakened the ability of the Scottish army to intervene effectively in English affairs. The successes of the English New Model Army revived confidence that the war could be won without the Scots and the complications which they brought to the negotiating table. The Scottish army was paid off and persuaded to leave England. With this influence removed, the Independents managed to seriously weaken Presbyterian organisation by denying the Church sessions and presbyteries the power of excommunication. The Accommodation Order was revived in November 1645, and protests from the London Common Council and the Westminster Assembly were overruled.

In June 1646, however, the English Church was re-established on a Presbyterian basis. Elders were appointed and a system of classes established in London. A later Act extended the system to Lancashire and several other counties set up their own system voluntarily. This was far from what the Presbyterians had wanted. Though powers of excommunication were granted to ministers and elders, their decision was subject to an appeal to a parliamentary committee. There was no compulsion for parishes to accept the Presbyterian system and Independent clergymen continued to minister and to receive their tithes. Attendance at the parish church was not enforced and there was no restriction on the formation of 'gathered churches': voluntary organisations of like-minded believers.

In addition to the very loose structure authorised by law, events in the Civil War years had made it unlikely that full Presbyterian unity would be attained. Gathered churches had appeared all over England and there had been a very wide toleration in the army. Even the national Church established in 1646 retained too much of the old ways for some. 'New Presbyter is but old priest writ large', said John Milton. Baptists referred to maintained ministers as 'priests of England' and to the services in parish churches as 'Church of England Worship'.

The army insisted strongly that there should be freedom to dissent from the Established Church. In December 1647, the Heads of the

Proposals submitted to the King permitted the establishment of Pres-byterianism, but demanded freedom for 'all such persons as shall not conform to the said form of government and divine service shall have liberty to meet for the service and worship of God, and for the exercise of religious duties and ordinances . . . so [long] as nothing be done by them to the disturbance of the peace of the kingdom'. This principle was accepted by the Rump in 1650 (by that time, the association of Presbyterianism with the King in the second Civil War had discredited its claims to exclusiveness) when the Elizabethan Act of Uniformity and most of the provisions of the recusancy laws affecting laymen were repealed (Cross in Aylmer, 1972, page 103).

The desirability of toleration in religion appears self-evident today. In the mid-seventeenth century many people shared the modern view, but there were rational and sincerely held reasons for wishing to limit toleration. The first reflects the same outlook which justified the burning of heretics in earlier times—that religious truth was known, fixed and eternal. Religious toleration would merely allow people to go to hell in their own way. Permitting the teaching of heresy was to imperil the immortal souls of all who might be infected by it. Surely it was better for a few heretics to suffer at the stake than for those they deluded to burn for all eternity in hell-fire? A second argument was more political than religious. Unless all people in a country professed the same religion, there could be conflicts between the demands of Church and State. Thirdly, there were the social consequences of allowing toleration. Sects might spring up which adopted, as part of their faith, doctrines of political and social revol-ution. Perhaps their teachings would be contrary to conventional morality and undermine the supernatural justification for fundamental laws.

Events in the Civil War and Interregnum seemed to justify the fears of those who wished to limit toleration. Indeed, they convinced some who had once been strong advocates of toleration that only a strong Church with extensive powers of discipline could prevent anarchy. One such man was John Tombes, active in the West Midlands during the Interregnum as a Baptist. He opposed both the national Church and the schemes for voluntary co-operation among parish churches. By 1660 he had been converted, by his horror at the heresies of some of the sects, to acceptance of the Anglican Settlement.

The Interregnum Church

Neither the Presbyterians nor those Independents who wanted a complete break between Church and State were to prevail during the

Interregnum. A series of Acts and ordinances continued to regulate Church organisation. Because of the pressure of other business in Parliament, it was not until 1650 that the Rump was able to turn its attention to religion. The Acts it passed were important, but they represented a moderate path rather than one committed to either Presbyterianism or the sects, one to which it was kept by the balance of pressure groups both in and out of the House.

Rather than abolishing tithes as the sectaries hoped, the Rump reinforced them. This reflected the comparatively conservative religious views of its members as well as their concern, as property owners, for the tithes in lay hands. The clergy were purged in some areas, but moderate Independent and Presbyterian clergymen were favoured in appointments to benefices and in invitations to preach before Parliament. The Presbyterian system of church government was allowed to continue. Indeed, a Bill to confirm it was defeated by only one vote.

The repeal of the Act of Uniformity and most of the recusancy legislation referred to above was a sop to the radicals. The Blasphemy Act and the formation of the Committee for the Propagation of the Gospel represented a Presbyterian reaction to the activities of the sects. The Act for the Propagation of the Gospel in Wales, however, was a measure on which virtually all could agree. It was also relatively easy to agree on an Act for the Propagation of the Gospel in the Four Northern Counties of England, but more difficult to reach consensus on its enforcement. The Welsh Act resulted in the ejection of 250 clergy for drunkenness, pluralism, incompetence or royalism. The commissioners appointed to administer the Act were very unpopular.

The Blasphemy Act was aimed at the more extreme sects. It lay down punishments for such things as declaring oneself to be God or equal to God, or arguing that offences such as murder, adultery and incest were not evil. There were only about twenty prosecutions under the Act and most, if not all, its victims seem to have been suffering from religious hysteria. The Act against sabbath-breaking, the notorious Act Against Incest, Adultery and Fornication, which imposed the death penalty, and the severe Acts against blasphemy and swearing were not, as has often been supposed, directed against the vices of immoral royalists, but against Antinomian sects such as the Ranters, who claimed that nothing was sinful to the truly religious. A further Presbyterian measure was the establishment of the Committee for the Propagation of the Gospel to counter the growing belief in Socinianism (a belief similar to Unitarianism involving a denial of the conventional Christian belief in the Trinity. Jesus was regarded as a good man and a prophet rather than as an eternal part of the Godhead). The same desire to root out doctrine regarded as heretical can be seen in the attempt to define fifteen fundamental beliefs, denial of which was regarded as intolerable heresy. It was partly this desire of the Rump to restrict toleration which induced Cromwell to dissolve it. As he said in his dissolution speech, 'Is it ingenuous to ask for liberty, and not to give it? What greater hypocrisy than for those who were oppressed by the Bishops to become the oppressors themselves, so soon as their yoke was removed?'

The *Instrument of Government* (the constitutional document establishing the Cromwellian Protectorate) continued the State Church, but no one was compelled to attend and there was liberty for all Christians to worship freely 'provided this liberty was not extended to Popery [Roman Catholicism] or Prelacy [Anglicanism], nor to such as under the profession of Christ hold forth and practise licentiousness'. (This last provision was obviously intended to restrict the Ranters.) Cromwell was to make toleration one of the 'four fundamentals' which had to be enshrined in any new constitution when amendments were discussed.

During the early months of the Protectorate, Cromwell took advantage of the constitutional provision enabling him to make laws, by issuing ordinances, counter-signed by the Council of State, in order to create two bodies known as the triers and the ejectors. The first was established to examine those who wished to be appointed as parish ministers. Only after they were reported, among other things, to be 'of holy and good conversation' could they be appointed. The rights of lay patrons were not affected as long as the candidate they preferred could qualify. However, though the institution of the triers might prevent unsuitable men obtaining office in the Church, it did nothing to remove those already there. In August 1654, county or regional commissions known as the ejectors were appointed to dismiss all unsuitable ministers and schoolmasters. They could be rejected on moral grounds, such as adultery, drunkenness, sabbath-breaking and excessive card playing, or professional incompetence: for example, ministers who could not preach and schoolmasters who could not teach. Those who used the Book of Common Prayer excessively could also be dismissed. Though many of those who lost their positions because of the ejectors were to be made martyrs after the Restoration, only a small number were dismissed for political reasons or for displaying too openly their preference for Anglican ways.

The national Church 1646–60

The position of the national Church during the Interregnum has often been questioned. Many historians have argued that it had no real existence. Claire Cross has demonstrated that this view is an exaggeration. Though the Presbyterian system was merely permitted by law rather than made compulsory, it did operate effectively: this is true of parish discipline, form of worship and church government. Presbyterian parish discipline was exerted in many parishes, though not necessarily in the rigid Scottish form. For instance, the institution of lay elders does not appear to have been popular in England: both ministers and laymen seem to have objected to it. The strongest resistance was to the Scottish Presbyterian custom of admitting to Holy Communion only those deemed worthy by the elders. Nevertheless, it was introduced in some parishes. In Bolton, for example, the two ministers and twelve lay elders examined those who wished to take communion and issued tickets to those they believed suitable. Ministers attempted to impose a similar discipline in other parishes, though their success varied. Some refused to celebrate Holy Communion when parishioners refused to be examined. Despite the limited extent to which Scots Presbyterian techniques were introduced, Puritan ministers such as Richard Baxter appear to have imposed a more rigid moral discipline than before the Civil War.

There does seem to have been a much greater acceptance of the Directory of Worship than of Presbyterian moral discipline. Its outline of service did not impose set prayers and it allowed considerable flexibility. In many parishes the form of service probably differed little from non-Laudian Anglican services.

The establishment of Presbyterian regional and national authority was never complete, but it was much more extensive than was once thought. It should be remembered that Elizabethan proto-Presbyterians had planned a system of classes, provincial synods and a national synod (see pages 271–2). Each 'classis' was to consist of representatives of parishes in a limited geographical area, a provincial city or part of a county. A classis met in London in November 1646 and organised fourteen parishes. The Presbyterian plan called for twelve classes in London and surviving records show that at least eight actually operated. The classes appear to have worked towards the establishment of Presbyterian parish government, strict catechising (religious teaching) and the use of the Directory of Worship. The Fourth London Classis, the one for which the fullest records survive, ordained ninety men between 1647 and 1659. Outside London, the classical system appears to have been most strongly established in Lancashire, where the classes of Manchester and Bury were particularly active. They operated in much the same way as the London classes, except that they called on the Justices of the Peace to enforce their rulings. Records are less well preserved elsewhere, but there is no doubt that classes operated in

Derbyshire, Nottinghamshire, Durham, Essex, Shropshire and Yorkshire.

The next tier of Presbyterian organisation operated only in London and Lancashire, as far as is known. The London Provincial Synod met regularly between 1647 and 1660. It supervised existing classes, set up new ones, and urged them to impose strict moral discipline. As no national synod was called, the London assembly assumed leadership. It acted as an advisory body for Presbyterians throughout England and Ireland and it issued several publications supporting Presbyterian principles. In the late 1650s it favoured schemes for greater unity with moderate Independents and Anglicans.

There can be no doubt that the Presbyterian national Church had a real existence and that it was a major force in religious affairs. Certainly, it was very different from the system of Presbyterianism enforced so rigidly in Scotland. Its comparatively loose structure probably made it easier for moderate Anglicans and Independents to remain within it. Between 1646 and 1660, Anglicans had the choice of remaining aloof from the national Church or compromising their principles (Anglican, in this context, means people who had a strong preference for Church government by bishops and the form of service laid down by the Book of Common Prayer). Their decision was partly a matter of attitude towards the divine right claims of the episcopate. Most Laudians believed that bishops were essential to a true Church: a Church could gain authority to preach the Word and minister the sacraments only by the apostolic succession (see page 292). Other Anglicans believed that bishops were essential to the well-being of the Church, but they accepted that a non-episcopal Church could be a true Church. The absence of bishops weakened a Church, but did not cut it off from God's grace nor turn its sacraments into blasphemous parodies.

The bishops and the Laudian clergy remained aloof from the Presbyterian establishment. They were forced to leave their livings: some joined Charles II in exile, while others existed as chaplains and tutors in the manor houses of Anglican gentlemen. During the Interregnum, Sir John Pakington's great house at Westwood in Worcestershire became a haven for dispossessed Anglican clergy and, indeed, something of a centre for Anglican intellectuals. Both the bishops in exile and those who remained in England continued to ordain priests and deacons, though they consecrated no additions to their own order. By 1659 there were only nine English bishops still living and it might not have been long until the English episcopate was extinguished by death.

Those Anglicans who did not not compromise continued to

celebrate Christmas, Easter and Whitsun, even though their recognition was forbidden in the Presbyterian Church, and they conducted services according to the Book of Common Prayer in private chapels. Except in the immediate aftermath of Penruddock's rebellion, they were not subject to serious persecution and the disabilities from which they suffered were a result of their pro-royalist political activities, rather than their religious views.

For more moderate Anglicans, clerical and lay, the choice was not so simple. For the clergymen, the decision to withdraw from a non-episcopal Church meant the loss of their right to preach and administer the sacraments in parish churches. In a sense, their position was like that of the Elizabethan Puritans who debated whether it was more important to reject vestments and ceremonies which smacked of popery, or to retain their authority to preach. Many moderate Anglicans accepted the Presbyterian Settlement as the best possible in the situation. They co-operated with it in public, but kept as far as possible to their accustomed ways, incorporating the old prayers in the new services. In some remoter areas, the Book of Common Prayer services seem to have been conducted in parish churches.

Many laymen who preferred Anglicanism could not bring themselves to withdraw from parish worship. To do so would be, they believed, socially subversive. A Presbyterian Settlement was better than religious anarchy. John Evelyn, who attended private Book of Common Prayer services in London, regularly worshipped in his parish church at Deptford. He wrote 'that though the minister were Presbyterially affected, he was, I understand, duly ordained and preached sound doctrine after their way, and beside was a humble, harmless and peaceable man'. (Quoted by Cross in Aylmer, 1972, page 111.) Richard Baxter commented on the benefits and drawbacks to his ministry in Kidderminster of the partial conformity of the neighbouring squire, Sir Ralph Clare, who had been one of the leading royalists in his county during the Civil War. He led a life as temperate as that of most Puritans and was a man who:

seldom would Swear any lowder than (By his Troth, & c.) and shewed me much Personal Reverence and Respect . . . yet (having no relish of this Preciseness and Extemporary Praying, and making so much ado for Heaven; nor liking that which went beyond the pace of Saying the Common Prayer . . .) his coming but once a day to Church on the Lord's days, and his Abstaining from the Sacrament, & c. as if we kept not sufficiently to the old way, and because we used not the Common Prayer Book, (when it would have caused us to be sequestered) did cause a great part of the Parish to follow him and do as he did; when else our Success and Concord would have been much more happy than it was. And yet Civility and yielding much beyond others of his Party, (sending his Family to be Catechized and personally Instructed) did sway with the worst almost among us to do the like.

While Anglicans either withdrew or adopted only a grudging and partial conformity, because they regarded Interregnum religious changes as too radical, the Independents were unhappy with them because they did not go far enough. The Independents, it will be recalled, were opposed to any national or regional organisation which restricted the freedom of the individual churches. There were, however, different types of Independent: indeed, so many variations that what is said here must be regarded as only a very broad and possibly oversimplified outline. The most conservative Independents differed from the Presbyterians mainly in their rejection of any religious authority superior to the individual parish. They accepted the principle of a publicly funded parish church which all should attend. Conservative Independents differed over the right to leave the parish church—they believed that all should attend their parish church and denied the right to withdraw and worship separately.

The more extreme Independents denied all links between Church and State. For them, Churches were purely voluntary associations of like-minded believers: they were not tied to any specific geographical area and no one was to be a member merely by right of residence. For the Baptists, full membership could not come by birth. The rejection of infant baptism was an assertion that Church membership was free from all earthly ties, even that of the family. As an Interregnum Baptist wrote, 'Once give over christening the whole parish [in] infancy and farewell that parish posture whch the Pope set up in all Christendom some six hundred years ago, yea then down falls the parochial church-steeple house, priesthood, pay and all. Amen, so be it'. (Quoted in C. Hill, *The World Turned Upside Down: Radical Ideas during the English Revolution*, Harmondsworth, 1974, page 99.)

Both types of Independency operated during the Interregnum. Parish ministers who refused to join the Presbyterian organisation of the national Church maintained fully self-governing congregations or joined in loose voluntary associations. The Baptists and Separating Independents lay between the mainstream and the radical sects. Such voluntarist churches often developed from a group within a particular parish, which believed or wished to worship in a particular way. For a time, it may have been able to reconcile membership of the parish church in the same way that Puritan or other particularly pious members of an Anglican parish before the Civil War had met for private devotions as well as the official services. Eventually, however, many came to a belief that they were called to establish a separate congregation which might either employ a minister or rely on laymen to officiate at its services. Some of the break-away Churches were motivated by strictly doctrinal considerations, while others simply wished to confine their religious fellowship to those whose faith and practice were as strict as their own. Some left open the question of infant or believer's baptism. In others, allowing a child to be 'sprinkled' (baptised in the Presbyterian fashion) was reason for excommunication.

Of the voluntarist groups, the Baptists were the largest. They shared attitudes to baptism, but differed in much else. The 'particular' Baptists accepted the orthodox Calvinist belief in predestination, while the 'general' Baptists adopted the Arminian view that salvation was available to all men. Both groups established strong regional and national associations. The general Baptists had well-developed associations in Kent and the East Midlands and they held a national conference to make recommendations on points of doctrine and discipline in 1656. The particular Baptists established five regional associations, for which that in London provided national leadership.

Other Independents found by experience that mutual support and co-operation were helpful. At first this was purely local and informal, but, in 1658, 120 Independent churches sent representatives to London to draw up the Savoy Confession of Faith.

In the later Protectorate, there were two divergent tendencies in the mainstream of English Protestantism. On the one hand, there was the development of greater distinction between groups such as Independents and Baptists and, on the other, there was an attempt to bring them together into a comprehensive and fairly tolerant Church. It was natural that distinctions should become clearer as time allowed different traditions to develop. The move towards unity can be explained by the unpleasant experiences of denominational strife and by belief that greater unity among the mainstream of English Protestantism would make it easier to combat Ranters, Quakers and Socinians. Presbyterian and Independent clergymen worked together in harmony from the early 1650s, and by the middle of the decade formal associations began to emerge. The best known is Richard Baxter's Worcestershire Association of seventy-two members. It included Presbyterians, Independents and those who would have preferred Anglicanism. There was a similar association in the north-western counties of Cumberland and Westmorland and this example was copied in many other parts of the country.

Baxter himself, and many other members of these associations, looked to a fully national Church combining the best elements of the three main traditions in English Protestantism. Baxter was often styled a Presbyterian, but he denied any denominational exclusiveness. He recognised the useful role that could be played by bishops, and he hoped that a system of Church government including bishops (though Baxter preferred the term superintendents) and synods might reconcile Anglicans and Presbyterians. One can envisage the possibility that Archbishop Ussher's scheme for limited episcopacy, discussed by Parliament in July 1641 and published in 1656, provided a basis for negotiation. The publication of the scheme a year after its author's death is surely an indication that many people thought that his was an idea for which the time was ripe. Had Cromwell lived longer, it is possible that a far more comprehensive national Church might have emerged. Clearly, with Cromwell as Protector, it would have had to be tolerant, but the type of Church envisaged by the ecumenists of the 1650s was one which could have encompassed most Englishmen: the bitter divisions between Church and dissenters which emerged after the Restoration might have been avoided.

Roman Catholics in the Interregnum

There was, however, one group for which no form of comprehension in an English national Church would have been possible in the 1650s: the Roman Catholics. The extreme hostility of the Puritans and the fears aroused by Catholic association with royalism in the Civil War might lead one to expect that they would suffer from harsh persecution. This was true only of the Civil War period itself— twenty-one priests were executed from 1641–6. In 1642 Catholics had to pay double subsidy rates and Catholic gentlemen who had assisted the royalist cause had to pay the maximum rate of fine to regain their estates. Though Roman Catholics were specifically excluded from toleration by the Instrument of Government, they were less persecuted during the Interregnum than in the 1630s. The repeal of the recusancy laws in 1650 freed Catholic laymen from fines for not attending their parish church. During the Interregnum, only two priests were executed. English Catholics living in London were allowed to attend mass in the chapels of foreign embassies. This *de facto* toleration of Catholics appears to have been the work of Cromwell himself. He was no keener on the persecution of Catholics than the members of any other religious group. In 1657, Parliament passed an Act requiring Catholics to swear an oath denouncing the temporal powers of the Pope, but Cromwell prevented the oath from being administered.

The sects

There were several consequences of the break-down of religious unity. Different groups emphasised, in extreme ways, tendencies which had been present within the religious mainstream. The doctrine of predestination, essential to orthodox Calvinism, could be interpreted in either a rigidly authoritarian way, granting the Elect sole right to rule, or in a much more liberal spirit which emphasised the equality of the Elect and their independence from the social and religious hierarchy. The best known group which applied the liberal version of Calvinism to religious and secular affairs was the Levellers. The authoritarian interpretation was upheld by Presbyterians and, indeed, by most Anglicans. Predestination was, however, applied not only in a socially and politically conservative manner, but, in the hands of the Fifth Monarchy men, turned into a justification for revolution.

The Levellers are not, strictly speaking, a religious group, yet they gained their inspiration from the democratic strain within Calvinism. The Protestant emphasis on the personal interpretation of the Bible made all men equal in the search for salvation. If men were free to choose in this, the most important of all matters, surely they were free to comment on secular concerns and, if necessary, to change the world until it accorded better with both Biblical teaching and commonsense. The Levellers first emerged as a group within the parliamentary army, determined to preserve religious freedom in the post-war years from the restrictions of bishops and Presbyterians alike. One of their leaders, Richard Overton, attacked Presbyterians as the 'brisk and spermatick sons of bishops', who had a 'godly care for their own guts'. This determination to protect religious freedom provoked the interest in constitutional reform, which was originally intended to prevent a settlement which imposed religious uniformity. Out of this concern, and the purely professional grievances of the unpaid soldiers, grew a movement which demanded sweeping constitutional and social reforms.

The Fifth Monarchy men (so called for reasons explained below) applied Calvinist predestinarian teaching and millenarian beliefs in a highly radical way. They have long been regarded by historians as figures of fun: fanatical, superstitious and insane. Contemporaries did not regard them in that light, but as dangerous radicals. They were right. It was not their millenarian beliefs which set them apart in the 1650s, but the revolutionary conclusions they drew from them. Millenarianism, the belief that Christ was soon to reappear on Earth and begin his thousand-year reign, was based, firstly, on the assumption that everything that happened in human affairs reflected the direct intervention of God and, secondly, on an interpretation of certain passages in the Books of Daniel and Revelations:

The vision of Daniel consisted of four beasts, representing world empires (generally accepted in this period as Babylon, the Medes and Persians, Greece, and Rome). The last beast had ten horns, or kings, and a little horn which destroyed several of the ten. After the destruction of the last beast, the kingdom was given to the saints for ever—the 'Fifth Monarchy'. No dates were given, but there were cryptic references to a time of woe lasting 1290 days, and a fullness of joy beginning after 1335 days. The prophecies of Revelation were still more involved. They described the reign of the Beast as lasting for 1260 days or 42 months. Two beasts persecute the saints, one from the earth with two horns, the other from the sea, with seven heads and ten horns. Two witnesses who testify against them are killed, lie dead for $3\frac{1}{2}$ days and then rise again. During this persecution, God encourages the saints by punishing His enemies—the opening of the seven seals, the blowing of the seven trumpets and the pouring out of the seven vials of wrath. After this, Satan is bound for a thousand years; Christ and the Saints reign for a thousand years, and then, at the end of the world, follows the battle of Armageddon, in which Satan is slain, and the Last Judgement begins. (B.S. Capp, *The Fifth Monarchy Men: A Study in Seventeenth-Century Millenarianism*, London, 1972, page 24.)

Belief that the millennium is near still exists today, but it is usually associated with minor sects rather than with the major denominations of twentieth century Christianity. In the seventeenth century the situation was very different. The millenarian expectations of the Fifth Monarchy men were not the preserve of isolated and semi-literate sectaries but part of the religious mainstream in England from the Reformation until at least the 1650s. Millenarianism was a fundamental characteristic of preaching before the Long Parliament, and of the seventy-eight clergymen who published three or more theological works in the 1640s, at least seventy per cent had millenarian beliefs. Royalists as well as parliamentarians explained the events of the Civil War in millenarian terms. At the Restoration some claimed Charles II as the fifth monarch.

What made the Fifth Monarchy men different and dangerous was the political implications that they drew from their theology. They believed that a revolutionary transformation of existing society was essential to purify and perfect the world for the Second Coming of Christ, and they saw the execution of Charles I as the first step. In 1649 they petitioned the army, expressing their hope that it would never be 'instrumental for setting up of a meer natural and worldly government'. They believed that the Rump might carry out the necessary transformation, but when they saw it hesitating and returning to conservatism, they placed their trust in Cromwell and the army. They reached their pinnacle of influence at the time of Barebone's Parliament. Many members of their movement, and men who were sympathetic to it, sat in this Parliament. Major-General Harrison, Cromwell's second-in-command, was a Fifth Monarchist and many other officers were supporters. In 1653 they were far from being a negligible sect and figures of fun—they seemed like men on the verge of taking over power. In the end, Cromwell drew back from social revolution and allowed Barebone's Parliament to dissolve itself: the Fifth Monarchists never forgave him. From the time he became Lord Protector, they saw him as their arch-enemy and he did his best to silence their preachers and pamphleteers. Officers who would not abandon their Fifth Monarchist notions were quickly dismissed from their posts.

One may ask why, in a time of radical change and religious debate, the Fifth Monarchy men were seen as so dangerous. The reason is mainly political rather than religious. Unlike the Ranters (see below), the Fifth Monarchy men were, in most respects, orthodox predestinarian Calvinists. They believed in the utmost moral strictness: indeed, it was part of their policy to extend the death penalty to a wide range of moral offences. Their services appear to have differed little from those of Baptists or Congregationalists. The enmity to them sprang from the belief that the Elect should rule on Earth. Presbyterians held this view, but tended to identify the Elect with those in authority. The Fifth Monarchy men did not. Despite the minority of university-educated ministers, officers, landowners and professional men who supported them, most of their members were urban workers and small traders. These people taught that the Elect should seize power from the corrupt ruling class, and do it by bloody revolution if necessary. Once in power, they should redistribute landed property, improve the lot of the poor and establish a new system of law and government based on the code of Moses and the Jewish Sanhedrin. It was their social radicalism which made them so hated and feared by their contemporaries. One of their leaders, Thomas Venner, was involved in a rising against Cromwell in 1657 and in another against Charles II in 1661, thus providing spectacular justification for suppression by the government of the day and their reputation for being fanatical and insane revolutionaries which has survived to this day.

One consequence of toleration was the way in which it allowed a reaction against orthodox Calvinism, especially among the poor.

Many rejected the whole idea of a State Church. They denied the need for an educated clergy supported by tithes and looked instead to the 'gifted' from among their own number who would work six days a week and preach on the seventh. This was an explicit denial of both the power of the ruling class and of the claims of its ordained representatives. The logical consequence of this declaration of independence from the upper classes in religious matters was a demand for much greater freedom in civil affairs. Religious radicalism played a very important role in the development of the Leveller and Digger movements. 'God made man and the devil made kings', sums up the anti-authoritarian element among the sects.

Anti-clericalism, that is opposition to the power and presumption of the clergy, was rife. In 1646 a trooper in Nottinghamshire laid his hand on his sword and said, 'This sword should never be laid down, nor many thousands more, whilst there was a priest [that is, a State Church clergyman or possibly any ordained minister] left in England'. When a group of Presbyterian ministers visited the New Model Army at Oxford, 'the multitude of soldiers in a violent manner called upon us to prove our calling . . . whether those that are called ministers have any more authority to preach in public than private citizens which were gifted'. The Quakers asserted that it was antichristian for 'such as are men of learning and have been at the university and have tongues' to 'be masters and bear rule in every parish, and none shall reprove or contradict what they say in public'. This last belief, held by many more than the Quakers, led to the custom of 'prophesying'. After the sermon, the congregation questioned the minister, discussed the sermon and allowed those of contrary view to express it. This practice was institutionalised in the Baptist churches.

The rejection of clergymen as the sole living religious authorities was followed by questioning of the literal accuracy of the Bible. For many, the Bible was to be interpreted allegorically. The Digger, Gerard Winstanley, spoke of the Virgin Birth and the Garden of Eden and the resurrection as allegories. The Ranter, Joseph Salmon, taught that the true Christian was not he who believed in the historical truth of the Bible, 'but he that by the power of the spirit believes all this history to be verified in the mystery; the history is Christ for us, the mystery is Christ in us'. Bible stories were viewed as symbols of the battle between good and evil which went on within the individual personality. Winstanley wrote, 'There is no man or woman needs go to Rome nor to hell below ground as some talk, to find the Pope, Devil, Beast or power of darkness; neither to go up into heaven above the skies to find Christ the work of life. For both these powers are to be felt within a man, fighting against each other'.

Emphasis on the internal struggle was reinforced by the myth of the Everlasting Gospel which divided human history into three stages. The first was the age of the Father or of the Law, from the Fall of Man (that is, when Adam and Eve succumbed to the temptation to eat the forbidden fruit) to the death of Christ. The second was the time of the Son or of the Gospel, the third the age of the Spirit in which the Holy Spirit came directly into the hearts of men and took precedence over both Law and Gospel. (Hill, *World Turned Upside Down*, pages 107–50.)

A further development in some sects was a rejection of belief in sin and hell. 'Sin and transgression is finished . . . . Be no longer so horridly, hellishly, impudently, arrogantly wicked as to judge what is sin and what is not', wrote Abiezer Coppe. One development from the emphasis on following 'the Light Within' was Antinomianism, the belief that nothing was sinful to the Elect, an idea which was given political implications when it was said that religion was a fable invented to 'keep the baser sort in fear' once private property, the family and the State were invented. It was used to further anti-clericalism in the statement about the clergy, 'Their trade is for money to declare against sin, yet they must preach it up and talk for it a little too, and do their work not too hastily, all at once, lest there be no more work for them ere long to do, but such as they were never bred up to live by'.

Rejection of sin was followed by denial of hell. There was a rising belief that hell was just a bad conscience. Many believed that God would not be so cruel as to condemn anyone to eternal punishment 'for a little time of sinning in the world'. Winstanley denied the existence of any localised heaven, hell or devil. The influence of the newly popular Copernican astronomy may be seen in the cruder rejection of the 'three decker' universe by John Boggis of Great Yarmouth, who asked in January 1646, 'where is your God, in heaven or in earth, aloft or below, or doth he sit in the clouds, or where doth he sit with his arse'.

Of all the sects it was probably the Ranters who most shocked conventional Puritans. Of all groups, they were the one which most strongly and openly adopted Antinomianism and rejected the idea that the Elect could sin. Some Ranters even adopted the position that 'those are most perfect . . . which do commit the greatest sins with the least remorse', but this was an extreme position stressed by their enemies. Perhaps more typical was Abiezer Coppe, who played down, rather than totally rejected, the traditional sins of the flesh, while stressing pride, covetousness, hyprocrisy, oppression, tyranny, unmercifulness and despising the poor. Ranters symbolised their rejection of conventional morality by meeting in alehouses, drinking heavily (remember that seventeenth century Puritans were not total abstainers—it was the heavy drinking, not the consumption of alcohol, which was shocking), smoking and blaspheming. They made a habit of parodying religious language. One of them 'let a great fart, and as it gave report, he muttered these words, let everything that hath breath praise the Lord' (Russell, 1971, page 363).

Inevitably, perhaps, the Ranters were associated with sexual sins. Thomas Webbe, a Ranter who had become rector of a parish church, was tried for adultery in 1650. Winesses claimed he had said 'there's no heaven but women, nor no hell save marriage' and 'that it was lawful for him to lie with any woman'. Ranters allowed free divorce and some attacked the whole institution of the family. Clarkson, a Ranter who changed his views, admitted that he had once seen little difference between prayer and adultery. 'No man could be freed from sin, till he had acted that so-called sin as no sin . . . Till you can lie with all women as one woman, and not judge it sin. You can do nothing but sin . . . No man can attain to perfection but in this way' (Hill, *World Turned Upside Down*, page 315). The Ranters existed as a significant force only until 1651. Even Independents who believed in toleration for virtually every other sect drew the line at the Ranters—people who rejected not only the authority of landlords and clergymen, but the supernatural sanctions of sin and hell. Though Christopher Hill has traced the continuation of their ideas into the 1660s, perhaps their greatest influence was negative. By shocking their contemporaries, they contributed to the renewal of conservatism, to the belief that a strong Church hierarchy was necessary and, in so doing, to the Restoration.

Ranters were not, of course, the only sect which shocked the orthodox. This could hardly be so when there may have been as many as 200 sects in London alone. Another radical group were the Muggletonians, founded by the London tailor, Ludovic Muggleton, who taught that he was one of two heavenly messengers foretold in the Book of Revelation sent to decide who would be saved and who would be damned. Though the Muggletonians survived until the nineteenth century, they were much less important than the Quakers.

Though they did not share the Ranters' rejection of conventional morality, the Quakers were a product of the questioning and sceptical attitude which frequently led to a rejection of the religious views of the upper classes and the ordained clergy. Their enemies accused them of Ranter views and, in the 1650s at least, they had much in common with them. Quakers shared the radical emphasis on the inner word or the Light Within. In the early days, they may have gone as far as to deny the Bible and the literal application of its teachings. By 1655, however, Quakers were specifically stating that they did not deny the existence of God, the historic Christ, heaven and hell. The Quakers did continue to reject much of the social order. They refused to have a separate ministry or a form of service: their meetings were and are without formal organisation. Members speak as they feel moved, otherwise all remain silent. Quakers refused to take off their hats to anyone. This was a total rejection of the main means by which social deference was shown. Indeed, as Conrad Russell has written, it was like a private soldier in a modern army refusing to salute his commanding officer. The use of 'thee' and 'thou' may seem merely quaint today. In the 1650s it was a revolutionary repudiation of yet another outward symbol of hierarchy, whereby superiors were addressed as 'you', equals and inferiors in the now obsolete forms. Quakers did not invent these protests against the social order, which were part of a radical tradition extending back at least to the Marian martyrs. To be consistent, they refused to address J.P.s as 'worshipful'. Their refusal to take oaths, based on the Biblical command 'swear not at all', removed the supernatural sanctions against lying without which contemporaries believed truth could not be guaranteed. Quaker pacifism was a post-1660 development.

Quakers particularly annoyed the orthodox by their custom of disrupting church services. They shared the anti-clericalism of many other radical groups: 'As for these men called ministers in this nation, the way of their setting up and sending forth, and the way of their maintenance, . . . they are the greatest and most woeful oppression in the nation. The earth is oppressed by them, the inhabitants groan under them', wrote the Quaker Edward Burrough. A result of such views was the belief that they were entitled to enter the 'steeple houses' and challenge the minister, especially to denounce his greed in taking tithes, once the sermon was over. George Fox, who became the Quaker leader, believed he had the legal right to speak once the sermon proper was over. The Lord's Day Act of 1656 was passed to make it clear that Quakers did not have this right.

It is clear, then, that the removal of controls had allowed sects of all types to emerge. Some simply held to the tenets of orthodox Calvinism with such intensity that they wished to worship only with like-minded people. Others held aloof on some small points of doctrine and became the precursors of modern denominations. Few of these presented any challenge to the foundations of society. Fifth Monarchists, Ranters and Quakers did. The fear they aroused was probably out of all proportion to their numbers, but in it lay the strength of the counter-attack against toleration.

The Restoration settlement, Anglicanism and dissent

The pattern of a loosely structured and Presbyterian national Church competing for support with mainstream Independents, Anglicans, Roman Catholics and fanatical sectaries was to be disrupted by the fall of the Protectorate. The restored Rump was willing to accept almost total freedom in religion. Its replacement by the recalled Long Parliament was followed by an attempt to enforce a more rigid Presbyterianism. All laws passed since 1648 were declared invalid, the Westminster Confession was to be imposed, presbyteries established and the penal laws against Roman Catholics were to be rigorously enforced. In 1659 there was no hope of such a policy succeeding. The dominant group among the gentry would settle for nothing less than Anglicanism. On the other flank, the Independents were unwilling to forfeit the toleration they had enjoyed for fourteen years.

The Convention Parliament, which met on 25 April 1660, showed little concern with religious issues. It knew it had to bring back the King while the army was divided. If restoration was delayed until all the details were settled, it might be delayed forever. Most doubts about the King's good intentions towards his religious opponents were, in any case, stifled by his Declaration of Breda promising 'liberty to tender consciences'.

Once the King returned, two powerful and conflicting power blocks confronted each other in the religious negotiations. On one side were the Presbyterians and moderate Independents, on the other, the Anglicans. The first had many advantages. They were a large proportion of the population, they had a majority in the Convention Parliament, they held almost all the positions of power in the Church, the universities, the armed forces and in the civil service. There was also the trump card—the King had promised toleration. They were, however, subject to a number of disadvantages. In the first place, they suffered from their association with revolution and the Interregnum government; they were also divided among themselves, between the Presbyterians, on the one hand, drawn largely from the gentry and the wealthier merchants, and, on the other, the Independents and the sects, whose social base lay in the lower ranks of society. In any case, many Presbyterians, especially those of the landowning class, were ready to accept Anglicanism as a bulwark against social revolution and religious anarchy. Venner's Rising helped convince many waverers that it was essential to preserve the unity of the propertied classes against dangerous sectaries. In addition, the rise of Laud had shattered the Calvinist unity of English Protestantism; the Civil War and Interregnum had seen Calvinism's eclipse as the essential belief of Puritanism. Denial of orthodox predestinarianism and the growth of rationalism were increasing. (On this last point see G.R. Cragg, *From Puritanism to the Age of Reason*, 1966, *passim*.)

The Anglicans, too, had a mixture of strengths and weaknesses. They had been defeated in the Civil War and they had been able to keep the active support of only a minority of the population. On the other hand, they could parade their undoubted loyalty to both Charles II and his martyred father. Perhaps their greatest strength was the party they had created among the gentry. Anglican clergymen who had lost their livings in the Interregnum had often gained positions as chaplains or tutors in the households of wealthy landowners. There they influenced the rising generation into acceptance of their beliefs. This was one of the factors which made Restoration Anglicanism into a pillar of conservatism, the ecclesiastical equivalent of the rule of law and the rights of property. In English country houses, Anglican scholars such as Henry Hammond and Gilbert Sheldon had written elaborate and intellectually impressive justifications for Anglican ritual and for the necessity of bishops in a true Church. While in exile, Anglican leaders such as Cosin, Bramhall and Morley had retained full Laudian ceremonial in their services and resisted alike the temptations of Roman Catholics and the Continental Reformed Churches. This generation of Anglicans was hardened by misfortune and given confidence in the rightness of their beliefs by Charles II's seemingly providential restoration.

The churchmen of the Interregnum and their Anglican opponents met in the Savoy Conference, April–July 1661. The issues were similar to those faced during every major religious upheaval—comprehension, toleration or rigid uniformity enforced by persecution. There were two other problems: should the orders of those clergymen who had not been ordained by a bishop be regarded as valid, and should ministers holding livings from which Anglicans had been ejected be themselves turned out to make way for their predecessors? There is no doubt that Charles himself wanted a national Church which was as inclusive as possible, coupled with toleration for those who could not in conscience worship within it. The Earl of Clarendon, his chief minister, is usually credited with similar views, though at least one major historical study presents the view that his real intentions, if not his public utterances, coincided with those of the High Churchmen.

In the situation of 1660, most Presbyterian leaders were prepared to accept some form of compromise. Indeed, leaders such as Richard Baxter, it will be recalled, had long been pressing for reconciliation between Anglicans, Presbyterians and mainstream Independents, perhaps by adopting something like Archbishop Ussher's scheme for modified episcopacy. Such plans, which recognised episcopacy as only a convenient method of church government rather than an essential feature of a true Church, were quite unacceptable to the High Churchmen. The difference in attitude to bishops was the major stumbling block to settlement. Baxter's refusal to accept anything which smacked of *de jure* episcopacy (that is of the belief that bishops were esential to a true Church) probably hardened the Anglican line on other issues. Regrettably, the Anglicans conducted the negotiations in a narrow and partisan spirit. No compromise was offered and men such as Baxter—who had been offered a bishopric as incentive to accept the virtually unmodified Anglicanism of the 1662 Settlement—reluctantly withdrew from the national Church.

Even before 1662, the Anglicans assumed that their religion had been restored along with the King. Dean Cosin of Peterborough immediately resumed full choral services in the cathedral and reinstituted the Church courts. Convocation met simultaneously with the Cavalier Parliament and the bishops were almost immediately restored to the House of Lords. It was the revived convocation rather than the Savoy Conference which made the final recommendations to Parliament. Despite pressure from the King, convocation and Parliament devised a harsh, uncompromising and intolerant Act of Uniformity. Neither in church government, nor in the form of service were any significant concessions made to supporters of the Interregnum Church. Comprehension had been ruled out.

Was there to be any toleration of dissenters or were they to be persecuted? The Cavalier Parliament both recognised their existence—in itself a sort of toleration—and imposed penalties on them. The Corporation Act of 1661 set up commissioners empowered to displace all officials in the towns who would not take an oath of allegiance, who would not swear that they believed resistance to royal power to be contrary to the will of God, declare that the Solemn League and Covenant (which had established Presbyterianism) was invalid, and take Anglican communion. This Act was designed to remove non-Anglican Protestants (hereafter referred to as dissenters) from positions of power in the towns and cities, their areas of greatest strength.

A series of Acts known collectively as the Clarendon Code were passed between 1662 and 1665 to restrict and penalise dissenters. The Act of Uniformity of 1662 declared that all clergymen, schoolmasters and university teachers were to take oaths that they accepted the Anglican Settlement by St Bartholemew's Day (24 August) 1662 or lose their positions. It is probable that about 1900 left their livings rather than conform. This deprived the Church of England of many ministers of the highest calibre, driving them into opposition when relatively small concessions might have retained their services, with incalculable benefit to the Church and the nation. The Conventicle Act (1664) prohibited the holding of any religious services which were not conducted in accordance with the Book of Common Prayer, if more than five persons from outside a single household were present. The Five Mile Act of 1665 forbade all ministers and teachers, deprived for refusing the oaths and declarations laid down by the Act of Uniformity, from coming within five miles of any town or city. None were to travel within five miles of the place where they had once held office.

Needless to say, the 'interlopers'—clergymen appointed to take the place of ejected Anglicans during the Civil War and Interregnum— were forced to return their livings to their former holders. During 1660, 290 sequestered Anglican ministers were restored and 695 Commonwealth clergy displaced. The question of non-episcopally ordained clergymen is one which bedevills negotiations for union between churches with bishops and those without to this day. In the situation at the time of the Restoration, it was to be expected that ministers who had not been ordained by a bishop, and who would not be re-ordained, should lose their position. Though the official Anglican position was that ministers ordained in the Presbyterian manner would have to undergo only 'conditional' ordination by a bishop in case their former orders should be invalid, many saw this requirement as a slur on their former ministry. Along with those who refused to accept other aspects of the Settlement, they were deprived on St Bartholemew's Day 1662.

The Church Settlement had both political and religious consequences. Its intolerance and rigidity were the result of an alliance between the High Church clergymen and the landed gentry. The latter had come to see the closest association between the Crown, the gentry and the Church as an essential bulwark against social revolution. Both Anglican clergymen and the gentry emphasised their loyalty to the King. Dr South proclaimed in 1666:

The Church of England glories in nothing more than she is the truest friend to kings, and to kingly government, of any other church in the world; that they were the same hands and principles that took the crown from the King's head and the mitre from the bishops'. (Beddard in Jones, 1979, page 167.)

Events were to show that gentry and Church were the most irrevocably united pair in the conservative trinity. Attempts to break or to strengthen this alliance provide a key—perhaps *the* key—to understanding the politics of the next thirty years.

There were important religious consequences. The Anglican Church was restored much as it had been before the Civil War, and with nearly all its problems still unsolved, its weaknesses apparent to all. Clergymen continued to be appointed by the lay owners of advowsons, bishops were political nominees chosen at least as much for their politics as for their religious virtues, appropriated tithes continued in lay hands and the Church was under-financed. In addition, its funds were distributed very unevenly. Holders of the wealthier bishoprics and deaneries were very well paid: the Bishop of Durham, for example, received £3000 per annum, a peer's income, while even the comparatively poor sees of Lichfield (£750) and St Davids (£450) provided economic status equivalent to that of prosperous gentlemen. At the other extreme, the poorer vicars and curates struggled to maintain standards on an income no greater than a farm labourer's. Despite the few rich plums in the Church, it no longer provided an attractive career for many sons of the manor house. Between 1660 and 1714, most clergymen were drawn from the homes of substantial farmers or provincial merchants rather than from the nobility or gentry. Unlike the Laudians, who had tried to compensate for similar social origins by emphasising their priestly office, the Restoration clergy acknowledged the superior status of the gentry as a precondition for their support against dissenters.

Despite these weaknesses, and the challenge that it was to face from both dissent and the Roman Catholics, the Church of England remained a powerful force in national life. The hierarchy of Church courts still existed and continued to exercise an often resented jurisdiction over laymen in both moral matters and in civil suits involving wills, matrimonial disputes and oaths. True, the Court of the High Commission was not revived, but the penalty of excommunication was far from trivial. For example, those subject to it could not make wills, instigate law suits or hold office under the Test and Corporation Acts. The authority of the ecclesiastical courts was much less challenged at Common Law than had been the case before the Civil War and the secular authorities were usually willing to imprison people 'signified' (that is, brought to their notice for contempt) by the Church courts. Religious discipline at the local level was imposed to a remarkable degree, especially in periods when the political objectives of the government required a strong Anglican Church. In Clayworth, Nottinghamshire, 200 of the 236 adults in the village received Easter Communion in 1676 and this level was maintained until at least 1686. In the Kentish village of Goodnestone in 1676, 128 persons made Easter Communion out of 144 (Bennett in Holmes, 1969, page 157).

Though the religious census drawn up in 1676 was designed to show the King that the Anglicans constituted the vast majority of the nation and must therefore be treated with caution, it is worth citing. Of the adult population over sixteen, nearly two and a half million were Anglicans, nearly 109 000 dissenters and 13 500 Roman Catholics. Even if the figure for dissenters needs to be increased, the numerical predominance of Anglicans is undoubted. Unless the continuing strength of the Anglican Church under the leadership of Gilbert Sheldon, Archbishop of Canterbury 1663–1677, and William Sancroft, Archbishop of Canterbury 1677–91, is recognised, it is almost impossible to understand many of the political developments of the time.

Anglicans were not totally united in the conservative and authoritarian attitude outlined above. A group of scholars known as the 'Cambridge Platonists', men such as Ralph Chudworth, Henry More, Benjamin Whichcote and John Smith, offered an alternative position known to its enemies as Latitudinarianism. Its adherents rejected alike ideas of predestination and direct revelations by God to individuals. They played down faith as the basis of Christian belief and stressed the importance of reason. Many were associated with new scientific ideas. Unlike the High Churchmen, they were willing to co-operate with dissenters, and many hoped for a more comprehensive national Church, which could combat Roman Catholicism and unbelief more effectively (Cragg, 1966, page 37–86).

After 1662 the dissenting denominations had to adapt to new circumstances. In many ways, the Presbyterians were in the most difficult position. They believed in the principle of a national Church, but they disagreed on particular points with the body re-established at the Restoration. Like a considerable proportion of the Episcopalians who had found themselves in the same position during the Interregnum, many who were Presbyterian at heart conformed outwardly. Some such men conducted their services as nearly as possible according to the Presbyterian Directory by racing through the Book of Common Prayer to allow time for long and often extemporary 'pulpit prayers'. Use of the surplice was widely evaded and in some parishes it was a long time until all knelt to receive communion.

Presbyterians who left the Church of England established congregations throughout the country, but they did not attempt to re-establish full Presbyterian organisation and discipline. In practice, there was little to distinguish them from the Independents. Unlike them, however, they hoped for changes in the national Church which would allow them to re-enter it. Indeed, this desire was so strong that it was not until 1673 that they conducted any ordinations. Until the 1680s many Presbyterians regularly attended Anglican services as well as their own. Though the Presbyterians were the largest of the non-conforming bodies in 1662, their ambivalent attitude towards separation may have been responsible for the gradual disappearance of Presbyterians as their members either returned to the national Church or adopted the principle of separation and became congregationalists. By the eighteenth century, many former Presbyterian chapels had become Unitarian and others had adopted the Arminian view that Christ had died for all men, not only the Elect.

The Independents had fewer psychological difficulties in accepting the new situation, especially if they were 'separating' Independents who had believed all along in 'gathered' Churches. The amorphous Independent bodies gradually emerged by the 1680s as the ancestors of the modern Congregational Churches. Though they clung to the principle of congregational independence, the trend toward cooperation and a national organisation which had begun during the Interregnum was continued. In addition, schemes for closer relations with the Presbyterians were considered in 1669 and 1689.

The Baptists continued as two separate bodies, the particular and the general Baptists. Both were subject to persecution as they were associated in the public mind with Quakers and Continental Anabaptists. Both subdivisions maintained national organisations, but were hampered by persecution until 1686. The general Baptists called a general assembly in 1668, 1672 and 1678, regularly from 1686. The particular Baptists did not attempt a general assembly until 1689. By the end of the century, the general Baptists were declining in number. Some congregations became Unitarian and members who did not accept this joined the particular Baptists.

The other significant dissenting body was that of the Quakers. After the Restoration, they continued their policy of denouncing the paid ministry, oaths and symbols of social hierarchy. As a result, they were subject to greater persecution than other dissenters. Nevertheless, George Fox was able to establish a system of meetings which ranged from the weekly meetings of individual congregations to yearly meetings in London to decide national policy.

Many developments within Anglicanism can be understood only in relation to the challenge presented by Roman Catholics and dissenters. These groups had an influence in English life out of all proportion to their numbers. Danby's census of 1676, it will be recalled, was probably an underestimate in its figure of 110 000 dissenters, about 4.5 per cent of the population. In the period 1715–1718, when numbers might have fallen a little from those in the late seventeenth century, dissenters appear to have made up 6.21 per cent of the English population and 5.74 per cent of that of Wales. In England, the Presbyterians were the most numerous with 3.3 per cent of the population, the Independents second with 1.1 per cent, the particular Baptists next with 0.74 per cent and the general Baptists 0.35 per cent. The importance of the dissenters lay in: the steadfastness with which they resisted persecution; their ability to expand in some of the remoter rural areas, where the established Church had made poor provision of buildings, clergy and services; and in their influence in the towns, where many wealthy merchant families attended non-conformist worship, as well, perhaps, as putting in occasional appearances at Anglican worship in order to quality for public office. On the other hand, dissent had little support among the gentry.

Persecution of dissenters was intermittent between 1660 and 1688. The desire for revenge among Anglican clergy and gentry for their own sufferings and humiliations during the Interregnum provided a motive, as did the equation of dissent with rebellion that lasted until the 1670s. Perhaps as important was a realisation that dissenters were a group who did not defer to the Anglican ruling class in the same way that lower class conformists did. In addition, the lower clergy of the Anglican Church felt that they and their Church were constantly threatened by a non-conformist tide.

Persecution of dissenters took many forms. One was the application of the Elizabethan recusancy laws, originally intended to be applied only to Catholics, to Protestant dissenters. In the period before the Popish Plot (1678), more than half those convicted may have been Protestants. In the years immediately after the Exclusion Crisis, there was a sharp increase in the conviction of Protestant dissenters as part of the policy of revenge for their support of Exclusion (Miller, 1973, pages 265–68).

Probably more common, though, was the application of the Conventicle Acts of 1664 and 1670. The earlier Act provided penalties of a £5 fine or three month's imprisonment for worshipping in an illegal conventicle (that is, more than five people not of the same household holding a religious service other than that of the Book of Common Prayer). The 1670 Act reduced the minimum penalty for a first offence to a five shilling fine, but it allowed the registration of a conviction without the accused offering a defence if one or two magistrates were presented 'notorious evidence and circumstance of the fact'. This allowed hearsay to be accepted and presumption of guilt, based on the most circumstantial of evidence, to lead to a conviction. For example, people were sometimes found guilty on the grounds that they were known dissenters and that they had entered a wood in which conventicles were known to be held, even though there was nothing to prove that one was conducted at the time of the alleged offence, let alone that they attended it. In addition, the 1670 Conventicle Act allowed dissenting ministers to be fined £20 for each service they conducted for more than five people.

There can be no doubt that the group most subject to persecution was the Quakers. Under the Quaker Act of 1662 they were subject to the same penalties extended to other dissenters in the Conventicle Act. In addition, they could be subjected to fines, imprisonment or transportation for refusing to take an oath legally tendered. In the aftermath of Venner's Rising, Quakers, who in the popular mind were closely associated with Fifth Monarchy men, were imprisoned in large numbers: 535 in Yorkshire alone. Because of their refusal to show the authorities the accustomed respect, especially in taking off one's hat and using the formal 'you' instead of 'thou' in speech, Quakers were more likely to be subject to vindictive punishments than were other dissenters.

Though there were certain times, the early 1680s for example, in which dissenters were subject to particular pressure, their fate depended very much on the attitude of their neighbours, who could either act as informers or shield them from the authorities, and on the magistrates themselves. In 1663 the assize judges were instructed to punish vigorously 'seditious meetings of sectaries and to convict the papists'. Nevertheless, the intensity of persecution depended on the personality and opinions of the individual judges. In the Oxford circuit, Judges Wyndham and Rainsford refused to try the Quakers who had been arrested on suspicion of being involved in Venner's Rising, but at the Hertford assizes Chief Justice Bridgeman bullied the grand jury into returning bills against a group of Quakers whom he then sentenced to transportation. Once arrested or fined, their treatment could be either humane or brutal, depending on the officials involved. Though considerable time was often given to pay fines, some officials delighted in distraining the goods of those who could not pay in ready money, in such a way as to cause maximum inconvenience: carters' horses were seized, workmen's tools, and ministers' books. Stories of minor atrocities abound: the throwing out of milk being heated for a sick child so that the saucepan could be seized, for example, and more major ones, such as a woman in childbirth having her bed and all her clothes taken, she being left naked on the bare floor.

In prison, fortunate prisoners were treated more leniently than would be possible today. They were allowed their own furniture, books, writing materials, unlimited visiting and even day passes to go into town. Others were thrown in with the common prisoners who robbed and abused them at every opportunity. At times of mass arrests, horrific overcrowding was common. Prisoners who angered the authorities were likely to be chained or locked in filthy dungeons for days at a time. At Launceston, George Fox and his companion would not pay the jailer the excessive fees demanded to look after them. As a result, they were consigned to a dungeon called Doomsdale:

a nasty stinking place where they used to put witches and murderers, after they were condemned to die. The place was so noisome, that it was said very few that went in ever came out alive . . . the excrements of prisoners had not been carried out for . . . many years, so that it was like mire and in some places to the tops of the shoes in water and piss . . . we burnt a little of our straw to take away the stink . . . which put [the jailer] in such a rage that he took pots of excrements of the thieves, and poured them through a hole upon our heads . . . whereby we were so bespattered that we could not touch ourselves or one another . . . In this manner were we fain to stand all night, for we could not sit down, the place was so full of filthy excrements.

Persecution was inconsistent owing to royal efforts to keep the promises made in the Declaration of Breda and, in Charles's later years and under James II, to gain the support of dissenters for royal policies. From 1660–62 the situation was unclear and only groups such as the Fifth Monarchy men faced persecution. Once the Act of Uniformity had been passed in 1662, Charles strove to protect dissenters. He made plans to suspend the operation of the penal clauses and tried to get the Lords to agree that he had the power to do so. Charles attracted additional opposition by offering toleration to Catholics as well as dissenters, something which was opposed even by Presbyterians such as Richard Baxter, who would have benefited from the action. Owing to almost unlimited opposition in Parliament, Charles was forced to abandon, for the time being, his attempts to gain toleration by the use of prerogative. Throughout the 1660s, however, Charles used his influence with moderate Anglicans and dissenters in an attempt to build a more comprehensive Church and gain a greater measure of toleration. In 1672 Charles issued the Declaration of Indulgence suspending the operation of most penal laws in religion. Dissenters were to worship freely if their ministers and meeting houses were licensed. Roman Catholics were allowed free exercise of their religion in private. (For the political reasons for this Declaration see chapter 7, pages 451–2.)

The uproar which followed forced Charles to withdraw the Declaration and to adopt policies which would gain the support of the Anglican Church and gentry; 1672 to 1678 was a period of persecution for the dissenters. After 1678 the fear of papists aroused by the Popish Plot led many members of the ruling class to adopt a pan-Protestant view and to seek the co-operation of dissenters against Catholics. The influence of such views on magistrates led to a reduction in persecution until the defeat of the Exclusion Bill, which most dissenters had supported, made them the objects of both royal and Tory revenge in the early 1680s. The penal laws of the Clarendon Code were rigorously enforced by both the ecclesiastical and the secular courts and England was reduced to greater outward conformity in religion than had been seen since the days of Laud.

The accession of James II cannot have been greeted with enthusiasm by the dissenters. Many must have thought that their lot would become worse under a follower of the Roman Antichrist, yet, paradoxically, it was to make their situation much more tolerable (in the short term) and lead to freedom from persecution in the future.

James's attempt to gain religious freedom for Catholics was not accompanied by any corresponding measure for Protestant dissenters in 1685–6. There were 300 convictions for breaches of the Conventicle Act in Middlesex alone in six months of 1686 and an uncertain number suffered monetary penalties under the recusancy laws. However, once James realised that the Anglican gentry were implacably opposed to his steps favouring Catholicism, he decided to turn to the dissenters for support. This was a reluctant change of attitude, because James regarded them as natural rebels and opponents of monarchy. In March 1686 he overcame his scruples and granted a general pardon to religious offenders. He even gave particular protection to the Quakers. When a group of Baptists petitioned for relief from the religious laws, he made it clear that any congregation which petitioned him would be granted exemption. In general, Quakers and Baptists accepted the King's good faith and took advantage of his offer. Presbyterians were more dubious and many were unwilling to accept toleration if it meant that religious freedom would be granted to Roman Catholics.

Eleven months later, in February 1687, James turned from offering mere toleration to those dissenters who would petition for it to granting full dispensation from the penal laws and a favoured place in society. The Declaration of Indulgence of 18 March 1687 suspended all laws limiting religious freedom and James set out to make it effective by dismissing Anglican J.P.s and borough officials who openly opposed his Declaration and appointing dissenters and Catholics in their place. As in 1686, the Presbyterians suspected the King and held back, but many of the radical sects accepted his offer. In Buckinghamshire, for example, thirteen dissenters were J.P.s in 1688, none of whom had been on the Commission before the Declaration of Indulgence. However, the large number of Catholics appointed to positions of power in local and central government—many more than their proportion of the population warranted—convinced most dissenters that James was merely using them as tactical allies whom he would discard when he had achieved his objective of strengthening the Roman Catholic Church in England. By the time of the Revolution in 1688, a majority of dissenters were firmly linked with Anglicans in opposing James II's religious policies.

Restoration Catholicism

During the reign of Charles II and James II, Catholics constituted much the same section of society and had about the same numbers as in the early seventeenth century. The size of the Catholic community is not known exactly: estimates have ranged from 50 000 to 540 000, though figures between 100 000 and 200 000 are most common. There is good reason to believe, however, that John Miller's calculation of about 60 000, 1.1 to 1.2 per cent of the population, is fairly accurate. It is clear that neither the Catholic threat perceived by Protestants, nor the hopes of Charles II and James II of basing policies on Catholic support, were realistic in the light of these numbers. Socially, however, Catholics constituted something of an élite. In the rural areas, they were led by peers and gentlemen. Between 1660 and 1678 the number of Catholic peers ranged between twenty-nine and thirty-two. Miller (1973, page 13) has summarised the spirit of rural Catholicism as 'aristocratic, rural and Royalist'. The strongholds of Catholicism, as before the Civil War, were in the north, especially Lancashire, and the West Midlands, especially Herefordshire and Monmouthshire. Catholic peers and gentlemen were able to support and shelter priests and gather around them pockets of Catholicism on their estates. The Catholic gentry usually lived on good terms with their Protestant neighbours, who often protected them in time of persecution.

Urban Catholicism was weak outside London, its adherents usually dependents of the Catholic gentlemen living near the town. London Catholics had the advantage of being able to attend mass in the chapels of the Catholic Queens and in certain foreign embassies. These chapels were very popular—in 1671 the Venetian resident reported that the four ambassadorial chapels could not hold all those wishing to attend and, even in 1680, two or three hundred people attended the Queen's chapel. The concentration of Catholics in Westminster and the western suburbs was probably explained by the proximity of places of worship. In the early 1680s there were fifty-one convicted recusants and seventy-seven papists or reputed papists in the City, 1169 in Westminster and the western suburbs. These included 191 gentlemen, but the proportion of non-gentle Catholics was much higher than in the rest of the country.

Perhaps the most important feature of Catholicism in greater London was its association with the royal Court. Charles I married a Catholic, Henrietta Maria, and this tradition was continued by his sons. Charles II's queen, Catherine of Braganza, was a Catholic. James II's first wife, Anne Hyde, converted shortly before her death and his second wife, Mary of Modena, was a life-long Catholic. As the Queen's servants were exempt from prosecution for recusancy, notable figures around the Court and wealthy merchants became technically the Queen's servants to benefit from this protection. There was a marked difference in attitude between the rural Catholics, who wanted merely *de facto* freedom from persecution, and the Court Catholics, who often talked unrealistically about the reconversion of England. At the very least, they wished to make political capital out of their loyalism during the Civil War to regain repeal of the penal laws and end their exclusion from political office. This divergence was a major weakness when James II set out to favour Catholics.

The government of the Roman Catholic Church in England was still beset by internal differences which, to some extent, mirrored the split between Court and country Catholicism. The majority of priests were chaplains to noblemen or wealthy gentlemen living in their houses and conducting the seasonal cycle of services for the master, his family, servants and tenants. This was an introspective type of Catholicism concerned mainly with protecting an existing community and its accustomed ways. Missionary priests travelled around, providing for independent congregations wherever they could find them. These missions were most common in London and in remote rural areas.

The Roman Catholic community was weakened by bitter divisions between the regular and the secular clergy: the regular clergy were members of monastic orders, and the secular were those who did not belong to orders, but worked within the ordinary diocesan and parochial system. These divisions were not solved in 1622 by the appointment of a bishop responsible for English affairs. Quarrels between the two groups of priests continued after the Restoration. The regular clergy looked to the head of their order in the English province, rather than to the bishop, for guidance. In the 1660s there were approximately 230 secular priests, 120 Jesuits, eighty Benedictines, fifty-five Franciscans and a small number of Carmelites and Dominicans. Jesuit numbers rose to a peak of 337 in 1689, but the others appear to have fluctuated little. Though most priests were dedicated men operating in hostile territory at considerable personal risk, some were unable to maintain standards. 'One seduced his host's wife and murdered the resultant child, another had to be treated for venereal disease; another was killed in a duel' (Miller, 1973, page 41).

A further division continued after the Restoration. Some priests were willing to accept, in return for toleration, an oath of allegiance denying the Pope's power to depose heretical rulers. Those who did were known as Blackloites after the priest, Thomas Blacklo. He had suggested such an arrangement in 1647. As in the case of the debate over the oath at the turn of the century, willingness to accept was more common among laymen than priests and it was eventually condemned by Rome. Again, like the earlier controversy, it involved a conflict between the secular priests and the Jesuits. The seculars, or at least a minority of them, were willing to accept an oath which the Jesuits repudiated utterly.

After the Restoration, however, one tradition of earlier Catholicism was dead. The militants who had looked to Mary Queen of Scots, to Philip of Spain, to the murder of Queen Elizabeth or the blowing up of James I and his Parliament as a step towards forced reconversion had no spiritual descendents. Those who believed that a Catholic England was possible saw it as a long-term process to be brought about by the grace of God, not the force of arms, by persuasion rather than the edict of a Catholic king. Even those who favoured the policies of James II looked only for opportunities for missionary work and the removal of their own political disabilities.

In the years immediately after the Restoration, Catholics were less subject to persecution than before the Civil War. Attitudes to Catholicism among Protestant Englishmen had changed a little. Archbishop Sheldon had shocked his contemporaries at Oxford by denying that the Pope was necessarily Antichrist—he admitted the possibility of other contenders for the title. Christopher Hill has argued that belief in Antichrist disappeared after the Restoration, a finding which ties in well with William Lamont's contention that beliefs in the imminence of the millennium declined at much the same time (C. Hill, *Antichrist in the Seventeenth Century*, Oxford, 1971, pages 146–54, 158–60; W. Lamont, *Godly Rule: Politics and Religion, 1603–1660*, London, 1969, pages 19–20). Such beliefs may have weakened, but they did not disappear. Certainly many of the old attitudes to Catholicism were to revive at the time of the Exclusion Crisis, and with them the cult of Queen Elizabeth.

See here she comes, the great ELIZABETH
Who the great Romish Babylon with her breath
Threw to the ground Rome's daubers ne'er were able
Since her blest reign yet to rebuild their Babel
Rome's terror still is great Elizabeth.

'A Poem on the Burning of the Pope', 1679

Your Popish Plot and Smithfield
We do not fear at all
For lo, beneath Queen Bess's feet
You fall, you fall, you fall.

'London's Defiance to Rome', 1679 (Quoted in Miller, 1973, page 74.)

Atrocity literature in the tradition of Foxe was updated by reference to the St Bartholemew's Day massacre in France, the Gunpowder Plot, the Irish massacres of the 1640s and the persecution of Piedmontese Protestants in the 1650s. It may be significant, however, that Foxe's emphasis on the part played by Protestant martyrs and the Godly Prince in preparing the way for the millennium was stressed less than stories of popish cruelty told for their own sake. Samuel Clarke's *General Martyrology* included drawings showing eighty-seven different ways in which Protestant martyrs had been put to death.

Though anti-Catholic attitudes were perhaps less pronounced in the 1660s, there was an enormous potential for their revival once Protestant Englishmen perceived a threat. Open anti-Catholicism was strong enough to prevent Charles II from removing the penal laws affecting life and limb. Many Catholics, especially those who had been associated with the Court in exile, seriously believed that it was possible to obtain full legal toleration, especially if agreement could be reached on a loyalty oath. A Bill offering toleration on those terms was introduced in the Lords in June 1661, but it had little hope of passing. In 1662 Catholics hoped to benefit from the King's plan to suspend the penal clauses of the Act of Uniformity, but once more Charles was unable to gain the toleration he desired for Catholics and Protestants alike.

Though Charles was unable to suspend the penal laws or have them repealed, he was able to ensure in the 1660s that they were not rigorously enforced. Between 1660 and 1671 only £147.15s.7d had been paid in recusancy fines, even though a committee of the House of Commons estimated the amount due at between four and five million pounds. Though the actions of anti-Catholic J.P.s, in presenting Catholics to the judges for recusancy, were producing convictions, royal policy was protecting them from the financial consequences.

From 1663 to 1672, Catholicism was not a major factor in English politics. Certainly, Catholics were blamed for the Fire of London in 1666, adding 'a belief in Popish pyromania . . . to the anti-Catholic tradition' (Miller, 1973, page 105), and the destruction of the English fleet by the Dutch in 1667 was regarded as the fault of papists, but these were isolated manifestations of anti-Catholic feeling, which was usually dormant in this period.

In 1672 Charles II's Declaration of Indulgence and his treaty with France brought fear of Catholicism to the surface. The conversion to Catholicism of the heir to the throne, Charles's brother, the Duke of York and future James II, had long been suspected and these suspicions were strengthened when he failed to take Anglican Communion at Easter 1673, and confirmed when he resigned his offices rather than swear the anti-Catholic oaths required by the Test Act. James's conversion made attitudes to Catholicism the central feature of political life. The old fear of the association between popery and arbitrary government was revived and there was an outburst of anti-Catholic literature. There was a marked increase in the number of Pope burnings each 5 November.

The failure of the policy embodied in the Declaration of Indulgence resulted in a return to co-operation with the Anglican ruling class, in a government dominated by Danby (the King's leading minister, see chapter 7, page 453). Under Danby, there was both a substantial increase in recusancy convictions and a real, though not especially successful, effort to collect the fines. The revival of anti-Catholic fears was, of course, responsible for the belief in the Popish Plot (see chapter 7, pages 455–6). 'There were two inchanting terms', wrote Bishop Parker, 'which could like Circe's intoxicating cups, change men into beasts, namely Popery and the French Interest'. During the panic which followed the plot, Catholics were placed under a great deal of pressure. In November 1678, Charles ordered the enforcement of the penal laws, commanded all papists except householders and tradesmen to move at least ten miles from London, prohibited Englishmen from attending mass in ambassadors' chapels, reinforced the five mile limit on papists' movements imposed by the Act of 1593 and revived the laws against priests, offering rewards for their capture. At the local level, there was a large increase in the number of Catholics convicted for recusancy. Many were ordered to take the oaths of allegiance and supremacy, swearing that they accepted the King as supreme governor of the English Church. The penalty for refusing these oaths was *praemunire*, the forfeiture of all goods and perpetual imprisonment. Though the administration of the oaths was limited, several Catholics were imprisoned. Undoubtedly the worst result of the panic was the execution of priests: none had been sent to the gallows between 1660 and 1678; eighteen were executed between 1678 and 1681 and others died in prison.

From 1681, pressure on the Catholics was reduced. The government ordered that priests were not to be executed, except at the King's command. In the aftermath of the Exclusion Crisis, religious persecution was concentrated on dissenters rather than on Catholics. In the county of Norfolk, for example, forty to sixty per cent of convicted recusants were Catholics in 1676–9; this figure was only six and a half per cent in 1684. Collection of fines from convicted recusants gradually became less rigorous, though substantial amounts were collected in the early 1680s.

Once James II came to the throne in 1685, the Catholics experienced better times, until the appointment of Catholic government ministers, J.P.s and army officers aroused such revulsion against Catholicism that James lost his throne (see chapter 3, page 232). The consequences of James's religious policy for the Catholic community have been given less attention by historians than the fact of the loss of his throne. The change from penalties to official encouragement had naturally led to a big increase in Catholic activity. At least eighteen new chapels were opened in London, six in York and at least one in most of the larger provincial towns. In addition, there were a number of Catholic schools and colleges founded. James was the main, though not the only, provider of funds for this expansion of missionary activity. Indeed, it was one of the cornerstones of his policy. He believed that once Protestants had an opportunity to observe Catholic worship and hear an exposition of Catholic beliefs from trained priests, they must be converted.

The Catholic mission was, however, faced not only by the hostility of Protestants, but by serious internal difficulties. In the first place, James was usually in conflict with Pope Innocent XI over appointments within the English Roman Catholic Church, diplomacy, and attitudes to France and the Jesuits. The most bitter quarrel concerned the Pope's refusal to appoint Father Edward Petre bishop on the grounds that he was a Jesuit and pro-French. Within England, the old hostilities between the Jesuits and the secular clergy remained. In addition, there was the practical problem of finding enough priests for the expanded level of activity. Priests require long training and, in a missionary situation, those who do not speak the language of the country are of little use. The number of English priests could not be expanded quickly enough to meet the demand for them and most of the foreign priests sent to supplement them were unsuitable.

Given both the hostility to Catholicism of the majority of Englishmen and the difficulties of the Catholic mission, it is not surprising that the number of converts was limited. There was only a slight increase in conversions between 1685 and 1688. Certainly, some ambitious courtiers were converted—the Earls of Sunderland, Yarmouth, Perth and Melford, for example, as well as important gentlemen such as Sir Thomas Stradling, Herbert Masters and Sir Nicholas Butler. At least ten, perhaps as many as thirty, Anglican clergymen became Roman Catholics and at least eight fellows of Oxford colleges. However, some of these were converts of convenience whose self-interested change of religion did nothing for the Catholic cause.

After the Revolution of 1688, most fruits of the missionary endeavour were swept away. A small number of genuine converts retained their faith. The merely ambitious quickly apostasised once more. The Catholic chapels were, for the most part, closed or physically demolished. James's belief that the tiny Catholic minority could reconvert England if only they could state their case was totally unfounded. His actions were to strengthen further the anti-Catholic tradition in England. They led to the passage of one of the few discriminatory laws remaining in the English statute book: the Act of Succession of 1701, which prohibited any Catholic or person married to a Catholic from succeeding to the throne.

Religion in the Revolution Settlement

The Revolution led to a number of important changes in religion. The most obvious was the passage of the Toleration Act of 1689, often seen as a reward to dissenters for the way the majority joined with Anglicans to oppose James II, rather than accepting the toleration he offered them. William III intended to give the dissenters more than bare toleration. He planned changes in the Church of England which would allow most dissenters to rejoin it, as well as toleration for the minority which would continue to remain outside. He received the leaders of the dissenting bodies and suggested establishing comprehension by making those beliefs and practices 'wherein all the Reformed Churches do agree' the basis of the national Church. William was a Dutch Calvinist who felt far more affinity for Presbyterianism than Anglicanism. He frightened the English bishops by consenting to an Act of the Scottish Parliament abolishing bishops and establishing Presbyterianism in that country. The fact that his decision was based on the realities of Scottish politics, rather than his personal opinions, did not ease Anglican fears.

William fanned the suspicions he had created, by his discussions with dissenters and his actions over the Scottish Church, by entering the House of Lords and demanding the repeal of the Test and Corporation Acts. This was a political error. As a result, the Comprehension Bill failed and only the Toleration Bill became law.

The toleration offered dissenters under this law was very limited in scope. They were freed from the operation of the penal laws on certain conditions: they had to take the oaths of supremacy and allegiance and make a declaration against transubstantiation; their meeting houses had to be registered with the bishop or quarter sessions, and their ministers had to subscribe to those parts of the thirty-nine articles which did not concern Church government; they were still subject to the Test and Corporation Acts, which excluded from any position of trust under the Crown, and any office in local government, all those who were not prepared to take Anglican communion and obtain a certificate from the minister; in addition, they were ineligible to attend the universities or to enter most of the professions.

With the compromise settlement, the dissenters seemed to lose their earlier zeal. Christopher Hill has argued that post-Revolution dissent retained only the dry bones of old Puritanism: its outward forms rather than the living spirit (Hill, *Society and Puritanism in Pre-Revolutionary England*, London, 1969, pages 485–95). Even if this is too harsh a judgement, there can be no doubt that dissent lost much of its missionary spirit, its sense of destiny, and its belief in the role of the mouth piece of God, urging the Elect nation to prepare for the millennium. Instead, there emerged small inward-looking denominations, concerned with personal piety, survival of their community and, increasingly, the pursuit of success in business.

Anglicanism, too, was profoundly changed by the Revolution: it had lost its legal monopoly. Between 1691 and 1710, 2536 places of worship for dissenters were licensed. As well as this, it suffered from internal division. Archbishop Sancroft, five bishops and 400 clergymen refused to take the required oaths of loyalty to William and Mary, arguing that it would be hypocritical for those who had preached for so long against resistance to Kings to accept a revolution. The willingness of the Nonjurors (those who refused to take an oath of allegiance to William and Mary on the grounds that James II was the true king) to suffer for their principles created much unease among the much greater number of clergymen who had taken the oath with the mental reservation that they were accepting William only as a *de facto* king not as a *de jure* (rightful) one. The Revolution altered the balance of power within the Church. The leadership of the High Church party was broken by the dismissal of the Nonjurors, and Latitudinarians were appointed to take their place—John Tillotson, Archbishop of Canterbury 1691–4, Thomas Tenison, his successor until 1715, Edward Stillingfleet, Bishop of Worcester 1689, Simon Patrick, Bishop of Chichester 1689, and Bishop of Ely 1691, are some notable examples. With the appointment of the Latitudinarian bishops, intolerant High Churchmanship became much more common among the ordinary parish clergy, men whose economic situation deteriorated after the Revolution and who were in the frontline of competition with dissenters.

The High Churchmen still looked to alliance with the State and repressive legislation to improve the lot of the Church. Men such as Tenison, however, accepted that the Church of England had to look to itself. He set out to remedy abuses, to stamp out pluralism and to further missionary work at home and abroad by supporting organisations such as the Society for the Promotion of Christian Knowledge and the Society for the Propagation of the Gospel. Vigorous leadership by the Latitudinarian bishops did produce something of a spiritual revival, though they were unable to convert the High Churchmen to their belief in comprehension. At the end of the century, and for many years afterwards, there was to be division in the Church.

Despite the continuing conflict, the Revolution Settlement had established a pattern of religious life which was to last for more than a century and which, indeed, has considerable influence to this day. Its consequences extend far beyond England to all parts of the world which were once part of the British Empire. The Anglican Church had lost its monopoly, but its rivals obtained only a partial toleration, which left them outside the mainstream of national life. This was, however, a major change from the situation of 1558. The unity of Church and society had been broken irretrievably. Throughout the whole period 1558–1700, there were four possible methods of organising religion—to rejoin the international Church, to retain a national and Episcopalian system, to create a national Presbyterian Church, or to allow fully independent bodies to exist. The system which emerged after 1689 was a combination of all four. England and Wales had an Episcopal church, Scotland a Presbyterian one: all three countries had Protestant dissenters and an increasingly tolerated Catholic minority. Ireland's established Episcopal Church was challenged by both Protestant dissenters and the Catholics who made up most of the population. Except in Ireland, the national Churches retained both political power and the adherence of the majority of the population, but there *is* a sense in which the Independents had won. The joining of any Church, even the national one, had become an essentially voluntary activity.

CHAPTER SIX

Parliament: its business and politics, 1558–1629

The historians' view of Elizabethan/early Stuart parliaments

It is impossible for historians to be totally objective. They are influenced, like anyone else, by the world in which they live and by their own personal beliefs and prejudices. For example, in the 1940s and 50s, when Marxism was fashionable, it was applied to the origins of the English Civil War. Marxist theory was concerned with the three steps to the rule of the working class: government by a feudal aristocracy; its overthrow by a bourgeois (middle class) revolution; and finally a second, proletarian (working class) revolution. Some historians enthusiastically applied this to the early seventeenth century. They proved, to their satisfaction, that the old nobility was declining, whereas the gentry and merchants were rising. The Civil War was the victory of the new middle class over the old aristocracy. Twenty years later Marxism is no longer fashionable. The Marxist explanation of the English Civil War is as dead as a dodo and the evidence on which it rested has been rejected as unreliable, selected to suit the argument, or misinterpreted.

There is a lesson to be learned in this. Historians are to some extent victims of their evidence, and of the times in which they write. The volume of surviving records for the period 1558–1629 is very small; the gaps are enormous, and it is very easy to misinterpret or to attach far too much importance to the bits and pieces which have come down to us. Secondly, historians are swayed by contemporary attitudes, and by the fads and fashions, the social and political norms of the day. They are even tempted to read back into an earlier age the ideals which matter most to them and their contemporaries. This is precisely what has happened in the study of Elizabethan and early Stuart parliaments. A number of English and American historians researched and wrote on that period at a time when two important developments were taking place in England. First, the Reform Acts of the nineteenth century, together with the Acts of 1918 and 1928 (which gave women the vote), transformed the English electorate. From a small property-owning 'élite' it became a democracy in which every adult exercised a vote. Secondly, while Parliament remained, in constitutional fact and theory, a trinity of monarch, Lords and Commons, it ceased to be so in practice. Since 1707, no king or queen had vetoed a Bill passed by the two Houses. In the nineteenth century, the monarch lost the power to choose a prime minister. Then, in 1911, the House of Lords' role in the making of law was severely limited. It could no longer alter or reject any Commons' Bill which involved the expenditure of public money, and any other Bill which it rejected automatically became law after two years. The House of Commons had become the dominant member of the parliamentary trinity.

The historians who, at that time, were studying Elizabeth I and the first two Stuarts were deeply affected by these changes. The House of Commons' supremacy within Parliament, and the choice of its members by a democratic electorate, were cherished contemporary ideals. They saw the Civil War and Revolution of the 1640s and 1650s as the first dramatic step towards the achievement of those ideals. Indeed, convinced that such an earth-shaking upheaval must have deep-seated and long-term causes, they went one step further back in time and searched for the origins of these events in the sixteenth century. There is no need to refer to more than three of these historians here: A.F. Pollard, whose career spanned the 1890s to the 1940s, Sir John Neale, who was his student and successor, and W. Notestein, an American working along the same lines, but on the early seventeenth century.

Pollard, a Tudor specialist, looked forward. (A.F. Pollard wrote a number of articles on particular aspects of Tudor parliamentary history, but his general interpretation is incorporated in one important and almost unreadable volume: *The Evolution of Parliament*.) He viewed the history of Parliament as a long-term evolutionary process towards the ideals of Commons' supremacy and democracy. Neale (1949, 1953, 1957; see Bibliography) looked in the other direction. He honestly and openly declared that it was his intention to seek out the origins of the Stuart conflict in the sixteenth century. He drew a picture of dramatic change. Parliament's power increased: within it there was a shift in authority from the Lords to the Commons. The Upper House (the Lords) lost its age-old superiority. Its independence vanished and it became a dutiful, obedient servant of the monarch. In Elizabeth's reign its prime function was 'to assist [the Crown] in controlling the Commons' (Neale, 1953, page 41). In contrast, the Lower House (the Commons) became more willing to assert itself, to question royal policies, and to oppose the government. On occasions it even tried to impose its own policies on the Crown. Implicit in all this was the development, between 1558 and 1640, of a struggle for supremacy between Crown and Parliament. In the short term, the result was that, in the later sixteenth century, there was a growth of conflict (this is the central theme of the two volumes of Neale's *Elizabeth I and her Parliaments*). More serious for Elizabeth was the emergence of a persistent, troublesome Puritan opposition which was organised to implement its own programme of Bills. Neale portrayed this opposition as the 'apprenticeship' of the early Stuart assemblies: it devised and passed on its techniques and practices to the parliamentary opponents of James I and Charles I (Neal, 1957, page 436).

The work of Notestein added little to this picture (1924; see Bibliography). He adopted the same approach as Neale, but concentrated on the development of procedures in the Commons. Procedures are no more than the methods of conducting business: they are simply designed to improve efficiency and to speed up the handling of business. However, Notestein detected a more sinister political motive behind their development and refinement. They were actually intended to weaken the grip of the monarch's Privy Councillors on the Commons and so to give greater freedom to the opponents of royal policies. Notice that these historians focussed their attention on parliamentary politics and constitutional issues. They were concerned with opposition, conflict and the jousting for power. However, political activity is always designed to fulfil certain ends. So we ought to ask ourselves what men hoped and expected to achieve through Parliament—not only the Privy Councillors sitting in the Lords or elected to the Commons to work on the Crown's behalf, but also the gentry and burgesses who came up to Westminster from their counties and towns, and the bishops and peers riding in from their dioceses and country estates. In brief, what were the legitimate and accepted functions and purposes of Parliament? And what were the expectations of Crown and community when it met?

The functions of Parliament

The prime function and purpose of any Parliament in this period was to serve the Crown. After all it was the monarch who decided when it should be called and naturally it was only summoned to satisfy some pressing need of government. With two exceptions, Elizabeth's parliaments met to grant her money. The monarchy was expected to subsist 'of its own' (that is, to finance its normal governmental responsibilities from its hereditary revenues, which were *not* voted by Parliament), except in emergencies, which usually meant war. However, this was proving difficult in the 1560s. Inflation, past mismanagement, and the costs of wars had seriously weakened the Crown's financial condition. Elizabeth needed supplements of money even in peacetime, and Parliament invariably responded with grants of fifteenths and tenths (levies on property and moveables in country and town) and subsidies (an income tax). In 1566–7 Elizabeth graciously cancelled one-third of the grant in order to put members in a grateful frame of mind and so ease their pressure on her to marry. In 1593 the Lords considered the Commons' grant to be too niggardly and successfully pressured it to increase the sum (Neale, 1953, pages 160–1; 1957, pages 298–312). But no Elizabethan Parliament refused or reduced the sum requested, as it had done occasionally in the earlier reigns of Henry VII and Henry VIII.

On two occasions the Queen called Parliament specifically to consider non-financial matters. In 1559 it met to settle the order of worship, doctrine and government of the Church; in 1572 its task was to proceed against the captive Mary Stuart for her complicity in the treason and rebellion of the last three years. These exceptions illustrate the other essential functions of Parliament: to offer up advice when it was required and requested, and to make laws. Even if a Parliament was summoned specifically for money, the Privy Council seized the opportunity to push through measures to further State security or good government. In 1571 it was the Treasons Act; in 1581 it was the penal law against Catholics; or again a labour code (the Act of Apprentices) in 1563 and a measure against promoters (common informers) in 1576 (the first two of these have been described at length in Neale, 1953, Part 4, chapter IV and Part 7, chapter II. However, he devoted scant space [six lines] to the third, and none to the fourth, because they did not cause any 'trouble').

Money and laws were what the government wanted. However, that was not the end of the story. Parliament was a meeting-place of the Crown and representatives of the governing class. The bishops and peers who sat in the Lords were the élite of Church and Society respectively; the gentlemen and burgesses who sat in the other House—400 of them in 1559, increasing to 462 before the end of the reign—were also propertied men. They represented a numerous country gentry and the ruling merchant oligarchies of many (but not all) cities and boroughs (Neale, 1949, pages 27, 140–2). The members of the Upper House and those whom the Commons represented comprised the governing class, who managed the realm under the Queen. They monopolised the key posts in local government, especially the offices of Lord Lieutenant, Deputy Lieutenant, J.P. and sheriff. They knew the state of the communities in which they lived and served her. They had a first-hand knowledge of the political temper, the state of religion, the economic and social condition of their localities. Above all, they came armed with a knowledge of the opinions of their fellows and neighbours: their attitude to particular royal policies, what political abuses, security problems, economic and social ills required new laws.

Parliaments provided the Queen and her Councillors with an invaluable opportunity to sound out the governing class, discover its grievances and discuss how best to remedy current problems in the kingdom. Sometimes irritated members voiced their complaints or criticism in Parliament, and occasionally criticism could be heated, as in the monopolies debates of 1597 and 1601. However, Parliament was usually an exercise in communication and co-operation for mutual benefit, with the Crown receiving a feed-back of local information from members, and in return lending the weight of its support to remedial legislation. Even criticism and heated debate were useful. They were both safety valves, 'letting off steam', and they were forms of communication. They plainly told the government of discontent which required attention and resolution.

If Parliament rendered important services to the Crown in the process of government, it also aroused the expectations and hopes of those who attended and the communities which they represented in the Commons. Members came armed with Bills for themselves, their kin, friends, clients or constituencies. They were not often Bills of national importance. Even rarer was the Puritan Bill to reform the Church or the measure to put an end to misconduct or abuses by royal officials. The great majority were personal or private, and 'beneficial', in nature. These terms require definition:

1 Personal Bills were concerned with individuals (or perhaps their families). Their range was almost infinite in its diversity: for example, ratifying the young Duke of Norfolk's marriage (1559), allowing Lord Bergavenny and Viscount Bindon to lease lands (1563), guaranteeing to the Ladies Cobham and Stafford their jointures (estates settled on a wife to maintain her after her husband's death) in 1566. A number of Acts naturalised (granted citizenship) to Englishmen's children born overseas. Many more restored 'in blood' the heirs of traitors. When a man was convicted of treason, his family was 'outlawed'. They could not receive honours or the protection of the courts in defence of their property. In 1559, seven heirs were restored to the full protection of the law; in 1563, eleven; in 1571, two; and in 1593, one.

2 Private Bills varied in scope, but their distinguishing charac-

teristic was that they did not touch upon the entire realm. (Those which did were public Bills, which affected everyone's lives and treated of such matters as religion, crime, rebellion, treason and defence of the kingdom.) Their variety, too, almost defies description, but generally they were geographically restricted to a county, a town or port, or economically limited to a 'sectional interest', such as an industry, an occupation, or a trading company. As this class of Bills was so numerous and occupied so much of Parliament's time, it is worth devoting space to an illustration of its range and diversity. In 1559, for example, there were Acts concerning shoemakers and the manufacture of woollen cloth in Essex and the sale of tanned leather (that is, hides or skins converted into leather). Some measures regulated trade: two prohibited the export of horses and raw hides, and others concerned customs duties on imported sweet wines and the shipping of goods in 'Englishe Botomes' (vessels). Few Parliaments concluded their business without at least one Act regulating standards of manufacture and this was no exception: there was a statute against the 'deceiptfull using of Lynnen (linen) Clothe'. Fish spawn and 'frye of fyshe' (not fried fish but young fishes) were protected; a fair was revived at King's Lynn in Norfolk; a chapel in the Welsh county of Carmarthenshire was converted into a parish; the Staffordshire assizes (see chapter 3, pages 199–200) were appointed to be held in the county town; and Trinity Hall College, Cambridge, became a corporation (that is, it became an 'artificial' person, able to act in the law courts to protect its rights). Parliament could (and did) deal with every aspect of the nation's everyday life (saving the Queen's prerogative and, unless she consented, religion).

3 Obviously, as their name suggests, 'beneficial' Bills were designed to bring advantages to those who promoted them. Sometimes the benefits which they bestowed on their sponsors were offset by penalties and hardships inflicted on others. So the City of London was concerned to provide cheap fuel for its inhabitants, but it found its supplies in the neighbouring counties threatened by iron mills which converted timber into charcoal for smelting the ore. In 1581 it introduced a Bill to protect its dwindling fuel resources by prohibiting new iron mills near London and the Thames. It also forbade the ironmasters to convert wood to charcoal for such purposes within twenty-two miles (the Commons finally settled on eighteen) of either the metropolis or the River Thames. The 'iron interest', headed by Sir Henry Sidney, put up a fierce (albeit unsuccessful) resistance.

However, the majority of beneficial Bills were not contentious and it remains true that the sitting of Parliament was an optimistic occasion. It was a chance for both Crown and governing class to satisfy their needs and expectations, and not only by passing Bills into law. Ambitious gentry, men of humbler birth who had hopefully prepared themselves for royal service with an education at university and an inn of court (law school), lawyers who enviously eyed the fat incomes of the Queen's judges: all of them hoped to attract the attention and favour of the monarch or one of her Privy Councillors—in brief, to pick up a patron. What better place to do this than in the House of Commons? A display of loyalty, enthusiasm and skill there was often the first step to a career in the government or judiciary. Lawyers, such as Robert Bell, John Popham, John Puckering, Edward Coke and Christopher Yelverton, all became experienced members and served as Speaker before rising to high judicial office. For others, among them Sir Francis Walsingham and Dr Thomas Wilson, parliamentary service was the beginning of a road which led to membership of the Privy Council. Parliament was capable of satisfying so many needs, ambitions and appetites.

The authority of Parliament before Elizabeth's reign

The essential functions of Parliament had not altered dramatically since the early sixteenth century, but its authority certainly had. Before the Reformation, statute (Acts of Parliament: that is, the law enacted by Parliament) was limited in its scope. It did not, and it was generally held that it could not, deal in 'matters spiritual'. In other words, the doctrine, government, discipline and condition of the Church, which were based on the law of God, could not be judged or altered by a body of laymen sitting in Parliament. Christopher St German, a lawyer, wrote in about 1528, on the very eve of the Reformation, that 'if any statute were made directly against the said law of God, [then] that statute was void' (that is, it was no law). Statute also paid great respect to property rights. This was hardly surprising in a Parliament which consisted of property owners. In the past, Acts of Parliament had encroached upon such rights in the case of a few individuals, but they had never authorised a wholesale confiscation of property or the suppression of those privileges and rights which went with the ownership of land. Once statutes had been made, they were enforced, not in Parliament, but by the judges in the King's courts. Before the Reformation, those judges showed no great respect for statute, which they interpreted freely rather than strictly. After all, it was only one of a number of forms of law and, according to St German, its chief use was in cases where 'other grounds of the law seemed not to be sufficient to punish evil men and to reward good men'.

The Reformation changed all this. At first this was not apparent, even in 1533–4 when Henry VIII broke with Rome and used Parliament to transfer the Pope's authority to the Crown. True, Papal Supremacy was replaced by Royal Supremacy—a change of enormous importance. The King's servants who drafted the Acts by which this was carried through were careful not to state that it was done by *authority of Parliament*. The Act of Supremacy simply stated that:

the King's Majesty justly and rightfully is and oweth to be the supreme head of the Church of England, and so is recognised by the clergy of this realm ...

In other words the King was already Supreme Head: it was a title given to him by God not by Parliament, which did no more by its authority than declare that his subjects should accept and regard him as such, with full power to exercise spiritual authority. The Acts of the 1530s gave the King the necessary weapons to destroy the Papacy's power and to punish those who resisted him, but they did not actually authorise changes in spiritual matters. As the result of the skilful drafting of these Acts, only the King could do that.

However, the same care was not taken in the following reigns. The nobles who governed in the name of the boy-King, Edward VI, carried through a Protestant Reformation. Like Henry VIII they used Parliament, but there the similarity ends. In 1549 the first Act of Uniformity introduced a prayer book setting forth a new order of service, and required everyone to observe it. It was enacted 'by the authority of Parliament'. Three years later the same authority replaced it by a more uncompromisingly Protestant prayer book. Edward VI's successor, Mary I, was determined to reverse the Reformation process, by restoring the Catholic religion and papal supremacy. However, the Acts of Henry and Edward had recognised the royal supremacy and made Protestantism the only lawful religion. So Mary had no choice but to turn to Parliament: in 1553 it repealed the Edwardian Reformation, and in 1554–5 it restored the Pope to all his former rights and powers. Each step had to be:

enacted and established by the Queen's Highness, the Lords spiritual and temporal and the Commons in this present Parliament assembled, and by the authority of the same ...

There was no going back. Once alterations in Church government and religion had been made by parliamentary statute, only new statutes could reverse them. Therefore, the Elizabethan Church had to be created in the same way. By 1559 Parliament was accustomed to dealing with matters spiritual and authorising changes in religion and Church government.

This was not, however, the only way in which the trinity of Crown, Lords and Commons advanced in authority and competence. (Note that 'competence' means the range of business and the scope of human activity with which Parliament could legitimately deal.) In 1536 it passed three Acts which established its right to enact laws about property: the Statute of Uses, the suppression of franchises (also known as 'liberties' or 'honours') and the dissolution of the lesser monasteries. The first of these Acts burdened many landowners' estates with the obligation to pay feudal dues to the King (see Appendix I, pages 481–3). The second concerned semi-independent territories within the realm, whose owners rather than the King controlled administration, tax-collection, law enforcement and justice. These property rights, which operated over extensive stretches of land— especially in Wales, the Welsh marches (or border lands) and in the north, above all in the county of Durham—were now abolished. The third Act, however, did not merely suppress or alter property rights. It sanctioned a massive transfer of the property itself: from the Church to the Crown. Later Acts to dissolve the larger monastic houses (in 1539), and the chantries (whose prime function was to pray for the souls of dead benefactors and their families, although many were also schools) in 1547, simply confirmed Parliament's competence to make laws on such matters.

The crowded events between 1529 and 1559 must have bewildered many people, and probably those who lived through them did not perceive at the time all the implications of what was happening. In retrospect, we can see that three changes did occur. Statute became omnicompetent: that is, able to deal with anything, in every sphere of life. Secondly, statute became supreme, the highest form of law. It could override custom, judges' decisions and all the other elements of which the Common Law was comprised. Only one thing could overthrow a statute, and that was another one. Finally it was recognised that sovereignty, the ultimate power in the State, resided in Parliament. This should not be misunderstood: Parliament was a trinity and the King was the senior partner in it. Indeed, the King's role in the State took two forms. On the one hand, he was *rex solus* or the King alone. As such, he governed the realm by the exercise of his limited prerogative (the traditional powers of kingship which were beneath the law and defined by it; see chapter 2, pages 106–8). On the other hand, as King-in-Parliament he demanded his subjects' obedience and nothing whatsoever was outside his competence.

Henry VIII informed a delegation from the House of Commons in 1543:

[We] be informed by our judges that we at no time stand so highly in our estate royal as at the time of Parliament . . .

Sir Thomas Smith, writing early in Elizabeth's reign, was in no doubts about the post-Reformation state of affairs:

The most high and absolute power of the realme of Englande, consisteth in the Parliament.

As we arrive at Elizabeth's reign, it is an appropriate time at which to take stock of the situation. There are a number of fundamentals about contemporary parliaments, at this stage of their evolution, which must not be forgotten, and which apply equally to the reigns of the last Tudor and the first Stuart:

1 Parliament was not a permanent part of government and its practical importance should not be overrated. During Elizabeth's reign it averaged only one meeting every three-and-a-half years, and even then the longest session lasted no more than fifteen weeks, with the shortest a mere five weeks and the average only ten. Furthermore, it was a royal institution and its prime function was to provision the government with money and laws. It was summonsed, prorogued (when a 'prorogued' Parliament met again it did so without fresh elections to the Lower House, because it was another session of the same Parliament) and dissolved (or terminated; when another one was called, the sheriff of each county was instructed to set in motion the process whereby new elections were held in the parliamentary boroughs and county within his jurisdiction) according to the pleasure of the Queen. So the life of each Parliament, indeed its very existence, depended on the Crown's needs, and its willingness to use Parliament to satisfy those needs. As Charles I was to remind the House of Commons in 1626:

Remember that Parliaments are altogether in my power for their calling, sitting and dissolution; therefore as I find the fruits of them good or evil, they are to continue or not to be.

Furthermore, when Parliament met it rarely exercised an effective influence on the Crown's major policy decisions (and there are very few signs that it ever wanted to act in this independent and competitive way). It performed no executive role: in other words, it did not take part in the execution of policy and administration of the realm, which was the right and responsibility of the monarch, through her (his) Privy Council and civil service. It did not even supervise the spending of the taxes which it voted to the Crown, or conduct an audit (official examination) to ensure that the money had been spent on the projects for which it had been granted. Parliament remained no more than an occasional instrument, called into being by the Crown to equip it more adequately in the business of government. And the sovereignty of Parliament, coupled with the new power of statute, was a novelty which, in the short term, strengthened rather than weakened the Crown.

2 Parliament was a trinity. It was not a duet of Queen and Commons. However, Neale, Notestein and others wrote the parliamentary history of Elizabeth's reign as if this was, in fact, the case. Sir John Neale, in particular, dismissed the third partner in the trinity, the House of Lords, as an obedient tool of the Queen:

The lay peers were too intimately attached to the Crown and Court to be persistent critics of the Sovereign. For most of them a government bill which was known to have the backing of the Sovereign was tantamount to a royal command (Neale, 1958, page 41).

As for the bishops who solidly voted against every bill on religion in Elizabeth's first parliament:

[T]heir action ought perhaps to be regarded as an exercise of conscience and of the privilege of free speech, rather than an effort to defeat the government (Neale, 1958, page 41).

In a number of punchy *solar plexus* judgements, Neale put the Lords down for the count:
    i By Elizabeth's reign, a balanced history of Parliament would be almost as predominantly a history of the House of Commons as it is in early Stuart times (Neale, 1949, pages 15–16).
    ii It is as well to remember that the function of a Tudor House of Lords was less to impede the Crown than to assist it in controlling the Commons (Neale, 1953, page 41).
    iii We know little about the method of working of the Upper House, except for what can be deduced from the

... *Journal*, kept by the Clerk. ... No Lord that we know of kept a private diary of proceedings, nor were the proceedings interesting enough to excite much comment from foreign ambassadors or from letterwriters (Neale, 1953, page 40).

These statements are full of assumptions: for example, that Parliaments were all about politics and not business, that the Lords' business was unimportant because it did not arouse public interest, that its chief task was a political one—to manage the Commons—and even that the Lower House had to be kept under control.

Neale's many assumptions will be questioned in the following pages. However, it is relevant to consider one of them here: that the House of Lords was relatively unimportant in the Elizabethan and early Stuart parliaments. The assent of all three members of the parliamentary trinity was necessary in order to make a Bill into an Act. Indeed, in the 1540s and early 50s, more Acts (that is, successful Bills) began in the Lords, not in the Commons (in 1539–47, only 103 Acts began in the Commons, but 156 commenced in the Lords. In Edward VI's reign the totals were 65 and 101.). It is true that in the three Marian parliaments of 1553–5, the Upper House behaved in a politically irresponsible way, obstructing or rejecting important government measures and generally holding up parliamentary business. The result seems to have been a loss of royal and public confidence in it. Thereafter, the monarch and others who wanted Bills passed usually preferred to put them into the other House first. However, just because fewer Bills began in the Lords, it does not mean that it ceased to be important. Its consent was still necessary for a Bill to become law. And it was more productive than the House of Commons: a higher proportion of Bills which began there eventually became Acts (in 1563, it only initiated forty-five out of the 135 Bills before Parliament, but thirty-two became Acts. In contrast, only nineteen of the ninety Bills which began in the Commons passed into law).

There is a simple explanation for this: that the Lords was the more efficient chamber. It is hardly surprising: it was a much smaller assembly. Therefore, it was easier to organise for the conduct of business. The Elizabethan Lords, which numbered no more than about eighty (and on most days there were not more than forty or fifty present), was more like a cosy debating club. Everyone had time to have his say. Moreover, as fewer Bills started there, it was possible to give each one a closer examination, a more thorough scrutiny. This was vitally important in the making of a new law: to ensure that it did not harm the Queen's prerogative or the liberties (that is, privileges) of her subjects; and that it was carefully and precisely worded, leaving no loopholes for foxy lawyers to exploit.

To assist the Lords in this work, the judges of the Queen's courts, the serjeants (the élite of lawyers, also in her service) and her own legal advisers (the Queen's attorney and solicitor), attended, sitting on woolsacks in the centre of the Chamber. They could not participate in debates, nor could they vote, but they drafted and revised Bills, and frequently sat on committees with bishops and peers in order to do so. They provided a pool of skill and experience in the law which the Commons could not match, even though it had its share of ambitious and able lawyers, many of whom would rise high in the Queen's service. In any case, absenteeism plagued the Commons and among the worst offenders were the lawyer members. St Stephens Chapel, where the Lower House sat, was next door to the great law courts of the realm where there were fat fees to be made. Naturally the lawyers preferred to find clients, represent their causes there and fill their own purses with clinking coin—anything rather than endure the unprofitable boredom of the Commons, where hours were spent in the technical and tedious business of knocking Bills into shape, where self-important members puffed their cheeks, blew out their sails and launched into endless voyages of speech.

So lawyers, the experts in drawing up and revising Bills, frequently stayed away from the Commons. The fact was notoriously known. An experienced member once advised a Privy Councillor how to get rid of unwanted and troublesome business, especially private Bills, which might delay the passage of the government's legislation: appoint committees to consider them.

The more committees that you make . . . the longer it wilbe ere the matter come in againe, speciallie if you will appointe lawiers in terme time.

(Law terms were those periods when the courts were in session, and when practising lawyers might be expected to fail to attend committees.) One morning William Fleetwood, himself a lawyer, advised the Commons that other members of his profession were in the courts and not in the House. They were brought back (Neale 1949, page 415).

This was not the only problem to beset the Commons. Its membership was large and growing (see page 338). In each Parliament, many were novices, new men needing guidance and direction (see pages 364–5). In contrast, the Upper House, consisting of bishops and peers who were there for life, was a body experienced in parliamentary business.

The Upper House could also exert pressure on its partner. The peers were a 'social élite' with many followers (clients) and relatives in the Commons: in some cases the peers had secured their relatives' or clients' election through their possession of government offices or their social influence. So in 1584 the Privy Council instructed Lord Cobham 'to deal with all the boroughs within the Cinque Ports [and] to take that course which shall seem best unto you . . . whether it shall be in taking upon you the naming of the burgesses yourself, or by such

good advice and direction as you shall give to the said boroughs
....' (The Cinque [five] Ports actually numbered seven: Dover,
Hastings, Hythe, New Romney, Rye, Sandwich and Winchelsea.
Governed by a royal appointee, in 1584 Lord Cobham, the ports
enjoyed special trading privileges, but in return had to provide the
Crown with ships in time of war.) Although the city of Salisbury
proudly declared that alone it could and would choose its representatives, its resolve crumbled when the Earl of Pembroke requested the
election of one of his clients. The peers were an élite of power and
privilege, and so was their House in Parliament. One member of the
Commons warned against the practice whereby joint committees of
the two Houses met to iron out differences over Bills, because they
resulted in:

the terrifying of men's opinions. I meane not that the Lordes do terrify men,
but men of the Common House coming up among them at conferences learn
their inclinations and, knowing that in the Common House nothing is secret,
they change their opinions to suit the Lords.

Although the Commons had one unquestioned political advantage—its right to initiate grants of lay taxation to the Crown—even
here the House of Lords was not unimportant. Taxes voted by the
clergy always began there. And in 1593, when the Lower House
offered money to Elizabeth, the Lords was dissatisfied and forced it
to increase its offer. Thus, the Upper House should never be ignored
or underestimated.

3 Parliament was a place of business, not an arena of conflict.
Why else would Elizabeth have summoned it regularly throughout her
reign? Disagreements, criticism and disputes certainly occurred: this
is hardly surprising when an imperious Queen came together with over
500 members of her self-confident governing class in order to discuss
the affairs of the realm. Yet disagreement seldom escalated into
conflict. Why should it have done so? The two Houses represented
an aristocracy which was bound together in common loyalty to the
Crown, its present wearer, Elizabeth I, and (increasingly) to the established Church. Apart from those minorities of ideological 'drop-outs',
the Roman Catholics, and the exponents of extreme Protestantism
(that is, Presbyterians and Separatists), the governing class was
remarkably consistent in its beliefs, priorities and prejudices. Nobles
and gentlemen were raised in the conviction that the highest form of
occupation was service to the Prince. They were instructed to worship
God, revere and obey the Queen, and serve the commonwealth. With
few exceptions, and only occasional lapses, they faithfully followed
these precepts.

4 The interests which most members wished to advance in Parliament were narrow: sectional, personal or parochial. Their counties or towns marked the boundaries of their political horizons. Not for them the great political issues of the day, unless those issues threatened to impair or destroy the order and stability of their own little worlds. There was a general (and justifiable) conviction that Mary Stuart on the throne, a disputed succession, the re-establishment of Catholicism, or a Spanish invasion would do just that. No wonder that members of both Houses warmed to such fears. When they urged the Queen to marry or name a successor (for example, in 1563 and 1566–7), and when they pressed her to condemn Mary Stuart in 1572, they were doing no more than give vocal expression to the alarm of the governing class. However, the political consciousness of most men did not extend beyond this.

Thus, we must discard the image of knights and burgesses, bishops and peers riding up to Westminster with scrolls of grievances, constitutional declarations, complaints and lamentations about royal misgovernment. They did not seek to contest with the Crown in a power struggle; indeed, the reverse was the case. The Queen's prime managerial problem was not conflict but absenteeism, not opposition but apathy. The notion that Parliament (and especially the Commons) wanted some kind of participation and control of Elizabeth's government must be discarded, once and for all.

5 Tudor Parliaments have become an obsession: for historians, teachers and students alike. They need to be cut down to size and observed in their right perspective. Lords and Commons simply voiced the concerns, fears and expectations of the governing class and promoted the Bills of some of its members. What really matters is the role of that class outside Parliament, in the country-at-large. After all, as we have seen, Elizabethan parliaments met infrequently, and then only for short sessions. The essence of the on-going relationship between the Crown and the aristocracy was in the counties, where Elizabeth and her Privy Council employed flattery, praise, persuasion, threats, sanctions and rewards to ensure 'good governance' by a class which was sometimes unpaid and always underpaid. It is here, not in Parliament, that the nexus, the nub, of that relationship is to be found.

The political record of Parliament

The discussion that follows is not a detailed chronological narrative of the Elizabethan parliaments—that is available in both the earlier writings of Neale and Notestein, and in the revised interpretation of more recent historians such as G.R. Elton, the details of which may be found in the text and Bibliography. This section is intended only to correct the errors of the earlier interpretation and to paint a more realistic picture of later Tudor parliamentary history. The thesis that opposition and conflict increased in Elizabeth's reign rests upon three considerations:

i The search for sixteenth century origins of the English Civil War.

ii The belief that Puritanism was just as much a parliamentary dynamic in Elizabeth's reign as it was to become in 1640–42.

iii 'Evidence' which supposedly substantiated both of these claims: on the one hand, the willingness of the Commons to challenge the royal prerogative over monopolies (in 1597 and 1601); and on the other, the emergence of an organised and persistently troublesome Puritan opposition in both the early Elizabethan parliaments and those of the 1580s.

We must be cautious about accepting claims for the existence of either of these phenomena. Certainly a war-weary Parliament expressed its irritation when the Queen's economies, forced upon her by war, extended to 'shoe-string patronage': in other words, grants of monopolies in trade and industry which cost her nothing (but which cost the nation dear, see chapter 2, page 160). Yet, this apart, the old machinery of management continued to operate confidently. During Elizabeth's last parliament one member, Sir Edward Hoby, attempted to sit near the Speaker's chair, while Sir Robert Cecil was addressing the Commons. Such seats were reserved for Privy Councillors (who could whisper advice and instructions to the Speaker) and so Hoby was duly rebuffed. He retired to sulk by the door of the chamber. It was duly noticed by Cecil who added insult to injury:

If any that sit next the door be desirous to sit next the Chair to give his opinion, I will not only give him my place, but thank him to take my charge. We that sit here, take your favours out of courtesy, not out of duty (Neale, 1949, page 412).

Sir Robert Cecil, who often hectored and scolded the House, was not a popular manager. Nevertheless, his retort reflects the managerial confidence of the Queen's servants. Elizabeth might respond to the Commons' grumbles by promising to cancel the most harmful of the monopolies, but her prerogative remained untouched. As always she knew when to bend with the wind and make concessions in the face of governing class discontent. It was all part of the give-and-take of parliamentary meetings.

The monopolies issue can only be understood if we remember that, politically, England was a kind of federation of localities, in which local loyalties and interests were powerful sentiments. Parliament must always be considered in the context of this structure of politics and society-at-large. Early modern English society was very parochial. As mentioned above, the county was what mattered most to landed gentlemen (who occupied the majority of borough and county seats in Elizabeth's parliaments): the Wentworths were of Buckinghamshire, the Knollys identified themselves with Oxfordshire, the Carews were men of Devon. Indeed, each one referred to his home-county, not England, as his 'country'. It provided him with his source of income, social influence and political prestige. There, he became involved in local faction politics, competition for office and property disputes. And there he served as J.P. or Deputy Lieutenant, collected the parliamentary subsidy, and served the Crown in such mundane but essential activities as supervision of sewage, drainage, highways and poor relief. The county was his continuing political world and his power base.

When the landed gentleman rode up to Parliament or the Court he carried his county priorities and politics with him. He brought with him a dilemma as well. Most gentlemen were anxious, or at least not averse, to using the event of a parliament to promote their own ambitions and concerns. They were also conscious of their duty to serve the Queen—and, moreover, most members were clearly willing to do so. However, they were, at the same time, elected and answerable to a community. That community varied enormously from numerous electorates in the larger counties, such as Yorkshire and Norfolk, to the pocket boroughs such as Aylesbury, Gatton and Old Sarum, where it was not unknown for the head of the family to nominate and elect the members.

Whatever the size and nature of each electoral community, the elected members had to answer to it when they returned after the session. This could create a serious conflict of interests for individual members. Consider, for example, taxation, for which parliaments were usually called. An ambitious gentleman might seek credit with the Queen by industrious and enthusiastic support for a large grant of money—especially as he had (probably) disgracefully under-assessed his own income for tax purposes and consequently his purse would not seriously suffer. On the other hand, what would he say to his fellows, friends and neighbours, the men who made up his little social and political world, when he rode home: that he had burdened them with a heavy tax merely in order to attract official favour or to demonstrate his personal loyalty? Moreover, if he was a county member, his electorate had grown. Inflation had brought many more within the electoral compass, as the forty-shilling freehold franchise applied to more landowners.

So the interests which a member served were inherently divergent and often in contradiction to each other. The dilemma became much more acute if he was also a courtier and/or a civil servant at Westminster—above all if he sat on the Privy Council. If so, he was bound to be engaged in Court politics, a member of a Court faction, supporting his patron and advancing himself in a never-ending game of snakes and ladders. A Court faction might see Parliament as an opportunity to push its interests and embarrass its opponents. However, it might equally find itself driven onto the defensive and even discomforted. Whichever way the wind was blowing, the client of a powerful patron had to take into account yet one more commitment in his political spectrum: not only to monarch, 'self' and his 'country', but also to patron and faction.

All of these tugging loyalties applied no less to a Privy Councillor than to anyone else, but a new and vital dimension was added. His was a special place. He was a member of a small governing board, the very linch-pin which held the agencies and activities of Tudor government together in some kind of co-ordinated whole. Once again, as with Parliament, we come up against a common problem in describing Tudor and early Stuart government. At the formal, institutional level—in other words, its functions, powers and procedures—description of government is easy enough. But behind this neat, orderly description lie the untidy political realities: the competition for office, faction politics and rivalry between patrons, all of them operating at both Court and 'country' levels. At the centre of both of these pictures—the ordered bureaucratic world and the political kaleidoscope—is the same political organ, the Privy Council. Under Elizabeth (though less so under the early Stuarts), it was the political power house without equal. Membership was the ultimate objective of the ambitious: of a Sir Walter Raleigh or Earl of Essex under Elizabeth, Sir Edwin Sandys or Sir Robert Phelips under James I, and particularly Thomas Wentworth in Charles I's early years.

Once that ambition was fulfilled, imagine the combination of parliamentary pressures and obligations on the new appointee—after all, if he was not a bishop or peer he was expected to secure his election to the Commons. He sought not only to advance himself; he was bound to serve his King or Queen, placate and satisfy his constituents, retain the favour of his patron, promote and defend his policies at the Council board, and manoeuvre in a kind of political limbo between political principle and convenience. Sometimes, he offered his monarch unpalatable advice: in particular, this was the experience of Sir William Cecil (later Lord Burghley). Yet he had the conviction that his proposed course of action was right. What to do? He could not rely upon the backing of the Council, which was frequently divided by faction conflict. Indeed, this was how Elizabeth retained her freedom of action and control of the Councillors. On the basis of 'divide and rule' she encouraged competitive rivalry and maintained a balance of factions in her Council: Leicester versus Burghley, Essex against Robert Cecil, war party opposing peace party, conforming Anglican versus reforming Anglican (Puritan), and so on.

Nevertheless, the Privy Council was not always divided. It could close ranks. Rival factions collaborated, both on mundane administrative matters and major policy questions. The Councillors were even capable of a broad consensus on such important issues as the Queen's marriage, the succession, Mary Stuart, the treatment of English Catholics and, to a surprising extent (Archbishop Whitgift apart), the further reformation of the Church. However, it was precisely on these issues that Elizabeth stood apart and in opposition to her Councillors. When they wanted her to marry, she gave them 'answers answerless' and she threw up a smokescreen of promise and prevarication, until she became too old to bear children and it ceased to be an issue.

The Councillors wanted a settled succession, but the Queen preferred to keep her options open. They laboured for twenty years to overcome her obstinate refusal to kill Mary Stuart. Time and again she held out firmly against the harsher anti-recusant measures which her Council sought. And she displayed no sympathy whatsoever with the pro-Puritan temper of Cecil, Leicester, Mildmay, Knollys, Walsingham and other prominent Councillors. Throughout her long reign Elizabeth made no significant concession to reforming Anglicanism. The *status quo* and discipline through the bishops were her watchwords. This was repeatedly demonstrated in Parker's *Advertisements*, the suspension of Grindal, Whitgift's triple oath, and the use of the High Commission (see chapter 4, page 258). On all of these issues the Court was often united behind the Privy Council in its efforts to persuade the Queen to act in accordance with its wishes.

When such action failed, the Council turned to Parliament to muster governing class support and thereby pressure the Queen into submission. The precise roles of Elizabeth and her Council in the decision whether (and when) to call Parliament are often impossible to identify. The ultimate decision rested with her, but it is probable (and on occasions certain) that she acted on her Council's advice. And there is little doubt that sometimes, behind the ostensible reason, usually money, was the Councillors' hope of using Parliament to bend the Queen to its opinions. It was both a sensible and a realistic expectation. After all, both Councillors and members of the two Houses of Parliament were recruited from the same class. They were in broad agreement on the pressing issues of the day, above all the security of the Queen and her Church and realm. Events were to prove how amply the Councillors' expectations were rewarded with deep concern and enthusiastic support: over succession and marriage in 1563 and 1566–7, religious reformation in 1566–7 and 1571, and over Mary Stuart and the Catholic menace in 1572 and 1581. Again and again what Sir John Neale misread as conflicts between government and opposition were nothing of the kind. They were parliamentary campaigns, stage-managed by the Privy Council, to pressurise an isolated Queen who was resisting the concerted opinions of her Council, Court, bishops, and governing class.

When the 'high politics' of Parliament in a non-party age are correctly understood and modern concepts of party, government and opposition are discarded, then the traditional interpretation of such historians as Neale and Notestein becomes irrelevant. Behind the formal structure of Parliament—the trinity of Queen, Lords and Commons—was the fundamental political reality: that it was a meeting of Elizabeth, her Council and Court and representatives of her governing class. To some extent their interests and priorities harmonised, but Court factions might use Parliament to score off each other. Rival vested interests might clash over private Bills: thus, in 1571, when London attempted to seize control of the cloth trade in Kent, it was thwarted; but the City won a long battle to prevent the depletion of its fuel supplies by iron-smelting mills, and in James I's reign its cheap food policy compelled it to clash with the farming interest which sought to prohibit imports of corn and Irish cattle.

The Privy Council's task was unenviable: to push through official business; to persuade both Parliament and Queen to particular courses of action; to prevent time-consuming debate between economic lobbies and disputes between the two Houses. At all times it had to keep in mind that members, especially of the Commons, served in a dual capacity. Many held offices in local government. As such, they were the Queen's representatives in the counties. But as members of Parliament they also represented their 'countries' at the centre. It could be difficult, even impossible, to reconcile the two obligations. On each matter before them they had to sort into priority their duty to the Queen, their personal self-interest, and the fact that they were answerable to their 'countries'. Only when their constituencies were generally threatened by administrative abuses or royal policies did something like a government-opposition confrontation occur: for example, over the age-old grievance of purveyance (the right to purchase food and requisition transport at prices below the market rate) or, in 1597 and 1601, monopolies. And it was a rare phenomenon until the 1590s, when the demands of war imposed on local government a burden which it was incapable of bearing.

Let us begin at the beginning. It has been accepted (with Sir John Neale), that the first Elizabethan Parliament (1559) developed into a political tug-of-war. The contestants were a conservative Queen and a Puritan pressure group. And the issue was the government and doctrine of the new Church. It is generally agreed that the outcome of the contest was a compromise, in which Elizabeth conceded rather more than her Puritan opponents. However, this interpretation has always rested on a fundamental assumption: that there was a Puritan opposition in the House of Commons. It could not be tested because no known list of members had survived. Only recently, the discovery and analysis of such a list has established that there were hardly any Puritans at all in this Parliament. Therefore, the story of the Elizabethan Settlement has had to be entirely re-examined and re-assessed. This has now been done and the results are to be found in Dr Norman Jones' book *Faith by Statute* (see chapter 4, page 255). One thing is certain: Neale's version is no longer acceptable. All the indications are that, in 1559, Elizabeth got more or less what she wanted from her Parliament.

The same conclusion must be drawn about the parliaments of 1563–7 and 1571. According to Neale, the Commons in these three sessions included a vocal, vigorous and organised Puritan opposition. It was, he tells us, opposition in a significantly new sense. In the past, parliamentary opposition had been negative and obstructive. In other words, it restricted itself to hampering, obstructing or defeating unpopular royal measures. The new Puritan opposition, however, had a positive programme of its own: to settle a Protestant succession, to improve a 'halfly-reformed' Church and to demand free speech in order to advance these aims. It rehearsed tactics, drafted its own Bills and planned its campaigns with care. This was something novel, because it was trying to impose its policies on the Crown, and it was challenging the Queen's claims to govern the Church without interference. When it demanded unlimited free speech it threatened personal monarchy: after all, if members could discuss anything, they could criticise the Queen's actions, her policies, her ministers, every aspect of her government (Neale, 1953, pages 27–9, 91–217).

There was only one flaw in this interpretation: it did not fit the facts. Neale claimed to have discovered an organised opposition party which campaigned for the Queen to marry or settle the succession in 1563–7, and which promoted a legislative programme for reform of the Church in 1566–7 and 1571. His evidence is of three kinds:

1 The discovery of a 'lewde pasquil' (piece of doggerel) which listed forty-three members with descriptive labels and referred to them as 'our choir'. The list included many of those redoubtable men

whom we have come to accept as Puritans: Paul Wentworth, Thomas Norton, Robert Bell, William Strickland and Christopher Yelverton. But who has taught us that they are Puritans? Sir John Neale. Yet nowhere did he explain what a Puritan was, contenting himself with such tags as 'zealot' and 'fanatic', and he proceeded to use the lewd pasquil as a kind of Puritan party list, evidence of organised opposition. After all, the word 'choir' implies organisation, unison, everyone marching to the same Puritan battle hymn. Or does it?

A careful analysis of the pasquil tells a different story. The list covers a broad spectrum of members, but very few, apart from Paul Wentworth, could be regarded as doctrinaire Protestants and hotheads. If by 'Puritans' we mean men who hated Popes, feared Catholicism and wanted to improve standards in their new Anglican Church, then most of those named in the pasquil qualify as Puritans: in the sense of anti-Catholic 'reforming Anglicans'. But then, by the same yardstick, so were the bishops, the Privy Councillors, courtiers, and the great majority of the governing class. Three minorities apart— Catholics, Presbyterians and Separatists—the government, order of worship and doctrine of the new Church were universally accepted. With only two possible exceptions—Paul Wentworth and William Strickland—the views of the 'Puritan choir' were indistinguishable from the Privy Council. Thomas Norton, the choir's supposed leader, William Cecil and Archbishop Parker thought alike on essentials.

But this is not the end of the story. The pasquil includes members who by no stretch of the imagination could be called 'Puritan'. Francis Alford was a religious conservative whose wife was a Catholic recusant. Again and again, he brought down on his head the anger of other members: when he opposed harsh measures against Catholics and counselled caution and a respect for justice when dealing with Mary Queen of Scots. What is Alford doing in a 'Puritan choir'? And what of Henry Goodere, imprisoned for assisting the Duke of Norfolk's plan to marry the deposed Scottish (and Catholic) Queen? Consider too Robert Newdigate, who curried favour with the Council by advising the House not to hunt after malpractices by civil servants, but to vote money to the Queen instead. (The correct form was for a Privy Councillor to propose taxation. Until then no action was taken by the House. Any member who anticipated the Council's request for money was treated with contempt as a 'bootlicker'.)

The explanation is a simple one. The pasquil is not a party list. It is not even a roll call of Puritans. It is a piece of scribble, probably written by some bored back-bench M.P. about men who caught his eye, or rather his ear: the spokesmen, the persuasive debaters, the orators. Look at their descriptions:

Bell the Orator
Wentworth the Wrangler
Saint John the Jangler
Brown the Blasphemer
Arnold the Accuser
Pares the Pacifier
Newdigate the Crier
Norton the Scold
Hales the Hottest

Clearly these are references to their oral parliamentary performance: what they were like as debaters. 'Choir' refers, not to harmony and organisation, but to the fact that these men were noisy and vocal, not silent. They were natural leaders of the Commons. This is revealed by the reference to other members at the end of the document:

As for the rest
they be at devotion
and when they be prest
they crye a good motion.

In other words, the remainder of the House looked to these men for a lead in debate. Being 'at devotion' means at prayer (that is, absorbed and silent) and like sheep they echoed the proposals of others with bleats of approval (that is, they cried 'a good motion'). But *nowhere* is there a single hint that this document has any connection with Puritanism or organised parliamentary politics. (There are only two references to religion and they concern conservatives: Nicholas L'Estrange, the Duke of Norfolk's steward, is 'the Relygous' and Francis Alford is 'the bolde'.) The anonymous author of this piece of scribble is usually sympathetic to the more conservative and cynical, and becomes almost scathing about the more ardent Protestants: so Lawrence Withers of the London Salters Company is described as 'Judas the worst merchant' and 'the wrynger', while Strickland is dubbed 'the styngere'. Whoever the author was, he amused himself by devising a rhyming scheme, so that we have:

Sequarston the mery
Wrothe the aspyrere
Warncombe the werye
Carewe the Cruell
Bartewe the indytor
Chichester the fooll
Gryce the backbyter

How can one create an organised Puritan political party out of this trivial matter? Neale showed the way. Which brings us to the second form of evidence.

2 On the basis of this document Neale erected his Puritan choir and supported it with a framework of inference and assumption. Again and again, he tells us that a provocative or obstructive action was 'surely', 'undoubtedly' or 'probably' the work of 'our choir of forty-three'. Slowly, but indelibly, he associates every sign of disharmony, disagreement and conflict, with this band of Puritan warriors—especially where he intimidates us with such expressions as, 'it would be childish to assume otherwise', or, 'it would take a simpleton not to suspect a planned drive' by the choir (Neale, 1953, pages 95–166). Fortunately, once the 'Puritan choir' evaporates, so does this framework of aggressive assumption.

3 This leaves us with a third, and unquestionable, form of evidence of organised parliamentary politics. In the opening days of the 1571 Parliament, William Strickland, in concert with Thomas Norton, seized the initiative and introduced a reforming programme. We should be impressed because it was certainly an impressive programme. In content it was thoroughgoing and in technique it was sophisticated. First Strickland recommended to the House what is known as the *Reformatio Legum Ecclesiasticarum*. Once we have digested this Latin mouthful, we may consider what it was all about. Before Henry VIII's break with Rome, England had been divided into two provinces, Canterbury and York. Each had been served by its own ecclesiastical assembly or convocation. Convocations served two functions: they voted money (to the Papacy before 1533–4, and thereafter to the Crown) and enacted Canon Law—ecclesiastical laws appropriate to that particular society. The *Reformatio* was an attempt by Archbishop Cranmer and his fellow bishops to update Canon Law, first in Henry VIII's reign and then under his son. However, the government did not implement it and it was shelved. In 1571 Strickland and Norton revived it. The former advised the Commons that the latter had it 'about his person'. Norton produced it and presented it to the House. Then Strickland recommended a series of Bills, labelled A to F. Most of them concerned standards: educated clergy, simony (the buying and selling of offices) and suchlike. Once again, Norton had the drafts of these Bills in his possession.

There is no doubt that it was a pre-planned, co-ordinated campaign. Yet do we have to assume that this was a grand Puritan conspiracy? The surviving evidence admits of only two conclusions: that two men, Strickland and Norton, sought to improve the condition of the Church, and that, so far, they were in agreement with the Council, the bench of bishops, and the representatives of the governing class in the Commons. Indeed one wonders whether there was a 'conspiracy', in which these two members were simply 'front men' for a concerned aristocracy manipulated by Councillors who wanted to coerce their Queen. If so, Norton was the right man for the job. He was an acquaintance of Archbishop Parker, a client of Sir William Cecil and son-in-law of Cranmer, who had bequeathed to him his library (including the *Reformatio*).

However, Strickland let the side down. He introduced a Bill to reform the Prayer Book. This was not designed just to improve standards: it touched a fundamental, the order of worship. The bishops found it unpalatable, so did the Councillors. Thomas Norton did not support it. It must have dismayed them all. It could sabotage the entire programme of reform, and it did so, because of the Queen's 'hardline' conservatism, her insistence on no change. It is just conceivable that she might have accepted some of the reforming programme, but for Strickland's tactical blunder. In the end one of the ABC Bills passed into law, and nothing else.

Always there was the ultimate obstacle: Elizabeth. Of course, political circumstances were never static: the Queen's brush with death when she had smallpox in 1562; Leicester's marriage suit to her; her proposal that he marry Mary Stuart; the Scottish Queen's flight from Scotland and the Duke of Norfolk's liaison with her; the English Queen's protracted diplomatic courtships with Continental princes. But Elizabeth was always the constant factor. She would not marry or name a successor. She would not succumb to pressure to reform her Church. The Queen would yield to no one. So, in the matter of marriage, she resisted the joint pressure of Lords and Commons (in 1563 and 1566–7), rejecting the advice of her frustrated Councillors, and reprimanding the Earl of Pembroke, the Duke of Norfolk, and even Leicester, for applying pressure at Court. The heat engendered in the early Elizabethan parliaments had nothing to do with Puritanism. It was the story of an obstinate and formidable Queen fighting (and defeating) a parliamentary coalition of bishops, peers, gentry and burgesses; a coalition which was orchestrated by a Privy Council driven by desperation about questions of national security to enlist the help of parliamentary representatives of the governing class.

The Council did not always go home empty-handed. If it failed to persuade the Queen to approve its parliamentary Bill for the condemnation of Mary Stuart in 1572, it wrung from her a severer Treason Act in 1571, the Duke of Norfolk's death in 1572 and harsher penalties against recusants in 1581. Such fruits of parliamentary labours were a tribute to the Council's dedication, its energy, its skill in 'recruiting' governing class support and, above all, to devoted loyalists such as Thomas Norton. Neale casts him as the leader of a Puritan opposition, but he was, in fact, a brilliant 'Parliament-man': client of Lord Burghley, Sir Francis Walsingham and Sir Christopher Hatton, and devoted to the related causes of God, Queen, Country and Council. These were his simple, uncomplicated and unswerving ideals. If you want to look at a typical moderate Puritan (for which read 'reforming Anglican') cast your eye over Thomas Norton.

Do not, however, take Peter Wentworth into account. Although he was one of Sir John Neale's heroes, he does not merit such attention. He was out of joint with the times, and a heavy moralising exhibitionist, not a standard bearer of personal liberties. Unlike Thomas Norton, who contributed so much to the development of more efficient procedures and the transaction of a drastically increased volume of parliamentary business, Wentworth was a parliamentary parasite. Narrow-minded and burdened with an inflated notion of his own importance, he paraded his personal brand of virtue, insulted the Queen and tired the House with his moral strictures. In 1576 he rehearsed a crude, ill-mannered attack on Elizabeth which was launched at the opening of the session. Fortunately the Speaker, Council and House (not the Queen) promptly despatched him to the Tower before he had reached the full flood of his insolent assault. Wentworth was not an advocate of liberty. Quite the reverse. His intolerance would have endangered personal liberties. He was little more than a parliamentary nuisance.

What Elizabeth's private thoughts were, we shall never know. Did she regard parliaments as a necessary evil? Who can tell? The important point to remember is that she continued to call them, despite all kinds of irritations and provocations: for example, new laws pressed upon her, such as that which, in 1581, demanded from recusants a monthly penalty of £20 for non-attendance at the Anglican Church; a pocket-Presbyterian agitation for a new order of worship in the established Church (in the 1580s); and the ever-tedious advices of that parliamentary dinosaur Peter Wentworth.

Between 1585 and 1603, however, there was a new set of circumstances. England was at war with Spain, the Queen was ageing, and policies had become fossilised. This was a novel, difficult, even unworkable combination. Some of the old issues—Puritan (reforming Anglican) agitation and the Queen's marriage (a woman in her sixties had no prospect of producing a child)—were dead. But one was very much alive: war. War demanded money, regularly and promptly. And Parliament voted it. Between 1587 and the end of the war in 1604, taxation was granted by five parliaments and collected in annual instalments. This was a novelty. Over a seventeen-year period the governing class became accustomed to the State's regular demand for assistance, although, of course, it was never enough. We might well feel envious of a golden age when the governing class assessed its own income for taxation purposes, when the upright, moralistic Lord Burghley was earning perhaps £5000 a year, but declared his income as £200. We, however, are used to a constant and heavy tax burden. The Elizabethans were not. Suddenly they were burdened with the responsibility of a long war. Members of the Commons had to answer to their constituents for annual taxation. All this occurred in an atmosphere of growing war-weariness, and irritation with official devices to extract more money.

The Queen was endeavouring to make ends meet: economising in every direction, cutting back on traditional sources of patronage and trying to give rewards 'on the cheap'. One effective way of doing this was to grant monopolies in the regulation, supervision or production of particular commodities. The Crown spent nothing in making such grants; indeed, it received a 'rake-off' from the monopolists' profits. But there was another by-product: the Commons rebelled against the effects of such monopolistic patents. In 1597 Parliament grumbled and rumbled, and Elizabeth chose to ignore it. In 1601 she paid for her neglect with a House of Commons quite out of hand, a powerful warning expression of governing class discontent. In the end, she made concessions and came to terms, because government was only workable in the context of a Crown-governing class alliance. This was a lesson learned by both Elizabeth and James I.

Parliament's business record

Parliament's concern was business, legislative business, and the key to an understanding of Parliament is a knowledge of how it went about that business. When it 'legislated', what precisely did it do? There were variations in the procedure by which a Bill became law, but, for the most part, the two Houses agreed on the best way to enact laws and, by a process of cross-fertilisation, their procedure developed on parallel lines. By the end of the sixteenth century, most measures underwent three readings. This was a realistic process, which was designed to meet the basic requirements of an assembly of amateur lawmakers. First, members had to be informed of the contents of a Bill. There were no printed copies, and the text was literally read to them. This was the first reading. Members then had the opportunity to discuss the contents—the substance and principles—of the Bill. This was the second 'reading'. At that stage, it might be rejected, or approved without amendment to await its third reading. Alternatively (and more frequently as the century progressed), it was referred to a committee (nominated by the House) for scrutiny and revision. Eventually (that is, if members bothered to turn up—always an unknown factor), the committee would complete its business and its chairman reported back to the House with proposed alterations. Once these had been approved and incorporated in the Bill, it was ready for its third and final reading. The substance of the Bill would have been chewed over at the previous reading. What remained was an examination of its wording. This was an exercise in precision, and depended on how carefully the text had been drawn. Only when the Bill had passed all these tests satisfactorily was the House prepared to acclaim its assent with (literally) a united voice. However, if some members still harboured doubts the House would go to a division. (The Commons normally voted by acclamation, with the Speaker deciding whether the 'ayes' or the 'noes' had the greater volume of support. However, if his decision was challenged, the House would divide. The supporters of the measure would file out, while opponents remained seated, and their numbers would be counted by tellers. The Lords was more sedate. Each member, from the most junior baron to the most senior duke, stood individually and said 'Content' or 'Not Content'.) If it survived that, it would be carried to the other House where more or less the same procedure would be repeated.

It is important to realise that this is an idealised description of what gradually became the standard legislative procedure for Bills of an uncontentious nature: that is, measures which raised no technical problems and encountered no hostility or conflict. But no matter whether a Bill was contentious or not, two considerations must be noted: first, members had to know its contents, discuss it, if necessary scrutinise it in detail, and finally assent or reject, and second, the Bill still had to receive the approval of the other House and, finally, of the Crown, though it should be added that it was not uncommon for the other House to reshape or reject, or for the Queen to veto, Bills which had sailed through the House of origin.

This raises a vital, indeed fundamental legislative characteristic: usually the House which first scrutinised a Bill played the major part in its enactment. A Bill entered Parliament like a lump of unrefined metal ore. It needed to be refined, honed and tempered, and to have its rough edges knocked off. Many of the Bills submitted to Parliament were drafted by amateurs or incompetents. They needed the professional touch, and that they seldom received until they were handed in to the Speaker of the Commons or the Lord Chancellor in the Upper House.

The House of origin, then—the House which first received a Bill—was the chief formative influence in the process of hammering it into shape. By the time it proceeded to the second chamber, the Bill had been scrutinised, its substance and language had been examined, and possible impediments, breaches of the Common Law and encroachments on the royal prerogative had been removed. So the Bill was almost certain to pass into law unless, in some way, it aroused the prejudices or still harmed the interests of the other House or the Crown. Such occurrences were not unknown. The dramatic increase in the volume of Bills after the 1530s increased the possibility of resistance.

So far as the government was concerned, the flood of Bills which inundated Elizabethan parliaments posed a serious problem. The magnitude of that problem should not be underestimated. In 1563, for example, there were 135 bills before Parliament, in a session of just under thirteen weeks, and thereafter there was an Elizabethan sessional average of between 110 and 120. Official business had to compete for time with this spate of private legislation. Moreover, the Queen compounded the Council's problems with her preference for short sessions: in 1563 Parliament sat for thirteen weeks, in 1572 for eight, in 1576 only five and in 1581 nine.

As if this was not enough, precious time was wasted by the simple fact that Elizabethans had a great stomach for listening: a sermon of an hour, for instance, might be viewed as a 'niggardly thing'. Rhetoric, the art of public speaking, was a prescribed subject in the universities and a growing number of nobles and gentlemen (as well as most bishops) had attended Cambridge or Oxford, though whether they were all serious students is another matter. The judges on the woolsacks in the Lords, the lawyers in the Commons, and many other members in both Houses, had attended the Inns of Court (law schools). There they had been trained in oral exercises, especially the moot (the mock trial). In the Common Law courts, evidence was oral—the spoken word—not written. In the 'reformed' religion (that is, Protestantism) the sermon was the instrument of Truth. It was an age of the spoken word.

Parliament was no exception to this tradition of the spoken word. Two Privy Councillors, Sir Walter Mildmay and Sir Christopher Hatton, occupied an entire morning session of the Commons (perhaps three hours) with their speeches. And the House had its share of windbags: William Fleetwood with his rambling and irrelevant anecdotes, those tedious moralists the Wentworths, and Sir Francis Knollys, so much respected by the Commons, but often putting it to sleep. Bored diarists and clerks jotted wearily on their scribble pads that he was tedious, irrelevant and seemingly never-ending. One observer noted, for instance, 'a longe tedious discourse on the subsidy'. We can almost hear the listener's yawns as he struggled to remain conscious. Again and again, however, the reporters of interminable speeches were full of praise for such performances. The House of Commons seems to us to have been remarkably tolerant: Fleetwood could tell it with confidence, 'You would be content to hear me these two hours'.

That was all very well, but the over-indulgence of the House posed a problem for the Privy Council. We can reconstruct its dilemma without resorting to imagination or invention. Consider the 1563 session: money was needed and the Queen's recent near-fatal bout of smallpox had frightened Councillors, courtiers and the rest of the governing class. She must be persuaded to marry or name a successor. But how to achieve these ends in the face of the host of private Bills which members of both Houses were bound to bring with them to Westminster? How to persuade Parliament to give priority to the subsidy? How to manoeuvre official Bills through before an impatient Queen ended the session? How to marshal governing class opinion so that Elizabeth married and gave birth to a successor or at least named one? And how to discourage time-wasting speeches and petty disputes over privilege?

Disputes over privilege were not conflicts between Crown and Commons—most privilege disputes concerned the privilege of freedom from arrest for debt during the time of Parliament, and they usually occurred when a member (or one of his servants, who were also protected) was arrested by a creditor during the parliamentary session. Two of the most important privilege cases of the reign concerned Arthur Hall (in the Commons) in 1576 and Henry Lord Cromwell in 1572. Hall was punished by the Commons for abusing the privilege and insulting the House (Neale, 1953, pages 333–45, 407–10). Cromwell behaved in an irresponsible and contemptuous manner towards the law. His eventual arrest served him right. But the House of Lords was very sensitive about noble privilege and he received its protection.

These privilege cases produced no dramatic political confrontation between Crown and Parliament. Elizabeth did not directly interfere in either of the cases described above. Still, the point is that they consumed time. So did inefficiency: how to organise over 400 knights and burgesses when at least half of them in each Parliament had not a clue about how to conduct themselves, or what to do? In 1584 William Fleetwood painted a vivid picture of the twin curses of the

Council: green, ignorant novices and the chattering gasbags who liked nothing more than the sound of their own voices (a touch of hypocrisy on Fleetwood's part?). He described not only the opening day in the Commons, with 'the knightes and burgeses out of all order, in troops standing upon the floore, making strange noises, there being not past (7 or 8) of the old parliamentes', but also a committee chaired by Mildmay. It numbered sixty, all young gentlemen. '[A]t our metyng in the afternoone [20] at ones did speak and there we sate talking and dyd nothing untill night. So that Mr Chaunc [ellor Mildmay, the chairman] was werie and then wee departed home.'

However, the Council never shirked its responsibilities as it understood them. The Councillors organised, toiled and exerted their managerial skills in order to obtain the money and laws required for the Queen's government; they coaxed, caressed and persuaded the two Houses to this end; they planned and stage-managed in the interest of speed and efficiency; and they used Parliament to sway and bend their formidable and obstinate royal mistress. In simple practical terms, how was this done? The old practices, well-tried in many previous parliaments, were still used. First, the government's programme was prepared before the session began. This might mean drafting Bills to put before Parliament, and naming spokesmen to advance them. Always it meant choosing the Speaker of the Commons. (This was not necessary in the Lords, where the Speaker, or chairman, was always the Queen's Lord Chancellor, or Lord Keeper.)

In theory, the Lower House chose its Speaker, but in practice it did not: the monarch and Council decided on the man for the job beforehand. When Parliament met, a Councillor would recommend him, another Councillor would second him, and the House almost always agreed. For example, on 28 January 1593, Queen and Council chose Sir Edward Coke. When Parliament met on 19 February, the Commons chose him as Speaker and Elizabeth 'graciously' agreed. Only once was the choice disputed: in 1566 and then it was for technical reasons, not, as Neale suggests, a political action by a Puritan opposition kicking against conciliar control (Neale, 1953, page 134).

There were two reasons for 'choosing' the Speaker before Parliament met. One is obvious: he was the man who decided the order of business in the House, and the Council needed to be sure that *its* business took priority over all those petty, personal and local Bills which plagued the Lower House. Secondly, the Speaker's 'election' by the Commons was followed by his presentation to the Queen. There followed one of those ceremonies which Tudor Englishmen loved: a long elaborate oration by the new Speaker. For the elected Speaker it was one of the great moments of his life. Long hours and days he sweated over this elaborate oral gem which held his audience enthralled and earned him praises, but would probably bore us to tears or drive us to sleep. They all had a similar form: praise for their beautiful virtuous Queen and then a conventional description of society, in which Elizabeth was the head, her nobility the arms and her Commons the feet—et cetera, *ad nauseam*. Naturally, time was needed for the Speaker to prepare this jewel of oratory. Thus, though the Commons formally chose Sir Edward Coke as its Speaker on 19 February 1593, the Queen and her Council had already selected him on 28 January. During the session, the Speaker was assisted in his parliamentary performance by the Councillors who actually sat around his chair and advised him. This was blatant management, but no one objected. There was nothing sinister in management. It was not a means to tread on the liberties of members, but simply to make Parliament speedier, more efficient and productive.

During the earlier Elizabethan parliaments a small group of Councillors shouldered the chief burden of management. They included Mildmay and Knollys in the Commons, and Lord Keeper Bacon and the Earl of Leicester in the Lords. The co-ordinator, initiator and leader was William Cecil—no one could match his energy, his attention to detail, his moderation and tact, and his ceaseless watch over the Queen's affairs in the Commons, where the pressure of business was greatest. However, in 1571 he was created Lord Burghley and henceforth sat in the House of Lords: the mastermind and managerial expert had gone from the Lower House. As a consequence of this, 1571 marks a turning point in the Elizabethan parliaments. How to cope with the continued spate of private Bills in the Commons? There were two solutions pursued. First, Burghley used the Lords, and even enlisted the Queen, to harry and push the Lower House on to a conclusion. In 1571 Elizabeth admonished them to:

leave long tales . . . and to deal with those things which were there to be proposed; that they might despatch that they were sent for and that they might the sooner return home.

During the session the Lords warned that:

as the Season of the Year waxed very hot, and dangerous for Sickness, so they desired that this House would spend the Time in proceeding with necessary Bills for the Commonwealth, and lay aside all private Bills in the meantime.

In the following year the Upper House repeated the Queen's instruction that the Commons 'do proceed in . . . weighty Causes, leaving apart all private Matters'.

Burghley did what he could from his remote place of control in the Lords. However, he was obliged to place increasing reliance on those men who can only be described as the Council's 'men-of-business'—knights and burgesses who gave devoted service to Elizabeth and her advisers. They were Burghley's eyes and ears, telling him what was happening in the Commons and devising ways of speeding up the passage of official business. Among them were Burghley's cousin, Thomas Dannet, his client Thomas Digges and, above all, the City of London members, who included more of his clients, in particular William Fleetwood and Thomas Norton. The latter was a skilled debater, much admired by the Commons. He collaborated with Councillors, especially Sir Walter Mildmay, in pushing through Council Bills. He played Burghley's game, hustling the Lower House on to pressure the Queen into action against Mary, the English Catholics and the Jesuits. Thomas Norton also laboured to make the House more efficient. He proposed afternoon sittings to deal with private legislation and to leave the mornings free for important (and official) business; and he suggested rules for joint meetings with the Lords to settle disagreements between them over Bills. Norton was not the only man-of-business, but he was the most important and successful of them.

An examination of Thomas Norton, a loyal reforming Anglican and Lord Burghley's client, sheds new light on developments in the late Tudor and early Stuart parliaments. According to Notestein, between the 1580s and the 1620s the Crown lost control of Parliament. There were several reasons for this. First, it took less trouble than before to secure the election of Privy Councillors to the Commons—in one Jacobean Parliament Sir Julius Caesar was its sole representative there. Secondly, the Crown lost the 'legislative initiative': in other words, when the Council ceased to prepare its business beforehand and to draw up a programme of Bills, the initiative for proposing and drafting new Bills passed to members of Parliament. The government also allowed the development of a new procedure which further loosened its control. On a growing number of occasions, the Commons went into a 'General Committee', later known as the 'Committee of the Whole House'. When this happened, the Speaker, a royal appointee, was replaced by a chairman chosen by the House (Notestein, 1924, page 37). The pieces of the picture fit together—a government becoming slack and sloppy about management and so allowing others (especially its critics and opponents) to take over effective control of the Commons. However, this does assume that there were men who conspired to seize control from the Crown. And of this there is no evidence, at least before Charles I's reign. So what is the true meaning of these developments?

The answer is to be found in the perennial problem which faced Lord Burghley and succeeding parliamentary managers: how to get through essential government business in short hectic sessions. Burghley had discovered how valuable were his clients, those unofficial men-of-business. This opinion must have been reinforced by the advice of an experienced Commons man in 1581. He wrote that official business should be well prepared, and that 'some other privie informed of it' (before it was submitted to Parliament)—by which was meant Norton and the other men-of-business in the House. He went on to point out that the Commons would more willingly follow the guidance of a respected 'private' or 'independent' member than that of a courtier or Councillor. The author of these advices was, one suspects, over-sensitive and ultra-cautious. However, the effective services of the unofficial men-of-business certainly explains a gradual change in managerial techniques. It became less important to elect a sizeable body of Councillors to the Commons. Burghley's control of the Commons through his men-of-business, while he sat in the Lords, proved to be effective enough.

Attitudes to law-making were also changing—in government circles, at least. Official opinion, expressed by the Queen herself, by Burghley and other Councillors, and endorsed by Thomas Norton, was that England already had too many laws. Rather than adding more, Norton preferred the effective enforcement of existing laws by the Privy Council, 'because it is the wheels of the Council that hold the chariot of England upright' (a perceptive comment on the key role of the Privy Council in government). Such attitudes harmonised with the opinions of the Queen. She was politically conservative and preferred to govern without alteration, change or novelty. James I had the same views. Therefore, the disappearance of official programmes of Bills did not indicate a falling-away of standards, a decline in thoroughness or a loss of initiative to some kind of opposition lobby in the Commons. It simply reflected the growing official conviction that there could be too many laws. Enforcement was more important than enactment.

As for the Committee of the Whole House, it was yet another device to cope with the flood of business in the Elizabethan-Jacobean parliaments. There were too many private Bills, and they were often drafted in a shoddy amateurish manner. The formal, elaborate rules of debate (in which a member could speak only once for or against a Bill on any one day) ate up time and sometimes hindered a thorough scrutiny of such Bills. Removing the Speaker and replacing him with a chairman was not a sinister political move. It was part of a process designed to get through more business more quickly. The 'Committee of the Whole' dropped the formal rules of debate, enabling members to speak more than once, to change their minds and announce their 'conversion'. Informality, in the cause of productivity, was its purpose. If you listen to the laboured, slow, formal and procedure-bound debates of any parliamentary assembly and then talk informally with a circle of friends, the difference soon becomes apparent. Informality permits a speaker more efficient discussion and examination of problems, formulation of ideas, and resolution of outstanding differences.

The transition from Elizabeth I to James I

The parliamentary problems of Elizabethan government were not fundamentally different under her successor. There were bound to be differences in emphasis and style which reflected the contrasting personalities and qualities of the two monarchs. However, one important political change had occurred in the last fifteen years of the Queen's reign, and in this respect 1603 produced, not a sudden, dramatic change, but only gradually deepening shades under James I. Elizabeth's ability to balance factions, to distribute patronage widely and to allow no monopoly of power to any one faction at Court, crumbled during the 1590s. The young Earl of Essex was the catalyst of change. He challenged the political authority of Lord Burghley and his son Sir Robert Cecil and he sought to monopolise power and patronage for his own faction (see chapter 2, pages 122–3). He ripped the romantic veil of mystique from the wrinkled Virgin Queen when he told her that her policies were as twisted as her old body ('[A]s crooked as her carcass', were his reported words). And he forced the Court to take sides in either the Cecil or Essex camp. There were no immediate parliamentary consequences of this bitter winner-take-all conflict in the twilight years of Elizabeth's rule. However, the Essex-Cecil rivalry set the tone for Court conflict in the next reign, when factions did carry their rivalries into Parliament: in 1614, 1621 and 1624. Nevertheless, the change was a gradual and undramatic one.

Elizabeth's death meant a change at the top, but surprisingly little else. Some familiar faces disappeared from the political scene, notably Sir Walter Raleigh, and some new ones became prominent, especially Robert Carr and other Scots who had come south with the new King.

But the political system underwent no startling change. The old problems of an antiquated administration and inadequate revenue bedevilled everything as before. The counties were growing restive and chafing at the restraints and controls of central government, but here too the process was a slow one. Most of all, the priorities, prejudices and interests of the governing class in Parliament showed little alteration.

Furthermore, if we examine the conduct of Jacobean parliaments, first, in terms of business and, secondly, in terms of Court-Parliament relations, it becomes clear that 1621 and 1624 were not very different from 1597 and 1601. The basic new ingredient, James in place of Elizabeth, was not the fundamental change which was once supposed. The Queen, remarkable though she was, enjoyed less success, and the new King was more competent, realistic and perceptive than the traditional view suggests. The decline in both public morality and administrative efficiency was already well advanced by the time Elizabeth died. Therefore, the Jacobean political world did not represent a dramatic transformation, a sudden collapse in standards—just a continuation of the downward progression which had become apparent in the last ten or fifteen years of the old Queen's reign. Parliament was similarly afflicted with the creeping disease of inadequacy which was overtaking the State machine. And here, as well, the two reigns are less divided by contrast than bound together by threads of continuity. Not that we should extend this and assume an inevitable slide towards Civil War. That thought had entered no one's mind, at least before 1640. And we are talking primarily of administrative decline, not some revolution in political habits, thoughts, priorities which suddenly destroyed veneration for monarchy.

It is true that there were novel and disturbing elements in the Jacobean parliamentary scene. Parliament was dissolved in 1614, without a single Act passed, and in 1621 with nothing more than the subsidy to its credit. Nothing of that kind had occurred in Elizabeth's reign. Nor had the Elizabethan Commons ever debated a constitutional document like the Apology and Satisfaction of 1604, when the Lower House protested that, while the power of princes continued to grow, the 'liberties' (privileges) of subjects did not. (Protests about infringements of privileges, however, had occurred in Elizabeth's reign: for example, the Wentworth brothers in 1566 and 1576. See Neale, 1953, pages 152–3, 318–32.) Neither had any Tudor monarch experienced the parliamentary trial and conviction of any of his ministers—James saw his Lord Chancellor (Bacon in 1621) and Lord Treasurer (Cranfield in 1624) impeached. Nevertheless, these episodes should not colour our picture of the parliamentary history of the reign. Novelty was the exception and there is much that is familiarly Elizabethan in James I's parliaments. As we have seen, James and his Council were of much the same mind as his predecessor, her advisers and their men-of-business, such as Thomas Norton: like them, they felt that there were already too many laws on the statute book. Consequently, the government had lost interest in the initiation of more. In 1593 Elizabeth's Lord Keeper had advised the assembled Parliament that its 'calling' was not 'for making of any more new laws and statutes, for there are already a sufficient number'. Rather than burden the Queen's subjects with more it would be preferable that 'an abridgement were made of these that are already'. Her successor's government echoed these sentiments. The Crown did not lose the inititative in legislation to a parliamentary opposition. It simply lost interest in legislation.

Not that legislation ceased to be an important function of Parliament, which continued to be flooded with the petty Bills of members and their constituents. Parliament remained a market place for the transaction of business and the fulfilment of members 'expectations'. The trouble was that it was so successful in attracting business that it could not find the time to transact more than a small proportion of it. Yet, while the petty Bills are much less dramatic and exciting than 'high' constitutional issues, they were the prime concern of many members, who were still pledged to serve their constituencies, as they had been in the past. Indeed the impeachments, first of monopolists and later of ministers in 1621 and 1624, irritated some members. They watched in frustration as the Commons absorbed itself in the far more exciting game of impeachment and neglected the Bills which they were anxious to pass. So, in the first session of 1621, only nineteen of about 100 Bills before the House struggled through to the Lords. Impeachment alone is a too simple explanation. There were just too many Bills to cope with, even without that particular diversion. John Chamberlain (in 1621) and Sir Francis Nethersole (in 1624) commented that the volume of pending legislation was too much, 'by reason thereof there are not near so many passed as might have been'. Parliament's very attractiveness to the promotors of Bills ensured its failure as a legislative body. Lord Burghley would have sympathised with their dilemma: he had had to live with it himself for twelve sessions in the previous reign (Russell, 1979, pages 35–6, 42, 45–8).

There were attempts to combat that dilemma, notably the procedural innovation of the Committee of the Whole House. Its origins were Elizabethan, as we have seen, but the Jacobean parliaments resorted to it more frequently. The purpose of the committee remained the same: parliamentary efficiency, not a political 'take-over'. As Conrad Russell points out, it was also designed to reach a consensus, a general agreement, rather than a vote which indicated disagreement and disunity. Formal speech-making and debate is always less likely than informal discussion to end in consensus. This makes sense if it is remembered that consensus politics lay at the heart of the political system. Government rested on Crown-governing class co-operation. Parliament was an important occasion when these two parties to the governing process sought areas of agreement and avoided, if possible, disagreement, divisive ideas and confrontation. G. R. Elton has described Parliament as a 'point of contact': it facilitated communication and discussion in order to find common ground on every major issue. Sometimes James I's government used the opportunity to seek information (Elton, 1974 article, pages 183–200; Russell, 1976 article, pages 16–17).

Any Parliament which experienced a communication breakdown was a failure, and everyone concerned laboured to avoid that. They did not always succeed. Indeed, it would be a gross distortion of the truth to suggest either that James was an able parliamentary manager, or that his parliaments were joyous occasions. On the other hand, Conrad Russell points out:

Members then did not come to Westminster in order to move the pieces on a constitutional chessboard. They were not in training for the civil war or for the Bill of Rights. (Russell, 1979, page 35.)

The reverse was, in fact, true: they wanted only a 'Parliament of union' and a productive session. This is not surprising. Members of the Commons in particular had divided loyalties. A 'Parliament of union' was an ideal which sprang naturally from their devotion to monarchy. However, they were also answerable to their friends and neighbours in the constituencies which they represented and in which they often lived. In 1621 members were worried about the reactions of their 'countries' if they returned home empty-handed, with no Bills passed. How would they justify their expense and their failure to satisfy the confidence reposed in them (Russell, 1976 article, pages 25–6)? 'No Acts, just more taxes' was the accusation which they feared as they rode the homeward trail from Westminster.

Yet how just would such a charge have been in the most lightly taxed country in Europe? James, like Elizabeth, called Parliament primarily for money. However, they both found that it either could not, or would not, deliver the goods—for all kinds of reasons. Apart from 1614, it always voted money on request. However, the governing class, including members of both Houses of Parliament, continued the Elizabethan practice of under-assessing their incomes for tax purposes. Some managed to evade the tax altogether. At the same time, inflation was eroding the real value of the taxes granted.

When Parliament attacked administrative abuses (and especially monopolies), it threatened to rob the Crown of a lucrative source of money. And when, in 1614, it offered supply to the King in return for his surrender of impositions (additional customs duties), it promised a 'once only' grant. In return, he would have to give up a guaranteed annual revenue, which was worth much more than the average annual revenue he received from Parliament. It is hardly surprising, then, that after the 1621 Parliament it was reported that James was toying with the idea of dispensing with parliaments altogether (Russell, 1979, page 52). After all, they could not satisfactorily fulfil the one function required of them by a monarchy which had lost interest in legislation.

There is a danger of misreading this development. Parliament, and in particular the Commons, was not flexing its political muscle. It was not growing more powerful, or attempting to coerce the Crown in a bid for sovereignty. The House of Lords continued to play an important role in the life of Parliament, both in its legislation and politics. In any case, the Commons was usually unaware of (or unwilling to use) its power of initiating taxation as a political lever. In 1606 it voted a large supply without a murmur. In 1610 it sent up a petition of grievances with a grant of money, but it was content to wait upon the King's 'gracious answer'. Eleven years later, the House showed an acute anxiety to retain James's favour and, with it, the continuation of parliaments in the future—indeed the subsidy was the only measure passed in this session. Once again, in 1624, money was voted before grievances were considered.

In only one parliament, that of 1614, was there a determined attempt to link redress with supply. Even then it was not a 'government-opposition' confrontation, but a conflict in Court and Council, which factions carried into Parliament. It must be admitted that the issue was not as simple as this. There was a constitutional element, indeed the only important constitutional conflict of the reign: impositions (see chapter 2, page 165–6). The issue—whether James could impose customs duties on previously untaxed commodities—had already reverberated throughout the session of 1610. In 1614 the King had the whip-hand. He threatened to dissolve Parliament if he did not receive supply, and finally he did just that. He was not going to forgo the certainty of £70 000 per annum from impositions for the sake of the smaller, occasional parliamentary grant. Conrad Russell (1976 article, page 9) writes that, '[T]he result had been such an over-whelming victory for the King that there can hardly be said to have been a contest.' This event not only demonstrated the limited nature of parliamentary authority, it also threw into question whether parliaments would survive. As one member wrote, in a moment of sober reflection after the assembly of 1614, this was 'a dissolution, not of this, but of all Parliaments.'

He was over-pessimistic, but his point should be taken. Parliament was not providing for the King's needs. It was afflicted with the same malaise which had crept through the entire structure of government since the 1580s. Why should the King summon a Parliament which grumbled rather than voted money, and which was niggardly when it did vote it? Collection was slow and the yield continued to decline as nobles and gentry under-assessed themselves in a shameless manner. On the other side, parliaments discovered that they could not force the King to bow to their wishes. He was ready to dissolve it and use extra-parliamentary sources of revenue which bought more into the Treasury than the sums which Parliament was prepared to vote— or its members dared to vote, because they had to answer to their constituents. The two Houses had only one recourse. They had to persuade the King not to make excessive demands, and to convince him of the justice of their case; at the same time they must convince their neighbours of the justice of his cause. How to fulfil the monarch's need and protect their 'countries' from frequent excessive taxation was just as much a dilemma for the Jacobean members as it had been for their Elizabethan predecessors.

Conrad Russell has already pointed the way in this area. It is just as impossible and absurd to write early Stuart parliamentary history in terms of 'conflict' between government and opposition as it is to treat Elizabethan assemblies in this way. An opposition must hope to alter policy or coerce the King. Parliament could do neither. Moreover, the parliamentary leaders so often represented as members of an opposition—Edwin Sandys, John Pym, Dudley Digges and Thomas Wentworth—were not separated from the government by policy differences. On all the great policy issues of the day, some members of the Council were in agreement with them; and they had no hope of lobbying the King successfully without support in the Council. So divisions in the Commons tended to reflect conciliar divisions: for instance, between the clients of Buckingham and his allies and those of the Earls of Pembroke and Arundel and Archbishop Abbot.

It is important to see Jacobean parliaments in the context, not of the modern two-party system, with the two Houses divided into government and opposition, but of contemporary faction politics which encompassed Court, Council and Parliament. This explains, for example, the supposedly dishonest, hypocritical and even treacherous conduct of Thomas Wentworth. The old version is that, after years of parliamentary opposition to the Crown, while at the same time seeking royal office, he deserted his old allies in 1629 when a tempting offer came from a King anxious to buy him off. In fact it was natural and acceptable that Wentworth should constantly seek office, because he was not 'in opposition'. He wanted to join his allies at Court where he could more effectively lobby the King on important issues. There were no cries of 'Judas' or 'blackleg' when he entered Charles I's service.

Indeed, in most respects the political and parliamentary structure of Jacobean England reveals little change from the previous reign. It has already been indicated that there were novelties, but for the most part an Elizabethan peer or gentleman would have been at home in the parliaments of James, where a major preoccupation of members was to gratify and conciliate their King. Their other great concern was to reconcile this effort with the protection of the interests of the counties from which they came. In these parliaments, the monarch still held most of the trump cards and divisions and contentions were not between royal government and an opposition but between competing factions in a divided Court and Council. Impositions became a genuine constitutional issue, but the Addled Parliament of 1614, the 'lawless' session of 1621, and the impeachments of royal ministers must not be seen as the product of constitutional conflict. They represent no more than the transfer of Court faction politics onto the floor of Parliament. If the level, frequency and intensity of parliamentary disagreement seems much greater than, say, in the Elizabethan parliaments of the seventies, this may simply reflect the much fuller documentation of James's assemblies. But it may be, to some extent, an accurate picture—if so it probably indicates a greater willingness on the part of Court factions to exploit parliaments in the pursuit of their policies, power struggles and quarrels.

If the Court projected itself into Parliament, did the 'country' as well? In other words, although Parliament did not split into government and opposition, was there a division between the Court and men of the country? Once again the answer must be a negative, at least in the divisive sense of conflicting positions and interests as depicted by Zagorin. In this respect, too, the change of monarchs was not accompanied by profound political change. Although a member of Parliament had to wear several caps—as Privy Councillor, royal servant, or plain M.P. and loyal subject anxious to gratify his King— these were all really Court hats. But such a member was also possessed of a country cap, as an elected representative there to protect his neighbours, friends and those whom he represented. In the sense of conflicting loyalties, the Court and country split was very real, but it carried no sinister political connotations of confrontation between King and Commons (see P. Zagorin, *The Court and the Country*, London, 1969).

The early parliaments of Charles I, 1625–1629

Between 1625 and 1629, the Englishman's political world was rapidly transformed. The events in Parliament in 1629 would probably have been inconceivable to most men in James I's last parliament in 1624. The catalyst of change in the political climate was war, first against Spain, and then simultaneously with France: the two most powerful military States in Europe. Strategically, financially and militarily, it was utter folly.

Quite apart from these considerations, however, it rapidly became apparent that England could not conduct a successful war against even one foreign enemy. War exposed the administrative decline and financial incapacity of royal government; the inability of the local bureaucracy to impress men for the army, to organise defences and levy money; the declining value of Parliament as a source of revenue; and the increasing concern of its members about the response of constituencies to the King's war demands. Into the fractious parliamentary climate generated by war were introduced new and explosive issues, in particular, Charles I's patronage of High Church Anglicanism (Arminianism) and his favourite, the Duke of Buckingham. Parliament's reluctance to provide realistic war revenues compelled Charles to resort to a forced loan, the imprisonment of gentlemen who refused to pay, and the shoe-string practice of billeting unruly soldiers on private families. These expedients led in turn to the constitutional crises of the Petition of Right in 1628 and the three resolutions of 1629—a novel concentration of political energy on the authority of the King and the liberties of the subject. Moreover, these short years saw early glimpses of what was to become, by 1640, a polarisation of Court (pro-King) and country (pro-governing class and localities) positions.

However, the extent of this division by 1629 should not be exaggerated. Nor, on the other hand, should it be attributed in the first place to the conduct of Charles I and his favourite, Buckingham. The seeds were sown in James I's last Parliament and they were sown, unwittingly, by the King himself. The central issue then was the projected war with Spain. Prince Charles and Buckingham were its ardent advocates. Indeed, the Duke manipulated Parliament with considerable skill in order to achieve his ends: in particular, to secure political and (therefore) financial support for the war, but also to impeach Lionel Cranfield, Earl of Middlesex, his arch-rival at Court. He had to overcome resistance from two quarters. One source was quite understandable: members of the Commons who, in the previous Parliament, had voted no laws for 'the ease of the subject', but burdened them with taxation, were fearful of the reception they would receive on their return home this time. One after another, they protested the poverty of their countries and asked protection for the poor. It was clear that, whatever they settled upon, it would be inadequate for the effective conduct of war.

However, the other source of resistance was even more formidable. It was the King himself. James was not averse to war in principle, but he would not embark on it unless he was guaranteed sufficient supply. Therefore, he wanted a promise of adequate funding before he declared war, and he told a parliamentary delegation his precise needs: five subsidies and ten fifteenths, together with additional annual revenue to meet his debts. The wisdom of his caution was confirmed when a week later the Commons decided to offer a mere three subsidies and three fifteenths. Buckingham feared that the King did not intend, in any case, to promote a war, but simply to divert the money to pay his debts. To a great extent these fears were justified. James limited his military activities to the financing of one mercenary force on the Continent, but he would not mount an all-out war. He scored over his son and his favourite because his commonsense told him that he could not afford a full-scale war.

Thus, when James's son's first parliament met in 1625, it distrusted the declared intention of the Crown to fight Spain. This was unfair to both Charles I and Buckingham. Yet the fractiousness of that parliament was a political reality which they had to face and overcome if they were to activate the war. The new regime compounded its problems. Charles's negotiations for marriage to the French princess, Henrietta Maria, were complicated by France's demand that he relax the penal laws against recusants (Catholics who refused to attend the Anglican Church). In 1624 he had promised Parliament that he would not do so. The French threatened to terminate the negotiations if he did not. Charles needed the alliance with France and the princess's dowry of £120 000. He not only conceded the point; he even lent ships to assist the French King in the suppression of a Huguenot (Protestant) rebellion.

These were not auspicious circumstances for the opening of a new King's first parliament. Nor was the severe plague epidemic in

London, which must have raised the hypochondria level of members and heightened their awareness of their own mortality—a most unsettling effect. The presence of Algerian pirate fleets off the southern coast must also have caused members to ponder on the efficiency of Lord Admiral Buckingham. Therefore, Parliament met in a tense, disturbed environment. Charles had called if for one simple reason: money for war, not only subsidies, but also the traditional life grant of tunnage and poundage. Members, however, were pressed from two sides: not just the King but also their constituents. Could they justify yet more money for a war which had not happened? In any case, with people dropping like flies around them, all they wanted to do was to get out of plague-ridden London in the deadly months of June and July. So they offered the King two subsidies—a pathetic handout in war-time. And, although they recognised that it was desirable to give Charles a bigger, more secure income, the pressure of time and the bubonic plague caused the Commons to hastily pass a temporary Bill granting him tunnage and poundage for one year only.

Thus, the Commons intended simply to defer to a less dangerous season the complex question of such a Bill. The House of Lords disapproved of a grant for only one year and so did not proceed with it. The upshot was that Charles had to levy these additional customs duties without parliamentary authority—an action which would only cause future parliaments to focus their constitutional sensitivity on impositions once more. Therefore, the consequent decline in King-Parliament relations derived from an external agent: the hand of God, or the plague flea on the black rat.

In such a brittle and tense atmosphere, when Parliament was beseiged in a disease-ridden city, other troubles were likely to ensue. So the Commons took issue with Richard Montague, an Arminian who had attacked the doctrine of predestination. The King promptly rushed to his rescue, warning the Commons not to meddle and even surprising his own Councillors with the advice that Montagu was his servant. Here, so early in the reign, we must recognise a new ingredient: Charles. He was willing to engage in confrontation politics, unlike his 'canny', lazy and cynical father or the elusive, evasive Elizabeth. And so, on 8 July, when members of Parliament were about to pack their bags, he dropped a typically insensitive bombshell: Parliament would be prorogued, almost immediately, to the plague-ridden city of Oxford, where he would ask for another instalment of money.

The Oxford session lasted no more than twelve days in the heat of August. Predictably, it produced no more cash for the King. The patience of members was frayed; they wanted only to escape an early death. Charles's support of the Arminians and his continued levy of impositions further irritated them. And when they escaped the unhealthy environment of Oxford, they would still have to explain their conduct to their 'countries'. Cornered in an unhealthy city, and trapped in their dual loyalties to King and constituency, members of the Commons may have sought a scapegoat. They found one in Buckingham. Some of his accusers were playing Court politics, but others genuinely questioned the Duke's management of the war and his failure to drive off the Algerian pirates. The criticisms and attacks were haphazard and unco-ordinated, but they were a portent of things to come. When Parliament was dissolved on 12 August 1625, the script for the next one had already been written.

In 1626, war compelled a new assembly. The situation was even less favourable to the King and especially to Buckingham. The embargo on trade with Spain had hit the cloth trade hard, and, as relations with France deteriorated, privateering and trade reprisals had dislocated the wine trade and fishing industry. Administrative mismanagement, but also Parliament's inadequate funding, had resulted in the military fiasco of the Cadiz expedition in 1625. And now Buckingham was faced with the prospect of war with France. The French mounted a diplomatic campaign at Charles I's Court in order to discredit the Duke. The household of Queen Henrietta Maria was the natural focal point of a powerful Court conspiracy to bring him down. Its leaders, the Earls of Arundel and Pembroke, were not averse to using Parliament in their cause. They could tap so many sources of discontent: decayed trade, harrassed local officials, financially burdened 'countries', disgruntled opponents of Buckingham, anti-Catholic and anti-Arminian phobias. Now was clearly the time to strike. Why then, we must ask, did Charles call Parliament at this time? The simple answer is that he was at war. He desperately needed money, and, being politically blind, he could not see that the price would be Buckingham's downfall. It took the Commons nearly two months to draw up a catalogue of charges against the Duke, but in their final form they stood as a damning commentary on his responsibility for contemporary misgovernment.

Conrad Russell claims that Charles (and Buckingham too) displayed great patience in their relationship with Parliament: in particular, they did not treat it merely as a source of revenue. The King's patience was to be eroded in these early years. Yet even now, with his favourite under threat of impeachment, he kept Parliament in existence for another eleven weeks. Why did he not dissolve it when, on 8–10 May, the Commons presented their accusations to the Lords? If Russell is right, it is because the King was pursuing his own vendettas. He wanted the Lords to condemn the Earl of Bristol for misconduct while ambassador in Spain, and to accept his imprisonment of the Earl of Arundel for a personal offence against himself. In other words, the King was more concerned with the response of the Lords than of the Commons—a reminder, once again, that we must keep the two Houses in their right perspective. Eventually, Charles made concessions to his Upper House. He did not proceed against Bristol and he ordered Arundel's release. The Lords, for their part, did not proceed with Buckingham's impeachment. When the King dissolved Parliament on 15 June, no grievances had been righted and no problems solved. Instead, his lack of sufficient supply drove him to impose a forced loan—the first step in the chain of events which led to the Petition of Right.

Yet, in the short term, the forced loan was a financial success. It produced almost as much as the subsidies which Charles had failed to obtain from Parliament (Russell, 1976 article, page 11). This must have encouraged him to regard Parliament as more of a nuisance than an aid to the process of 'good governance'. On the other hand, the forced loan did not produce enough and the English war effort continued to be bedevilled by lack of money. Whether the source of revenue was a parliamentary tax or a forced loan, the problem did not alter or diminish: amateur administrators operating local government would not or could not apply too much pressure to their friends, kin and neighbours. English government was too decentralised, too dependent on unpaid officials and the goodwill of the governing class to mount a successful, professionally conducted war.

Moreover, as England and France muddled their way into hostilities in 1626–7, Charles found himself in conflict with the two greatest military powers in Europe. His Lord Admiral, Buckingham, was undeterred. The Duke attempted to join forces with the Huguenots, who were besieged in the port of La Rochelle. This summer campaign achieved nothing, but it was expensive in men and money. The dead could be written off, but not the mounting costs or debts. Hand-to-mouth government was the order of the day: the Ditchfield grant (a massive sale of Crown lands) and the forced loan were the most dramatic expedients adopted at this time. The former simply depleted Charles I's capital resources, but the latter eroded aristocratic goodwill and provoked parliamentary conflict in 1628. This is understandable. Prominent gentlemen who were entrusted with the task of collecting the loan were torn by conflicting loyalties to their King and to their counties. What was worse, they had to perform their duties in a growing atmosphere of irritation and alarm. Charles had not only arrested five knights for refusing to pay the loan, he had even overridden the law courts, claiming the right to imprison without any reason given. At the same time, he was billeting fractious, unruly and unpaid soldiers on civilian households. This saved him money but, like the forced loan, it raised the question of the rule of law. Could the King disregard the liberties of the subject in this way?

To do him justice, there is no evidence that Charles was consciously bent on an absolutist course. Despite the parliamentary frustrations and provocations of recent sessions, he had not yet given up the traditional policy of Crown-governing class co-operation, although one suspects that his patience was becoming frayed. He was simply determined to wage war and needed the money to do so. However, he sadly misjudged the public mood. The governing class groaned under the multifarious financial and administrative burdens of wars in which it had no interest. Instead, it was addressing itself to what it saw as the more serious immediate consideration: the threat to the rule of law.

The new Parliament which assembled in 1628 sharply reflected an isolationist spirit and a deep concern about the subject's liberties. There was no general agreement on the best course of action, and there was no concerted attempt to force a confrontation with the King. Still, the sense of grievance was general, because most members' 'countries' were grumbling about the same things: forced loans, arbitary imprisonment, martial law, forced billeting and unpopular levels of taxation. This unity of grievance expressed itself in a novel way, when members set aside their private Bills which usually had been their top priority. For almost twelve weeks, the Commons pursued one hare—the Petition of Right. For the first time, a single-minded assembly neglected everything else and concentrated on a single issue. Members were, however, trapped in an inextricable, if familar, dilemma. They were still anxious to serve the King, but they were also bound to serve those who had chosen them. They could not vote Charles enough for his war effort, and in any case they regarded his foreign adventures as too costly and even irrelevant. Charles too was in a dilemma, because the five parliamentary subsidies which he was offered would only provide for a fraction of his military needs.

The scene was set for a constitutional crisis. Not that anyone sought change: all of those involved in the crisis were conservative in temper. They made their appeals to ancient precedents, above all to Magna Carta. Since England was a conservative society, the only way to win wider public support was to demonstrate that the objective was not innovation, but a return to a past golden age. However, when the King refused to confirm old laws against such practices as unparliamentary taxation and arbitrary imprisonment, the Commons was driven to demand a new law which forbade them. Gradually a consensus of opinion emerged: the King's actions were arbitrary, and they were the consequence of an unwanted war. War had been the catalyst of the late Elizabethan decline, and now, once again, within a few years, it was the catalyst which transformed the essentially co-operative spirit of Elizabethan-Jacobean parliaments into the Caroline crisis of the late 1620s. The Court-country conflict was also becoming a political reality.

A symptom of the crisis was the Commons' decision to seek 'redress before supply': not to vote money until the King had guaranteed the liberties of the subject. This was not quite the novelty it might be supposed. It had been mooted as long ago as 1566, and again in 1610. However, it had not been earnestly and successfully pursued. In 1624 Parliament had presented a petition of grievances, but it had voted the subsidy without waiting for a satisfactory answer. However, on occasion—for example, in 1614, 1625 and 1626, and over the two issues of impositions and the power of Buckingham—the Lower House had pressed the matter with more vigour and sense of purpose. Twice the monarch dissolved Parliament without obtaining supply, while in 1625 he did not receive the customary life-grant of tunnage and poundage. Meanwhile, no concessions were made to Parliament on the subjects which so agitated it.

However, in 1628 the time was ripe for success. The King was desperate for money to continue his war on two fronts. What better time to force him to curb the recent and arbitrary tendencies of the government? The promise was not realised. Charles's resistance to any new law binding him compelled the Commons to opt instead for his written acceptance of a parliamentary petition. As members debated this, attention focussed on the royal prerogative. Was it limited and under the law, or was the monarch answerable only to God? Sir Edward Coke played a constant incessant theme: that the law was sovereign and that the rule of law must be known, defined and certain. Charles and his Councillors set against this the 'needs of State'. In emergencies, it required a residue of flexible, indeterminate power, enabling the King to act promptly without waiting for a Parliament. Recent events suggested to many members that this was a mere pretext for arbitrary actions.

Charles stood firm, refusing to surrender the power of arbitrary imprisonment. In answer to Coke's appeal to the rule of law he called up God in his defence:

God has trusted the King with governing the while. He hath therefore trusted him with ordering of the parts; and there are many cases, of infinite importance to the subject, and of *undoubted trust* . . .

But, perhaps for the first time, trust of the King was being called into question. He was claiming extra-parliamentary taxes and arbitrary imprisonment as expressions of an emergency power, outside the law and sanctioned by God. Naturally he would accept no new law which pared down or defined this emergency prerogative. Deadlock loomed, until Coke hit upon a compromise: a petition which bore the King's assent and protected the liberties of his subjects, rather than a law which specifically limited royal authority. It would add up to the same thing in the end.

There was one snag: the House of Lords, which shuffled uncomfortably when it was required to play the role of umpire between King and Commons. Nevertheless, after protracted debate it agreed to accept the Petition of Right without alteration. In doing so, it deserted its usual Stuart position of loyalty to the monarch, who ought to have taken heed of this ominous development. Instead, he continued to wriggle. On 2 June he delivered a vague, woolly, unsatisfactory answer to the Petition. In this tense situation, other fears and grievances bubbled to the surface. Buckingham was once again attacked; so were the Arminians and their growing influence in the State and Church (see chapter 4, pages 281–3). The outcome looks, at first sight, like a double defeat for the King. He gave his assent to the Petition of Right as if it was an Act of Parliament, and he was also obliged to receive a Remonstrance which criticised him for promoting Arminianism, acting in an arbitrary manner and neglecting both shipping and national defences. To add injury to insult, the Commons failed to pass either the Bill of Arms (which would have empowered him to raise a militia in order to defend the realm) or the Tunnage and Poundage Bill (which was vital in the financing of his wars).

Yet, when Parliament ended, what had it achieved? Charles warned members, when he gave his more precise answer to the Petition, that it meant no more than his first answer. They had no power to hurt his prerogative. And he dismissed the Remonstrance with the words, 'I see you are fallen upon points of state which belongs to me to understand better than you . . .': words reminiscent of Queen Elizabeth. The two Houses did not realise it at once, but they had lost. Parliament could not make effective the provisions of the Petition of Right—no forced loans without parliamentary consent, no arbitrary imprisonment, no forced billeting, no martial law—without the ability to enforce them at law. The judges of the Common Law courts were servants of the King. Moreover, the five subsidies eventually voted provided a meagre return and were totally inadequate. Tunnage and poundage had not even been granted, thus obliging the King to collect it without parliamentary authority. By the end of this session he must indeed have been pondering whether parliaments were worth the trouble. He had been humiliated by wide-ranging criticism of his government, financial blackmail and a pathetically inadequate cash handout. At the same time that his government was being accused of the neglect of England's defences and its Channel shipping, he was denied the laws and financial means to fulfil these responsibilities. As early as 1626 he had issued a warning:

Remember that Parliaments are altogether in my power for their calling, sitting and dissolution: therefore as I find the fruits of them good or evil, they are to continue or not to be. And remember, that if in this time, instead of mending your errors, by delay you persist in your errors, you make them greater and irreconcileable. Whereas on the other side, if you go on cheerfully to mend them ... you shall encourage me to go on with Parliaments.

By the end of the 1628 session, Charles must have been discouraged. The future of Parliament lay under a lengthening shadow. Yet once again it was called, in the following year. His motives for this are obscure: perhaps taxation, or parliamentary authority to levy tunnage and poundage (although he was successfully collecting it without parliamentary consent). Conrad Russell suggests that he summoned it 'because, like other prominent Englishmen of his day, he had a strong attachment to the proper, traditional, and legal way of doing things' (Russell, *Parliaments and Politics*, page 395). If this was the case, we may admire Charles's integrity, but not his tact or his tactics. He had ignored the 1628 Remonstrance, promoted Arminians to his Privy Council and continued to levy tunnage and poundage illegally. Here was fuel enough to stoke the parliamentary fires. Yet he persisted in his efforts to work with Parliament, even though the taxes which it had voted in 1628 had not eased his financial difficulties. One reason is that members of Parliament, and the rest of the governing class, consistently and grotesquely under-assessed themselves for taxation purposes. It was nothing new: the Elizabethans had done it to their Queen. Now the Carolines were repeating the performance. Whatever the reason, Parliament was not meeting the King's wartime needs. In any case, it met under a dual pressure: members' 'countries' demanded protection of their liberties and purses, and the King demanded authorisation of tunnage and poundage.

Even Buckingham's assassination in the previous year failed to ease the tensions provoked by this pressure from both sides. Any issue could have led on to crisis. As it happened, it was the seizure of the goods of John Rolle for non-payment of tunnage and poundage which provided the spark. Rolle was a member of the Commons. Here was a tailor-made issue: it enabled knights and burgesses to rise to the defence of the subject's liberties and in protest against illegal taxation. In the midst of this tense situation, religion provided another source of discord. Arminians were supposedly bent on the destruction of Parliament. John Pym, Sir Nathaniel Rich and others enthusiastically pursued this issue, which they had failed to settle in 1628.

Unfortunately, realistic tacticians like Pym did not guide the House. The impulsive Sir John Eliot assumed an irresponsible leadership and led the Commons members towards the possible destruction of their assembly. Eliot attacked Privy Councillors, smelled Arminianism everywhere, and whipped up his followers against the treatment of Rolle. He also instigated the violent action of holding Speaker Finch in his chair (thereby preventing him from standing and so ending the sitting) while the House passed three resolutions: that whosoever 'shall . . . seek to extend or introduce Popery or Arminianism . . . [who] shall counsel or advise the taking and levying of . . . Tunnage and Poundage, not being granted by Parliament' or who 'shall voluntarily . . . pay the said subsidies' would be adjudged 'a capital enemy to this Kingdom . . .'. The very wording of these resolutions marked the King as the ultimate target. No wonder he dissolved Parliament and resolved on no more for the time being.

On the other hand, members of the Commons had always had to live with a difficult problem: they had to balance their priorities of service to the King and obligations to their 'countries'. Their problems, and the King's, had been compounded by war, which had exposed the incapacity of the English State to fight a war (let alone two wars) without desperate expedients or realistic parliamentary grants. The former provoked conflict (and in any case proved inadequate) and the latter were not forthcoming. It only remained for Sir John Eliot to lead Parliament into such turbulent courses that its very survival was threatened.

CHAPTER SEVEN

The rise of Parliament, 1629–1700

The 'eleven years' tyranny'

In 1629 Charles I determined to rule for a time without Parliament: to turn away from co-operation with the parliamentary classes to a policy of strict enforcement of government decisions at the expense of local initiative, flexible interpretation and customary ways. Such a policy involved a self-conscious decision to continue the concentration of power in the hands of a narrow group of courtiers. It is certainly untrue that Charles I planned to introduce absolute monarchy on the Continental model, but it can hardly be denied that he gave an impression of Continental influence, of wanting to change the balance of power within the English State in favour of greater centralisation, more discretionary power for the monarch and a powerful Church made more independent of lay control.

The exact nature of Charles I's intentions has never been made clear. Charles was by nature secretive, vacillating and, once his mind was made up, stubborn. His policies have often been identified with those of Strafford and Laud, the two architects of 'Thorough'. However, neither Charles nor the other members of his Privy Council were ever totally committed to their aims, nor to the ruthless methods by which they pursued them. Most members of Charles I's government did, however, share certain aims. They wished to make government more efficient, to extend the control of central over local government, to strengthen the power of the Church, to reinforce the social hierarchy and to regulate the economy. The objectives of economic control were largely old-fashioned in both economic and social policy—enforcement of monopolies, restrictions on occupational mobility by the continuation of apprenticeship laws, and the maintenance of social stability in the countryside by anti-enclosure laws.

In his attempt to impose a more centralised State which allowed a large extension of personal rule by the monarchy, Charles was faced by a number of problems. One of the most important was the way in which his policies alienated virtually the whole of the politically important classes. The concentration of power offended those peers who were excluded from Charles's government, and the way in which that power was exercised turned some into leaders of the opposition groups which began to form. To make things worse, Charles's economic and religious policies offended the lower ranks of the political nation as well. During the period 1629–40, those who opposed the policies of Charles I could look for redress neither to Parliament nor, in most cases, to a Court group which shared their views. The way was closed to any but extra-constitutional opposition. And while the government was too narrowly based to offer representation to the main interest groups in the country, it was itself disunited. Plans for administrative reform were thwarted by courtiers and bureaucrats who benefited from the old system. For example, Lord Cottington (Master of the Court of Wards) was often, though rather unfairly, identified with 'Lady Mora', which was Strafford and Laud's expression for corruption and inefficiency. There was also considerable difference of opinion over religion.

It is probably typical of Charles that he succeeded in offending the paid officers in central government without reforming them adequately. Charles's Commission into Fees revealed that posts were often held by sinecurists, who received substantial payments for duties which were carried out by deputies. In some cases there was a whole chain of deputation, in which a succession of parasites shared the payment with the nominal office-holder and the person actually doing the work. There was a large body of under-employed officials, who tried to increase their fees in any way they could. Clerks in the Court of Common Pleas, for instance, were paid for the number of pages they wrote in legal proceedings. Not surprisingly, the clerks 'drew pleadings at "an extraordinary length". . . . The sheets were described as small, the margins large, the lines few and the number of words to a line even fewer . . .' (W. J. Jones, *Politics and the Bench: The Judges and the Origins of the English Civil War*, London, 1971, page 112). Though corruption and inefficiency were found throughout all government departments and the law courts, Charles merely fined the offenders and allowed them to continue acting as before.

During the 1630s Charles I was faced with a number of specific problems. The first of these was economic. It was a decade of poor harvests. There was only one good harvest in ten years, a situation which was to be repeated only once in the next 120 years. In a society dependent on good harvests, not only for food, but as a stimulus to the level of economic activity, this was a particularly serious situation. The largest non-agricultural component in the economy, the cloth trade, had not recovered fully from the disastrous slump of 1620–1 and it was unable to cope with the alteration of consumer preferences and the growth of foreign competition in the main export markets. A combination of the worst harvest of the decade, and a particularly depressed export market for cloth in 1630, created a crisis which left its mark on the country for years to come (Stone, 1973, page 131; Supple, 1959, *passim*).

A related and conspicuous problem for Charles I was that of finance. He was perennially short of money and, in the absence of parliamentary grants, he turned to a wide range of dubiously legal and politically disastrous devices for raising funds. Monopolies, knighthood compositions, forest fines and, above all else, ship money alienated most of the governing class (see chapter 3, pages 172–3, 212–14).

A more specialised difficulty, and one which few people of the time appreciated, was that posed by the contraction of employment opportunities for graduates. The usual shortage of educated clergymen faced by Elizabethan bishops had been replaced by a glut. Highly qualified young men faced a long period in an ill-paid curacy with little prospect of promotion, unless they had family connections. There were few openings outside the Church. The result was a sense of alienation among the intellectuals, which turned many of them into vocal critics of government and society. Paradoxically, the policies which Charles might have put into effect had his finances permitted— appointing many more professional bureaucrats along the lines of the Continental monarchies—might have solved the problem of graduate under-employment and turned the intellectuals into his avid supporters. (For religious policies and their consequences, see chapter 5, pages 294–5.)

Many of Charles I's critics saw events in Ireland as a dress rehearsal for his intentions in England. Charles appointed Thomas Wentworth, later Earl of Strafford, Lord Deputy of Ireland in 1633, and he was to retain that position until 1640. During that time, he strengthened the authority of the Dublin government, humiliated the Irish peerage, repossessed Crown and Church lands at the expense of both native Irish and the established English settlers, introduced Arminianism into the official Irish Church, a body with too little support to be able to afford divisions in its ranks, and purged the Irish officials if they showed any signs of disaffection. This rigid and authoritarian policy was outwardly successful, as long as Strafford's strong hand was in control. Once it was removed, the simmering discontent became outright rebellion. English authority in Ireland was challenged in a way it had not been since the time of Elizabeth I. The rebellion resulted in atrocities and, even more, in atrocity stories. For the war of reconquest and revenge, a strong army was needed.

Had it not been for events in Scotland, it is possible, even probable, that Charles could have mobilised the wave of Protestant and nationalist fervour in support of a royal army raised and commanded in the traditional way. However, conflict in Scotland was to arouse even more suspicion of the King's intentions. The problem began as a religious one—the King introduced into Scotland a number of Laudian religious practices—but it became constitutional as well. If the King could ignore both the General Assembly of the Church of Scotland and the Scottish Estates (Parliament), and introduce a new liturgy merely by proclamation, what could he not do? In addition, Scottish nationalism was offended.

The increased power given to the Church courts in Scotland, and the greater role in both Church and State to be exercised by the bishops, were provocative and widely resented moves, made worse by the order that the Scottish clergy accept both a new Book of Canons (Church laws) and a new liturgy (order of service). The latter, which appeared in 1637, was regarded by the Scots as 'Popish in its frame and its forms'. There were riots at its introduction and a woman, one Jenny Geddes, has been raised from historical obscurity by her act of flinging a stool at the head of the minister who was reading it in St Giles Cathedral, Edinburgh. The result was an organised protest movement against the new service. In February 1638, opponents signed the National Covenant to 'labour by all means lawful to recover the purity and liberty of the Gospel as it was established and professed' before the introduction of the Canons and the new service. Faced with this widespread opposition, Charles allowed the General Assembly of the Church of Scotland to settle Scotland's religion. It proceeded to denounce the new service, the Canons, the Church courts and to excommunicate the bishops. It refused to disperse when Charles dissolved it.

The Scots raised an army of 22 000 under the veteran soldier General Leslie. Charles could not face such a force without calling on Parliament for funds. The elections to the Parliament which was to meet in April 1640 were marked by intense political campaigning. In nearly all parts of the nation, the attitudes of the candidates to the policies of the King, and the way they were affecting both the country as a whole and the local community, were more important than social status. Once the new Parliament met, it became apparent that, for a majority of its members, the King's methods of raising money since the last Parliament met, his support for Laudian religious policies, his attitude towards local government and his perceived constitutional intentions constituted a greater danger than the Scots. The Short Parliament, as it has become known, refused to vote funds for the King until he granted them redress of grievances. In May, the King dissolved Parliament.

Still determined to suppress the Scots, the King succeeded in raising money from courtiers and, with considerable difficulty, from the City. Charles raised an army of sorts: the retainers of noblemen and courtiers, gallant and otherwise unemployed young gentlemen— these made up the romantic element in an army which consisted mainly of those trained bandsmen without the wit or the money to escape service, together with the untrained substitutes bribed or conscripted to take the places of those who had. In August 1640 the English army was soundly defeated by the Scots. Under the terms of the peace (Treaty of Ripon) which followed, the Scots were to continue occupying Newcastle and receive a payment of £850 a day until permanent settlement was made. Charles could not borrow sums of the magnitude required. He had to summon Parliament once more.

The elections to the Long Parliament were even more heated than those to the Short Parliament, and the supporters of the King fared even worse. About sixty per cent of the commoners elected had served in the Short Parliament, and it was men known to oppose the Court who had the greatest chance of election. In its social composition, the Long Parliament was typical of its predecessors. Between one-half and two-thirds of its members were landed gentlemen, eighty were lawyers and between fifty and seventy were merchants, 310 are recorded as having been enrolled at one of the Inns of Court, 169 had matriculated at Oxford and 111 at Cambridge. Of the 493 M.P.s elected to the Long Parliament, about 400 were opponents of the Court. The remainder were courtiers, men with a strong vested interest in the existing government (for example, monopolists and associates of customs farmers) or those who had a very strong sympathy with Laud's religious innovations. Office-holders were far from unanimous in supporting the Court, something which may be explained by the Commission into Fees and other pressures placed on them in the 1630s.

The first session of the Long Parliament

The anti-Court group was led by John Pym in the Commons and by men such as Francis Russell, the Earl of Bedford, and Robert Greville, Lord Brooke, in the Upper House. Other prominent opponents were Denzil Holles, John Hampden, Oliver St John, Walter Earl, Benjamin Rudyard and Edward Hyde. Despite widespread differences over detail, most members of the Long Parliament agreed that it was necessary to change the King's ministers—his 'evil counsellors'—to remove the machinery of prerogative government, and to ensure that the King could not dispense with Parliament in the future. Above all else, they were agreed in their fear that the King might use force to sweep away their assembly and with it, they believed, the liberties of England. It was this terror that the King might destroy them by force which explains so many of the the drastic moves taken by the Long Parliament. It is uncertain whether the King did not realise the depth of these fears, or whether he was oblivious to their consequences. The known policies of Strafford, the Army Plot of May 1640 to put down Parliament by force, Charles's attempt to replace the Governor of the Tower of London with a man more favourable to his cause on 5 May 1640, and the King's own actions in attempting to arrest the Five Members (five prominent members of the opposition) on 4 January 1642, all aggravated the situation.

Terror explains the ruthlessness with which Parliament turned on Charles's ministers. The most hated was undoubtedly 'Black Tom Tyrant', the Earl of Strafford. There can be no doubt about Strafford's attitude. If Parliament challenged the ultimate authority of the King, it must be removed by force. The parliamentary leaders should be charged with treason for their correspondence with the Scots. Strafford was seen as a danger to both the aspirations of the parliamentarians and to their very lives. No wonder the Earl of Essex exclaimed 'Stone dead hath no fellow' when Parliament debated the action to be taken against Strafford. Early in 1641, Strafford was impeached (that is, charged by the Commons, with the Lords as judges and jury) with 'endeavouring to subvert the fundamental laws and government . . . and to introduce arbitrary and tyrannical government against the law'. This charge was impossible to sustain. Treason was an act against the Crown, not against vague and undefined fundamental laws. As Strafford argued brilliantly in his defence, the King's ministers must be free to give him advice according to their judgement and conscience, or else government would be impossible. The Lords adjourned proceedings indefinitely. Urged on by rumours of further army plots, and backed by violent demonstrations by London citizens, the Commons now moved to destroy Strafford by a medieval device which had long lain dormant, an Act of Attainder. Attainder required no judicial procedure. It was a nakedly political weapon, requiring only an Act of Parliament declaring that its victim had committed an act for which he deserved to die. Though reluctant at first, Parliament was urged on by mob violence to pass the attainder. On 12 May 1641, Strafford was executed.

The other members of Charles's government were also under

attack. Laud was arrested at the same time as Strafford and impeached, although he was not executed until 1645. Lord Keeper Finch fled to France rather than face a treason trial for his conduct as a judge in the Ship Money Case. The Secretary of State, Sir Francis Windebanke, also fled into exile rather than face impeachment on a charge of favouring Catholic recusants. This accusation was more true than his enemies realised, as Windebanke had been negotiating with the Pope for men and money to crush opposition in England. The judiciary came under attack, especially for their conduct in the Ship Money Case. Sir Robert Berkeley was arrested and charged with treason; six other judges were bound over in £10 000 each to appear before the Commons once charges against them had been prepared. Other judges were arrested who had found for the King in political cases, and by October 1642 every King's Bench judge was either with the King's army or in prison (Jones, *Politics and the Bench*, pages 137–43).

Once the immediate threat imposed by Strafford was removed, Parliament proceeded to dismantle the machinery of prerogative rule. First, the Triennial Act of 1641 removed the King's sole prerogative of summoning, adjourning or dissolving Parliament. The King was to summon Parliament at least once every three years and it was not to be dissolved or prorogued without its own consent until it had sat for at least fifty days. In case the King should fail to call Parliament, the obligation to do so was placed, firstly, on the Lord Chancellor, then on the Lords collectively and, finally, on the sheriffs. There was no maximum length for Parliament laid down. In May 1641, the Long Parliament passed an Act to prevent dissolution without its own consent. The main reason for this was to ensure that good security could be given for the loan which was being negotiated by Parliament to pay the Scots. Once Parliament had been dissolved, the King could have repudiated this debt.

On 5 July 1641, the Act for the abolition of Star Chamber swept away not only its main object, but the equivalent jurisdiction of the Councils of the North and of Wales, the special Court of the Duchy of Lancaster and the Court of Exchequer of the County Palatine of Chester. The Privy Council lost its power of judgement in both civil and criminal cases and its power of committal to prison was subject to judicial review in Kings Bench or Common Pleas. The Court of the High Commission was abolished on the same day and the creation of any similar court was prohibited. The other Church courts lost most of their powers of punishment.

Charles's unparliamentary taxation was condemned. On 22 June 1641 the Tunnage and Poundage Act legalised past impositions but prohibited them in future. It was made clear that customs duties, however traditional, could be collected only on the authority of Parliament. On 7 August 1641, ship money was declared illegal. A further Act of the same day fixed the boundaries of the royal forests at those of 1622. The demolition of the King's methods of financing personal rule was completed by the Act of 10 August 1641 which ensured that there would be no more knighthood compositions (Roots, 1968, pages 32–42; Ashton, 1978, pages 129–56).

Up until August 1641, the vast majority of M.P.s supported the measures taken to destroy prerogative government. Public opinion, certainly in London and probably in the rest of the country, was on the side of the reformers. Parliament's actions had been backed and sometimes driven on by rowdy and often violent demonstrations in London. The crowds included not only apprentices and the poor, but solid and prosperous citizens. It might be supposed, then, that in passing these popular measures which had eliminated both the ministers of the period of personal rule and the mechanism by which that rule was enforced, Parliament had achieved its objectives; that it would be able to settle to a period of mild reformation and reconstruction when it resumed after its six week recess. This was not to be.

Despite their many successes, the parliamentary opposition had failed in one essential objective, without which all the rest would be useless. The men whom Morrill calls the 'official country' had not persuaded the King to take them into his government, to make them his ministers, to grant them the power to introduce the policies in which they believed. The nearest they had come was in May 1641 when it appeared that the King was willing to take the moderate country peer, the Earl of Bedford, into his service and even to advance Pym and Lord Saye and Sele in return for their agreement to spare Strafford's life. The death of Bedford and failure to agree to saving Strafford ended such hopes and, during the first session of the Long Parliament, none of the country leaders attained more than honorific appointments. None was placed in a position of power sufficient to enable him to bridge the gap between King and country. If the ministers of personal rule had gone, those who replaced them were seen as little better. With power in the hands of these men, the 'official country' could not introduce its own policies, and even what it *had* achieved was in danger of a counter-revolution.

The second session of the Long Parliament

When Parliament reassembled on 20 October 1641, the atmosphere was poisoned by Charles's attempt in Edinburgh to arrest the Earl of Argyle and the Duke of Hamilton. This added even more to the suspicion that he would use the army, raised to suppress the rebellion in Ireland, against Parliament. This turned an Irish question into an English crisis. No one suggested that Ireland be abandoned. The atrocity stories aroused cries for revenge. Nearly everyone believed that the Irish planned a general massacre of all British settlers and that they had already murdered many thousands. English Protestants believed that priests were the ringleaders. They were said to have preached that such killings were meritorious acts. Pamphlets of the time enlarged upon the cruelty of the Irish. For example, *The Rebels' Turkish Tyranny* accused them of ravishing women and of toasting children on spits before their parents' eyes, burning them to ashes, or mutilating them. In the excitement of the times, there were even rumours that Charles had encouraged the rebels.

The existing royal army in Ireland, already regarded by Parliament as a danger to England, would have to be enlarged in order to suppress the Irish rebellion. Parliament was well aware that the sword they were obliged to help the King forge against the Irish was double-edged. News of the Irish revolt reached Westminster on 1 November. On 5 November Pym moved that Parliament should not vote money or in any way assist the King in the reconquest of Ireland until he changed his policies and his advisers. Probably because of antipathy to the Irish, hatred of their religion and the desire for revenge whipped up by atrocity stories, Parliament refused to accept this proposition. Three days later an even more radical proposal was passed, that Parliament itself should raise the necessary forces unless the King agreed with its request.

While the King did not agree with this proposal, one which would have taken from him the free exercise of his prerogative to command all the armed forces of the kingdom, he still had no 'party' and was unable to do anything except play for time. At this point, cracks began to appear among the hitherto united parliamentarians. Their greatest difference of opinion concerned religion. Virtually all were opposed to Laud's religious policies which, it cannot be stressed too much, had offended not only Puritans, but virtually all English Protestants. There were, however, divisions between the moderate Episcopalians, who wanted to return to something like the English Church of the 1620s and the radical reformers, who introduced the Root and Branch Bill for the total abolition of episcopacy. The King attempted to foment this division by stating in October 1641 that he intended to maintain the 'doctrine and discipline of the Church of England as it was established by Queen Elizabeth and my father' (Kenyon, 1969, page 194).

Pym's answer was to press on with the Grand Remonstrance, a list of grievances against the King, which had been in preparation throughout the first session, but left incomplete owing to the pressure

of other business. In its revised form, the Grand Remonstrance criticised the King's past actions, especially introducing Arminianism and
favouring Roman Catholics, and stated that it was essential to ensure
that the 'malignant party' did not use force to destroy the liberty of
Parliament. All this would have retained the support of most members. However, Pym and his associates added clauses which would
have given Parliament the power to ratify the King's appointment of
ministers and to remove them by a mere motion of 'no confidence'
rather than the judicial procedure of impeachment. Acceptance of
these proposals would have made government responsible to Parliament generations before it happened. In addition, church reform
was to be effected by a synod of clergy which included foreign
Protestants.

The debate over the Grand Remonstrance was fierce and
prolonged. For the first time, there was a significant body of opinion
in Parliament which felt that Pym and the radicals were going too far.
On 22 November, the Commons passed the Grand Remonstrance by
only eleven votes. The split in Parliament went beyond mere opposition to the Grand Remonstrance. Now, the group of moderates who
had supported the attack on the King's government in the first session
of the Long Parliament made a conscious decision to support the King.
Their leader was Edward Hyde, the future Earl of Clarendon.

In December 1641 and January 1642, the situation was tense and
volatile. There was widespread rioting in London and the King
believed that it was deliberately fomented by the radical leaders in
Parliament in order to force his hand by the implicit threat to the safety
of the Queen: the fear of violence by one's opponents was not
confined to Parliament. On 29 December a motion to move Parliament
to a place of safety away from the rioters was lost only because the
rioters had succeeded in keeping the bishops away from Parliament.
When the bishops returned the following day, they tried to have the
ruling reversed, only to be impeached for their pains. Faced with this
reversal, the King followed a dual policy. On 2 January, he made a
belated effort at bridge-building by offering the Chancellorship of the
Exchequer to Pym. It was too late. An offer which would have been
accepted eagerly a few months before was refused. The increasing
division between the moderates and the radicals in Parliament was
confirmed by the appointment of Culpepper to the Exchequer and of
Falkland as a Secretary of State. Both were supporters of Hyde.

With the refusal of conciliation by the radicals, the King, egged
on by the Queen and angered by the impeachment of the bishops, was
provoked into his ill-advised attempt on 4 January 1642 to arrest by
force the five members: Pym, Hampden, Strode, Holles and

Haselrig. He proposed to charge them with endeavouring 'to subvert the fundamental laws of the Kingdom' and with aiding the Scots. The members had fled to the City, where they were sheltered by Puritan radicals. The situation was dangerous, yet war was not inevitable. The consitutional moderates, such as Hyde and Culpepper, remained in London and attended Parliament, where they acted as the King's agents in the search for a settlement. At this stage, it was only a few royalist militants centred on the Queen who sought a violent solution.

Unfortunately, lack of trust in the King and the army being raised for Ireland provided the catalysts of Civil War. The moderates argued that the King had to be trusted. Pym and his group could not trust him. The remark of the Queen that concessions made by the King under duress were not binding was well known. Even if the King had no present intention of using the Irish army against England, he might be driven to it by the Queen, in the same way that she had provoked the attempted arrest of the five members. Modern feminists might like to reflect on the fate of three kings driven to repressive measures against dissent by their wives—Charles I, Louis XVI of France and Nicholas II of Russia.

The only force which could have thwarted an army which had conquered Ireland and returned to impose its will on the home country was the militia. After earlier attempts to obtain some form of parliamentary control had failed, on 5 March 1642 both Houses passed the Militia Ordinance, declaring that the parliamentary plan for placing the trained bands under Lords Lieutenant it appointed was to be obeyed as if it was an Act of Parliament. This was a step to revolution, and both sides prepared for war. Forces loyal to Parliament refused to admit the King to Hull, where munitions gathered for the Scottish war were stored. In June, Parliament issued the Nineteen Propositions, acceptance of which would have constituted a humiliating defeat for the King. He was to accept the Militia Ordinance, agree to the reformation of the Church by a synod, hand over the education and marriage of his children to Parliament and surrender all rights of appointment to office or nobility (Kenyon, 1969, pages 196, 244–7).

Though still without any significant party, the King held out. Hyde advised the King that he would need to strengthen his position if he was to get better terms than the dictated settlement of the Nineteen Propositions. The King had already (27 May) forbidden obedience to the Militia Ordinance. In June he went further by issuing Commissions of Array to the Lords Lieutenant and a group of prominent gentlemen in each county, ordering them to take control of the trained bands in his name. The King's reply to the Nineteen Propositions, issued on 18 June, was a brilliant statement of the constitution, which confirmed the constitutional Acts of the first session, but claimed that any further encroachment on the King's powers would lead to anarchy and disorder. On 22 August, at Nottingham, the King performed the action which created a state of war—he raised the royal standard.

The immediate cause of the war should be plain in the preceding pages. In the first session of the Long Parliament, the King agreed to nearly all the demands made by the vast majority of both Houses. In the second session, the parliamentarians gradually split between those who wanted to trust the King's intentions and those who believed that his failure to appoint as ministers the leaders of the parliamentary opposition proved that he was not sincere, and that he would strive to reverse the measures he had accepted. Driven on by the Queen, they believed he might use the Irish army to achieve this by force. Thus in order to protect the achievements of the first session, it was necessary to go further and ensure that the power of counter-revolution was seized from the King. To do this, they had to trespass on royal prerogatives never questioned before. Many moderates came to see Pym and the radicals as a greater danger to the constitution than was the King. By August 1642, the almost unanimous demand for moderate reform of two years earlier had been replaced by strident cries from almost equal groups: one demanding sweeping incursions into the prerogative, the other shouting, 'Stop'.

The historiography of the Civil War

It is almost mandatory for a student of British history to have an opinion on the causes of the Civil War. In this section, it is proposed to examine the views of selected contemporary writers and later historians in an attempt to isolate those elements of interpretation which have remained constant and those which have evolved with the years. Where possible, the position taken by a writer will be related to his personal philosophy and circumstances. According to the Oxford philosopher of history, R.J. Collingwood, each generation must rewrite its history so that it can ask its own questions of the past. On the other hand, Howard K. Beale found that there was no interpretation of the American Civil War known in 1946 which had not been foreshadowed by writers working during or even before it (R.G. Collingwood, *The Idea of History*, Oxford, 1961; H.K. Beale, 'What Historians Have Said about the Causes of the Civil War', *Theory and Practice In Historical Study*: *A Report of the Committee on Histo-*

riography, Social Science Research Council Bulletin, 54, New York, 1946).

A full analysis of the causes of the English Civil War could examine the opinions of historians in four main areas: political and constitutional conflict, the role of religion, social and economic factors, and the decisions of individual leaders, both at the national and the local level. To these four should, perhaps, be added a discussion of the impact of international affairs and the influence of any Europe-wide trends or general crisis. In this chapter, the opinions of historians about the political and constitutional issues and the part played by social and economic developments will be given most attention.

Political and constitutional conflicts provided the traditional reasons for war. The historiographical disputes in this area revolve, for the most part, around the question of whether it was the King or the parliamentarians who were the real revolutionaries. For many contemporaries, this was the central issue at stake. Even before the war, there were mutual accusations of attempting to change the balance of the constitution. During the war, there was an overwhelming body of ephemeral literature on this point, as well as some works still worth reading to this day. Of these, one of the most interesting parliamentarian accounts is that by Lucy Hutchinson, the wife of Colonel Hutchinson, a parliamentarian and regicide who died in prison after the Restoration. She expressed the view that Charles I was attempting to subvert the English constitution until it was like that of France:

The example of the French king was propounded to him, and he thought himselfe no Monarch so long as his will was confin'd to the bounds of any law. But knowing that the people of England were not pliable to an arbitrary rule, he plotted to subdue them to his yoke by forreigne force . . . for he was a prince that had nothing of faith or truth, justice or generosity in him: he was the most obstinate person in his selfwill that ever was, and so bent upon being an absolute uncontrowlable Soveraigne that he was resolv'd to be such a King or none. (Lucy Hutchinson, *Memoirs of the Life of Colonel Hutchinson*, [edited by J. Sutherland], Oxford, 1973, pages 46–7.)

The most eloquent exponent of the ultra-royalist position was Thomas Hobbes, who published his philosophical justification of despotism based on fear in *Leviathan* (1651). He applied himself to the problem of the Civil War in *Behemoth* (1668, published in 1679), in which he defended the traditional powers of the monarchy and claimed that the people were seduced from their duty by a faction of papists, Presbyterians, sectaries and Parliament men, who had fallen in love with the popular governments of Greece and Rome. The people themselves he blamed for their lack of duty towards their King, whom they thought of merely as the highest nobleman in the land, rather than as an absolute, God-given sovereign. Finally, he joined a long line of right-wing opinion in his condemnation of the universities, which, he claimed, 'have been to this nation, as the wooden horse was to the Trojans'. In his advocacy of royal despotism, Hobbes expressed the view of a small minority of royalists. He was certainly more royalist than the King.

More judicious was Edward Hyde, Earl of Clarendon, whose massive history of the Great Rebellion, begun in 1641 and completed in 1667, is something of a justification for his own actions. He was very critical of all the actions of the King which were condemned in the first session of the Long Parliament. Likewise, he regretted Charles's failure to make bridge-building initiatives by taking into office some of the parliamentary leaders. In the end, however, the Grand Remonstrance and the Nineteen Propositions represented such a breach of the existing constitution that the blame for the war must be placed primarily on the shoulders of Pym and his associates (Clarendon, *History of the Rebellion and Civil Wars in England*, [edited by W.D. Macray], Oxford, 1888).

From the early nineteenth century came the great tradition of 'Whig' historiography which cast Charles as the villain. The Whig version of history can be described simply (if crudely) in this way: many, indeed most, nineteenth century Englishmen believed that the highest achievement of their country had been the attainment of a parliamentary government and constitutional monarchy. To this, they attributed personal liberty, the triumph of Protestantism, economic growth and imperial glory; they felt very sympathetically toward Continentals who were still struggling to attain a parliamentary constitution. It is hardly surprising that nineteenth century scholars made heroes of parliamentarians and denigrated the actions of their opponents. While this is quite understandable, it did result in a distorted view of history. The objectives and achievements of men in the past were evaluated only according to the contribution they had made to Parliament.

In the present work, no detailed analysis and evaluation of the Whig historians is possible, but some should be mentioned by name. Henry Hallam, author of *Constitutional History from the Accession of Henry VII to the Death of George II* (London, 1827) was the first major nineteenth century historian to consider the constitutional issues raised by the Civil War. Hallam was a lawyer by profession and in politics a Whig. It is hardly surprising that he was sympathetic to Parliament rather than the King, yet he expressed his views with such moderation that he was vigorously attacked by the next great historian who interpreted the Civil War. Thomas Babington Macaulay adopted a strongly partisan approach in his *History of England from the Accession of James II* (London, 1848). (Despite the title, there is a chapter on the Civil War.) He argued that the events of the 1630s justified the parliamentary leaders' distrust of the King, a man personally faithless and 'impelled by an incurable propensity to dark and crooked ways', whose actions led men to choose ultimately between a Turkish despotism or a republic. Macaulay's Whig bias comes through particularly strongly when he brushes aside claims that the Grand Remonstrance demanded that the King accept a revolutionary change in the constitution, by pointing out that it asked little more than was achieved in 1688.

Probably the greatest foreign student of the English Civil War was the German founder of modern 'scientific history', Leopold von Ranke. His *History of England, Principally in the Seventeenth Century* (Oxford, 1875, published in German between 1859 and 1868) is based on a preconceived principle of selection. In his preface, he stated that his intention was to 'direct his eyes to those epochs which have had the most effectual influence on the development of mankind'. For Ranke, the great role of the English in world history was their constitutional progress, 'the legal settlement of their home affairs'. For a German living at a time when his own nation was faced with the problems of unification and devising a constitution, this was a natural position to take. Though not as antagonistic to Charles personally as most English Whigs, Ranke sided with the men who, he believed, had shown the world the way to constitutional government. Nevertheless, he saw Pym as a revolutionary; but a revolutionary whose cause was just.

Of the later Victorians, S.R. Gardiner was undoubtedly the greatest historian of the Civil War. He was a man of incredible industry, whose *History of England from the Accession of James I to the Outbreak of the Civil War, 1603–42*, in ten volumes (London, 1883–4) and its companion work on the Civil War itself, are still the basic sources of narrative for present-day historians. Though his conviction that Parliament was on the side of the future was equal to that of his great Whig predecessors, he differed from them in a number of ways. Unlike most of them, he denied that Charles I was attempting to establish autocracy in place of the mixed constitution. He recognised that there were no clear precedents establishing the ultimate authority of the King or Parliament. However, he placed the chief blame for the conflict on Charles. While Pym's demands in the Grand Remonstrance and the Nineteen Propositions were revolutionary, they were provoked by Charles's dishonesty.

Very similar views were carried into the twentieth century by G.M. Trevelyan. His *England Under the Stuarts* (London, 1904) reveals the same rational judgements as those of Gardiner, but a stronger emotional identification with the cause of Parliament. More recently, D.L. Keir's *Constitutional History of Modern Britain* (London, 1938) provides a specialist's interpretation of the legal and constitutional problems of 1642. He argues that, on balance, the King had the better constitutional case.

Throughout the nineteenth century, Tory response to the Whig charges was surprisingly muted. Perhaps the dominance of liberal democratic, if monarchical, ideals left no place for the defence of a King who wished to retain real power. In this century, however, the distaste felt by some intellectuals for Nazi and Communist revolutionaries alike, may have made possible the defence of Charles expounded in the works of Esme Wingfield-Stratford: *Charles, King of England, 1600–1637*, and *King Charles and King Pym, 1637–1643* (London, 1949). He denies strongly that Charles had any intention of imposing tyranny on England: while he was not perfect, he was making a genuine attempt to rule England in the interests of all his subjects, rather than those of the rapacious landlords and merchants who desired a land dominated by the rich. The King adopted means of dubious legality only when the illegal opposition of the selfish opponents of his paternalistic policies took steps to hinder the normal working of government. He praises the success of paternalistic rule and claims that Charles was popular with the common people.

Very different was the state of things after the overthrow of King Charles's 'tyranny'. The possessing classes got firmly into the saddle, and proceeded not only to scrap the whole attempt to intervene on the poor man's behalf to secure him a job of work and a fair deal with his employer, but also, two years after the Restoration, to pass one of the most shameless acts of class tyranny ever devised ... the Act of Settlement (*Charles, King of England*, page 331).

It is interesting to note how closely this High Tory interpretation of the motives of the parliamentarians coincides with those of the Marxists.

The most important line of research since the Second World War has involved consideration of the extent to which men of the mid-seventeenth century understood such concepts as sovereignty and the mixed constitution. G.L. Mosse has argued that the seventeenth century inherited the ideal of mixed monarchy from the Middle Ages. This theory saw the King as possessing certain absolute rights by Common Law and the ancient customs of the realm, just as the people had certain absolute rights, especially those concerning property. What was to be done if either side attempted to exceed its rights? Mosse claims that by the seventeenth century an idea of sovereignty existed and was widely known through the work of Sir Thomas Smith. Once law was regarded as something which could be made by man, it was necessary for one person or organisation to have final authority or sovereignty in all fields. The Civil War was an attempt to determine by force where sovereignty lay. Rather similar views have been put forward by R.W.K. Hinton, who argues that in the early seventeenth century, the idea of mixed monarchy was gradually giving way to that of sovereignty (G.L. Mosse, 'Change and Continuity in the Tudor Constitution', *Speculum*, 22, 1947, pages 18–28; R.W.K. Hinton, 'English Constitutional Theories from Sir John Fortescue to Sir John Eliot', *English Historical Review*, 75, 1960).

On the other hand, Margaret Judson argues, with a wealth of evidence, that men of all shades of opinion, before and in the early stages of the Civil War, thought in terms of a mixed monarchy made possible by the rule of law. What caused the war, in her view, was the political failure of the King and his advisors to reach a satisfactory solution to the problems which confronted them. There was no constitutional or legal way to resolve a problem when the partners in mixed monarchy could not agree. The Civil War began as an attempt to demarcate royal and popular powers and to determine the exact nature of the balance (M.A. Judson, *The Struggle for the Constitution*, New Brunswick, 1949).

In the discussion of the problem of whether King or Parliament was the real revolutionary during the Civil War, contemporaries and modern historians have, for the most part, fallen into one of four camps. They have adopted either the royal conspiracy theory, which saw Charles as a crypto-tyrant; the opposite viewpoint, which saw Pym and his followers as men who provoked rebellion in their own interests; or one of the two constitutionalist positions. The constitutional royalist position regards the King's actions from 1629 to 1641 as improper, though not necessarily constituting a deliberate attempt to create a despotism, and sees Parliament as the constitutional aggressor after 1641. The fourth view agrees with most of the points made in the third, but argues that Parliament was forced into demanding radical constitutional changes because the King had given good cause for distrust of his motives.

Probably the position of Gardiner and Judson is closest to the truth. The ideal of the mixed monarchy provided no clear-cut answer to the problem of resolving constitutional disputes, and the law had no certain answer to the relative rights of King and Commons. In any case, the search for historical precedents and constitutional ideas was largely an attempt by traditionally minded contemporaries and historians to justify political actions.

Neither all contemporary writers, nor all twentieth century historians, were willing to explain the Civil War in exclusively political, religious and constitutional terms. Many saw the political debates, the constitutional changes and the arguments over legal niceties as mere superstructure on the underlying realities of economic and social change. As Hugh Trevor-Roper said, 'Every great revolution has both its profound social content and its immediate political cause' (H.R. Trevor-Roper, *Historical Essays*, London, 1957). The revolt against explanations based on political and religious principle can be based either on the Marxist assumption that such ideals are merely a product of a particular type of society and the class interests within it, or on the so-called Namier method, which explains political actions in terms of personal and family interests. Marxists argue, for example, that both Protestantism and the ideals of constitutional government are ideologies formulated in the interests of the middle class. Sir Lewis Namier examined the structure of English politics in 1760 and found that membership of the various political factions, and the expression of particular principles, could be justified in nearly every case by economic motives. Many other historians have attempted to explain political alignments in other periods of history by applying the techniques of analysis which he developed.

Both Sir John Oglander and the Earl of Clarendon saw a major cause of the Civil War as the decline of the 'mere' gentry: those with no income other than that from land. Desperate to improve themselves and jealous of their more successful rivals, these men turned to revolution. On the other hand, James Harrington (*Oceania*, 1656) and Henry Neville (*Plato Redivivus*, 1681, but written in the 1650s) argued that the economic rise of the gentry at the expense of Crown, Church and peerage had been insufficiently recognised by the constitution.

The Civil War resulted from the armed struggle of the gentry to seize the political power warranted by their new economic status (see L. Stone, 1975; P.A.M. Taylor, *The Origins of the English Civil War: Conspiracy, Crusade, or Class Conflict*, Boston, 1965).

In the twentieth century, disagreement over these rival interpretations gave rise to one of the most bitter historiographic conflicts of our age. This is the so-called 'gentry controversy'. In its simplest form, it consisted of two parts: first, were the gentry rising or falling economically, and second, did the fate of the gentry play any significant part in causing the Civil War? The long debate was conducted in scores of books and hundreds of learned articles. Its ramifications extended to hundreds of examination questions and even more answers. Happily, this protracted dispute is now dead, and the oversimplified assertions of the original protagonists now forgotten by even the most unimaginative examiners. It cannot be ignored in historiography, however, because of its central role in the development of new research and, indeed, new research techniques.

The gentry controversy developed from the application of Marxist ideology to the problems of the Civil War. Writing in the late nineteenth century, Engels reinforced Marx's view that the English Civil War was a bourgeois (middle-class capitalist) revolution. To many historians who wrote or grew up in the 1920s and 1930s, the Marxist version of history was irresistibly attractive. For men such as Christopher Hill, R.H. Tawney and Lawrence Stone, Marxism showed the cause of the First World War, a personally traumatic experience for those of their generation; it forewarned of events in Nazi Germany and it offered an explanation and a cure for the Depression and for the manifest inequalities of Britain between the wars. Most intellectuals of the 1920s and 1930s were influenced by Marxism. Many became Communists. At the end of the nineteenth century, Engels briefly expressed what is still the orthodox Marxist interpretation of the Civil War. He regarded the parliamentarians as representing an alliance between the rising middle class and the ex-feudal landowners. Following the extinction of so many old noble families during the Wars of the Roses, the feudal ideals declined and many landowners became, for all practical purposes, part of the bourgeoisie. The Civil War was caused by a rising of the merchants and those landowners who had adopted bourgeois ideals and practices, against the King and the minority of landlords who were still genuinely feudal (Engels in Stone, 1975, pages 3–6).

Writing half a century later, Christopher Hill (*The English*

Revolution, 1640, London, 1940) expounded in more detail the Leninist ideas expressed above. Still a leading authority on the period, Hill has now modified his views, but this work of his youth is regarded by many historians as the best short exposition of the Marxist case. Hill argued that the King represented the landowning nobles, aristocratic commercial racketeers and their hangers-on. The commercial middle class and the progressive landowning bourgeoisie sought its own selfish interests, but in so doing performed the important historic function of clearing the way for the development of capitalism. The ideological component, both political and religious, was merely a reflection of the struggle between the dying feudal society and the rising bourgeoisie. Hill developed at greater length than Lenin the idea that the gentry had taken over monastic and aristocratic lands and that this altered the economic balance of society. Even more important than the actual change in land ownership was the dropping by the new landlords of feudal ideals in return for those of capitalist profiteering. Land they regarded as a source of money profit, while Puritanism was the religion of advancing capitalists.

A rather less orthodox, but still basically Marxist interpretation, is that of R.H. Tawney. In his study of Harrington and in his 'Rise of the Gentry' article (1940–1), Tawney argued a case which stressed the role of the rising gentry in causing the war. Tawney took his cue from Harrington and traced the transfer of property from aristocracy and Church to the gentry.

The facts were plain enough. The ruin of famous families by personal extravagance and political ineptitude; the decline in the position of the yeomanry . . . the loss not only of revenue but of authority by the monarchy, as Crown lands melted; the mounting fortunes of the residuary legatee, a gentry whose aggregate income was put even in 1600 at three times that of peers, bishops, deans and chapters . . . (Tawney, 1941, page 5).

In short, Tawney believed that Puritanism was the ideology of capitalism, that 1540–1640 was a period of economic advance by capitalist and Puritan classes, that the gentry were a rural branch of the bourgeoisie—a rising class using new methods—while the Crown and aristocracy were a debtor class dependent on loans from merchants and gentry. 'It was discovered, not for the last time, that as a method of foreclosure, war was cheaper than litigation'. Tawney's basic ideas were similar to those of the pure Marxists, but he stressed more than they the importance of the gentry class. His most important advance was methodological. He attempted, by counting the number of manors transferred from peerage to gentry, to provide a statistical basis for his claim that the gentry were rising, but as will be shown later, he ran into serious problems of definition.

Support for Tawney has been provided by the numerous writings of Lawrence Stone. Once the expounder of ideas almost identical to those of Tawney, he now emphasises the importance of the relative decline of the aristocracy (he has been criticised for the use of this word rather than 'peerage'), rather than the rise of the gentry. He argues that the revolution was made possible because the peerage lost its military power to the centralising State, and allowed its authority in local matters to be taken over by the gentry. In addition, for a short period, the peerage declined economically. 'The rise of the gentry is to some extent—though certainly not entirely—an optical illusion, resulting from this temporary weakness of the aristocracy' (Stone, 1975, page 64).

Just as the events of the early twentieth century had strengthened Marxist influences, those of the Cold War reduced them; and indeed, for many people, made anti-Marxism an article of faith. It was in this new world of anti-Marxist revisionism that the attacks of H.R. Trevor-Roper and J.P. Cooper burst forth. They denied the statistical basis of Tawney's 'rise of the gentry' claim with such ruthless zeal that Tawney was moved to reply that 'an erring colleague is not an Amalekite to be smitten hip and thigh'. In his works published in 1953, 1957 and 1967, Trevor-Roper has adopted a very different interpretation from that of Tawney. In the first place, he denied every one of Tawney's basic tenets. For him, the period 1600–1640 was not one of economic advance, but rather one of stagnation or even decline for the landowning classes; he asserts that Puritanism, especially in its more extreme forms, was the religion not of rising capitalists but of 'backwoods' squires, such as those of Scotland; he argues that the mere gentry were not rising economically, and that every example of a rising gentry family cited by Tawney had in fact made its money from Court connections, trade or the law; and finally, that the great city merchants and advanced capitalists were on the side of the King, and that it was the lesser merchants and small tradesmen who were generally on the side of Parliament. Using the findings of J.P. Cooper, Trevor-Roper attacked Tawney's statistics, pointing out that a manor was by no means a uniform piece of property, but rather a bundle of legal rights, privileges and responsibilities; that Tawney assumed a far greater distinction between gentry and aristocracy than was warranted in fact; that much of the decline in noble land-holding could be explained by the extinction of families between the beginning and the end of his study; and that he did not credit, to the peerage, land held by families which obtained their titles during this period.

In 1958 J.H. Hexter's 'Storm over the Gentry' (*Encounter*, 1958) article criticised both Tawney and Trevor-Roper for:

[Piling] on their evidence a burden of hypothesis heavier than their evidence can sustain. [W]e may suspect that their judgement has been clouded by over-addiction to some general conception of the historical process.

Though he explained the rise of the gentry in terms of the economic and military decline of the peerage, Hexter argued that the choice of sides in the Civil War was determined more by political and religious beliefs than by economic and social factors. After 1958, however, no one but examiners and their victims took the gentry controversy seriously, at least in the terms it was originally stated. If the wordy battles of the 1950s had generated excessive heat, they were also responsible for much light, especially on social, economic and local history.

A study of the historiography of the English Civil War reveals both constants and trends. Contemporary writers foreshadowed, even if only in embryonic form, virtually every modern interpretation. Though they were not unbiased—and we should not expect them to be—they have their uses as well as their limitations. As Thomas Fuller said:

I must treat tenderly, because I go not, as before, on men's graves, but I am ready to touch the quick of some yet alive. I know how dangerous it is to follow truth too near to the heels. (R.C. Richardson, *The Debate on the English Revolution*, London, 1977, page 8.)

Despite their obvious weaknesses, contemporaries first expressed not only the nineteenth century political, constitutional and religious interpretations, but also expressed, in the person of Richard Baxter, the connection between religion and the rise of capitalism; the idea of the rise of the gentry (Harrington); and the importance of the declining gentry (Clarendon). In some ways contemporary thought was in advance of the nineteenth century, which, in line with the political preoccupations of that age, largely ignored the social and economic factors in the revolution.

The main historiographical achievements of the nineteenth century historians were methodological. Macaulay relied on his prodigious memory and a limited range of documents. Hallam was his superior in this respect, but he too was not a really scientific historian.

Ranke advanced beyond them, as he used a very wide range of sources, including the dispatches of the Venetian Ambassador, a neutral source. The trend towards the use of the widest possible range of sources reached its height in the work of Gardiner, whose study of the Civil War is still regarded as the definitive narrative history of the period. According to E.P. Gooch:

. . . his volumes form the most solid and enduring achievement of British historiography in the latter half of the nineteenth century. . . . His work was the first narrative based on an exhaustive study of the vast mass of authorities reposing in public and private archives. The evidence of newspapers and pamphlets was freely used. Memoirs, however illustrious their author, were treated as secondary, not primary authorities. (E.P. Gooch, *History and Historians in the Nineteenth Century*, Boston, 1962, page 235.)

The principal weaknesses of the nineteenth century historians were their pre-occupation with the purely political and, perhaps even more serious, their tendency to view the past through the spectacles of the present. For many, the past was not to be studied for its own sake; their ancestors were not men living to achieve their own ends. The past was rather a source of information about how we became the fine fellows that we are today. Though writing about the past, they had not really escaped from time-bound parochialism.

In the twentieth century, the stream of largely political narrative has not run dry, but there has been a change of focus from the political, constitutional and religious to the social and economic. The Marxist and neo-Marxist interpretations discussed above, and the alternative theories of economic determinism expounded by Trevor-Roper and his followers, have occupied the centre of the historiographic stage. The first half of this century saw the publication of general theories, often based on an inadequate factual basis. More recently, we have seen both critical analyses of them and a flood of narrow specialised studies, many designed to find support for one of the general theories. Frequently they have used social science concepts and statistical methods. However, they have been unsuccessful in providing adequate proof of general interpretations, and failure has led to a questioning of their appropriateness (Hill in Stone, 1975, page 90).

The historiography of the English Civil War provides support for both Collingwood and Beale. Historians have, as Collingwood claimed, imposed the preconceptions and preoccupations of their own age on the past. On the other hand, the findings of Beale on the historiography of the American Civil War (see page 398) can be duplicated in the English case. Despite advances in methodology, in the use of sources, in the establishment of ideals of scientific accuracy and impartial detachment, in the use of social science concepts and twentieth century quantitative methods, the explanations that historians give for the Civil War today would not be alien to the men of the seventeenth century if they could rise from their graves.

The Civil War

The Civil War is one of the most significant episodes in English history. For the first time since the Wars of the Roses, large and organised armies with a national, rather than a regional or factional, base were to face each other. It has been estimated that as many as ten per cent of the adult male population fought in the Civil War, a remarkably high proportion for the seventeenth century. On the other hand, consciousness of war filtered down slowly to some ranks of society. As the battle of Edgehill was about to start, an old farm labourer was advised to leave the field. When told that the armies of King and Parliament were about to fight, he is said to have replied, 'What! Has them two fallen out, then'.

The war years display a continuous tension and interaction between political and military considerations. Military successes and reverses influenced the political attitudes and war aims of both sides. Changing political patterns in turn affected army command and military objectives. Within both the King's Council and Parliament, moderates struggled with those who wanted to achieve outright victory and a dictated settlement. On the parliamentarian side, the army developed as a centre of political power which was to rival that of its employer, but it too consisted of competing groups. The Scottish Presbyterians were divided between those who wished to intervene on the side of the English Parliament and those who did not. It is the interaction of all these groups, not just the conflict of armies, which determined the outcome of the Civil War.

Parties in Parliament

The majority of the Commons and the minority of the Lords who remained at Westminster after the Civil War broke out were not united. At least from the late nineteenth century, when Gardiner's books were published, until 1940, when J.H. Hexter's revisionist work caused historians to think again, students believed that most

Sites of the major battles in the Civil War, 1642–1646

members of Parliament during the Civil War could be divided into two groups: the Independents, or war party, and the Presbyterians, or peace party. Hexter and the historians who have followed him see a third party, the middle group, holding the balance of power between the other two. Furthermore, they deny that there was any necessary connection between the religious Independents and the war party on the one hand, and the peace party and religious Presbyterians on the other. Though the correlation between the two was high for a time in the later part of the Civil War, this was a product of a particular set of circumstances, not the result of any logical alliance between the two.

The peace party, led by Denzil Holles, John Maynard and William Lewis, wanted peace at almost any price. Most of the peace party was prepared to abandon or substantially modify the Grand Remonstrance and the Nineteen Propositions, and to give up the idea of controlling the militia and the executive. It was content to settle for an end to Laudianism and prerogative government. As Clarendon wrote of peace party members, 'they desired the same peace that the King did'. Peace party members were afraid of arousing the lower classes to the support of Parliament, in case they should demand radical reform; in particular, they were afraid of religious disorders. In addition, some were parliamentarians mainly because their estates were under the control of Parliament's armies.

In contrast to the peace party, the war party followed Henry Marten in believing that, 'There is another and more natural way of ending a war than by agreement, namely by conquest' (Underdown, 1971, page 46). Other important leaders were Sir Arthur Haselrig, William Strode and Sir Henry Vane. The war party wanted victory, a peace dictated by Parliament, and radical reforms. Whereas the peace party tended to gain additional support when the King's forces were in the ascendant, it was determined to resist any settlement reducing the terms of the Nineteen Propositions. Its commitment to parliamentary victory became even stronger when the royalists appeared to be winning the war.

The war party was not, however, a totally united group. Most of its members intended to restore and preserve the constitution, which they believed the King's innovations in Church and State had threatened. Their victory would be used only to 'maintain the laws and true religion'. One of the war party members said, 'I will fight to maintain a law but never to get a [new] law'. However, a small minority of men, such as Sir Henry Vane and Henry Marten, intended all along to achieve sweeping changes. The smallness of this group is suggested by Marten's suspension from the House in 1643 for advocating republicanism.

The middle group between these two was led by John Pym, the man Gardiner wrongly believed to have headed the Independent (war) party. The middle group sometimes allied with the war party in 1642–4, and on other occasions with the peace party. It was, however, consistent in so-doing. It voted with the war party in calling for active military measures and in authorising taxation to make them possible, and it voted with the peace party to keep negotiating with the King and seek an end to the war by agreement. In general, the middle group had the same conservative views as the peace party and an identical desire to restore and protect the traditional constitution. It shared with the war party the belief that the gains of 1641 had to be protected by the King's acceptance of the Grand Remonstrance and the Nineteen Propositions. The role of the middle group was critical: as long as it maintained its strength, it could prevent either of the other parties from gaining total predominance in Parliament. If this happened, there was a real threat that the party defeated in Parliament would join with outside groups in an attempt to regain its position by force.

One of the major issues which revealed differing attitudes in Parliament was the support given to rival generals. Even in 1642, many of the war party believed that Essex, the Lord General (that is, Commander-in-Chief of all Parliament's forces), was insufficiently active, and even that he did not want to win the war. In this they were correct, as Essex shared the peace party's belief that the war was purely defensive and nothing more than a preliminary to negotiations. For this reason, Essex was supported by the peace party and, usually, by the middle group. The war party, on the other hand, wished to divert men and supplies from Essex to the commander of Parliament's army in the west, Sir William Waller, a man whose early successes had gained him the nickname 'William the Conqueror'. In 1643 the changed military situation convinced the middle group that drastic measures were necessary if the war was to be ended. The royalist victory over Lord Fairfax's army at Adwalton Moor, and over Sir William Waller at Roundaway Down, created a real threat of ultimate royalist victory and certainly strengthened the negotiating position of the King, who was able to reject the Oxford Propositions: terms more favourable than he had been offered before.

The month of August 1643 marked a turning point. The Scots agreed to send troops to take Parliament's side, but only if the English would undertake a religious reformation along Presbyterian lines. By the treaty of November 1643, the English agreed in return to give the Scots an equal voice in the making of a treaty with the King, to pay £66 666. 13s. 7d to the Scottish army in Ulster, and to place the parliamentary army in Ireland under a Scottish commander. In return, the Scots were to send 21 000 men into England.

The events of 1644–5 created a new political alignment: the middle group gradually split until it ceased to exist, the majority of its members joining the war party; and the old peace party of Holles and Stapleton increasingly identified itself with the Scots. The war party was associated with an army of Independents, the peace party with Scottish Presbyterians. This association of the war party with Independency was strengthened by the tendency for war party members and religious Independents to share radical political views. On the other hand, Presbyterianism was associated with social conservatism. Many moderate Episcopalians, whose views differed little from a large proportion of the country gentlemen on the King's side, accepted Presbyterianism as the best option available. Thus, by the end of 1645 the three-party division of Parliament had been replaced by a largely two-party one. For the first time, it was proper to refer to the two parties as Presbyterians and Independents.

The two parties were, however, far from united. The correlation between religion and political views was incomplete. The Presbyterian party was a loose coalition of religious Presbyterians, Erastians and conservatives. The Independents were the products of the radical-middle group alliance. It was the survival of this alliance which was to be so critical to the settlement which would be achieved. If it collapsed, 'The Army and the radicals would be out of control, and the result would be revolution' (Underdown, 1971, page 75).

The problems of peace

The end of the first Civil War in April 1646 settled only one issue: it was no longer possible for the King to impose his will by force. Virtually all the other Civil War issues were still alive. The outstanding points of disagreement included the control of the militia, the fate of the King's closest ministers and advisers, the structure of the English Church, and the relationship between Crown and Parliament. In addition, there were a number of disputed points between those on the winning side: in particular, those relating to the disbanding of the army and the payment of its arrears.

In 1646 there were several different power groups capable of influencing a constitutional settlement. In the first place, there was the King himself. Defeated in war, he could still negotiate and have a very considerable influence. There was still very little republican feeling. The Scots had a great deal of influence, though this was declining in 1646, due to the strength of the New Model Army, their disappointingly meagre contribution to the war, the cost of supporting the Scottish army in England, and the fact that they were no longer needed now that the war was won. They were, however, still a force to be reckoned with. Their capacity to influence English affairs was strengthened by the King's decision to surrender to them in 1646, but they used this trump card only to gain payment of their arrears. They then withdrew from England and were able to influence events only from a distance.

Parliament was, of course, nominally the controlling force once the war was won. It was, however, divided about the settlement for which it would strive. After the withdrawal of the Scots, the conservative influence of the English Presbyterians came to predominate. Their position was strengthened further by the so-called Recruiter elections, held in 1646 to replace deceased, resigned and royalist M.P.s.

Parliamentary authority to effect a settlement was to be challenged increasingly by a politically conscious army. The army was, however, made up of men with a wide range of political views. One can usually distinguish the opinions of the senior military commanders, often known as the grandees, from the generally more radical opinions of the junior officers and the men in the ranks. The army's effectiveness as a political force would be limited unless it could be united in support of a single programme.

The City of London had an influence which could not be ignored. It controlled a great part of the nation's money supply. Its large population and its proximity to Parliament in nearby Westminster gave it very considerable political power. Of course, the nearness of the City to Westminster was a two-edged sword—it also provided central government with both the opportunity and the motive to exercise a great deal of influence on London's affairs.

Though able to influence events at the centre less directly, the opinions of the counties and provincial towns had also to be taken into account. Although short-term solutions might be made without reference to them, it was unlikely that any settlement to which a substantial body of provincial opinion was opposed could be permanent.

The events of 1646–8 resemble the story of the ten little Indians. One by one the power centres were eclipsed, until only one remained. It was by no means clear at first which power centre would dominate. Broadly speaking, it can be said that the majority of the power centres, and the greater part of the country, favoured a moderate settlement, with the constitutional arrangements existing at the end of the Long Parliament's first session providing the basis for agreement. Most accepted that there would have to be some further restrictions on the power of Charles I, though not necessarily on his successors, and that there should be a national Church. Owing to the association of episcopacy with the defeated royalist cause, Church organisation would have to involve some form of Presbyterianism. Finally, the new constitution would be guaranteed by a personal treaty between the King and Parliament. Such a settlement was the wish of the so-called

Presbyterian majority in Parliament, of the ruling élite in the City of London, of the Scots, of the majority in the counties, and of all but a few of the provincial towns. Only among a small articulate body of townsmen, in the army, and among the parliamentary independents was there significant support for anything more radical.

In 1646 the desire for a more democratic settlement was found among a group of mainly urban radicals known as the Levellers. There is considerable controversy among historians about how radical the Levellers were. Some claim that they wanted something very close to manhood suffrage (that is, the vote for all adult men), while others believe that they aimed only at a greater share of political power for farmers, small businessmen and, perhaps, independent skilled workers. This issue is still unsettled, but it is probable that both strains existed within the broad Leveller movement.

Parliament and the army

In March and April 1647, Parliament tried to remove the army as a centre of power by disbanding it. This attempt to pave the way to a purely civilian settlement was thwarted because Parliament refused to meet the army's purely professional demands for payments of arrears, an indemnity for acts committed in the war (that is, freedom from prosecution) and an opportunity for officers and men alike to join the army which was to be sent to Ireland. Parliament made few concessions. In March and April 1647, several regiments elected spokesmen known as agitators to negotiate with the parliamentary commissioners responsible for organising disbandment. They demanded payment of arrears, indemnity and pensions for the dependents of soldiers killed in the war. Though these were purely professional grievances, Parliament condemned their petition as an unjustified meddling in government by a purely mercenary army.

Once the army realised its political power it could not be stopped from using it. Parliament tried to make amends for its earlier shabby treatment of the army by offering to pay six weeks' arrears. This no longer sufficed. Political consciousness was growing. Parliament decided that it had to make further concessions: three agitators were allowed to address the Commons on 29 April and the senior officers were instructed to draw up a report on the complaints of the army. Parliament drew up plans to meet the grievances of the army, but it was still determined to allow the army no part in the political settlement. Some Presbyterians proposed the creation of a new force of Scots and English conservatives to impose by force the political and religious system they wanted. By this time it had become clear that the victorious armies of the Civil War, especially the New Model Army, were no longer the instruments of Parliament. For Parliament to impose its will, the old armies would have to be disbanded and a new army created which would act as the parliamentary majority wished.

The army, on the other hand, realised that, if it was disbanded, a conservative and Presbyterian settlement would be imposed on England. On 2 May Parliament decided once more that the army should be disbanded and it ordered demobilisation of different units in different places. The army refused to disband: on the contrary, the regiments met at Newmarket, and on 3 June the army improved its negotiating position by seizing the key piece on the political chess-board, the King himself. Cornet Joyce and his cavalry troops seized him from Holdenby House and took him into the custody of the army. Then, emboldened by Parliament's inability to coerce them, on 6 June the radical elements in the army persuaded it to accept the Engagement not to disband until its grievances were redressed. A General Council of the Army was formed, consisting of all the generals, together with two officers and two privates from each regiment. The General Council took the fateful step of moving beyond purely professional grievances to the advocacy of its own scheme for constitutional reform: this was the *Representation from the Army*, issued on 14 June.

Parliament could not, of course, resist the army on its own. The plans to bring back the Scots were still not complete and the Scottish army was too far away. A group of leading Presbyterians, the so-called eleven members, planned to use the London militia and the forces being raised in London as an army for Ireland as a counter to the New Model Army. Their scheme was defeated only by the army's entrance into London on 6 July. The eleven members were ejected from Parliament. The threat to the political and military power of the army had been removed, at least for the time being. However, it was far from securing political supremacy. In any case, its political demands were no longer presented with a united voice. Only when it had established internal unity could the army have any hope of imposing its will.

Divisions in the army

The basic division was between the senior officers, or grandees, and the political activists among the junior officers and in the ranks. Men such as Cromwell and Ireton were landowners: they wanted reform, not revolution. They dreaded the anarchy which would follow a breakdown of military discipline just as much as they feared the unconditional return of the King to his traditional powers. On the other hand, many junior officers and soldiers had adopted Leveller ideas. To them, the political aims of the military grandees were nothing but a 'sell-out' of all they had fought for. Differences within the army came to a head when it undertook direct negotiations with the King.

In 1647 the army officers and their parliamentary allies placed before Charles the *Heads of the Proposals* as a basis for a constitutional settlement. Based on the Representation of the Army of 14 June, this document called for a purge of Parliament, a dissolution followed by regular elections, the right to petition, the rule of law, religious toleration, redistribution of constituencies, clearly defined powers for the Council, appointment of officials and control of the militia by Parliament for ten years. Daring as they were, these plans did not go nearly far enough for the army radicals. The growth of Leveller influence in the army was shown by the publication of the tract, *The Case of the Army Truly Stated* in October 1647. The Army Council meeting at Putney thrashed out the policies they wished to endorse. Their most important product was the petition to Parliament styled the *Agreement of the People*. This document was remarkably radical for its time. It declared that the people were the true source of all power, called for a major redistribution of parliamentary seats, elections every two years, and the supremacy of Parliament over all other authority, except that of the people who elected it. There was to be freedom of conscience in religion, an end to military impressment, indemnity for actions taken during the Civil War, equality before the law and law reform.

The generals were alarmed at these proposals and determined to suppress the radicals. The agitators were ordered to return to their regiments. This was the end of the Council of the Army. In future, the senior officers were to make all the decisions. A near-mutiny of radical soldiers at Corkbush Field was quickly suppressed by Oliver Cromwell and one of the ring leaders was executed on the spot after a court martial. The threat to the unity of the army was over. The sword was firmly in the hands of the generals.

The second Civil War

The King's negotiations with the army over the Heads of the Proposals were of dubious sincerity. He seemed to believe that he could get better terms from Parliament than from the army. His real intention was to divide his enemies and restore himself to his full powers. Seeing the division between Parliament and the army, Charles decided that the time was ripe to overthrow his English enemies in alliance with the Scots. In November 1647 he escaped from military custody and took up residence in Carisbrooke Castle on the Isle of Wight. There he made an agreement with the Scots to establish Presbyterianism in England for three years and to persecute the Independents during that time. The Scots would make this possible by invading England and acting with English Presbyterians and royalists to defeat the New Model Army.

These terms were, of course, secret, but fortified by them the King stalled on the negotiations with both Parliament and the army. Annoyed by the King's intransigence and suspicious of his motives, the radicals in Parliament imposed the Four Bills on the King, saying that no settlement was possible until he agreed to, first, parliamentary control of the militia for twenty years, second, an annulment of his past declarations against Parliament, third, the cancellation of all titles and honours granted to royalists since the outbreak of the Civil War and, fourth, the acceptance of Parliament's right to meet in any place of its own choosing. It is significant that the Four Bills contained no religious clause, probably because Parliament was unable to agree on one. The King refused to accept the Four Bills and Parliament responded by passing the Vote of No Addresses on 3 January 1648. By this vote, Parliament agreed to end all negotiations with the King until he accepted the Four Bills.

It was at this point that the second Civil War broke out. It was an attempt by the Scottish Engagers, led by the Duke of Hamilton, to combine with a rising of former cavaliers and Presbyterians in England and Wales to impose a politically conservative, monarchical and ecclesiastically Presbyterian settlement. Unfortunately for their cause, the Scots and their English allies did not co-ordinate their actions well. Poor timing allowed the New Model Army to pick off the rebels one at a time. Fighting began in March, and was over in August.

Backed by the City of London, the Presbyterians in the Commons strengthened their position during the second Civil War. In September 1648, men of the middle group, left to negotiate with the King in the Isle of Wight, initiated the Treaty of Newport negotiations, in which the King made some major concessions, especially his agreement on 9 October that Parliament should control the militia for twenty years. Religion was the principal barrier, as the King refused to abandon episcopacy as resolutely as the extreme Presbyterians demanded their own form of church government. It was clear, however, that any treaty between King and Parliament could be vetoed by the army. There was no longer any force able to prevent the New Model Army from imposing its will by force. All that restrained it was the constitutional beliefs of its officers and the reluctance to seize power by no right but that of the naked sword.

In November a new General Council of the Army, this time made up only of officers, met in St Albans Abbey. Under the leadership of Henry Ireton, the army gradually adopted a position of total opposition to the Treaty of Newport. On 29 November the *Army Remonstrance* against the Treaty was ready to be presented to the Commons. The Remonstrance argued for punishment of the King and sweeping constitutional reform. Parliament postponed consideration of the Remonstrance for a week, by which time it was hoped that the Treaty would be an established fact.

The army leaders debated their next course of action, but their discussion was cut short by events in Parliament. The majority there were still determined to make a settlement with the King on terms most unacceptable to the army. The army leaders felt they had no option but to act. So they arrested the King on 30 November. Despite this, Parliament continued to debate the King's reply to the Treaty of Newport. On 4 December, the day the army entered Westminster, Parliament voted to accept the King's answer to its proposals. A conservative constitutional settlement could now be made—unless the army stopped it.

On the night of 4 December, Ireton, Harrison, Ludlow and other senior officers decided to purge from Parliament all who had voted for the Treaty or who had voted against the August motion declaring those who had assisted the Scots in the second Civil War to be rebels and traitors. Two days later Colonel Pride and a large force of soldiers attended the House and prevented approximately 100 members from entering. Eventually, the number of those forbidden by the army to sit in Parliament rose to 231. Forty-five of these were imprisoned. The army was now in charge. Pride's Purge did not, however, make inevitable the trial and execution of the King. Cromwell, who had arrived in London only after the Purge, strove to reach a settlement. The King was given three preconditions for settlement. He had to abandon the power to veto legislation, agree to the sale of bishops' lands (something it was believed would make impossible a return to episcopacy) and he was to break all contact with the Scots.

Charles continued to believe that he was indispensible and that no settlement could be made without him. He refused the ultimatum. On 23 December the Commons appointed a committee to recommend a way of bringing the King to justice and the army council agreed that there was no alternative to a trial. The more conservative officers were being pushed on by the radical demands of the soldiers. With the failure of negotiations, Cromwell was forced to accept the trial though he was still opposed to execution.

On 4 January, the Commons passed an ordinance setting up a high court of justice to try the King. This was in itself a radical act without precedent. It was accompanied by another departure from the traditional constitution, for which both sides had claimed to be fighting: when the Lords refused to pass the ordinance, the Commons declared that it alone could pass Acts with the full force of law as 'the people are, under God, the original of all just power' (Underdown, 1971, page 173).

The court began the trial in Westminster Hall on 20 January. The King was charged before 135 judges with attempting 'to erect an unlimited and tyrannical power to rule according to his will and to overthrow the rights and liberties of the people ... [and] he hath traitorously and maliciously levied war against the parliament and people therein represented'. The trial was, of course, political, and the verdict a foregone conclusion. In some respects it can be compared to the show trials of totalitarian regimes in the twentieth century. The sentence was another matter. Even when the court began its preliminary sessions, there was hesitation among the generals about whether to depose Charles and continue the monarchy with the Duke of Gloucester (his third son—the older two, the future Charles II and James II were believed to have been corrupted already by their father's influence) or whether to proceed to execution and republicanism. To begin with, Cromwell had advocated the former course, but at some time during the trial he changed his mind and adopted the policy of destroying not only the King but the monarchy too. 'We will cut off his head with the Crown upon it', he is reputed to have said.

Despite his earlier reservations, Cromwell was the man who pressured and hounded the other judges to sign the death warrant: he was only partially successful. On 30 January, Charles was executed on a special scaffold built outside the Banqueting House in Whitehall. The central act of revolution was complete. The execution was followed by further radical measures. Within two months, monarchy was formally abolished as 'unnecessary, burdensome and dangerous', the House of Lords was dissolved as 'useless and dangerous' and on 19 May the republic was formally proclaimed.

The Rump

The remnant of Commons' members left after Pride's Purge was nick-named 'the Rump': it was not a flattering description, meaning as it does 'tail-end' or backside. The Revolution and the execution of the

King left the country without a government. There was no proper executive and no clear-cut division of authority between the Rump and the Council of Officers. This was quickly remedied on 13 February 1649, when all the functions of monarchy were handed over to a Council of State with forty members, thirty-one of whom were members of Parliament. On 19 May England was declared to be a Commonwealth or Free State. Councillors were to be elected annually by Parliament. As the Rump of Parliament remained in constant session until its dissolution, the Council of State was under constant scrutiny. Although the Rump was dependent for its continued existence on the sufferance of the army, the Commonwealth was the most parliamentary system of government ever established. All legislative power was vested in a unicameral (single chamber) Parliament and the executive was subject to it.

The radicals had high hopes for a sweeping reform programme. This was not to be. In the first place, the new government had to establish itself against its internal and external enemies. The Purge and the execution of the King had alienated numerous supporters of Parliament in the Civil War. There was a very real risk that they would unite with the old royalists in a bid to bring in Charles II. Charles was waiting on the Continent for just such an opportunity, supported by the European monarchs who were horrified at the execution of one of their fellows. In addition, there was widespread support for him in both Scotland and Ireland. His main problem was to decide whether to strike first in Scotland or Ireland.

The decision was made for him when an army under Cromwell was despatched to Ireland. Cromwell acted with ruthlessness, though in accordance with contemporary rules of war, in storming the west coast towns of Drogheda and Wexford and putting the entire garrison to the sword. By early 1650, Ireland was safely in English hands and Cromwell returned to England, leaving the mopping up operations in the hands of his radical son-in-law, Henry Ireton. Scotland presented a more serious problem in two ways: first, Cromwell did not wish to fight the Scots. Though he could not stomach their rigid Presbyterianism, he recognised them as co-religionists and (the Covenanters at least) as old allies in the first civil war. In contrast, the Catholic Irish were regarded as barbarians and idolaters. Second, the Scots were able to raise stronger military forces.

Charles landed in Scotland on 23 June 1650. He gained the support of the Presbyterians by taking the Covenant and even denouncing his Catholic mother as an idolater. The first army raised in his name was defeated by Cromwell at Dunbar in September 1650, but he did not despair and a year later he had another army, strong enough to invade England. It proceeded south, attracting little English support. The county militia remained loyal to the government and assisted Cromwell's army in defeating the Scots in 'God's crowning mercy at Worcester'. Charles escaped to France, but it was clear that he was no longer an immediate threat.

With the defeat of Charles II and the Scots, the external danger receded. The initial horror at Charles I's execution had faded and the disturbed state of European diplomacy made England a valuable ally. The way was clearly open to radical reform. But the radical's hopes were dashed. The reforms carried out by the Rump were extremely limited and were usually considered only under pressure from the army. The main areas of reforming activity can be considered in turn: religion, the law, social and economic matters, and parliamentary elections.

Religious reform was expected both by those for whom the prospect was a nightmare, and by the sectaries who saw it as a cause which made the suffering of the war worthwhile. The religious reforms undertaken by the Rump, however, were limited in scope and moderate in intent (see chapter 5, pages 300–1). Even after the Battle of Worcester (September 1651), no major changes were effected.

The hopes of major reforms in the legal system were just as surely dashed. To many radicals, the law and the lawyers represented injustice and oppression. Colonel Pride declared 'that it would never be well in England until . . . the mercenary lawyers' gowns were hung up by the Scotch trophies'. The House did, in fact, *consider* major reforms. The general principle of law reform was discussed in June and August 1649, and specific proposals came before it in November 1649 and March 1650. As in other matters, the victories of Dunbar and Worcester provided renewed impetus to reforming activity. Potentially, the most important period for law reform was the first half of 1652, when the Commission on Law Reform headed by Mathew Hale, a prominent lawyer, put forward its proposals to reform abuses and anachronisms (for example, English was to be used rather than Latin or French in all legal proceedings) and partly reconstruct the court system. One particularly resented legal fee was abolished, while peers and M.P.s lost certain legal privileges. Shortly before dissolution, an Act for the probate of wills was passed. The right to imprison for debt was restricted, though not, as the radicals wished, abolished. Major proposals to decentralise the legal system, to simplify the law and to codify it into volumes comprehensible to laymen all failed. These failures resulted from the strength of the lawyers in the House, resentment at the way in which the army tried to force the Rump to take action and the lack of interest of most of the propertied members in remedying the social abuses caused by defects in the law.

Talk of social reform resulted in little action, most of it within traditional bounds. Plans for a northern university at Durham were discussed, but not implemented. No sweeping legislation to attack the causes of poverty was enacted, though pragmatic measures were taken to bring down the price and increase the supply of food and fuel in the famine years of 1648–9. The steps taken differed little, if at all, from those one would have expected from a pre-war government. The recommendation of the Hale Commission that the law be changed to protect tenants and copyholders was not passed. On the other hand, Acts for fen drainage, for reducing law costs for landlords and for enclosure quickly became law. As Underdown has said, 'It is difficult to resist the conclusion that the Rump was more protective of the rich and powerful than the poor and oppressed' (Underdown, 1971, page 284).

The Rump was widely expected to reform the electoral system, both in the distribution of seats and in the franchise. In fact, it discussed at least four major proposals. The first was the Levellers' plan, put forward in the second *Agreement of the People*. Another was the modification of this scheme submitted to the Rump by the officers in January 1649; the third was the proposal put forward by the Rump's own committee in 1650 and, finally, the fourth was the Bill, based on the committee's recommendations, which the Rump was close to passing at the time of its dissolution. Though there were significant differences between these drafts for constitutional reform, they all had in common an intention to reduce the number of seats, to eliminate rotten boroughs, and to redistribute seats on a rational basis. The Leveller scheme envisaged redistribution in proportion to population; the others, more realistically in those pre-census days, wanted representation to be based on the amount of tax paid by each county. The franchise appears to have been regarded as less important than redistribution, as it was debated only when the rest of the Bill was virtually settled. The forty shilling freeholder qualification was replaced by one requiring voters and candidates in county elections to own property valued at £200. This change obviously disenfranchised some smaller freeholders, but it also would have given the vote for the first time to many prosperous men whose wealth lay in lease-hold land or commercial property. It would, for example, have retained the franchise for prosperous inhabitants of those boroughs which were to lose independent representation. Though often seen as conservative, the new electoral qualification was probably a rationalisation, a response to the emerging situation in which economic status did not depend only on freehold land. It made all types of property equal before the electoral law. It is uncertain whether the new qualification would have expanded or contracted the size of the electorate. Owing to the limited contemporary comment on this measure, it is probable that there would have been little change.

One may now ask the question—why did the Rump fail to live up to the hopes and the fears of those who expected revolutionary change? The answer can probably be found by considering, first, the composition of the Rump; second, the practical problems it faced; and, third, the unhappy relationship between the Rump and the army. The older view of the Revolution saw in Pride's Purge the sweeping away of the moderate Presbyterians and the retention in Parliament only of radical Independents as intent on sweeping change as the army that had allowed them to stay in power. Underdown has shown that the Rump was made up not only of men he chooses to regard as revolutionaries, but also of conformists, people who lacked any real commitment to revolution. Blair Worden has gone even further than this. He believes that Underdown has overestimated the radical commitment of many whom he describes as revolutionaries. Both before and after the Revolution, Worden claims, men served in Parliament for all sorts of reasons: loyalty to any *de facto* government as a better alternative to anarchy, the belief that they had an obligation to serve their constituents, and personal ambition. He points out, furthermore, that enthusiasm for political revolution, a belief that the execution of the King was necessary to protect the gains of the first Civil War, or even a commitment to republican government, did not necessarily correlate with a commitment to social reform or radical religious views.

Until the battle of Worcester, there were further obstacles, too. The Rump and the Council of State had to concern themselves too much with the pressing practicalities of war at home, war with the Dutch, foreign policy, famine and the establishment of control in the localities. Once the immediate military threat from Charles II had receded after Worcester, the officers returned and the Rump was freed from some of its pressing practical concerns, and there was no longer the same need to conciliate the moderates. Surely the time for reform had come.

Cromwell thought it had; so did the Council of Officers and the urban radicals. The Rump, however, did not. Some of the reasons for their opposition to particular reforms have been outlined above. In addition to these, there was a resentment of the army. Many Rumpers were never to forgive it for Pride's Purge and, for most, the proper relationship between Parliament and the army was that of master and servant. The very fact that reforms were being pressed by the army was a good reason for holding back.

Relations between the army and the Rump grew steadily worse. Cromwell came under increasing pressure from his own officers and the civilian sectaries to effect a further coup and dissolve the Rump by force. For a long time, the constitutionalist element in Cromwell's complex personality predominated. He encouraged demands for reform, but tried to persuade the Rump to carry them out. The Rump paid so little heed to the army's demand that it has been said to have been possessed of a collective death wish. Finally, on 20 April 1653, Cromwell attended the House and forcibly dissolved it with the words, 'You are no parliament, I say you are no parliament. I will put an end to your sitting.' A file of musketeers added weight to these words. The reply of John Bradshaw, uttered when he evicted the Council of State later the same day, provided warning that a military regime would be unacceptable. 'You are mistaken to think that this parliament is dissolved; for no power under heaven can dissolve them but themselves; therefore take you notice of that'.

Cromwell stated at first that his reason for dissolution was the intention of the Rumpers to perpetuate their own position by calling for 'recruiter' elections to fill vacant places in the House, rather than by completely new elections according to the new franchise and distribution. This explanation was accepted by almost all historians until recently. However, Worden has demonstrated that the Rump did not plan to perpetuate itself in the manner charged, but intended a full dissolution and new elections. In any case, Cromwell's motive for forced dissolution was not designed to prevent self-perpetuation. He had recently arrived at the conclusion that the time was not ripe for free elections. Any newly elected Parliament was likely to be as unrevolutionary as the Rump. What was needed, Cromwell believed, was a period of time between dissolution and the new election, in which a government of some forty officers and former Parliament men should carry out reforms and educate the people into a way of thinking which would encourage them to elect godly and reformist members to the next Parliament. Although he genuinely believed, for a time, that the Rumpers intended to keep their own seats and simply co-opt new members, it was their rejection of his own scheme for a delay between dissolution and the new election to which he most objected.

The Rump has had a bad press. To the Levellers and other radicals it was an obstacle to reform. To the royalists it was the instrument which provided a constitutional facade for the execution of the King. To these and other observers it appeared corrupt, faction-ridden, and dilatory. The first two charges cannot be denied, if examined from the standpoint of those making them. A few Rumpers were corrupt on a large scale, and others can be charged justly with minor financial offences. However, there is nothing to suggest that they were more venal than other parliamentarians of their day, or than the army officers who made many of the charges. Certainly, the assembly was far from popular. As Cromwell said when he dissolved it, 'There was not so much as the barking of a dog'. In retrospect, however, it can be seen that the Rump had many redeeming features. It played a very useful role in settling the country after the execution of the King, its administration in England was effective and the systems of government it established in Scotland and Ireland were in advance of anything either had experienced before.

Yet, on balance, the Rump had failed. It had not established a firmly based civilian government which could maintain power without the protection of a large army capable of turning it out. Perhaps its failure was inevitable. The gentlemen, lawyers and merchants of the Rump may have been of slightly lower social status, and rather less conservative, than typical members of earlier Parliaments, but they were still members of the ruling class, men who, for the most part, could share few of the radical aspirations of the army and the sects.

Barebone's Parliament

In Cromwell's decision to expell the Rump, his Puritan idealism gained ascendency over his constitutionalism. In particular, the victory over the Scots had strengthened his belief that he was God's chosen instrument, of whom great things were to be expected. The expulsion left him, as Commander-in-Chief, the only visible authority in the country. There was no Parliament to obstruct radical reform. To Cromwell, as to most other Englishmen, direct military rule was totally alien. Cromwell had dissolved the old Council of State with the Rump, but he quickly replaced it with a new thirteen-member body. He had, however, eventually to turn to a more permanent solution.

Within the army there was a major difference of opinion. Major-General Lambert, representing the more conservative and the (usually gentlemen) officers, wanted a small council of ten or twelve, which would be assisted by an elected Parliament. They were opposed by the religious radicals, led by Major-General Harrison, who wanted to dispense with parliaments altogether and rule the country through a large council of seventy members, modelled on the Jewish Sanhedrin. For Harrison, a Fifth Monarchist, the reign of Christ on Earth was about to begin. Parliamentary constitutions were irrelevant. Cromwell decided on a compromise between the two. He would call a new representative assembly of godly persons. It was uncertain whether he intended it to be a parliament or a constituent assembly called to advise on the structure of the country's future government. In any case, once the assembly met, it declared itself to be a full parliament.

The new Parliament consisted of 140 members, with five representing Scotland and six Ireland. It was thus the first Parliament of Great Britain. The method of its choosing is uncertain. The traditional view, expressed by Gardiner, is that the members were selected by the sectarian churches. More recently, the significance of London politics has been stressed and the desire of Cromwell and Harrison to pack the new assembly with relatives and close personal friends. What *is* certain is that its members were not elected either in the traditional way, or according to any of the reformed constitutions which had been proposed.

Over the centuries, as well as in their own time, members of this Parliament have been held up to ridicule. The name generally given to it is obviously chosen to be derogatory. It is derived from one Praise-God Barbon, a London leather seller who played a fairly minor part in its proceedings. Clarendon said of its members that they were mostly 'inferior persons, of no quality or name, artificers of the meanest trades . . . [with] only some few of the quality and degree of gentlemen, and who had estates'. This is an exaggeration. Nearly half of its members had been elected to Parliament in the past, or were to be in the future. There were, however, fewer of the greater gentry than was normal, and no lawyers.

The charge that the members of this Parliament were a collection of impractical fanatics is untrue of the majority, though certainly there were some in the assembly who qualified for that description. In fact, members can be divided into a relatively conservative group, concerned with practical reforms, and a smaller, though very active, body of men whose main concern was the furtherance of their unorthodox religious ideas. (See chapter 5, pages 308–10, for a discussion of the influence of Fifth Monarchists.)

Reforms introduced or discussed in this Parliament were sane and probably even sensible, when considered in the abstract, though not always advisable in terms of practical politics, because of the vested interests they offended. The introduction of civil marriage and the registration of births, deaths and marriages has a precociously modern ring. The attempt to codify the law was based on the successful scheme carried out in the colony of Massachusetts, though a Parliament without lawyers lacked the professional expertise necessary to carry it out. Certain to arouse the antagonism of the legal profession was the decision to abolish the Court of Chancery, an institution long charged with delays and high fees: some of the cases before it had been introduced thirty years earlier and still had not been brought to conclusion. Dissolution of this unpopular institution was not, however, accompanied by any practical proposal to deal with the cases before it. Other legal reforms showed a humanitarianism in advance of that of contemporary lawyers. The debtor's law was condemned, and a committee recommended a sensible solution to debt. Genuine bankrupts would be released and the goods of fraudulent debtors should be seized and sold. The death penalty was to be abolished for some first offences, such as horse stealing and picking pockets; the penalty of pressing to death for those who refused to plead should be done away with, and the mode of executing women who murdered their husbands changed from burning at the stake to simple hanging. A proposal to allow three magistrates to pronounce divorce in cases of proven adultery by husband or wife was a little radical for even this Parliament, and divorce, other than by Act of Parliament, had to wait until the nineteenth century.

In Parliament itself, the split between the moderates and the radicals was becoming greater. The former introduced further practical reforms of the Treasury, taxation, education and Commissions of the Peace. The radicals tempted fate by insulting Cromwell as the 'old Dragon', because he would not accept their Fifth Monarchist notions, such as replacing English law with the Mosaic code. It was the moderates who were to win the day. They managed to pass through the House an Act to erect a special High Court of Justice for political offences (something which was obviously aimed at radical extremists, even more than at royalists) by putting it to the vote while the radicals were at a prayer meeting.

By December 1653, Cromwell despaired of the Parliament he had called with high hopes six months before. This time, however, a military coup could be avoided. On 12 December the moderates attended the House early and voted its dissolution and the surrender of their power to Cromwell. A group of radicals attended the House later in an attempt to carry on, and were removed by soldiers. The colonel in command asked them what they were doing: 'We are seeking the Lord.' 'Then', he said, 'you may go elsewhere, for to my certain knowledge he has not been here these 12 years' (quoted in Roots, 1968, page 169).

The Protectorate

The Commonwealth was at first governed, in theory, by Parliament alone. The men who still sat in Parliament had a monopoly of legislative and executive authority. Parliament sat full-time and the executive was responsible to it. This was a far cry from the old pre-Civil War trinity of King, Lords and Commons, but at least an important part remained. All the decisions modifying the constitution had been made or at least ratified by Parliament. That these changes were possible only because they were instigated or backed by the army is quite apparent, but the military sword was decently obscured in a civilian scabbard. The dissolution of the Rump, however, marked an end to constitutional pretences. There is no way that Barebone's Parliament could be regarded as legitimate under the old constitution. It was purely the creation of the army.

Cromwell the revolutionary, it must be remembered, was also Cromwell the country gentleman. If it was not possible to retain government by an institution possessing organic continuity with the old regime, it was necessary to set up a new system of government which resembled that of the past. Well before the resignation of Barebone's Parliament, Cromwell was moving to belief in the need for a constitution with a monarchical element in it. In a conversation with his friend, the lawyer, judge and later Ambassador to Sweden, Bulstrode Whitelocke, Cromwell asked, 'What if a man should take it upon him to be King?'.

The new constitution did not make Cromwell king, but it did contain something of the monarchical in it. The Council of Officers, led by John Lambert, produced England's first written constitution, the *Instrument of Government*. It was much influenced by the Heads of the Proposals of 1647, adapted to the conditions of 1654. Executive authority was to be held by a Lord Protector, assisted and restricted by a Council of State appointed for life. There was no Upper House. This makes it possible to see the Council of State as an oligarchical element in legislation as well as executive government. Parliament was to be called at least every three years and had to sit for a minimum of five months before it could be dissolved. It was to be elected by a revised franchise similar to that under consideration by the Rump at the time of its dissolution. The parliaments of England, Scotland and Ireland were united, the latter two kingdoms having thirty seats each. By a single clause in an army-imposed constitution, James I's aim of a united Great Britain was achieved. In England a large number of small boroughs were disenfranchised when borough seats were reduced from 398 to 133. The number of county M.P.s was increased from ninety to 265. The remaining boroughs elected their representatives in the traditional way. The county franchise was changed from the forty shilling freeholders' qualification to the ownership of real or personal property with a capital value of £200. Anglicans were excluded from the first four parliaments and Roman Catholics forever.

The Protector had extensive powers, more restricted in some ways than those of his royal predecessors, and more extensive in others. He did not have the King's absolute veto over parliamentary bills: he could delay them for only twenty days unless they were contrary to the Instrument, and his appointment of the chief officers of State was subject to 'the approbation of Parliament'. On the other hand, Cromwell was granted an income of £200 000 a year for civil government, and for the maintenance of an army of 30 000 men, which was not subject to parliamentary control. As long as an army existed on this scale, it would be the ultimate authority. As long as Cromwell could retain its loyalty, his power was secured. The kingly power to issue proclamations was reinforced by the provisions giving the Protector power to issue ordinances with the force of law at any time Parliament was not sitting: such ordinances were to remain in force until the matter could be considered by Parliament.

In many ways, the power of Parliament was more restricted than in the traditional constitution. The provisions of the Triennial Act were continued and the Protector had not inherited the royal power of absolute veto over Bills, but Parliament was restricted by constitutional provisions for which no machinery for amendment was provided. The large permanent revenue and the constitutional establishment of a large army were serious restrictions on parliamentary authority. The demand that Parliament control the armed forces of the country had been the most important reason for the outbreak of war in 1642. The constitution of 1654 placed in the hands of the Protector the power which Parliament had most wished to deny Charles I. The power of appointing officers had been another important issue. As outlined above, the Protectorate parliaments were to have some vaguely defined powers over the appointment of listed high officers, and none at all over the rest. In short, it can be concluded that though the role allotted to Parliament showed both gains and losses when compared with the pre-war situation, it fell far short of parliamentary demands in the Civil War, demands for which the army officers who imposed the Instrument of Government had claimed to be fighting.

The Instrument of Government had a number of strengths and weaknesses. The greatest need of the country in 1654 was a stable government with a broad social base of support. The Instrument was only partly successful in attaining this goal. The return to a more traditional type of government pleased some conservatives alienated by the Commonwealth, but the exclusion of royalists from the first four parliaments and the denial of religious toleration to Anglicans limited its role in reconciling the landed gentry. Local studies show, however, that the Instrument was partially successful in persuading Presbyterians and even the sons of royalists to accept county offices which they had spurned during the Commonwealth. On the other hand, the Protectorate was a denial of the radical aspirations of people such as the Levellers and Diggers and it alienated the republicans who wanted government by Parliament alone.

The first Protectorate Parliament was not called until 3 September 1654, nearly ten months after the declaration of the Protectorate. During this time, Cromwell made full use of his power to legislate by ordinance. Taxes were continued, the Act imposing the Engagement (to be true and faithful to the Commonwealth) was repealed, the Treason Ordinance of 19 January 1654 made it treason to assert in public that the Lord Protector and Parliament were not the supreme authority and a religious settlement was attempted (see chapter 5, page 301). A total of eighty-two ordinances were issued. Twenty of these were financial, many were simple extensions of legislation which would expire unless renewed, and a few were directed at internal security. Only comparatively minor social and economic measures were passed. One of the few major changes contemplated at this time was law reform: in August 1654 an ordinance made alterations in the Court of Chancery. Foreign policy was exercised without the need for ordinances. The Protector had inherited the royal prerogative to negotiate with foreign powers.

When the first Protectorate Parliament met in September 1654, constitutional issues were to dominate its proceedings. Parliament protested against the imposition of a constitution by the army and claimed for itself the right to determine how the country should be governed. The Protector and Council declared their willingness to agree to constitutional amendments in 'circumstantials', provided that four 'fundamentals' were maintained. These were: first, government by a Single Person and Parliament; second, the inability of Parliament to make itself perpetual; third, religious toleration; and, fourth, power over the armed forces was to be shared by Protector and Parliament. All members were to take the 'Recognition', an undertaking to accept government by a Single Person and Parliament. Ninety members, mainly the extremer republicans led by Sir Arthur Haselrig, withdrew rather than sign.

The members who signed did not necessarily accept the other three fundamentals of the Instrument. The majority were determined to increase the power of Parliament and whittle away that of the Protector, Council and army. Parliament demanded that the position of each Councillor be subject to parliamentary confirmation in each session, something which would have made the executive responsible to Parliament, and it strove to reduce the size of the standing army from the 57 000 at which it stood to the 30 000 guaranteed by the Instrument. The militia was to be strengthened to supplement the reduced regular forces and the Protector's control over the latter was to be restricted to Cromwell's lifetime. Perhaps even more controversial was the plan to limit religious freedom by listing 'damnable heresies' which would not be tolerated.

The conflict between Parliament's demands and the Protector resulted in deadlock: no legislation was passed. The essential problem was that Parliament's demands were directly contrary to the wishes of the army and the sects. Partial disbandment would reduce the political power of the army and it might tempt disaffected gentlemen to risk a new civil war. In addition, there were professional considerations: disbandment would end the military careers of many officers and men who had known no other. Finally, the list of 'damnable heresies' would have made illegal many sects influential in the army. To have agreed to Parliament's specific demands would have been to hand all power back to that institution. That is, of course, what Parliament wanted and what the Protector was determined not to do. It is scarcely surprising that the very day the five months' sitting guaranteed by the Instrument expired, Cromwell dissolved Parliament.

Cromwell had failed to manage Parliament. Given the contrast between his desires and those of the traditional ruling class who still provided the majority of members, this is no surprise. Cromwell, however, did not see it that way. He dismissed Parliament with bitter words. Just as the failure of Barebone's Parliament had pushed him back towards moderate constitutionalism, his inability to gain the support of the first Protectorate Parliament returned him once more towards Puritan repression, to authoritarianism rather than conciliation. Royalist activity provided a justification for more direct military rule. In March 1655 a small-scale rising in the western county of Wiltshire was led by John Penruddock. Penruddock's rising was easily suppressed, but it was significant in being the first rising since the Civil War in which royalists alone were involved.

A further incentive to direct rule by the sword was the need to maintain large armed forces on land and sea, and to pay for extensive diplomatic representation in Europe. This created a perpetual financial crisis, while doubts about the stability of the regime made it difficult to borrow (see chapter 3, page 179).

It was apparent that the way to cut expenditure most quickly was to reduce the size and pay of the army, but to do so was to threaten security. A solution was attempted in mid-1655. As reductions in the regular forces were made, the militia was to be strengthened and placed, together with the regular armed forces of a particular region, under one of the ten (later eleven) major-generals whose main task was to preserve internal security. The cost of the new militia and the administration of the major-generals was met by the imposition of a decimation tax (a tax of ten per cent) on the incomes of known royalist sympathisers with estates worth more than £100 a year. However, this did not solve Cromwell's financial problems. Mounting deficits forced the calling of an 'emergency' Parliament in 1655, well before one was made necessary by the triennial provisions of the Instrument.

Despite the attempts of the major-generals to influence the elections, the new M.P.s were a mixed bunch. Popular anti-government feeling was shown by the electoral slogan, 'No Courtiers, No Swordsmen'. Nevertheless, Major-General Goffe was able to say for the government that the electoral results were 'not so good as we would have wished them . . . and not so bad as our enemies would have had them' (quoted in Roots, 1968, page 198). Many officials and supporters of the government were elected, but open opponents were excluded by Cromwell and included both conservative and radical enemies, royalists and rigid Presbyterians as well as republicans. The exclusion of about 100 members aroused much anger. One writer asked whether the exclusion of 100 members was not 'a crime twenty-fold beyond that of the late King's in going about to seclude the five members'.

After this inauspicious beginning to the first session of the new Parliament, a period of particularly good relations with the Protector was to follow. Parliament began by introducing sumptuary legislation restricting dress and roundly condemning such feminine frivolities as the use of beauty spots and cosmetics. Legal reform was discussed once more and Bills were introduced to improve the administration of the law in the provinces. A Court of Equity was to be set up in Yorkshire as a substitute for the civil jurisdiction of the now defunct Council of the North. Anxious to remain on good terms with the

Protector, Parliament attacked the major-generals only indirectly by refusing to pass a confirmation of the decimation tax. As keen to remain on good terms with Parliament as its members were with him, Cromwell decided to sacrifice the major-generals. On the same day that they failed to confirm the decimation tax, members voted £400 000 for the Spanish war. Cromwell had now attained the object for which he had called Parliament.

Following the grant of war finance, Parliament turned to more controversial matters. Despite Cromwell's objection to the persecution of Catholics who presented no political threat, he decided to accept Bills reviving and strengthening anti-Catholic penal laws. This move towards religious intolerance against Catholics was followed by a demonstration of revulsion at radical sectarianism. Still not willing to alienate the Protector by calling directly for restrictions on the sects, Parliament took up the case of James Naylor who had ridden into Bristol on a donkey claiming, they chose to believe, that he was Christ. His explanation that his was merely a re-enactment of Christ's entry into Jerusalem was rejected and, after prolonged debate, Parliament declared Naylor guilty of blasphemy and ordered him to be twice humiliated, branded, flogged and subject to tongue boring. Cromwell, who was opposed to these proceedings, asked Parliament on what authority it had exercised this judicial power. None had been granted it by the Instrument of Government. It could only claim that it had inherited the authority of earlier parliaments. This was an undefined authority and therefore dangerously capable of indefinite expansion, especially where there was no check provided by a second chamber.

The constitutional implications of the Naylor case provided an excuse for bringing forward an idea entertained by some supporters of Cromwell. If he would become King and restore something like the old constitution, then there would be a system of checks and balances. The power of each institution would be clear. This is, of course, a somewhat rosy and inaccurate view of the ancient constitution. However, this was ignored or forgotten in the desire to find an answer to the problems of the present.

The decision to offer Cromwell the Crown was the product of a number of factors. In the first place, it represented the rise of a new and mainly civilian group of Cromwellian supporters. They can be considered as the representatives of those country gentlemen who believed in the pre-war ideals of balanced government, social conservatism and religious moderation, rather than sectarian enthusiasm.

Secondly, the civilian Cromwellians and many of the country gentlemen, wanted to replace the Instrument of Government, a document military in inspiration and imposition, with a creation of

Parliament. This would symbolise a return to truly parliamentary authority. Once more power would be in the hands of the traditional ruling class, rather than in those of upstart officers. This was not an altogether fanciful view. If a new and 'civilianised' regime was widely accepted, the need to preserve a large army for internal security would disappear. A smaller army would mean lower taxes, and lower taxes greater acceptance of the regime. This would allow the army to be further reduced and so the cycle would continue. The small army would clearly lose much of its political influence, a factor which would itself make the Cromwellian government more acceptable to many country gentlemen.

Perhaps the most important single factor in the desire to press for kingship in 1656 was the realisation that Cromwell was ageing. At fifty-seven he was showing signs of the tensions and strains which he had experienced in the last fourteen years. There was no guarantee, in any case, that he would die a natural death. In January 1657, the discovery of Sindercombe's plots reminded all that Cromwell's life could easily be cut short by a bullet. One of Sindercombe's plans had miscarried only because an unexpectedly large crowd had blocked the would-be assassin's planned escape route. Unwilling to face the virtual certainty of his own capture and execution, he had abandoned the attempt. Cromwell's death at this time would probably have led to renewed civil war. One M.P. said of Sindercombe's plot, 'I believe none of us that sit here had been safe if this design had prospered'. Once Cromwell was named king, the succession, and hence political stability, would be secure.

The constitution which Parliament proposed to Cromwell came to be known as the *Humble Petition and Advice*. Its essential features were the elevation of Cromwell to the kingship, and the creation of a second chamber to take the place of the House of Lords. The sole authority to bar its own members was to be held by each House, Parliament was to have direct control over appointment to the Privy Council and other specified offices, and there was to be a stricter control over religion. Though this proposal would have reduced some of his powers, Cromwell was very tempted to accept. It offered the way to the moderate constitutionalist settlement he, or at least part of him, had always wanted. In the end, he refused the kingship, substituting the power to name his successor, but accepted the other parts of the proposals. His repudiation of the throne reflected two things: first, army opposition and, second, personal doubts. In the army there was widespread belief in the providential destruction not only of Charles I but of monarchy itself. Though the ranks of the army had been repeatedly purged to turn it into a purely professional and non-political force, talk of kingship was followed by dissension and moves to revive agitators and councils of the Army.

In the eyes of many soldiers, to restore the monarchy would be to oppose God's will. It was obvious, too, that Cromwell's coronation would reduce the power of the military grandees. The interests of the grandees and the beliefs of the soldiers united the army. Cromwell's acceptance of the throne would probably have resulted in a military coup. He might, nevertheless, have risked it if it had not been for his own doubts about whether Providence had actually called him to be king. These doubts and his realistic appraisal of the dangers involved combined in his decision to decline the throne. At last, on 25 May 1657, Cromwell accepted the Humble Petition and Advice except for the kingship. On 26 June he was installed as Protector for the second time in an elaborate ceremony resembling a coronation. It seemed that Cromwell lacked only the name of king.

With the acceptance of the new constitution, the first session of Parliament ended. It did not reassemble until 20 January 1658. By then the second chamber had been created, though it was still known only as the 'other House'. Sixty-four members were summoned (sixty-three with one late addition) including seven 'old' peers, of whom only two were prepared to sit, peers' sons and baronets, relations of Cromwell, army officers, and thirty members of the Commons. Forty-two were willing to sit and thirty-six actually sat.

Unfortunately for Cromwell, the happy relations he had experienced with the first session of this Parliament were not to continue. The new constitution did not allow him to purge Parliament and the entry of the republicans, together with the elevation to the 'other House' of thirty of his leading supporters, completely changed the character of the Commons. Republican M.P.s made bitter attacks on the existence of the 'other House', organised petitions, and expressed the grievances of the army. Recall of the Rump and a return to complete religious freedom was urged. Tension in Parliament was accompanied by renewed royalist activity and rumours of military plots and mutinies. Only fourteen days after the commencement of the second session, Cromwell dissolved Parliament. His bitter dissolution speech was ended with the words, 'and let God judge between you and me', to which republican members were heard to reply, 'Amen'.

The government struggled to contain army restlessness and renewed threats of royalist insurrection. A few militant officers were sacked, and the troops calmed by pay. A special High Court of Justice tried known royalist conspirators, executing a number of the leaders. A tenuous control was maintained while the Council struggled with the problem of the succession and debated the desirability of calling another Parliament. On 3 September, the anniversary of the battles of Dunbar and Worcester, Oliver Cromwell passed quietly into death, the problem of permanent settlement still unresolved.

From Richard to Restoration

The period between the death of Oliver Cromwell and the Restoration is often depicted as one of inevitable collapse. In fact, the transfer of power to Richard Cromwell was smooth and uneventful. As Clarendon wrote, 'the King's condition never appeared so hopeless, so desperate'. Despite this it was only twenty-one months until Charles Stuart was to return as king.

Richard Cromwell had both advantages and disadvantages , when compared with his father. On the positive side, he was not associated with either the Civil War or the execution of the King. This made him acceptable to many who could not forgive Oliver his past. Under Richard, the Protectorate had an excellent chance of reconciling the Presbyterians and moderate royalists who made up such a large part of the landed gentry. On the other hand, Richard was quite unprepared by experience for this sudden thrust into the highest levels of public life. Though intelligent and amiable, he lacked the strength of personality possessed by his father and his younger brother, Henry. Lucy Hutchinson (wife and biographer of an army officer) said of him, 'Richard was a peasant in his nature, yet gentle and vertuous, but he became not greatnesse'. His greatest disadvantage was his lack of military experience and consequent low standing with the army.

The steps to restoration can be given only in outline here. Richard's Parliament, elected on the traditional franchise and distribution, met in January 1659. There were bitter disputes between the conservative majority and the army, supported by the radical minority in Parliament. On 21 April a struggle between Richard and the military grandees for the loyalty of the army left Richard a mere figurehead. The generals forced him to dissolve Parliament the following day. The Rump was recalled on 7 May and on 25 May Richard resigned.

The shaky co-operation between the recalled Rump and the army was temporarily strengthened by the premature royalist rising in Cheshire: Booth's rebellion. The forces which suppressed this rising were led by one of the rival grandees, John Lambert, whose prestige was, of course, raised by his victory. The Rump was unwilling to recognise Lambert's achievement by promotion and it was proving itself incapable of finding a solution to the problems of permanent settlement. Lambert dismissed it in October. At this point, the armies of Lambert and Desborough, unpaid, mutinous, and politically agitated, ceased to be reliable military forces. Disunity among the senior commanders was followed by the growth of faction among their subordinates. Only General George Monck's army in Scotland remained reliable. It was paid regularly from Scottish sources, its commander-in-chief had served with it throughout the occupation and he had purged it of any unreliable elements, while taking steps to promote officers loyal to him. When Monck's army moved south, there was nothing to stop it. Realising that they could claim no more right to rule than could Monck, Lambert, Fleetwood, and Desborough recalled the Rump once more. On arrival in London, Monck insisted that all former members of the Long Parliament should be readmitted. Pride's Purge had now been reversed. The majority of members were now monarchists.

Supported by the navy, which Admiral Montague had brought back from the Baltic, and by the City of London, Monck was able to ensure that there was no interference from the other generals with the steps being taken towards Restoration. The recalled Long Parliament recognised that it was unrepresentative: eighteen very eventful years had passed since it had first been summoned. Elections were called. The new body was styled a convention rather than a parliament, as it had not been summoned by the King or, as in Cromwell's parliaments, by a quasi-monarchical authority. On 1 May the Convention declared for monarchy, on 8 May it pronounced Charles king, and on 25 May he landed at Dover. The Interregnum was over.

In order to understand why the governments of the Interregnum collapsed and allowed restoration of a Stuart king, one may look at the problem in three main ways: first, the viability of the system of government created by Oliver Cromwell; second, the importance of particular events between Oliver Cromwell's death and the Restoration; and third, the role of royalists in England and the court-in-exile.

The system of government established by Oliver Cromwell depended on the army. His government was established by the sword, it was maintained by the sword and it was to perish because it could not dispense with the sword. He was still a constitutionalist who hoped to rule through a parliament, but only one which would accept his views on essential issues. The problem lay in Cromwell's inability to win over the majority of the gentry, prosperous farmers and merchants, the men who constituted the political nation, to accept his rule or his wishes. For Cromwell to establish his regime permanently, he had to do one of three things. His ideal was to find a way of gaining the support of both the traditional ruling class and the army. The vast difference between the two made this a virtually impossible task. Second, he could abandon the army and pursue reconciliation with the gentry at all costs. As his refusal of the kingship offered by the Humble Petition and Advice was to show, neither his personal ideals nor the army would let him do this. The third possibility was much more revolutionary. He could break with the past and abandon both the traditional ruling class and its machinery of government. Perhaps less radically, he could adopt Leveller parliamentary notions and swamp the gentry by admitting to the political nation large numbers who had formerly lain outside it. Parliament could be made amenable to reform by changing the social basis of its election. The political revolution could have been made permanent by a social revolution which would have changed the social basis of power. This is the solution which many radicals of later ages believe Cromwell should have adopted.

There are two main reasons why he did not, or why he made only tentative moves in this direction, as in the calling of Barebone's Parliament and in the rule of the major-generals. In the first place, once more, one must consider Cromwell's personality. He believed in no more than limited social reform, certainly not in social revolution. One must never forget his dual role in securing the success of the political revolution and stopping the Levellers in their attempt to maintain the momentum from political to social revolution. In the second place, there is no guarantee that massive extension of the franchise would have gained parliamentary support. Though many commentators, both among seventeenth century writers and later historians, believe that the farmers, the labourers and the townsmen favoured radical reform, most of the detailed local studies written in the last twenty years throw doubt on that belief, except for some of the towns. If the local studies are correct, only a revolutionary regime which possessed all the machinery of a modern totalitarian state could have succeeded in imposing its will.

What Cromwell succeeded in doing during his lifetime was to maintain the conflicting forces in uneasy balance. While he lived, the precarious balance was safe. He could find no permanent solution. The reasons for his failure as a parliamentary manager lie partly in the problem outlined above. Despite the somewhat less socially élitist character of Cromwell's parliaments compared with others in the previous fifty years, they were still dominated by members of the traditional ruling class. There would always be conflict between their conservative views and those of the radical army officers.

Secondly, the fact that Parliament was granted a subordinate part in a constitution imposed by the army was an overwhelming source of dissension except, in contrast, in the second session of the second Protectorate Parliament when opposition of republicans to the creation of a second chamber, and army antagonism to a new constitution not of its making, combined to replace the grievances of the old ruling class as the main cause of dissatisfaction.

Thirdly, Cromwell was not a legitimate hereditary king. Despite the many conflicts between Charles I and his parliaments, no one challenged his position as Head of State until late in the Civil War. The ancient constitution, which determined the relationship between Charles and his parliaments, was open to different interpretations, but no one challenged its legality.

Fourthly, Cromwell had even less skill than his Stuart predecessors in planning for parliaments and building up a pro-Court faction within them. This inability to gain the consent of Parliament on issues he believed crucial was in part due to problems already outlined; but lack of tactical skill was an important contributory factor. Inability to gain agreement left only the alternatives of surrendering or using force.

The major weakness of the system of government existing at Cromwell's death was that it depended on the skills of one man. To say that Henry, Oliver Cromwell's young son, or John Lambert might have preserved the Protectorate is, unless one regards Richard Cromwell as uniquely unsuitable, to support this contention: that the system depended on the man. Oliver Cromwell's greatest achievement was his preservation of army unity during his lifetime. With his death, this was soon lost. The army grandees, Fleetwood, Desborough and Lambert, could not, however, keep in bounds their jealousy and ambition. Below them, the junior officers and the other ranks were becoming political once more. Once army unity was broken, Restoration was at last possible. In a sense, Cromwell's greatest success was also a failure. His inability to solve the problem of succession to his position as commander-in-chief, by grooming a man who would both continue Cromwell's policies and have the respect of his fellow generals, was to precipitate the rapid return to royal government.

Standing apart from the other ambitious and political generals was George Monck in Scotland. A professional who had begun his career in the Netherlands, and a former royalist, he believed that soldiers had no political role. He said that obedience was his great principle. Monck had kept his army almost entirely free of political activity. When the armies in England fragmented and collapse threatened,

Monck was able to go south and, whether or not this was his intention from the first, restore the King.

Little has been said about royalist plots. They make for interesting and romantic stories—arms smuggling, conspiracies in country houses, steadfast loyalty and courageous death. In fact, they did little or nothing which helped the King directly. Indeed, one can argue that they prolonged the last stages of the Interregnum by creating unity among those who had nothing in common except opposition to armed royalism. On the other hand, royalist activity may have hindered the acceptance of a permanent Cromwellian settlement by making necessary the large army and the concomitant high taxation both so resented by conservative civilians. Perhaps too, they contributed to the generally unsettled air of 1658–1660 and helped create the belief that stability would return only with Charles II.

The Restoration Settlement

The Restoration was a whole complex of changes which brought back the hereditary monarchy, Parliament, the Anglican Church, the unchallenged pre-eminence of the Common Law and a restoration of most alienated land to the Crown and the Church. It was not, however, the return to pre-war conditions which many people ardently desired.

The first and most obvious part of the Restoration was the return of the legitimate and hereditary monarchy. In law, the Interregnum did not exist. Charles II had automatically ascended the throne at the moment of his father's execution and 1660 was, technically, the eleventh year of his reign. The powers of the restored monarchy were not, however, those of 1640. Charles II accepted the Acts restricting royal power passed in the first session of the Long Parliament. He did not, however, have to accept any further limitations. Two crucial issues of the Civil War, control over the militia and appointment of royal ministers, were settled entirely in the monarchy's favour.

The makers of the Restoration Settlement were criticised afterwards for bringing back the King without conditions, but their failure to impose any was a product of the situation in 1660. Delays caused by negotiating conditions could have shattered the fragile unity of Anglicans and Presbyterians in Parliament and given time for the army to reunite. The conditions of 1660 had not been expected, and if this opportunity had been lost, it might have gone forever.

The Restoration was just as much a restoration of Parliament as of the monarchy. Parliament returned in its traditional constitutional form as an institution of two Houses. The Commons were to be

elected according to the traditional franchise and by the old constituencies. Interregnum reforms were ignored. Parliament became
purely English and Welsh once more as the Scots and the Irish regained
their own parliaments. The Upper House again became the House of
Lords, occupied by the hereditary peers and, from 1661, the bishops,
assisted as before by the non-speaking and non-voting Law Lords.
The restored Parliament was to be dominated by the old élites. The
Act Against Tumultuous Petitioning restricted the presentation to
Parliament of most petitions not approved by a J.P. The Corporation Act provided a means of strengthening the influence of conservative townsmen and the neighbouring gentry in the parliamentary
boroughs. The Anglican Church was a very important part of the new
order and the system of Common Law was strengthened at the
expense of its rivals (see chapter 5, pages 315–20 and chapter 3, pages
236–7).

The land settlement saw the return of Crown and Church lands,
as well as those confiscated from royalist gentlemen by statute.
Lands sold by royalists to pay composition fines were not returned.
However, neither return nor non-return was as important to most
families as the protests of some would suggest. Most purchasers of
Crown and Church lands were allowed to remain as long-term tenants
on favourable leases, and a large proportion of the lands sold to pay
fines had been repurchased by their owners prior to the Restoration.
Despite the dramatic consequences for some individuals and families,
neither the post-Civil War period nor the Restoration land settlements
produced large social changes.

One of the most important aspects of the Restoration is that it
returned England to civilian rule. In later times, there were to be fears
that Charles II or James II might use troops raised for foreign wars
to establish absolute government either on the Continental model, or,
like Cromwell, to act as the ultimate check on parliaments which
pressed for policies unpopular with the government. It is significant,
indeed crucial, that for most of the Restoration era no such force
existed and that when it did, in the last year of James II's reign, it
proved politically unreliable. The restored Stuarts could reign only if
they retained the consent of their subjects. The Restoration is just as
important for what it failed to restore as for what it did. In the first
place, it could not and did not return England to the pre-war situation.
The execution of the King was the central event of the century: its
effects and those of Civil War, military rule and a decade of constitutional experimentation could not be erased from the collective mind.
It was probably too much to expect that any constitutional arrangement could provide the settled and stable government for which the

country craved after two decades of war and revolution. Despite the assumptions of those responsible for the Restoration, that some mythical golden age would return with the King, too much had been left unsettled. The age which followed was one of insecurity, corruption and fear. A major source of uncertainty and conflict was the poorly defined division of power between King and Parliament and, indeed, between the two Houses of Parliament. The Restoration constitution was based on the assumption of harmony and co-operation between King and Parliament. In the honeymoon period immediately after the Restoration, enough of this existed to prevent serious conflict. As time went on, the emergence of serious political disagreements over foreign policy, religion and the succession led to different interpretations of the constitution.

As mentioned above, the relationship between King and Parliament established by the Restoration was based on that existing in 1641, after the reforming legislation of the Long Parliament. Parliament was made a permanent part of the constitution by statute. The Triennial Act of 1664 placed on the King the obligation to summon Parliament every three years. Unlike the 1641 Act, which created machinery to ensure that it met if the King did not perform his duty, the Triennial Act of 1664 was based on the assumption that the King could be trusted. This allowed Charles II to avoid summoning Parliament between 1681 and 1685.

A stronger protection for the continued existence of Parliament was the extension of its role in finance, public legislation and private Bills. The King no longer had the power to collect taxes without parliamentary sanction. Revenue from the remaining Crown lands was a small part of governmental expenditure. The permanent revenue granted to cover the ordinary expenses of government was set at a level which ensured the need for Parliament to meet and vote extra funds in most years. Parliament's legislative function was increased by the sweeping away of the prerogative courts. The King now had no way of punishing those who disobeyed proclamations: they could be charged in a Common Law court only if the proclamation was a reminder of existing law. It was clear that new laws could be created only by statute. The abolition of the judicial powers of the Privy Council and the prerogative courts also created a need for more private legislation. Defects in existing law could be remedied after the Restoration only by Parliament. Finally, the Lords inherited some of the appeal court functions of the Privy Council. (The Judicial Committee of the Privy Council remained the final Court of Appeal for the colonies, as it does to this day. Some self-governing countries within the Commonwealth now voluntarily retain appeal to the Privy Council as the ultimate legal remedy. Within England and Wales the highest court of appeal is, and has been since the Restoration, the House of Lords.)

At a less tangible level, the development, especially during the Interregnum, of the doctrine of the separation of powers had become widely, indeed almost universally, accepted. This required that laws be made by a body quite separate from the institution which administered them, or from the courts which decided disputed points of law and tried offenders. Associated with this belief was the view that executive government should be accountable to the elected law-making body. In other words, government policies and the actions of ministers were open to query and criticism in Parliament. Events in the Interregnum had made this far more than a theory. It is quite clear that the ideals of balanced government, separation of powers and accountability could be attained only if Parliament was to meet regularly.

However, the King was still very much the centre of government. He was the head of the executive, his consent was essential to legislation and he had extensive powers over Parliament. He was head of the Church and all the law courts acted in his name. He had the sole right of appointing and promoting peers and bishops. Subject only to the unenforceable Triennial Act, the King retained the powers of summoning, proroguing and dismissing Parliament. His ability to influence elections in many boroughs, and the royal power to recall borough charters, could and did have a crucial effect on the elections of the 1680s. The royal veto over legislation was also untouched. The King retained the power to dispense certain persons from the effects of legislation and, more arguably, to suspend the enforcement of particular laws. All government was carried out in the King's name. The Privy Council, barring only the loss of its judicial powers, had the same range of functions as it had had under Charles I, or, for that matter, Elizabeth I. The officers of State appointed by the King could be removed only by him or by the complex and protracted procedure of parliamentary impeachment. The King or his high officers appointed all the important officials in county government. The King also retained sole authority over foreign relations. This could have important consequences in domestic politics: for example, Charles II probably hoped to make a sufficient profit from the Third Dutch War (1672–4) by capturing enemy ships, and by the increase in customs duties which would result from the seizure of Dutch trade by the

English, to reduce his dependence on Parliament. By the secret Treaty of Dover in 1670 he obtained a foreign subsidy which was intended to make it unnecessary for him to summon Parliament.

The King had sole command over all the armed forces in the kingdom, though he was expected to keep only a small force of regular soldiers in peacetime and to place command of the militia in the hands of leading county gentlemen. These expectations made his military prerogative of very limited use in the establishment of absolutism; unless, of course, he was in a strong enough position to ignore them.

Despite the very real constitutional authority which the King possessed at the Restoration, his specific legal powers were less important than the attitude of the people toward them. He was granted this authority because they thought it necessary for the exercise of government. In a reaction against the Interregnum governments, the landed classes were prepared to trust Charles II in a way they had been unwilling to trust Charles I. The existence of a strong and independent monarchy was seen as a bulwark against revolution.

Weaknesses in the royal position

Despite this array of powers, the King had a number of constitutional weaknesses. The first was a lack of money. Only for comparatively brief periods did the permanent revenues allow the possibility of ruling without recourse to further parliamentary finance. Secondly, the King had only a small central bureaucracy. Though this was improving in efficiency, there was no possibility of it expanding to take over local administration. The abolition of the prerogative courts had played an important part here—there were now few openings for civil lawyers, the men whose training, unlike that of the common lawyers, specially fitted them for royal service by making them look at all problems from the point of view of advancing the King's interests (Jones, 1979, page 18).

Thirdly, it is significant that Charles and James II had little ability to control and exploit economic activity. Their role in this was far smaller than either that of Charles I or their fellow monarchs abroad. It was Parliament rather than the Court which attempted to resolve the conflicting interests of rival economic groups, and Parliament which laid down the foundations of national economic policy.

Finally, the small size and unpopularity of the standing army ruled out the possibility of a coup, at least until James II succeeded in expanding it in the last years of his reign. Without the power to coerce his subjects by force of arms, Charles II could follow only those policies which were enforceable by constitutional means, and which would not provoke armed rebellion.

Party and parliamentary management

Once sustained conflict arose between Crown and Parliament, the ill-defined nature of their relationship made necessary some fuller definition of their spheres of responsibility. It was, perhaps, inevitable that each should attempt to extend its powers at the expense of the other.

There were three main ways in which government-Parliament deadlocks could be resolved. The first was for the King to dispense with Parliament altogether and establish a system of absolutism modelled on that of Louis XIV. Charles II was suspected of wishing to follow a Catholic and absolutist policy as early as 1663. The weaknesses in the King's position, in particular his finances and the lack of a large standing army, made this policy impracticable, especially as it was opposed by all but a tiny minority of the King's subjects.

The second was more subtle. It involved keeping the existing parliamentary system but, by the control of elections and manipulation of members, rendering the majority in both Houses of Parliament subject to the King's will: Parliament would exist only to legitimate his decisions. It would have no independence and would cease to be a centre of opposition. The third possible resolution is the converse of the second. Parliament could seize, from the King, authority over government, and his ministers would then be responsible to Parliament. Though parliamentary government was to emerge as the winner among the options, it took a long time for this to happen. In the 1660s and 1670s, few members of Parliament wanted it to. To a large extent, the first steps towards parliamentary control of the executive (government) were defensive, designed to ensure the continued existence of a free and independent Parliament.

Conflict between King and Parliament was to involve many different techniques, most used by both sides. The first was an attempt by Charles II's ministers to build a pro-Court faction in Parliament by the use of bribes, pensions, office and promises. This was a technique appropriate to the Cavalier Parliament, which did not face a general election for eighteen years. During the Exclusion Crisis, however, three elections in quick succession established electoral manipulation as the more appropriate technique. This was a more radical approach, in that it involved an appeal to the electors, not just to those already elected to Parliament, and it opened the way to pamphleteering and attempts to control the only 'mass medium' of the age, the Press. Following the success of the opposition in the elections, the Crown turned to the manipulation of the borough franchises in order to ensure a majority in the Commons favourable to royal policies.

There can be little doubt that the important feature of political life in the years after the Restoration was the development of parties. This can be attributed to two men: the first was Thomas Osborne, successively Earl of Danby, Marquis of Carmarthen and Duke of Leeds (he is most frequently referred to as Danby). Danby built up the Court party in the 1660s and the Tories in the late 1670s. The second man closely involved in the creation of political parties was Anthony Ashley Cooper, Earl of Shaftesbury, the leader of the first Whigs.

The development of party was a new phenomenon. In the past there had been factions, regional groupings and alliances of men likely to benefit from particular policies. What differentiated a party from the other types of political organisation was the commitment of its members to particular points of principle, its existence over long periods of time, its attempts to formulate a common policy over a wide range of issues and the willingness of its members to submit to some form of discipline. Fully fledged parties of this type did not emerge suddenly in the reign of Charles II, but organisations developed which were without doubt the ancestors of not only the modern party system, but also of two of the modern parties.

The importance of parties and their growth can be assessed in relation to elections, their connections with government, the extent to which they dominated other political relationships and their association with particular social classes. However, parties did not develop in a vacuum. Their emergence was an integral part of the political struggles, and of the constitutional issues which grew out of them.

The rise of conflict

The period from 1660 to 1700 was one of rapid constitutional change. The vagueness of the Restoration Settlement, and the unwarranted assumption of continued identity of interest between the monarch and the ruling class, resulted in a period of turmoil and instability. Both King and Parliament strove to impose their own interpretation of the constitution on the other, once the effects of the post-Restoration honeymoon had been dissipated. Constitutional issues rarely attract heated debate when considered in the abstract. They usually rise to prominence only when associated with some burning political issue in which they may affect the outcome. Between 1660 and 1688, the main political issues were the interrelated ones of foreign policy and religion. From the differing views over these two issues sprang bitter disputes over the relative powers of King and Parliament, which culminated in the successful attempt by Parliament to regulate the succession. From 1689 to 1700, foreign policy, the war with France and the financial needs created by war provided the focus for most political and constitutional disputes, though for some the events of 1688–9 remained a controversial issue. The conflicts between William III and his parliaments were to contribute to the most far-reaching assertion of the power of Parliament over the monarchy in the Act of Settlement. Though constitutional theory played some part in all these changes, it was small compared with the influence of particular conflicts over specific issues.

One such issue was religion. Charles II was a genuinely tolerant man who did not wish to persecute for the sake of religion. Indeed, he saw his Declaration of Breda, promising 'liberty to tender consciences' both as an ideal and a promise he wished to keep. In addition, the admission of Protestant dissenters and Roman Catholics to a share in public life would reduce his dependence on the Anglican landed class. An increasingly important factor in religious policy was Charles II's gradual drift towards Roman Catholicism, which was to culminate in his deathbed conversion. Apart from Charles's reluctance to accept the restrictions imposed on dissenters by the Clarendon Code, religion was not to become a fundamental issue in *domestic* politics until the 1670s. Charles's pro-Catholic religious policies were, however, of considerable importance in *foreign* policy. Charles favoured the Catholic French over the Protestant Dutch. As the Dutch were England's great rivals in maritime trade, both in Europe and in the colonies, wars against them had some popularity with the merchant community. By the 1660s, however, this was increasingly offset by fear that defeat of the Dutch would lead to an increase in French power. As well as being Catholic, France was turning to protectionist economic policies at home and expansion overseas. In addition, the excellent fighting qualities of the Dutch in the second Dutch War of 1665–7 produced a grudging respect and a preference for having them as friends. These factors, and mutual exhaustion, combined to produce the Treaty of Breda in 1667.

Charles remained hostile to the Dutch and a friend of Louis XIV. After 1667, Parliament was usually pro-Dutch and anti-French. Foreign policy was, however, still a royal prerogative. Even the right of Parliament to express an opinion about foreign policy was as uncertain as it had been under Elizabeth. The application of foreign policy could, however, be checked by Parliament if it involved the expenditure of additional funds. After a brief combination with Sweden and the Dutch in the anti-French Triple Alliance of 1668, Charles returned to his policy of friendship with France. In any case, his signature of the Triple Alliance was probably intended only to show Louis that England's friendship was worth having and not to be taken for granted, rather than to do France any real harm.

The age of Clarendon

Even in these early years, the undefined boundaries between the authority of the King and that of Parliament were to cause problems. Their resolution was not helped by the character and policies of the King's chief minister, the Earl of Clarendon. In some ways Clarendon is an appropriate symbol of the immediate post-Restoration years— backward-looking, determined to restore the golden age of balanced government which he believed had existed before the Civil War. He was unwilling to accept that times had changed and that new problems must be faced with new methods. His fellow ministers also represented the past, though admittedly rival parts of it. The Earl of Ormonde and the Earl of Southampton were, like Clarendon, former Cavaliers; their colleagues, the Earl of Manchester, the Duke of Albemarle (General George Monck) and Anthony Ashley Cooper were old Cromwellians. This was a union of old opponents and it represented a resolution of past battles. There was little understanding of how to approach the future.

Though honest, sincere and hardworking, Clarendon, both as a man and as a statesman, was a bad choice as first minister. As a man he had an old-fashioned and near puritanical morality, which he constantly preached to the annoyance of both King and courtiers. The marriage of his daughter, Anne, to James, Duke of York, the future James II, gave him an unjustified reputation for ambition. His construction of a vast mansion in Piccadilly, built, symbolically enough, from material so riddled with woodworm that the building soon became unsafe and had to be demolished, led to suspicions of corruption. He was, furthermore, associated with three very unpopular policies: the sale of Dunkirk to the French, the marriage of Charles to the Catholic and barren Catherine of Braganza, and the acceptance of Tangier and its concomitant costs of defence as part of Catherine's dowry. It was widely believed that it was French bribes given him to agree to the sale of Dunkirk which had paid for his mansion. A symbol of the unpopularity Clarendon gained in this way was shown by an incident reported by Pepys. Graffiti at Clarendon's gate included a sketch of a gibbet (gallows) and the rhyme, 'Three sights to be seen, Dunkirk, Tangier and a barren Queen'. As a statesman, Clarendon recognised neither that there was a permanent split in English society, which would have to be recognised in techniques of parliamentary management, nor that a major reorganisation in government administrative methods was necessary.

From the first suspicion that Charles had toyed with the possibility of following Catholic and absolutist policies, which suspicion was aroused by the Declaration of Indulgence of 1662 (a statement from the King suspending all penalties for religious dissent), Charles was to have difficulty in getting Supply Bills through Parliament. Charles saw at once that it would be necessary to have 'undertakers' build up a pro-Court group by the use of favours, and to promise what amounted to bribes. Clarendon regarded this as a breach of the principle of free parliaments. Acting on the King's instructions, however, Bennet, Clifford and Coventry built up a King's party and succeeded in getting royal measures through Parliament. It was now clear that Clarendon had lost control and that he was isolated. He was seen as an obstacle to promotion by ambitious younger men, he was detested by the King's favourites and mistresses and he was obviously ineffective. Paradoxically, it was as scapegoat for the unsuccessful Dutch War, a war which Clarendon had not wanted, that he met his (political) end. His decision to lay up part of the fleet as a preliminary to peace had made possible the successful Dutch attack on the naval base at Chatham. The Dutch sailed their navy up the Medway and destroyed many English ships. Their most humiliating act from the English point of view was their capture of the flagship, the *Royal Charles*. In the angry session of Parliament which followed, Charles was forced to dismiss Clarendon from office. An attempt by his enemies to follow his fall by his execution caused him to flee into exile.

The Cabal

Between 1667 and 1673 Charles followed a pro-Catholic policy both at home and abroad. He ruled with the assistance of the Cabal, a group of ministers, the initials of whose surnames or titles spelled the word— Clifford, Arlington, Buckingham, Ashley Cooper and Lauderdale. Though they were his appointees and his alone, Charles did not make them into a united team. He consulted them individually and conducted his foreign policy himself, sometimes without informing the ministers of the agreements he had made.

The essential features of Charles II's policies—religious toleration at home and the French alliance abroad—were closely associated. The Treaty of Dover signed between Charles II and Louis XIV in June

1670 committed Charles to a war with the Dutch and the grant of toleration to the English Catholics, in return for a French pension of £150 000 a year. When the time was right, Charles was to declare himself a Catholic and Louis was to send him 6000 soldiers to suppress any opposition. Except for the war clause, all of the Treaty was secret, not only from Parliament, but also from all the ministers except Clifford and Arlington. That the subsidy and promise of troops was intended to help Charles at the expense of Parliament and the Anglican ruling class is self-evident, but there were more subtle connections as well. By defeating the Dutch, Charles hoped to open to English merchants a large part of the trade held by the Dutch. Indirect taxation would then rise and lessen his dependence on Parliament. It might also be expected to increase the relative importance of city merchants and financiers, thus creating a rival social base for political power to that of the Anglican landowners.

Charles II was defeated both at home and abroad. The Dutch turned back the invading armies and organised a powerful coalition. Charles's foreign policy had gained him no quick victory, but rather entry into a long war. At home, Charles issued the Declaration of Indulgence in 1672, suspending the penal laws against both Protestant dissenters and Roman Catholics. This use of the suspending power was both constitutionally dubious and politically unwise. The power to suspend the operation of a law was a debatable part of the King's prerogative which, if it was accepted at all, was understood to allow him only to suspend a law in an emergency: for example, a law prohibiting the importation of grain could be suspended during time of famine. There was almost total repugnance to the idea that the King could thwart the clear intention of a statute by suspending it, simply because it was contrary to his policies.

When Parliament met in 1673, it voted £1 200 000 for the war, but forced Charles to withdraw the Declaration of Indulgence. The Declaration had been an obvious attempt to extend the power of the Crown by exploiting an ill-defined area of the constitution. Parliament's reply to this underhand form of constitutional aggression by the King was a frontal assault on his power to appoint whomsoever he chose as ministers. The Test Act of 1673 required all holders of public office to receive communion in the Anglican Church, to take the oath of supremacy and to condemn the doctrine of transubstantiation. As Roman Catholics would refuse to do this, the King was unable to appoint them to office. This was a serious restriction on the royal prerogative.

The defeat of the policy of religious indulgence was followed by defeat in foreign policy. The Third Dutch War ended by the Treaty of Westminster in 1674. The war, which had cost England £6 000 000 to fight, had gained only £180 000 from the Dutch. The events of 1673 and 1674 constituted the heaviest and most humiliating defeats of Charles II's reign. He had challenged both Parliament and the Anglican ruling class and had failed. Perhaps he would be able to attain his ends more easily by working through Parliament and in alliance with the ruling class.

The rise of Danby

The parliamentary attack on Charles's policies in 1673–4 had been largely unco-ordinated and it lacked clear leaders. Likewise, the Cabal had not prepared any parliamentary defence. The King himself and Clifford, the minister most associated with his unpopular policies, had hoped to dispense with Parliament for the time being and had not seen any need to control it. If, however, royal policies were to be backed by Parliament, it was essential to cultivate a following within it. It is obvious that if the government was to build up a party in Parliament, those who opposed royal policies would find it necessary to do the same.

Following the collapse of the Cabal as a result of the Test Act (see also page 330), Thomas Osborne, Earl of Danby, became Charles's chief minister. His intention was to follow policies acceptable to the majority of the landed gentry and to organise a pro-government group in Parliament. He reconciled most of the ruling class by following pro-Anglican policies at home and by repudiating pro-French foreign policies. Danby's position was extremely complex. His pro-Anglican and anti-French policies were perfectly genuine, but they were not accepted by Charles and were openly opposed by his brother James and some of Danby's ministerial colleagues. He never had the full support of Charles, and he held his position only because of his ability as an administrator and a parliamentary manager. His position in Parliament was weakened because of rumours about the true royal policies which constantly came to the ears of members and he was frequently charged with supporting royal absolutism. This charge showed a misunderstanding of Danby's position. Once the King found a means of dispensing with Parliament, Danby's authority would become much weaker and, indeed, he himself could be dispensed with:

he probably would have been, in such circumstances, as Charles did not like him personally. Danby's alternative to outright absolutism was a managed Parliament. However, it needed to be reasonably strong in order to make important his own role as mediator between it and the Crown.

Danby became Lord Treasurer in July 1673 and, in the absence of strong competition, the King's chief minister by April 1675. A few months later, the King withdrew from the Dutch war under strong parliamentary pressure. Danby hoped that once peace was made, he could balance the budget by policies of honesty and economy, and gain support for a government which followed Protestant and anti-French policies. He also appealed to Anglican bigotry against dissenters by instigating a new wave of persecution.

In the parliamentary session which began in April 1675, Danby set out to weaken the parliamentary opposition to royal ministers by imposing on all M.P.s and government officials an oath not to attempt any alteration in the government of Church and State. Despite a long and heated debate, the Bill passed the Lords after seventeen days. Leadership of the opposition to it came from Shaftesbury, who led a counter-attack which included an unsuccessful attempt to impeach Danby. The Bill failed in the Commons largely because of a jurisdictional dispute between the two Houses. Danby knew that Louis had promised Charles an annual subsidy of £100 000 to enable him to dissolve Parliament in the next session, if it refused supply or pressed for anti-French policies. Dissolution would weaken or eliminate Danby's influence. He was determined to control the next session.

Before Parliament met again, Danby encouraged Court supporters to attend Parliament early, worked on M.P.s through patrons, built up the number of government pensioners, transferred the payment of compensation to former excise farmers into the control of the ministers, and increased the use made of secret service funds to bribe members. These methods did build up support for the Court, but they provoked an equal, and opposite, response from the country opposition. Until the dissolution of the Cavalier Parliament, there was a constant and close battle in Parliament between Danby's Court party and the country party led by Shaftesbury. It was Louis XIV who funded some of Danby's most bitter opponents, in the hope that the more extreme country party members would make unworkable Danby's policy of managing Parliament and force Charles to dissolve it and rule as a dependent of France. Nevertheless, Danby succeeded in leading a reasonably successful government until 1678.

Despite its temporary success, Danby's policy of governing through a Court party in Parliament was to fail in the end. He had pursued two overriding objectives: first, to make government possible, and, second, to keep his own power. In order to do so, he had deliberately followed policies which he believed acceptable to the Anglican ruling class. He believed that once this class had no grounds in principle for opposing the government, it should be possible to use official influence to ensure that he had a permanent core of supporters in Parliament. There is no doubt, however, that he hoped to make government stronger and more authoritarian by these means. If he failed to gain the necessary co-operation of Parliament, he was prepared to dispense with it and rule with the backing of an army. For reasons outlined above, this was never his first choice.

Danby's failure in 1678 resulted from a number of factors. In the first place, he did not have the support of the King for his policies. He was always conscious that he could be dismissed at any time, especially as Charles did not like him personally, and there were always rivals for his position. Secondly, the King's secret negotiations with France could not be kept totally unsuspected. Rumours of them constantly leaked out and created an atmosphere of doubt and uncertainty. Thirdly, the King's Declarations of Indulgence in 1663 and 1672, as well as the leaks about his secret policies, created a fear of Catholicism which was intensified when James's conversion to Catholicism became generally known in the early 1670s. Finally, Danby's methods of parliamentary management worked only in a Parliament of long duration, something which was recognised by the opposition in their constant demands for a dissolution. When elections came, the tactics by which Danby had secured support in Parliament would reduce the likelihood of his parliamentary friends being re-elected.

The fall of Danby and the dissolution of the Cavalier Parliament were to follow from one of the most unsavoury episodes in English history, the so-called Popish Plot. In August 1678, two disreputable adventurers, Titus Oates and Israel Tonge, announced that they had unearthed a popish plot to murder Protestants, introduce a Catholic army from the Continent, burn London again and place James on the throne. Such absurd charges were commonplace and were usually given only a cursory examination by the authorities. In this case, however, two unfortunate accidents encouraged belief. One was the sudden death of Sir Edmund Berry Godfrey, the magistrate before whom the information had been laid. He was found impaled on his own sword and was generally believed to have been murdered by papists in order to suppress evidence. The second was the discovery that James's secretary, Edward Coleman, had been corresponding on English political matters with French Catholic leaders. In a country long unsettled by the news of the heir to the throne's conversion to Catholicism, this seeming corroboration of the plot brought about almost universal belief in its reality. More false witnesses came forward and thirty-five Catholics were executed.

On 1 November 1678 both Houses passed a unanimous resolution:

that there hath been, and still is, a damnable and hellish Plot, contrived and carried on by the Popish recusants, for the assassinating and murdering the King, and for subverting the government, and rooting out and destroying the Protestant religion.

In the panic which followed the publication of the Popish Plot, Danby fell from power and was impeached. At last Charles was forced to dissolve Parliament and call new elections.

Exclusion and the rise of party

Such fears led to the demand that James and other Catholics be excluded from the throne. Charles hoped to deflect the demands for Exclusion by offering to agree to a Limitation Bill, which would have placed restrictions on the powers of any Catholic king; in particular, by denying him any power over the Church of England. The Bill of Limitations diverted very few adherents of Exclusion: most saw it as an inadequate safeguard against James, who could not be trusted. As a Catholic he could, Protestants thought, repudiate any agreement, even any oath, with a clear conscience, if to do so would further his religion. Statute would be helpless to restrain him. Once King, he could throw aside any restrictions on his powers as Henry VII had done in 1485. Alternatively, he could use the suspending and dispensing powers to nullify inconvenient restrictions.

A more drastic variation on the theme of limitations was that of regency. This policy was advocated by some of the Duke of Monmouth's supporters (Charles's illegitimate son), as it provided a possible way to make him effective Head of Government. The weakness of the regency plan was that it might create the embarrassing spectacle of the English King fighting, with Continental backing, against troops of a Regent who was acting in his name.

There were important tactical reasons for the policy of Exclusion. Those who had angered James by opposing him could protect themselves against revenge only by taking the strongest possible steps to see that he never came to the throne. Finally, the Exclusion Bill had the advantage of being short and easily comprehensible. It could not be misunderstood and it could not be stalled by lengthy debates on each of a large number of complex clauses. Exclusion, it seemed, was the only safe policy. But Exclusion was also a very radical measure. It represented a move by Parliament to alter hereditary succession. It was a claim that the King must be acceptable to the political nation, and in this it cut across contemporary assumptions about the hierarchical nature of society and the God-given character of monarchical authority. Only fears such as those aroused by Catholicism could have produced such a revolution in thinking only twenty years after the Restoration.

The struggle for and against Exclusion was of such magnitude that it produced new tactics and new methods of political organisation. The Exclusion Crisis is usually, and correctly, seen as a parliamentary struggle. It was, however, far more than just a tactical conflict of competing factions at Westminster. The struggle for and against Exclusion centred on the gaining of a majority in each House of Parliament, and on persuading or pressuring the King to agree to the Bill. Both the attempts to gain a majority in the Commons, and to force the King to agree to Exclusion, resulted in a major split within the political nation.

The Exclusion Crisis brought the electorate back as an important part of the political scene. During 1679 and 1681, elections were to have an importance which had been denied them by the duration of the Cavalier Parliament and which, in any case, they had rarely possessed before. Especially in the autumn election of 1679, the issue of Exclusion dominated the electoral process, with local issues playing only a minor role. Whig writers asked voters to put national politics before local issues or ties to friends and kinsmen. To do so was a reversal of the whole pattern of the past. The Whig Press held up, as examples to be followed, the actions of the freeholders in Buckinghamshire and Essex in resisting the pressures of the Tory gentry and clergy to vote for their nominees. This had been a significant step for the freeholders to take. Many of the tenants who possessed sufficient freehold to qualify for the vote were 'plumpers', using both votes (in two-member constituencies) as directed by their landlord. Others customarily cast one for the candidate favoured by the squire, the other at their own discretion. For tenants to use both votes against the express wishes of their landlord was an act of social insubordination which panicked many gentlemen into thinking that a revolution was at hand. In fact, this breach of custom was encouraged by leading Whig peers, who visited the hustings to weigh their influence against that of the Tory clergy and gentry.

The press campaign was made possible by the lapsing in 1679 of the first Licensing Act, which had imposed censorship controls. Both sides were now free to appeal to the political nation. Not only journalistic 'hacks' (the term dates from this period and refers to the custom of less successful journalists of living in cheap lodgings at Smithfield among the butchers or 'hacks'), but writers of such note as Andrew Marvel and John Dryden, engaged in writing vituperative political propaganda. The latter's assault on Shaftesbury in 'Absalom and Achitophel' is a masterpiece of character assassination.

Associated with the press campaign was the rise of petitioning. Petitions to the King begged him to accept the policy of Exclusion. They served a two-fold purpose: first, to act as propaganda to the nation as a whole and gain further support for the movement by persuading waverers that Exclusion was inevitable and that they would be well-advised to join the winning side, and, second, to convince Charles that in granting Exclusion he would be bowing to the wishes of the nation. These petitions were, however, challenged by counter-petitions known as abhorrences which expressed revulsion at any change in the succession.

In London, a further mobilisation of popular exclusionist sentiment was made by the Green Ribbon Club, which made the annual bonfires and Pope burnings on 5 and 17 November (Guy Fawkes Day and the anniversary of the accession of Elizabeth I—the first commemorates the unsuccessful attempt of Roman Catholic conspirators to blow up James I's Parliament while he was opening the second session on 5 November 1605) into massive demonstrations in favour of Exclusion. Violence was not part of Shaftesbury's plan of action, nor of that of most of his followers. His campaign focused entirely on Parliament, elections and persuasion of the King. However, after the failure of their object, a few of his party turned to violence: notably the Rye House Plot to murder Charles and James on their way back from Newmarket in 1683, and the western rising under Monmouth in 1685.

The tactics of the campaign are probably less significant than the development of the party organisation which put them into effect. Nothing like the parliamentary parties of 1679–81 had ever existed before, and it is important to remember that party was, at this time, a term of abuse. Both sides declared the other to be a party, but denied being one itself. Despite the importance of party, some prominent politicians succeeded in remaining aloof. One of the most prominent men who did so was Lord Halifax, 'the Trimmer' (that is, one who maintains the 'trim' or balance of the ship of State). He was determined to prevent either side gaining an exclusive hold on power.

The Whigs stood for Exclusion and all their activities centred around this cause. Their leader, the Earl of Shaftesbury, indicated that all other problems could be solved once this goal was achieved. More generally, the Whigs had inherited the policies of Danby's opponents. These included greater individual freedom, for example, habeas corpus (which was the right to be charged in court with a specific offence known to law if one had been arrested, and making illegal indefinite imprisonment by government order, a tactic sometimes resorted to in the past to suppress political rivals); opposition to electoral malpractices; a broad interpretation of the franchise; frequent parliamentary elections and regular parliamentary sessions. The Whigs were anti-Catholic because they believed that Catholicism and arbitrary government were associated inseparably, but they were willing to offer at least partial toleration to Protestant dissenters. They were opposed to standing armies as a danger to liberty. In short, the Whigs were associated with mildly liberal and anti-authoritarian views. There was, however, no unanimity among them on any policy except Exclusion, something which reflects their mixed social origins.

The Whig leaders were aristocrats, such as Shaftesbury, and greater country gentlemen. They were supported by wealthy London merchants, probably by a majority in the City. They had the support of townsmen, something which reflected both dissenter influence in urban centres, and resentment in the boroughs at interference in their affairs by Tory gentlemen. In the counties, the most solid source of Whig support was freeholders below the rank of gentlemen. It is important, however, not to see the Whigs as a mainly lower class group, despite their undoubted appeal to those who lay in the lower ranks of the political nation. The Whigs were reputed to have the best horses and they controlled the race course at Newmarket.

The Whigs were known as petitioners at first, from the petitions they organised in favour of Exclusion. But their enemies' identification of them with dissent and rebellion resulted in their being given the name 'whiggamores', after the Presbyterian rebels of south-western Scotland, the name which in its shortened form was to be that of a political party until the nineteenth century. Contemporary satirists emphasised the links between the Whigs and the more fanatical sectaries. 'These Geneva Whigs', wrote one, 'are demure, conscientious, prick-eared vermin' and Judge Jeffreys referred to Whigs as 'snivelling saints'. According to another writer, everything a Whig said was emphasised by a 'zealous twang of his nose' and he opposed everything commanded 'for no other reason than that it was commanded'.

His prayer is a rhapsody of holy hickops, sanctified barkings, illuminated goggles, sighs, sobs, yexes, gasps and groans. He prays for the King, but with more distinctions and mental reservations than an honest man would have in taking the covenant.

The Tory party rose in response to the policies and methods of the Whigs: their aim was to stop Exclusion. Committed to the principle of Cavalier loyalty, they were determined to end this campaign, which they believed would lead to rebellion and civil war: 'Forty-one is here again' was a favourite slogan. They claimed to be the 'soundest part of the nation' and there can be little doubt that they constituted the greater part of the landed gentry. Their particular principle was loyalty to the Anglican Church which, they believed, was not only the teacher of true religion, but an effective shield against both papist absolutism and dissenter rebellion.

The Tories were noted for rather anti-intellectual views. Many condemned the growth of free schools, where boys remained until they were sixteen or seventeen and were then fit only for an 'idle trade' or, worse still, to go on to university. In popular stereotype, all good Tories were beer drinkers, while many Whigs preferred coffee, something which explains the antithesis of 'plotting ' and 'sotting' in the following rhyme:

And better it is to honestly sotting
Than live to be hanged for caballing and plotting.

A Whig tract described a Tory in the following terms:

A Tory is a monster with an English face, a French heart and an Irish conscience. A creature of a large forehead, prodigious mouth, supple hams and no brains. They are a sort of wild boars, that would root out the constitution . . . that with dark lanthorn policies would at once blow up the two bulwarks of our freedom, Parliaments and Juries; making the first only a Parliament of Paris, and the latter but mere tools to echo back the pleasure of the judge. They are so certain that monarchy is *jure divino*, that they look upon all people living under Aristocracys or Democracys to be in a state of damnation; and fancy that the Grand Seignor, the Czar of Muscovy and the French King dropt down from Heaven with crowns on their heads, and that all their subjects were born with saddles on their backs.

Why did Exclusion fail?

Some historians have seen the defeat of the Exclusion movement as a defeat of Parliament, or as evidence that the King was more powerful than the Commons. This conclusion can be upheld only in a narrow, technical and institutional sense. The collapse of Exclusion marked the failure of a well-organised majority in the Commons, which was probably not representative of the political nation, by the King and the Tories. It was not the King alone who defeated the first Whigs, but a growing movement within the political nation.

In the narrower arena of Westminster, and of Oxford in 1681, the defeat can be explained partly, even mainly, in terms of constitutional powers. Indeed, the King's power to dissolve, summon, and prorogue Parliament was used to great effect. Each of the Exclusion parliaments was dissolved when the pressures became too great for the King to cope with them in any other way. The calling of the third Exclusion Parliament at Oxford denied the Whigs massive demonstrations of support from the London crowds. It is important to remember, however, that the Whigs never had a majority in Parliament, only in the Commons. Charles was never put in the position of having to veto an Exclusion Bill which had passed both Houses.

Had the Exclusion Movement been representative of the vast majority of the nation, it is probable that it would have succeeded, though perhaps only after a civil war. If fear of Catholics was responsible for the origin of the Exclusionist cause, then terror of civil war determined the course of the conflict. The majority of the aristocracy and gentry believed that the English were prone to civil war and they had a cyclical view of history, believing that events occured in ever repeating patterns. They knew how much they had to lose if civil war broke out again.

It is, of course, true that it takes two to fight. Total unity in the cause of Exclusion would certainly have avoided war; as would destroying the Exclusion Movement. In 1681 there were two factors preventing a bloodless rebellion in favour of Exclusion. Firstly, the King controlled a standing army and a militia which was generally believed loyal to him. If such forces could be defeated at all, it would involve realisation of the gentry's worst fear, a protracted war. Secondly, fear of civil war had created a situation in which the majority of the political nation had turned against Shaftesbury's methods and his objective. The case for Exclusion was based on the dangers of a Catholic King. These were, however, in the future and uncertain.

Charles might outlive James; if James succeeded he might not be a tyrant. In any case, the next in line of succession, James's daughter Mary, was a Protestant. The Exclusion Movement created an immediate danger which, in the eyes of the Tories, took precedence over hypothetical problems in the future. Once the Exclusion Movement created a reaction, the King was able to use his prerogative powers to strengthen and reward the Tories.

Finally, one must consider the role played by Charles himself. J.R. Jones stresses his importance. Not only did he encourage the emerging Tories to adopt the same electoral techniques and propaganda methods as their opponents, but he made correct decisions on tactics. Jones concludes:

in the last resort the defeat was Charles's achievement. Throughout the crisis his judgement was almost faultless. In 1679 he rejected advice from Danby and James that he should refuse to make any concessions and suppress the opposition, a course of action which would have infallibly caused a new civil war. Instead he tricked Shaftesbury by giving him the false hope of being eventually converted to Exclusion [and] ... waited until it was safe to use his prerogative powers. Only when the time was ripe did he put an end to the quite unprecedented dependence [on Parliament] that had existed since 1660. (Jones, 1978, pages 215–6.)

In contrast, John Miller states 'Charles II is often credited with great political skill in handling the Exclusion crisis, but I suspect that such credit is undeserved.' He claims that Charles was frequently irresolute and that he did not see, until after James did, that he must throw all his resources behind the Tories if Exclusion was to be avoided. Only after the failure of the Oxford Parliament in March 1681, did he realise that compromise was impossible. Charles, Miller claims, won the conflict because of good luck and the inherent strength of his position (J. Miller, *James II, a Study in Kingship*, Hove, 1978, page 94).

Perhaps the truth lies somewhere between the two. Charles did have a strong position, in terms of both constitutional authority and popular fears, and he was lucky that neither Scotland nor Ireland rose in revolt. He may have considered surrender. On the other hand, his actions, if not his thoughts and private conversations, were consistently resolute and, in the event, well advised. It was the combination of the man and the powers available to him which defeated Exclusion.

The Tory triumph, 1681–6

The failure of the Exclusion Movement left Charles in a very strong position. He was in close alliance with a powerful section of the ruling class. His opponents were discredited and dispirited. Many were only too willing to acknowledge defeat and seek readmission to royal favour. Charles and the Tories set out to consolidate their position by using royal prerogative powers and the judiciary. Both King and Tory gentry considered this not as a work of revenge, but as an essential step to preserve national security. Even the King's failure to obey the Triennial Act was accepted by the Tory gentry.

The first move to secure the alliance of King and Tories against the Whigs was the prosecution of Shaftesbury for treason in 1681. He was saved by the elected Whig sheriffs of London and Middlesex who selected a Whig grand jury which refused to commit him for trial. This was a defensive victory, but Shaftesbury had to flee abroad to avoid renewed prosecution before a partisan Tory jury. He died in Amsterdam in 1683. In the same year the Rye House Plot, a plan by a few fringe Whigs to assassinate Charles and James, allowed the government, thanks to perjured witnesses and the cooperation of the Chief Justice, Jeffreys, to execute not only the plotters, led by Lord Russell, but other prominent Whigs. Another group of leading Whigs was forced into exile. The Rye House Plot further discredited the Whigs as subversives in the eyes of the country.

Charles and the Tories set out to ensure that the Whigs lost their urban power base. Fifty-one corporation charters were called in by the legal process of *quo warranto*. Cities and boroughs had to justify their claims to local self-government by submitting their charters (documents recording grants of self-government, which laid down their constitution). If any technical flaws could be discovered, and none were perfect, the charter was forfeit. Even London lost its charter and small centres voluntarily surrendered them when they were challenged, thus avoiding an expensive and vain defence. The new charters invariably strengthened the royal power to appoint officials or veto those who were elected. In most cases, the authority of the county magistrates in borough affairs was increased. There was also renewed persecution of the dissenters, a mainly urban group (see chapter 5, page 322).

When James II succeeded his brother in February 1685, all was calm. The majority of the political nation greeted his peaceful accession with relief. Civil war had been avoided. Both the new King and the Tories were, however, afraid of what would happen when Parliament met. Though there had been no session of Parliament since 1681, the conflicts and the Whig dominance of the Commons in the Exclusion parliaments were a horrifying thought to King and Tories alike. A new Parliament was, however, essential: the revenues voted to Charles II lapsed at his death. James hurriedly recalled and revised forty-seven charters in an attempt to ensure that the boroughs did not elect Whigs. This last minute safeguard was scarcely necessary. Only about forty former Whig M.P.s, and perhaps twenty who had been Whig supporters from outside the House, were elected. Of 195 members elected by boroughs with remodelled charters, only nine were Whigs.

In the counties, the Tory gentry united to ensure that they agreed on sound Tories as candidates. Where there was significant Whig strength in a county, it was often circumvented by the electoral tricks of Tory sheriffs. With this combination of popular support and electoral organisation, it is scarcely surprising that James's Parliament was so overwhelmingly Tory. It had no sooner met than it was driven even closer to the King by Monmouth's rising in the south-west (June 1685). Though it was quickly suppressed, the rising created genuine horror: the spectre of civil war had risen again. In the aftermath, Parliament voted James II such generous permanent revenue that he had no financial need to call it again (see chapter 3, pages 188–9). A Bill of Attainder was rushed through Parliament and used to execute Monmouth without trial. The prosecution—one might say persecution—of former Exclusionist leaders was revived.

The success with which James had met in the first year of his reign convinced him that he had the power to further the project dearest to his heart, the removal of political disabilities on Catholics. James believed that the destruction of the first Whigs had left a political nation of Tories, who really accepted the sermons of their clergy about the necessity of non-resistance to Kings. He thought that Tory claims of loyalty were unconditional. He did not see that they depended on two unspoken assumptions: that he would continue to protect the interests of the Anglican Church, and of the landed gentry. James also over-estimated the importance of electoral techniques. These were very effective in eliminating a weak opposition, when the majority of the political nation was on his side. The Whigs had shown the usefulness of such techniques to a large and well-organised minority. Their effectiveness in support of policies which were detested by the vast majority had never been put to the test. Finally, James greatly over-estimated the strength of Catholicism. Like many fearful Protestants, he believed that there were vast numbers of secret Catholics, and that there were many more waverers who would be convinced of the Truth once they could hear it from the lips of a Catholic priest.

This does not mean one must accept the view of Whig historians that James intended to convert England to Catholicism and arbitrary government based on that of France. When examined rationally, the whole idea is ridiculous. The two per cent of the English population which was Catholic could not persecute the rest into Catholicism, even if the secret Catholics and the expected converts expanded the number five-fold. James had an army of no more than 20 000, in which the proportion of Catholic officers never exceeded an eighth. Until 1688, his heir was the Protestant daughter of his first marriage, Mary. In 1685, James was fifty-one: he and his second wife had been married for eleven years, and although she was still in her twenties, her almost constant pregnancies had resulted only in a succession of miscarriages and babies dead at, or soon after, birth. The chances of a healthy male heir seemed slim. James's objective was only to save Catholics from persecution and to make them eligible for public office on the same terms as other Englishmen. He believed that he could, within his lifetime, give Catholics such an established position in English society that it could not be denied them in the future. In the longer run, he believed, Englishmen would be voluntarily converted when they became aware of the undoubted superiority of the one true faith.

James received an early warning that he would be faced with strenuous opposition. In the second session of his Parliament, which met again in November 1685, he requested funds for a standing army in which there would be Catholic officers. The so-loyal Parliament which had welcomed James showed unexpected opposition—opposition led by men who had been staunch in the battle against Exclusion. Funds for the army were eventually voted but, in both Lords and Commons, there was consistent and organised opposition to the appointment of Catholic officers. A committee of the Lords took the lead in co-ordinating the activities of the two Houses. James was infuriated. He prorogued Parliament in November. It was never to meet again.

James intended to persuade and coerce the Tories into accepting his pro-Catholic policies, while using his prerogative powers and his control over the judges to attain his short-term ends. In 1686 he began the policy of closeting M.P.s and peers: that is, having private meetings with them in an attempt to persuade them to agree to the repeal of the Test Act and the other anti-Catholic laws. Those who did not agree were dismissed from their offices. However, pressure on M.P.s and peers, even if successful, could not change the law until Parliament met again. James did not want to wait. In November 1685 he used his dispensing power and appointed Catholics to positions they were ineligible to hold under the Test Act, and he took steps to stop the collection of recusancy fines. In June 1686 this use of the dispensing power was declared legal in the collusive action of Godden *v.* Hales. Catholics were appointed to other offices, and those who refused to agree that James had the right to appoint them were dismissed. James's attempt to control the Church by establishing the Court of Ecclesiastical Commission was openly opposed by most bishops and clergymen. By the end of 1686, it was clear that the alliance between James and the Tory gentry was at an end.

The road to revolution

James was determined to attain his ends regardless of the opposition of the Tories. This involved three major steps. The first was simply a continuation of what he had been doing in 1685–6: the use of his prerogative and the law courts to free Catholics from the operation of the penal laws. Secondly, he set out to undermine the local power of the Tory gentry by dismissing them from office and replacing them with men, often Catholics or dissenters, who would support his policies. This aspect of his policy belongs to the 'Problems of government' (chapter 3) section of this book, but it must be mentioned here as a companion policy to his third major campaign, the attempt to create a parliamentary majority from the dissenters, Catholics and former Whigs. James's policy was to transfer political power from the Tory gentry, who made up the traditional ruling class, to the townsmen and freeholders. This was a revolutionary step, perhaps as radical as any of the Interregnum constitutional schemes. Like them, it was a revolution from the top. The ending of the Tory gentry's virtual monopoly of power may be seen as a move towards democracy, but that was not James's intention. His desire was to entrench in power men who owed their position to him and who were not steeped in the traditions of Parliament. It was, in short, an attempt to establish absolutism.

The details of James's Catholicising policy require only passing mention in this chapter: they included the appointment of Catholic army officers and civilian officials, the encouragement of leading statesmen to convert to Catholicism and the dismissal of those who, like Rochester, refused. Clergymen who converted to Rome were allowed to keep their Anglican Church incomes and Magdalen

College, Oxford, was turned into a Roman Catholic institution. The penal laws against Catholic and dissenters were negated by the use of the dispensing power. Finally, in 1687, the Declaration of Indulgence gave a blanket exemption from penalties and restrictions to Catholics and Protestant dissenters alike. There was a clear challenge to Parliament in all these actions. If the King could thwart the obvious intention of Parliament by either massive use of the dispensing power, or by the administratively simpler process of suspension, parliamentary statutes were in force only at the will of the King. A packed Parliament was even worse—it would give royal absolutism a constitutional form.

In 1688 James began extensive preparations for his next Parliament, intended to meet in October. His object was to pack it with Catholics, dissenters, and those Anglicans who accepted toleration. His first step was to have agents organise addresses in support of his Declaration of Indulgence. These addresses were issued mainly by corporations where dissent was strong. His second step was to undertake a systematic purge of local officials. In the third phase, a further remodelling of charters was carried out. A considerable number were recalled, this time to remove the Tory influence which had been strengthened since 1681.

In 1688 the Tories were almost totally united against James's policies. The dissenters were divided: some, like William Penn, believed that James's call for toleration was sincere, and others that it was merely a front for the furthering of Catholicism and that the dissenters would be abandoned once his objective had been achieved. Once more, French precedents encouraged distrust of James. The rest of the Whig party were divided also. At first some were only too happy to see their Tory rivals humiliated, but gradually the majority came around to their old view that James's change of political alliances was merely another way of establishing Catholicism and absolutism. There can be no certainty about the result of the election planned for 1688.

Three factors were to bring the crisis to a head. The first was the Seven Bishops' Case. Seven bishops who had refused the King's order to have the Declaration of Indulgence read from the pulpit, and had published their reasons for doing so, were tried for libel. They were acquitted. This apparent attack on the Anglican Church aroused the worst fears of popery. The second critical change was the birth of a healthy son to James and the Queen, an event which completely transformed the situation. James was a middle-aged man with indifferent health. Many opponents were willing to accept his policies in the belief that they would be reversed under his Protestant successor. His son, however, would now displace the Protestant heirs, Mary and Anne, in the succession. He would be brought up a Catholic and England could be faced with a line of Catholic kings. Policies which could be tolerated when there was a foreseeable end to them were at once regarded as an intolerable burden. The third factor was provided by William of Orange. Though he had long played a role in English affairs, he was not interested in them for their own sake. Rather he wanted to make use of England in the long struggle by the Dutch against the French. William believed, until the birth of James's male heir, that he had only to wait for the throne to pass to his wife, Mary, in the normal course of events.

Realising that William's English ambitions now seemed as desperate as their own hopes of a Protestant successor, seven leading men wrote to William and invited him to invade England, in order to protect Protestantism and political liberty. William accepted the invitation and in late October the 'Protestant wind' (an easterly) brought his fleet and his army safely to the west of England. West countrymen detested James for his bloody revenge after Monmouth's rising and they flocked to William. There were risings in Cheshire and Nottinghamshire. In Yorkshire the former leader of the Court Party and strong opponent of Exclusion, Danby, led the revolt against James. Finally, William's success was made certain when John Churchill, the future Duke of Marlborough, and most of the English army, changed sides. James fled, was caught and taken back to London, only to escape a second time and make his way to France.

The speed of James's fall resulted, paradoxically, from exactly the same consideration which had led to the shattering defeat of Exclusion—fear of civil war. In 1681 waverers among the gentry had swung behind the Tories to prevent the minority of the political nation from plunging the nation into war. In 1688 they sensed that the situation had changed. The opposition were in the majority and they were determined to have their way. To support the government was to vote for civil war. Once William had invaded, the die was cast. Only the destruction of James's government could prevent civil war.

The Revolution of 1688 has often be seen as the 'Whig Revolution', as the 'Bloodless Revolution', and as a victory of Parliament over the King. It was none of these things: rather, it was made by Whigs and Tories alike. If Whig theories could justify the deposition of kings for breaking their implicit contract with the nation, these theoretical considerations were still largely unpublished and, in any case, were given scant consideration by the practical and pragmatic statesmen who made the Revolution. True, the Revolution was bloodless in England; but it was far from that in Scotland and Ireland. Neither can it be seen as a victory of Parliament, as an institution, over the monarchy. Parliament was not in session and James's careful preparations for its next meeting might well have gained him the sort of Parliament, or at any rate, the sort of Commons, he wanted.

The 1688 Revolution was a victory of the governing class over a government which had isolated itself from the mainstream of the nation. In future, both King and Parliament would have to reflect the views of that class on the fundamental issues over which it was united.

The Bill of Rights

The basis of the Revolution Settlement was established by the Convention Parliament, a body summoned by a group of nobles in the same way that normal parliaments were called. It differed only in that the writs were not issued by the King. Its first and most important session was the three weeks sitting in February 1689. It performed two main tasks. It passed the Bill or Declaration of Rights and, after a long debate, it offered the Crown to William and Mary jointly, with William exercising all executive authority.

The Bill of Rights was not a sweeping or innovative constitutional document, nor was it one which settled in detail all the points in conflict between Crown and Parliament. It was certainly not a statement of Whig political theory. Rather it was a list of grievances against James II's government, which members of the Convention had found intolerable, together with practical measures to ensure that no future King erred in the same way. No more could be expected. Members of the Convention Parliament were still Whigs and Tories, men who had been and were to be in future bitter political opponents. The Bill of Rights was the lowest common denominator of their agreement and a set of rules within which future political conflicts would be fought.

The Bill of Rights gives the impression that it strengthened the power of Parliament against the King. It certainly condemned the abuse of prerogative powers: the suspending power was prohibited altogether, and the dispensing power 'as it hath been exercised of late'; no standing army was to be kept without the consent of Parliament; the Court of Ecclesiastical Commission was abolished and there were provisions against cruel and unusual punishments. Parliament was to meet frequently and elections were to be free. All these provisions restricted the power of the King to rule arbitrarily, and they also provided a means by which Parliament could be made accountable to the electorate.

It was not, however, a means of constitutional aggression against monarchical power. Despite the desire of some Whigs to extend the power of Parliament at the expense of the King, the majority of the Convention Parliament wanted only a defensive victory: a specific statement defining the relationship between Crown and Parliament and making explicit those restrictions on royal power which they believed had been understood in 1660. The consensus of the Convention Parliament was to condemn constitutional aggression by James II and to ensure that future kings accepted their understanding of the constitution . In any case, a significant alteration of the balance of constitutional authority in favour of Parliament would have been bitterly resented by the new king. He had accepted very real risks in invading England and he had done so in order to make England part of his alliance system against France, not to strengthen the power of Parliament. No one who had studied William, and indeed the whole House of Orange's history of conflict with the popular movements in the Netherlands, could have made the mistake of thinking that William would voluntarily relinquish any significant part of the royal prerogative.

It could hardly be expected that this hasty justification of rebellion would solve all England's constitutional problems. It did not. The 'balanced' constitution of the eighteenth century, which, at least in its idealised form, represented a clear balance of power and a system of checks and balances, took several more years to emerge. (It was this eighteenth century constitutional ideal which was adapted to the needs of a federal republic by the newly independent United States.) The 1688 Revolution left the King as head of government. He appointed all ministers, he commanded all the armed forces in the kingdom and foreign affairs were his sole prerogative. Subject only to the provisions of the Triennial Act, he could still summon, dissolve and prorogue Parliament. He was still the fount of honour, able to appoint to the peerage and promote within it at his sole discretion. William created twenty-seven temporal peers and promoted sixteen: by the end of his reign thirty-six of 162 lay peers owed their present titles to him. He named twenty-one bishops, including fourteen in 1689–91. In addition, he transferred five of his appointees and two pre-Revolution bishops to richer sees. By 1702, eighteen of the twenty-six bishops were William's nominees.

There was no restriction on favouring foreigners, though he was to be much criticised for the honours and material rewards he bestowed on Dutchmen. Virtually the only part of the Settlement which specifically strengthened the powers of Parliament in relation to the King was the Coronation Oath Act, which required William and Mary to swear they would respect the laws made by Parliament.

Further changes to the constitution owed much to war. England was to be at war with France for almost all of William's reign. The first consequence of this was the government's need for money. William was granted a permanent revenue of £7 000 000, but this was sufficient only to meet the cost of civil government and a peacetime military establishment. During this war William's army expanded from 8000 to over 88 000, and its cost rose to over £2 500 000 a year. This vast sum required frequent meetings of Parliament to vote taxes. It was the financial need created by war which established the custom of annual sessions of Parliament. Under William, the longest period during which no Parliament met was ten months.

Parallel with the growth in the frequency of parliaments was the development of a much larger and more efficiently organised bureaucracy. As Parliament was not inclined to trust this extension of executive power, the custom of appropriating funds for particular purposes became the norm. From 1690 a committee of the House of Commons examined accounts to ensure that the terms of the appropriating Act had been observed and that the funds had been spent without dishonesty, waste or inefficiency. As a result, M.P.s gained considerable administrative skill. Though many M.P.s remained 'country' at heart, concerned only with the needs of their constituents and with keeping down taxation, many came to appreciate both the problems and the true cost of government.

One of the decisions William had to make at the beginning of his reign, and from time to time thereafter, was the extent to which party considerations should influence his choice of ministers. The temporary unity achieved against James lasted only until the immediate objective had been attained. The Whigs felt that it was they and their principles which had brought William to the throne. They expected a monopoly or near-monopoly of offices at first and they hoped to use their new power to gain a partisan revenge on the Tories who had persecuted them under James. The Tories, however, also expected at least a substantial share of office. They saw themselves as the natural party of government and representatives of the traditional ruling class.

William was determined to avoid giving a monopoly of power to either party. He followed a policy of 'trimming', of balancing factions. In fact, William had no reason to be tied to either party. He took almost as high a view of his prerogative as had his predecessors and he was unhappy with the Whigs, as he believed that they were near-republicans who wished to make him a mere 'Doge of Venice'. In addition, he was disgusted by their narrow and vengeful spirit. However, William overestimated their strength in 1689 and gave them a greater share of office than their support warranted, though a share which fell well short of their demands.

The Tories were supporters of strong government led by an effective monarchical power. For them, like William, good government, law and order took precedence over individual freedom and parliamentary debate. On the other hand, the Tories were lukewarm supporters of William. A considerable number had voted against his kingship in 1688. Some were secret Jacobites (that is, people who wished to bring James back to the throne) and many more were willing to accept William and Mary as only *de facto* sovereigns. This feeling was so strong that the loyalty oath was amended to allow the swearing of fidelity to William and Mary as sovereigns rather than as 'rightful and lawful sovereigns'. Perhaps the Earl of Sunderland, one of William's leading ministers, summed up the situation best when he said, 'it is very true that the Tories were better friends to monarchy than the Whigs were, but his majesty was to consider that he was not their monarch'. (Quoted in Lockyer, 1976, page 372.)

Mixed ministries had two main advantages: first, they avoided driving parties into total opposition and, second, they reduced the King's dependence on party. It should be remembered that even in the 'rage of parties' in the 1690s, 'party' was still a pejorative term, a synonym for faction. As E.L. Ellis has written:

Party activity in the late seventeenth century was like sin, universally condemned and widely indulged; it remained almost as formally undefended as fornication and was usually denounced with the same vehemence. (Ellis in Holmes, 1969, page 119.)

In the conditions of the 1690s, it was very important to avoid driving the Tories into outright opposition. Had this happened, their Jacobite inclinations might have asserted themselves. Especially in 1690, when England was closer to defeat than at any other time in the series of wars against France that ended at Waterloo, a Jacobite rising, or even a Jacobite obstruction of government, could have brought an end to William's reign. It should be remembered, too, that the system of alternating party governments lay far in the future. The concept of His Majesty's loyal opposition was still inconceivable in the 1690s. Certainly the nation was used to a multitude of factions clamouring for office, but the few instances of fully polarised politics, such as the conflict between Essex and Cecil a century earlier, or that between the

Whigs and Tories at the time of the Exclusion Crisis, had led to violent rebellion, armed risings, executions, imprisonment and exile for the defeated party. Only a change in the conventions under which politics were conducted would allow the development of peaceful and non-lethal alternation of party governments.

For the King, there was a major disadvantage in party government. He would become dependent on a party. He did not wish to be 'King of the Whigs' or 'King of the Tories'. Single-party government would also deprive the King of a choice of ministers. In practice, however, William had to take party considerations into account in the formation of governments. In the long run, party government was to leave the monarch only as formal Head of State, with the leader of the party in power as the head of government.

A most important development in the 1690s was the increase in the amount of legislation handled by Parliament. Between 1689 and 1702, 809 bills were introduced, compared with 533 from 1660 to 1684, a period nearly twice as long. This is mainly a reflection of the increased time Parliament was sitting: fifty-three and a half months in twelve and a half years under William, and forty-one months in Charles II's twenty-four years as effective Head of State. The longer sittings reduced the pressure of business which had resulted in the failure of many Bills in the past. Under William, half the Bills initiated passed into law, a figure which was to improve to two-thirds under Anne. Perhaps, too, it was the greater availability of Parliament which made statutes rather than royal charter the most common means of establishing such institutions as major overseas trading companies after the Revolution.

Parliament expanded its constitutional authority by taking advantage of the King's financial needs. It was able to extend its influence over policy, even in foreign affairs. As discussed below, William could obtain support for the Grand Alliance and the renewal of the war after the Treaty of Ryswick only by allowing and encouraging free debate on foreign policy in Parliament and in the country as a whole. There was also a more direct assertion of the power of the purse in the tacking onto money Bills prohibitions: on the election to Parliament of holders of new revenue posts in 1694, excise officials in 1700 and customs officials in 1701.

Paradoxically, it was the much resented placemen (that is, holders of official government positions who were also members of Parliament) who were doing much to extend the links between Parliament and government. The country opposition saw only the opportunity for the government to influence the voting behaviour of its employees, not the significant role of these men in expressing the views of Parliament on the Privy Council and in government departments. In the 1690s many placemen were appointed precisely because of their standing in Parliament.

The party system in the 1690s

Despite the frequent use of party labels, historians are far from unanimous about their meaning and their importance. Nineteenth century writers generally assumed that the terms Whig and Tory meant much the same as they did in their own day. Party was believed to be the basis of political conflict. In the 1920s, however, there was a reaction against seeing the politics of the 1690s in purely party terms, and writers such as W. T. Morgan, K. Feiling and G. M. Trevelyan pointed out that other factors, such as the personal role of the monarch, Court-Country feeling and the looseness of party ties, had to be taken into account as well as party alignments. Party was, however, regarded as the most important factor in political life.

The idea that the Whig-Tory conflict dominated politics was challenged in 1941 and 1956 by R. Walcott who extended back into the 1690s the complex pattern of politics Sir Lewis Namier had discovered to exist at the accession of George III. In 1760, Namier found, the Whig-Tory dichotomy had to be discarded in favour of a scheme which recognised the existence of a group of politically minded men who fought the Whig-Tory battles, a substantial body of office-holders in Parliament who nearly always voted for the government of the day, and their opposites, the independent country gentlemen, who were generally to be found on the side of the opposition. Within all these categories, family and regional ties were of considerable importance. Walcott claimed he had discovered a similar pattern of politics in the 1690s. In his view, the most significant groups in William's parliaments were seven family connections.

Most recent research has not supported Walcott. The discovery of a number of voting lists unknown to Walcott, as well as the reinterpretation of familiar documents, has led present-day historians to adopt a position not very different from that of the 1920s. H. Horwitz has summed up the present historiographical position. He argues, first, that parties had an effective existence and that their rivalry was the prime factor in politics; second, that contemporary political conditions limited the role of the parties and distorted the conflict between Whigs and Tories; and, third, that the structure of parliamentary politics was fluid. He cites as evidence for the first conclusion the general consistency of voting patterns in the recently studied division lists, the way in which disputed elections were decided in the House of Commons on party political lines, the evidence that lords who appointed proxies to vote for them when they had to be absent from a division almost always nominated a member of the same party, and the way in which disputes between the two Houses usually reflected party conflict (Horwitz in Holmes, 1969, pages 96–114; Horwitz, *Parliament, Policy and Politics*, Manchester, 1977. For a contrary, though minority view, see D. Rubini, *Court and Country 1688–1702*, London, 1967, especially pages 259–78).

Three main factors limited the exclusive importance of party. The first was the existence of a substantial proportion of the Lords and a smaller proportion of the Commons who held offices of profit under the Crown. Such positions could be lost for opposition to Crown policies. Members who did not hold office were bitterly critical of those who did and were, regardless of party, likely to attack the government for corruption, administrative abuses, electoral irregularities and for undermining the independence of Parliament. Finally, neither party had a strong discipline and both were made up of shifting power groups, to which members might have a stronger loyalty than to the party as a whole.

The operation of party can be observed when one studies the makeup of William's ministries and the influence of parliamentary elections. In 1689–90 William had a mixed Whig-Tory ministry in which the Whigs had a rather greater share of office than their strength really warranted. They were, however, disappointed, as they believed that it was they who had brought William to power and that they should have had a monopoly or near-monopoly of office. In addition, they wished to use their position to gain revenge on the Tories for their sufferings between 1681 and 1688. In disgust, William called a new Parliament in 1690 and appointed a mixed ministry with a predominance of Tories, a balance which seems to have reflected that in Parliament. The leading minister in this government was Danby, now elevated to the earldom of Carmarthen. Despite the liberal use of place and pensions and the large number of officials elected, this ministry could not gain sufficient backing for the King's war policies. The war was going badly, especially on land, and there was considerable pressure to adopt a predominantly naval strategy and scale down the operations of the army on the Continent. The role of officials and pensioners was much resented in what was often known as the Officers' Parliament, and the government was faced with a succession of Bills demanding annual elections. A Triennial Bill passed both Houses, only to be vetoed by the King. It was clear that the Tory leaders were no more successful in delivering stable government acceptable to the Crown.

As a result of the Tory failure, William turned again to the Whigs and gradually increased the number of offices held by a group known as the Whig Junto, led by the Earl of Sunderland, together with Somers, Montague and Wharton. There was, however, a Whig predominance rather than a Whig monopoly. The 1695 election increased Whig strength in the Commons and there was considerable pressure on the King to hand over virtually all offices to them. In 1696 the discovery of a plot to assassinate William, led by Sir John Fenwick, precipitated a Whig scheme to weaken the Tories (who still had reservations about William's right to be King) by demanding that all office-holders join an association which required an oath to William as rightful sovereign. This backfired when Fenwick revealed that some of the Whig leaders had made secret contacts with James to ensure their safety if the war was lost or a Jacobite rebellion succeeded.

The revelations which came out of Fenwick's plot discredited both parties. In 1697 the Peace of Ryswick gave relief from war. These two factors combined to weaken the Whig and Tory following, and a succession of weak ministries followed, constantly under attack from a revived country party. The so-called new country party had as its leading spokesman Robert Harley, a former Whig. It is probably a misnomer to call it a party. It was a conglomeration of many groups: Whigs disappointed that the 1688 Settlement had not gone far enough, anti-war Tories, embittered former placemen, perennial critics of all government, and country gentlemen who simply wanted lower taxation. The opposition grew out of war weariness and dislike of William, as a foreigner, alien courtiers and Continental policies.

The country seized control of the Commons and pressed for policies diametrically opposed to those of the King. In particular, William regarded the Peace of Ryswick as a truce before the battle which would secure a favourable balance of power in Europe. To this end, William wished to retain in readiness a force of 20 000 men. The Commons would agree to only 7000. William was forced to send home his Dutch guards and disband to poverty in a foreign land the regiment of French Huguenot exiles who had served their adopted country so well. His Whig Junto ministers were attacked and they had no effective party backing. Several were expelled from office. The Commons introduced a Bill to force William's Dutch favourites to hand back the land they had been granted in Ireland. This was a personal humiliation to William and he dropped broad hints that he was considering abdication. By 1701 it was clear that effective government was impossible while the opposition dominated the Commons. William decided that he had no choice but to bring the opposition leaders into the government.

It was in 1701 that the Act of Settlement was passed. It is often regarded as a great constitutional statement, as a further refinement of the Bill of Rights. It strengthened the prohibition on a Catholic successor by specifying that the throne should pass on the death of Anne, should she die childless, to the descendants of James I's daughter Elizabeth, the so-called Winter Queen, who had married the Elector Palatine. Several members of Continental royal families in a more direct line of descent were passed over on account of religion. In addition to the omission of Catholics from the throne, any person married to a Catholic was also excluded.

Apart from this, however, the Act of Settlement was mainly a country catalogue of protest against William's government practices since 1689. A much more direct attack on William's methods was made in the Place Act which disabled holders of an office of profit under the Crown from election. This was part of the country programme of purifying Parliament from government influence. A requirement that governmental decisions be made in full Privy Council reflected disquiet at the making of decisions in secret cabinet councils. This made it difficult for the opposition to identify and impeach ministers responsible for policies of which it disapproved. The requirement that the King must have the permission of Parliament to go abroad was a product of William's custom of spending, on average, half the year overseas. The final major section of the Act, which denied that the royal power of pardon could be used to bar impeachment, was an obvious part of country policy.

Conclusion

The parliaments of Elizabeth and the parliaments of William—could they be the same institution? In procedure, in ceremony and in traditions, much had stayed the same, but their function was quite different. Under Elizabeth, parliaments were occasional, brief and called to meet specific needs. The House of Commons was occupied, for the most part, by men elected on the basis of their local status, in order to serve the Crown and represent the sectional needs of their constituents. Under William, Parliament was a partner in government, essential to its finance: an institution with an accepted role as advisor, critic, accountant and watchdog. Though local considerations were still important in elections, they were increasingly fought on the basis of party and attitudes to national political issues.

These changes had not taken place overnight. One must not forget that the accession of Elizabeth was as remote from men living in the last year of William's reign as 1842 is from 1984. During that time, society, the role of government, the economy, foreign affairs and the role of England in the world had all changed dramatically. In 1558 Britain was an offshore island at the periphery of world affairs, neglected, weak and seen as a pawn in the great struggle between France and Spain. In 1558 the English parliamentary system was, to foreign eyes, an archaic relic of the medieval past, suited only to a dreamy backwater. The European trend was to strong, centralised, efficient and bureaucratic government. Yet by 1700 the rise of the backward State had been accompanied by the development of the once derided institution into an essential part of government.

The further development of Parliament lies outside the timespan of this work, but in that development lies part of the proof of the relevance of parliamentary history today. The full-blown balanced constitution of the eighteenth century was the starting point for the system of government in the United States as well as a model for European liberals. The later development of full parliamentary control of government and the progressive expansion of the franchise made Parliament representative of the whole people, not just of the ruling class. In the later evolution of Parliament one may find the origin of the system of government adopted and adapted by New Zealand, Australia, Canada and many other Commonwealth countries. What seventeenth century Englishmen had proved was that effective government and parliamentary participation could go hand in hand. Indeed, the verdict of the war of the 1690s, which England survived in much better shape than her allies or her enemies, was that Parliament was a great aid to, or even a prerequisite for, efficient government.

Though 1700 marks the end of a century and 1702 the end of a reign, neither represents the terminal date of parliamentary development. It is , however, a critical date. In 1558 Parliament was not really a part of government, but rather just an aid to efficient government. In the 1630s its role, indeed its very existence, was under threat. In the 1640s and 1650s Parliament faced the possibility of extinction as anything other than an ornamental relic, first, at the hands of the King, and second, at the hands of its own armies. The Restoration of 1660 gave Parliament a permanent place in the constitution, but did not define it. The parliamentary history of the next two reigns contains the story of the attempt to establish a balance between King and Parliament, until, in the 1690s, the aftermath of the 1688 revolution, when the demands of war gave Parliament an essential place in government. From the 1690s onwards, government without the participation of Parliament was unthinkable. Parliament had become the central institution of public life.

APPENDIX I

The finances of the English State, 1558–1629

Note that the term 'royal revenues', as it is used here, is not synonymous with 'taxation'. Taxes could only be raised by consent of Parliament, and were only an irregular supplement to Crown income (that is they were extraordinary income). The ordinary revenues of the Crown were permanent hereditary revenues, which it possessed by right, and did not have to be voted to it by Parliament. They were derived from four sources:

The ordinary revenue of the Crown

Crown lands

As most royal estates were leased out, the income therefrom took the form of lease rents. A number of royal farms were retained to provide the Court with foodstuffs, either when it was at Whitehall or on progress. Royal lands consisted of the ancient demesne of the Crown, augmented by the confiscated estates of attainted felons and traitors (for example, the Duke of Buckingham in 1521 and the Earl of Westmorland in 1569), and the property of the dissolved monasteries.

Customs revenue

The greater part of this revenue was obtained from export duties on wool, cloth and leather, and from import duties on a variety of products. In theory, the Crown was only empowered to levy customs duties for the regulation of trade and the protection of native industry; such income as the Crown derived from the practice was incidental. But the Tudors were pragmatic monarchs and what mattered in practice was the income they could squeeze from trade. While the Crown could increase or suspend duties on commodities originally specified by Act of Parliament, it was doubtful if it could impose duties on other goods without parliamentary consent.

Feudal dues

These were revenues to which the King was entitled as feudal overlord. They consisted of dues owed by those who were tenants-in-chief of the Crown: in other words, by those whose ancestors had held their land directly from the Crown. The most important of these payments were:

    i the relief (paid when an heir succeeded to his property); escheat (reversion of property to the Crown if there was no heir);

    ii wardship of a minor heir (the right to administer his property and receive its profits, and to marry off the heir or heiress to a 'suitable' partner designated by the Crown);

    iii custody of the property of widows and idiots.

The profits of justice

These consisted of fees paid by suitors for writs and letters in civil cases, the fines levied both in the Common Law and prerogative courts, and the profits from penal legislation: for example, against enclosers and smugglers.

The Church

In addition to these sources of ordinary income were the revenues due to the King as Supreme Head from 1534 on:

    i *First fruits*: the new incumbent of any ecclesiastical living, whether bishopric or parochial benefice, had to pay one year's income to the Crown.

    ii *Tenths*: thereafter each member of the clergy had to pay ten per cent of his annual income to the Supreme Head.

Extraordinary revenues voted to the Crown

Tunnage and poundage

This was a problem levy, because it was a semi-permanent, or at least a long-term source of revenue. Under the Tudors it was levied, in the first Parliament of the reign, for the life of the reigning monarch. It was originally a levy upon tuns of wine (one tun equals two pipes or four hogsheads, containing 252 old wine gallons!), wool and woolfells (sheepskins), and leather, although it had been extended to embrace a number of other commodities by the sixteenth century.

Fifteenth and tenth

This was a levy on moveable property, one-fifteenth in rural areas and one-tenth in urban. The amount to be levied on each county had for long been fixed by what was known as a 'composition'. This meant that in each county and borough it yielded a fixed amount, the real value of which fell during the inflation which began in Henry VIII's reign. To compensate for this, Parliament sometimes voted more than one fifteenth and tenth.

Subsidy

Introduced by Wolsey in 1514, the subsidy was a primitive form of income tax, levied at a rate of one to four shillings in the pound (five to twenty per cent). Unfortunately for the monarchy it too became a fixed levy based on county 'compositions'.

Clerical subsidy: voted by the convocations of Canterbury and York.

APPENDIX II

Common Law procedure

The Common Law courts followed a system of oral pleading before judge and jury. In criminal trials a formal charge known as an indictment was laid. It was first placed before a grand jury of up to twenty-four persons, who decided whether there was real suspicion and enough evidence to send the accused for trial.

Once the grand jury declared the indictment a 'true bill', the accused was tried before a judge and a twelve member jury (petty jury). Witnesses were heard. Prosecution witnesses were put on oath but defence witnesses were not. Persons charged with treason or felony, for which the penalty was death, were not allowed a lawyer to defend them. Those charged with misdemeanours (offences often punishable with no more than a fine) were allowed counsel. All evidence was given orally in open court, though any written confession made by the accused could be read. All witnesses were liable to be cross-examined, though it can hardly be expected that effective cross-examination could be carried out by an illiterate prisoner on trial for his life. After all evidence had been heard, and both sides had summed up, the jury retired to consider its verdict and its foreman pronounced the accused either 'guilty' or 'not guilty'.

In civil cases, the plaintiff obtained a writ from Chancery which enabled the case to commence. The procedure for bringing a civil action to court was slow and cumbersome. Counsel (lawyers) for both sides prepared documents, but once the suit came to court, oral pleadings were used as well. The case was heard by judge and jury. Except in complex cases or those involving particularly valuable property, the Westminster courts usually assigned civil cases to the Assizes by a writ known as *nisi prius*. This writ ordered the parties to a dispute to appear in Westminster on a certain day unless it had already been settled at the Assizes.

GLOSSARY

It is one of the shortcomings of most history text books that terms are often used without adequate explanation. This is particularly true of religious terms. We live in a secular age when few people go to Church, except to be baptised, married or buried, or to hear the Christmas carol service. Nor are many people instructed in Christianity, whether it be of the Roman Catholic, Anglican or Presbyterian variety (or any of the other religious brands available to a market of dwindling interest). It can no longer be assumed that transubstantiation, communion, Eucharist or sacraments are terms naturally familiar to most examination candidates. The authors have attempted to resolve this problem in two ways:

1 Short definitions have been inserted in the text in brackets.

2 Longer and more technical terms have been explained in the brief selective glossary below.

In addition there are glossaries in a number of other works: for example, F. Heal and R. O'Day (editors), *Church and Society in England: Henry VIII to James I*, London, 1977, page 177; P.L. Hughes and J. Larkin, *Tudor Royal Proclamations*, 3 volumes, New Haven and London, 1964–9.

Archdeacon
A bishop's chief subordinate official.

Chantry
A small monastic institution. Its prime function was to say prayers for the chantry's founder and his descendants, though sometimes it also included a school.

Clerks of the Parliaments
The clerks were the professional civil servants of Parliament. The clerk of the Parliaments (the senior clerk) served the House of Lords and the underclerk served the Commons. They compiled the journals (records of business) of the two Houses, held draft Bills in their custody and, at the first reading, read

aloud the text of the Bill to the House. They wrote out copies of Bills for interested members (at a price, of course), they drafted neat copies of amendments, and they transcribed paper Bills onto parchment when they were likely to pass the House. The Lords' clerk had additional duties relating to Parliament as a whole: in particular, at the end of Parliament he transcribed the text of public Acts on to a 'Parliament roll'. This served as a record for law courts if they wished to consult a statute.

Communion
A term usually used in the Anglican, Presbyterian and other Protestant Churches. Like the Eucharist it is a sacrament celebrating the Last Supper. However, it embodies a rejection of the Roman Catholic doctrine of transubstantiation, whereby a miraculous transformation of the bread and wine occurs. To the extremer Protestants, communion was no more than a token act of remembrance.

Convocation
The Church of England was divided into the two provinces of Canterbury (south) and York (north). Each province had its own assembly or convocation, which consisted of two Houses: the upper (bishops) and the lower (representatives of the lower clergy). The Canterbury convocation met at the same time as Parliament, whereas York assembled after the end of Parliament. The function of the convocations was to enact canon law (decrees of the Church).

Escheator
A royal official, usually a local gentleman, who was responsible for the protection of the King's right to feudal dues in his county.

Eucharist
The Roman Catholic sacrament which celebrates the Last Supper and embodies the doctrine of transubstantiation (see below).

Excommunication
An official sanction against offenders, denying them the sacraments and cutting them off from the Church.

Impeachment
A parliamentary process, whereby the House of Commons drew up charges against a 'public enemy' (who, in the seventeenth century, was often a minister or other great royal official) and presented him to the House of Lords, which tried him and passed judgement.

Jesuits

Members of the Roman Catholic Society of Jesus who were noted for their missionary and educational work, especially the conversion of non-Christians or the reconversion of lapsed Catholics.

Journals of Parliament

The clerks of the two Houses kept personal records of business for their own use. By James I's reign they had become official records. The Commons' journal reported the progress of Bills and, occasionally, debate. The Lords' journal also recorded business, but in addition it included a daily attendance register.

Lord Chancellor

He performed many roles. As a senior civil servant, he was the head of the department of Chancery, which was the Crown's secretariat. It drafted State documents, especially the more formal and solemn ones. And he was Keeper of the Great Seal, which was attached to them in order to confirm that they were genuine. He was also Speaker of the House of Lords, head of the judiciary (the law courts) and presiding judge in Star Chamber and the Court of Chancery. His administrative and judicial authority was enormous and, in prestige, he remained the first officer of State under the Crown. However, by Elizabeth's reign he had, in practice, ceased to be the chief formative influence in government. The most trusted political adviser was now appointed to the office of Secretary.

Lord Keeper

He was the Lord Chancellor by another name. Elizabeth used the title frequently. The Lord Keeper was burdened with the same powers and responsibility as someone who had been given the title of Lord Chancellor. For the Queen it had two advantages: she did not have to pay him as much, and it was a title which could be granted to a commoner without raising him to the peerage.

The mass

The central religious ceremony of the Roman Catholic Church, in which the Eucharist (the Last Supper) is celebrated.

Prayer Book

The Elizabethan Prayer Book, which set forth the liturgy (order of worship) of the new Church, was a modified version of that of 1552. The modifications were conservative: that is, in a Catholic direction. The most important change concerned communion. It was phrased ambiguously so that the ceremony could be read two ways: as a simple act of commemoration or as a ritual which acknowledged the real presence of Christ in the bread and the wine.

Presbyterian
A Calvinist who sought a Church governed by assemblies (presbyteries) of clergy and lay elders, rather than by bishops and a supreme governor. He also wanted to replace the Anglican prayer book by the Directory (order of worship) of Calvin's Geneva.

Sacraments
Religious ceremonies of symbolic or theological significance. Roman Catholics and some Anglicans accepted that there were seven: the **Eucharist** or **communion** (celebration of the Last Supper), **baptism** (the act of sprinkling with water as a token of admission to the Church), **confirmation** (the rite confirming the vows made on their behalf as infants at baptism), **penance** (the act of penitence as a punishment for sins), **extreme unction** (the death-bed rite of anointing), **ordination** (the act of conferring holy orders: that is admitting a man to the priesthood) and **matrimony** (the marriage rite). See also **communion, mass** and **transubstantiation**.

Seals
Three seals (which made impressions on wax) were used to confirm that royal documents were genuine. The wax impression of the Great Seal was attached to very formal documents, such as charters and peace treaties. The Privy Seal was affixed to all ordinary administrative documents, especially letters to royal officials. The signet was the most private seal. It was used for confidential advices and instructions, and for the King's personal correspondence with favoured servants and friends.

Separatism
Separation from the Church by those who wanted to use their own order of service and organise their own religious communities.

Thirty-nine articles
These embodied the theological doctrine of the Church, as established by the Elizabethan Settlement of 1559. They were devised by the 1563 convocation, which took as its model the forty-two articles of Edward VI's reign and proceeded to modify them.

Transubstantiation
The Roman Catholic doctrine of the Eucharist. During the celebration of the Last Supper the bread and the wine are transformed into the flesh and blood of Christ.

BIBLIOGRAPHY

This is not intended to be a comprehensive bibliography: that would be both a futile and unrealistic exercise. It is intended to be a working bibliography, rather than a compendium of what has been written on the period. The authors have adopted the following terms of reference:

1 Each chapter, or pair of chapters, has been allocated one section of the Bibliography.

2 Where possible, books have been selected because they are cheap enough for a school to purchase and readily accessible.

3 A supplementary bibliography of articles has been included. These can usually be interloaned through the public library system.

4 Each work cited here is accompanied by brief critical comment covering its weaknesses and strengths, and the particular thrust of its interests and its omissions.

The books and articles cited in the text do not necessarily figure in this select bibliography: where they do not do so, we have provided a full reference in the text. Where they *do* figure in the Bibliography, we have cited the author's name and date of publication in the text, along with the relevant page number. The items recorded below are recommended as further reading on the grounds of relevance, value, accessibility and (in most instances) reasonable cost.

General

Aylmer, G.E. *The Struggle for the Constitution, 1603–1689*. Blandford Press, 1965. Published also as *A Short History of Seventeenth Century England* in Mentor paperback.

> This is an exercise in economical writing. The narrative is clear and concise and the book has a nice balance between description and evaluative comment. However, it is important to remember that it is primarily concerned with constitutional, political and religious history.

Aylmer, G.E. (editor) *The Interregnum: The Quest for Settlement, 1646–1660*. Macmillan, London, 1972.

> Part of a series. An invaluable collection of essays, some of which are listed separately here. A relatively inexpensive paperback.

Bindoff, S.T. *Tudor England.* Penguin, Harmondsworth, 1950.

Still a minor classic. A useful introduction, with the added virtue that it is relatively cheap. However, it is important to remember that in some respects (for example, Parliament and religion) it has become out-of-date.

Elton, G.R. *England Under the Tudors.* Methuen, London, 1974.

This book embodied the first full statement of Elton's thesis of the 'Cromwellian revolution' of the 1530s. However, it is unsatisfactory for students of the period 1558–1700. The Elizabethan section is probably the weakest in the book (although it is certainly worth reading) and it tends to be political and constitutional in its emphasis. If it is used, the 1974 edition is recommended. It contains an additional chapter which revises certain aspects of the book.

Elton, G.R. *The Tudor Constitution.* Cambridge University paperback, 1960 (revised edition, 1982).

The classic study of Tudor government, which replaces J.R. Tanner's earlier volume on the same subject. It consists of a combined commentary and select documents. It has one disadvantage: that its language and technical detail are often too difficult for all but the brightest school students. Moreover, it is primarily concerned with institutions and administration—their functions and how they worked. Politics—that is, how men operated the machine of government, exploited it, and used it to satisfy their ambitions—play little part. To learn about the political realities of the system, such as faction and the patron-client relationship, it is better to look at **Penry Williams**, *The Tudor Regime*, Oxford University Press, 1979. However, both books cover the entire Tudor period. They are thematically, not chronologically, structured and one has to mine them in order to unearth the relevant material about Elizabeth's reign. Yet Elton remains invaluable on the subjects of the Crown, Parliament (especially in the revised edition of 1982), central government and the law courts; less so for religion and local government.

Hill, C. *The Century of Revolution, 1603–1714.* Sphere paperback, London, 1974.

Ignore his sketchy superficial narrative, but use his stimulating, often provocative, study of government, religion and economics. This book works well in harness with Aylmer's *The Struggle for the Constitution.* (See page 491.)

Holmes, G. (editor) *Britain After the Glorious Revolution, 1689–1714.* Macmillan, London, 1969.

As for Aylmer, *The Interregnum.*

Hurstfield, J. *Elizabeth I and the Unity of England.* English Universities Press, London, 1960.

A very clear, concise, compact account of the reign, which has two particular virtues: first, it charts the decline of Elizabethan government in the nineties and, second, it departs from the tradition of uncritical praise of Elizabeth, epitomised in Neale and Rowse, and offers tentative criticism of her, especially in the last years of the reign.

Jones, J.R. *Country and Court: England 1658–1714.* Edward Arnold, London, 1978 (paperback).

Essential reading for the Parliament and government themes. This work summarises its author's massive and often pioneering researches into the late seventeenth century, and much else besides. Not as strong on the religious and social and economic themes. It includes an extremely useful annotated bibliography which is organised thematically and has references to specialised works not mentioned here.

Jones, J.R. (editor) *The Restored Monarchy, 1660–88.* Macmillan, London, 1979.

As for Aylmer, *The Interregnum.*

Kenyon, J.P. *The Stuart Constitution: Documents and Commentary.* Cambridge University Press, 1969.

A first-rate source of documents with a valuable commentary.

Loades, D.M. *Politics and the Nation, 1450–1660.* Fontana paperback, 1974.

One of the better general texts which, unfortunately, ends in 1660, not 1700. It is constitutional and political in emphasis, and, like so many text books, it gives insufficient attention to economic matters. Nevertheless, it is a useful introductory 'overview' of two-thirds of the period covered by this book.

Lockyer, R. *Tudor and Stuart Britain, 1471–1714.* Longman, London, 1976 (1964).

Now available in paperback. A clearly written narrative. A good general text widely used in schools and deservedly so.

Russell, C. *The Crisis of Parliaments: English History 1509–1660.* Oxford University Press, 1971.

Perhaps the best text book on the period up to the Restoration. It incorporates the results of much recent research before its publication—especially on Parliament, religion, and the causes of the Civil War. Unfortunately, its title over-emphasises the role of that institution in the history of the period.

Russell, C. *The Origins of the English Civil War.* Macmillan, London, 1973.
As for Aylmer, *The Interregnum.*

Stone, L. *The Causes of the English Revolution, 1529–1642.* Routledge and Kegan Paul paperback, London, 1973.

A logically structured book which attempts to provide a pattern of causation. Its arguments and analysis are not universally accepted—no explanation of the Civil War ever is—but it does attempt to explain a very complex process in a simple, clear and logical way.

The social and economic structure

This section of the Bibliography covers works of particular relevance to chapter 1. After a list of general texts, applicable to the whole chapter, the list is divided according to the sub-sections of the chapter.

Clarkson, L.A. *The Pre-Industrial Economy in England.* Batsford, London, 1971.

A very useful introductory text.

Coleman, D.C. *The Economy of England 1450–1750.* Oxford University Press, 1977.

Shorter and more simply written than Wilson's *England's Apprenticeship* (see below), it could be consulted with profit by many seventh formers.

Ramsay, P. *Tudor Economic Problems.* Victor Gollancz, London, 1972.

Still the most convenient and economical text book on the Elizabethan economy, especially for agriculture, trade, industry and inflation.

Rowse, A.L. *The England of Elizabeth: the Structure of Society.* Cardinal paperbacks, London, 1973.

Despite the adulation of Elizabeth, his male prejudice against women and his hostility to Puritans (a strange contradiction), this is a readable impressionistic portrayal of Elizabethan society.

Seaver, P.S. (editor) *Seventeenth Century England: Society in an Age of Revolution.* New Viewpoints, a division of Franklin Watts, New York, 1976.

This volume includes Lawrence Stone's 'Social Mobility in England, 1500–1700' and Joan Thirsk's 'Seventeenth Century Agriculture and Social Change'.

Stone, L. *The Crisis of the Aristocracy, 1558–1641.* Clarendon Press, Oxford, 1981.

The size and cost of the hardback version (1965) make it unrealistic for school purposes. Its thesis and conclusions are controversial, but it is a goldmine because of its wealth of detail. Use the paperback edition which is of more manageable length and will not bankrupt the school.

Supple, B.E. *Commercial Crisis and Change in England 1600–1642.* Cambridge University Press, 1959.

A theoretical explanation of booms and slumps in trade during the early seventeenth century, which disabuses us of the idea that they were caused by anything resembling the trade cycles of a more developed capitalist economy. Mainly for teachers, but it could be handled by enthusiastic seventh form economists.

Wilson, C. *England's Apprenticeship, 1603–1763.* Longman paperback, London, 1971.

Essential reading for the seventeenth century. It is logically structured, which makes it easy to locate material relevant to particular themes. The chapters on trade and industry are particularly sound, and the book also contains a very useful bibliography.

The social structure and social mobility

Campbell, M. *The English Yeoman under Elizabeth and the Early Stuarts.* Yale University Press, New Haven, 1942. (Reprinted by The Merlin Press, London, 1962 and 1967.)

A thorough coverage of a romanticised class often neglected by historians. A desirable rather than a necessary purchase.

Hill, C. 'The Many-Headed Monster in Late Tudor and Early Stuart Political Thinking' in C.H. Carter (editor), *From the Renaissance to the Counter Reformation.* Random House, New York, 1965.

An insight into governing class fears of those whom they governed. Interesting interloan material.

Hoskins, W.G. *Provincial England: Essays in Social and Economic History.* Macmillan, London, 1965.

A very useful book which provides specific studies to supplement some of Laslett's generalisations (see below).

Laslett, P. *The World We Have Lost.* Methuen University Paperbacks, London, 1971. (The first edition, 1965, has been extensively revised.)

An excellent, though controversial, work, which could provide the starting point for the course by making it possible for young adults to attempt an answer to the question, 'What would it have been like to have lived as an ordinary man or woman 300 years ago?'. It is a useful corrective to many misconceptions about the nature of pre-industrial society. Essential reading for teachers and very highly recommended for pupils.

Stone, L. *Social Change and Revolution in England, 1540–1640.* Longman paperback, London, 1975.

A useful combination of the author's commentary and extracts from contemporaries and historians. The 'rise of the gentry' debate is summarised here—no need to go further on that worn-out controversy. A note of caution: this book looks at the century before 1640, not in its own right, but with an eye to the Civil War to come.

Tawney, R.H. *The Rise of the Gentry, 1588–1640.* Economic History Review Supplements, 11, 1941.

Trevor-Roper, H.R. *The Gentry, 1540–1640.* Economic History Review Supplements, 1, 1953.

The size of the community

Glass, D.V. and D.E.C. Eversley (editors) *Population and History.* Edward Arnold, London, 1965.

Glass, D.V. and R. Revelle *Population and Social Change.* Edward Arnold, London, 1972.

Wrigley, E.A. *Population and History.* World University Library, London, 1969.

For most schools, these are books to be borrowed on inter-library loan rather than purchased. By using the chapters and articles in the works cited above, which are relevant to sixteenth and seventeenth century England, one can obtain a fund of fascinating material and gain some insight into the technical complexities of calculating population before the days of census.

Agriculture and agrarian problems

Kerridge, E. *Agrarian Problems in the Sixteenth Century and After*. Allen and Unwin, London, 1969.

A long introduction and a collection of documents. Invaluable for teachers and pupils.

Kerridge, E. *The Agricultural Revolution*. Allen and Unwin, London, 1967.

Did the real agricultural revolution take place a century earlier than has been supposed? Kerridge gives a strongly affirmative answer. For most schools this is a book to borrow on inter-library loan.

Thirsk, J. (editor) *The Agrarian History of England and Wales, Volume IV, 1500–1640*. Cambridge University Press, 1967.

This massive collaborative work is a goldmine of information about the social structure, tenures, techniques, life-styles and housing of rural England. An expensive, but highly desirable reference book.

Thirsk, J. 'Seventeenth Century Agriculture and Social Change', in Seaver (editor), *Seventeenth Century England*. (See page 494.)

An excellent short study.

Trade and industry

Coleman, D.C. *Industry in Tudor and Stuart England*, in the Studies in Economic History series. Macmillan paperback, 1975.

A useful, brief (and therefore cheap) and tolerably interesting monograph on a subject which is often presented in an excruciatingly dull way.

Davis, R. *English Overseas Trade, 1500–1700*, in the Studies in Economic History series. Macmillan paperback, 1973.

Brief, palatable and useful.

Jack, S.M. *Trade and Industry in Tudor and Stuart England*. Historical Problems, no. 27. Allen and Unwin paperback, London, 1977.

A very competent text, accompanied by an illuminating collection of documents.

Inflation

Outhwaite, R.B. *Inflation in Tudor and Early Stuart England*. Macmillan, London, 1969.

A first-rate study which is within the grasp of able seventh formers, especially those taking economics. A concise and inexpensive paperback.

Ramsay, P.H. (editor) *The Price Revolution in Sixteenth Century England*.

Methuen University Paperbacks, London, 1971.

> An extremely useful collection of articles, most of which can be read by pupils.

Poverty, vagrancy and poor relief
Beier, A.L. *The Problem of the Poor in Tudor and Early Stuart England.* Methuen, London, 1983.

> A very clear, brief, up-to-date and cheap survey, with a useful bibliography.

James, M. *Social Problems and Policy During the Puritan Revolution.* Routledge and Kegan Paul, 1966 (1930).

> Lengthy description and justification of Puritan social policy. Inter-library loan material for enthusiasts.

Jordan, W.K. *Philanthropy in England 1480–1668: A Study of the Changing Patterns of English Social Aspirations.* Allen and Unwin, New York, 1959.

> Worth consulting despite the deliberate, but incomprehensible, decision not to correct for inflation the data on giving. This has invalidated many of his conclusions. The book should be read with 'Inflation and Philanthropy in England: A Re-Assessment of W.K. Jordan's Data' by **William R. Bittle** and **R. Todd Lane**, *Economic History Review*, second series, 39, 1976, pages 203–210, which provides a useful corrective. However, note further comments and criticism in subsequent issues of this journal.

Pound, J. *Poverty and Vagrancy in Tudor England.* Longman, London, 1971.

> An excellent short study which includes several interesting documents as well as a concise and lucid introduction. Essential reading.

Taylor, G. *The Problem of Poverty 1660–1835.* Longman, London, 1969.

> This is a companion volume to the work by Pound.

Colonisation
Parry, J.H. and P. Sherlock *A Short History of the West Indies.* Macmillan, London, 1981.

> Brief, but the best survey.

Simmons, R. *The American Colonies from Settlement to Independence.* Longmans, London, 1976.

> It is big, expensive and much of it is on the eighteenth century, but it is recent and readable.

The early modern state: problems of government
This section of the Bibliography covers chapters 2 and 3.

Carter, J. 'Law, Courts and Constitution', in Jones (editor), *Restored Monarchy.* (See page 493)

> An excellent summary.

Carter, J. 'The Revolution and the Constitution', in Holmes (editor), *Britain After the Glorious Revolution*. (see page 492.)

Well worth consulting.

Coakley, T.M. 'Robert Cecil in Power: Elizabethan Politics in Two Reigns' in H.S. Reinmuth Jr. (editor), *Early Stuart Studies*. University of Minnesota Press, 1970.

Useful as evidence for the fact that 1603 marked, not a sudden change, but rather a step in a longer-term transition from Elizabethan to Caroline politics. Cecil provided the strongest thread of continuity between the two dynasties.

Everitt, A.M. *Change in the Provinces in the Sixteenth Century*. University of Leicester, Department of English Social History Occasional Papers, second series, 1, 1969, paperback.

A study of the local communities and their relationship with the nation-at-large.

Foster, C.C.F. 'The English Local Community and Local Government, 1603–1625', in A.G.R. Smith (editor), *Reign of James VI and I*. Macmillan, London, 1973.

A good short introduction to county government.

Foster, F.F. *The Politics of Stability*. Royal Historical Society, London, 1977.

This compact and informative work has a rather uninspiring pedestrian style, but it is, nonetheless, an important study of the government of the Elizabethan City of London. As the governmental structure did not substantially change in the following century, Foster's work has a value well beyond 1603.

Hill, L.M. 'County Government in Caroline England, 1625–1640', in Russell (editor), *Origins of the English Civil War*. (See page 493.)

Another good short study of the structure and problems of county government.

Jones, W.J. *Politics and the Bench: The Judges and the Origins of the English Civil War*. Allen and Unwin paperback, 1971.

A combination of text and documents. It is important as the only digestible, accessible, and relatively cheap study of the political role of the early Stuart judges.

MacCaffrey, W.T. 'Place and patronage in Elizabethan Politics', in S.T. Bindoff *et al.*, *Elizabethan Government and Society*. Athlone Press, London, 1961.

Important as a study of the relationship between office, other forms of royal patronage and the patron-client mechanism under Elizabeth.

Morrill, J.S. *Revolt of the Provinces: Conservatives and Radicals in the English Civil War, 1630–1650*. Allen and Unwin, London, 1976.

A summary of most of the research done in local history of the Civil War period. Very valuable. Readable by students, but mainly for teacher use.

Russell, C. 'Parliament and the King's Finances', in Russell (editor), *Origins of the English Civil War*.

Includes material hard to find elsewhere.

Smith, A.G.R. *The Government of Elizabethan England*. Arnold paperback, London, 1972.

Essential reading. The best introduction to the subject, because it combines a study of institutions with the political realities which lay behind them, and it does so in a cheap, compact book. Referred to in a Bursaries Examiner's Report as a 'dangerously good book'. Includes an excellent summary of the workings of the patronage system.

Tomlinson, H. 'Financial and Administrative Developments in England, 1660–1688', in Jones (editor), *Restored Monarchy*.

An excellent summary written by a school teacher.

Underdown, D. 'Settlement in the Counties, 1653–1658', in Aylmer (editor), *The Interregnum*. (See page 491.)

An excellent study.

Woolrych, A. 'Last Quests for Settlement, 1657–1660', in Aylmer (editor), *The Interregnum*.

Carries on where Underdown finishes.

Religion

This section of the Bibliography covers chapters 4 and 5.

Beddard, R.A. 'The Restoration Church', in Jones (editor), *Restored Monarchy*.

Undoubtedly the best starting point for a study of this topic.

Clifton, R. 'Fear of Popery', in Russell (editor), *Origins of the English Civil War*.

Essential reading.

Collinson, P. *The Elizabethan Puritan Movement*. Cape, London, 1971.

Expensive, but unfortunately essential. The classic study of Elizabethan Puritanism.

Cragg, G.R. *Puritanism in the Period of the Great Persecution 1660–1688*. Cambridge University Press, 1957.

Much good material, but very sympathetic to the Puritans. Hagiography rather than history.

Cragg, G.R. *From Puritanism to the Age of Reason*. Cambridge University Press, 1966.

A short book. A very useful and interesting discussion of the changes taking place in theology and, indeed, in intellectual life generally.

Cross, C. *The Royal Supremacy in the Elizabethan Church*. Historical Problems, no. 8. Allen and Unwin paperback, London, 1969.

Excellent on Elizabeth's government of the Church.

George, C. and K. *The Protestant Mind of the English Reformation, 1570–1640*. Princeton University Press, 1961.

A fairly large and expensive book. In contrast to **New** (see below) its authors stress the common elements in the theology of 'Anglicans' and 'Puritans' before the Laudian revolution. The debate between New and the Georges is summarised very well in **McGrath**, *Papists and Puritans under Elizabeth I*, Blandford Press, London, 1967, pages 35–41.

Heal, F. and R. O'Day *Church and Society in England. Henry VIII to James I*. Macmillan, London, 1977.

This is a good example of the relatively recent and more balanced approach to religion. It devotes much of its space and time to the condition of the new Church, rather than to expressions of dissent. The most important articles are those by R. Houlbrooke ('The Protestant Episcopate, 1574–1603'), C. Cross ('Churchmen and the Royal Supremacy') and F. Heal ('Economic Problems of the Clergy'). See also *Continuity and Change, 1500–1642*, by the same editors and in the same series (1976).

Miller, J. *Popery and Politics, 1660–1688*. Cambridge University Press, 1973.

An excellent and relatively short book which contributes greatly to our knowledge of both religion and politics in the Restoration era.

New, J.F.H. *Anglican and Puritan: The Basis of their Opposition, 1558–1640*. Stanford University Press, California, 1964.

This work has one important weakness: the distinction it makes between Puritans and Anglicans, as if the former were in some essential way separate from the latter.

Tyacke, N. 'Puritanism, Arminianism and Counter-Revolution', in Russell (editor), *Origins of the English Civil War*.

Concise, interesting, essential.

Parliament

This section of the bibliography covers chapters 6 and 7.

Ashton, R. *The English Civil War: Conservatism and Revolution, 1603–1649*. Weidenfeld and Nicolson, London, 1978 (1979, paperback).

A fairly specialised work, but it summarises much of the recent research into the Civil War and its causes. For teacher reference and the most able students.

Neale, J.E. *Elizabeth I and her Parliaments*. 2 volumes, Cape, London, 1953 and 1957.

Important, because it held the field for twenty years. Now it is under heavy attack from the revisionists; it is also very long and expensive. Better, perhaps, to read **Elton's** article. 'Parliament: Functions and Fortunes' (see page 502), which summarises and criticises many of Neale's arguments.

Neale, J.E. *The Elizabethan House of Commons*. Cape, London, 1949.

Neale's institutional study of the Commons. However, half the book is concerned with disputed elections and the quality (education, experience, kinship connections) of members. As with all of Neale's work, it is primarily concerned with politics and personnel, rather than with the functions and business of Parliament (although there are sound chapters on procedure).

Notestein, W. *The Winning of the Initiative by the House of Commons*. Proceedings of the British Academy, Volume XI, London, 1924.

Like Neale, Notestein is politically orientated. This is a classic statement of the thesis that, in the forty years before the Civil War, the Crown's opponents attempted to wrest control of Parliament from it. Historiographically it is important, but no longer to be accepted without question.

Roots, I. *The Great Rebellion, 1642–1660*. Batsford, London, 1968 (1966).

An excellent narrative with a considerable amount of interpretation.

Russell, C. *Parliaments and English Politics, 1621–1629*. Oxford University Press, 1979.

Too expensive to be a realistic purchase for most schools. However, it is an important 'revisionist' statement on the early Stuart parliaments. It argues that the crisis which developed in 1625–9 was not a constitutional one. The first part of the book is a useful, detailed structural analysis of government and politics.

Smith, A.G.R. 'Constitutional Ideas and Parliamentary Development in England, 1603–1625', in A.G.R. Smith (editor), *The Reign of James VI and I*. Macmillan, London, 1973.

An excellent summary by a leading scholar.

Underdown, D. *Pride's Purge: Politics in the Puritan Revolution*. Clarendon Press, Oxford, 1971.

A very important specialist work, putting forward an interpretation which was revolutionary when first devised. Though still not unchallenged, it has achieved acceptance by a majority of scholars. Mainly teacher reference.

Worden, B. *The Rump Parliament, 1648–1653*. Cambridge University Press, 1974.

A very important work which has revolutionised understanding of its subject. Mainly for teacher use.

Articles

Elton, G.R. 'Tudor Government: the Points of Contact: Parliament', *Transactions of the Royal Historical Society*, fifth series, XXIV, 1974.

Very important. It looks at Parliament in a socio-political context and especially as a vital communications link between Crown and governing class.

502 Revolution, Reaction and the Triumph of Conservatism

Elton, G.R. 'Parliament in the Sixteenth Century: Functions and Fortunes', *Historical Journal*, 22, 2, 1979, pages 255–78.

This is essential reading. It is the first full-scale attack on the Neale-Notestein interpretation of parliamentary history.

Graves, M.A.R. 'Thomas Norton the Parliament Man: an Elizabethan M.P., 1559–1581', *Historical Journal*, 23, 1, 1980, pages 17–35.

This article is a step in the demolition of Sir John Neale's thesis that there existed a Puritan opposition in the Elizabethan parliaments.

Roskell, J.S. 'Perspectives in English Parliamentary History', *Bulletin of the John Ryland Library*, 46, 2, 1964, pages 448–75.

The first criticism of the Pollard-Neale-Notestein thesis that Parliament (and within it the Commons) rose in power during the sixteenth and early seventeenth century.

Russell, C. 'Parliamentary History in Perspective, 1604–1629', *History*, 61, 1976, pages 1–27.

A cheaper (though earlier and, perhaps, less accessible) alternative to his book. It also has the advantage that it covers the whole of James I's reign. It represents an early 'revisionist' statement on the early Stuart parliaments.

Index